American Premium Guide to
Knives & Razors
Identification and Value Guide

Sargent

Published by

700 E. State Street • Iola, WI 54990-0001
Telephone: 715/445-2214

Please call or write for our free catalog.
Our toll-free number to place an order or obtain a free catalog is 800-258-0929
or please use our regular business telephone 715-445-2214
for editorial comment and further information.

Library of Congress Catalog Number: 99-61890
ISBN: 0-87341-754-2

Printed in the United States of America

ACKNOWLEDGMENTS

It is never possible to acknowledge all who contribute to works of this sort. There are always so many helpful and cooperative people in an endeavor such as this that to thank them all in print would be impractical. To those of you who worked so hard on my behalf, my heartfelt thanks. I hope the finished work meets with your approval.

Without photographs, the book would be unfinished at best, so many thanks to the following for their cordial hospitality and permission to photograph their collections: Joe Chance and Paul Davis. A special thanks to Jean Sargent for her contribution. Other contributors who made this update possible are: Rich Kupillas; Billy Bums—Case Knives, Texas; G.A. Miller—Remington Knives, Wisconsin; Fred Fisher—Queen Knives, Ohio; Ralph Scruton—Hawbakers, Rare Case (supplied Old Case photos), Pennsylvania; Charlie Noyes—Robesons, Alabama; Gerald Witcher—photos, Tennessee; Bill Wright—Remington sheath knives, Indiana; Wayne Robertson—Old Case photos, Texas. A special thanks to Elmer Kirkland for letting us photograph his Case Sheath knives. A special thanks to Tony Foster for his time and effort in helping price the Case Pocket knives. J.L. Johnson III, Case photos, Virginia; John Lussier, Queens, R.I.; Howard J. Drake, Queen's photos and information, Pennsylvania. Thanks to Ronnie Sizemore for his contribution of photos of Case sheath knives in Edition three and four. Ronnie's collection was sold to Jim Sargent. A special thanks to Charlie Noyes for revising the Robeson section, from his personal collection. Special thanks to Gerald Witcher for the many case photos from his personal collection.

Without the interest and knowledge of the people listed above, and many others involved with cutlery, it would be impossible for any one person to author a book of credibility without the assistance of other expertise. Thanks to all.

We need your help

Should you come across a knife that you feel should be included in our next book, please send a clear, black and white photograph, along with the pattern number (if there is one), handle material, length (closed), and stamping to Jim Sargent in care of Krause Publications, 700 E. State St., Iola, WI 54990-0001.

CONTENTS

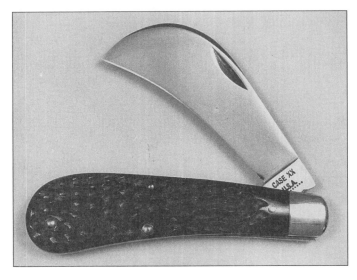

61011, Hawkbill, jigged wood scales, 4", 10 Dot, $35.

A mint "Genco, Bradford, Pa., Easy Aces," (1930-55).

R15, 3-1/4", 2 blade, small leg, gray swirl pyremite, 3-1/4", Remington Circle UMC; $300.

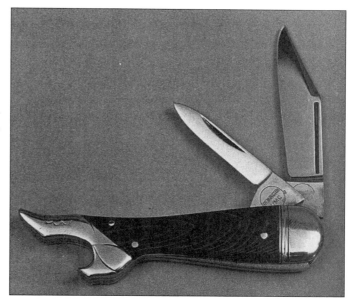

PREFACE

In considering my approach to this guide, there were several things that I wished to bring to the collector. First and foremost was to have the most realistic values available; next was to photograph as many knives as possible and to have them so distinct that the reader could see the smallest details. Last, but certainly not least, was to produce a guide for the novice, as well as the expert knife fancier.

The reader will also see that emphasis was placed on older knives, such as Case's "older knives and Tested XX through 1984 (6 Dot),"—anything after that usually carries the suggested retail price.

There are still a lot of old knives out there that haven't been discovered or just haven't been brought forward. Hopefully we can encourage the folks who possess those Remington Bullets and other rarities to join us in the camaraderie of knife collecting.

This fifth edition now includes a revised section on Robeson Pocket Knives. We have also included more than 140 new photos of Case, and reinstated the Winchester, USA section. There are also 50 new additional Queen photos.

The prices quoted in this book are as accurate as possible in reflecting current market value. Keep in mind that the prices are a guide, not hard fact. Prices will vary depending on many factors including: economic trends, collector interests, rarity, location, condition, exceptional handles, cash prices, trades, popularity of patterns, and buyers' willingness to pay the quoted price.

The prices included in this book were arrived at by comparing numerous knife lists, knife-show prices, dealer inquiries, and discussions with numerous collectors. Obviously, prices will vary from those quoted. Dealers will generally pay 60 to 70 percent of the prices quoted when purchasing knives. The older and rarer knives may bring a higher percentage, and the more common or recent production knives may bring a lower percentage.

Every possible effort was made to make this book the most complete and accurate one ever published on pocket knives. It was a true labor of love, taking more than a year of work to revise and expand. I appreciate the many letters and conversations that led to the vast new material, patterns, variations, photos, historical notes, and information in this new volume.

Jim Sargent
Florence, AL

AROUND THE SHOWS

Charlie Burns examines a knife. Serious business, eh Charlie?

John Martin, left, and Joe Chance chat at one of the knife shows. Do you have a clue as to who's the "good" guy? (Hint: Joe is wearing the white hat).

Spectators browse at all the different knives featured at a show.

Eddie Moreland, left, and Tony Foster. Who's going to let go of the knife first?

Three super-nice folks: Frank, Frank and Lisa.

Professor Gerald Witcher speaks at the Chattanooga show.

NKCA Museum entrance, Chattanooga, TN.

George and John—trading knives for apples.

INTRODUCTION

A crude cutting tool, or knife, was probably one of the first tools used by primitive man. From the first moment he used a sharp rock to crack a pterodactyl egg, man has never stopped looking for ways to improve on the knife. In reality, it has not been a man's search for a better mouse trap that helped shape society, but rather his search for a better knife.

Some 175,000 years ago, give or take a century, man dropped down out of the trees, stood on his own two feet, picked up a sharp stone and went out to search for dinner. He moved to a cave for warmth and protection. Then, he discovered fire.

The discovery of fire, followed by the innovation of cooked foods, created a need for more refined tools (knives). To coin a phrase, "Necessity is the mother of invention"—and so, the flint knife was born. Flint was a more pliable medium than stone and man found he could shape and fashion a more efficient tool. He also found that by heating this tool in a fire, it became tougher and more durable.

During this period, the family or tribal unit was coming into its own. Man had begun to settle down. He had his cave and his fire, he hunted food and prepared it with his greatly improved knife. Yet, instinctively he knew things had just begun.

Metal was the next great step toward a more durable and pliable resource with which to ease his daily chores. With the introduction of iron around 3000 B.C., man had truly reached a "Golden Age" that would revolutionize his life.

Once iron was a routine part of the tool maker's materials, steel was not far away. Steel was truly the one material that revolutionized our lives. The steel industry, as we know it today, which is actually the basis for all modern day industry, came about because of man's search for the "better knife."

By the 14th century, advances in the steel industry, and therefore in the cutlery industry, caused a great deal of romance and fantasy to spring up around certain forges. The skill of some steel makers was cloaked in more secrecy than surrounded the invention of the atom bomb. Mythology speaks of King Arthur's Excalibur, the Singing Sword. It tells us of Balmung, the knife with which Sigfried split the anvil with one stroke.

Metals for the famous Damascus weapons were forged in India. Damascus weapons were produced by laminating high carbon steel with milder steel in layers. This process is still in use today.

During the early Christian era, production of the dagger, or sheath knife, was a forge's major product. The dagger was not just a form of protection, but a utensil important to good table manners.

By the 15th century, England emerged as the center for fine steel and cutlery. London, Hallamshire and Sheffield were known then, as they are today, for their knowledge of the cutler's art. The cutlery guilds began here, and formed the basic models for our present day trade unions.

Caring for your knives

Rust is as old as iron and finding a cure for rust is like finding a cure for the common cold. There are some precautions that should be taken so your collection of knives will not diminish in value.

Cleaning

Use a soft, all-cotton cloth or chamois to clean your knives, then apply a coat of Simichrome Polish—put on and wipe off (leaves protective film) on the entire knife. Vaseline should never be used because it allows moisture to seep beneath its coat and cause rust. It is a good idea to check your knives often for possible trouble spots.

Storage and handling

The most recommended method of storing knives is in vinyl rolls with a cloth interior. These rolls are also a very convenient way to transport knives. Leather rolls have a small degree of tanning acid in them and this can cause rust. If it is possible, leave your knives unrolled during storage; this allows air movement and cuts down on moisture.

Display cases with felt interiors are another way to store knives and also allows a collection to be exhibited easily. Some collectors use elastic bands to attach their knives to the display while others choose to use wire. Elastic makes it easier to slip knives in and out for closer inspection, while wires must be cut and replaced each time. A Plexiglas top will also cut down on dust and possible theft.

Transporting your knives from cold to warmth will cause condensation which will result in rust. In other words, don't leave your collection in your car trunk over night during the cold season and then bring it into the show the next day without expecting some condensation. Keep your knives at a constant temperature or at least within a few degrees at all times.

A word about celluloid: Celluloid was made from a petroleum base and does give off fumes; these fumes will cause rust. Keep celluloids stored separately.

A word about sunlight: Direct sunlight fades anything!

Knife handles are fragile, especially bones, stags and pearls, so don't toss around carelessly and DON'T DROP. Broken or cracked handles reduce value.

What to collect

There are some who collect everything, as long as it is of excellent quality and brand. Then there are other schools of thought such as collecting by:

> Pattern—Trappers, Peanuts, Gunstocks, etc.
> Handle Materials—Goldstone, Pearl, Rogers bone, etc.
> Manufacturer—Cases, Queens, Schrade-Waldens, etc.
> Specialties—Advertising knives.

It would be wise for a beginner to come to a decision before too much is invested in his or her collection.

Knives as investments

There are knife dealers and there are knife collectors and it is most important to choose your direction before jumping in with both feet. Some people are both, but they know when to turn their hat around when it comes to dealing. So, if your main interest is turning a profit in knife marketing, there are a few things that affect the pricing structure and you must learn to recognize these.

General economic conditions—When times are bad, individuals and dealers are willing to take less than they would during the previous "good times" in order to obtain some badly needed ready cash. As a dealer, this may be the best time to pick up some collections at a depressed price, but you also know that your own inventory isn't selling at the previous higher prices. If you have the staying power, your purchases at this time can reap benefits when times are better.

Sudden increases in numbers of knives available—Sometimes large collections are broken up and introduced back into the knife market. A company will announce that it will no longer produce knives with a certain handle material, in turn driving up that particular handle material; however, several years later you may find that the company that

stopped producing with that material is going to release another several thousand limited edition with the same material and this may tend to level off prices. There have been warehouse discoveries of large numbers of certain patterns with these being dumped into the market. You can imagine what this will do to prices.

Remember, not all knives continually go up in value. In short, playing the knife market is like playing the stock market: keep your finger on the pulse and stay up with it on a daily basis by reading newsletters, monthly knife publications and by keeping your ears open.

Then there is the investor that purely enjoys his or her collection and the price is inconsequential if that certain Peanut will finally fill out that treasured display. The collection is then thought of as part of the family and no one thinks of selling their children, right?

Finding pocket knives

The days of wandering the backroads in search of general stores and hardware stores in order to relieve the owner of his outdated and overburdened knife displays are over. Some of the reasons that these fertile hunting grounds are a thing of the past are that the owners of these emporiums grew wise to the fact that they themselves already had a decent start on their own collections; another reason is that as knife collecting grew in popularity, it didn't take long for the collectors to clean these sources out; and still another is the sad fact that so many of these popular gathering places have been pushed aside for more modern convenient stores, discount stores and malls.

Don't be disheartened though; there are still excellent sources for a would-be serious collector.

Join a nearby club and become a student of knives. Get your hands on as many knife publications as possible and learn. (Many knife clubs have swap meets.) Attend Knife Shows. These are excellent places to find knives, and the prices are usually very reasonable due to very competitiveness of the dealers. Several other sources are antique shows, flea markets, estate auctions and dealers' direct mail lists.

Also, don't forget that there are still those mystical, dark, cluttered corners of attics, barns, garages and workshops. One never knows what lurks in the bottom of that tattered old cardboard box.

Condition

Mint—Never been carried or sharpened, straight from the factory and sometimes in the original box.

Excellent—Handles are in good shape, blades still close with a snap and also blades show only slight wear.

Very Good—Blades show approximately 25% wear, handles in good condition, one blade may snap weakly, blades can't have been repaired or changed, stamp can still be seen clearly with the naked eye.

Fair—Blades show 50% wear, blade closing is mushy, cracked handles, replaced handles, blades repaired or changed stamp is weak.

Poor—These are used mostly as parts knives and will have well worn or broken blades, handles are broken or completely missing, the stamp is barely visible, if at all.

Restoration

There is absolutely nothing wrong with restoring a knife by using original parts that are available. Most of the time it makes the knife even more desirable than one in worn condition.

We can draw a parallel here with the restorations of antique and classic automobiles. When one of these is restored with original parts you can be sure it is more valuable so don't worry whether a knife has been restored. Of course, if you find an old knife and you are positive that it is in original mint condition and it's still in the original box you are better off.

COUNTERFEITING

Counterfeit: "Something made to imitate another thing with a view to defraud."

With the explosion in popularity of knife collecting, there comes the unscrupulous individual who preys on the uninformed and novice collector. Some of these individuals have the equipment and skills to produce nearly perfect copies of existing patterns, while others do jobs that stick out like a sore thumb.

The following are some obvious things to look for, plus photos that will point out a few of the counterfeiter's tricks:

- Handle materials that don't match up with the proper number in the factory numbering system. Modern technology has recently supplied some handle materials that look very close to some of the old originals. If you are not sure get a second and third opinion.

- Knowing dates and when materials were no longer used; for instance, Christmas Tree, gold stone, candy stripe and multi-colored celluloid were only used prior to 1940; yellow celluloid with a white liner was used by Case until the mid-'50s prior to 1940, while the compositions are still being used today, such as yellow, black, and white. It will take a little "schooling" to become knowledgeable in this.

- Stampings that have been altered either by completely grinding off the old stamp and new ones applied; this is also time to discuss that the tangs and backsprings should be of the same thickness because grinding will make the tang thinner. Look for numbers that are of different size than the factory numbers; they will probably be of poorer quality and spaced differently than the other numbers— the black within a factory stamp is hard to come off while it is easier to remove from a counterfeit.

- There should be no protruding rivets inside of the liner.

- Some shields are obviously amateurishly made and are glued on.

Counterfeits that show up are usually more than $100, so it is a good idea to ask for a bill of sale or an invoice. Reputable dealers are always happy to supply these. If you find yourself with a counterfeit knife and can't locate the seller, don't put it back in the market but have it displayed somewhere so it may save someone else a loss.

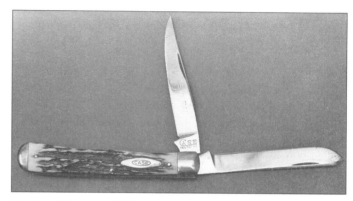

B. Case trapper, with stag handle. Stag has been installed, master blade milled and too narrow, stamp cold stamped, appears to be on a K-Bar Frame.

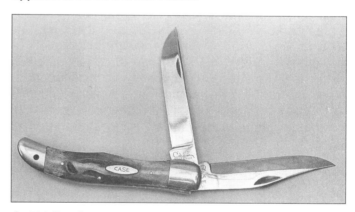

C. Folding hunter, 5265SAB, TESTED XX, handles have been installed, cold stamp, blade ground to fit backspring, pull is in wrong placed drilled for lanyard, but lanyard holes were not drilled until 1964.

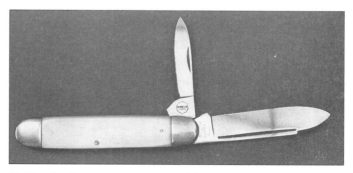

E. Remington stamp put on with electric pencil (circle is fuzzy and ragged), blade is too narrow for backspring.

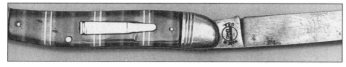

A. Remington, wrong number R1615L, bullet shield on a candy-stripe handle, stamp is etched; Remington.

D. Winchester 1936, new handles installed, cold stamp, 6 is longer than other numbers.

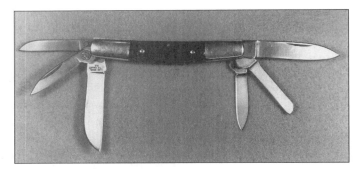

F. Case Bros. Little Valley; six-blade Congress.

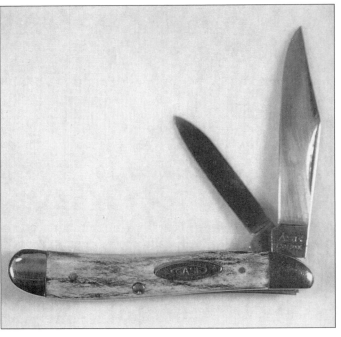

H. Case Tested XX; 5220.

Case never made this pattern, nor did it make a six-blade congress knife. Blades are stainless steel. Stamps on each blade are counterfeit. Bone handle material is not Case jigging pattern. Blades ground to fit backsprings. (See photo F).

This frame is slightly smaller than a tested '65 frame (probably a Queen folding hunter). Lanyard holes were not drilled until 1964 and the rivets are in a straight line. The stripe in the middle of the handle was never used by Case (this was probably done to take the place of a shield and because large pearl slabs of handle material are difficult to get). Cold stamped. Blades are stainless steel. Pull on master blade is too far forward for tested period. (See photo G).

The blades and shield have been changed on this knife. (Notice the space around the upper left-hand corner of the shield. The replacement was

glued in). The stag is like new and the blades are stainless steel. Clip blade is the wrong shape and the pull is too wide. (See photo H).

The handles on this doctor's knife are new candy-stripe material, the blade stang has been shaved and restamped, and the metal is new. Donated to the National Knife Museum by Curtis Turner of Georgia. (See photo I).

This is a copy of Tested 6488 with bone handles and counterfeit stamp—stainless steel blades. Blades have been ground to fit backsprings, and the bone and jigging are from a relatively new knife. It appears that no part of the knife was made by Case and even the shield is counterfeit. (See photo J).

Copy of a XX5392. Stamp is cold stamped and

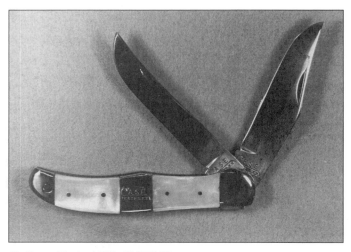

G. Case Tested XX; 8265SAB.

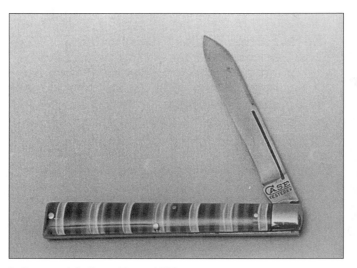

I. Counterfeit Case Tested XX.

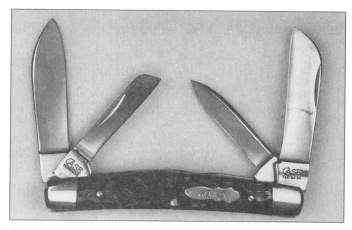

J. Congress four-blade.

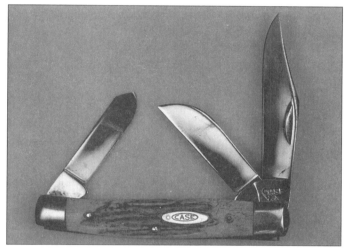

K. Three-blade Stockman.

counterfeit (note the different size letters and Xs). The stag is not original for XX era and appears to be artificially aged. (See photo K).

Copy of a R165 tested with Christmas Tree handles. When compared to the real thing, the frame is about 1/16" shorter and narrower. Christmas Tree han-

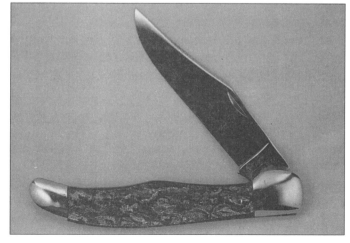

L. Folding hunter.

M. Five-blade Case stag.

dles are old original material, which means the knife was probably a Kabar or Queen pattern. The blade is one of the counterfeit flat blades made some time after 1950. The stamp appears to be good, which means this knife would fool many collectors. (See photo L).

This counterfeit was intended to be a very rare XX 5547. To begin with, Case never made a five-blade 47 pattern. The number stamped on the back of the master blade is 5347. The 3 indicates that blade came from a three-blade knife. Everything else seems to be original Case parts. The craftsman of this knife added an additional backspring and two more blades. A close inspection of the backspring indicates the knife has definitely been taken apart and reassembled. (See photo M).

This was intended to be a Case Tested 9151, but the stamp is counterfeit. The blade is stainless steel shaped wrong for a 51 pattern. The swedges and thumb pull are not correct. The frame is shorter than a 51 pattern and the bolsters are not the correct lengths. The handles, intended to be cracked ice or imitation pearl, are cheap plastic. The handles have been glued on (note there are rivets in the handle material). The blade has also been ground to fit the backspring. (See photo N).

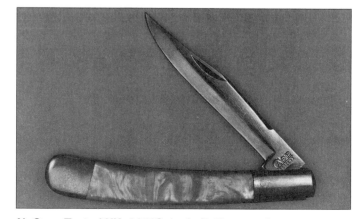

N. Case Tested XX; 9151Sab., imitation pearl.

HANDLE MATERIALS
and
DESCRIPTIONS

Appaloosa—brown and light colored spots (smooth bone)

Black bone—smooth bone dyed black

Birdseye—not a handle material, but refers to large rivets on handle

Bone—shin bone of cattle

Bone stag—same as bone with different jigging

Brass—brass metal

Brown bone—dyed bone

Buffalo horn—can be horn from any animal

Burnt orange—brownish orange delrin

Buttermilk—two-color cream celluloid

Candy stripe—red and white stripe celluloid

Celluloid—man-made material (translucent appearance)

Christmas Tree—celluloid of mingled red, green and black

Cocobolo—hard wood

Composition—man-made material, dull (solid appearance)

Cracked ice—off-color white (appearance of frosted window)

Delrin—man made plastic, petro base

Ebony—ebony wood

Engine turned silver—metal with uniform knurl lines

Genuine pearl—mother of pearl shell

Genuine stag—antlers of deer

Gold—self explanatory, 14K, 12K, 10K and plated

Gold stone—gold glitter celluloid

Green bone—bone dyed shades of green

High art—photos under clear celluloid

Horn—horn from various animals

Imitation ivory—composition resembling ivory

Imitation onyx—yellowish marble appearance

Imitation pearl—man-made white composition

Ivory—animal tusk

Jigged bone—machine notched bone

Laminated wood—layers of wood pressed together

Marine pearl—imitation pearl

Mother of pearl—same as genuine pearl

Mottled—mingled colors

Multi-color—many colors in stripes or mingled, comp.

Nickel silver—self explanatory, also known as German silver

Pakkawood—man made, pressed-wood appearance

Peachseed—jigging on bone appears pitted like a peach seed

Pyralin—man made, petro base such as celluloids

Pyremite—same as pyralin

Red bone—bone dyed various shades of red

Red stag—stag dyed various shades of red

Redwood—wood from redwood tree

Rogers bone—bone processed by the Rogers Co.; dark to brilliant red, also green, brown; heavier than most bones

Early type—brown tan or yellow color; late type—reddish brown to bright red

Rough black—man made plastic "PLASTAG"-1940

Saw cut—bone or comp. has been sawn and left marks

Scales—anything used as handle materials

Second-cut stag—pieces of stag with little or no character or grooves that have been specially jigged and dyed to give the material a stronger stag appearance

Slick black—man-made composition

Smoked pearl—dark bluish gray in either genuine pearl or imitation pearl

Smooth bone—self explanatory

Stag—same as genuine stag

Staglon—imitation stag

Stained bone—dyed bone

Stainless steel—self explanatory

Sterling silver—self explanatory

Tortoise—actual tortoise shell; illegal to use now

Tortoise (celluloid)—imitation of actual tortoise shell

Walnut—wood of walnut tree

Waterfall—translucent material that resembles a waterfall as knife is rotated

Winterbottom bone—bone processed by Winterbottom Co.

Wire—knife frames made from #9 wire

Wood—various wood, walnut, ebony, redwood, maple, etc.

GLOSSARY

Bail (shackle)—metal ring attached to the bolster so the knife can be put on a key ring or tied to a belt

Drilled—hole drilled in bolster in order to put a lanyard through

Jigging—machine notching

Lanyard—cord or line (usually braided)

Pull—thumbnail groove on blade for opening (regular pull or long pull)

Rockwell hardness test—a diamond cone being impressed into metal; the deeper the penetration, the softer the metal

Scale—another term for man-made handle materials

Serrated—saw toothed edge

Shackle—see bail

Shadow—no bolsters

Springer—spring operated (switchblade)

Zipper—switchblade with square release button set into handle

PATTERN NAMES ENCOUNTERED THROUGHOUT THIS GUIDE

Baby Copperhead
Banana
Bark Loosener
Barlow
Bartender's
Birdseye—large rivets on handle
Bowtie
Butterbean
Canoe
Carpenter's
Cattle
Citrus—melon tester
Coke Bottle
Congress
Copperhead
Daddy Barlow
Doctor's (Phys.)
Dog Leg Jack
Easy Opener
Elephant's Toe—also Sun Fish
Equal End
Fish Scaler
Fisherman's
Florist's Knife
Folding Hunter

Grafting
Greenskeeper
Gunboat
Gunstock
Half Hawkbill
Half Whittler
Hammerhead
Hawkbill
Hobo
Humpback
Jack
Leg
Lineman's
Lobster
Maize
Mako
Moose
Muskrat
Navy
Office
One Arm Man
Peanut
Press Button—switch blade
Pruner
Riggers

Rope
Senator
Serpentine
Shark's Tooth
Shroud Cutter (Paratrooper's)
Sleeveboard
Sod Buster
Sowbelly
Stabber
Stockman
Sun Fish—also Elephant Toe,
    Toenail
Swell Center
Swell End Jack
Timberscribe
Toledo Scale
Toothpick
Trapper
Utility—Camp or Scout
Whaler
Wharncliffe
Whittler—master blade folds
    between two other blades

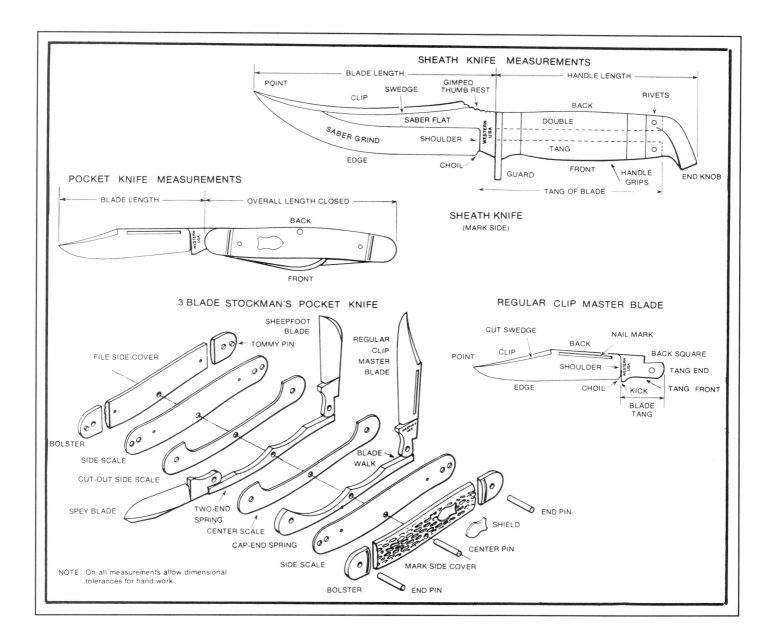

SHEATH KNIFE MEASUREMENTS

POINT — BLADE LENGTH — HANDLE LENGTH
CLIP — SWEDGE — GIMPED THUMB REST — BACK — RIVETS
SABER FLAT — DOUBLE
SABER GRIND — SHOULDER — WESTERN USA — TANG
EDGE — CHOIL — GUARD — FRONT — HANDLE GRIPS — END KNOB
TANG OF BLADE

SHEATH KNIFE
(MARK SIDE)

POCKET KNIFE MEASUREMENTS

BLADE LENGTH — OVERALL LENGTH CLOSED
BACK
WESTERN USA
FRONT

3 BLADE STOCKMAN'S POCKET KNIFE

SHEEPFOOT BLADE
TOMMY PIN
FILE SIDE COVER
REGULAR CLIP MASTER BLADE
BOLSTER
SIDE SCALE
CUT-OUT SIDE SCALE
SPEY BLADE
BLADE WALK
TWO-END SPRING
CENTER SCALE
CAP-END SPRING
SIDE SCALE
END PIN
SHIELD
CENTER PIN
MARK SIDE COVER
BOLSTER
END PIN

REGULAR CLIP MASTER BLADE

CUT SWEDGE — NAIL MARK
POINT — CLIP — BACK — BACK SQUARE
SHOULDER — WESTERN USA — TANG END
EDGE — CHOIL — KICK — TANG FRONT
BLADE TANG

NOTE: On all measurements allow dimensional tolerances for hand work.

BLADE STYLES

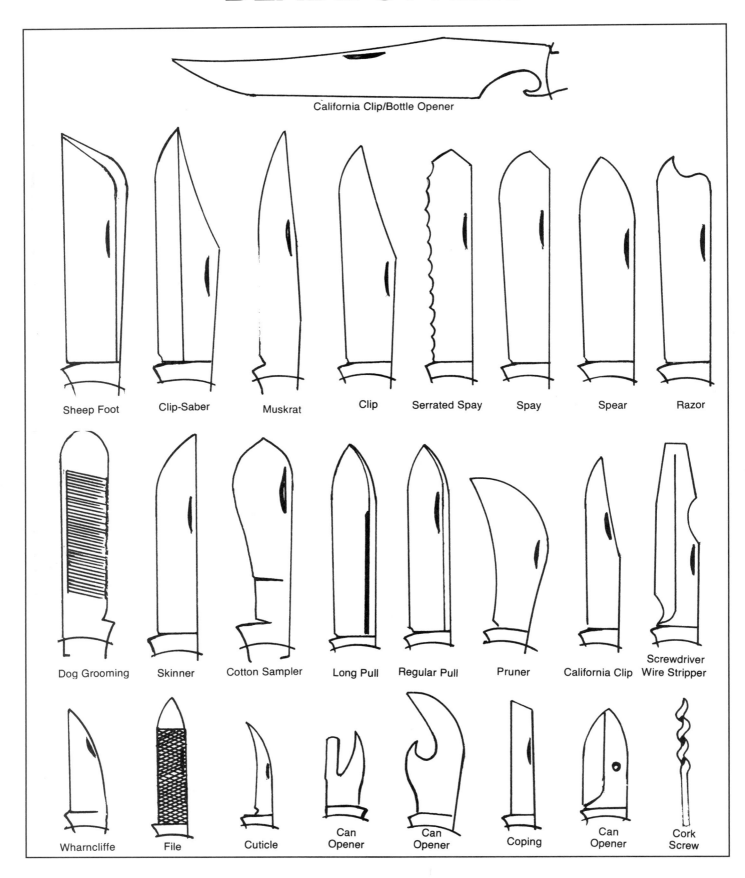

California Clip/Bottle Opener

Sheep Foot Clip-Saber Muskrat Clip Serrated Spay Spay Spear Razor

Dog Grooming Skinner Cotton Sampler Long Pull Regular Pull Pruner California Clip Screwdriver Wire Stripper

Wharncliffe File Cuticle Can Opener Can Opener Coping Can Opener Cork Screw

BLADE STYLES

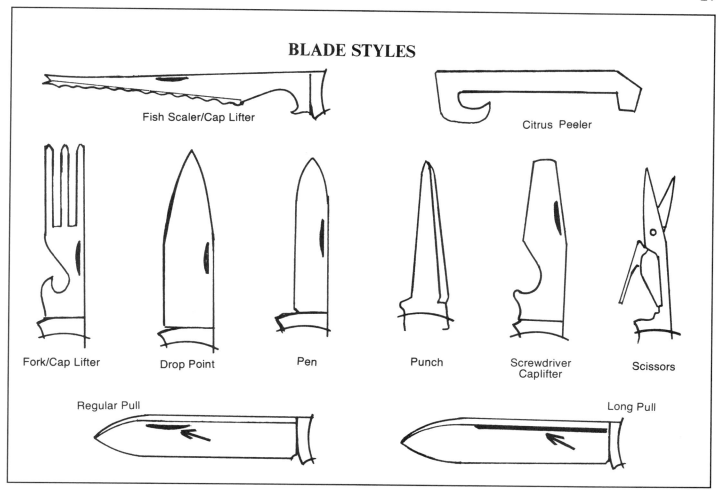

Fish Scaler/Cap Lifter

Citrus Peeler

Fork/Cap Lifter Drop Point Pen Punch Screwdriver Caplifter Scissors

Regular Pull Long Pull

COMMON ABBREVIATIONS and SYMBOLS

1/2	master blade is clip blade
B	budding
B&G	budding & grafting
EO	easy opener
F	file
J	long spay blade
K	corkscrew
L	lock back
LP	long pull
LR	electrician's knife
M	metal
P	pakkawood
PEN	pen blade
PU	punch blade

R	bail in handle (shackle)
R	candy stripe
RAZ	razor blade (one arm man)
RM	Christmas tree or red mottled
S	sterling silver
SAB	Saber blade
SCI	scissors
SH	sheep-foot blade
SHAC	shackle (bail)
SHAD	no bolsters
SP	spay blade
SSP	stainless steel, polished blade edge
SS	stainless steel
T	tip bolsters

CASE NUMBERING SYSTEM

First digit denotes the handle material.
Second digit tells the number of blades.
Last two digits are the factory pattern numbers.
An "O" at the first or the third digit indicates a variation
  in that particular knife; for example, 06263S.S. or 62048SP.

Number and Letters of Handle Material

1	Walnut	B	Imitation onyx, waterfall
2	Black composition (slick black)	RM	Red mottled or Christmas tree
3	Yellow composition	BM&H	Brown mottled
4	White composition	CI	Cracked ice (imitation pearl)
5	Genuine stag, second-cut stag, red stag, white stag	G	Green bone, green delrin
		GS	Gold stone celluloid
6	Bone, green bone, red bone, delrin, laminated wood, rough black Rogers bone, Appaloosa	HA	High art
		IV	Imitation ivory
7	Tortoise, imitation tortoise, curly maple (1970s)	SS	Stainless steel
		W	Wire
8	Genuine pearl	GPY	Variety of celluloid colors
9	Imitation pearl (cracked ice)	SR	Smooth rose bone
A	Appaloosa	SG	Smooth green bone

Case Blade Types

PEN	Pen blade	J	Long spay blade
RAZ	Razor (one arm man blade)	L	Locks open
K	Cork screw	EO	Easy open
PU	Punch blade	K	Cap lifter or bartender's knife
CC	Concave ground	SCIS or SC	Scissors
SAB	Saber ground		
SP	Spay blade	LP	Long pull
B&G	Budding and grafting blade	DG	Dog grooming
SH	Sheep-foot blade	SKW	Skate wrench
1/2	Master blade is clip style	SER	Serrated edge
F	File blade	FK	Fork

Miscellaneous Abbreviations

BOLS	Bolsters	SHAD	No Bolster or S
R	Bail in handle	SSP	Stainless blades and springs with polished blade edge
DR	Bolsters drilled		
T	Tip bolsters	SB	Spring blade

Stamping Positions Help Date Bulldogs

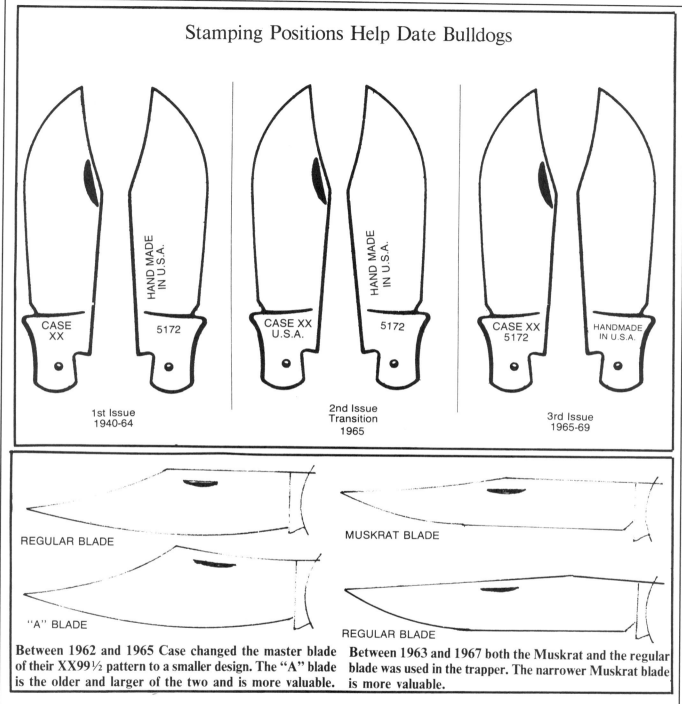

1st Issue
1940-64

2nd Issue
Transition
1965

3rd Issue
1965-69

REGULAR BLADE

"A" BLADE

MUSKRAT BLADE

REGULAR BLADE

Between 1962 and 1965 Case changed the master blade of their XX99½ pattern to a smaller design. The "A" blade is the older and larger of the two and is more valuable.

Between 1963 and 1967 both the Muskrat and the regular blade was used in the trapper. The narrower Muskrat blade is more valuable.

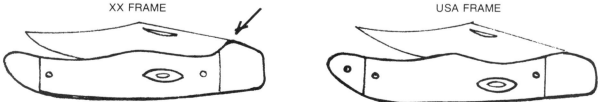

XX FRAME

USA FRAME

1965 brought a change in the Folding Hunter. The XX frame has a larger front bolster that has a more pronounced curve where it joins the handle on top. The XX frame was last used in 1964 and the lower bolster was drilled for a lanyard in only the 1964 knife. The USA frame took over in 1965 and the drilling for a lanyard is standard. (See page 61 for more illustrations.) In the mid 80's Case stopped drilling the lanyard holes again.

CASE STAMPINGS

Used until 1915

Used until 1915

**CASE'S
BRADFORD**
Used until 1920

**W.R. CASE & SONS
CUTLERY CO
BRADFORD, PA**
Used until 1920

**CASE & SON'S
BRADFORD
PA**
Used until 1920

CASE XX
Used until 1920

**CASE
BRADFORD
PA.**
Used until 1920

**STANDARD
KNIFE CO**
1920-23

1920-40

1920-40

1920-40

TESTED XX
1920-40

25¢
1935-40

50¢
1935-40

**CASE XX
METAL STAMPINGS
LT.D.**
1942-45

1947-52

**CASE'S
TESTED XX**
1940-50

**CASE
XX**
1940-64

**CASE XX
STAINLESS**
1950-64

**CASE XX
U.S.A.**
1965-69

**CASE XX
STAINLESS
U.S.A.**
1965-69

**CASE XX
U.S.A.**
· · · · · · · · · ·
1970-79

**CASE XX
STAINLESS
U.S.A.**
· · · · · · · · · ·
1970-79

CASE XX
· · · · · · · · ·
U.S.A.
Used from 1980
(Lightning S)

CASE XX
· · · · SS · · · ·
U.S.A.
Used from 1980
(Lightening S Stainless)

**CASE XX
BRADFORD, PA.**
19 U S A 91

U.S.A.
· · · · · · ·
1993

EXPLANATION OF CASE "DOT" SYSTEM

In 1970 Case began stamping the tang with 10 Dots underneath the U.S.A. and for each year thereafter, a dot was eliminated until 1979 had only 1 Dot. In 1980 they went back to 10 Dots but with the "lightning S". The Dots are between "Case XX and U.S.A." Again, a Dot is omitted for each new year.   * Beware of Case 75¢ & 1.00 knives, never made.

W.R. CASE & SONS CUTLERY CO.
ALGONGUIN
BRADFORD, PA. U.S.A.
(Clippers Stamp)

CASE BROS. & CO.
GOWANDA N.Y.

Ca. 1896

L. V. KNIFE ASSN.
LITTLE VALLEY
N.Y.
1900

CASE MFG. CO.
LITTLE VALLEY
N.Y.

circa early 1900's

W R CASE
&
SONS
MADE IN USA

1900-1903

W R CASE
&
SONS
MADE IN U.S.A.
1900-1910

W.R. CASE & SONS
GERMANY
1900-1915

W. R. CASE
& SON
BRADFORD PA
1902-1905

W.R. CASE
& SON
LITTLE VALLEY
N.Y.
1902-1905

W R CASE & SON
CUTLERY
CO
1902-1905

C. PLATTS & SONS
ELDRED, PA.
1904

J. D. CASE
CO.
KANE, PA
c. 1905-1910

CASE
KANE, PA.
1907-1909

KANE CUTLERY
CO.
KANE, PA
1907-1909

KANE CUTLERY
CO.
1909

W R CASE & SON
Little Valley, NY
c. 1910

CASE BROS.
CUT.
CO.
1912

W R CASE
& SONS
BRADFORD, PA

1916-1920
Military Stamp Used WWI

XX
1940-1946

CASE STAMPINGS

```
W.R. CASE & SONS
   CUTLERY CO.          FRONT
  BRADFORD, PA.


 GS197 SOLINGEN          BACK
    GERMANY
```

1989. This stamp can be found on four different knife patterns, 1,000 of which were made in four different handle materials. These knives were made on contract for Jim Parker in 1989. These knives can easily be identified by looking on the rear side of the tang. You will find the pattern number and the words, "Soligen Germany."

```
    CASE
  BRADFORD, PA.
   19 USA 90
```

1990-1996. In 1990, Jim Parker first introduced an exclusive line of knives called "Case Classics." These knives were authorized under a licensing agreement with Case. Blue Grass Cutlery actually manufactured most of these knives on contract. However, four of the patterns were made by Case. They were the 54 Trapper pattern, the 94 Gunboat pattern, the four-bladed 88 Congress pattern, and the two-bladed 52100 Saddlehorn pattern. Each of these knives has the date stamped on the tang. This is the "Case Bradford" version. Smoky Mountain Knife Works has a special agreement to continue production of the Case Classics 6340 pattern during 1997 through 1999.

```
    CASE
   19XX94
```

c. 1993-1996. This is the "Case XX" Case Classics stamping.

c. 1994 ONLY. This is the "Case $1.00" version. (Case Classics).

```
CASE XX
BRADFORD, PA.
 19USA91
```

c. 1990-1993. For the first four years (1990-93), Case stamped its knives this way. Each year the two numbers on the right were changed.

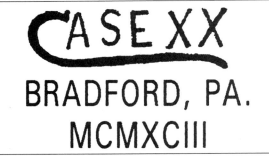

c. 1993. This stamp uses Roman numerals to indicate the year the knife was made. This stamp was used on special-order knives for a period of two or three years.

c. 1993-present. In late 1993, Case returned to

the dot dating system, removing one dot each year. This knife is a six-dot; thus, it was made in 1994. A few patterns may have been stamped with this stamp as early as 1990.

CASE XX
USA
XX CHANGER

1996-present. This stamp is used today for the "Changer" series, which has a handle with interchangeable blades.

CASE XX
USA
61549 L SS

1997-present. This is the current stamp used for patterns with lock-back blades like 51225Lss. When the Copperlock (51549LSS) was introduced in 1997, Case made what was termed a "mistake." The initial stamp was made to indicate a lock-back blade, which it has. However, the intent was to have the standard stamp on this knife. So the first blades were used and now the standard stamp will be used on blades put in the Copperlock produced in the future. This is just one example of the many variations which have occurred throughout Case's history. Several years from now, one version of the Copperlock stamp will be worth more than the other, depending on how many of each were made.

M. S. L^{TD} XX

c. 1948-1952. In 1948, W.R. Case & Sons, at the request of the Canadian government, purchased the PICTOU Cutlery Company in Pictou, Nova Scotia. Case changed the name to R. Case & Sons LTD.

CASE XX
METAL STAMPINGS
LT.D.

c. 1948-1952. This is another version of the stamp. Both are difficult to find in the U.S.

CASE XX
U.S.A.

c. 1965-1969. Many "USA"-era knives can be found in mint condition today.

c. 1920-1940. This stamp is similar to the previous one, but the "E" turns outward on the far right side.

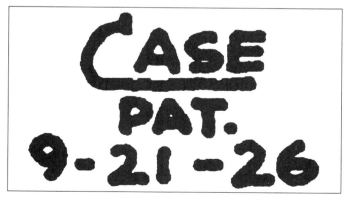

c. 1920s. This stamp is on a wire knife which was patented by another manufacturer and was probably made on contract.

c. 1920-1940. This stamp is sometimes called a "circus" stamp. Note the box-like "C." It was not commonly used, but a few patterns have been seen with this stamp.

c. 1916-1920. I have only seen this stamp on one pattern. It is a two-bladed goldstone senator pattern. It has a unique "S" shield for stainless. The back of the master blade also has a "U.S." stamped on it. All but one of the half-dozen or so I have seen have both blades broken about halfway up. This probably means they were some type of contract knives that were returned and never sold.

c. 1932-1940. This stamp is generally on large folding hunters and Coke-bottle patterns. This is a very rare version. Most have "TESTED XX" under the word "Case."

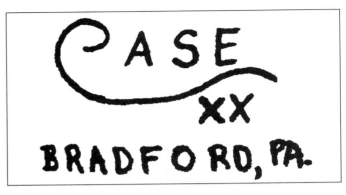

c. 1932-1940. This stamp is also used on larger knives in most situations. This knife is a switch-

blade. There are similar stamps, but note the bottom of the "C." This is where the difference is.

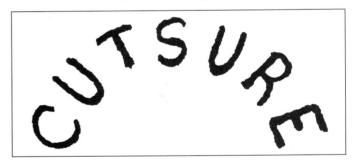

c. 1930s. This is a stamp found only on scissors.

PRIMBLE
BELKNAP

c. 1930s. Case made this contract knife for Primble. It is C61050 pattern with greenbone handles.

c. 1920s. CUTSURE was a brand name used by Kruse & Bahlmann Hardware Company, in business from 1894-1962. Case made some of its patterns on contract. This particular knife is a 6214 pattern with greenbone handles.

WHITE
HOUSE

c. 1920s. White House was a brand used by McWhorter-Weaver Hardware in Nashville, TN in the early '20s. Case made many of its knives on contract. This stamp is on a celluloid-handled barlow.

c. 1920s. Winchester contracted with Case in the late '20s to manufacture a one- and two-bladed 91-pattern (large sleeveboard). These knives have green-bone handles.

c. 1915-1940. Case made many knives for Clauss in Freemont, OH. They generally have greenbone handles and are identical to Case knives except for the shield, tang stamp, and unique pattern numbers which are usually stamped on the back of the master blade tang.

c. 1925-1948. This stamp is frequently found on fixed-blade knives, as well as pocket knives.

c. 1925-1948. This is another version which has the word "Incorporated" instead of "U.S.A."

c. 1925-1948. Here you see a slightly different version which has neither "Incorporated nor "U.S.A." under "Kinfolks."

STANDARD KNIFE CO 2

c. 1925-1948. A few of the Standard stamps have the number "2" under the words "Knife Co." No documentation exists to explain this variation. However, it is a much rarer version of the stamp.

STANDARD KNIFE CO.

c. 1925-1948. This version of the stamp has all the words in a straight line and is less common than the two-line version.

STANDARD

c. 1925-1948. Some fixed-blade knives are stamped with the single word "STANDARD." Generally STANDARD knives were made to be a less expensive line than Case knives. The shields are slick, but if you take the shield off a STANDARD knife, it will usually have CASE on the reverse side. It was not uncommon to simply reverse CASE shields for the STANDARD brand.

CASE KNIFE NAMES and PATTERNS

Over the years, a number of knife patterns have been given names by manufacturers and collectors. Listed here are some of the more common names and their pattern.

Barlow	62009	Hobo	6251 FK
Bean	62131	Lady's Leg	R297
Bird's Eye	33044	Little Copperhead	62109X
Boss	P172L	Lobster	83090 SR
Bow Tie	61051	Mako	P158L
Buffalo	P172	Melon Tester	4100 SS
Bull Dog	5172	Mini Trapper	6207 SP
Canoe	62131	Moose	6275 SP
Cheetah	5111-1/2L	Muskrat	Muskrat
Citrus Knife	6296X	One Arm Man	6205 RAZ
Coke Bottle	6225-1/2	Peanut	6220
Big Coke Bottle	C61050	Riggers Knife	6246R
Congress	6488	Rope Knife	6250
Copperhead	6249	Scout	6445R
Cotton Sampler	1119	Shark's Tooth	P179L
Daddy Barlow	6143	Sidewinder	Sidewinder
Doctor's Knife	6185	Sleeve Board	82079-1/2
Easy Opener	3199 EO	Sod Buster	2138
Elephant's Toe Nail	6250	Sow Belly	G3039
Fisherman's Knife	32095F	Sunfish	6250
Folding Hunter	6265	Texas Jack	6292
Green's Kepper	4247K	Texas Toothpick	61095
Gun Boat	53131	Trapper	6254
Gunstock	6215	Viet Nam	6249
Half Hawk Bill	6217	Whaler	1199 SH R
Hawk Bill	61011	Wharncliffe	32051
Hammer Head	P159L	Whittler	6308

ALLIANCE OF LOCAL KNIFE CLUBS

Membership in the Alliance of Local Knife Clubs is free; just send the name, address and phone number of your club representative to G. T. Williams, 4499 Muddy Ford Road, Georgetown, KY 40324-9280.

If you would like to start a local club, contact the Alliance of Local Knife Clubs for a free starter package: 4499 Muddy Ford Road, Georgetown, KY 40324-9280.

If your club is inadvertently omitted or is a newly formed club, please notify the author and it will be included in future editions.

ALABAMA

Heart of Dixie Cutlery Club
1436 Timberland Dr. SE
Cullman, AL 35055

Wheeler Basin Knife Club
P.O. Box 346
Hartselle, AL 35640
(205) 773-4257
Rep: Bill Carroll

ARIZONA

Arizona Knife Collectors
14822 S. Gilbert Rd.
Gilbert, AZ 85296
(602) 812-8529
Rep: Tom Bryan

CALIFORNIA

Southern California Blades
23204 Falena Ave.
Torrance, CA 90501
(310) 326-3869
Rep: Lowell Shelhart

COLORADO

Rocky Mtn. Blade Collectors
P.O. Box 324
Westminster, CO 80230
(303) 426-9004
Rep: Fred Clark

FLORIDA

Deep South Knife Collectors
P.O. Box 9001
Pensacola, FL 32513
(904) 477-2202
Rep: Robert Lewis

Florida Knife Collectors
5321 Holden Road
Coca, FL 32927
(407) 636-1876
Rep: Louie Prothman

Fort Meyers Knife Club
P.O. Box 706
St. James City, FL 33956
(813) 543-3473
Rep: Stanley Thomas

GEORGIA

Chattahoochee Cutlery Club
P.O. Box 568
Tucker, GA 30084
(770) 963-6406
Rep: Michael Cowart

Ocmulgee Knife Collectors Club
RT 27 Box 185
Macon, GA 31211
(912) 746-3181
Rep: Joseph P. Wilson

Three Rivers Knife Club
783 NE Jones Mill Road
Rome, GA 30165
(706) 234-2540
Rep: Jimmy Green

IDAHO

Miniature Knifemakers Society
1900 W. Quinn #153
Pocatello, ID 83202
Rep: Terry Kranning

ILLINOIS

American Edge Collectors Association
P.O. Box 2565
Country Club Hills, IL 60478
Rep: Mike Kightly
(630-759-0749)

Bunker Hill Knife Club
RR2
Bunker Hill, IL 62014
(618) 278-4356
Rep: Cecil M. Turner

INDIANA

Indiana Knife Collectors
RR #3 Box 348
Alexandria, IN 46001
(317) 754-7082
Rep: Gordon Kinnaman

IOWA

Hawkeye Knife Collectors
628 Washington St.
Madrid, IA 50156
(515) 266-0910

KANSAS

Kansas Knife Collectors Association
P.O. Box 1125
Wichita, KS 67201
(316) 838-0540
Rep: Bill Davis

KENTUCKY

Central Kentucky Knife Club
4499 Muddy Ford Road
Georgetown, KY 40324-9280
(502) 863-4919
Rep: G. T. Williams

Kentucky Cutlery Association
4914 Bluebird Ave.
Louisville, KY 40213
(502) 933-2737
Rep: Alden Gibbons

MARYLAND

Chesapeake Bay Knife Club
939-I Beards Hill Road #122
Aberdeen, MD 21001
(410) 272-2959
Rep: Glenn Paul Smit

MASSACHUSETTS

Northeast Cutlery Collectors
P.O. Box 624
Mansfield, MA 02048
(508) 226-5157
Rep: Cindy Taylor

MICHIGAN

Jackson Area Knife Collectors
575 Lantern Circle
Hanover, MI 49214
(517) 565-8002
Reps: Joe and Joann Russ

Marble Plus Knife Club
P.O. Box 228
Gladstone, MI 49837-0228
(906) 428-9180
Rep: Mack McDonald
Mid-Michigan Knife Club
212 McDonald St.
Midland, MI 48640
(517) 636-2626

Rep: Greg Moe

Wolverine Knife Collectors Club
14543 Yale Ct.
Sterling Heights, MI 48313
(313) 247-5883
Rep: Pat Donovan

MINNESOTA

North Star Blade Collectors
P.O. Box 20532
Bloomington, MN 55420
(507) 287-9254
Rep: Richard Gustafson

MISSOURI

Gateway Area Knife Club
#5 Cedar Park
Florissant, MO 63031
(314) 839-3895
Rep: John Brown

NEW YORK

Empire Knife Club
1203 E. 98th St.
Brooklyn, NY 11236
(718) 763-0391
Rep: Jan Muchnikoff

NORTH CAROLINA

Bechtler Mint Knife Club
P.O. Box 149
Rutherfordton, NC 28139
Rep: Larry Lattimore (704 287-5432)

Tar Heel Cutlery Club
2730 Tudor Rd.
Winston Salem, NC 27106
(919) 725-1016
Rep: Clyde Ranson

OHIO

Fort City Knife Collectors Club
P.O. Box 18686
Fairfield, OH 45018-0686
(513) 574-0899
Rep: Bob Wurzelbacher

Johnny Appleseed Knife Collectors
668 Lenox Ave.
Mansfield, OH 44906
(419) 747-7551
Rep: James Webb

Western Reserve Cutlery Assoc.
P.O. Box 355
Dover, OH 44622
Rep: Glenn Graham

OREGON

Oregon Knife Collectors
P.O. Box 2091
Eugene, OR 97402
(514) 484-5564
Rep: Dennis Ellingen

PENNSYLVANIA

Allegheny Mtn. Knife Collectors
P.O. Box 23
Hunker, PA 15639
(412) 925-2713
Rep: Don States

Case Collectors Club
P.O. Box 4000
Bradford, PA 16701
(800) 523-6350
Rep: Jean Cabisca

Keystone Blade Association
P.O. Box 46
Lewisburg, PA 17837
(717) 966-9209

Mason-Dixon Knife Club
914 Hykes Rd.
Greencastle, PA 17225
(717)-597-8511
Rep: Ralph Scruton

SOUTH CAROLINA

Palmetto Cutlery Club
P.O. Box 1356
Greer, SC 29652
(803) 578-3533
Rep: Johnny Perry

TENNESSEE

Fight'n Rooster Cutlery Club
Box 936
Lebanon, TN 37087

Memphis Knife Collectors Club
1439 Elmgrove
Burlison, TN 38015
(901) 476-3834
Rep: Wayne Koons

North East Tennessee Knife Club
P.O. Box 562
Kingsport, TN 37660
Rep: Bobby Beuris

Soddy Daisy Knife Collectors
Box 1224
Soddy Daisy, TN 37379
(423) 842-3794
Rep: Fred Rohr

TEXAS

Gulf Coast Knife Club
P.O. Box 265
Pasadena, TX 77501
(281) 479-3072
Rep: Mike Moeskau
Permain Basin Knife Club
4309 Roosevelt

Midland, TX 79703
(915) 682-8683
Rep: Fred Nolley

Texas Knife Collectors Assoc.
P.O. Box 4754
Austin, TX 78765-4754
(512) 837-2590
Rep: Tommy Nolley

VIRGINIA

Northern Virginia Knife Collectors
Box 501
Falls Church, VA 22040
(703) 790-1960

Old Dominion Knife Collectors
4236 Lakeridge Circle
Troutsville, VA 24175
(703)-977-0242
Rep: John Riddle

Shenandoah Valley Knife Collectors
P.O. Box 924
Harrisburg, VA 22801
(703) 833-2047
Rep: Wes Shrader

WISCONSIN

Badger Knife Club
P.O. Box 511
Elm Grove, WI 53122
(414) 479-9765
Rep: Robert G. Schrap

CASE CUTLERY HISTORY

The Case family's interest in the cutlery business goes well beyond the present facilities located in Bradford, Pa. It all started back in the late 1800s, with six of the nine children of Job Russell Case and Deborah Milks Case: Theresa, Emma, Jean, John, Andrew, and William Russell, better known as W.R. Job Russell Case was never involved with the cutlery business. He was a horse trader, farmer, and freighter. It was these six children who first introduced the cutlery business into the case family.

It is not known for sure how the Case family became interested in the cutlery business, but Theresa may have been the first of the children to become associated with the industry. Sometime in the late 1800s, Theresa married J.B.F. Champlin, who was a cutlery salesman at the time. The Champlins had a son and later, around 1882, they formed J.B.F. Champlin & Sons Cutlery Company in Little Valley, N.Y. About four years later, and still in Little Valley, J.B.F. Champlin & Sons Cutlery Company and the four Case brothers mentioned above joined Cattaraugus Cutlery Company.

The only one of the six children mentioned who did not become directly involved with the family cutlery business was Emma. However, Emma Case married John W. Brown and their son, Wallace, and grandson, Dansforth Brown, were connected with Union Cutlery and later Kabar.

While on the topic of companies related to the Case family, there is another one that should be mentioned. Jean Case had a daughter, Addie May, who married William Burrell and had a son, Dean. Dean later went on to form Burrell Cutlery Co. in Ellicottville, N.Y.

W.R. Case had three children: Debbie, J. Russell, and Theresa. Debbie and J. Russell went to work for Cattaraugus Cutlery Company. Theresa married Herbert Crandall, founder of Crandall Cutlery Company, which was located in Bradford, Pa. Around the turn of the century.

While at Cattaraugus Cutlery, Debbie married H.N. Platts, son of Charles W. Platts who emigrated from England in the 1860s. Charles Platts learned the cutlery business in Sheffield, England, and after coming to this country traveled through New England before coming to New York state. H.N. Platts, with his wife Debbie and the rest of the Platts family formed C. Platts & Sons Cutlery Company in 1896. This company was first located in Gowanda, N.Y., but later moved to Eldred, Pa. During the same time (1896), Jean, John, and Andrew Case left Cattaraugus Cutlery Company and formed Case Brothers Cutlery Co., also located in Little Valley. It is reported that when Case Brothers Cutlery Co. first began, it purchased its knives from C. Platts & Sons Cutlery Co. in Gowanda. This would account for the "Case Brothers and Co. Gowanda NY" found on some older Case knives. Soon after the Case brothers formed their own company, J. Russell Case (son of W.R.) left Cattaraugus Cutlery Co. and joined his uncles as a salesman for Case Brothers Cutlery Co.

Around 1903, J. Russell left Case Brothers Cutlery Co. and, backed by his father, formed W.R. Case and Sons Cutlery Co. in Little Valley. J. Russell used a photograph of himself and his father and grandfather on all company literature and advertising. This gave the new company a three-generation image that helped the company to compete with the larger, more established, businesses of the day.

After a couple of years of prosperous business, W.R. Case and Son Cutlery outgrew its rented facilities in Little Valley and moved to Bradford, Pa. in 1904. After it moved to Bradford, the company merged with

C. Platts & Sons Cutlery Co. and became W.R. Case & Sons Cutlery Co., which was incorporated in 1905. Around 1911, H.N. Platts left W.R. Case & Sons and moved to Colorado.

After H.N. Platts left, Crandall Cutlery Co. joined W.R. Case & Sons. Herbert Crandall, Theresa Case's husband, was W.R. Case's son-in-law, so they were still keeping it in the family.

It was around 1911 that W.R. Case acquired the equipment and trademark from Case Brothers in Little Valley. A few years earlier, Case Brothers was destroyed by fire. Even though the company rebuilt in Springville, N.Y., it never recovered the status it once had. It was also at this time that Case Brothers Cutlery Co. ceased to exist. Therefore, W.R. Case & Sons was able to produce its knives with the famous "XX" trademark.

Also around 1911, after Case Brothers went out of business in Little Valley, Jean Case formed Jean Case Cutlery Company in Kane, Pa. This company was in business for several years before selling out to the Hollingsworth family.

W.R. Case & Sons Cutlery Co. was first located on Bank Street in Bradford. Under the leadership of J. Russell Case, the company continued to prosper and finally outgrew its facilities. In 1929, Case moved to its location on Russell Boulevard. The coincidence of the Case Company move and the Stock Market Crash still prompts quips and chuckles today.

Even though the Depression that started in 1929 brought despair and ruination to many companies, W.R. Case & Sons survived. It did so by staying with its commitment to produce a quality knife, yet at a price the average man could afford. These were the years of the 10-, 15- and 25-cent knife. These prices were actually incorporated into the tang stamping. When the country finally started to pull itself out of the Depression, W.R. Case & Sons acquired the equipment to produce household cutlery and in 1936, patented Concave Ground Household Knives. It was also in 1936 that Case bought the Genco Company, manufacturers of straight razors. Also around this time, Adolph Hitler was beginning to mount his offenses on Eastern Europe. By the early 1940s, Case' reputation for quality had grown tremendously—to the extent the U.S. government came directly to the company to manufacture fighting and survival knives for the military without putting the project up for competitive bidding.

In May 1944, W.R. Case & Sons Cutlery Co. and E. W. Smiley of Sturgis, MI purchased the Schaaf and Good Company, manufacturers of scissors and shears. From this purchase, they formed Case-Smiley Corporation, located in Fremont, Ohio. In 1949, Smiley sold his interest to Case and the company changed its name to Case Shear Corporation. In 1952, Case Shear Corp. leased a newly built factory building in Nashville, Arkansas. By 1953, Case Shear Corp. moved to Nashville and the Fremont plant was sold. After several years, Case Shear Corp. purchased the building and remains there today.

In 1952, Case set up a corporation in Nashville named Case-Nashville. It took a lease on a modest building and began manufacturing Case pocket knives. This corporation continued producing pocket knives until 1975 when the pocket knife plant was built in Bradford. At the end of 1975, Case-Nashville Corp. was absorbed and became part of the W.R. Case & Sons Cutlery Co.

In 1941, representatives of Wear-ever pots and pans, a subsidiary of Alcoa, approached W.R. Case & Sons to discuss having it produce a nine-piece cutlery set under the Wear-ever brand. They were to be sold to housewives at demonstration dinners in conjunction with Wear-ever pots and pans. The proposal was agreed upon and soon after, Case received an order for 40,000 sets. This operation had just begun when the attack on Pearl Harbor occurred and within weeks it had to be abandoned to permit rapidly increasing production for the war effort.

In 1945, shortly after the war, Wear-ever and Case met to review the proposal. The original sets had sold so readily and the rapidly increasing demand for Case's own products plainly indicated Case did not have enough capacity. After reviewing several alternatives, Case and Alcoa decided to form a separate corporation, in 1948, for the production of these sets. After reviewing several locations, Olean, N.Y. was selected as the site for the new company, named Alcas Cutlery, a combination of Alcoa and Case. Case sold its interest in the company in 1972. However, Alcas still operates today, subcontracting for other manufacturers.

A busy year for Case was 1948. It was in that year that J. Russell Case and John O'Kain were approached by the minister of trade and industry for the Province of Nova Scotia, Canada. The minister proposed that Case could try to salvage a cutlery company in Picton, Nova Scotia. That same day, Mr. O'Kain was told to accompany the minister back to Nova Scotia and set up a new company called W.R. Case & Sons of Canada Ltd.

An inspection of the plant was a disaster, with most of the equipment being antiquated and outmoded. However, Case decided to give it a go. Unfortunately, the company was short lived. Aside from the facilities, Case was faced with another problem. Lobster fishing was a big business in that area and for three months out of the year, employees expected to go out on the lobster boats. Consequently, it was decided to return the plant to the province and dissolve the corporation.

When J. Russell Case died in 1953, he was succeeded by O'Kain, who had joined the company in 1940. His wife, Rhea, was J. Russell's niece. Previous to her marriage to O'Kain, Rhea was married to Harold Osborne, a salesman for Case until his death.

In 1972, John O'Kain retired and W.R. Case & Sons Cutlery Co. was purchased by American Brands Inc. It was also in 1972 that J. Russell Osborne, great nephew of J. Russell Case and Rhea O'Kain's son, became operating head of the company.

Through the years, Case's reputation for quality continued to grow. By the early 1970s, the demand for Case products grew to such proportions, the company was only able to fill a fraction of its orders. With American Brands as its new parent company, Case was able to expand to meet this demand. In 1975, a new pocket knife manufacturing facility was built in South Bradford on Owens Way and all pocket-knife operations were relocated there. It was also in 1975 that J. Russell Osborne died. Upon his untimely death, R.N. Farquharson, V.P. sales, assumed leadership of the company, a position he held until his retirement in 1981.

Chronology

The "Case" name has been a standard bearer in the cutlery industry for more than 90 years. Although there are many cutlery related businesses to carry the "Case" name, Case Brothers and W.R. Case and Sons are the pivotal corporation and all others seem to revolve around them. A popular misconception among collectors of both knives and razors is that "Case Brothers" was the parent company of W.R. Case and Sons. In truth, they were two competing cutlery manufacturers, and for periods of time unfriendly rivals.

Case Brothers Cutler Co.

1881-86: John D. Case Co. Little Valley, N.Y. John D. Case awarded patent for his butterfly razor on Feb. 8, 1881.

1886-87: Jean, John and Andrew Case were involved with Cattaraugus Cutlery Co., Little Valley, N.Y.

1890-1900: Case Bros.; Wholesalers of Cutlery, Spring Green, CO.

1896: John, Jean and Andrew Case form Case Brothers Cut. Co. in Little Valley, N.Y. (jobbers)

1900: Case Brothers Cutlery Co. incorporated in Little Valley, N.Y. (manufacturing company)

1901: Elliot and Dean Case left Case Brothers to form Standard Knife Co., Little Valley, N.Y.

1902: J. Russell Case leaves Case Brothers

1903: Standard Knife Company went out of business

1907: Case Brothers open a second factory in Kane, PA

1909: Andrew J. Case leaves Case Brothers to join Union Cutlery Co.

Case Brothers purchased the Smethport Cutlery Company in Smethport, PA

Case Brothers Kane, PA reorganized under the name Kane Cutlery Co.

Smethport factory burns to the ground in June 1909

1910-11: Case Brothers build new factory in Warren, PA to replace Smethport works.

1912: Case Brothers Cutlery Co., Little Valley, NY burns to the ground

On March 27, 1912, Case Brothers Cutlery Co. reach an agreement to rebuild in Springville, NY

1913: Case Brothers, Springville, NY goes into operation

1914: Late 1914 Case Brothers Cutlery Co. unable to recover from two devastating fires (Smethport, PA & Little Valley, NY) goes out of business. Oct. 21, 1914, Case Brothers Cutlery Co. sells its trademark "Tested XX" to W.R. Case and Sons

W.R. Case and Sons

1900: Little Valley Knife Ass'n. incorporated in Little Valley, NY. (H. Crandall, jobber)

1902: J. Russell Case forms W.R. Case and Son in Little Valley, NY (jobber)

1904: Late 1904, H.N. Platts in an agreement to form merger with W.R. Case & Son.

H.N. Platts purchases his brothers' shares of C. Platts Sons Cutlery Co., Eldred, PA

1905: C. Platt's Sons and W.R. Case and Son are merged to form W.R. Case and Sons, Bradford, PA Crandall Cutlery Co. incorporated as a manufacturing company in Bradford, PA (formerly Little Valley Knife Association)

1907-09: Plaits Brothers Cutlery Co., Andover, NY (in operation for less than 2 years)

1911: H.N. Plaits leaves W.R. Case and Sons to form Western States Cutlery Co., Boulder, CO. The actual separation of the two companies took several years to complete (1911-1914)

1912: W.R. Case and Sons acquire Crandall Cutlery Co. of Bradford, PA

1914: W.R. Case and Sons first acquire "Tested XX" trademark from Case Brothers Cutlery Co.

1915: W.R. Case and Sons first use of "Tested XX" trademark. During this period (1914-20) W.R. Case and Sons reorganize their entire product line due to World War I and the departure of H.N, Platts

1917: Start of World War I

1920: W.R. Case and Sons "Tested XX" line in full production

Case introduces a second (less expensive) line under the Standard Knife Co., Bradford, PA mark

1923: W.R. Case end use of Standard Knife mark 1926 Kinfolks incorporated in Little Valley, NY (Kinfolks razors are manufactured by W.R. Case and Sons)

1936: W.R. Case and Sons acquire razor stocks and trademark of Genco corporation

1940: W.R. Case change their line stamping to "Case XX" (full implementation is delayed for several years due to World War II)

1941: Start of World War II

1942: Although Case has been cutting back on razor production since the mid-1930s, in January 1942, W.R. Case effectively ended razor production (relying on existing stocks and razors acquired from Genco) and begin tooling up for the war effort

1945: World War II ends

1955: Case introduces a new line of razors to replace exhausted stocks (marked "Made in USA by Case") (approx. 1955-60) Kinfolks Incorporated, Little Valley, NY goes out of business

Case Cutlery Works, Bradford, PA

Case Bros. Cutlery Works, Springville, NY

1962: W.R. Case manufactures the genuine mother-of pearl "CASE ACE" as mementos for its officers and salesmen; W.R. Case and Sons formally ended 57 years of straight razor production

1965: W.R. Case changes product line marking to "Case XX USA"

1970: Case changes product line marking to the Dot system

1972: W.R. Case and Sons sold to American Brands Inc.

1980: Case changes product line marking to lightning SS with Dots system

1988: American Brands sold W.R. Case & Sons to James F. Parker, Chattanooga, TN.

1990: W.R. Case & Sons was sold to River associates, Inc., of Chattanooga, TN.

1990: Case changes product line marketings to W.R. Case & Sons, Bradford USA, PA, and the year.

1993: W. R. Case & Sons was sold to Zippo Mfg. Co. of Bradford, PA.

1993: W.R. Case & Sons changed the product line to a long tail C, USA Dots underneath

Case-American Made

Knife collecting is perhaps the fastest-growing hobby in America. It provides plenty of enjoyment, as well as being an excellent investment for the future.

Of the thousands of knives collected, and the undisputed manufacturing behind them, the W.R. Case & Sons Cutlery Company has more dedicated followers than any other company. Case continues to produce fine quality cutlery items today.

In my opinion, a carefully assembled collection of selected Case knives will continue to grow in value year after year. Many Case knives that have sold for $100 a year or two ago, have doubled or tripled in value. The demand for older knives is a definite reality. I felt that collectors needed a realistic price guide to judge the current value of their knives. This guide contains carefully prepared prices that reflect the current market and scarcity of many Case knife patterns.

Knife collecting is a very personal hobby, where each individual can select his or her specialty. There are Case collectors who search for certain patterns, such as trappers, whittlers, canoes, muskrats, peanuts, folding hunters, etc. Some collect certain handle materials such as stag, bone, pearl, yellow, rough black, green bone, etc. Many collect certain blade stampings, such as Case Tested, Case XX, Case XX USA, Case XX USA 10 Dots, etc. And, of course, there are the collectors who want any knife as long as it has a case marking. Regardless of your desires for a case specialty, you will find willing buyers, sellers, and traders at any knife show.

I have endeavored to give each knife a fair market price for the knife in 100 percent mint condition.

If your preference is for used knives, you will have to use your own judgment as to a fair value. As a general rule, used knives bring between 25 percent to 50 percent of this book's value. Make no mistake about it: used knives can have considerable value, but for a sound investment, it is more desirable to collect only mint Case knives. Knives that have exceptionally beautiful handles in bone and stag will bring a premium price that is usually $5 to $20 more than the book price.

Remember to take excellent care of your collection, as you are the curator during your lifetime for future generations to enjoy. Moisture and finger prints are the prime villains to avoid. Check your collection periodically and keep your knives in a dry location. Make an asserted effort to wipe your knives at least once a month. You can very quickly have a sizable amount of money invested in your collection and just as quickly lose money if you allow your knives to deteriorate from lack of care and maintenance.

Beyond the shadow of a doubt, the best teacher and lessons for learning about Case knives are to attend as many knife shows as possible. Most dealers and collectors are very patient about explaining the many variations and subtleties that make some knives rarer than others. The more knives you examine, the more familiar you will become with them. This experience will also make it easier to spot counterfeits or altered knives. If you are just starting out, take the time to mostly look and talk, rather than buy. Don't start out hoping to collect every Case knife, as it would be virtually impossible. Set your goals at a more realistic level such as one particular pattern, a certain type of handle or one particular blade stamping. A collection with a theme or direction will be easier to sell than one that is simply a conglomeration of everything.

Above all, when you reach the point where you are purchasing knives costing hundreds of dollars, make sure that you buy only from reputable dealers who will stand behind the authenticity of the knife. Beware of a bargain, as in all probability, you are being taken. As in any hobby, there are always those unscrupulous few who will make a fast dollar in any way they can. Many counterfeiters are very good and only an expert can tell. Simply be as careful as you can and familiarize yourself with Case manufacturing methods and details.

In any event, get your feet wet at a knife show: look, ask questions, read books and articles, become a Case knife collector, and join thousands of us who enjoy this great hobby. It is advisable to join the National Knife Collectors Association as well as any of the many local and individual knife clubs throughout the country. The Case Company has its own "Case Collectors Club" for those of us who will collect nothing else. Its newsletter contains valuable information on both new and old Case knives.

All prices listed are for knives in mint condition.

Case Bros., Little Valley, NY, Tested XX, rare Cotton Sampler.

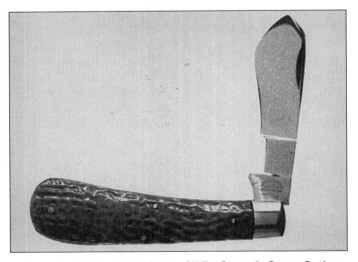

Cotton Sampler, green bone, W.R. Case & Sons Cutlery, Bradford, PA., rare. Photo courtesy Walter Nelson.

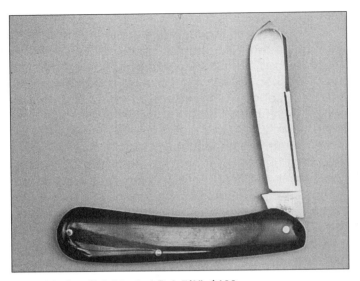

Spay blade, slick black, LP, 3-5/8", $160.

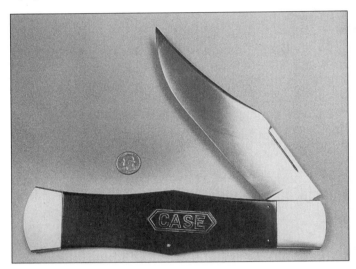

Display knife, approx. 500 made (note size in relation to quarter), $1,000.

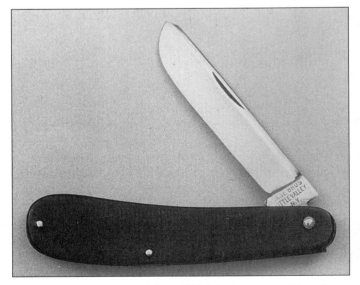

Case Brothers, Little Valley, NY, black composition (castrating knife), 3-1/2", $200.

M100, Red Cracked Ice, 3-1/4", XX, $130.

M100, All Metal, 3-1/4", XX, $110.

B100, imitation onyx, 1920-40, Tested XX.......... 160
B100, Christmas tree, 1920-40, Tested XX 250
G100, celluloid, 1920-40, Tested XX 160
M100, metal, 3-1/4", 1920-40, Tested XX 130
M100, blue celluloid, 3-1/4", 1920-40,
   Tested XX 160
M100, cracked ice, 3-1/4", 1920-40, Tested XX.. 140
M100, green bone, 3-1/4", 1920-40, Tested XX.. 175
M100, gold, 3-1/4", 1940-64, XX 175
P100, asst. celluloid, 1910-40, Tested XX 175
M101R, metal, 2-7/8", 1920-40, Tested XX 125

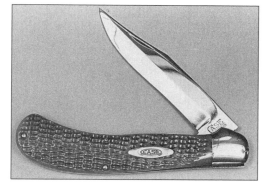

6100SAB, green bone, 4-1/2", Tested XX, $800.

3100, yellow comp., 4-1/2", 1920-40,
   Tested XX 700
4100SS, white comp., 5-1/2", 1965-69, USA...... 125
4100SS, white comp., 5-1/2", 1970, 10 Dot........ 140
4100SS, white comp., 5-1/2", 1970, 10 Dot,
   serrated edge, rare 600

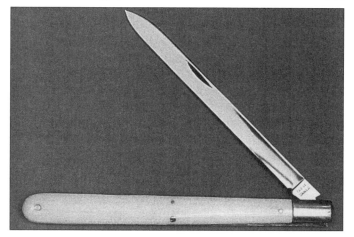

4100SS, Melon Tester or Citrus, White Comp., 5-1/2", XX, $75. Has both small stamp and large stamp, each $75.

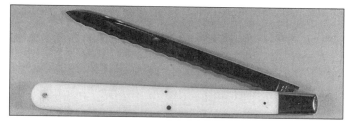

4100SS, White Comp., 5-1/2", 1965-1969, U.S.A., serrated edge, $400.

2103SP, slick black, 3-1/4", 1920-40,
   Tested XX 325
3103SP, yellow comp., 3-1/4", 1920-40,
   Tested XX 325

6001, Green bone, 4-3/4", W.R. Case & Sons, Bradford, PA, $700. Not shown: W.R. Case & Sons, (same knife in Rogers Bone, $800); GS001, W.R. Case & Sons, (same knife, with gold stone handles, $700.)

4103B&G, white comp., 3-1/4", 1920-40,
   Tested XX 325
5103SP, stag, 3-1/4", 1920-40, Tested XX.......... 500
6103B&G, green bone, 3-1/4", 1920-40,
   Tested XX 500
7103SP, tortoise, 3-1/4", Tested XX.................... 500
8103SP, pearl, 3-1/4", Tested XX........................ 600
6104B, green bone, 3-3/8", 1920-40,
   Tested XX 350
6104B, bone, 3-3/8", 1940-55, XX...................... 275
61005, green bone, 3-3/8", 1920-40, Tested
   XX, bolsters stamped..................................... 450

Top: 61005-1/2, green bone, 3-1/8", bolsters stamped, 1920-40, Tested XX; $500. Bottom: 61005, Rogers bone, 3-3/8", bolster stamped, 1915-20, Case Bradford, Pa.; $500.

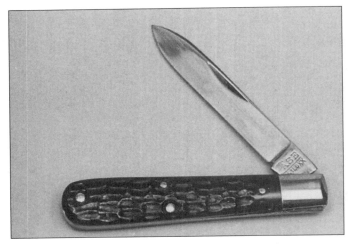

6106, Green Bone, 2-5/8", 1920-40, Tested XX, $250.

6106, green bone, 2-5/8", 1920-40,
Tested XX, 25-cent knife 500
7106, tortoise shell, 2-5/8", 1920-40,
Tested XX 260

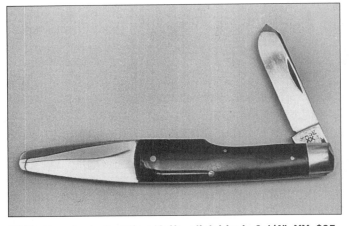

2109, Gunstock, Budding Knife, slick black, 3-1/4", XX, $95.

2109B, slick black, 3-1/4", 1920-40, Tested XX .. 125

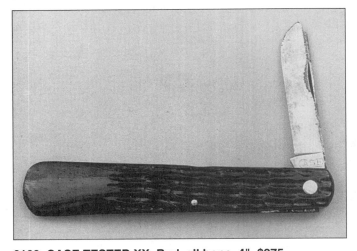

6109, CASE TESTED XX, Bud, all bone, 4", $275.

6109B, bone, 3-1/4", 1920-40, Tested XX 260

2109B, slick black, 3-1/4", 1965-69, USA........... 100

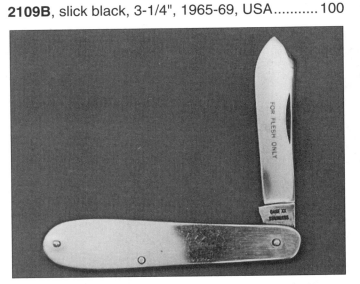

M110, all metal, spay blade, stainless, 3-1/8", XX, $110.

M110, metal spay, 3-1/8", 1920-40, Tested XX ... 135
6110SP, spay or budding knife, imitation
bone, 3-1/8", 1920-40, Tested XX 225

91210-1/2, switchblade, onyx, 3-3/8", Tested XX, $500.

91210-1/2, cracked ice, 3-3/8", 1920-40,
Tested XX 500
11011, walnut, 4", 1920-40, Tested XX 110

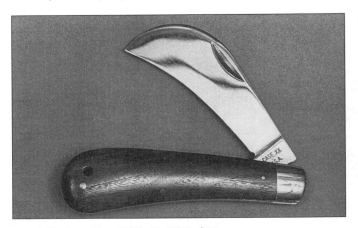

11011, Walnut Hawkbill, 4", USA, $35.

61011, green bone, 4", 1920-40, Tested XX 200
61011, Rogers bone, 4", 1920-40, Tested XX 225
11011, walnut, 4", 1940-64, XX 60
61011, green bone, 4", 1940-55, XX 175
61011, red bone, 4", 1940-64, XX 150
61011, laminated wood, 1940-55, XX 125
61011, bone stag, 1940-64, XX 100
61011, laminated wood, 1965-69, USA 40
61011, bone stag, 1965-69, USA 125
11011, walnut, 1970, 10 Dot 40

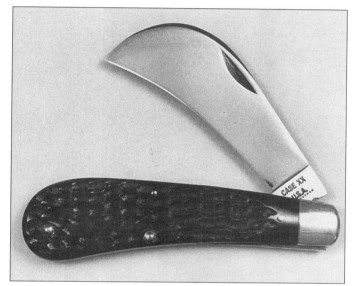

61011, Hawkbill, jigged wood scales, 4", 10 Dot, $35.

H1211-1/2, mottled comp., 4", 1920-40,
Tested XX, switch blade 750
31211-1/2, yellow comp., 4", 1920-40,
Tested XX, switch blade 700

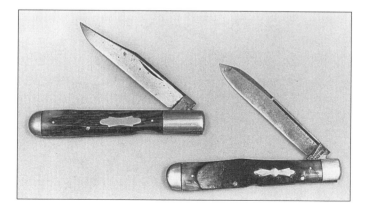

Left: 5111-1/2, Stag, 4-3/8", Case Bros., Little Valley, $1,200.
Bottom: 5111L, Stag, long pull, 4-3/8", W.R. Case & Son, Bradford, PA; $1,200.

3111-1/2, yellow comp., rare, 1920-40,
Tested XX 750
6111L, fine bone jig, spear, 4-1/2",
Case & Son 900

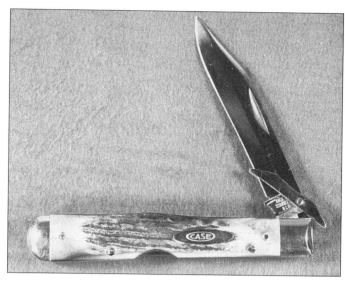

5111-1/2L, Gen. Stag, saber blade, 4-7/16", 1970, 10 Dot, $1,250.

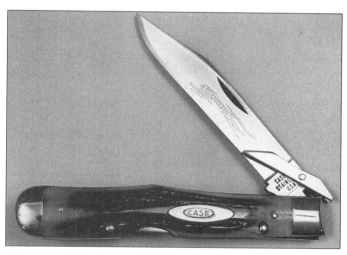

5111-1/2 LSSP, Cheetah, lockback, Genuine Stag, 4-7/16", large or small stamp, $325.

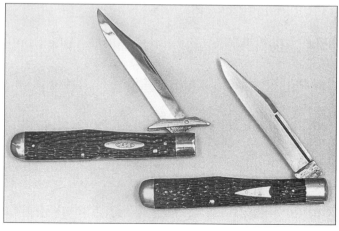

Left: 6111-1/2L, Green Bone, 4-3/8", Tested XX, $1,000.
Bottom: 6111-1/2, Green Bone L.P., 4-3/8", Case's Bradford, Pa., $1,000.

6111-1/2L, green bone, 4-3/8", 1920-40,
    Tested XX 700

6111-1/2LP, green bone, 1920-40,
    Tested XX 1,200

6111-1/2, green bone, 1940-55, XX................. 1,000

6111-1/2L, green bone, 1940-55, XX............... 1,000

6111-1/2L, bone, 1940-64, XX............................300

61111-1/2, bone, 1965-69, USA..........................400
    Extra 1 was factory error.

6111-1/2L, red bone, 1940-55, XX......................400

6111-1/2L, bone, 1965-69, USA 150

6111-1/2, with error: knife shows an extra 1.

R1212-1/2, switchblade, candy stripe, 4", 1920-40, Tested XX, $900. Not shown: 3121 2-1/2, Yellow Comp., 4", 1920-40, Tested XX, $800.

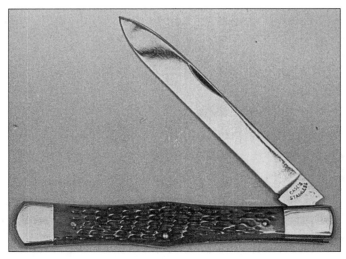

61213, Green Bone, 5-3/8", Case's Stainless, $800.

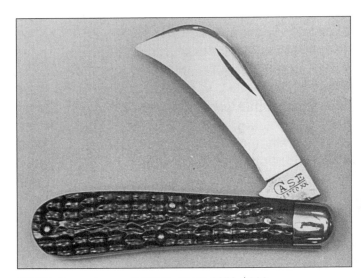

61013, Green bone, 3-9/16", Tested XX, $300.

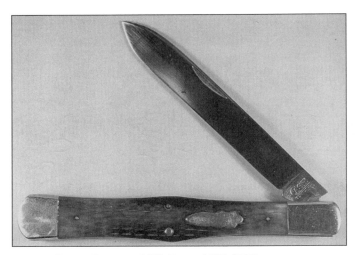

61213, Green Bone, 5-3/8", Tested XX, $750.

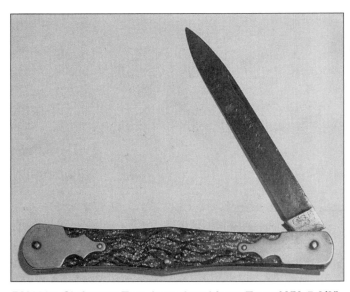

RM1213, Christmas Tree, barn door hinge, Tested XX, 5-3/8", $1,200. Photo courtesy Dave Dempsey.

5111-1/2L, stag Cheetah, rare, 1970, 10 Dot ..1,000

6111-1/2L, bone, 1970, 10 Dot 150

31213, SAB., yellow comp., 5-3/8", Tested XX...650

31213, yellow comp., spear, 5-3/8", 1920-40,
Tested XX 650

61213, green bone, 5-3/8", 1920-40,
Tested XX 750

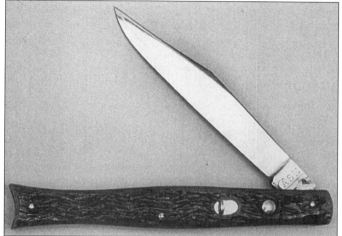

61213-1/2, Rogers bone S/B, 4", Tested XX, $1,200.

61214-1/2, bone, 4-1/8", 1920-40, Tested
XX, switch blade 1,600

51215-1/2F, stag, 5", 1920-40, Tested XX,
switch blade 2,500

51215-1/2G, stag, 5", 1920-40, Tested XX,
switch blade 2,500

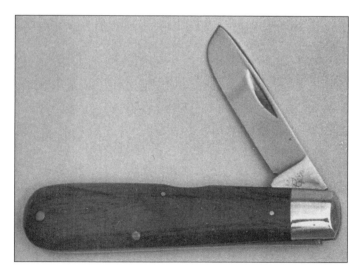

1116SP, Walnut, 3-1/2", XX, $55.

1116SP, bud walnut, 3-1/2", 1965-69, USA 35

1116SP, bud walnut, 3-1/2", 1970, 10 Dot 40

W1216K, wire, 3-1/8", 1920-40, Tested XX 150

W1216, wire pruner, 3-1/8", 1920-40,
Tested XX 150

6116, spear, green bone, 3-3/8", 1920-40,
Tested XX 225

6116SH, green bone, 3-3/8", 1920-40,
Tested XX 250

6116-1/2, Green Bone, 3-3/8", Tested XX, $150.

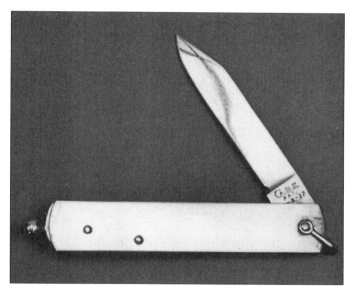

M1217, All Metal, 2-7/8", Tested XX, $300. Made for Case by Schrade (contract late 1930s).

1117SHR, walnut, 1920-40, Tested XX...............100

M1218K, metal, 3", 1920-40, Tested XX.............135

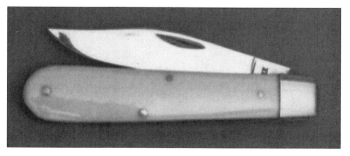

31024-1/2, Yellow, 3", XX, $60.

31024-1/2, flat yellow, 3", Tested XX 150

3124, yellow comp., 3", 1920-40, Tested XX 150

3124-1/2, yellow comp., 3", 1920-40,
Tested XX 150

6124, green bone, 3", 1920-40, Tested XX 175

6124-1/2, green bone, 3", 1920-40, Tested XX .. 175

61024, green bone, 3", 1920-40, Tested XX 175

31024, yellow comp., 3", 1920-40, Tested XX 150

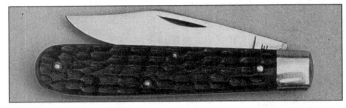

61024-1/2, Bone, 3", XX, $55.

61024-1/2, red bone, 3", XX 85

61024-1/2, bone, 3", 1965-69, USA 40

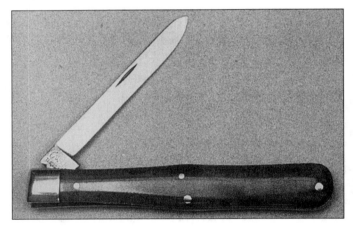

B1025, Waterfall, 3", Tested XX, $300.

7129-1/2, tortoise shell, 1920-40, Tested XX 250

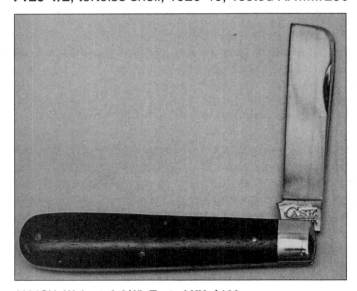

1131SH, Walnut, 3-3/4", Tested XX, $100.

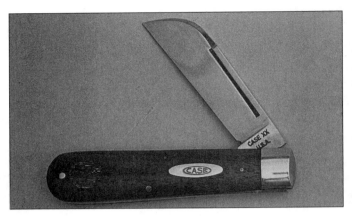

11031SH, Walnut, LP, 3-3/4", USA, $30.

1131EOSH, walnut, 3-1/16", 1920-40,
Tested XX 135

11031SH, walnut, 3-1/16", 1920-40, Tested XX .. 110

11031SH, walnut, 3-1/16", 1920-40,
Tested XX, Concave ground blade 150

11031SH, walnut, 3-1/16", 1940-64, XX 40

11031SH, walnut, 3-1/16", 1940-64, XX,
Concave ground blade 60

11031SH, walnut, 3-1/16", 1970, 10 Dot 30

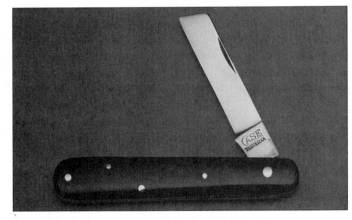

2136, Black Composition, 4-1/8", Tested XX, $160.

2136B, slick black, 4-1/8", 1940-55, XX 160

2137, black comp., 3-5/8", 10 Dot, 1970 35

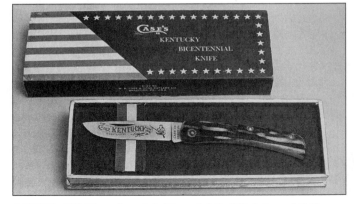

5137SS, KY. Bicentennial, Stag, 3-1/2, "Stainless," $45.

2137, Sod Buster Jr., Black Comp., 3-5/8", 7 Dot, 1983, $20.

G137, green delrin, 3-1/2" 35
P137, pakkawood, 3-1/2" 35
5137, stag, carbon, 3-1/2" 40

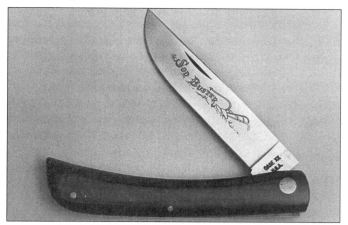

2138, Black Comp., 4-5/8", USA, $30.

2138, black comp., 5-5/8", 1970, 10 Dot 30
2138SS, black Comp., 5-5/8", 1970, 10 Dot 30
2138LSS, black comp., 5-5/8", 1970, 10 Dot 75

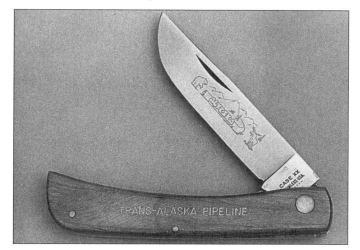

P138LSS, pakkawood, 500 made, 4-3/4", Case 5 Dot, 1975, Lockblade, Alyeska Pipeline, $175.

1139, Walnut Banana Knife, 4-1/4", Case XX, $185.

1139, walnut, 4-1/4", 1920-40, Tested XX 185

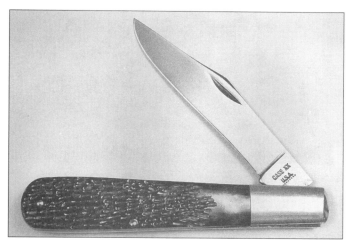

6143, proto model, jigged bone, 5", 8 Dot, 1972, $150.

6143, red fiberloid, rare, 1940-45, Tested XX 300
5143, stag handles, Case Founders 85
6143, brown bone, 5", 1920-40, Tested XX 200
6143, green bone, 5", 1920-40, Tested XX 250
6143, green bone, 5", 1940-55, XX 200
6143, jigged bone (rare), 5", 1970, 10 Dot 175

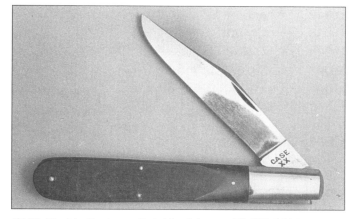

6143, Daddy Barlow, slick black bone, 5", XX, $125.

6143, red bone, 5", 1940-64, XX 110

6143, bone, 5", 1940-64, XX 85

6143, bone, 5", 1965-69, USA 55

6143, bone, 5", 1970, 10 Dot 55

RM1048, Christmas tree, 4-1/8", 1920-40, Tested XX 350

G.S. 1048, gold stone, 4-1/8", 1920-40, Tested XX 300

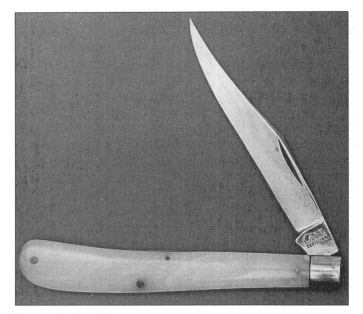

B1048, imitation onyx, 4-1/8", Tested XX, $300.

R1048, candy stripe, 4-1/8", 1920-40, Tested XX 310

31048, yellow comp., 4-1/8", 1940-64, XX 75

31048, flat yellow, 4-1/8", 1940-64, Tested XX 90

31048, yellow comp., 4-1/8", 1965-69, USA 40

31048, yellow comp., 4-1/8", 1970, 10 Dot 40

61048, green bone, 4-1/8", 1920-40, Tested XX 300

61048, Rogers bone, 4-1/8", 1920-40, Tested XX 325

61048, green bone, 4-1/8", 1940-55, XX 250

61048, red bone, 4-1/8", 1940-64, XX 125

61048, bone, 4-1/8", 1940-64, XX 85

61048, late Rogers bone, 4-1/8", 1940-64, XX ... 150

61048, delrin, 4-1/8", 1965-69, USA 30

61048, bone, 4-1/8", 1965-69, USA 55

61048SSP, bone, 4-1/8", 1965-69, USA, Stainless, polished blade 75

61048SSP, delrin, 4-1/8", 1965-69, USA, Stainless, polished edge 30

61048SSP, bone stag, 4-1/8", 1965-69, USA, blade etched "Tested XX Stainless" (1st mod.) 90

61048SSP, bone stag, 4-1/8", 1965-69, USA 75

61048, delrin, 4-1/8", 1970, 10 Dot 30

61048SSP, delrin, 4-1/8", 1970, 10 Dot, Stainless, polished edge 30

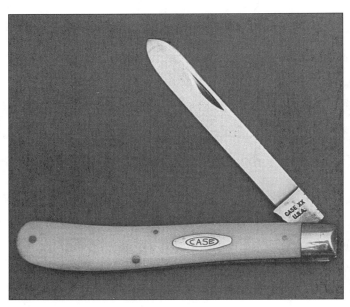

31048SP, Yellow, 4-1/8", USA, $75.

31048SP, flat yellow, 4-1/8", 1940-64, XX 95

31048SP, yellow comp., 4-1/8", 1940-64, XX 85

61048SP, green bone, 4-1/8", 1940-55, XX 350

61048SP, bone, 4-1/8", 1940-64, XX 75

61048SP, red bone, 4-1/8", 1940-64, XX 125

61048SP, Rogers bone, Late, 4-1/8", 1940-64,XX 150

61048SP, delrin, 4-1/8", 1965-69, USA 30

61048SP, bone, 4-1/8", 1965-69, USA 75

31048SP, yellow comp., 4-1/8", 1970, 10 Dot 50

61048SP, delrin, 4-1/8", 1970, 10 Dot 30

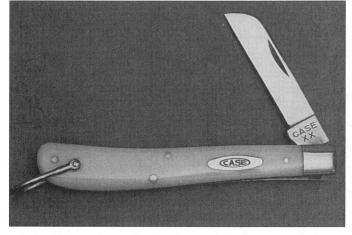

31048SH-R, florist knife, Yellow, 4-1/8", XX, $85.

61049, green bone, 4-1/16", 1920-40, Tested XX 500

61049L, Rogers bone, 4-1/16", 1920-40,
Tested XX 800
R1049, candy stripe, 4-1/16", 1920-40,
Tested XX 800
R1049L, candy stripe, 4-1/16", 1920-30,
Tested XX 1,000

GS10050, gold stone, 5-1/8", Tested XX 1,000
910050, C.I. French pearl, 5-1/8", Tested XX 550

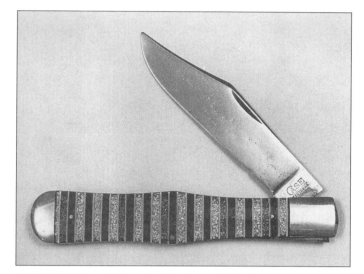

B10050, Glitter Stripe, 5-1/4", Tested XX, $1,200.

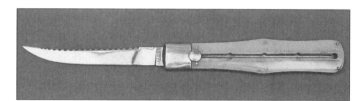

PB1050F, Push-Out, onyx, 5-3/8", Tested XX, $650.

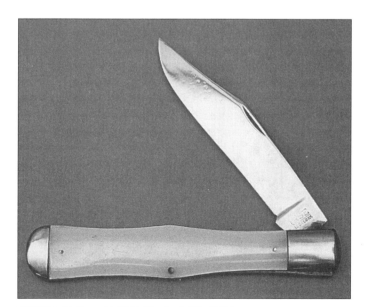

310050, Yellow, 5-1/8", Tested XX, $500.

GS10050, flat blade, goldstone, 5-1/4",
Tested XX 900

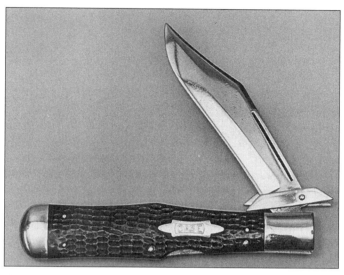

C61050L, SAB LP, Green Bone, 5-1/4", Tested XX, $2,500.

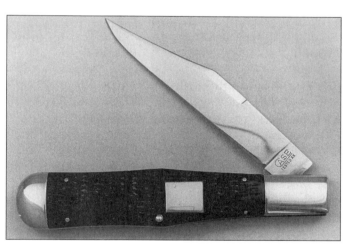

Switchblade-"Zipper Release." The knife shown is **C61050L, Bone Flat Blade, 5-1/8", 1920-40, Tested XX, $2,500.** Not shown: **C61050L, Green Bone, Rare, 5-1/8", no lower bolster, 1920-40, Tested XX, $3,500.**

RM1050SAB, Christmas tree, 5-1/8",
1920-40, Tested XX 1,000
RM1050, Christmas tree, 5-1/8", 1920-40,
Flat blade, Tested XX................................... 1,000
HA1050, high art, 5-1/8", 1920-40 1,000
PBB1050, 1920-40, Tested XX........................... 600
PB31050F, yellow celluloid, 1920-40,
Tested XX 650
C31050SAB, yellow comp., 1920-40,
Tested XX 600
C31050, yellow comp., 5-1/8", 1920-40,
Flat ground, Tested XX 600
C51050SAB, stag, 5-1/8", 1920-40,
Tested XX 1,000

C91050SAB, French pearl, 5-1/8", 1920-30,
Rare handle, Tested XX 700

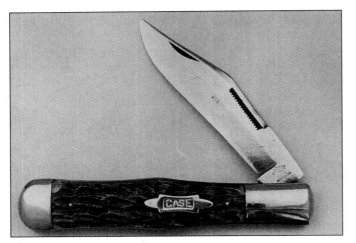

C61050, SAB, Rogers Bone, 2 Pulls, 5-1/4", W.R. CASE & SONS, Made in U.S.A., $1,200.

61050, flat blade, green bone, 5-1/8",
1920-40, Tested XX 600
610050, flat blade, green bone, 5-1/8",
1920-40, Tested XX 500
710050, flat blade, tortoise, 5-1/8", 1920-40,
Tested XX 650
C91050SAB, onyx, 5-1/8", 1920-40,
Tested XX 650
C61050SAB, green bone, 5-1/8", 1940-55,
XX, Coke Bottle 550
C61050SAB, wood, 5-1/8", 1940-64, XX,
Coke Bottle 125
C61050SAB, bone, 5-1/8", 1940-64, XX,
Coke Bottle 225
C91050, flat blade, cracked ice, 5-1/8",
1920-40, Tested XX 600

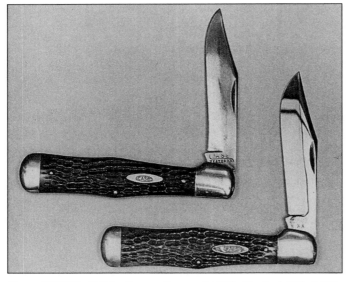

Top: C61050, SAB, Green Bone, 5-3/8", Tested XX, $450.
Bottom: C61050, SAB, Red Bone, 5-3/8", XX, $300.

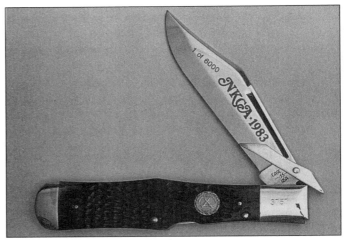

C61050L, 1983 NKCA Club Knife, SAB SS, Bone, 5-1/2, $125

C61050SAB, wood, 5-1/8", 1965-69, USA,
Coke Bottle 60
C61050SAB, bone, 5-1/8", 1965-69, USA 300
C61050SAB, wood, 5-1/8", 1970, 10 Dot,
Coke Bottle 60

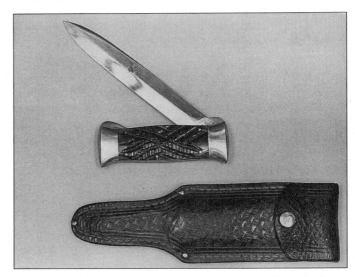

651, Green Bone w/sheath, Tested XX, $1,000. 551, Stag with sheath, Tested XX, $900. - Not Shown

M1051L, SSP, Aluminum, 3-3/4", 8 Dot, 1982, $20.

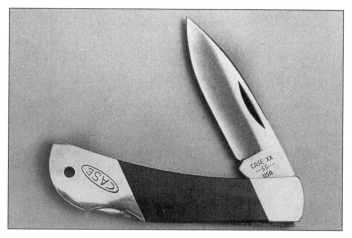

P10051L, SSP, pakkawood, Brass Bolsters, 3-3/4", $30.

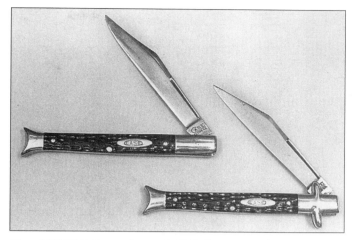

Top: 61051LP, Green bone, 3-7/8", Tested XX, $500. Bottom: 61051LP, Green bone w/guard, 3-7/8", Tested XX, $550.

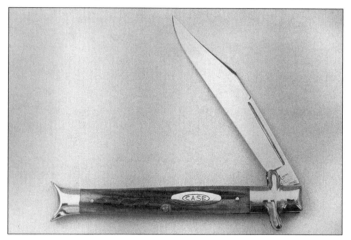

51051LP, Bow Tie, second cut stag, rare, 3-7/8", Case Tested XX, $700.

551, stag with sheath, Tested XX 900
RM1051, Christmas tree, 1029-40, Tested XX ... 500
GS1051, gold stone, 1920-40, Tested XX 450
R1051, candy stripe, Tested XX 450
81051, pearl, Tested XX 600
31051, yellow celluloid, 1920-40, Tested XX 600
R1051L, candy stripe, 1920-40, Tested XX 650

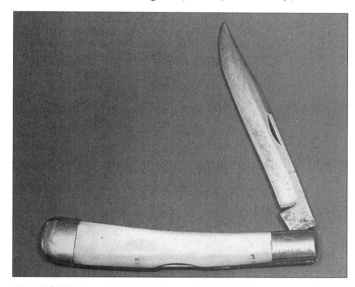

8151LSAB, Pearl, 5-1/4", Tested XX, $1,500.

8151SAB, pearl, 5-1/4", Tested XX 1,350
9151SAB, onyx, 1920-40, Tested XX 600
B151LSAB, imitation onyx, 1920-40,
    Tested XX 600
3151SAB, yellow, 1920-40, Tested XX 600

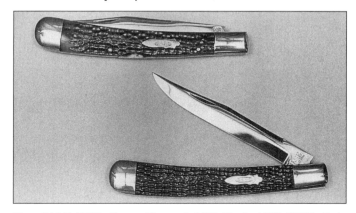

Top: 6151LSAB, Green Bone, 5-1/4", Tested XX, $800. Bottom: 6151SAB, Green Bone, 5-1/4", Tested XX, $700.

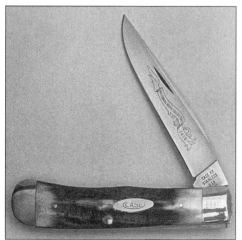

5154SSP, 1979 NKCA Trapper, stag (year knife), 4-1/8", $60.

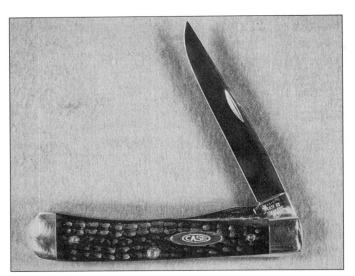

6154LSS, Muskrat blade, (proto model), rare, USA, $500. John Osborne Collection.

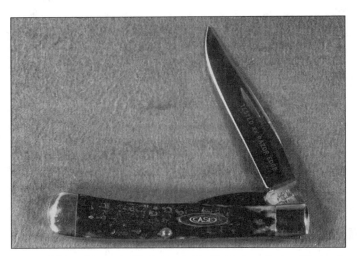

6154LSSP, Glazed Finish, 2nd Model, Blade Etched, USA, Brass Liner Lock (proto model), $500. John Osborne Collection.

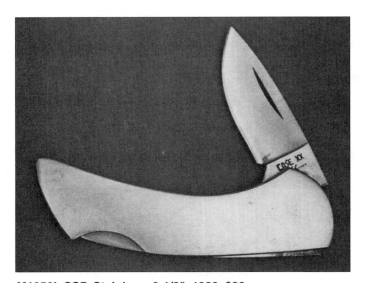

M1056L SSP, Stainless, 2-1/2", 1980, $20.

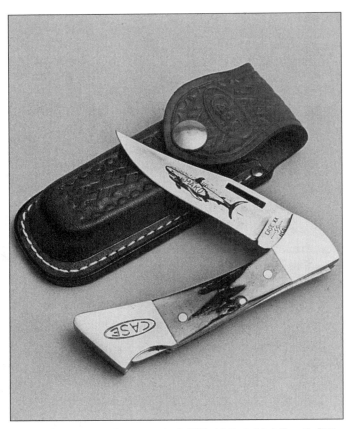

5158L, SSP, Mako, Stag, 1980, 4-1/4", 10 Dot, Lighting S, $55.

P158LSSP, pakkawood, Dots 40
P158LSSP, pakkawood, Dots 40
7158LSSP, curly maple, Dots 45

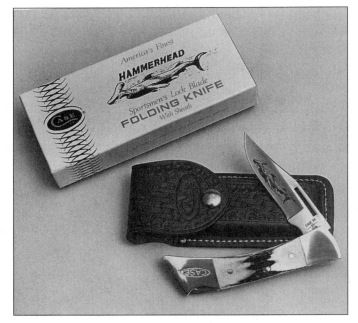

5159L, SSP, Hammerhead, Black Stag, 1980, 5", 10 Dot, Lighting S, $70.

P159LSSP, pakkawood, 5", Dots 45

2159LSSP, black comp., 5", Dots 35

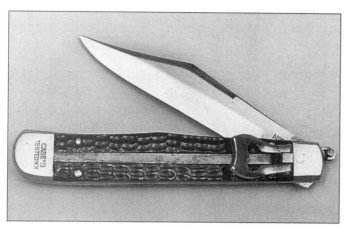

6161L, Green bone, 4-3/8", **hinge-type release, Tested XX, $2,000.**

5161LSAB, genuine stag, 4-3/8", 1920-40,
Tested XX 2,000

5161L, genuine stag, 4-3/8", 1920-40,
Flat blade, Tested XX 2,000

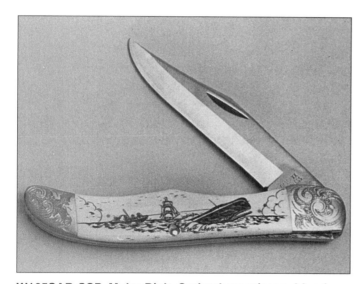

W165SAB SSP, Moby Dick, Scrimshaw w/case, blue box, 5-1/4", $150.

W165SABSSP, scrimshaw with case,
Nantucket Sleigh Ride, 5-1/4", Red Box 135

RM165, Christmas tree, 5-1/2", 1920-40,
Tested XX 1,200

GS165, gold stone, 5-1/2", 1920-40,
Tested XX 1,000

3165SAB, yellow comp., 1920-40, Tested XX 500

5165SAB, genuine stag, 1920-40, Tested XX 450

5165, genuine stag, flat blade, 1920-40,
Tested XX 500

5165, second-cut stag, flat blade, 1920-40,
Tested XX 600

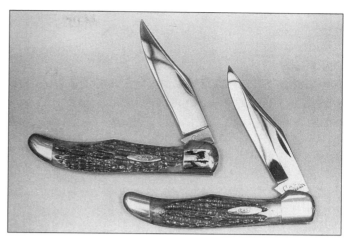

Top: 6165, 2nd Cut Bone, flat blade, 5-1/4", Tested XX, $600.
Bottom: 6165SAB, 2nd Cut bone, 5-1/4", Tested XX, $550.

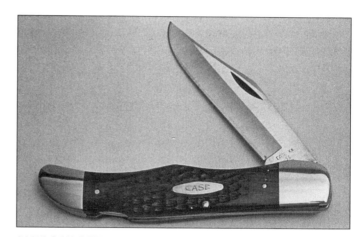

6165LSAB SSP, Wood, 5-3/4", 3 Dot, $45.

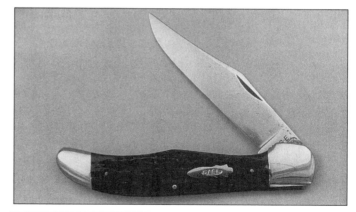

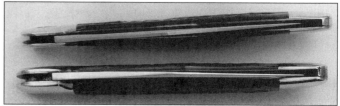

6165, Flat Blade, Green Bone, bottom photo shows thinness of knife bolsters compared to another 6165SAB Tested XX, which is considered rare; thin bolster, 5-1/4", $750.

6165SAB, green bone, 1920-40, Tested XX 500

6165, green bone, 1920-40, flat blade,
Tested XX 550

6165SAB, rough black, 1940 Tested XX 450

6165SABDR, laminated wood, 1979-80, 1 Dot 40

6165SABDR SSP lockback, laminated wood,
1979-80, 1 Dot 45

6165SABDR, laminated wood, 1978-78, 2 Dot 40

6165SABDR SSP lockback, laminated wood,
1978-79, 2 Dot 45

6165SABDR, laminated wood, 1977-78, 3 Dot 40

6165SABDR SSP lockback, laminated wood,
1977-78, 3 Dot 45

6165SABDR, laminated wood, 1976-77, 4 Dot 40

6165SABDR, laminated wood, 1975-76, 5 Dot 40

6165SABDR, laminated wood, 1974-75, 6 Dot 45

6165SABDR, laminated wood, 1973-74, 7 Dot 50

6165SABDR, laminated wood, 1972-73, 8 Dot 50

6165SABDR, laminated wood, 1971-72, 9 Dot 60

6165SABDR, laminated wood, 1970-71, 10 Dot ..75

6165SABDR, laminated wood, 1965-70,
U.S.A., small pattern number 75

6165SABDR, laminated wood, 1965-70,
U.S.A., large pattern number 75

6165SAB, laminated wood, 1965-66, U.S.A.,
XX frame, not drilled for Lanyard 85

6165SABDR, laminated wood, 1965-1966,
U.S.A., XX frame 85

6165SAB, laminated wood, 1965-66, XX 140

6165SAB, bone, 1950-65, XX, small pattern
number 175

6165SAB, bone, 1950-65, XX, large pattern
number 175

6165, red bone, 1940-60, XX, Master blade,
flat ground 400

6165SAB, bone, 1950-65, XX, worm groove 350

6165, green bone, 1940-55, XX 400

6165SAB, green bone, 1940-50, XX,
Master blade, flat ground 500

6165SAB, rough black, 1940-51, XX 350

5165SSP lock, stag, "custom made" 200

5165SABSSP, stag, 1976, 4 Dot, "American
Spirit," SN #1906 150

4165SABSSP, white composition, 1977,
3 Dot, "Texas Special," SN #1906 75

4165SAB, white composition, "custom made" 75

IV165SAB, elephant ivory, "custom made" 125

5165SAB, stag, 1949-65, XX, low pull,
Not drilled for Lanyard 175

5165SAB, stag, 1949-65, XX, low pull 175

5165SAB, stag, 1949-56, XX, high pull 225

5165, stag, 1949-55, XX, Master blade,
flat ground 450

5165, stag, 1920-40, Case XX Tested,
Master blade, flat ground, bomb shield 500

5165SAB, stag, 1920-40, Case XX Tested 450

6165, green bone, 1920-40, Case XX Tested,
Master blade, flat ground, bomb shield 500

6165SAB, green bone, 1920-40, Case
XX Tested 500

6165SAB, rough black, 1920-40, Case
XX Tested 450

3165, yellow composition, 1920-40, Case
XX Tested 450

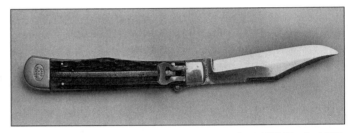

5171L, switchblade, Stag-bolster stamped, 5-3/8", Tested XX, $2,700.

5171L, genuine stag, 5-1/2", 1920-40,
Tested XX, lower bolster not stamped 2,700

6171L, green bone, 5-1/2", 1920-40,
Tested XX, lower bolster not stamped 3,000

6171L, green bone, 5-1/2", 1920-40,
Tested XX, lower-bolster stamped 3,000

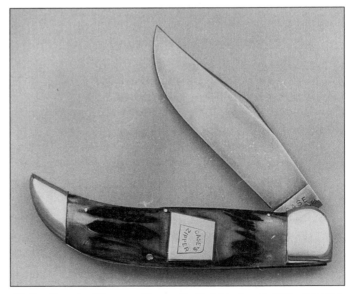

**5172, Case's Zipper, Clasp Switchblade, 5-1/2", $6,500.
6172, Case's Zipper, Clasp Switchblade, Green Bone, 5-1/2", $6,500. Not Shown.**

5172, USA Bulldog, engraved bolsters, probably a proto-type, $350. Photo courtesy Earl Howard.

5172, Stag, 5-1/2", 1965-69, USA, $200.

5172, genuine stag, 5-1/2", 1920-40,
Tested XX 1,500
5172XX, genuine stag, 5-1/2", 1940-64............. 325

P172, Buffalo, pakkawood, 5-1/2", USA, $100.

H172, mottled brown, 5-1/2", 1920-40,
Tested XX 1,500
RM172, Christmas tree, 5-1/2", 1920-40,
Tested XX 2,500
2172, slick black, 5-1/2", 1920-40,
Tested XX 1,200
3172, yellow comp., 5-1/2", 1920-40,
Tested XX 1,200
GS172, gold stone, 5-1/2", 1920-40,
Tested XX 2,100
P172, pakkawood, 5-1/2", 1970, 10 Dot was not made.
There were a few 1980 10 Dots. Dots were on top of tang backside.

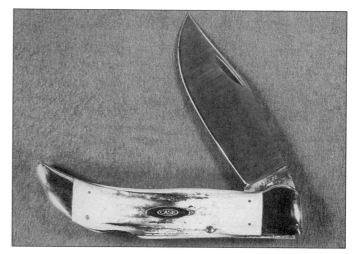

5172LSSP, No Etching, 4 Dot, 1976, $400. John Osborne Collection.

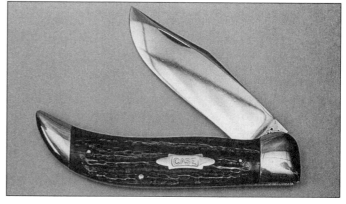

6172, Green Bone, 5-1/2", Tested XX, $1,500.

5172, stag, 5-1/2", 1965-69, USA 200

5172, stag, 5-1/2", 1965, USA, transition stamp
  and pattern number on same side of blade 300

5172, stag (plain), 5-1/2", 1965, USA,
  Bulldog etch-no handmade stamp, rare 600

6185, Dr.'s knife, bone, 3-3/4", XX, $175.

R6185, candy stripe, LP, 3-3/4 ", Tested XX 500

Y6185, green pyremite, 3-3/4 ", Tested XX 500

RM185, Christmas tree, 3-5/8", 1920-40,
  Dr.'s knife, Tested XX 550

3185, yellow comp., 3-5/8", 1920-40
  Tested XX 350

6185, red bone, Pat. No., 3-5/8", Tested XX 500

6185, green bone, 3-5/8", 1920-40, Tested XX .. 550

3185, yellow comp., 3-5/8", 1940-64, XX 175

6185, red bone, 3-5/8", 1940-64, XX 300

3185, flat yellow, 3-5/8", 1965-69, USA 150

3185, yellow comp., 3-5/8", 1965-69, USA 125

6185, bone, 3-5/8", 1965-69, USA 125

3185, flat yellow, 3-5/8", 1970, 10 Dot 200

6185, bone, 3-5/8", 1970, 10 Dot 125

6185, delrin (rare), 3-5/8", 1970, 1 0 Dot 250

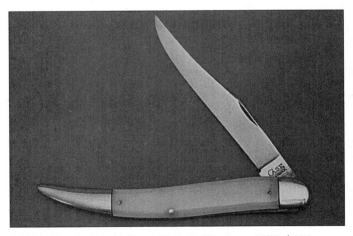

31093, Toothpick, Yellow, Hi-Pull, 5", Tested XX, $300.

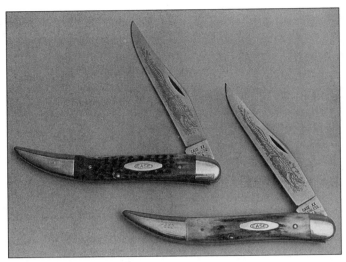

Gator Set (Toothpicks): Top: 61093S.S.P. Bottom: 51093S.S.P., 2,750 Sets made. Each set is $175.

RM1093, Christmas tree, 5", 1920-40,
  Toothpick, Tested XX 450

GS1093, gold stone, 5", 1920-40, Tested XX 350

HA1093, high art, 5", 1920-40, Tested XX 400

P1093, swirl celluloid, 5", 1920-40, Tested XX ... 350

R1093, candy stripe, 5", 1920-40, Tested XX 400

RM1093, mottled red, 5", 1920-40, Tested XX ... 400

31093, yellow comp., 5", 1940-64, XX 160

31093, yellow comp., rare, 5", 1965-69, USA 300
  Caution: may not have been made.

61093, green bone, 5", 1920-40, Tested XX 450

61093, green bone, 5", 1940-55, XX,
  Toothpick 450

61093, red bone, 5", 1940-64, XX 225

61093, bone, 5", 1940-64, XX 150

61093, bone, 5", 1965-69, USA 125

61093, bone, 5, 1970, 10 Dot 125

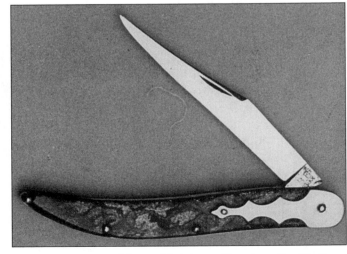

RM193, barn door hinge, Christmas Tree handle, 5", Case Tested XX, $600.

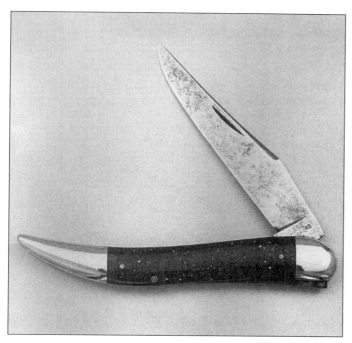

GS1094, gold stone, 4-1/4", Case Bradford, PA, $450.

B1094, onyx, 1920-40, Tested XX 350
R1094, candy stripe, 1920-40, Tested XX 400
61094, Rogers bone, 1920-40, Tested XX.......... 400

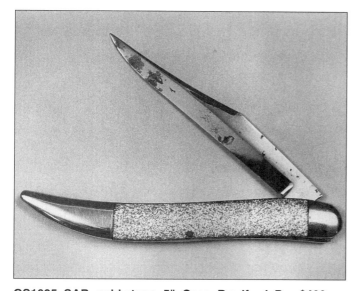

GS1095, SAB, gold stone, 5", Case, Bradford, Pa., $400.

RM1095, Christmas tree, 5", 1920-40,
    Tested XX 450
B1095, waterfall, 1920-40, Tested XX 400
B1095, imitation onyx, 1945, Case's Stainless ... 350
R1095, candy stripe, 5", 1920-40, Tested XX 400
31095, yellow comp., 5", 1920-40, Tested XX 300
61095, green bone, 5", 1920-40, Tested XX 450
4196X, white comp., citrus knife, 1920-40,
    Tested XX, Case's Stainless 500

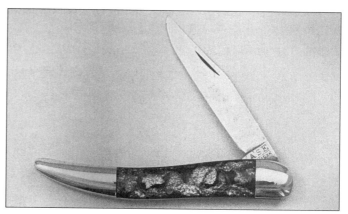

RM1096, Christmas Tree, 3-1/8", Case Tested XX, $400.

61096, green bone, 3-1/8", 1920-40,
    Tested XX 400
R1096, candy stripe, 3-1/8", 1920-40,
    Tested XX 400

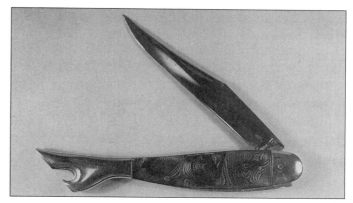

GM1097, leg knife, Green Mottled, 5", Tested XX, $400.

GS1097, gold stone, 1920-30, Tested XX 400
31097, yellow comp., leg, 1920-40, Tested XX... 310
RM1097, Christmas tree, 1920-30, Tested XX ... 450
R1097, candy stripe, 1920-30, Tested XX 400

5197L SSP, Stag, 5", $75.

7197LSSP, pakkawood...55

P197LSSP, pakkawood 45

7197LSSP, curly maple 90

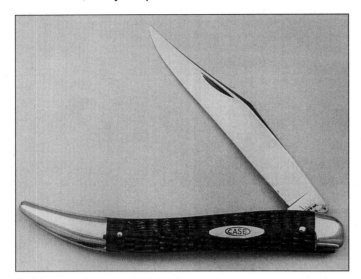

61098, Green Bone, 5-1/2", Tested XX, $450.

RM 1098, Christmas tree, 5-1/2", 1920-40,
  Tested XX 500

R1098, candy stripe, 5-1/2", 1920-40,
  Tested XX 450

B1098, waterfall, 5-1/2", 1920-40, Tested XX.....500

61098, Rogers bone, 5-1/2", 1920-40,

Tested XX 550

3199EO, yellow comp., 4-1/8", 1920-40,
  Tested/XX 260

1199SHRSS, walnut, 4-1/8", 1940-64, XX............60

1199SHRSS, walnut, 4-1/8", 1965-69, USA 40

1199SHRSS, walnut, 4-1/8", 1970, 10 Dot 40

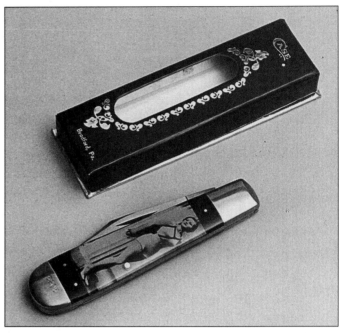

HA199-1/2SSP, Hi-Art with box, 4-1/8", 7,500 made, $90.

Case Two Blade

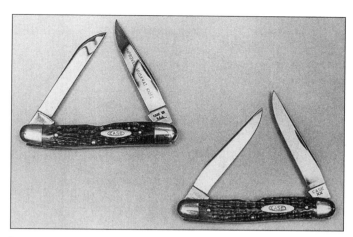

Top: Muskrat, Bone, Hawbaker's Special, 3-7/8", 1970, 10 Dot, $600. Bottom: Muskrat, Green Bone, 3-7/8", 1940-55, XX, $700.

Muskrat, green bone, 3-7/8", 1920-40,
Tested XX 1,500
Muskrat, yellow celluloid, 3-7/8", 1920-40,
Tested XX, rare 1,500
Muskrat, Rogers bone, early, 3-7/8",
1920-40, Tested XX 1,600
Muskrat, rough black, 3-7/8", 1940-50, XX 700
Muskrat, red bone, 3-7/8", 1940-64, XX 350
Muskrat, Rogers bone, late, 3-7/8",
1940-64, XX 450
Muskrat, Rogers bone, early, 3-7/8",
1940-50, XX 1,000
Muskrat, bone, 3-7/8", 1940-64, XX 225
Muskrat, bone, 3-7/8", 1965-69, USA 150
Muskrat, bone, 3-7/8", 1970, 10 Dot 75

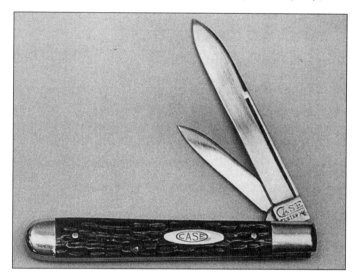

Unknown, Green Bone, LP, Tested XX, $200.

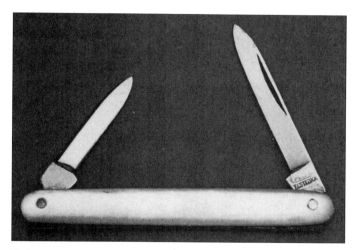

Unknown, Pearl, 2-1/8", Tested XX, $150.

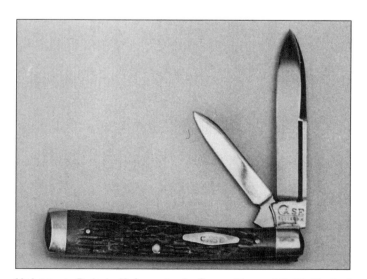

Unknown, Dr.'s knife/gunstock, Green Bone, LP, 3", Tested XX, $450.

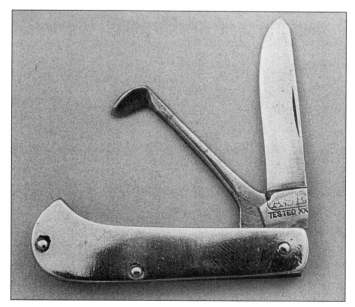

Unknown, metal castrating knife, Cord Cutter, 2-5/8", Tested XX, $175.

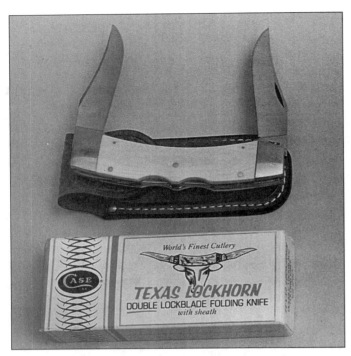

Texas Longhorn, double lock back, micarda, imitation ivory, (discontinued), 4-1/2", $145.

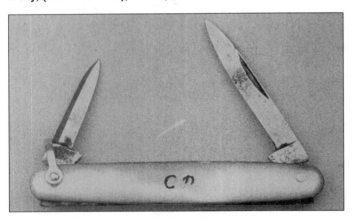

Watch Fob, Pearl with Bail, 1-3/4", Tested XX, $175.

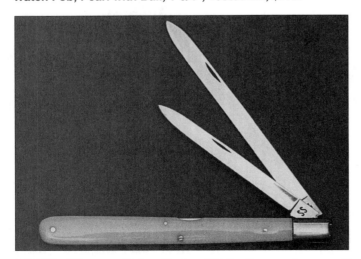

4200SS, Citrus or Melon Tester, White Comp., has small and large stamp, 5-1/2", USA, $175.

4200SS, melon tester, white comp., 5-1/2", 1940-64, XX 700

4200SS, white comp., 5-1/2", 1965-69, USA, Melon tester, serrated master blade 800

4200SS, white comp., 5-1/2", 1970, 10 Dot, melon tester 175

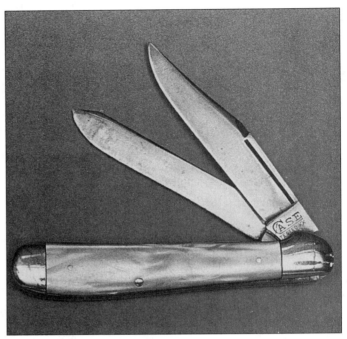

9200LP, Cracked Ice, Imi. Pearl, 4", Tested XX, $700.

6200LP, green bone, 3-15/16", 1920-40, Tested XX 1,200

3200LP, yellow comp., 3-15/16", 1920-40, Tested XX 700

5200LP, stag, 3-15/16", 1920-40, Tested XX... 1,200

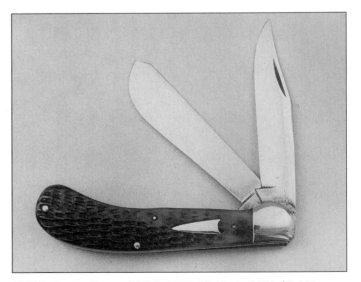

62100, Green Bone, 4-5/8", 1920-40, Tested XX, $1,200.

32100, yellow comp., 4-5/8", 1920-40, Tested XX 1,000

92100, imitation pearl, 4-5/8", 1920-40,
Tested XX 1,000

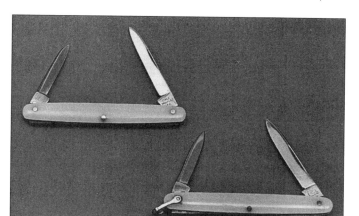

Top: **3201**, Yellow, 2-5/8", Case Bradford, $110. Bottom: **3201R**, Yellow with Bail, 2-5/8", Tested XX, $100.

6201F, Green Bone, 2-5/8", Tested XX, $150.

RM201, blue/cream mingled, 2-5/8",
1920-40, Tested XX 225

22001R, slick black, 2-5/8", 1920-40,
Tested XX 125

3201, yellow comp., 2-5/8", 1920-40,
Tested XX 125

6201, green bone, 2-5/8, 1920-40, Tested XX.... 150

62001, green bone, 2-5/8", 1920-40,
Tested XX 150

7201, tortoise shell, 2-5/8", 1920-40,
Tested XX 225

82001, genuine pearl, 2-5/8", 1920-40,
Tested XX 160

82101R, genuine pearl, 2-5/8", 1920-40,
Tested XX 150

9201, imitation pearl, 2-5/8", 1920-40,
Tested XX 100

9201R, imitation pearl, 2-5/8", 1920-40,
Tested XX 110

92101R, imitation pearl, 2-5/8", 1920-40,
Tested XX 100

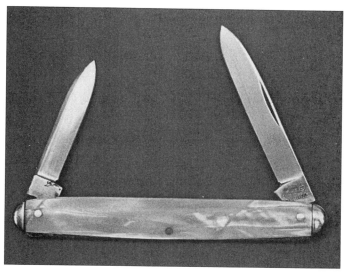

92001T , Cracked Ice, 2-5/8", Tested XX, $110.

3201, yellow comp., 2-5/8", 1940-64, XX 40
6201, bone, 2-5/8", 1940-64, XX 55
8201, pearl, 2-5/8", 1940-64, XX 110
9201, imitation pearl, 2-5/8", 1940-64, XX 35
9201, cracked ice, 2-5/8", 1940-64, XX 35
9201R, imitation pearl, 2-5/8, 1940-64, XX 40
9201R, cracked ice, 2-5/8", 1940-64, XX 40
3201, yellow comp, 2-5/8", 1965-69, USA 30
6201, bone, 2-5/8", 1965-69, USA 35
9201, imitation pearl, 2-5/8", 1970, 10 Dot 30
3201, yellow comp., 2-5/8", 1970, 10 Dot 30
3201, flat yellow comp., 2-5/8", 1970, 10 Dot 45
6201, bone, 2-5/8", 1970, 10 Dot 30

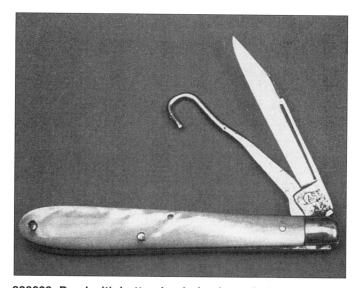

820028, Pearl with button hook, (no lower bolsters), 2-7/8", Case Tested XX, $350.

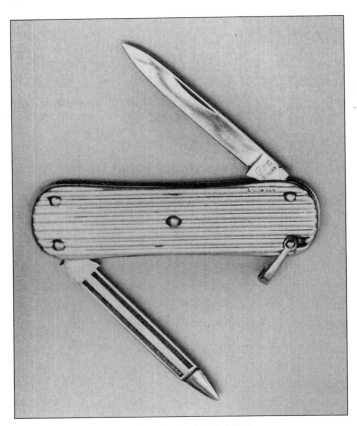

S2, Sterling Silver, 2-1/4", Tested XX, $175.

S2 L.P., sterling silver, 2-1/4", XX 125
S2, sterling silver, 2-1/4", XX 125
S2 LP, sterling silver, 2-1/4", U.S.A..................... 150

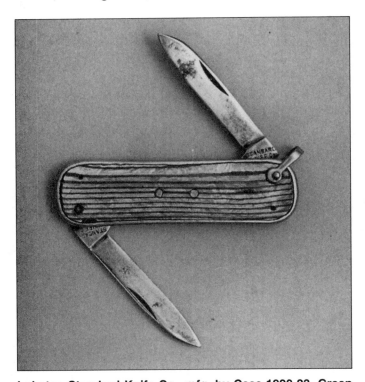

Lobster, Standard Knife Co., mfg. by Case-1920-23, Green Stripe Celluloid, 2-1/4", $55.

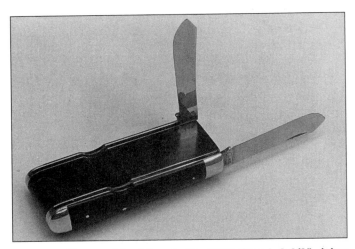

1202, grafting and budding knife, G&B Wood, 3-3/8", (also made in 3" Long Pull), Tested XX, $500.

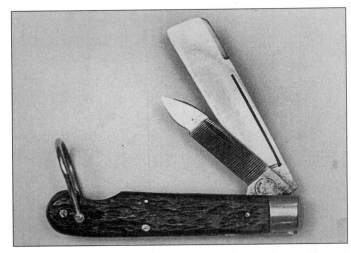

6202SHR, Rogers bone, with bail, WWI Navy Issue, 3-1/4", WR Case & Son, $200.

5202RAZ, stag, 3-3/8", 1920-40, Tested XX.......360
6202, green bone, 3-3/8", 1920-40, Tested XX...200

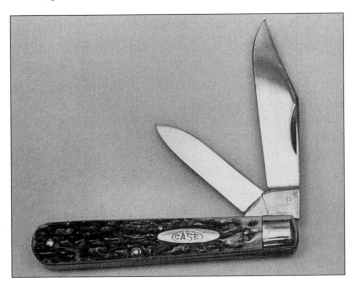

5202-1/2, Stag, 3-3/8", Tested XX, $225.

2202-1/2, slick black, 3-3/8", 1920-40,
Tested, XX 135
6202-1/2, green bone, 3-3/8", 1920-40,
Tested, XX 200
6202-1/2, rough black, 3-3/8", 1920-40,
Tested, XX 150
6202-1/2EO, green bone, 3-3/8", 1920-40,
Tested, XX 225
6202SHREO, bone, 3-3/8", 1920-40,
Tested, XX 225
6202-1/2, rough black, 3-3/8", 1940-50, XX........ 100
6202-1/2, green bone, 3-3/8", 1940-55, XX........ 150
2202-1/2, slick black, 3-3/8", 1940-64, XX.......... 150
6202-1/2, bone, 3-3/8", 1940-64, XX 50
6202-1/2, bone, 3-3/8", 1965-69, USA 40
6202-1/2, delrin, 3-3/8", 1970, 10 Dot.................. 30
6202-1/2, bone stag, 3-3/8", 1970, 10 Dot........... 40
62103, green bone, 2-7/8", 1920-40,
Tested XX 200
62103R, green bone, 2-7/8", 1920-40,
Tested XX 200
82103, genuine pearl, 2-7/8", 1920-40,
Tested XX 200
82103R, genuine pearl, 2-7/8", 1920-40,
Tested XX 200

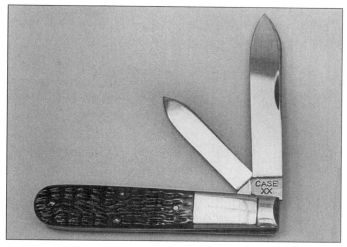

6205, Green Bone, 3-3/4", XX, $200.

6205, green bone, 3-3/4", 1920-40, Tested XX...450
6205, red bone, 3-3/4", 1940-55, XX 300
6205, bone, 3-3/4", 1940-55, XX 200

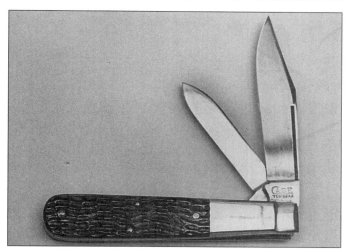

6205-1/2, Green Bone, LP, 3-3/4", Tested XX, $500.

5205-1/2, stag, 3-3/4", 1920-40, Tested XX........ 550
62005-1/2, green bone, 3-3/8", 1920-40,
Bolsters, stamped, Tested XX......................... 500

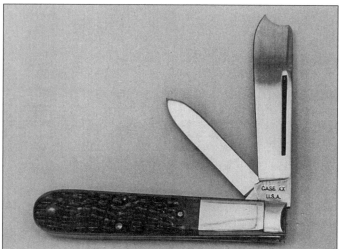

6205RAZ, Bone, LP, 3-3/4", USA, $125.

5205RAZ, stag, 3-3/4", 1920-40, Tested XX....... 600
5205, stag, 3-3/4", 1920-40, Tested XX.............. 550
62005, spear, green bone, 3-3/8", 1920-40,
Tested XX 550
6205RAZ, green bone, 3-3/4", 1920-40,
Tested XX 600
6205RAZ, rough black, 3-3/4", 1940-50, XX 500
6205RAZ, green bone, 3-3/4", 1940-55, XX....... 500
6205RAZ, red bone, 3-3/4", 1940-64, XX........... 300
6205RAZ, Bone, 3-3/4", 1940-64, XX................. 200
6205RAZ, bone, 3-3/4", 1970, 10 Dot 125

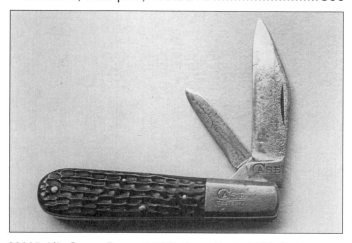

62005-1/2, Green Bone, 3-3/8", Case Tested XX, $500.

5206, stag, 2-5/8" 1920-40, Tested XX 250
6206, green bone, 2-5/8", 1920-40, Tested XX .. 225
8206, pearl, 2-5/8", 1920-40, Tested XX 300

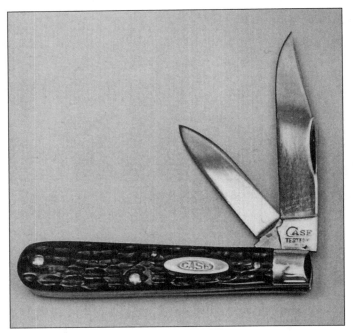

62061/2, Green Bone, 2-5/8", Tested XX, $175.

6206-1/2, rough black, 2-5/8", 1920-40,
Tested XX 160
5206-1/2, stag, 2-5/8", 1920-40, Tested XX 250
8206-1/2, genuine pearl, 2-5/8", 1920-40,
Tested XX 250
6206-1/2, rough black, 2-5/8", 1940-50, XX 140
6206-1/2, green bone, 2-5/8", 1940-50, XX 175

6207LP, Green Bone, 1920-35, 3-1/2", Clauss, Fremont, Ohio, U.S.A., Case contract knife, $300.

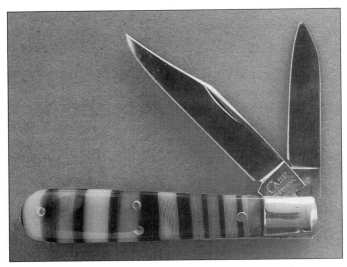

B206-1/2, Butter-Molasses, Waterfall Handle, 2-3/4", rare, $350.

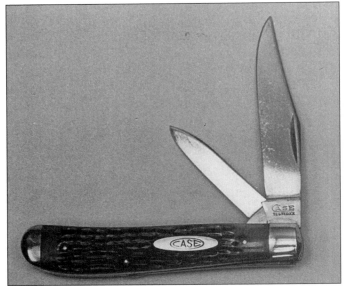

6207, Green Bone, 3-1/2", Tested XX, $300.

6207LP, green bone, 3-1/2", Tested XX 400
6207, green bone, 3-1/2", Tested Frame XX 400
RM207LP, Christmas tree, 3-1/2", 1920-40,
Tested XX 450
2207, slick black, 3-1/2", 1920-40, Tested XX 350
3207, yellow comp., 3-1/2", 1920-40,
Tested XX 350
5207, stag, rare, 3-1/2", 1920-40, Tested XX 450
6207LP, rough black, 3-1/2", 1920-40,
Tested XX 350
6207, rough black, 3-1/2", 1940-50, XX 250
6207, green bone, 3-1/2", 1940-55, XX 300
6207, red bone, 3-1/2", 1940-64, XX 150
2207, slick black, 3-1/2", 1940-64, XX 250
6207, bone, 3-1/2", 1940-64, XX 75
6207, Rogers bone early, 3-1/2", 1940-64, XX ... 350

6207, bone, 3-1/2", 1965-69, USA........................55
6207, bone, 3-1/2", 1970, 10 Dot........................60

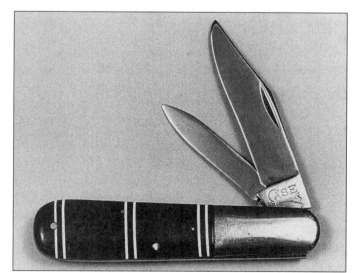

6208, Bone, 3-1/4", 10 Dot (1970), $40.

5208, stag, 3-1/4", 1920-40, Tested XX..............200
6208, green bone, 3-1/4", 1920-40, Tested XX ..150
6208, rough black, Tested XX............................150
6208, rough black, 3-1/4", 1940-50,
 XX, half whittler...125
6208, green bone, 3-1/4", 1940-55, XX..............150
6208, red bone, 3-1/4", 1940-64, XX....................85
6208, bone, 3-1/4", 1940-64, XX..........................50
6208, bone, 3-1/4", 1 965-69, USA......................40
2209, slick black, bud folding blade, rare,
 3-1/4", XX...250

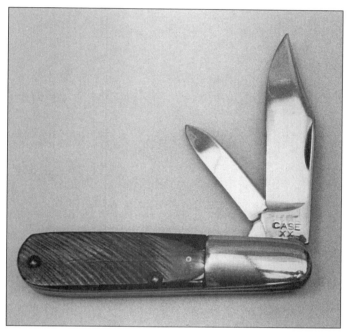

62009-1/2, Green Bone, Clip Blade, Round Bolster, 3-3/8", XX, $150.

62009-1/2, green bone, 3-5/16", 1940-55, XX....150
62009-1/2, red bone, 3-5/16", 1940-64, XX..........65
62009-1/2, bone, 3-5/16", 1940-64, XX 45
62009-1/2, bone, 3-5/16, 1 965-69, USA,
 Master blade in back......................................40
62009-1/2, bone, 3-5/16", 1965-69, USA,
 Master blade in front 40
62009-1/2, delrin, rare, 3-5/16", 1970, 10 Dot 100
62009-1/2, bone stag, 3-5/16", 1970, 10 Dot........40

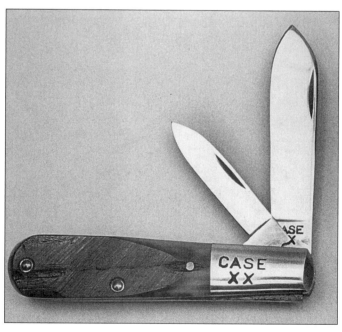

62009, Bone, Spear Blade, 3-3/8", XX, $50.

R2009-1/2, Candy Stripe Scales, 3-3/8", Tested XX, $350.

62009-1/2, green bone, 3-5/16", 1920-40,
 Tested XX 200
92009-1/2, cracked ice, 3-5/16", 1920-40,
 Tested XX 300
62009-1/2, black comp. 3-5/16", 1940-50,
 XX saw marks...125

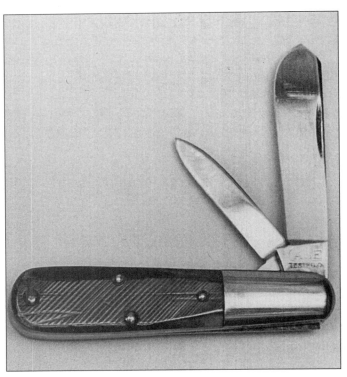

62009, Barlow spay blade, Green Bone, 3-3/8", Tested XX, $250.

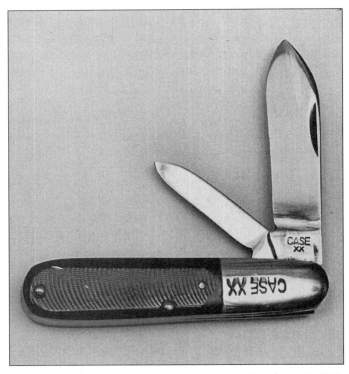

62009, Black Comp., Bolster Stamped upside down, 3-3/8", 1940-50, XX, $100.

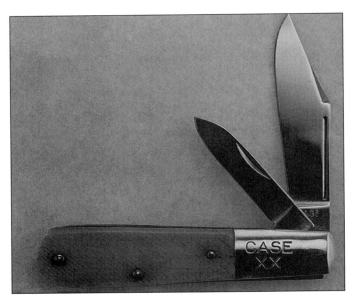

62009-1/2, LP, green bone, 3-3/8", 1940-55, XX, $175.

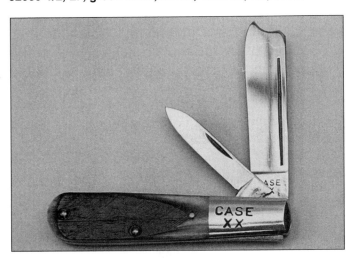

62009 RAZ, Bone, LP, 3-3/8", 1940-55, XX, $85.

62009, bone 3-5/16", 1965-69, USA,
Master blade in front 45

62009RAZ, bone, 3-5/16", 1965-69, USA

62009, spear, Delrin, USA 65
Master blade in back..50

62009RAZ, bone, 3-5/16", 1965-69, USA,
Master blade in front 50

62009, delrin, 3-5/16", 1970, 10 Dot....................40

62009, bone stag, 3-5/16", 1970, 10 Dot.............50

62009RAZ, delrin, 3-5/16", 1970, 10 Dot.............50

62009RAZ, bone, 3-5/16", 1970, 10 Dot 50

62109, Spear, Baby Copperhead, Green Bone, 3-1/8", (rare), $400.

62109X, green bone, 3-1/8", 1920-40,
Tested XX 325

62109X, rough black, 3-1/8", 1920-40,
Tested XX 200

62109X, rough black, 3-1/8", 1940-50, XX 140

62109X, green bone, 3-1/8", 1940-55, XX..........250

62109X, red bone, 3-1/8", 1940-64, XX...............90

62109X, bone, 3-1/8", 1940-64, XX......................75

62109X, bone, 3-1/8", 1965-69, USA 50

62109X, bone, 3-1/8", 10 Dot, (1970)...................50

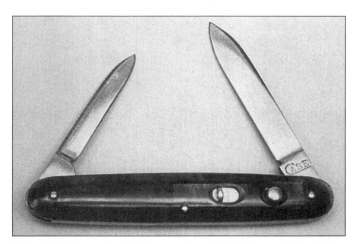

T7210, double switchblade, tortoise, 3-3/8", Tested XX, $700.

H2210, mottled, 3-3/8", 1920-40, Tested XX 700

62210, bone, 3-3/8", 1920-40, Tested XX...........700

92210, cracked ice, 3-3/8", 1920-40,
Tested XX 700

2210, Slick Black, plain shield, 3-1/8", Tested XX, $150.

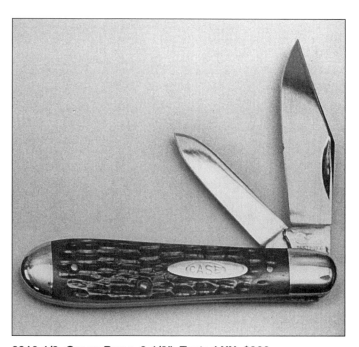

6210-1/2, Green Bone, 3-1/8", Tested XX, $200.

3210-1/2, yellow comp., 3-1/8", 1920-40,
Tested XX 150

5210-1/2, stag, 3-1/8", 1920-40, Tested XX........200

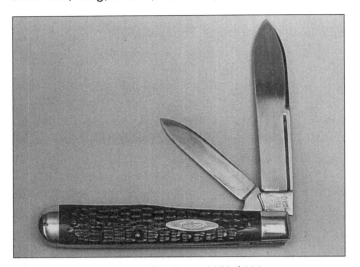

6211LP, Green Bone, 4-1/2", Tested XX, $600.

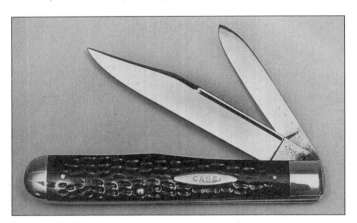

6211-1/2, Green Bone, LP, 4-1/2", Tested XX, $600.

6212 L.P., red Winterbottom 3-3/8",
W.R. Case...250

6213, Rogers bone, 4", 1920-40, Tested XX 600

6213, green bone 4", 1920-40, Tested XX..........400

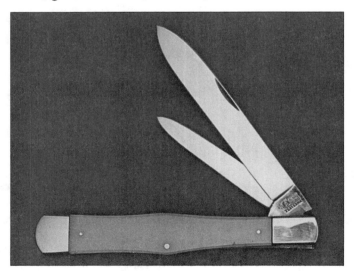

32213, Spear, Yellow, 5-1/4", rare, Tested XX, $800.

62213, spear, Rogers bone, 5-3/8", rare,
Tested XX 1,000

62213, spear, green bone, 5-3/8", 1920-40,
Tested XX 800

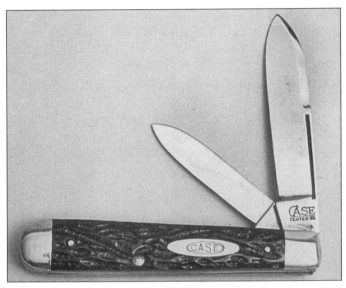

6214, Rough Black, LP, 3-3/8", Tested XX, $150.

6214, green bone, 3-3/8", 1920-40,
Tested XX 165

6214, rough black, 3-3/8", 1940-50, XX,
with shield...100

6214, rough black, 3-3/8", 1940-50, XX,
without shield 90

6214, green bone, 3-3/8", 1940-55, XX 150

6214, red bone, 3-3/8", 1940-64, XX 75

6214, Rogers bone late, 3-3/8", 1940-64, XX.....125

6214, bone, 3-3/8", 1940-64, XX 45

6214, bone, 3-3/8", 1965-69, USA......................40

6214, delrin, 3-3/8", 1970, 10 Dot........................30

6214, bone stag, 3-3/8", 1970, 10 Dot.................45

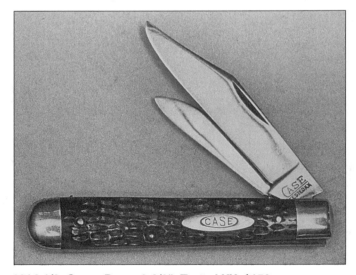

6214-1/2, Green Bone, 3-3/8", Tested XX, $150.

5214-1/2, stag, 3-3/8", 1920-40, Tested XX 225

6214-1/2, Rogers bone, 3-3/8", 1920-40,
Tested XX 200

6214-1/2, rough black, 3-3/8", 1940-50, XX........100

6214-1/2, green bone, 3-3/8", 1940-55, XX........150

6214-1/2, red bone, 3-3/8", 1940-64, XX.............60

6214-1/2, bone, 3-3/8", 1940-64, XX....................45

6214-1/2, bone, 3-3/8", 1965-69, USA 35

6214-1/2, delrin, 3-3/8", 1970, 10 Dot...................30

6214-1/2, bone stag, 3-3/8", 1970, 10 Dot............45

6216, green bone, 3-3/8", 1920-40, Tested XX ..250

6216EO, Green Bone, with chain, 1 of 100, 3-3/8", 1920-40, Tested XX, $500. Photo courtesy Ralph Scruton.

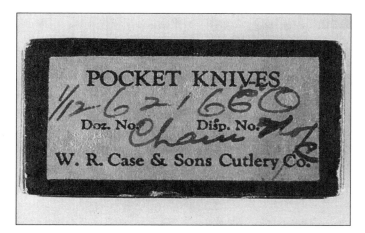

End of Box, marked 6216EO, 1/12 doz., very rare, $1,000-$2,000. Photo courtesy Ralph Scruton.

6216EO, green bone, 3-3/8", 1920-40,
Tested XX 300

6216, bone 3-3/8", 1940-64, XX 90

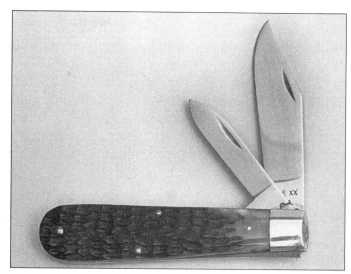

6216-1/2, bone, 3-3/8", USA, $40.

6216-1/2, green bone, 3-3/8", 1920-40,
Tested XX 200

6216-1/2, bone, 3-3/8", 1940-64, XX 50

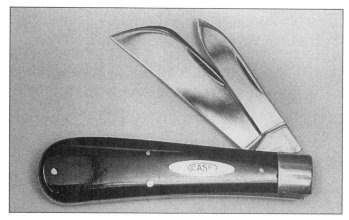

2217, Slick Black, 3-7/8", Tested XX, $250.

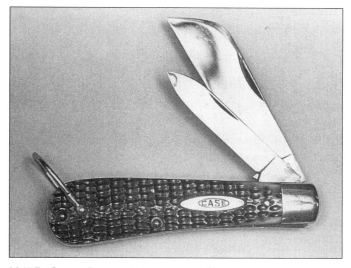

6217R, Green Bone, 4", Tested XX, $325.

6217, green bone, 4", 1920-40, Tested XX.........325
6217, green bone, 4", 1940-55, XX 250
6217, red bone, 4", 1940-64, XX 150
2217, slick black, 4", 1940-64, XX 250
6217, bone, 4", 1940-64, XX 125
6217, wood, 4", 1965-69, USA 50
6217, bone stag, 4", 1965-69, USA 85
6217, bone stag, 4", 1970, 10 Dot 85
6217, laminated wood, 4", 1970, 10 Dot..............50

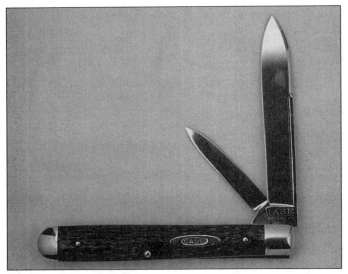

62019LP, Green Bone, 4", Tested XX, $400.

6219, green bone 4-1/8", 1920-40, Tested XX ...400
62019, green bone 4-1/8", 1920-40,
      Tested XX 400

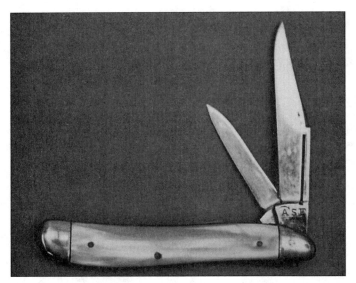

9220, Peanut, Cracked Ice LP, 2-7/8", Tested XX, $250.

RM220, Christmas tree, 2-3/4", 1920-40,
      Tested XX 450
RM220SAB, Christmas tree, 2-3/4", 1920-40,
      Tested XX 500

2220, slick black, 2-3/4", 1920-40, Tested XX 225
3220, yellow comp., 2-3/4", 1920-40,
      Tested XX 225
5220, stag, 2-3/4", 1920-40, Tested XX 300
6220, rough black, 2-3/4", 1920-40,
      Tested XX 225
6220, Rogers bone, 2-7/8", Tested XX 350
6220, green bone, 2-3/4", 1920-40, Tested XX...350
6220SAB, green bone, 2-3/4", 1920-40,
      Tested XX, long pull 450
8220, genuine pearl, 2-3/4", 1920-40,
      Tested, XX 450
9220, imitation pearl, 2-3/4", 1920-40,
      Tested, XX 250
2220, slick black, 2-3/4", 1940-64, XX 75
3220, yellow comp., 2-3/4", 1940-64, XX.............75
5220, stag, 2-3/4, 1940-64", XX...........................85
6220, rough black, 2-3/4",
Peanut, 1940-50, XX 175
6220, green bone, 2-3/4", 1940-55, XX 350
6220, red bone, 2-3/4", 1940-64, XX 125
6220, Rogers bone, 2-3/4", 1940-64, XX............150
6220, bone, 2-3/4", 1940-64, XX 75
9220, imitation pearl, 2-3/4", 1940-64, XX..........150
9220, cracked ice, 2-3/4", 1940-64, XX 150
2220, slick black, 2-3/4", 1965-69, USA 60
3220, yellow comp., 2-3/4", 1965-69, USA...........55
5220, stag, 2-3/4", 1965-69, USA 70
6220, bone, 2-3/4", 1965-69, USA........................60
6220, delrin, 2-3/4", 1965-69, USA 100
2220, slick black, 2-3/4", 1970, 10 Dot 55
3220, yellow comp., 2-3/4", 1970, 10 Dot.............55
3220, flat yellow, 2-3/4", 1970, 10 Dot 100

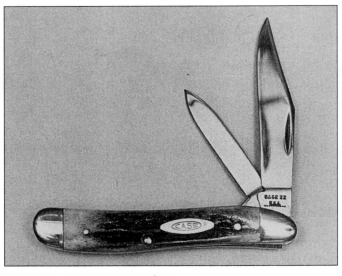

5220, Stag, 2-7/8", 10 Dot, $85.

6220, bone, 2-3/4", 1970, 10 Dot............................70
6220, delrin, scarce, 2-3/4", 1970, 10 Dot 125
6220, bone, 2-3/4", 1971, 9 Dot..........................100
3221, spear, yellow, 5-3/8", rare, Tested XX.......800

06221-1/2, Green Bone, 3-1/4", Tested XX, $400.

06221-1/2, green bone, long pull, Tested XX......450
02221-1/2, slick black, 3-1/4", 1920-40,
   Tested XX 350
07221, tortoise, 3-1/4", 1920-40, Spear,
   Tested XX 450
06221, Wharncliffe, green bone, 3-1/4",
   1920-40, Tested XX 450

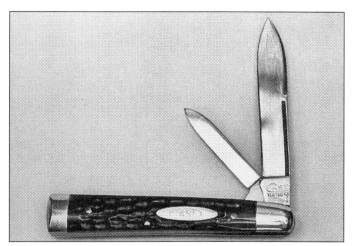

6222, Green Bone, 3-3/8", LP, (Phys.), Tested, $600.

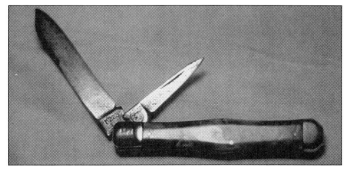

P223, green-swirl celluloid, 3-1/2", 1920-40, Tested XX, $300.

6223, green bone, 3-1/2", 1920-40, Tested XX...350
9223, imitation pearl, 3-1/2", 1920-40,
   Tested XX 300

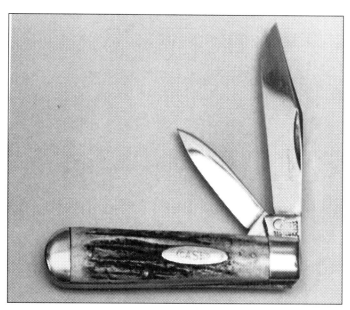

5224-1/2, Stag, 3", Tested XX, $225.

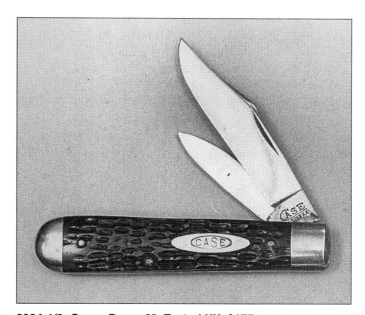

6224-1/2, Green Bone, 3", Tested XX, $175.

RM224-1/2, Christmas tree, 3", 1920-40,
   Tested XX 300
3224-1/2, yellow comp., 3", 1920-40,
   Tested XX 150
2224SH, slick black, 3", 1920-40, Tested XX......200
2224RAZ, slick black, 3", 1920-40, Tested XX ...300
3224, yellow comp., 3", 1920-40, Tested XX 150
6224, green bone, 3", 1920-40, Tested XX.........225
2224SP, slick black, 3", 1940-64, XX..................175
2224SH, slick black, 3", 1940-64, XX 175

2224RAZ, slick black, 3", 1940-64, XX 200

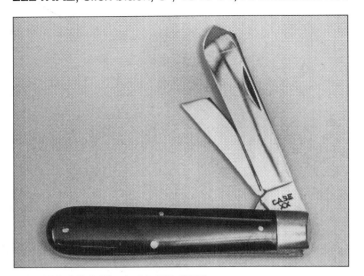

22024SP, Slick Black, 3", XX, $250.

52024, stag, 3", 1920-40, Tested XX 225

62024, green bone, 3", 1920-40, Tested XX 175

62024SH, green bone, 3", 1920-40, Tested XX .. 200

62024RAZ, green bone, 3", 1920-40,
Tested XX 225

220024SP, slick black, 3", 1940-64, XX,
"Little John Carver," (extremely rare, price
quoted is for knife in the original balsa
wood block and sleeve) 1,000

62024, green bone, 3", 1940-64, XX 150

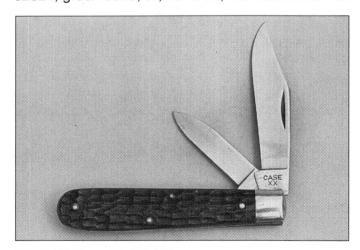

62024-1/2, Bone, 3", XX, $45.

52024-1/2, stag, 3", 1920-40, Tested, XX 200

62024-1/2, green bone, 3", 1920-40,
Tested, XX 150

32024-1/2, yellow comp., 3", 1940-64, XX............ 60

32024-1/2, flat yellow, 3", 1965-69, USA 70

62024-1/2, green bone, 3", 1940-55, XX 150

32024-1/2, yellow comp., 3", 1965-69, USA 55

62024-1/2, bone, 3", 1965-69, USA..................... 45

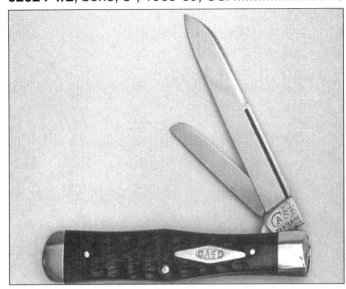

6225LP, Green Bone, 3", Tested XX, $300.

32025, yellow spear blade, 3", Tested XX 250

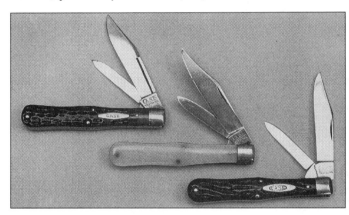

Top: 62025-1/2, Green Bone, 3", 1920-40, Tested XX, $300. Middle: 32025-1/2, Yellow Comp., 3", 1920-40, Tested XX, $225. Bottom: 62025-1/2, Rough Black, 3", 1920-40, Tested XX, $225.

22025-1/2, slick black 3", 1920-40, Tested XX ...225

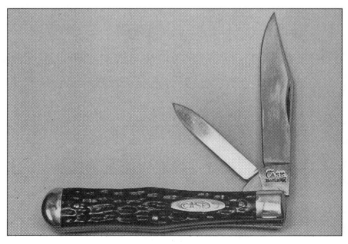

6225-1/2, Coke Bottle, Green Bone, 3", Tested XX, $300.

5225-1/2, stag, 3", 1920-40, Tested XX 300

6225-1/2, rough black, 3", 1920-40,
Tested XX 250

6225-1/2, rough black, 3", 1940-50, XX 175

6225-1/2, green bone, 3", 1940-55, XX 250

6225-1/2, red bone, 3", 1940-64, XX 110

6225RAZ, bone, 3", 1940-64, XX 300

6225-1/2, bone, 3", 1940-64, XX 75

6225-1/2, bone, 3", 1965-69, USA 60

6225-1/2, bone, 3", 1970, 10 Dot 60

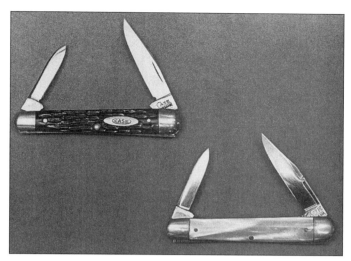

Top: **62027-1/2**, Bone, 2-3/4", Tested XX, $125. Bottom: **92027-1/2**, Imitation Pearl, 2-3/4", LP, Tested XX, $125.

RM2027-1/2, Christmas tree, 2-3/4",
1920-40, Tested XX 300

GS2027-1/2, gold stone, 2-3/4", 1920-40,
Tested XX 225

62027-1/2, green bone, 2-3/4", 1940-64,
Tested XX 150

82027-1/2, pearl, 2-3/4", Tested XX 225

62027-1/2, rough black, 2-3/4", 1940-64, XX 100

62027-1/2, bone, 2-3/4", 1940-64, XX 55

92027-1/2, cracked ice, 2-3/4", 1940-64, XX 80

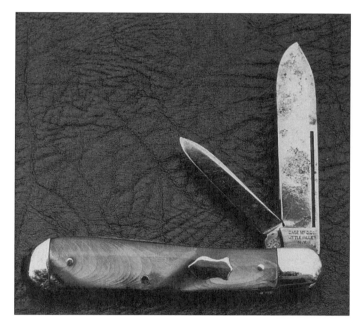

GPY2026, Pyremite, 3", $400. Photo courtesy Mark Nagle.

RM2026, Christmas tree, 3", 1920-40,
Long pull, Tested XX 360

82026, genuine pearl, 3", 1920-40,
Long pull, Tested XX 325

6226-1/2, green bone, 3", 1920-40, Tested XX .. 250

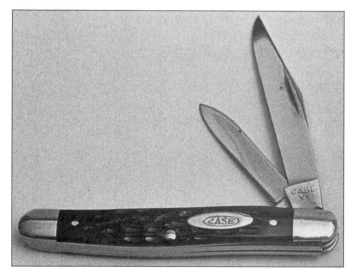

6227, Bone, 2-3/4", 1940-64, XX, $45.

6227, Rogers bone early, 2-3/4",
1920-40, Tested XX 225

6227, green bone, 2-3/4", 1940-55, XX 150

6227, red bone, 2-3/4", 1940-64, XX 65

6227, bone, 2-3/4", 1 965-69, USA 40

6227, delrin, 2-3/4", 1970, 10 Dot 35

6227, bone stag, 2-3/4", 1970, 10 Dot 40

H2027, mottled, 2-3/4", 1920-40, Tested XX 225

RM2027, Christmas tree, 2-3/4", 1920-40,
Spear, Tested XX 300

RM2027, red mottled, 2-3/4", 1920-40,
Tested XX 250

62027, green bone, 2-3/4", 1920-40,
Tested XX 150

92027, imitation pearl, 2-3/4", 1920-40,
Tested XX 140

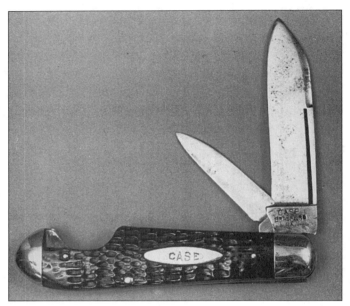

6228LP EO, Green Bone, 3-5/8", Case Bradford, PA, $250.

2228, slick black, 3-1/2", 1920-40,
Dog Leg, Tested XX 200

2228EO, slick black, 3-1/2", 1920-40,
Tested XX 225

2228PU, slick black, 3-1/2", 1920-40,
Tested XX 200

6228, green bone, 3-1/2", 1920-40, Tested XX ..225

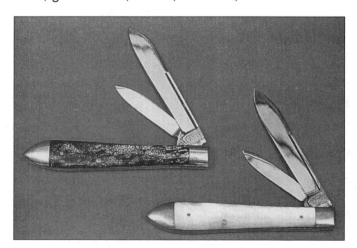

Top: RM2028, Christmas Tree, 2-7/8", LP, Tested XX, $400.
Bottom: 82028, Pearl, 2-7/8", LP, W.R. Case & Son, Bradford, Pa., $350.

22028, slick black, 3-1/2", Tested XX.................300

GS2028, gold stone, 3-1/2", Tested XX 350

62028, rough black, Tested XX........................200

62028, green bone, 3-1/2", 1920-40,
Tested XX 200

22028, slick black 3-1/2", 1940-64, XX 150

22028-1/2, Slick Black, 3-1/2", XX, $110.

M2028-1/2, metal, 3-1/2", 1920-40, Tested XX...125

22028-1/2, slick black, 3-1/2", 1920-40,
Tested XX 160

62028-1/2, green bone, 3-1/2", 1920-40,
Tested XX 225

62028-1/2, rough black, 3-1/2", 1940-50, XX......150

62028-1/2, bone, 3-1/2", 1940-64, XX 150

62028-1/2, early Rogers, 3-1/2", 1940-50, XX....250

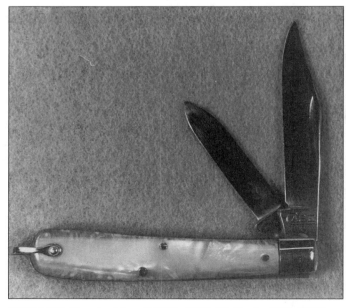

9229-1/2R, Cracked Ice, 2-1/2", 1920-40, Tested XX, $200.

6229-1/2, green bone, 2-1/2", 1920-40,
Tested XX 250

6229-1/2, rough black, 2-1/2", Tested XX 200

7229-1/2, tortoise, 2-1/2", 1920-40,
Tested XX 300

8229-1/2, pearl..300

2229-1/2, slick black, 2-1/2", 1940-64, XX............85

6229-1/2, bone, 2-1/2", 1940-64, XX 75

2229-1/2, slick black, 2-1/2", 1965-69,
rare, USA 200

6229-1/2, bone, 2-1/2", 1965-69, USA 85

6230, green bone, 3-1/4", 1920-40, Tested XX ..200

02230, black comp., 3-1/4", 1920-40,
Tested XX 200

05230LP, stag, 3-1/4", 1920-40, Tested XX........250

06230, green bone, 3-1/4", 1920-40,
Long pull, Tested XX 250

06230SH, green bone, 3-1/4", 1920-40,
Tested XX 225

06230SP, green bone, 3-1/4", 1920-40,
Tested XX 225

09230, imitation pearl, 3-1/4", 1920-40,
Tested XX 225

02230-1/2, black comp., 3-1/4", 1920-40,
Tested XX 175

05230-1/2, stag, 3-1/4", 1920-40, Tested XX......225

06230-1/2, green bone, 3-1/4", 1920-40,
Tested XX 225

09230-1/2, imitation pearl, 3-1/4",
1920-40, Tested XX 225

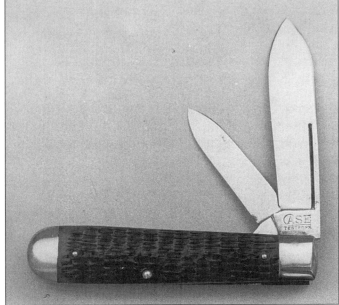

6231, Imi. Bone, 3-3/4", LP, no shield, Tested XX, $200.

6231LP, red bone, Shield, 3-3/4", Tested XX......225

6231, bone, 3-3/4", 1940-64, XX 125

6231, rough black, 3-3/4", 1940-50, XX 150

6231, green bone, 3-3/4", 1940-64, XX 250

6231, red bone, spear, 3-3/4", 1940-64, XX 200

6231, bone, rare, 3-3/4", 1965-69, USA 300

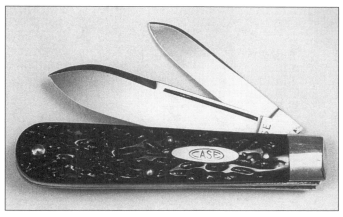

62031, Rough Black, 3-3/4", LP, 1940-49, XX, $175.

22031, slick black, 3-3/4", 1920-40,
Tested XX 200

52031, stag, 3-3/4", 1920-40, Tested XX 300

62031, green bone, 3-3/4", 1920-40,
Tested XX 300

62031, rough black, 3-3/4", 1920-40,
Tested XX 175

62031, rough black, 3-3/4", 1940-49, XX............150

62031, bone, 3-3/4", 1940-64, XX 125

62031, green bone, 3-3/4", 1940-55, XX 250

62031, green bone, 3-3/4", 1940-55, Long,
Pull, XX 275

62031, red bone, 3-3/4", 1940-64, XX 175

12031LR, Walnut, 3-1/4", Electrician's Knife, XX, $45.

12031L, walnut 3-3/4", 1920-40, Tested XX 125

12031LR, walnut, 3-3/4", 1965-69, electrician's
knife, USA, ...30

12031LR, walnut, 3-3/4", 1970, 10 Dot,
Electrician's knife 30

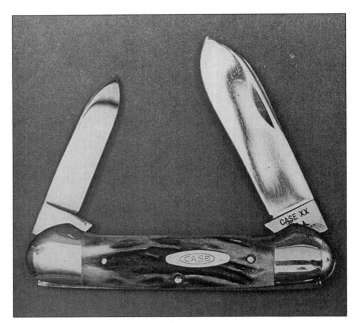

52131, Stag, 3-5/8", 1970, 10 Dot, $150.

52131, stag, 3-5/8", 1920-40, Tested XX 600
52131, stag, long pull, 3-5/8", 1920-40,
Tested XX 700
92131, cracked ice, 3-5/8", 1920-40,
Tested XX 650
52131, red stag, XX 450
52131LP, red stag, XX 750
52131, stag, 3-5/8", 1940-64, XX 300
52131, stag, long pull, 3-5/8", 1940-55, XX 500
52131, stag, 3-5/8", 1965-69, USA 150
62131, bone, 3-5/8", 1965-69, USA 75
62131, bone, 3-5/8", 1970, 10 Dot 75
62131, bone, 3-5/8", 1964, XX 300

Beware: A few made in 1964, but not sold in
production; however, a few could have gotten to the
collector market.

2231-1/2, slick black, 3-3-/4", 1920-40,
Flat blade, Tested XX 200
6231-1/2, green bone, 3-3/4", 1920-40,
Tested XX 250
6231-1/2, rough black, 3-3/4", 1920-40,
Tested XX 175
6231-1/2, bone, 3-3/4", 1920-40, Tested XX 200
2231-1/2, slick black 3-3/4", 1940-64, XX,
Long pull is standard 65
2231-1/2SAB, slick black, 3-3/4", 1940-64,
XX, Long pull is standard 65
42311-1/2, white comp., 3-3/4", 1940-64,
XX, Long pull is standard 210

6231-1/2, bone, 3-3/4", 1940-64, XX,
Long pull is standard 85
6231-1/2, red bone, 3-3/4", 1940-64, XX 150
6231-1/2, green bone, 3-3/4", 1940-55, XX 225
6231-1/2, rough black, 3-3/4", 1940-50,
Long pull, XX 125
2231-1/2SAB, slick black, 3-3/4", 1965-69,
USA, Long pull is standard 45
6231-1/2, bone, 3-3/4", 1965-69, USA,
Long pull is standard 65
2231-1/2SAB, slick black, 3-3/4", 1970,
10 Dot, Long pull is standard 45
6231-1/2, bone, 3-3/4", 1970, 10 Dot,
Long pull is standard 65

62031-1/2, Rough Black, 3-3/4", Tested XX, $225.

22031-1/2, slick black, 3-3/4", 1920-40,
Tested XX 175
52031-1/2, stag, 3-3/4, 1920-40, Tested XX 300
52031-1/2SAB, stag, 3-3/4, 1920-40,
Tested XX 350
62031-1/2, green bone, 3-3/4, 1920-40,
Tested XX 300
22031-1/2, slick black, 3-3/4, 1940-64, XX,
Long pull is standard 100
62031-1/2, green bone, 3-3/4, 1940-55, XX 250
62031-1/2, red bone, 3-3/4, 1940-64, XX 200
62031-1/2, bone, 3-3/4, 1940-64, XX,
Long pull is standard 110
62031-1/2, rough black, 3-3/4, 1940-50, XX 125

62031-1/2, rough black, 3-3/4, 1940-50,
long pull, XX.. 125

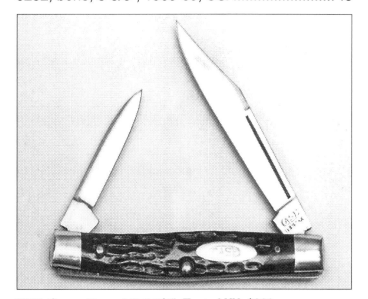

3232, Yellow Comp, 3-5/8", XX, $125.

3232, yellow comp., 3-5/8", 1920-40,
Tested XX 150
5232, stag, 3-5/8", 1920-40, Tested XX 225
6232, green bone, 3-5/8", 1920-40, Tested XX ..225
6232, Rogers bone, late, 3-5/8", 1940-64, XX....125
6232, rough black, 3-5/8", 1940-50, XX..............125
6232, green bone, 3-5/8", 1940-55, XX 175
6232, red bone, 3-5/8", 1940-64, XX 125
5232, stag, 3-5/8", 1940-64, XX 110
6232, bone, 3-5/8", 1940-64, XX 65
5232, stag, 3-5/8", 1965-69, USA........................ 75
6232, bone, 3-5/8", 1965-69, USA.......................45

6233, Green Bone, LP, 2-5/8", Tested XX, $200.

5232, stag, 3-5/8", 1970, 10 Dot..........................85
6232, bone, 3-5/8", 1970, 10 Dot.........................45
3233, yellow comp., 2-5/8", Tested XX,
long pull 135
3233, yellow comp., 2-5/8", XX, long pull 135
3233, yellow comp., 2-5/8", (large) XX,
regular pull 50
3233, yellow comp., 2-5/8", (small) XX,
regular pull 50
3233, yellow comp., 2-5/8", USA, regular pull 50
3233, yellow comp., 2-5/8", 10 Dot, regular pull ...50
3233, yellow comp., 2-5/8", 9 Dot, regular pull 40
3233, yellow comp., 2-5/8", 7 Dot, regular pull 30
3233, yellow comp., 2-5/8", 6 Dot, regular pull 30
9233, cracked ice, 2-5/8", XX, long pull 50
9233, cracked ice, 2-5/8", Tested XX, long pull 50
9233, cracked ice, 2-5/8", (large) XX,
regular pull 50
9233, cracked ice, 2-5/8", (small) XX,
regular pull 50
9233, cracked ice, 2-5/8", USA, regular pull.........35
9233, cracked ice, 2-5/8", 4 Dot, regular pull........30
9233, cracked ice, 2-5/8", XX, rare,
no bolsters 250

8233, letter opener, Pearl, 6-3/4", $250.

8233, pearl, 2-5/8", (large) XX, regular pull 85
8233, pearl, 2-5/8", USA, regular pull 85
8233, pearl, 2-5/8", 10 Dot, regular pull 85
8233, pearl, 2-5/8", 9 Dot, regular pull 75
8233, pearl, 2-5/8", 8 Dot, regular pull 75
8233, pearl, 2-5/8", 7 Dot, regular pull 75
8233, pearl, 2-5/8", 6 Dot, regular pull 75
9233, imitation pearl, 2-5/8", XX, long pull..........135
9233, imitation pearl, 2-5/8", (large) XX,
regular pull 50
9233, imitation pearl, 2-5/8", 10 Dot, regular pull..45
9233, imitation pearl, 2-5/8", 9 Dot, regular pull....40
9233, imitation pearl, 2-5/8", 8 Dot, regular pull....40
9233, imitation pearl, 2-5/8", 7 Dot, regular pull....40
9233, imitation pearl, 2-5/8", 6 Dot, regular pull....30
9233, imitation pearl, 2-5/8", 5 Dot, regular pull....30

9233, imitation pearl, 2-5/8", 4 Dot, regular pull....30

9233, Shad Cracked Ice, 2-5/8", rare, no bolsters, XX, $250.

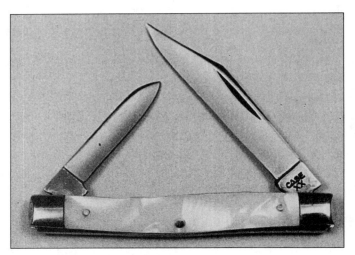

9233, Cracked Ice, 2-5/8", XX, $50.

6233, rough black, 2-5/8", Tested XX, long pull..175

6233, rough black, 2-5/8", XX, long pull..............150

6233, rough black, 2-5/8", XX, regular pull 100

5233SS, stag, 2-5/8", Tested XX,
Centennial, regular pull......................................45

GS233SS, gold stone, 2-5/8", Tested XX,
Centennial, regular pull......................................45

R6233SS, red, 2-5/8", Tested XX, Centennial,
regular pull 40

RM233, Christmas tree, 2-5/8", Tested XX,
long pull 325

GS233, gold stone, 2-5/8", Tested Bradford,
long pull 325

5233, stag, 2-5/8", (large) XX, regular pull..........100

5233, stag, 2-5/8", USA, regular pull 90

5233, stag, 2-5/8", SS USA, razor edge,
regular pull 50

5233, stag, 2-5/8", 10 Dot, regular pull 100

5233, stag, 2-5/8", SS #507 4 Dot, regular pull 50

5233, stag, 2-5/8", SS USA 3 Dot, regular pull 50

6233, green bone, 2-5/8", Tested XX, long pull ..250

6233, green bone, 2-5/8", XX, long pull 250

6233, bone, 2-5/8", (large) XX, regular pull 60

6233, red bone, 2-5/8", XX, regular pull..............100

6233, bone, 2-5/8", USA, regular pull 50

6233, red bone, 2-5/8", USA, regular pull 75

6233, bone, 2-5/8", 10 Dot, regular pull 50

6233, delrin, 2-5/8", 10 Dot, regular pull 60

6233, delrin, 2-5/8", 9 Dot, regular pull 45

6233, delrin, 2-5/8", 8 Dot, regular pull 40

6233, delrin, 2-5/8", 7 Dot, regular pull 35

6233, delrin, 2-5/8", 6 Dot, regular pull 30

6233, delrin, 2-5/8", 5 Dot, regular pull 30

6233, delrin, 2-5/8", 4 Dot, regular pull 30

2234, Dr.'s knife, slick black, LP, 3-5/8", Tested XX, $600.

5234, stag, doctor's knife, 3-5/8", 1920-40,
Tested XX 1,000

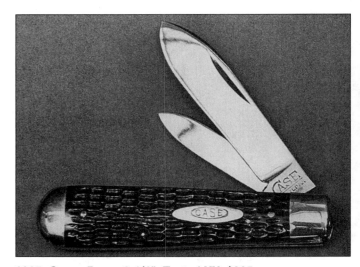

6235, Green Bone, 3-1/4", Tested XX, $225.

6235EO, green bone, 3-1/4", 1920-40,
Tested XX 300

6235SH, green bone, 3-1/4", 1920-40,
Tested XX 225

6235, rough black, 3-1/4", 1940-50, XX.............90

6235, green bone, 3-1/4", 1940-55, XX 200

6235, bone, 3-1/4", 1940-64, XX 65

6235EO, bone, 3-1/4", 1940-64, XX 225

6235, red bone, 3-1/4", 1940-64, XX 125

6235EO, rough black, 3-1/4", 1940-50, XX.........250

6235, early Rogers, 3-1/4", 1940-50, XX............250

6235, bone (rare), 3-1/4", 1965-69, USA............225

6235EO, black imitation jigged bone, 3-1/4", XX, $50.

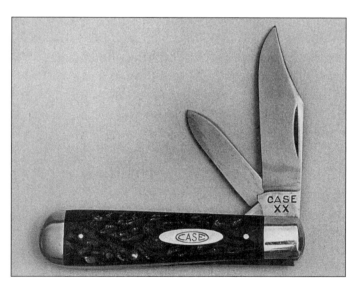

6235-1/2, Rough Black, 3-3/8", XX, $75.

3235-1/2, yellow comp., 3-3/8", 1920-40,
Tested XX 200

5235-1/2, stag, 3-3/8", 1920-40, Tested XX........250

6235-1/2, green bone, 3-3/8", 1920-40,
Tested XX 250

6235-1/2PU, green bone, 3-3/8", 1920-40,
Tested XX 275

6235-1/2, bone, 3-3/8", 1940-64, XX 60

6235-1/2PU, bone, 3-3/8", 1940-64, XX 175

6235-1/2, green bone, 3-3/8", 1940-55, XX........175

6235-1/2, red bone, 3-3/8", 1940-64, XX 110

6235-1/2, bone, 3-3/8", 1965-69, USA,
Master clip blade in back 45

6235-1/2, bone, 3-3/8", 1965-69, USA, master
clip blade in front; also with no shield 45

6235-1/2, bone, 3-1/4", 1970, 10 Dot...................45

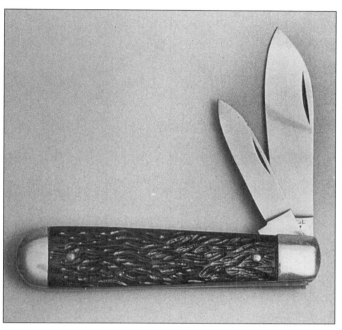

620035, Imitation Black Bone, 3-1/4", XX, $35.

620035LP, black plastic, 3-1/4", 1940-64, XX.......35

620035EO, black plastic, 3-1/4", 1940-64, XX......50

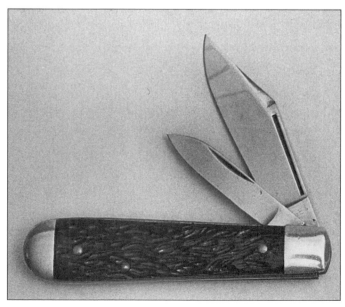

620035-1/2, Black Imi. Bone, 3-1/4", XX, $40.

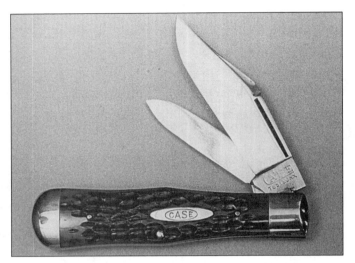

6237-1/2, Green Bone, LP, 3-1/2", Tested XX, $650.

6237 LP, green bone, 1920-40, Tested XX 650

6237-1/2, Rogers bone early, 1920-40,
    Tested XX 750

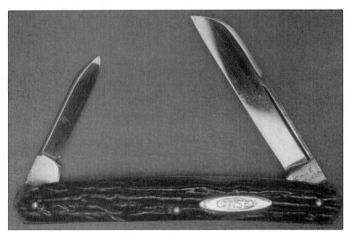

5238, Rogers Bone, 3-5/8", Case Bradford, PA-Pattern number on Pen blade, $350.

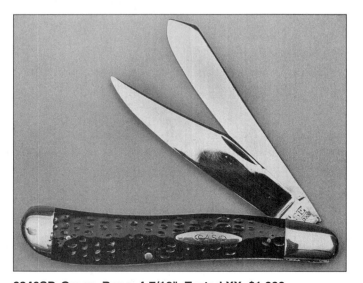

6240SP, Green, Bone, 4-7/16", Tested XX, $1,000.

3240SP, yellow comp., 4-7/16", 1920-40,
    Tested XX 700

6240Pen, green bone, 4-7/16", 1920-40,
    Tested XX 700

9240SP, imitation pearl, 4-7/16", 1920-40,
    Tested XX 700

62042, Imitation Black Bone, 2-7/8", XX, $50.

52042LP, stag, 3", 1920-40, Tested XX,
    Slant bolsters 250

52042, stag, reg. pull, 3", 1920-40,
    Tested XX 200

62042, green bone, 3", 1920-40, Tested XX 175

8042, genuine pearl, 3", 1920-40, Tested XX,
    slant bolsters 325

92042, imitation pearl, 3", 1920-40, Tested XX... 100

92042LP, imitation pearl, 3", 1920-40,
    Tested XX 125

62042, rough black, 3", 1940-50, XX 50

62042, green bone, 3", 1940-55, XX 125

62042, red bone, 3", 1940-64, XX 100

62042, bone, 3", 1940-64, XX................................ 60

62042R, bone, 3", 1940-64, XX 60

92042, imitation pearl, 3", 1940-64, XX 40

92042, cracked ice, 3", 1940-64, XX 40

92042R, imitation pearl, 3", 1940-64, XX.............. 45

92042R, cracked ice, 3", 1940-64, XX.................. 45

62042, bone, 3", 1965-69, USA 40

62042R, bone, 3", 1965-69, USA 40

92042, imitation pearl, 3", 1965-69, USA.............. 35

92042R, imitation pearl, 3", 1965-69, USA 35

62042, stainless, rare, 3-1/4", 1970, 10 Dot 200

62042, bone, 3", 1970, 10 Dot 40

62042R, bone, 3", 1970, 10 Dot 40

92042, imitation pearl, 3", 1970, 10 Dot................ 35

92042R, imitation pearl, 3", 1970, 10 Dot 40

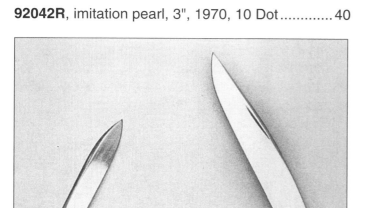

52044, 2nd Cut Stag, 3-1/4", rare, Tested XX, $250.

62044F, green bone, 3-1/4", 1920-40,
Tested XX 200

82044, genuine pearl, 3-1/4", 1920-40,
Tested XX 250

8044F, genuine pearl 3-1/4", 1920-40,
Tested XX 250

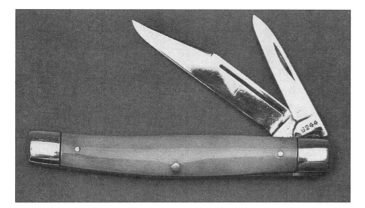

B244, Waterfall, LP, 3-1/4", Tested XX, $150.

2244, slick black, 3-1/4", 1920-40, Tested XX 135

3244, yellow comp., 3-1/4", 1920-40,
Tested XX 135

5244, stag, 3-1/4", 1920-40, Tested XX 200

6244, green bone, 3-1/4, 1920-40 Tested, XX 200

88244, genuine pearl, 3-1/4", 1920-40,
Tested XX 250

9244, imitation pearl, 3-1/4", 1920-40,
Tested XX 150

6244, green bone, 3-1/4", 1940-55, XX 125

6244, red bone, 3-1/4", 1940-64, XX 75

6244, bone, 3-1/4", 1940-64, XX 50

6244, bone, 3-1/4", 1 965-69, USA 40

6244, bone stag, 3-1/4", 1970, 10 Dot 40

6244, delrin, rare, 3-1/4", 1970, 10 Dot 125

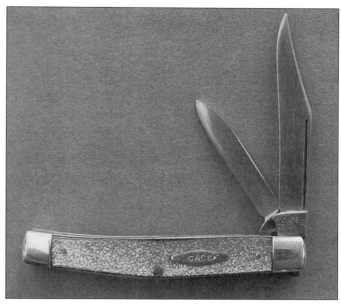

GS244LP, gold stone, 3-1/4", Case, Bradford, PA, $250.

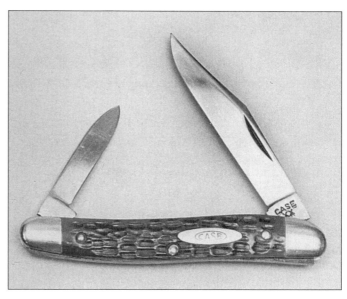

06244, Green Bone, 3-1/4", XX, $150.

02244, slick black, 3-1/4", 1920-40, Tested XX .. 120

05244, stag, 3-1/4", 1920-40, Tested XX 200

06244, green bone, 3-1/4", 1920-40,
Tested XX 175

06244, red bone, 3-1/4", 1940-64, XX 75

06244, bone, 3-1/4", 1940-64, XX 50

06244, bone, 3-1/4", 1 965-69, USA 40

06244, delrin, 3-1/4", 1970, 10 Dot 40

06244, bone stag, 3-1/4", 1970, 10 Dot 40

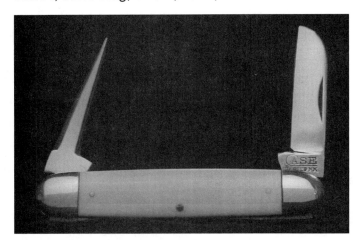

B245PU, Waterfall, Tested XX, 3-3/4", $250.

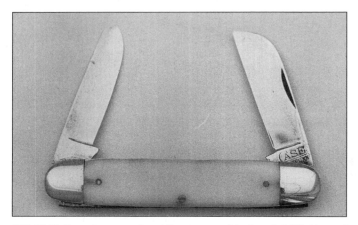

03245, Yellow Comp., sheep foot, spay blades, 3-3/4", Tested XX, $200.

06245, Dog Grooming Knife, large and small stamp, Green Bone, 3-3/4", 1920-40, Tested XX, $500.

02245, slick black, 3-1/4", 1920-40, Tested XX .. 160

04245B&G, white comp, 3-3/4", 1920-40, Tested XX 225

04245LP, white comp., 3-3/4", 1920-40, SH.FT., Tested XX 200

06245, green bone, 3-3/4", 1920-40, spear, Tested XX.. 275

06245, green bone, 3-3/4", 1920-40, dog grooming, Tested XX 500

06245, green bone, 3-3/4", 1920-40, Tested XX 225

06245, green bone, 3-3/4", 1920-40, dog grooming, Tested XX 450

02245-1/2, slick black, 3-3/4", 1920-40, Tested XX 160

05245-1/2, stag, 3-3/4", 1920-40, Tested XX 250

06245-1/2, green bone, 3-3/4", 1920-40, Tested XX 275

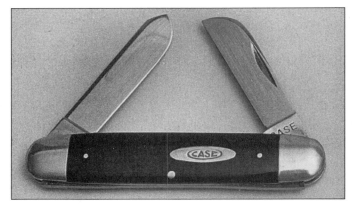

2245SHSP, Slick Black, 3-3/4", XX, $200.

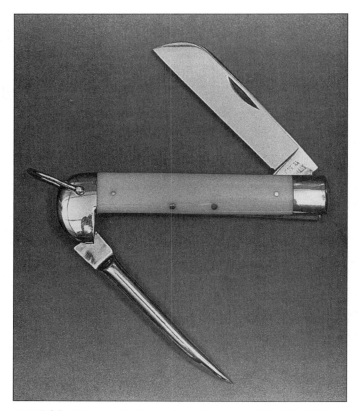

3246RSS, Rigger's Knife, Yellow Comp., 4-3/8", XX, $150.

3246R, yellow comp., 4-3/8", 1920-40, Navy knife, Tested XX.................................. 225

6246R, green bone, 4-3/8", 1920-40, Tested XX 400

3246R, yellow comp., 4-3/8", 1940-64, XX, Rigger's knife (none stainless)........................ 200

6246RSS, red bone, 4-3/8", 1940-64, XX,
stainless..275

6246RSS, bone, 4-3/8", 1940-64, XX,
stainless... 175

3246RSS, yellow comp., 4-3/8", USA.................300

These have never been made in USA stamp.

6246RSS, bone, 4-3/8", 1965-69, USA,
stainless..100

6246RSS, bone, 4-3/8", 1970, 10 Dot,
Stainless, rigger's knife..................................100

06246, Bone, W.R. Case & Sons, Brad. PA, $275.

05247J, stag, 3-7/8", 1920-40, Tested XX..........750
06247J, green bone, 3-7/8", 1920-40,
Tested XX 700

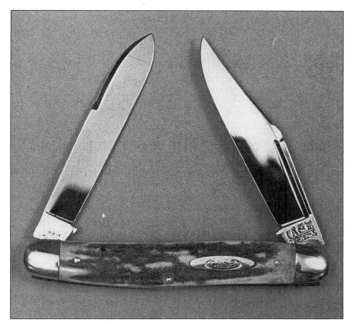

05247JLP, Red Stag, Tested XX, (rare), 3-7/8", $850.

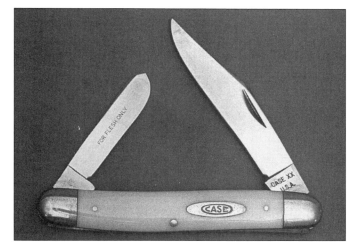

04247SP, White Comp., 3-7/8", USA, $150

04247SP, white comp., 3-7/8", 1920-40,
Long pull, Tested XX.......................................300
05247SP, stag, 3-7/8", 1920-40, long pull,
Tested XX 350
06247SP, Winterbottom bone, 3-7/8",
1920-40, Long pull, Tested XX........................750
06247SP, green bone, 3-7/8", 1920-40,
Long pull, Tested XX.......................................450
06247Pen, green bone, 3-7/8", 1920-40,
Long pull, Tested XX.......................................450
06247Pen, rough black, 3-7/8", 1920-40,
Long pull, Tested XX.......................................325
04247SP, L.P., white comp., 3-7/8",
1940-64, XX...225
04247SP, white comp., 3-7/8", 1940-64, XX.......150
05247SP, stag, 3-7/8", 1940-64, XX 200
05247SP, stag, 3-7/8", 1940-64, long pull, XX....300
05247SP, red Stag, 3-7/8", 1940-64, XX 450
05247SP, red Stag, 3-7/8", 1940-64,
long pull, 1940-64 500

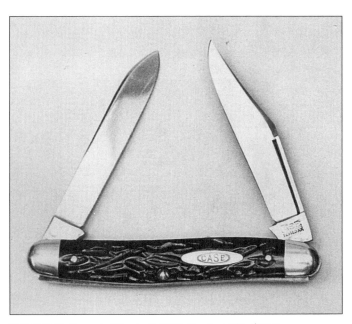

06247JLP, Rough Black, 3-7/8", Tested XX, $650.

05247Pen, stag, 3-7/8", 1940-64, XX 200

05247Pen, stag, 3-7/8", 1940-64, long pull, XX .. 300

05247Pen, red stag, 3-7/8", 1940-64, XX 400

05247Pen, red stag, 3-7/8", 1940-64,
long pull, XX 450

06247Pen, green bone, 3-7/8", 1940-55 XX 250

06247Pen, green bone, 1940-55, regular
pull, XX 225

06247Pen, rough black, 3-7/8", 1940-64, XX 225

06247Pen, rough black, 3-7/8", 1940-64,
Long pull, XX 250

06247Pen, red bone, 3-7/8", 1940-64 XX 125

06247 Pen, bone, 3-7/8", 1940-64, XX 90

06247Pen, red Rogers bone late,
3-7/8", 1940-64, XX 200

06247Pen, Rogers bone late, 3-7/8",
1940-64, XX 200

06247Pen, bone, 3-7/8", 1970, 10 Dot 75

4247FK, Greenskeeper, 1940-64, 3-7/8", Case XX, Spl. Dandelion Blade, $400.

4247FK, greenskeeper , 1965-69, USA 400

4247FK, white comp., 3-7/8", 1970, 10 Dot,
Greenskeeper's knife, (very scarce) 450

4247FK, white comp., rare , 3-7/8", 1973,
7 Dot 400

62048SP, Green Bone, LP, 4", Tested, XX, $350.

62048SP, green bone, 4", Easy Opener,
Tested XX 350

RM2048, Christmas tree, 4", 1920-40,
Tested XX 550

RM2048SP, Christmas tree, 4", 1920-40,
Tested XX 550

B2048, onyx, 4", 1920-40, Tested XX 300

GS2048, gold stone, 4", 1920-40, Tested XX 350

R2048, candy stripe, 4", 1920-40, Tested XX 350

32048SP, yellow comp., 4", 1940-64, XX 100

62048SP, green bone, 4", 1940-55, XX 250

62048SP, red bone, 4", 1940-64, XX 125

62048SP, Rogers bone, 4", 1940-64, XX 175

62048SP, bone, 4, 1940-64", XX 80

32048SP, yellow comp., 4", 1965-69, USA 55

62048SP, delrin, 4", 1965-69, USA 30

62048SP, bone stag, 4", 1965-69, USA 50

62048SPSSP, delrin, 4", 1965-69, USA 30

62048SPSSP, bone, 4", 1965-69, USA,
Stainless, polished, master blade etched
"Tested XX Stainless" (first model) 100

62048SPSSP, bone, 4", 1965-69, USA,
stainless polished edge 75

62048SPSSP, bone, 4", 1965-69, USA,
stainless polished blade 90

32048SP, yellow comp., 4", 1970, 10 Dot 60

62048SP, delrin, 4", 1970, 10 Dot 30

62048SPSSP, delrin, 4", 1970, 10 Dot,
stainless, polished edge 30

62049PEN, green bone, 4", Tested XX 800

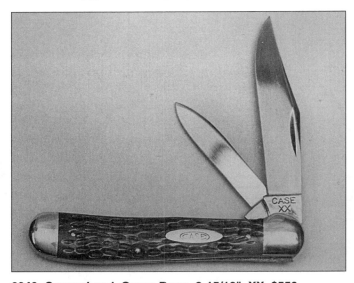

6249, Copperhead, Green Bone, 3-15/16", XX, $550.

P249, mottled brown, 3-15/16", 1920-40,
Tested XX 450

6249, rough black, 3-15/16", 1920-40,
Tested XX 350

6249, green bone, 3-15/16", 1920-40,
Tested XX 450

9249, imitation pearl, 3-15/16", 1920 40,
Tested XX 400

6249, red bone, 3-15/16", 1940-64, XX 300

6249, Rogers bone, early, 3-5/16", 1940-64,
XX 800

6249, rough black, 3-5/16", 1940-49, XX............450

6249, bone, 3-15/16", 1940-64, XX 150

6249, bone, 3-15/16", 1965-69, USA.................. 100

6249, bone, 3-15/16", 1970, 10 Dot................... 110

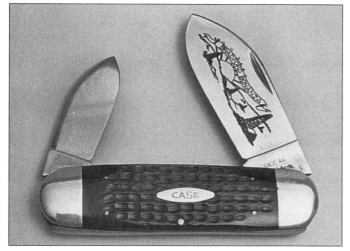

6250, Bradford Bonanza (scarce), laminated wood, 4-1/2",
10 Dot (1980), $100.

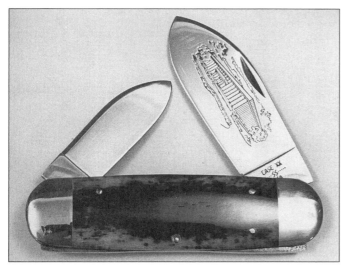

A6250, Museum Founders, Appaloosa Bone, 4-1/2", 1980
(Lightning S), $200.

6250, green bone, 4-3/8", 1920-40,
Tested XX 1,250

6250, green bone, 4-3/8", 1940-55,
Sunfish, XX 1,000

6250, red bone, 4-3/8", 1940-64, XX 400

6250, bone stag, 4-3/8", 1940-64, XX................ 325

6250, laminated wood, 4-3/8", 1940-64, XX 150

6250, laminated wood, 4-3/8", 1965-69, USA..... 100

6250, bone stag, 4-3/8", 1965-69, USA.............. 300

6250, laminated wood, 4-3/8", 1970, 10 Dot....... 100

6251, green bone, 5-1/4", 1920-40,
Tested XX, Knife-fork combo. 750

6251, Rogers bone, early, 5-1/4", 1920-40,
Knife-fork combo., Tested XX 800

9251, imitation onyx, 5-1/4", 1920-40,
Tested XX, Knife-fork combo. 750

8251, pearl, 5-1/4", 1910-15, knife-fork
combo. 2,500

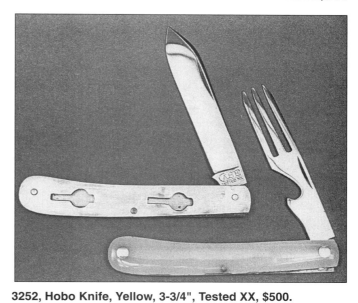

3252, Hobo Knife, Yellow, 3-3/4", Tested XX, $500.

6252, green bone, 3-3/4", 1920-40,
Knife-fork combo., Tested XX 650

52052, stag, 3-1/2", 1920-40, Tested XX 500

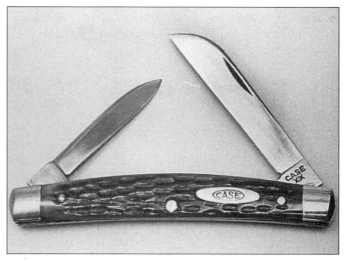

62052, Green Bone, 3-3/4", 1920-40, Tested XX, Knife-Fork
Combo, $500.

62052, green bone, 3-1/2", 1920-40,
Tested XX 500

62052, Rogers bone, early,
3-1/2", 1920-40, Tested XX............................600

62052, rough black, 3-1/2", 1940-50, XX............400

62052, green bone, 3-1/2", 1940-55, XX 300

62052, red bone, 3-1/2", 1940-64, XX 150

62052, bone, 3-1/2", 1965-69, USA.....................75

62052, bone, 3-1/2", 1970, 10 Dot........................75

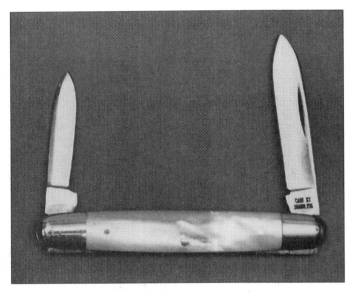

82053SS, Pearl, 2-1/4", with Bolsters, XX, $85.

82053SRSS, Pearl, 2-13/16", USA, $75.

GS2053, gold Stone, Tested XX 250

5253, stag, 3-1/4", 1920-40, Tested XX..............150

5253LP, stag, 3-1/4", 1920-40, Tested XX..........200

6253, green bone, 3-1/4", 1920-40, Tested XX ..175

62053, green bone, 2-3/4", 1920-40, Bolsters,
Tested XX 175

82053SR, pearl, 2 -13/16", 1920-40,
Tested XX 175

9253, imitation pearl, 3-1/4", 1920-40,
Tested XX 125

62053SS, bone, 2-3/4", 1940-64 XX, bolsters......75

82053SR, genuine pearl, 2-13/16", 1940-64,
XX 100

82053SS, genuine pearl, 2-13/16", 1940-64,
Stainless, XX 100

62053SS, bone, 2-3/4", 1965-69, USA,
Rare, with bolsters 175

82053SRSS, genuine pearl, 2-13/16",
1965-69, Stainless, USA................................. 75

6254SSP, Bone Trapper , (Pigs Eye Steel Pin), 1978, 2 Dot (special order), rare, $150.

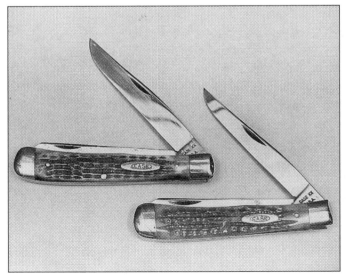

Top: 5254, 2nd Cut Stag, Reg. blade, 4-1/8", USA, $550. Bottom: 5254, 2nd Cut Stag, Muskrat, 4-1/8", USA, $600.

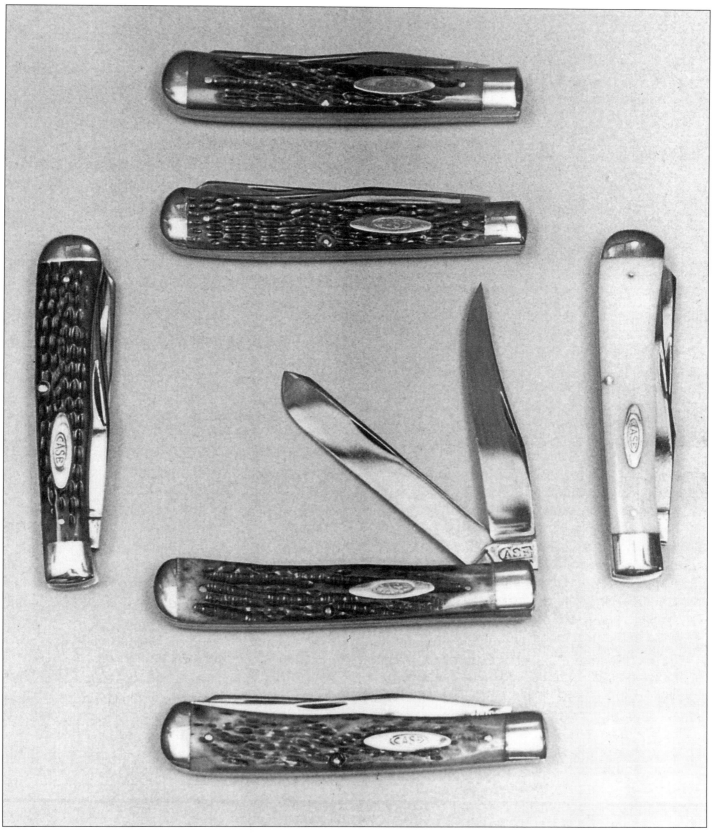

Trapper 54 Pattern: Top to bottom: 5254, Red Stag, 4-1/8", Tested XX, $3,000; 6254, Green Bone, 4-1/8", Tested XX, $3,000; 5254, (blades open) 2nd Cut Stag, 4-1/8", Tested XX, $3,000; 6254, Rogers Bone, 4-1/8", XX with Tested Frame, $3,000; 5254, Stag, 4-1/8", Tested XX, $2,500. Left: 6254, Red Bone, 4-1/8", Tested XX, $1,800; right: 3254, Yellow Comp., 4-1/8", Tested XX, $2,000.

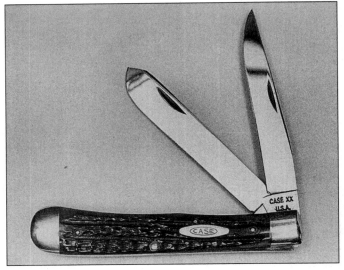

6254, Trapper, 2nd Cut Bone, 4-1/8", Muskrat Blade, USA, $600.

3254, yellow comp., 4-1/8",
1920-40, Rare, Tested XX 2,000

5254, red stag, 4-1/8", 1920-40, Tested XX,
rare 3,000

5254, stag, 4-1/8", 1920-40, Tested XX 2,500

5254, second-cut stag, 4-1/8", 1920-40,
Rare, Tested XX...3,000

6254, green bone, 4-1/8", 1920-40,
Tested XX 3,000

6254, red bone, 4-1/8", 1920-40, Tested XX,
rare 2,500

6254, Rogers bone, early, 4-1/8", 1920-40,
Rare, Tested XX...3,000

9254, imitation pearl, 4-1/8", 1920-40,
Tested XX 2,200

6254, Winterbottom bone, 4-1/8", 1920-40.....3,500

3254, yellow comp., 4-1/8", 1940-64, XX............175

3254, yellow comp., 4-1/8", 1940-64, XX,
Tested frame, first model 300

First models read "Tested XX Stainless" etched
lengthwise on clip blade. Second models read "Tested
XX Razor Edge" etched lengthwise on clip blade.

3254, flat yellow, 4-1/8", 1940-64, XX,
Tested Frame, First Model..............................325

6254, green bone, 4-1/8", 1940-55, XX,
Tested Frame, First Model, rare...................1,800

6254, red bone, 4-1/8", 1940-64, XX,
Trapper 600

6254, red bone, 1st Model, Tested Frame,
XX...1,000

5254, stag, 4-1/8", 1940-64, XX 350

5254, stag, 4-1/8", 1940-64, XX,
Tested Frame, First Model..............................450

5254, red stag, 4-1/8", 1940-64, XX, rare 1,500

6254, bone, 4-1/8", 1940-64, XX 350

6254, bone, 4-1/8", 1940-64, XX,
Tested Frame, First Model..............................500

6254, second-cut stag, 4-1/8", 1940-64,
XX, rare...2,000

6254, Rogers bone, 4-1/8", 1940-42, XX,
Rare, Tested Frame 2,500

3254, yellow comp., 4-1/8", 1965-69, USA 110

3254, flat yellow, 4-1/8", 1965-69, USA 125

3254, flat yellow, 4-1/8", 1965-69, USA,
Rare, Muskrat blade 350

3254, yellow comp., 4-1/8", 1965-69, USA,
Muskrat Blade...250

5254, stag, 4-1/8", 1965-69, USA 150

5254, stag, 4-1/8", 1965-69, USA, Muskrat
blade 300

6254, bone, 4-1/8", 1965-69, USA......................150

6254, bone, 4-1/8", 1965-69, USA,
Muskrat blade 300

6254, second-cut reg. blade, 4-1/8",
1965-69, USA 600

6254SSP, 4-1/8", 1965-69, USA, Both blades
stamped "Case XX, Stainless".......................550

6254SSP, bone, 4-1/8", 1965-69, USA,
polished blades 250

6254SSP, bone, 4-1/8", 1965-69, USA, polished
edge 135

6254SSP, bone, 4-1/8", 1965-69, USA,
Muskrat blade, polished edge 300

6254SSP, bone, 4-1/8", 1965-69, USA,
Muskrat blade, polished blade 300

6254SSP, bone, 4-1/8", 1965-69, USA,
First Model, ("Tested XX Stainless"
etched lengthwise on master blade)................275

3254, yellow comp, 4-1/8", 1970, 10 Dot............125

3254, flat yellow, 4-1/8", 1970, 10 Dot 225

5254, stag, 4-1/8", 1970, 10 Dot 150

5254, second-cut stag, 4-1/8", 1970,
10 Dot, Very rare...800

6254, bone, 4-1/8", 1970, 10 Dot.......................150

6254SSP, bone, 4-1/8", 1970, 10 Dot,
polished edge 125

6254SSP, bone, 4-1/8", 1970, 10 Dot,
large stamp 400

6254SSP, 4-1/8", 1970, 10 Dot, gut blade
proto (6 made) 600

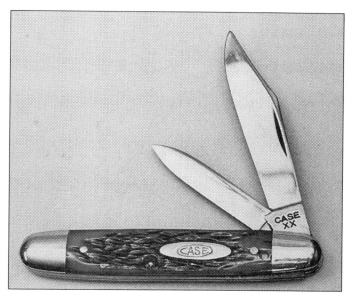

62055, Rogers Bone, 3-1/2", XX, $225.

22055, slick Black, 3-1/2", 1920-40,
Tested XX 200

22055LP, slick black comp., 3-1/2",
1920-40, Tested XX 250

32055, yellow comp., 3-1/2", 1920-40,
Tested XX 225

32055, yellow comp., 3-1/2", 1920-40,
Long pull, Tested XX 300

62055, green bone, 3-1/2", 1920-40,
Tested XX 275

62055LP, green bone, Tested XX 225

62055, rough black, 3-1/2", 1920-40, Long pull,
Tested XX 350

92055, imitation pearl, 3-1/2", 1920-40,
Tested XX 250

62055, rough black, 3-1/2", 1940-50, XX 150

62055, rough black, 3-1/2", 1940-50 XX,
long pull 200

62055, green bone, 3-1/2", 1940-55, XX 250

62055, green bone, 3-1/2", 1940-55, XX,
long pull 325

62055, red bone, 3-1/2", 1940-64, XX 125

22055, slick black, 3-1/2", 1940-64, XX 75

22055, slick black, 3-1/2", 1940-64, XX,
long pull 125

62055, bone, 3-1/2", 1940-64, XX 85

62055, bone, 3-1/2", 1940-64, XX, long pull 200

92055, cracked ice, 3-1/2", 1940-64, XX 225

92055, cracked ice, 3-1/2", 1940-64, XX,
long pull 300

22055, slick black, 3-1/2", 1965-69, USA 185

62055, bone, 3-1/2", 1965-69, USA 55

62055, bone, 3-1/2", 1970, 10 Dot 55

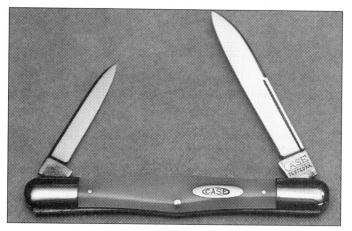

32056, Yellow/White Liner, 3-1/2", Case Tested XX, $250.

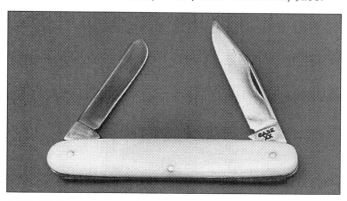

4257, White Comp., 3-3/4", XX, $45.

4257, white comp., 3-3/4", 1920-40, Tested XX .. 100

4257, white comp., 3-3/4", 1940-64, XX,
"Office Knife" on handle 125

42057, white comp., 3-5/16", 1920-40,
Tested XX 80

92057, imitation pearl, 3-5/16", 1920-40,
Tested XX 90

42057, white comp., 3-5/16", 1940-64, XX,
"Office Knife" on handle 125

42057, white comp., 3-5/16", 1940-64, XX,
Office Knife, plain handle 50

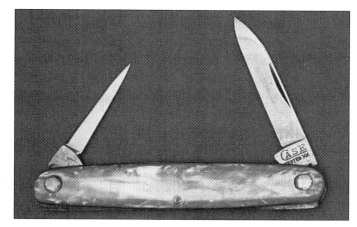

92058, Birdseye, French Pearl, 3-1/4", Tested XX, $125.

32058, yellow comp., 3-1/4", 1920-40,
Tested XX 125
92058, imitation pearl, 3-1/4, 1920-40,
Tested XX 125
92058, cracked ice, 3-1/4, 1940-50, XX 125

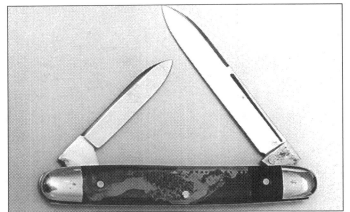

HA2058LP, High Art Handles, Regular Bolsters, 3-1/4", $400.

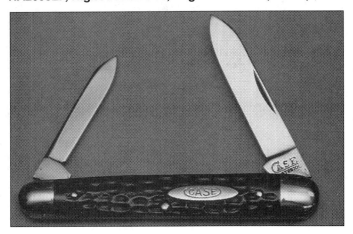

Senator Pen.

62059, green bone, 3-1/4", 1920-40,
Tested XX 150
62059SP, green bone, 3-1/4", 1920-40,
Tested XX 150
62059-1/2, green bone, 3-1/4", 1920-40,
Tested XX 150

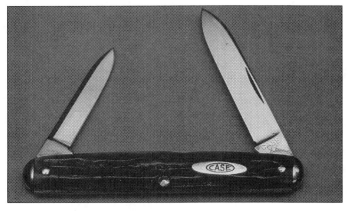

Equal End Gentleman's Knife.

5260, stag, 3-7/16", 1920-40, Tested XX 200
5260, red stag, 3-7/16", 1920-40, Tested XX...... 225
5260, stag, 3-7/16", 1940-64, XX........................ 175
5260, red stag, 3-7/16", 1940-64, XX 200

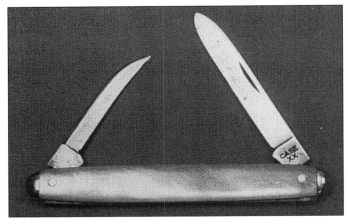

8261, Pearl, 2-78", 1940-64, XX, $55.

6261, green bone, 2-7/8", 1920-40, Tested XX... 120
6261F, green bone, 2-7/8", 1920-40,
Tested XX 135
8261, genuine pearl, 2-7/8", 1920-40,
Tested XX 145
8261F, genuine pearl, 2-7/8", 1920-40,
Tested XX 155
9261, imitation pearl, 2-7/8", 1920-40,
Tested XX 100
9261F, imitation pearl, 2-7/8", 1920-40,
Tested XX 120
9261, imitation pearl, 2-7/8", 1940-64, XX 35
9261, cracked ice, 2-7/8", 1940-64, XX 35
8261, genuine pearl, 2-7/8", 1965-6, USA 75
9261, imitation pearl, 2-7/8", 1965-69, USA 30
8261, genuine pearl, 2-7/8", 1970, 10 Dot 75
9261, imitation pearl, 2-7/8", 1970, 10 Dot 35

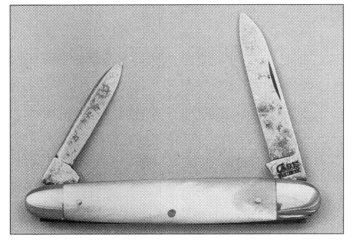

82063, Genuine Pearl, 3-1/8", 1920-40, Tested XX, $150.

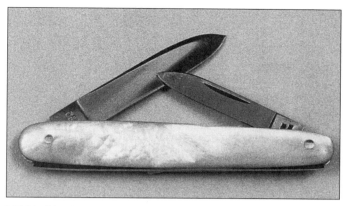

82063, Shadow, Pearl, 3-1/16", XX, $125.

82063, genuine pearl, 3-1/16", 1920-40,
No bolster, Tested XX 150
82063SHADSS, genuine pearl, 3-1/16",
1965-69, USA 225
62063SS, bone, 3-1/16", 1940-64, XX 75
62063, green bone, 3-1/16", 1940-55, XX 150

62063LP, Green Bone, 3-1/16", 1920-40, Tested XX, $175.

62063SS, red bone, 3-1/16", 1940-64, XX 100

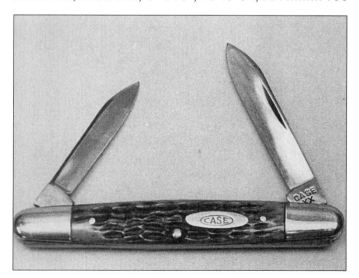

06263, Green Bone, Non Stainless, 3-1/8", XX, $125.

05263, stag, 3-1/8", 1920-40, Tested XX,
non-stainless.. 150
06263, green bone, 3-1/8", 1920-40,
Tested XX 150
08263, genuine pearl, 3-1/8", 1920-40,
Tested XX 150
06263SS, green bone, 3-1/8", 1940-55,
XX, Stainless 150
06263SS, red bone, 3-1/8", 1940-64, XX 90
05263, stag, non stainless, 3-1/8", 1940-64,
XX 200
05263SS, stag, 3-1/8", 1940-64, XX 75
06263, bone, 3-1/8", 1940-64, XX 80
06263SS, bone, 3-1/8", 1940-64, XX.................... 60
05263SS, stag, 3-1/8", 1965-69, USA 80
06263FSS, bone, 3-1/8", 1965-69, USA.............. 45
06263SSP, bone, 3-1/8", 1965-69, USA,
polished blade.. 45
06263SSP, bone, 3-1/8", 1965-69, USA,
edge, polished 45
06263SSP, bone, 3-1/8", 1965-69, USA, master
blade etched "Tested XX Stainless,"
first model, brushed finish.................................. 60
Also polished finish.
05263SS, stag, 3-1/8", 1970, 10 Dot 75
06263SS, bone, 3-1/8", 1970, 10 Dot.................. 45
06263SSP, bone, 3-1/8", 1970, 10 Dot,
polished blade.. 45
06263FSSP, bone, 3-1/8", 1970, 10 Dot,
polished blade.. 45
06263FS, bone, 3-1/8", 1970, 10 Dot 45

62063-1/2, Bone, 3-1/16", Stainless, XX, $75.

62063-1/2, green bone, 3-1/16", 1920-40,
Tested XX 150
82063-1/2, genuine pearl, 3-1/16",
1920-40, Tested XX 175

92063-1/2, imitation pearl, 3-1/16",
1920-40, Tested XX 150

62063-1/2, green bone, 3-1/16", 1940-55, XX 125

62063-1/2SS, red bone, 3-1/16", 1940-64, XX 90

92063-1/2, imitation pearl, 3-1/16", 1940-64, XX.. 85

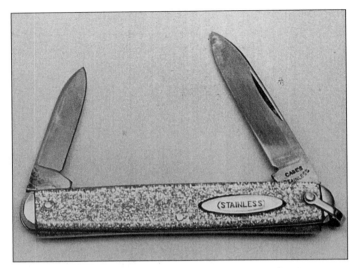

GS264R, Gold Stone, 3-1/8", Case's Stainless, $250.

6264T, green bone, 3-1/8", 1920-40,
Tip bolster, Tested XX 175

6264TF, green bone, 3-1/8", 1920-40,
Tested XX 175

8264T, genuine pearl, 3-1/8", 1920-40,
Tested XX 225

8264TF, genuine pearl, 3-1/8", 1920-40,
Tested XX 225

9264TF, imitation pearl, 3-1/8", 1920-40,
Tested XX 120

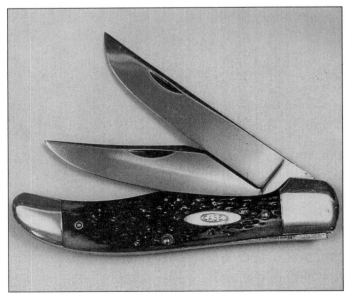

6265SAB, Folding Knife, Rogers Bone, late, 5-1/4", XX, $550.

6265LP, Green Bone, 3-1/4", Tested XX, Pattern No. stamped on back of master blade, $300.

3265SAB, yellow comp., 5-1/4", 1920-40,
Tested XX 500

3265, yellow comp., 5-1/4", 1920-40,
Flat blade, Tested XX 550

5265SAB, stag, 5-1/4, 1920-40", Tested XX 450

5265, stag, 5-1/4", 1920-40, Tested XX,
flat blade 500

5265, second-cut stag, 5-1/4", 1920-40,
Flat blade, Tested XX 700

6265, second-cut stag, 5-1/4", 1920-40,
Tested XX 600

6265SAB, green bone, 5-1/4", 1920-40,
Tested XX 500

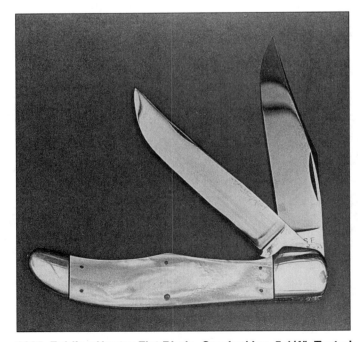

9265, Folding Hunter Flat Blade, Cracked Ice, 5-1/4", Tested XX, $650.

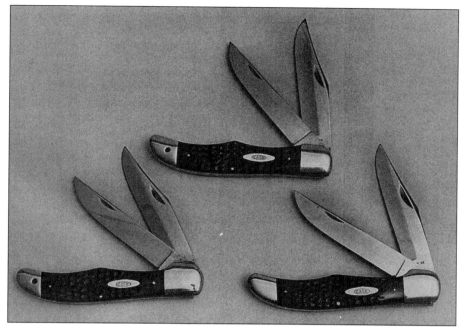

Folding Hunters: Top: 6265SAB, Pakkawood, 5-1/4", USA Frame/drilled bolsters, $55; left: 6265SAB, Pakkawood, 5-1/4", USA on XX Frame Drilled Bolster, $90; right: 6265SAB, Pakkawood, 5-1/4", USA on XX Frame/Bolster not drilled, $110. Pig's Eye Bolsters-Pin-made for Florida State Conservation Dept. 6265 for skinning alligators. Nickel Pins broke easy, so changed to steel pins. Not in production. Photo courtesy Ralph Scruton.

6265SAB, rough black, 5-1/4", 1940, Tested XX 450

6265, flat ground, 5-1/4", 1940, Tested XX 500

5265, stag, 5-1/4", 1940-64 XX, flat master blade 500

5265SAB, stag, 5-1/4", 1940-64, XX 175

5265SABDR, stag, 5-1/4", 1940-64, XX 200

5265SAB, second-cut stag, 5-1/4", 1940-64, XX 700

6265, green bone, 5-1/4", 1940-55, XX, flat blade 500

6265SAB, red bone, 5-1/4", 1940-64, XX 225

6265, red bone, 5-1/4", 1940-64, XX, flat blade 400

6265, bone, 5-1/4", 1940-64, XX, flat ground master 400

6265SAB, laminated wood, 5-1/4", 1940-64, XX 125

6265SAB, bone, 5-1/4", 1940-64, XX 300

6265SAB, Rogers bone, 5-1/4", 1940-64, XX 500

5265SABDR, stag, 5-1/4", 1965-69, USA 125

5265SAB, stag, bolsters not drilled, XX Frame USA 200

6165 and 6265 with bomb shield and all blades stamped bring a premium of approx. $100 or more.

5265SABDR, stag, 5-1/4", 1965-69, USA, XX Frame 200

6265SAB, bone, 5-1/4", 1965-69, USA, XX Frame 300

6265SABDR, bone, 5-1/4", 1965-69, USA, small blade serrated 300

6265SABDR, wood, 5-1/4", 1965-69, USA, XX Frame 90

6265SABDR, wood, 5-1/4", 1965-69, USA 60

6265, green bone, 5-1/4, Flat blade, 1920-40, Tested XX 550

9265SAB, imitation pearl, 5-1/4", 1920-40, Tested XX 500

9265, imitation pearl, 5-1/4", 1920-40, Flat blade, Tested XX 550

6265SAB, rough black, 5-1/4", 1940-50, Folding hunter, XX 400

6265, rough black, 5-1/4", 1940-50, Flat blade, XX 450

6265SAB, green bone, 5-1/4", 1940-55, XX 400

6265SAB-DR, bone, 5-1/4", 1965-69, USA, XX, Frame 300

5265SAB-DR, stag, 5-1/4", 1970, 10 Dot 125

6265SAB-DR, wood, 5-1/4", 1970, 10 Dot 60

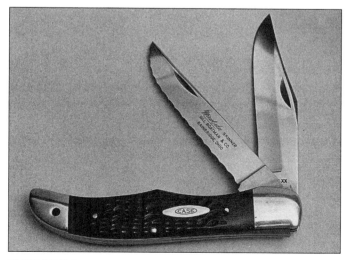

6265SAB/DR, Folding Hunter, Pakkawood, Serrated Edge, Bill Boatman, 5-1/4", USA, $200.

6265SAB, red bone, 5-1/4", 1940-64, XX,
Bill Boatman, serrated 350

6265SAB, laminated wood, 5-1/4", 1940-64,
XX, Small blade serrated, Bill Boatman
Special 200

6265SAB, bone, 5-1/4", 1940-64, XX, Small
blade serrated, Bill Boatman Special..............350

6265SAB DR, bone, 5-1/4", 1940-64, XX,
Small blade serrated, Bill Boatman Special 350

6265SAB DR, laminated wood, 5-1/4", 1940-64,
XX, Serrated small blade, Bill Boatman..........250

6265SAB DR, wood, 5-1/4", 1965-69, USA,
Serrated small blade, Bill Boatman.................250

6265SAB DR, wood, 5-1/4", 1970, 10 Dot,
Bill Boatman...250

Note: All Boatman serrated-blade folding hunters
are quite scarce.

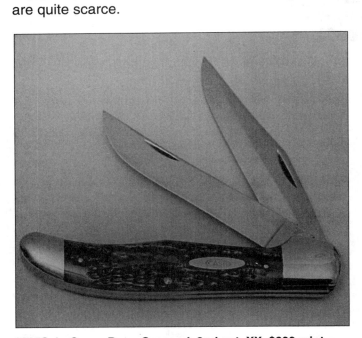

6265Sab, Green Bone Grooved, 2nd cut, XX, $600 mint.

6265SAB DR SSP, laminated wood, 5-1/4",
1979-80, 1 Dot...40

6265SAB DR SSP, laminated wood, 5-1/4",
1978-79, 2 Dot...40

6265SAB DR SSP, laminated wood, 5-1/4",
1977-78, 3 Dot...40

6265SAB DR SSP, laminated wood, 5-1/4",
1976-77, 4 Dot...45

6265SAB DR SSP, laminated wood, 5-1/4",
1975-76, 5 Dot...45

6265SAB DR SSP, laminated wood, 5-1/4",
1974-75, 6 Dot...45

6265SAB DR SSP, laminated wood, 5-1/4",
1973-74, 7 Dot...50

6265SAB DR SSP, laminated wood, 5-1/4",
1972-73, 8 Dot...50

6265SAB DR, laminated wood, 5-1/4",
1979-80, 1 Dot...40

6265SAB DR, laminated wood, 5-1/4",
1978-79, 2 Dot...40

6265SAB DR, laminated wood, 5-1/4",
1977-78, 3 Dot...40

6265SAB DR, laminated wood, 5-1/4",
1976-77, 4 Dot...40

6265SAB DR, laminated wood, 5-1/4",
1975-76, 5 Dot...45

6265SAB DR, laminated wood, 5-1/4",
1974-75, 6 Dot...45

6265SAB DR, laminated wood, 5-1/4",
1973-74, 7 Dot...45

6265SAB DR, laminated wood, 5-1/4",
1972-73, 8 Dot...50

6265SAB DR, laminated wood, 5-1/4",
1971-72, 9 Dot...55

6265SAB DR, laminated wood, 5-1/4",
1970-71, 10 Dot...75

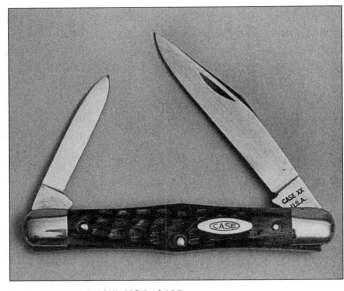

06267, Bone, 3-1/4", USA, $125.

06267, rough black, 3-1/4", 1940-50,
Tested XX 200

06267, cracked ice, 3-1/4", 1920-40,
Tested XX 200

06267, early Rogers bone, 3-1/4", 1920-40,
Tested XX 275

06267, green bone, 3-1/4", 1920-40,
Tested XX 250

06267, bone, long pull, 3-1/4", 1940-64, XX 125

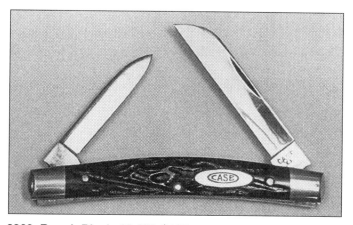

6269, Rough Black, 3", XX, $125.

6269, rough black, 3", 1920-40, Tested XX 175

6269, green bone, 3", 1920-40, Tested XX.........250

8269, genuine pearl, 3", 1920-40, Tested XX 325

9269, imitation pearl, 3", 1920-40, Tested XX.....200

6269LP, rough black, 3", 1940-50, XX...............200

6269, green bone, 3", 1940-55, XX 200

6269LP, green bone, 3", 1940-55, XX 250

6269, red bone, 3", 1940-64 XX 110

6269, bone, 3", 1940-64, XX 65

6269, bone, 3", 1965-69, USA 50

6269, bone, 1970, 10 Dot 50

6270F, bone, 3", 1920-40, Tested XX 300

8271, pearl, 3-1/4", reg. pull, 1940-64, XX.........200

8271, pearl, straight bolsters and pins,
    3-1/4", XX 200

RM271, red-black Christmas tree, 3-1/4",
    Case's Stainless 300

6271F, bone, 3-1/4", 1920-40, Flat bolsters,
    Tested XX 250

8271, genuine pearl, 3-1/4", 1920-40,
    Tested XX 250

8271F, genuine pearl, 3-1/4", 1920-40,
    Tested XX 250

9271, cracked ice, XX...150

6271, red bone, 3-1/4", 1940-64, XX 95

6271SS, bone, 3-1/4", 1940-64, XX 90

8271, genuine pearl, 3-1/4", 1940-64, XX,
    long pull 250

8271SS, genuine pearl, 3-1/4", 1940-64, XX..... 225

8271SS, genuine pearl, 3-1/4", 1940-64,
    XX, long pull..250

8271SSFLP, genuine pearl, 3-1/4", 1940-64,
    XX 225

8271F, genuine pearl, 3-1/4", 1940-64, XX.........200

8271F, genuine pearl, 3-1/4", 1940-64, XX,
    long pull 225

22074-1/2PU, slick black, 3-1/4", 1920-40,
    Tested XX 200

5275SP, stag, long pull, 4-1/4", 1920-40,
    Tested XX 650

6275SPLP, green bone, 4-1/4", 1920-40,
    Tested XX 600

6275SP, rough black, 4-1/4", 1920-40,
    Tested XX 400

6275SP, rough black, 4-1/4", 1940-50, XX,
    long pull 400

6275SP, red bone, 4-1/4", 1940-64, XX..............350

6275SP, red bone, 4-1/4", 1940-64, XX,
    long pull 450

6275SP, bone, 4-1/4", 1940-64, XX 125

6275SP, green bone , 4-1/4", 1940-64, XX,
    reg. pull 450

6275SP, bone, 4-1/4", 1965-69, USA 100

6275SP, bone, 4-1/4", 1970, 10 Dot 100

6276, green bone, 3-5/8", 1920-40, Tested XX...350

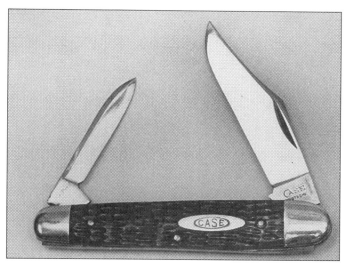

6276-1/2, Sleeveboard, Green Bone, 3-5/8", Tested XX, $300.

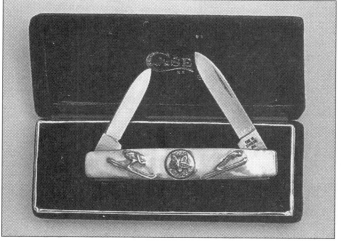

OL278SS Sterling, 1980 Winter Olympics, 3-1/16", (1,000 made), 1980, Serial No. 1000-2000, $200.

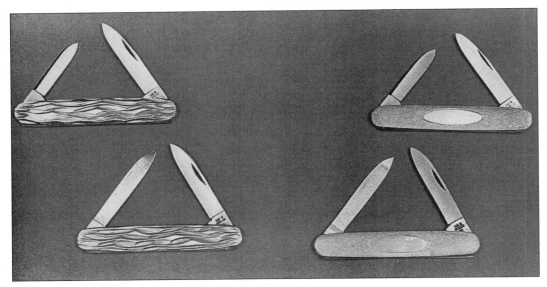

Proto Type, 250 of each produced: Left: M279, Bark, 3-1/16", Pen $35, File, $35. Right: M279, jewel, 3-1/6", Pen $35, File $35.

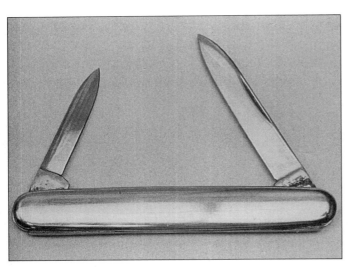

M279, All Metal, 3-1/8", Tested XX, $95.

6279F, Green Bone, 3-1/8", Tip Bolsters, Tested XX, $150.

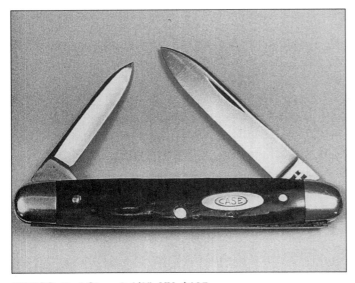

5279SS, Red Stag, 3-1/8", XX, $125.

RM279, Christmas tree, 3-1/8", 1920-40, Tested XX 225

GM279, green mottled, 3-1/8", 1920-40, Tested XX 200

M279R, metal, 3-1/8", 1920-40, Tested XX 90

2279, slick black, 3-1/8", 1920-40, Tested XX 100

3279, yellow comp., 3-1/8", 1920-40, Tested XX 100

3279R, yellow comp., 3-1/8", 1920-40, Tested XX 100

6279, green bone, 3-1/8", 1920-40, Tested XX...125

8279SHAD, genuine pearl, 3-1/8", 1920-40, Tested XX 200

82079, genuine pearl, 3-1/4", 1920-40, Tested XX 200

M279SS, metal, 3-1/8", 1940-64, XX....................30

627955, red bone, 3-1/8", 1940-64, XX 85

6279, Green Bone, 3-1/8", Tested XX, $175.

6279, bone, 3-1/8", 1940-64, XX 85
6279SSF, bone, 3-1/8", 1940-64, XX.................... 75
627955, bone, 3-1/8", 1940-64, XX 65

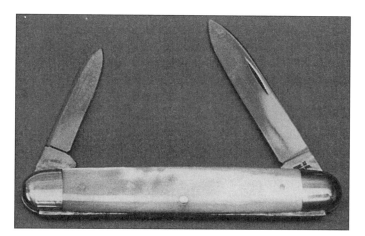

8279, Pearl, 3-1/8", Tested XX, $200.

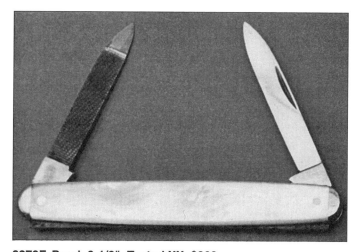

8279F, Pearl, 3-1/8", Tested XX, $200.

8279, genuine pearl, 3-1/8", 1940-64, XX............. 90
827955, genuine pearl, 3-1/8", 1940-64, XX......... 80
9279, imitation pearl, 3-1/8", 1940-64, XX 80
9279SSSHAD, cracked ice, 3-1/8", 1940-64,
    XX 35
927955, cracked ice, bolsters, 3-1/8",
    1940-64, XX 90
M279SC, stainless, 3-1/8", 1965-69, USA............ 40
M279SS, stainless, 3-1/8", 1965-69, USA,
    polished 30
M279SS, stainless, 3-1/8", 1965-69, USA 30
M279SSF, stainless, 3-1/8", 1965-69, USA 30
527955, stag, 3-1/8", 1965-69, USA 175
627955, bone, 3-1/8", 1965-69, USA 45
627955, bone, 3-1/8", 1965-69, USA,
    Transition (XX to USA) 90
M279SCSS, stainless, 3-1/8", 1970, 10 Dot 40
M279SSF, stainless, 3-1/8", 1970 10 Dot 30
627955, bone, 3-1/8", 1970, 10 Dot..................... 45
M279SS, metal, 3-1/8", 1970, 10 Dot 30
M279SSF, metal, 3-1/8", 1940-64, XX 35
2279SSSHAD, slick black, 3-1/8", 1940-64 XX 75

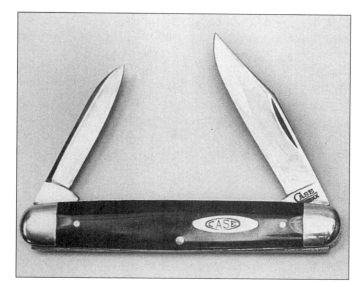

22791/2, Slick Black, 3-1/4", Tested XX, $125.

5279, stag, 3-1/8", 1940-64, XX.......................... 150
527955, stag, 3-1/8", 1940-64, XX...................... 150
6279, rough black, 3-1/8", 1940-50, XX................ 90
627955, rough black, 3-1/8", 1940-50, XX............ 75
6279SSF, rough black, 3-1/8", 1940-50, XX 75
6279, green bone, 3-1/8", 1940-55, XX 100
627955, green bone, 3-1/8", 1940-55, XX 85

6279SSF, green bone, 3-1/8", 1940-55, XX 110

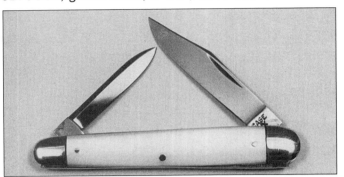

82079-1/2, Pearl, 3-1/4", XX, $85.

62079, spear blade, 3-1/4", Tested XX 150

62079-1/2, green bone, 3-1/4", 1920-40,
Tested XX 175

82079-1/2, genuine pearl, 3-1/4", 1920-40,
Tested XX 185

92679, imitation pearl, 3-1/4", Tested XX............ 140

92079-1/2, cracked ice, 3-1/4", 1920-40,
Tested XX 120

62079-1/2, bone, 3-1/4", 1940-64, XX 125

62079-1/2SS, green bone, 3-1/4", 1940-64,
XX 125

62079-1/2, rough black, 3-1/4", 1940-64, XX...... 150

82079-1/2SS, genuine pearl, 3-1/4", 1940-64,
XX 75

92079-1/2, imitation pearl, 3-1/4", 1940-64, XX.... 80

92079-1/2, cracked ice, 3-1/4", 1940-64, XX 90

82079-1/2SS, genuine pearl, 3-1/4", 1965-69,
USA 75

82079-1/2SS, genuine pearl, 3-1/4", 1970,
10 Dot 90

6281, bone, 3-1/8", 1920-40, Tested XX............. 800

8281, pearl, 3-1/8", 1920-40, Tested XX.......... 1,000

9281, imitation pearl, 3-1/8", 1920-40,
Tested XX 700

GS281, gold stone, 4", 1920-40, Tested XX 750

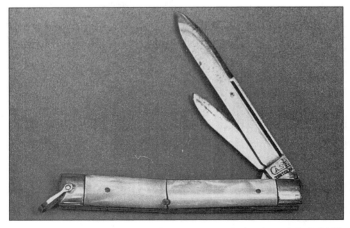

9282R, Physician's Knife, Cracked Ice, Imitation, LP, 2-3/4", Tested XX, (Handle Cracked), $500.

B282, Christmas tree, 2-3/4", 1920-40,
Doctor's knife, Tested XX 700

B282, imitation onyx, 2-3/4", 1920-40,
Tested XX 500

5282, stag, 2-3/4", 1920-40, Tested XX 700

6282, green bone, 2-3/4", 1920-40, Tested XX... 700

6282, early Rogers bone, 2-3/4", 1920-40,
Tested XX 700

8282, genuine pearl, 2-3/4", 1920-40,
Tested XX 750

62082, Dr.'s Knife, Green Bone, LP, 2-7/8", Tested XX, 1920-40, $700.

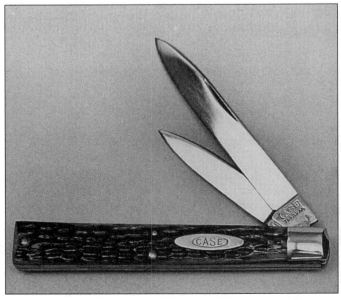

6285, Dr.'s Knife, Green Bone, 3-5/8", Tested XX, $850.

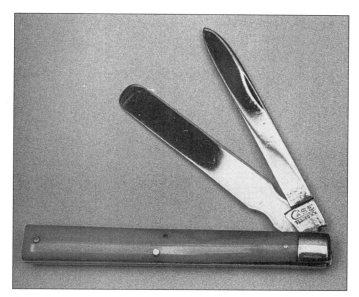

B285, Waterfall, Dr.'s Knife, 3-5/8", Tested XX, $850.

RM285, Christmas tree, 3-5/8", 1920-40,
  Tested XX 850
B285, waterfall, 3-5/8", 1920-40, Tested XX.......850
3285, yellow comp., 3-5/8", 1920-40,
  Tested XX 600
7285, tortoise, 3-5/8", 1920-40, Tested XX.........800

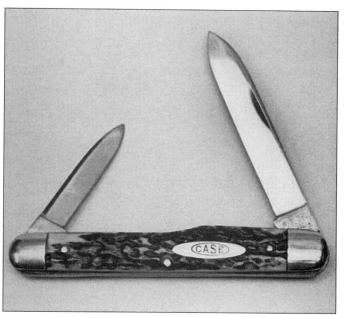

5287, Gunstock, Stag, 3-1/2", Tested XX, $800.

8287, pearl, 3-1/2", 1920-40, Tested XX.............900

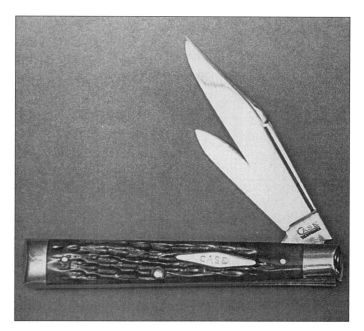

62086, Dr.'s Knife, Green Bone, 3-1/4", Tested XX, $700.

52086, stag, 3-1/4", 1920-40, Tested XX.............750
62086, Rogers Bone early, 3-1/4", 1920-40,
  Tested XX 800
82086, genuine pearl, 3-1/4", 1920-40,
  Tested XX 800
92086R, imitation pearl, 3-1/4", 1920-40,
  Tested XX 650

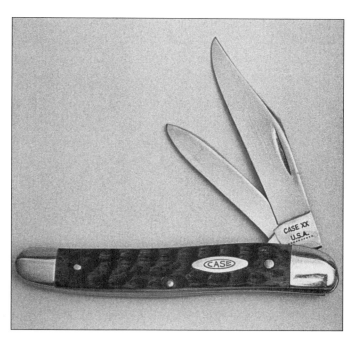

62087, Bone, 3-1/4", odd shield, 10 Dot, $50.

22087, slick black, 3-1/4", 1920-40, Tested XX ..135
42087, white comp., 3-1/4", 1920-40,
  Tested XX 150
62087, green bone, 3-1/4", 1920-40,
  Tested XX 150
22087, slick black, 3-1/4", 1940-64, XX................30
52087, stag, 3-1/4", 1940-64, XX.........................90

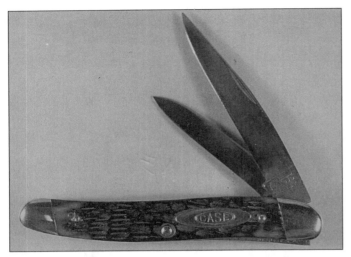

62087, Green Bone, 3-1/4", Slant Bolsters, 1920-40, Tested XX, rare, $250.

62087, bone, 3-1/4", 1940-64, XX	....	65
62087, rough black, 3-1/4", 1940-50, XX	....	100
62087, green bone, 3-1/4", 1940-55, XX	....	125
62087, red bone, 3-1/4", 1940-64, XX	....	85
22087, slick black, 3-1/4", 1965-69, USA	....	35
52087, stag, 3-1/4", 1965-69, USA	....	75
62087, bone, 3-1/4", 1965-69, USA	....	45
22087, slick black, 3-1/4", 1970, 10 Dot	....	40
52087, stag, 3-1/4", 1970, 10 Dot	....	75
62087, delrin, 3-1/4", 1970, 10 Dot	....	35

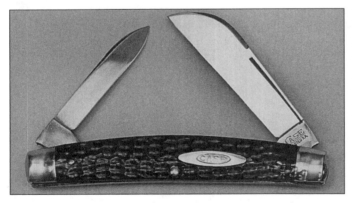

6288, Green Bone, LP, 4-1/8" 1920-40, Tested XX, $1,250.

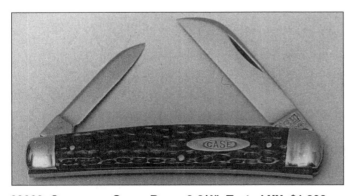

62089, Congress, Green Bone, 3-3/4", Tested XX, $1,300.

6288LP, Green Bone, no shield, 4-1/8", both blades stamped, Case Tested XX, spear master blade, $1,250.

6291, Green Bone, 4-1/2", contract made by Case for Winchester, $1,500.

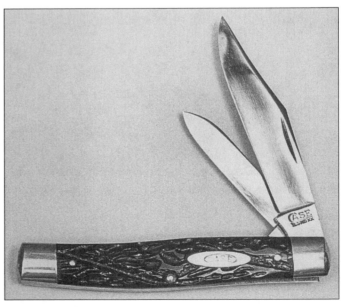

6292, Rough Black, 4" 1920-40, Tested XX, $250.

3292, yellow comp., 4", 1920-40, Tested XX 250

6292, green bone, 4", 1920-40, Tested XX.........250

6292, rough black, 4", 1940-50, XX....................200

6292, green bone, 4", 1940-55, XX 250

6292, red bone, 4", 1940-64, XX 150

6292, bone, 4", 1940-64, XX 90

6292, bone, 4", 1965-69, USA.............................55

6292, bone, 4", 1970, 10 Dot.............................55

32093F, yellow comp., 5", 1920-40,
Tested XX 300

62093F, green bone, 5", 1920-40,
Tested XX 350

32093F, yellow celluloid, 5", 1945, Case's
Stainless 300

62093F, green bone, 5", 1945, Case's
Stainless 350

6294, green bone, 4-1/4", 1920-40,
Tested XX 800

6294LP, green bone, 4-1/4", 1920-40,
Tested XX 850

6294LP, red bone, 4-1/4", 1920-40,
Tested XX 850

6294JL.P., green bone, 4-1/4", 1920-40,
Tested XX 1,600

6294LP, Rogers bone, early, 4-1/4",
1920-40, two-blade gunboat, Tested XX......2,000

6294, green bone, 4-1/4", 1940-55, XX 450

6294, red bone, 4-1/4", 1940-64, XX 450

6294L.P., red bone, 4-1/4", 1940-64, XX...........600

6294, bone, 4-1/4", 1940-64, XX 250

6294LP, bone, rare, 4-1/4", 1940-64, XX............400

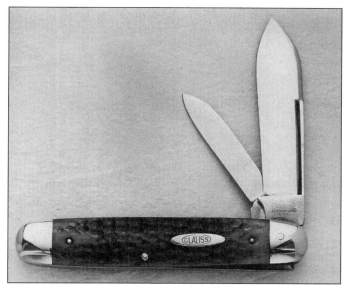

6294LP, Green Bone, 1920-40, 4-1/4", Clauss, Fremont, Ohio, U.S.A. Case Contract Knife, $450. Photo courtesy John Petzl.

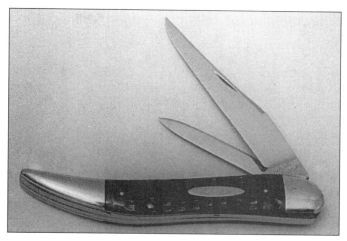

62094, Green Bone Handles, 4 -1/4", $450.

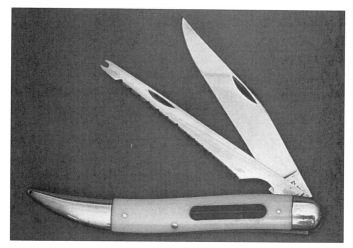

32095F, Fish Scaler, Yellow, 5", XX, $90.

32095F, flat yellow, 5", 1940-41, XX 100

RM2095F, Christmas tree, 5", 1920-40,
Fisherman's knife, Tested XX 400

32095F, yellow comp., 5", 1920-40, Tested XX ..250

32095FSS, yellow comp., 5", 1920-40,
Tested XX 250

32095F, yellow comp., Case's Stainless.............300

32095FSS, yellow comp., 5", 1965-69, USA 75

32095FSS, yellow comp., 5", 1970, 10 Dot 75

RM2096, Christmas Tree, 3-1/8", 1920-40,
Tested XX 450

R2096, candy stripe, 3-1/8", 1920-40,
Tested XX 450

62096, Rogers Bone, 3-1/8", 1920-40,
Tested XX 400

62096, Rogers bone, early, 3-1/8", 1920-40,
Tested XX 450

62096, green bone, 3-1/8", 1920-40,
Tested XX 400

Note: RM2096, R2096 and the three 62096s are Toothpicks.

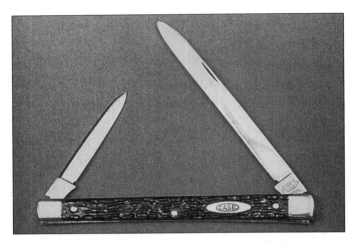

6296X, Green Bone, 4-1/4" Case's Stainless, $900.

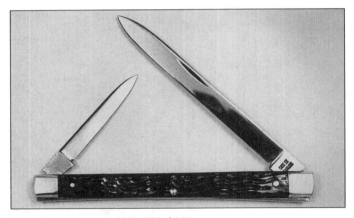

6296XSS, Bone, 4-1/4", XX, $300.

6296X, Clip point, rare, XX 400

6296XSS, red bone, 4-1/4", XX 350

6296X, green bone, 4 -1/4", 1920-40,
Half-oval, Stainless, Tested XX....................... 900

6296XSS, green bone, 4-1/4", 1940-55, XX....... 650

6296XSS, bone, 4-1/4", 1965-69, USA 400

R297, candy stripe, 1920-40, small leg,
Tested XX 400

B297, Christmas tree, 1920-40, small leg,
Tested XX 450

3297, yellow comp., 1920-40, small leg,
Tested XX 350

8297, genuine pearl, 1920-40, small leg,
Tested XX 450

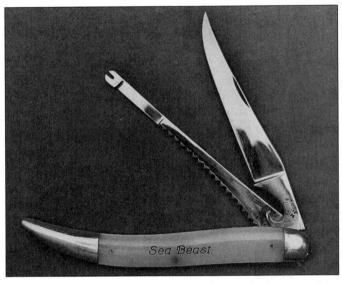

B2098F, Sea Beast, Imi Onyx, 5-1/2", Case's Stainless, $350.

RM2098F, Christmas tree, 5-1/2", 1920-40,
Tested XX 450

B2098F, imitation onyx, 5-1/2", 1920-40,
Tested XX 350

32098F, yellow comp. 5-1/2", 1920-40,
Tested XX 350

62098F, green bone, 5-1/2", 1920-40,
Tested XX 450

62098F, green bone, 5 -1/2", Case's Stainless... 450

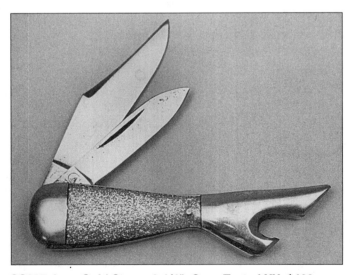

GS297, Leg, Gold Stone, 3-1/4", Case Tested XX, $400.

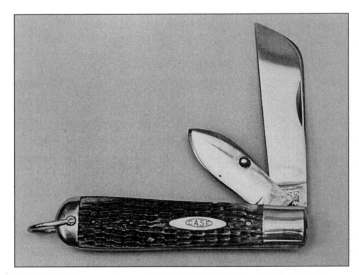

6299SHR, Green Bone, 4-1/8", 1920-40, Tested XX, $350.

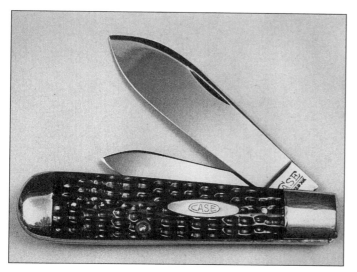

6299, Green Bone, 4-1/8", 1920-1940, Tested XX, $325.

6299, rough black, Tested XX 250
5299, stag, 4-1/8", 1920-40, Tested XX 450
6299, bone, 4-1/8", 1940-64, XX 225
6299, rough black, 4-1/8", 1940-50, XX.............. 175
6299, green bone, 4-1/8", 1940-55, XX 300
GM2099R, green mottled, 2-7/8", 1920-40,
    Tested XX 135
82099R, genuine pearl, 2-7/8", 1920-40,
    Tested XX 200

Note: GM2099R and 82099R are Senator/Lobster.

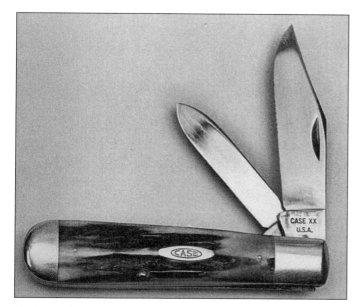

5299-1/2, Stag, 4-1/8", 1965-69, USA, $135.

3299-1/2, yellow comp., 4-1/8", 1920-40,
    Tested XX 250
5299-1/2, stag, 4-1/8", 1920-40, Tested XX........ 450
6299-1/2, green bone, 4-1/8", 1920-40,
    Tested XX 500

6299-1/2, green bone, 4-1/8", 1940-64, XX 400
3299-1/2, yellow comp., 4-1/8", 1940-64, XX 100
3299-1/2, yellow comp., 4-1/8", 1940-64,
    XX, "A" blade 125
3299-1/2, flat yellow, 4-1/8", 1940-64,
    "A" blade, XX 140
5299-1/2, stag, 4-7/8", 1940-64, XX 125
5299-1/2, stag, 4-1/8", 1940-64, "A" blade, XX... 175
3299-1/2, yellow comp., 4-1/8", 1965-69, USA..... 75
3299-1/2, yellow comp., 4-1/8", 1970, 10 Dot....... 75
3299-1/2, flat yellow, 4-1/8", 1970, 10 Dot 85
5299-1/2, stag, 4-1/8", 1970, 10 Dot.................. 125

Pattern Unknown, 3 blade, 3 Backspring, Whittler, Green Bone, 3-3/8", Tested XX, $450.

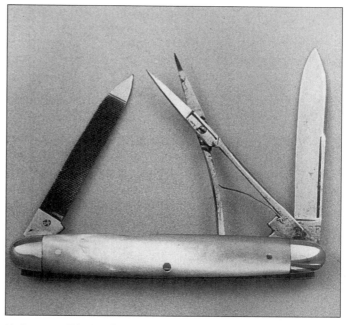

Unknown, Blade, Scissors, File, Equal End, Pearl, 3-1/4", Tested XX, $400.

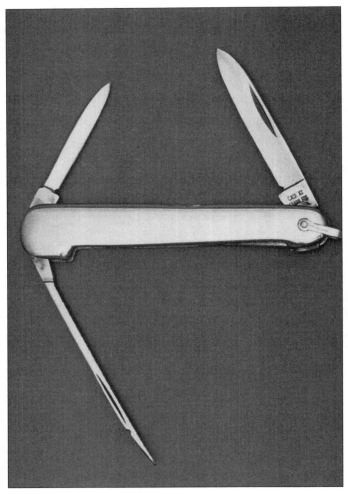

M3102R, All Metal, 2-3/4", XX, $40.

M3102R, metal, 1920-40, Tested XX.................. 110
M3102RSS, metal, 1965-69, USA 35
M3102RSS, metal, 1970, 10 Dot.......................... 35

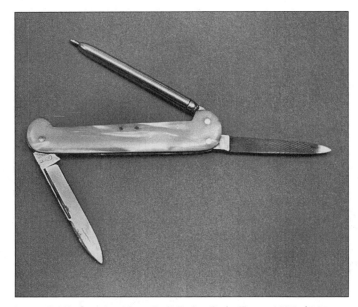

83102F LP, Cracked Ice, Ball Point Pen, Tested XX, $225.

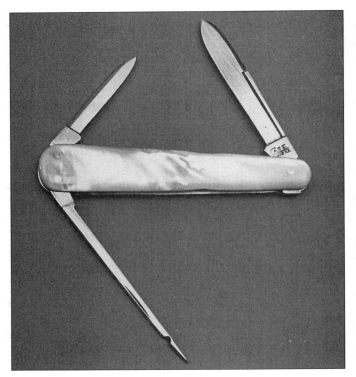

83102, Pearl, 2-3/4", 1920-40, Tested XX, $225.

63102, green bone, 1920-40, flat bolsters,
Tested XX 250
83102SS, genuine pearl, 1940-64, XX 200

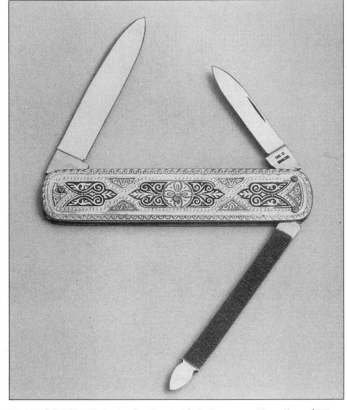

T3105SS File, Toledo Scale, 3-1/8", Dots on Handles, $75.

T3105SS, metal, 1940-64, XX 225
(Older knife has no dots on handle.)

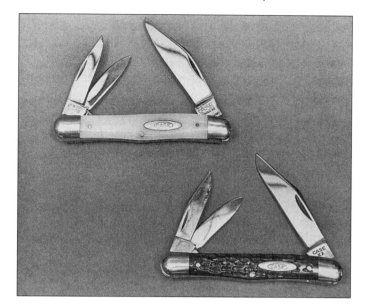

Top: 3308, Yellow Comp., 3-1/4", 1920-40, Tested XX, $350.
Bottom: 6308, Green Bone, 3-1/4", 1940-64, XX, $500.

6308, rough black, Tested XX 350
2308, slick black, 3-1/4", 1920-40, Tested XX 350
5308, stag, 3-1/4", 1920-40, Tested XX 600
6308, green bone, 3-1/4", 1920-40, Tested XX .. 550
8308, genuine pearl, 3-1/4", 1920-40,
   Tested XX 700
6308, rough black, 3-1/4", 1940-50, XX.............. 225
6308, red bone, 3-1/4", 1940-64, XX 200
6308, bone, 3-1/4", 1940-64, XX 135
6308, bone, 3-1/4", 1965-69, USA..................... 85
6308, bone, 3-1/4", 1970, 10 Dot........................ 85

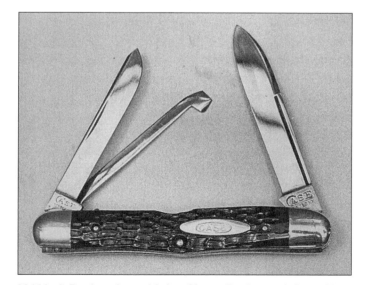

63109, 3 Backspring whittler Citrus Peeler and Cap Lifter, Green Bone LP, 3-5/8", Tested XX, $800.

63109, green bone, 1920-40, Tested XX 700
93109, cracked ice, 1920-40, Tested XX 700
RM3109, Christmas tree, 1920-40, Tested XX ... 800
83109X, pearl, 1920-40, Tested XX 700
GS3109X, gold stone, 1920-40, Tested XX 700

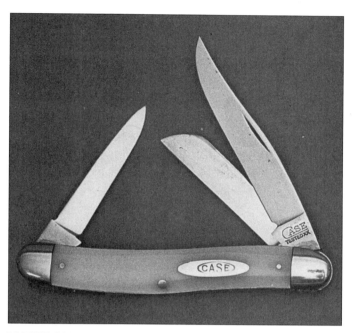

3318HE, Yellow Cell., 3-1/2", Tested XX, $225.

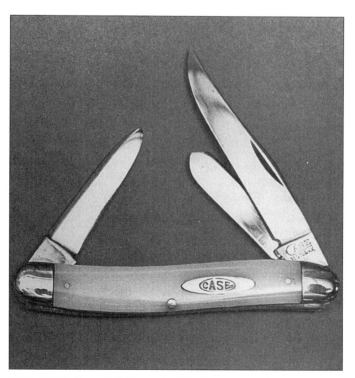

3318 HP, Yellow Cell Spay, 3-1/2", Tested XX, $225.

4318HP, White Comp, 3-1/2", XX, $75.

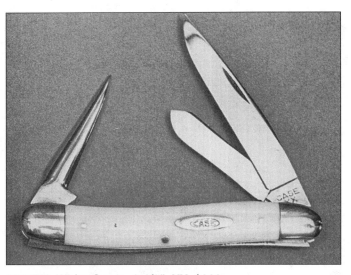

4318PU, White Comp, 3-1/2", XX, $200.

RM318HE, Christmas tree, Tested XX 500
RM318SHPEN, Christmas tree, 3-1/2",
   1920-40, Tested XX 500
3318SHPEN, yellow comp., 3-1/2",
   1920-40, Tested XX 200
3318SHSP, yellow comp., 3-1/2",
   1920-40, Tested XX 200
3318SPPEN, yellow comp., 3-1/2",
   1920-40, Tested XX 200
5318SHSP, stag, 3-1/2", 1920-40, Tested XX.....400
6318SHPU, green bone, 3-1/2", 1920-40,
   Tested XX 375
6318SPPU, green bone, 3-1/2", 1920-40,
   Tested XX 375
6318SPPen, green bone, 3-1/2", 1920-40,
   Tested XX 375

6318SHPEN, green bone, 3-1/2", 1920-40,
   Tested XX 375
6318SHPEN, green bone, 3-1/2",
   1920-40, Tested XX 375
5318Hpen, red Rogers bone, XX 200
8318SHSP, genuine pearl, 3-1/2",
   1920-40, Tested XX 500
9318SHPEN, cracked ice, 3-1/2",
   1920-40, Tested XX 250
9318SHPU, cracked ice, 3-1/2", 1920-40,
   Tested XX 250
3318SHPEN, yellow comp., 3-1/2",
   1940-64, XX 60
4318SHSP, white comp., 3-1/2", 1940-64, XX.......75
4318SH, white comp., 3-1/2", 1940-64, XX,
   master blade, California clip...........................85
6318SPPU, rough black, 3-1/2", 1940-50, XX....200
6318SHSP, rough black, 3-1/2", 1940-50, XX....200
6318SHPEN, rough black, 3-1/2", 1940-50, XX.200
6318SPPU, green bone, 3-1/2", 1940-55, XX....300
6318SHSP, green bone, 3-1/2, 1940-55, XX......300
6318SHSP, green bone, 3-1/2", 1940-55,
   long pull, XX..350
6318SHPEN, green bone, 3-1/2", 1940-55,
   XX 200
6318SPPU, red bone, 3-1/2", 1940-64, XX 150
6318SHSP, red bone, 3-1/2", 1940-64, XX.........150
6318SHPen, red bone, 3-1/2", 1940-64, XX.......150
6318SPPU, bone, 3-1/2", 1940-64, XX...............175
6318SHSP, bone, 3-1/2", 1940-64, XX.................90
6318SHSPSSP, bone transition, 3-1/2",
   1964, XX, XX to USA......................................200
6318SHPEN, bone, 3-1/2", 1940-64, XX..............90
9318HP, cracked ice, 3-1/2", 1940-64, XX..........200
3318SHPEN, yellow comp., 3-1/2", 1965-69,
   USA 55
4318SHSP, white comp., 3-1/2", 1965-69, USA...60
6318SPPU, bone, 3-1/2", 1965-69, USA..............55
6318SHSP, bone, 3-1/2", 1965-69, USA 55
6318SHPEN, bone, 3-1/2", 1965-69, USA 55
6318HPSS, polished blades, 3-1/2",
   1965-69, USA 65
6318HSSPSSP, bone, 3-1/2", 1965-69, USA,
   blade edge polished.......................................60
6318HP, polished stainless, 3-1/2", 1965-66,
   USA 65
6318SHSPSSP, bone, 3-1/2", 1965-69, USA,
   first model, edge etched "Tested XX
   Stainless" 85
3318SHPEN, yellow comp., 3-1/2", 1970,
   10 Dot 55

4318SHSP, white comp., 3-1/2", 1970, 10 Dot 65
6318SPPU, bone, 3-1/2", 1970, 10 Dot................55
6318SHPEN, bone, 3-1/2", 1970, 10 Dot 55
6318SHSP, bone, 3-1/2", 1970, 10 Dot 55
6318HPSSP, bone, 3-1/2", 1970, 10 Dot,
    blade edge polished...55

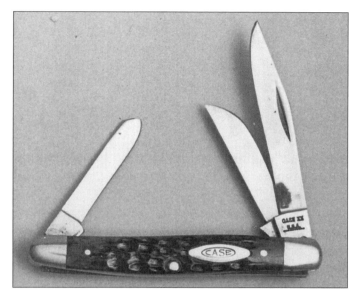

6327SHSP, Bone, 2-3/4", 1970, 10 Dot, $50.

6327SHSP, bone, 2-3/4", 1940-64, XX 75
9327SHSP, imitation pearl, 2-3/4", 1940-64, XX...65
9327SHSP, cracked ice, 2-3/4", 1940-64, XX.......65
6327SHSP, bone, 2-3/4", 1965-69, USA 50
9327SHSP, 2-3/4", 1965-69, USA 45
6327SHSP, delrin, scarce, 2-3/4", 1970,
    10 Dot 100
9327SHSP, 2-3/4", 1970, 10 Dot 45

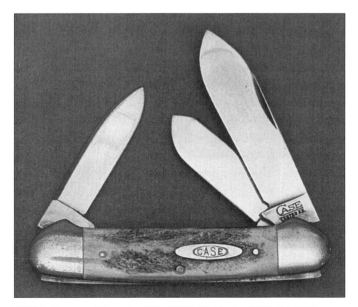

53131, Canoe, Stag, 3-5/8", 1920-40 Tested XX, $1,500.

13031LR, Electrician's Knife, Walnut, 3-3/4", XX, $50.

13031LR, walnut, 3-3/4", 1965-69, USA,
    Electrician's knife 45
13031LR, walnut, 3-3/4", 1970, 10 Dot,
    Electrician's knife 45

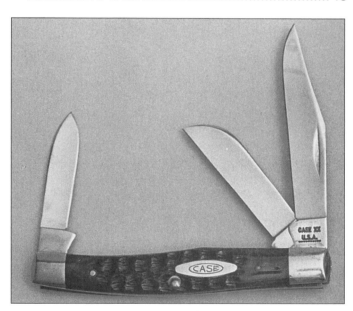

6332, Bone, 3-5/8", 1970 10 Dot, $75.

5332, stag, 3-5/8", 1920-40, Tested XX 400
6332, green bone, 3-5/8", 1920-40, Tested XX...300
5332, stag, 3-5/8", 1940-64, XX..........................135
5332LP, stag, 3-5/8", 1940-64, XX 225
6332, rough black, 3-5/8", 1940-50, XX..............200
6332, green bone, 3-5/8", 1940-55, XX 250
6332, red bone, 3-5/8", 1940-64, XX 125
6332, Rogers bone, late, 3-5/8", 1940-64, XX....150
6332, bone, 3-5/8, 1940-64, XX...........................90
6332, bone, 3-5/8, 1965-69, USA 55
5332, stag, 3-5/8, 1965-69, USA 85

5332, stag, 3-5/8, 1970, 10 Dot 85

6333, Rough Black LP, 2-5/8", 1940-50, XX, $150.

6333, rough black, LP, 2-5/8, 1920-40,
Tested XX 200

6333, green bone, 2-5/8, 1920-40, Tested XX 225

9333, cracked ice, 2-5/8, 1920-40,
Tested XX 140

6333, rough black, 2-5/8", 1940-50, XX 90

6333, green bone, 2-5/8", 1940-55, XX 175

6333LP, green bone, 2-5/8", 1940-55, XX 225

6333, bone, 2-5/8", 1940-64, XX 65

6333, Rogers bone, early, 2-5/8", 1940-64, XX .. 100

9333, imitation pearl, 2-5/8", 1940-64, XX 40

9333, imitation pearl, 2-5/8", 1940-64,
long pull, XX 125

9333, cracked ice, 2-5/8", 1940-64,
long pull, XX 125

9333, cracked ice, 2-5/8", 1940-64, XX 50

6333, bone, 2-5/8", 1965-69, USA 50

9333, imitation pearl, 2-5/8", 1965-69, USA 45

6333, delrin, 2-5/8", 1970, 10 Dot 40

6333, bone stag, 2-5/8", 1970, 10 Dot 50

9333, imitation pearl, 2-5/8", 1970, 10 Dot 40

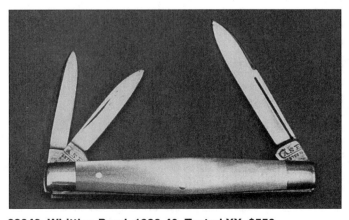

83042, Whittler, Pearl, 1920-40, Tested XX, $550.

93042, imitation pearl, 1920-40, Tested XX 400

63042, early Rogers bone, 1920-40,
Tested XX 550

Top: 3344PU, Yellow Cell. w/Shield, 3-1/4", 1920-40, Tested XX, $200. Bottom: 3344, Yellow Cell no Shield, 3-1/4", 1920-40, Tested XX, $150.

33044HP, Birdseye, Yellow Comp., 3-1/4", 1964, XX, $90.

33044HP, flat yellow, 3-1/4", 1964, XX, 100
made one year in XX 10

33044SHSP, yellow comp., 3-1/4",
1965-69, USA, Birdseye 70

33044SHSP, yellow comp., 3-1/4", 1970,
10 Dot, Birdseye 70

33044SHSP, flat yellow, 3-1/4", 1970, 10 Dot 85

GS344, 3-1/4", 1920-40, Tested XX 350

RM344SHSP, Christmas tree, 3-1/4",
1920-40, Tested XX 400

RM3044F, Christmas tree, 3-1/4",
1920-40, Tested XX 425

B344PU, imitation onyx, 3-1/4", 1920-30,
Tested XX 225

3344SPPU, yellow comp., 3-1/4",
1920-40, Tested XX 200
5344SHSP, stag, 3-1/4", 1920-40, Tested XX.....350
5344SHPEN, stag, 3-1/4", 1920-40, Tested XX..350

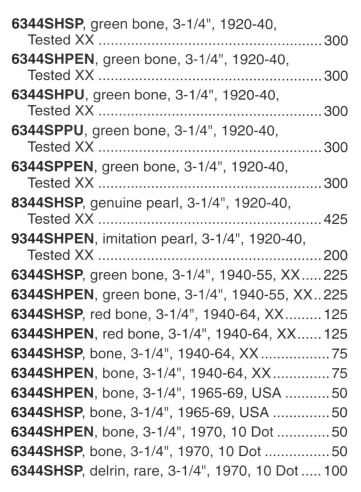

6344, Green Bone, 3-1/4", 1920-40, Tested XX, $300.

6344SHSP, green bone, 3-1/4", 1920-40,
Tested XX 300
6344SHPEN, green bone, 3-1/4", 1920-40,
Tested XX 300
6344SHPU, green bone, 3-1/4", 1920-40,
Tested XX 300
6344SPPU, green bone, 3-1/4", 1920-40,
Tested XX 300
6344SPPEN, green bone, 3-1/4", 1920-40,
Tested XX 300
8344SHSP, genuine pearl, 3-1/4", 1920-40,
Tested XX 425
9344SHPEN, imitation pearl, 3-1/4", 1920-40,
Tested XX 200
6344SHSP, green bone, 3-1/4", 1940-55, XX.....225
6344SHPEN, green bone, 3-1/4", 1940-55, XX..225
6344SHSP, red bone, 3-1/4", 1940-64, XX.........125
6344SHPEN, red bone, 3-1/4", 1940-64, XX......125
6344SHSP, bone, 3-1/4", 1940-64, XX 75
6344SHPEN, bone, 3-1/4", 1940-64, XX 75
6344SHPEN, bone, 3-1/4", 1965-69, USA 50
6344SHSP, bone, 3-1/4", 1965-69, USA 50
6344SHPEN, bone, 3-1/4", 1970, 10 Dot 50
6344SHSP, bone, 3-1/4", 1970, 10 Dot 50
6344SHSP, delrin, rare, 3-1/4", 1970, 10 Dot 100

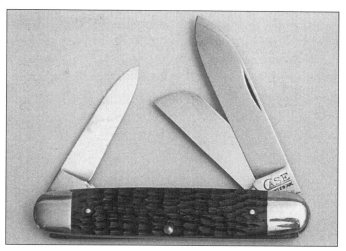

63045, Green Bone, 3-5/8", 1920-40, Tested XX, $300.

6345, green bone, 3-5/8", 1920-40, Tested XX...325
6345PU, green bone, 3-5/8", 1920-40,
Tested XX 350

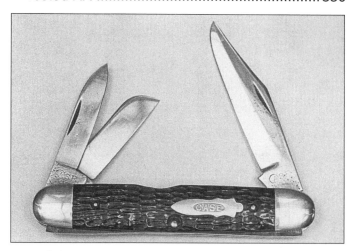

6345-1/2SAB, Whittler, Green Bone, 3-5/8", 1920-40, Tested XX, $1,200.

6345-1/2PU, red bone, XX.................................225

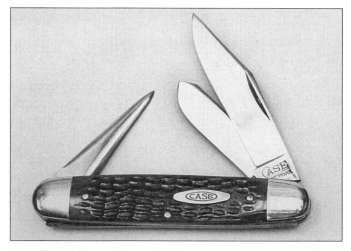

6345-1/2 PU, Green Bone, 3-3/4", 1920-1940, Tested XX, $375.

2345-1/2PU, slick black, 3-5/8", 1920-40,
Tested XX 275

6345-1/2, imitation bone, 3-5/8", 1920-40,
Tested XX 150

6345-1/2, green bone, 3-5/8", 1920-40,
Tested XX 350

6345-1/2SH, green bone, 3-5/8", 1920-40,
Tested XX 350

6345-1/2, rough black, 3-5/8", 1920-40,
Tested XX 250

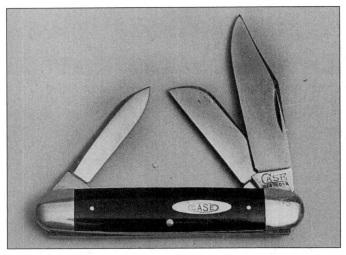

2345-1/2, Slick Black, 3-5/8", 1920-40, Tested XX, $250.

2345-1/2SH, slick black, 3-5/8", 1940-64, XX 100

2345-1/2P, slick black, 3-5/8", 1940-64,
long pull, XX.. 150

6345-1/2SH, rough black, 3-5/8", 1940-50,
XX 225

6345-1/2SH, green bone, 3-5/8", 1940-55, XX ... 325

6345-1/2SH, red bone, 3-5/8", 1940-64, XX 250

6345-1/2SH, bone, 3-5/8", 1940-64, XX 175

2345-1/2SH, slick black, 3-5/8", 1965-69, USA .. 150

6345-1/2SH, bone, rare, 3-5/8", 1965-69, USA .. 400

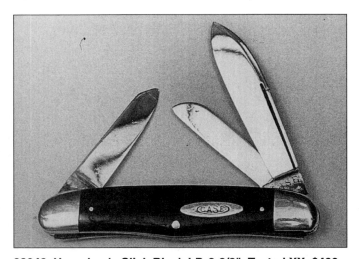

23046, Humpback, Slick Black LP, 3-3/8", Tested XX, $400.

33046, yellow comp., 3-5/8", 1920-40,
Tested XX 400

33046, white comp., 3-5/8", 1920-40,
Tested XX 400

M346, metal, 3-5/8", 1940-50, XX, "Metal
Stampings Ltd." English Navy contract 135

M346, metal, 3-5/8", 1940-64, XX "Case
XX Made For USA Navy" 125

M346, aluminum, 3-5/8", 1940-50,
"Canadian Navy contract," XX 150

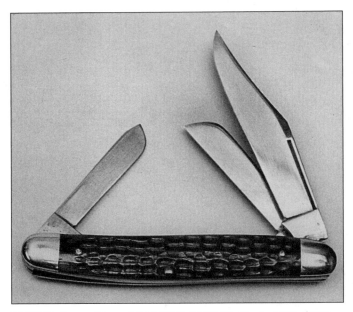

6347HP, Green Bone LP, 3-7/8", 1920-40, Tested XX, $450.

RM347SPPU, Christmas tree, 3-7/8",
1920-40, Long pull, Tested XX......................... 650

RM347SPPen, Christmas tree, 3-7/8",
1920-40, Long pull, Tested XX......................... 650

RM347SHPU, Christmas tree, 3-7/8",
1920-40, Long pull, Tested XX......................... 650

M347SPPen, metal, 3-7/8", 1920-40, Long pull,
Tested XX 250

M347SPPU, metal, 3-7/8", 1920-40, Long pull,
Tested XX 250

3347SHSP, yellow comp., 3-7/8", 1920-40,
Long pull, Tested XX... 350

3347SPPen, yellow comp., 3-7/8", 1920-40,
Long pull, Tested XX... 350

3347SPPU, yellow comp., 3-7/8", 1920-40,
Long pull, Tested XX... 350

3347SHPU, yellow comp., 3-7/8", 1920-40,
Long pull, Tested XX... 350

5347SHSP, stag, 3-7/8", 1920-40, Long pull,
Tested XX 500

5347SHPen, stag, 3-7/8", 1920-40,
Long pull, Tested XX... 500

6347-J, bone, 3-7/8", 1920-40, Long pull,
Tested XX 1,200

6347SHSP, green bone, 3-7/8", 1920-40,
Tested XX 500

6347SHSP, green bone, 3-7/8", 1920-40,
Long pull, Tested XX... 550

6347SHPen, green bone, 3-7/8", 1920-40,
Tested XX 500

6347SHPen, green bone, 3-7/8", 1920-40,
Long pull, Tested XX... 550

6347SHPU, green bone, 3-7/8", 1920-40,
Tested XX 500

6347SHPU, green bone, 3-7/8", 1920-40,
Long pull, Tested XX... 550

6347SPPen, green bone, 3-7/8", 1920-40,
Tested XX 500

6347SPPen, green bone, 3-7/8", 1920-40,
Long pull, Tested XX... 550

6347SPPU, green bone, 3-7/8", 1920-40,
Tested XX 500

6347SPPU, green bone, 3-7/8", 1920-40,
Long pull, Tested XX... 550

6347PUPen, green bone, 3-7/8", 1920-40,
Tested XX 500

6347PUPen, green bone, 3-7/8", 1920-40,
Long pull, Tested XX... 550

6347JSH, green bone, 3-7/8", 1920-40,
Long pull, Tested XX....................................... 1,200

6347JSPU, green bone, 3-7/8", 1920-40,
Long pull, Tested XX....................................... 1,250

6347SHSP, rough black, 3-7/8", 1920-40,
Long pull, Tested XX... 400

6347SPPU, rough black, 3-7/8", 1920-40,
Long pull, Tested XX... 400

6347SHPU, rough black, 3-7/8", 1920-40,
Long pull, Tested XX... 425

6347SHSP, Rogers bone, early, 3-7/8",
1920-40, Long pull, Tested XX......................... 650

9347SPPen, cracked ice, 3-7/8", 1920-40,
Tested XX 400

9347SPPU, cracked ice, 3-7/8", 1920-40,
Long pull, Tested XX... 425

9347JPU, cracked ice, 3-7/8", 1920-40,
Long pull, Tested XX....................................... 1,000

3347SHSP, yellow comp., 3-7/8", 1920-40,
Long pull, Tested XX... 275

3347SPPU, yellow comp., 3-7/8",
1920-40, Tested XX 300

3347SHSP, flat yellow comp., 3-7/8",
1920-40, Tested XX 125

5347SHSP, stag, 3-7/8", 1920-40, Tested XX..... 200

5347SHSP, stag, 3-7/8", 1920-40,
Long pull, Tested XX... 400

5347SHSP, red stag, 3-7/8", 1920-40,
Tested XX 400

5347SHSP, red stag, 3-7/8", 1920-40,
Long pull, Tested XX... 600

5347SHSP, stag, 3-7/8", 1940-64, XX,
Stainless Steel, all blades stamped 400

5347SHSP, red stag, 3-7/8", 1940-64, XX,
Stainless Steel, all blades stamped 500

6347SPPen, rough black, 3-7/8", 1940-64, XX ..300

6347SHSP, rough black, 3-7/8", 1940-64, XX 300

6347SHSP, rough black, 3-7/8", 1940-64,
Long pull, XX 400

6347SHPU, rough black, 3-7/8", 1940-64, XX....350

6347SHPU, rough black, 3-7/8", 1940-64,
Long pull, XX 400

6347SPPU, rough black, 3-7/8", 1940-64,
Long pull, XX 400

6347SHSP, green bone, 3-7/8", 1940-64, XX.....350

6347SHSP, green bone, 3-7/8", 1940-64,
Long pull, XX 425

6347SHPU, green bone, 3-7/8", 1940-64, XX 475

6347SHPU, green bone, 3-7/8", 1940-64,
Long pull, XX 475

6347SPPU, green bone, 3-7/8", 1940-64, XX 400

6347SPPU, green bone, 3-7/8", 1940-64,
Long pull, XX 450

6347SPPen, green bone, 3-7/8", 1940-64, XX...400

6347SPPen, green bone, Long pull, 3-7/8",
1940-64, XX.. 450

6347SHSP, green bone, 3-7/8", 1940-64, XX,
Stainless Steel, all blades stamped 450

6347SHSP, Rogers bone, late, 3-7/8",
1940-64, XX.. 300

6347SHPU, Rogers bone, late, 3-7/8",
1940-64, XX.. 300

6347SPPU, Rogers bone, late, 3-7/8",
1940-64, XX.. 300

6347SHSP, Rogers bone, late, 3-7/8",
1940-64, Stainless Steel, all blades
stamped, XX 350

6347SHSP, red Rogers bone, late,
3-7/8", 1940-64, XX 300

6347SHSP, red Rogers bone, late, 3-7/8",
1940-64, Stainless Steel, all blades
stamped, XX 350

6347SHSP, red bone, 3-7/8", 1940-64, XX......... 250

6347SPPU, red bone, 3-7/8", 1940-64, XX 275

6347SPPen, red bone, 3-7/8", 1940-64, XX....... 250

6347SHSPSSP, red bone, 3-7/8", 1940-64,
XX, Stainless Steel, all blades stamped 300

6347SPPU, second-cut bone, 3-7/8",
1940-64, Long pull, XX 600

6347SHSP, bone, 3-7/8", 1940-64, XX 150

6347SPPen, bone, 3-7/8", 1940-64, XX 150
6347SPPU, bone, 3-7/8", 1940-64, XX 175
6347SHPen, bone, 3-7/8", 1940-64, XX............. 150
6347SHPU, bone, 3-7/8", 1940-64, XX 175
6347SHSP, bone, 3-7/8", 1940-64, XX,
Stainless Steel, all blades stamped 300
3347SHSP, yellow comp., 3-7/8", 1965-69,
USA 65
3347SHSP, flat yellow comp, 3-7/8",
1965-69, USA 85
5347SHSP, stag, 3-7/8", 1965-69, USA.............. 125
5347SHSPS, stag, 3-7/8", 1965-69, USA,
Stainless Steel, all blades stamped 125
5347SHSPS, stag, 3-7/8", 1965-69, USA,
Stainless Steel, polished blades,
large stamp 140
5347SHSPS, stag, 3-7/8", 1965-69, USA,
All stainless-steel blades stamped.................. 375
5347SHSPS, stag, 3-7/8", 1965-69, USA,
Transition USA-XX... 400
6347SHSP, bone, 3-7/8", 1965-69, USA 100
6347SPPen, bone, 3-7/8", 1965-69, USA 100
6347SPPU, bone, 3-7/8", 1965-69, USA............ 125
6347SHSPSSP, bone, 3-7/8", 1965-69, USA,
first model, all blades stamped "Case XX
Stainless USA".. 300
6347SHSPSSP, bone, 3-7/8", 1965-69, USA,
First model brushed finish............................. 175
6347SHSPSSP, bone, 3-7/8", 1965-69, USA 100
6347SHSPS, bone, 3-7/8", 1965-69, USA,
Polished, all blades small stamped................ 400
6347SHSPS, bone, 3-7/8", 1965-69, USA,
Polished blades, small stamp 150
6347SHSPS, bone, 3-7/8", 1965-69, USA,
Polished blades, large stamp........................ 175
3347SHSP, yellow comp., 3-7/8", 1970, 10 Dot.... 65
3347SHSP, flat yellow comp., 3-7/8", 1970,
10 Dot 95
5347SHSP, stag, 3-7/8", 1970, 10 Dot.............. 125
5347SHSPS, stag, 3-7/8", Stainless, 1970,
10 Dot 300
5347SHSP, stag, 3-7/8", 1970, 10 Dot,
Transition 10 Dot-USA 325
6347SHSP, bone, 3-7/8", 1970, 10 Dot 100
6347SPPen, bone, 3-7/8", 1970, 10 Dot 100
6347SPPU, bone, 3-7/8", 1970, 10 Dot 110
6347SHSPSSP, bone, 3-7/8", 1970, 10 Dot 110
630047SPPen, green bone, 3-7/8",
1920-40, Tested XX, iron bolsters, iron
liners-no shield, wide backsprings 450
630047SHSP, green bone, 3-7/8", 1920-40,
Tested XX, iron bolsters, iron
liners-no shield, wide backsprings 450
630047SPPUJ, green bone, 3-7/8", 1920-40,

Tested XX, iron bolsters-iron liners-no
shield, wide backsprings 550

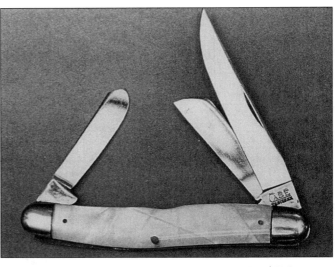

93047, Cracked Ice, 3-7/8", 1920-40, Tested XX, $450.

B3047, waterfall, 3-7/8", 1920-40, Tested XX..... 600
43047, white comp., 3-7/8", 1920-40,
Tested XX 325
53047, stag, 3-7/8", 1920-40, Tested XX 650
63047, green bone, 3-7/8", 1920-40,
Tested XX 600
93047, cracked ice, 3-7/8", 1920-40,
Tested XX 500
53047, stag, 3-7/8", 1920-40, Tested XX 200
63047, green bone, 3-7/8", 1920-40,
Tested XX 450
63047, rough black, 3-7/8", 1920-40,
Tested XX 400
63047, red bone, 3-7/8", 1920-40, Tested XX..... 300
63047, bone, 3-7/8", 1920-40, Tested XX........... 150
93047, cracked ice, 3-7/8", 1920-40,
Tested XX 400
53047, stag, 3-7/8", 1920-40, Tested XX 135
63047, bone, 3-7/8", 1920-40, Tested XX........... 110
53047, stag, 3-7/8", 1970, 10 Dot..................... 125

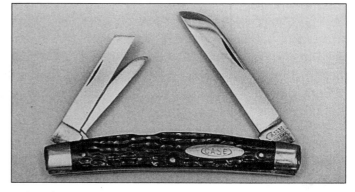

63052, Congress Whittler, Green Bone, 3-1/2", 1920-40, Tested XX, $1,600.

63047, bone, 3-7/8", 1970, 10 Dot...................... 110
3352, yellow hobo, 3-3/4", 1920-40, Tested XX,
    three-piece, knife, fork and spoon 450

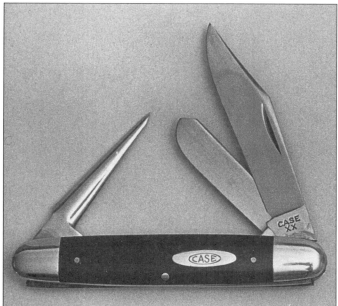

20355PU, Slick Black, 3-1/2", 1940-60, XX, $400.

23055, slick black, 3-1/2", 1920-40, Tested XX .. 350
23055PU, slick black, 3-1/2", 1920-40,
    Tested XX 400
8460SC, genuine pearl, 1920-40, Tested XX 250
Note: This knife is Equal End.

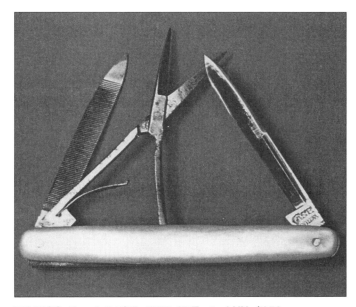

8361FSC, Pearl, 2-7/8", 1920-40 Tested XX, $350.

2361F, slick black, whittler, 2-7/8",
    1920-40, Tested XX 350
8361, pearl, whittler, 2-7/8", 1920-40,
    Tested XX 400

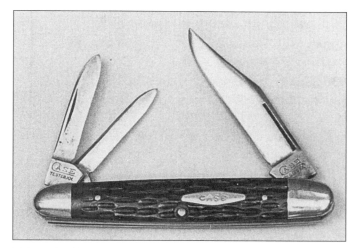

63063-1/2, Green Bone LP, 3-1/16", Tested XX, $400.

5364TF, Stag, 3-1/8", 1920-40 Tested XX, $300.

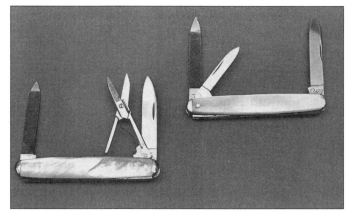

Left: 8364, TSCI SS Pearl, not a whittler, 3-1/8", 1940-64 XX, $125. Right: 8364TF, Pearl Whittler, rare, 3-1/8", 1920-40, Tested XX, $350.

8364T, genuine pearl, 3-1/8", 1920-40,
    Tested XX 300
8364SC, genuine pearl, 3-1/8", 1920-40,
    Tested XX 300

8364TSS, genuine pearl, 3-1/8", 1920-40,
Tested XX, Stainless, tip bolsters 150

8364SSSC, genuine pearl, 3-1/8", 1965-64,
USA, Stainless.. 125

8364SSSC, genuine pearl, 3-1/8", 1970,
10 Dot, Stainless... 135

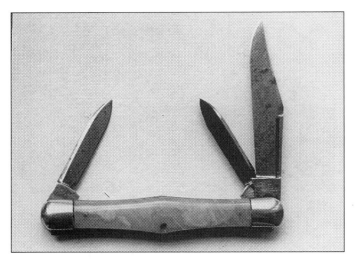

9367, Imitation Onyx, 3-1/4", Case Tested XX, $350.

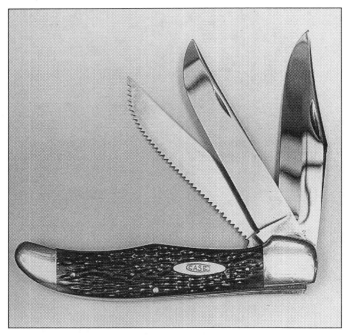

6365 SAB/SAW, Proto Type, 3-Blade Folding Hunter, Bone, 5-1/4", Very Rare, XX, 3 Back Springs (mid-'50s), $3,000.

6367, green bone, 1920-40, Tested XX 350
8367, genuine pearl, 1920-40, Tested XX 425
63067, green bone, 1920-40, Tested XX 350

6366, Clip, sheep foot, spay, 3-3/16", Green bone, Tested XX, $400.

6366, green bone, 3-1/8", 1920-40, Tested XX ..250
6366PEN, green bone, 3-1/8", 1920-40,
Tested XX 250
6366PEN, green bone, 3-1/8", 1920-40,
Tested XX 300

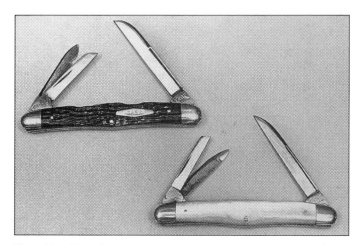

Top: 6370FLP, Green Bone, 3-1/8", 1920-40 Tested XX, $525.
Bottom: 8370FLP Pearl, 3-1/8", 1920-40, Tested XX, $550.

6370LP, green bone, 1920-40, Tested XX..........500

8370LP, genuine pearl, 1920-40, Tested XX 525

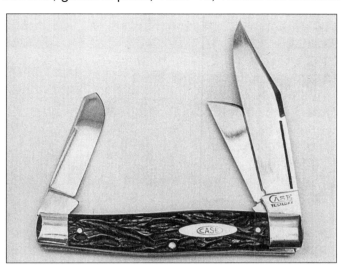

6375LP, Rough Black, 4-1/4", 1920-40, Tested XX, $600.

5375, stag, 4-1/4", 1920-40, long pull,
Tested XX 900

5375LP, second-cut stag, Tested XX...............1,500

6375, green bone, 4-1/4", 1920-40,
Long pull, Tested XX......................................900

6375LP, Winterbottom bone, 4-1/4",
1920-40, Tested XX 1,600

5375, stag, 4-1/4", 1940-64, Tested XX..............200

5375, stag, 4-1/4", 1940-64, Long pull,
Tested XX 400

5375, second-cut stag, 4-1/4", 1940-64,
Tested XX 650

5375, second-cut stag, 4-1/4", 1940-64,
Long pull, Tested XX......................................800

6375, rough black, 4-1/4", 1940-50,
Tested XX 350

6375, rough black, 4-1/4", 1940-50,
Long pull, Tested XX......................................400

6375, green bone, 4-1/4", 1940-55, Tested XX ..350

6375, green bone, 4-1/4", 1940-55,
Long pull, Tested XX......................................500

6375, red bone, 4-1/4", 1940-64, Tested XX 250

6375, red bone, 4-1/4", 1940-64, Long pull,
Tested XX 450

6375, bone, 4-1/4", 1940-64, Tested XX.............200

6375, bone, 4-1/4", 1940-64, Long pull,
Tested XX 350

5375, stag, 4-1/4", 1965-69, USA.......................150

5375, second-cut stag, 4-1/4", 1965-69, USA 700

6375, bone, 4-1/4", 1965-69, USA......................150

5375, stag, 4-1/4", 1970, 10 Dot........................150

6375, bone, 4-1/4", 1970, 10 Dot.......................150

6376SP, Rogers bone, early, 4", W.R.
Case & Sons..600

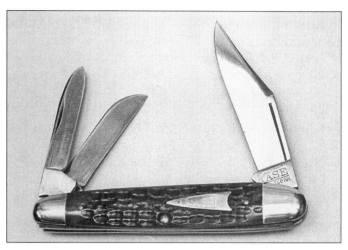

6376-1/2LP, Green Bone Whittler, 3-5/8", Tested XX, $650.

2376-1/2, slick black, 4", 1920-40, Tested XX 500

5376-1/2, stag, 4", 1920-40, Tested XX 600

6376-1/2, green bone, 4", 1920-40, Tested XX...600

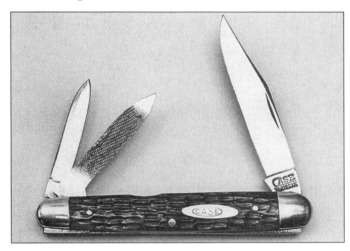

6379-1/2F, Green Bone, 3-1/4", 1920-40, Tested XX, $450.

6379-1/2, green bone, 3-1/4", 1920-40,
Tested XX 450

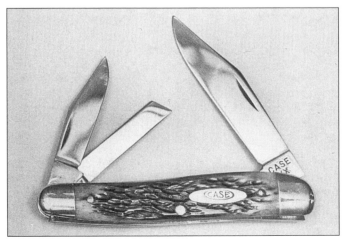

6380, Rogers Bone Whittler, 3-7/8", 1940-55, XX, $900.

6380, Rogers bone, early, 3-7/8", 1920-40,
flat blade, Tested XX 1,200

6380, green bone, 3-7/8", 1920-40,
Tested XX, flat blade, whittler 1,200

6380, green bone, 3-7/8", 1940-55, XX,
whittler 900

6380, red bone, 3-7/8", 1940-64, XX 350

6380, bone, 3-7/8", 1940-64, XX 225

6380, bone, 3-7/8", 1965-69, USA..................... 150

6380, bone, 3-7/8", 1970, 10 Dot........................ 150

83081, genuine Pearl, 3", 1920-40,
Lobster, Tested XX... 225

9383, Cracked Iced, 3-1/2", 1940-55, XX, $350.

9383SAB, cracked ice, 3-1/2", 1940-55, XX....... 450

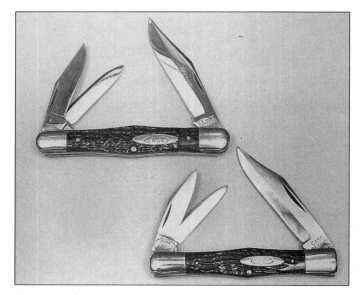

Top: 6383SAB, Green Bone, 3-1/2", 1920-40, Tested XX, $700. Bottom: 6383SAB, Green Bone, 3-1/2", Case Bradford, Square Bolsters, $800.

B383, imitation onyx, 3-1/2", 1920-40,
Tested XX 500

2383, slick black, 3-1/2", 1920-40, Tested XX 400

GS383, gold stone, 3-1/2", 1920-40,
Tested XX 600

5383, stag, 3-1/2", 1920-40, Tested XX 650

5383SAB, stag, 3-1/2", 1920-40, Tested XX 750

6383, green bone, 3-1/2", 1920-40, Tested XX... 600

6383LP, green bone, rare, 3-1/2", 1920-40,
Tested XX 800

8383, genuine pearl, 3-1/2", 1920-40,
Tested XX 800

9383, imitation pearl, 3-1/2", 1920-40,
Tested XX 550

2383, slick black, 3-1/2", 1940-64, XX 160

2383SAB, slick black, 3-1/2", 1940-64, XX 300

5383, stag, 3-1/2", 1940-64, XX......................... 250

5383SAB, stag, 3-1/2", XX 500

5383, red stag, 3-1/2", 1940-50, XX 450

6383SAB, green bone, 3-1/2", 1940-50, XX....... 800

6383, rough black, 3-1/2", 1940-50, XX 300

6383, green bone, 3-1/2", 1940-55, XX 500

6383, red bone, 3-1/2", 1940-64, XX 250

6383, bone, 3-1/2", 1940-64, XX 200

9383, imitation pearl, 3-1/2", 1940-64, XX 300

9383SAB, imitation pearl, 3-1/2", 1940-64,
XX 400

2383, slick black, 3-1/2", 1965-69, USA 175

5383, stag, 3-1/2", 1965-69, USA 160

6383, bone, 3-1/2", 1965-69, USA..................... 125

5383, stag, 3-1/2", 1970, 10 Dot 150

6383, bone, 3-1/2", 1970, 10 Dot........................ 125

63083, green bone, 3-3/16", 1920-40,
Tested XX 350

83083, genuine pearl, 3-3/16", 1920-40,
Tested XX 350

Note: 63083 and 83083 are both Lobsters.

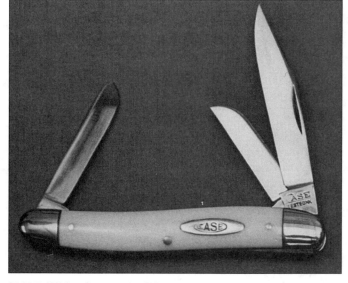

43087, White Comp., 3-1/4", 1920-40, Tested XX, $225.

23087ShPEN, slick black, 3-1/4", 1920-40,
Tested XX 150

63087SPPEN, green bone, 3-1/4", 1920-40,
Tested XX 250

63087SPPEN, rough black, 3-1/4", 1940-50,
XX 150

63087SPPEN, green bone, 3-1/4", 1940-55,
XX 225

63087PEN, red Rogers bone, 3-1/4",
1940-55, XX 125

63087SPPEN, red bone, 3-1/4", 1940-64, XX.... 140

23087SHPEN, slick black, 3-1/4", 1940-64, XX....60

53087SHPEN, stag, 3-1/4", 1940-64, XX 100

63087SPPEN, bone, 3-1/4", 1940-64, XX 80

23087SHPEN, slick black, 3-1/4", 1965-69,
USA 40

53087SHPEN, stag, 3-1/4", 1965-69, USA...........85

23087SHPEN, bone, 3-1/4", 1965-69, USA 65

23087SHPEN, slick black, 3-1/4", 1970, 10 Dot...50

53087SHPEN, stag, 3-1/4", 1970, 10 Dot............. 80

63087SHPEN, delrin, 3-1/4", 1970, 10 Dot.......... 45

63087SHPEN, bone, 3-1/4", 1970, 10 Dot 60

5387, stag, 1920-40, Gunstock whittler,
Tested XX 1,000

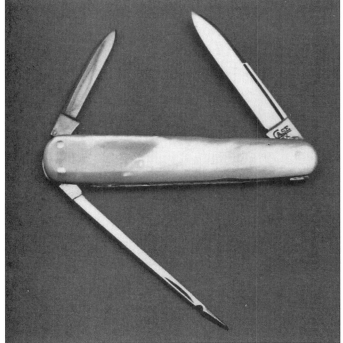

83088, Pearl Lobster LP, 3-1/8", Tested XX, $225.

83088SS, genuine pearl, 3-1/8", 1920-40,
Tested XX 225

83088SS, genuine pearl, 3-1/8", 1940-64, XX.... 150

83089SCI, genuine pearl, 3-1/16", 1920-40,
Tested XX 225

83089SCISSF, genuine pearl, 3-1/16",
1940-64, XX... 150

83089SCSSF, genuine pearl, 3-1/16",
1965-69, USA 275

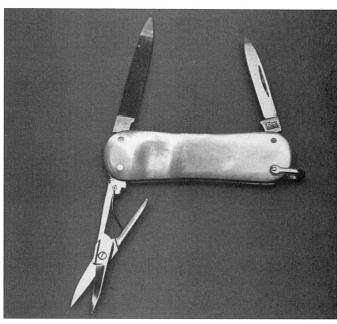

83090SCI, Pearl Lobster, 2-1/4", 1920-40, Tested XX, $200.

83090SCRSS, genuine pearl, 2-1/4",
1940-64, XX... 175

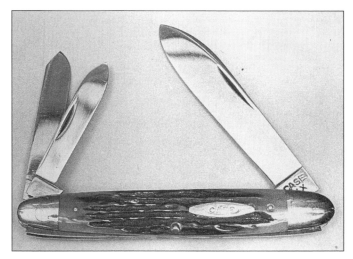

5391, Stag, 4-1/2", 1940-42, XX, $2,000.

3391, yellow comp., rare, 4-1/2", 1920-40,
Tested XX 2,500

5391, red stag, 4-1/2", 1920-40, Tested XX..... 2,500

5391, stag, 4-1/2", 1920-40, Tested XX 2,000

6391, green bone, 4-1/2", 1920-40,
Tested XX 2,700

6391, green bone, 4-1/2", 1940-42, XX 2,000

5391, red stag, 4-1/2", 1940-42, XX 2,200

Note: 83089SCI through 5391 are three-blade Lobster Scissors.

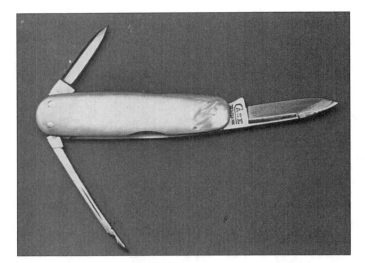

83091, Genuine Pearl, 2-1/4", 1920-40, Tested XX, $225.

GM3091, gold plate, 2-1/4", 1920-40,
Tested XX 250

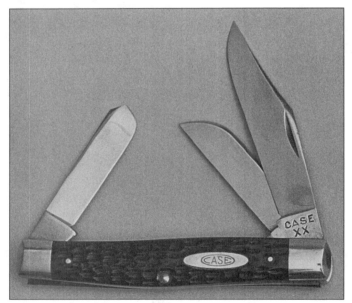

6392, Green Bone, 4", 1940-55, XX, $250.

B392PU, onyx, Tested XX 350
5392, stag, 4", 1920-40, Tested XX 500
6392, green bone, 4", 1920-40, Tested XX 550
6392PU, green bone, 4", 1920-40, Tested XX 600
6392HP, rough black, 4", 1920-40, Tested XX 350
5392, stag, 4", 1940-64, XX 200
6392, rough black, 4", 1940-50, XX 300
6392, rough black, 4", 1940-50, long pull, XX 450
6392, green bone, 4", 1940-55, XX 400
6392, red bone, 4", 1940-64, XX 225
6392, bone, 4", 1940-64, USA 140

5392, stag, 4", 1940-64, USA 125
6392, bone, 4", 1965-69, USA 80
6392, bone (transition), 4", USA,
(Master blade USA/spay blade 10 Dots) 200
5392, stag, 4", 1970, 10 Dot 125
6392, bone, 4", 1970, 10 Dot 90
6392, bone, 4", 1970, 10 Dot, to USA 200

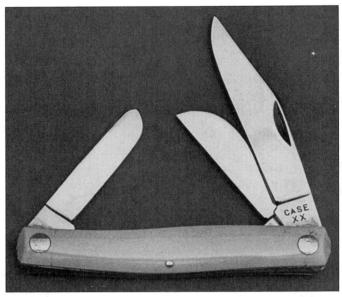

33092, Yellow w/o Shield, 4", 1940-64, XX, $100; with shield, $100.

33092, flat yellow, 4", 1940-64, XX 125

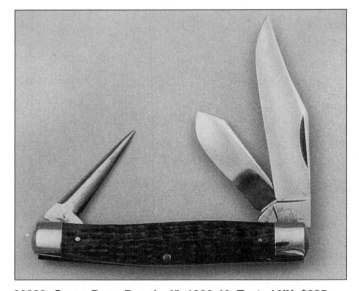

63092, Green Bone Punch, 4", 1920-40, Tested XX, $325.

33092, yellow comp., 4", 1920-40,
Birdseye, Tested XX 200
630092, green bone, 4", 1920-40, Tested XX 250
33092, yellow comp., 4", 1965-69, Birdseye,
USA 75

33092, yellow comp, rare, USA, Birdseye,
two blades stamped USA 150

33092, yellow comp, 4", 1970, Birdseye, 10 Dot .. 75

33092, flat yellow, 4", 1970, 10 Dot 100

5393, stag, 3-15/16", 1920-40, Tested XX 600

6393, green bone, 3-15/16", 1920-40,
Tested XX 600

6393R, green bone, 3-15/16", 1920-40,
Tested XX 600

9393, imitation pearl, 3-15/16", 1920-40,
Tested XX 450

93093, imitation pearl, 3-15/16", 1920-40,
Tested XX 500

Note: 5393 through 93093 are Stockman/Transition.

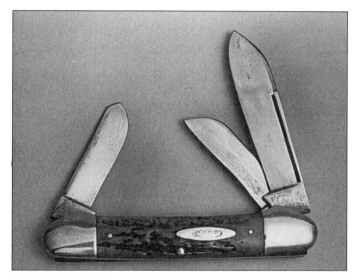

5394LP, Gun Boat, Stag, 4-1/4", 1920-40, Tested XX, $2,500.

6394, green bone, 4-1/4", 1920-40,
Tested XX 2,500

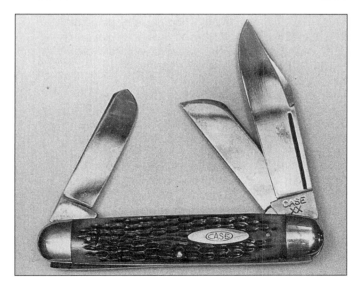

6394-1/2, Green Bone LP, 4-1/4", 1940-50, XX, $1,200.

5394-1/2, stag, 4-1/4", 1920-40, Tested XX 2,400

6394-1/2, green bone, 4-1/4", 1920-40,
Tested XX 2,000

6394-1/2, red bone, 4-1/4", 1940-64, XX 1,200

6394-1/2LP, red bone, 4-1/4", 1940-64, XX 1,500

6394-1/2, red bone, 4-1/4", 1940-64, XX,
Muskrat blade (rare) 900

6394-1/2, bone, 4-1/4", 1940-64, XX 1,000

6394-1/2LP, bone, 4-1/4", 1940-64, XX 1,000

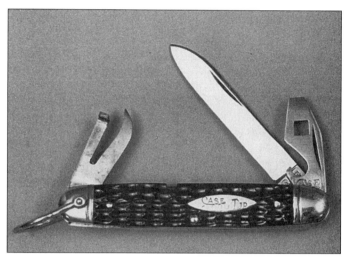

Scout Jr., Green Bone with skate wrench, or could be T-Model Ford Coil adjustment wrench. Scout shield, Tested XX, (rare), 3-3/8", $700.

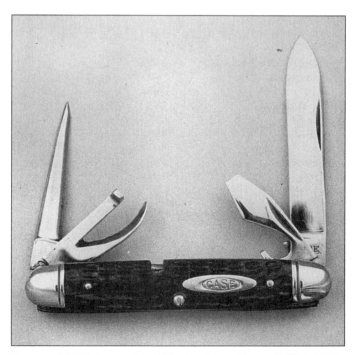

Shown: 64090, Scout Jr., 4 Blade, Green Bone, 3-3/8", 1920-40, Tested XX, $500. Not shown: 64090, Scout Jr., Gen. Pearl, 3-3/8, 1920-40, Tested XX, $600; and 64090, Scout Jr., Slick Black, 3-3/8, 1920-40, Tested XX, $400.

Current Values for Case Stag Sets
and other Miscellaneous Sets and Singles

Description	Yr. Made	# in set	# made	Price	Comments
#1 Stag Collector Set	USA-10 Dot	23	2,000	$3,000	Includes 5 sheath knives & 18 folders
#2 Stag Collector Set	USA-10 Dot	12	700	1,300	Includes 5 sheath knives & 7 folders
4 Dot Razor Edge Set	1976	7	15,000	550	No engraved bolsters sets made
3 Dot Blue Scroll Set	1977	8	19,000	650	Add $50 for 52033
3 Dot Mint Set, with engraved bolsters	1977	8	1,000	750	No 52033 engraved bolsters made
2 Dot Red Case Set	1978	7	14,000	350	
2 Dot Mint Set, with engraved bolsters	1978	7	1,000	500	Price includes wood display box
1 Dot Bradford Centennial Set	1979	6	7,500	295	
1 Dot Mint Set, with engraved bolsters	1979	6	1,000	400	Price includes wood display box
10 Dot 75th Anniversary Set	1980	7	7,500	375	
10 Dot Mint Set, with engraved bolsters	1980	7	1,000	450	Price includes wood display box
Set of four etched sheath knives	1976-79	4	?	250	For 1, 2, 3, & 4 Dot sets above
9 Dot Plain Set (no etch)	1981	6	5,000	325	
9 Dot Mint Set, with engraved bolsters	1981	6	1,000	400	Price includes wood display box
1983 2nd Cut Stag Set	1983	5	700	350	
1983 Mint Set, with engraved bolsters	1983	5	300	400	Price includes wood display box
1984 2nd Cut Stag Set	1984	5	600	350	
1984 Mint Set, with engraved bolsters	1984	5	400	450	Price includes wood display box
Congress Set-all have serial numbers	1984	3	2,000	225	With wood/glass display box
Mint Congress Set, with engraved bolsters	1984	3	500	325	With wood/glass display box
Whittler Set, with engraved bolsters	1983	3	2,500	350	With wood/glass display box
75th Anniversary Gunboat Set	1980	3	5,000	350	With wood/glass display box
Gunboat Set	1985	3	2,500	200	With wood/glass display box
Barlow Set	1982	3	5,000	175	With wood/glass display box
Pearl Set	1982	3	1,000	550	With wood/glass display box
Trapper Trio Set	1978	3	2,500	225	With wood/glass display box
Texas Toothpick Set	1984	3	2,500	225	With wood/glass display box
Gator Set	1979	2	2,750	160	With hardshell box
Double Eagle Bi-Cent (523-7)	1976	1	2,500	285	With wood chest
Chief Crazy Horse Kodiak	1982	1	5,000	285	With box & leather sheath
Foundes Knife (5143)	1979	1	20,000	85	With wood/glass display box
Moby Dick (W165)	1977	1	10,000	150	With wood/glass display box
Nantucket Sleigh Ride (W165)	1979	1	7,500	135	With wood/glass display box
Stag Mako (5158L SSP)	'70s-'80s	1	?	65	With leather pouch & box
Stag Hammerhead (5159L SSP)	'70s-'80s	1	?	75	With leather pouch & box
Stag Sharktooth (5197L SSP)	'70s-'80s	1	?	85	With leather pouch & box
Sidewinder	1980-82	1	?	175	With leather pouch & box
Texas Lockhorn	1980	1	?	145	With leather pouch & box
"Boss" (P172L SSP)	1980	1	?	85	With leather pouch & box
Buffalo (P172)	USA-1970	1	?	100	With wood box

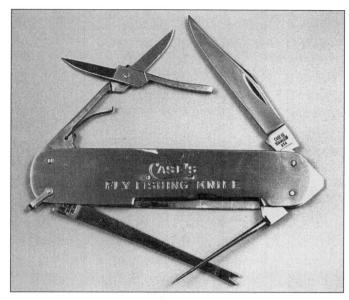

Fly Fisherman's Knife, Stainless Steel, 3-7/8", 1970, 10 Dot, $200.

Fly Fisherman, non SS, 3-7/8", 1920-40,
Tested XX 375
Fly Fisherman, stainless,
3-7/8", 1920-40, Tested XX 300
Fly Fisherman, stainless, 3-7/8", 1940-64, XX .. 275
Fly Fisherman, stainless, 3-7/8", 1940-64,
XX, (XX to USA) 275
Fly Fisherman, stainless, 3-7/8", 1965-69,
USA (USA to 10 Dot) 250
Fly Fisherman, stainless, 3-7/8", 1965-69,
USA 250
Fly Fisherman, stainless, 3-7/8", 1970, 10 Dot,
Transition (10 Dot to 9 Dot) 250
Fly Fisherman, stainless, 3-7/8", 1970, 10 Dot,
Transition 10 Dot to USA 250

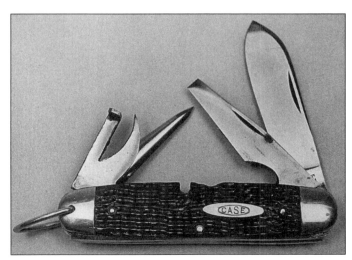

6445R, Camp Scout or Utility, Green Bone, 3-3/4", 1920-40, Tested XX, $325.

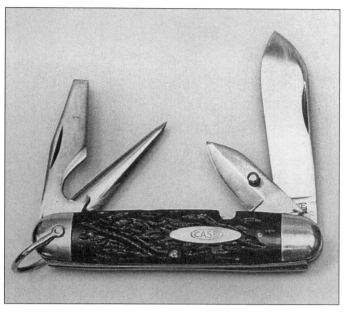

6445R, Rough Black, 3-3/4", 1920-40, Tested XX, $275.

B445R, imitation onyx, 3-3/4", 1920-40,
Tested XX 350
6445R, red fiberloid, 3-3/4", 1920-40, Navy
knife, Tested XX 300
9445R, imitation pearl, 3-3/4", 1920-40,
Tested XX 325

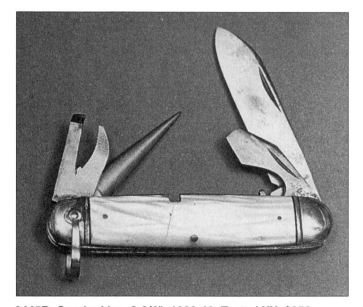

9445R, Cracked Ice, 3-3/4", 1920-40, Tested XX, $350.

6445R, rough black, 3-3/4", 1940-49, XX 200
6445R, imitation jig bone, 3-3/4", 1940-50, XX 75
6445R, red bone, 3-3/4", 1940-64, XX 150
6445R, bone, 3-3/4", 1940-64, XX 90
6445R, bone, 3-3/4", 1965-69, USA 75
6445R, bone, 3-3/4", 1970, 10 Dot 85
64045, rough black, 3-3/4", 1940-50, XX 100

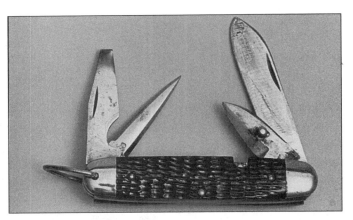

64045R, Scout, Green Bone, no shield, 3-5/8", Tested XX, $275.

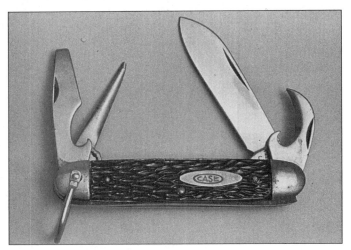

640045R, Scout, Black Plastic, 3-5/8", 1940-50, XX, $40.

640045R, green bone, 3-3/4", 1920-40,
Tested XX 275
640045R, brown plastic, 3-3/4", 1940-64, XX.......45
640045R, black plastic, 3-3/4", 1965-69, USA......35
640045R, brown plastic, 3-3/4", 1970, 10 Dot 45

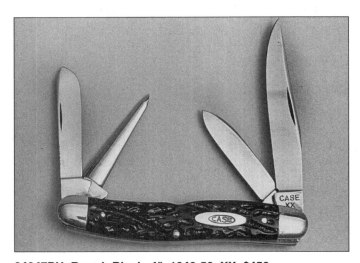

64047PU, Rough Black, 4", 1940-50, XX, $450.

64047PU, rough black, 4", 1920-40,
Tested XX 350

64047PU, green bone, 4", 1920-40,
Tested XX 400
94047PU, imitation pearl, 4", 1920-40,
Tested XX 400
64047PU, green bone, 4", 1940-50, XX 600
64047PU, red bone, 4", 1940-64, XX 350
64047PU, bone, 4", 1940-64, XX........................300
64047PU, bone, 4", 1965-69, USA 150
64047PU, bone, 4", 1970, 10 Dot.......................150

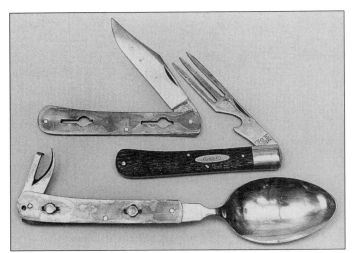

HOBO 6452, Green Bone, 3-3/4", Clip Blade, 1920-40, Tested XX, $450.

M452, metal, 4", 1920-40, Tested XX 385
GS452, gold stone, rare.................................1,000

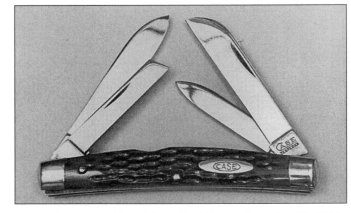

64052, Congress Transition, Red Bone, Rare, 3-1/2", XX to Tested XX, $1,500.

6452, green bone, 4", 1920-40, spear blade,
Tested XX 550

54052, stag, 3-1/2", 1920-40, Tested XX 1,600

64052, green bone, 3-1/2", 1920-40,
Tested XX 1,600

64052, Rogers bone, Tested XX 2,000

54052, stag, 3-1/2", 1940-64, XX 400

3452, yellow comp., 4", 1920-40, Tested XX 400

54052, stag, 3-1/2", 1940-64, XX
(XX To USA) 500

64052, green bone, 3-1/2", 1940-55, XX 400

64052, red bone, 3-1/2", 1940-64, XX 300

64052, bone, 3-1/2", 1940-64, XX 200

64052, bone, 3-1/2", 1940-64, XX (XX
To USA) 250

54052, stag, 3-1/2", 1965-69, USA 175

54052, stag, 3-1/2", 1965-69, USA (USA to
10 Dot) 250

64052, bone, 3-1/2", 1965-69, USA 140

64052, bone, 3-1/2", 1965-69, USA (USA
To 10 Dot) 200

54052, stag, 3-1/2", 1970, 10 Dot 200

54052, stag, 3-1/2", 1970, 10 Dot (10 Dot to
USA) 250

64052, bone, 3-1/2", 1970, 10 Dot 150

64052, bone, 3-1/2", 1970, 10 Dot (10 Dot To
USA) 175

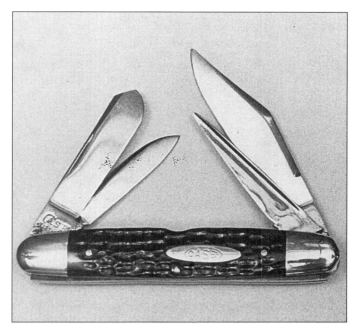

64055PU, Green Bone, 3-1/2", 1920-40, Tested XX, $650.

64055PU, green bone, 3-1/2", 1940-55, XX 700

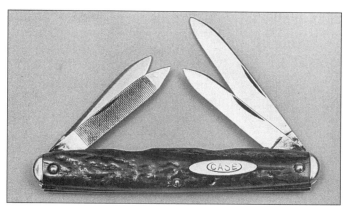

5460T, Stag, 3-3/8", 1920-40, Tested XX, $400.

5460T, red stag, 3-3/8", 1920-40, Tested XX 500

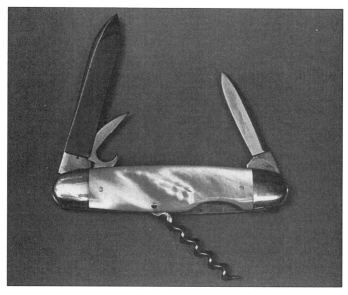

84062K, Pearl, 3-1/4", 1920-40, Tested XX, $450.

94062K, imitation onyx, 3-1/4", 1920-40,
Tested XX 400

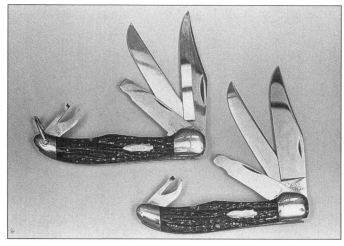

6465SAB-R, Folding Hunter, Saber Blade, Green Bone, 5-1/4",
Tested XX, $2,500.

6465, green bone, flat blade, Tested XX..........2,500

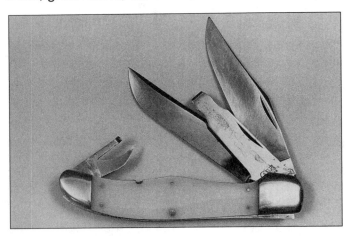

3465, Folding Hunter, Yellow Cell., 5-1/4", Rare, Flat Blade, 1920-1940, Tested XX, $2,500.

9465CI, French pearl handle, 1920-40,
Tested XX 2,500

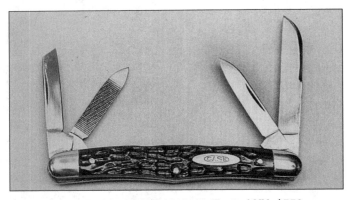

6470F, Green Bone, 3-1/8", 1920-40, Tested XX, $550.

6470, green bone, 3-1/8", 1920-40,
Tested XX 550

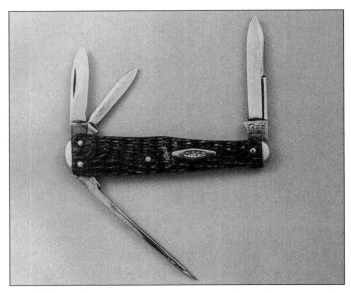

64081, Gunstock Whittler, Green Bone, 3", Lobster Claw File, Tested XX, $750.

5488, stag, 4-1/8", 1920-40, Congress, Tested XX 2,000

5488LP, stag, 4-1/8", 1920-40, Tested XX.......2,500

5488, Winterbottom bone, 4-1/8", 1920-40, Tested XX 3,500

6488, green bone, 4-1/8", 1920-40, Tested XX 2,000

6488LP, green bone, 4-1/8", 1920-40, Tested XX 2,500

6488LP, Rogers bone, 4-1/8", 1920-40, Tested XX 3,000

6488LP, rough black, 4-1/8", 1920-40, Tested XX 1,600

6488, rough black, reg. pull, rare, 4-1/8", 1940-50, XX...1,000

6488LP, rough black, 4-1/8", 1940-50, XX..........900

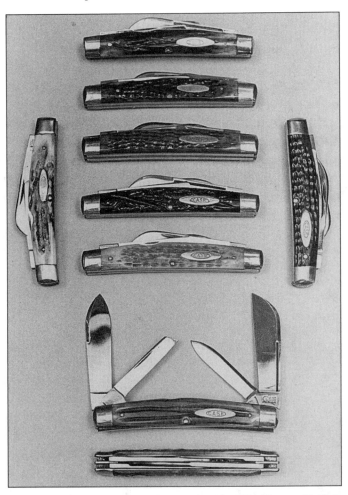

Top to bottom: 5488 Red Stag LP, XX; 6488 Bone, 10 Dot, RP; 6488 Green Bone, LP, XX; 6488, Rough Black, LP, XX; 5488 2nd Cut RP Stag, XX; 6488 Winterbottom Bone LP, Tested XX. Left: 5488 Stag, Tested XX, RP. Note: There are some opinions that the 88 pattern was not made in Regular Pull tested stamp; however, the author believes they were and they will be left in the book until proven wrong.

6488, rough black, 4-1/8", 1940-50, XX,
Transition-blades are regular and long pull..2,000

6488LP, green bone, 4-1/8", 1940-42,
recessed bolsters...2,500

6488, red bone, 4-1/8", 1940-64, XX 600

6488, red bone, 4-1/8", 1940-64, long pull,
XX 1,000

5488, stag, 4-1/8", 1940-64, XX 400

5488, stag, 4-1/8", 1940-64, XX (XX To USA) 500

5488, stag, 4-1/8", 1940-64, long pull, XX 1,200

5488LP, red stag, XX....................................... 1,800

5488, second-cut stag, 4-1/8", 1940-64, XX.......650

5488, second-cut stag, 4-1/8", 1940-64, XX,
(XX To USA) 700

5488, second-cut stag, 4-1/8", 1965,
Transition, USA-XX... 700

6488, bone, 4-1/8", 1940-64, XX 300

6488, bone, 4-1/8", 1940-64, long pull, XX......1,000

6488, bone, 4-1/8", 1940-64, XX,
(XX to USA-and USA to XX)..........................400

6488, second-cut stag, 4-1/8", 1940-64, XX.......600

5488, stag, 4-1/8", 1965-69, USA 300

5488, stag, transition, 4-1/8", 1970, (10 Dot
to USA, USA to 10 Dot); (caution: this
one may never have been made by
W.R. Case) 400

5488, second-cut stag, 4-1/8", 1965-69, USA 600

6488, bone, 4-1/8", 1965-69, USA......................200

6488, bone, 4-1/8", 1965-69, USA (USA To
10 Dot) 250

6488, second-cut stag, 4-1/8", 1965-69, USA 600

5488, stag, 4-1/8", 1970, 10 Dot........................350

6488, bone, 4-1/8", 1970, 10 Dot.......................200

6488, bone, 4-1/8", 1970, 10 Dot (10 Dot To
USA) 250

No 9 Dot 1971 6488 Congress Made.

64009OR, green bone, 1920-40, Tested XX.......300

949OR, imitation pearl, 1920-40, Tested XX 300

34009OR, yellow comp., 1920-40, Scout,
Tested XX 300

B529, imitation onyx, rare, 3-7/8",
Tested XX 2,500

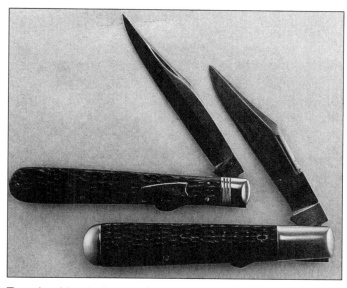

Top: Lockback, brown bone, 4-1/2", W.R. Case & Sons, $1,000. Bottom: Lockback, brown bone, 4-1/2", Case Bros., Springville, N.Y., $1,200.

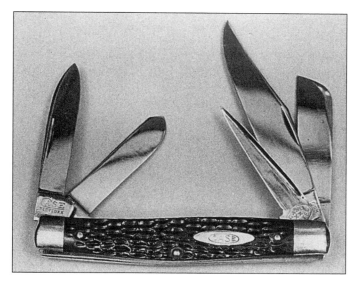

6592, Transitional, Green Bone, 3-7/8", Tested XX, $2,500.

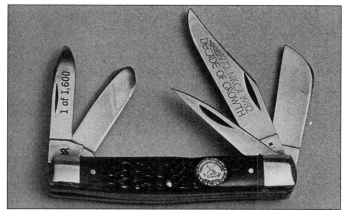

6592, NKCA 10th Anniversary, Bone, 4", 1983-1,600 made, $100.

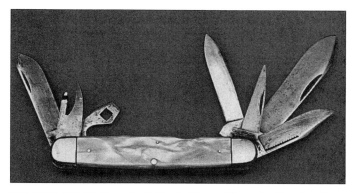

97145PU SK.W, Case's 7-Blade Skate Wrench, Cracked Ice, Very Rare, (only four have been seen by the author), 4", $5,000.

61009-3/4, Winterbottom, 3-3/8", flat-half saber, W.R. Case & Sons, $450.

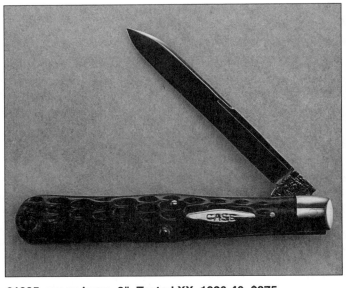

61025, green bone, 3", Tested XX, 1920-40, $275.

61214-1/2, brown bone, 4", Tested XX, $1,600.

61028EO, Winterbottom, 3-1/2", W.R. Case & Son, $275.

61215-1/2, Rogers bone, 5", 1920-40, Tested XX, $1,600.

6149, Rogers bone, 3-15/16, W.R. Case & Sons, 1905-1915, $375.

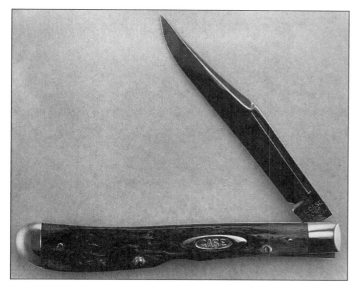

61049L, Rogers bone, 4-1/8", Case Bradford, Pa., 1915-1920, $900.

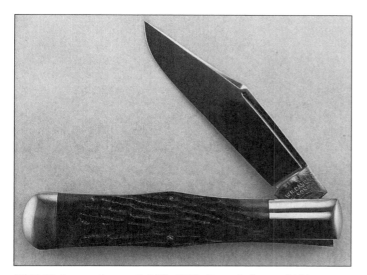

610050, brown bone, 5-1/8", W.R. Case & Sons, $600.

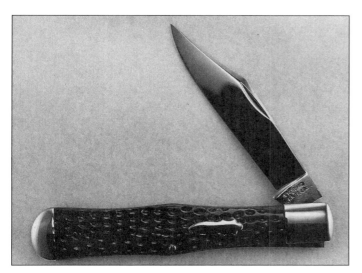

610050, green bone, 5-1/8", flat blade, Standard Knife Co., $350.

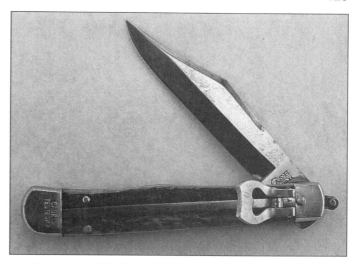

5161L, stag, 4-3/8", Tested XX, 1920-1940, $2,000.

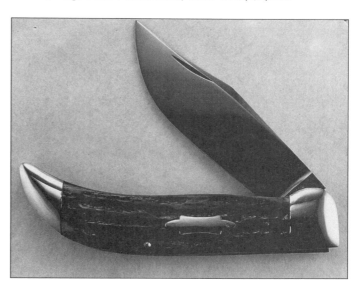

6172, green bone, 5-1/2", Kinfolks, $1,600.

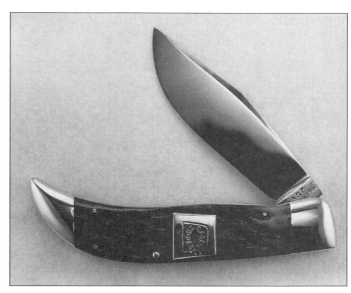

6172L, green bone, Case Zipper Switchblade, 5-1/2", Case Bradford, Pa., $6,500.

Top: 6185, physician's knife, green bone, 3-3/4", Tested XX, 1920-40, $600. Bottom: 6185LP, physician's knife, green bone, 3-3/4", Tested XX, $675.

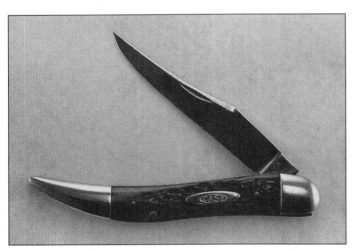

61094, Rogers bone, 4-1/4", Case Bradford, Pa., $400.

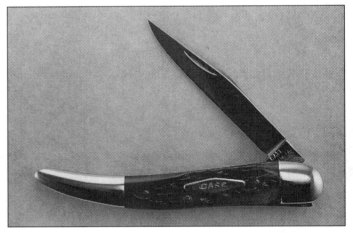

61096, Rogers bone, 3-1/8", Case Bradford, Pa., 1915-20, $400.

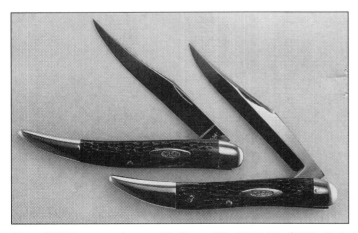

Top: 61095, green bone, 5", Case XX, 1940-55, $400. Bottom: 61095SAB, green bone, 5", Case Bradford, Pa., 1915-20, $500.

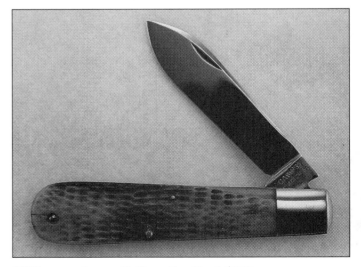

6199, green bone, 4", Case Bradford, $275.

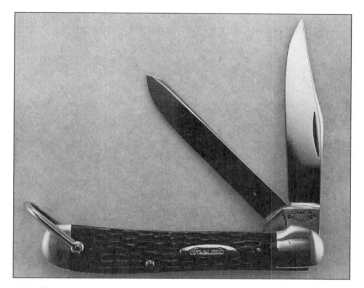

6200R, green bone, 3-15/16", Case's Stainless, $1,200.

6204, brown bone, 3-1/2", Case Bros., L.V., $400.

6202, green bone, 3-3/8", Tested XX, 1920-40, $175.

62005, green bone, 3-3/8", Case Tested, 1920-40, $450.

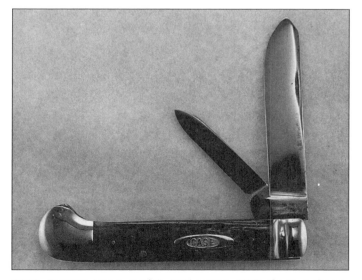

6203, Rogers bone, 3-5/8", half canoe, W.R. Case & Sons, $1,200.

6206, Rogers bone, 2-5/8", W.R. Case & Sons, $225.

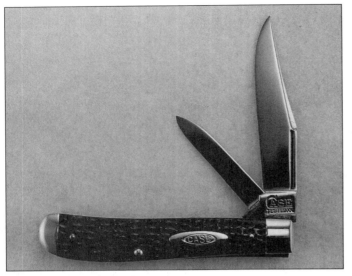

6207LP, green bone, 3-1/2", Tested XX, 1920-40, $425.

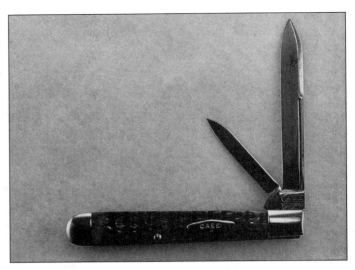

62019, green bone, 3-3/4", Tested XX, $550.

6206, Rogers bone, 2-5/8", W.R. Case & Sons, $225.

6220, Rogers bone, 2-3/4", W.R. Case & Sons, $300.

Top: 6220, green bone, 2-3/4", Tested XX, $400. Middle: 6220SABLP, green bone, 2-3/4", Tested XX, $450. Bottom: 6220LP, green bone, 2-3/4", Tested XX, $400.

62020-1/2, Rogers bone, 3-3/8", W.R. Case & Sons, $300.

5223, stag, 3-5/8", Case Bros., Little Valley, N.Y., $600.

6221, Rogers bone, 3-1/4", W.R. Case & Sons, $400.

6223, green bone, 3-1/4", Tested XX, $450.

06221-1/2, green bone, 3-5/8", Tested XX, $400.

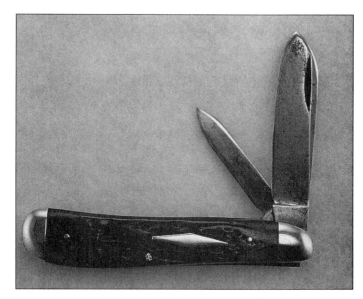

6226, Rogers bone, 3", W.R. Case & Sons, $250.

Top: 06230, green bone, 3-1/4", Tested XX, $300. Bottom: 6230-1/2, green bone, 3-1/4, Tested XX, $300.

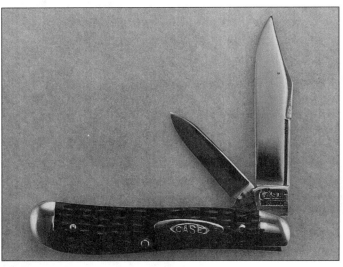

6226-1/2, green bone, 3V, Tested XX, $300.

6231-3/4, Winterbottom, 3-3/4", half sab., W.R. Case & Sons, $400.

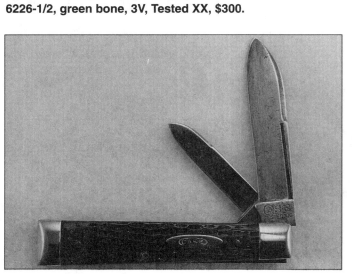

6234, green bone, 3-5/8", Tested XX, $800.

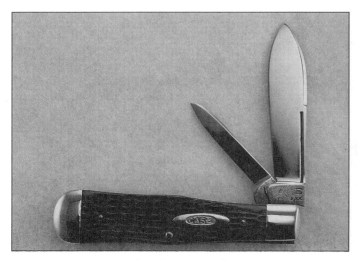

6237, green bone, 3-1/2", Tested XX, $500.

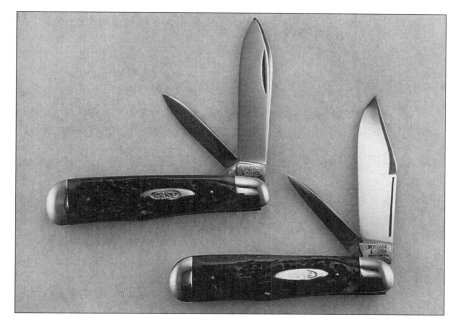

Top: 62035, Rogers bone, 3-1/4", W.R. Case & Sons, $300. Bottom: 62035-1/2LP, Rogers bone, 3-1/4", W.R. Case & Sons, $300.

Top: 6240SP, green bone, 4-7/16", Tested XX, $800. Bottom: 6240 Pen, green bone, 4-7/16", Tested XX, $900.

62035-1/2, bone, 3-1/4", Tested XX, $300. Photo courtesy Marlyn Kepner.

6238, green bone, 3-5/8", Case Bradford, Pa., $350.

Unknown, cracked ice, 2-3/4", oval Tested XX, cam operated automatic, $250. Photo courtesy Marlyn Kepner.

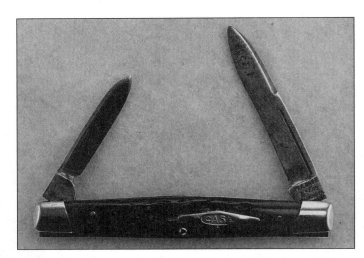

62042LP, Rogers bone, 3", slant bolsters, W.R. Case & Sons, $250.

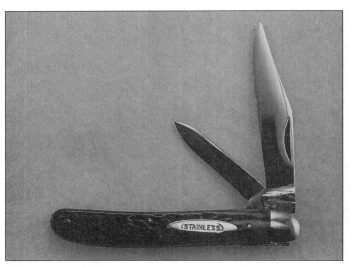

6242, Rogers bone, 2-3/4", Case's Stainless, $400.

6287, Rogers bone, 3-1/8", flat bolsters, W.R. Case & Sons, $250.

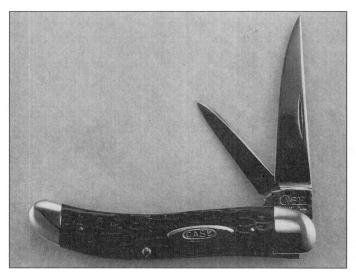

62039, green bone, 3-3/8", small sow belly, Tested XX, $500.

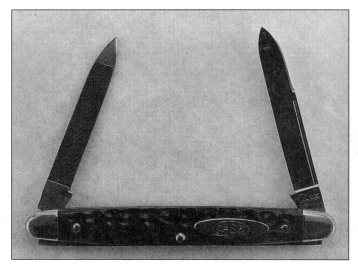

6271FLP, green bone, 3-1/4", Tested XX, $300.

Top: 06245-1/2LP, green bone, 3-3/4", Tested XX, $350. Bottom: 06245, green bone, 3-3/4", Tested XX, $350.

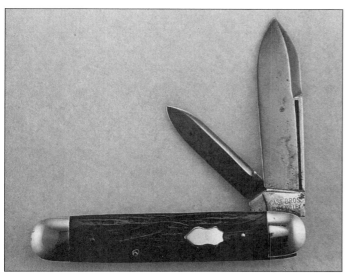

6245LP, brown bone, 3-3/4", Case Brothers, $350.

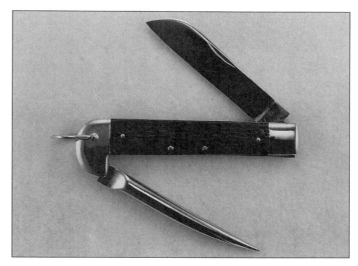

6246R, green bone, 4-3/8", Tested XX, $400.

6254, brown bone, Wharncliffe blade, 3", Case Brothers, Springville, N.Y., $550.

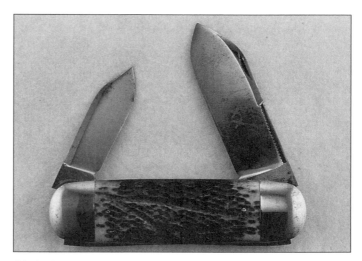

6250, brown worm groove bone, 4-5/8", Case Brothers, L.V.N.Y., $3,000.

Top: 62048SPLP, green bone, 4-1/8", Case Bradford, Pa., $400. Bottom: 62048 Pen LP, Rogers bone, 4-1/8", Case Bradford, Pa., $450.

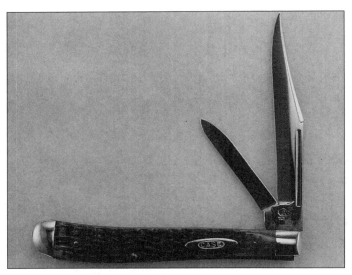

62049LP, green bone, 4-1/8", Tested XX, $700.

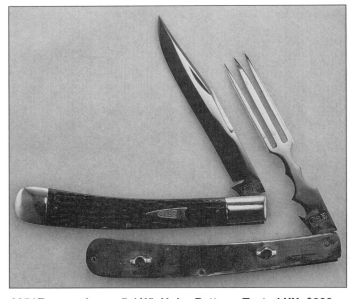

6251F, green bone, 5-1/4", Hobo Pattern, Tested XX, $800.

6273, brown bone, Wharncliffe blade, 3-3/4", Case & Sons, $400.

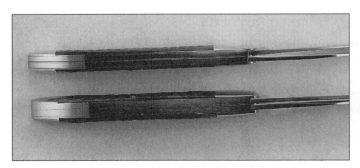

6265, top: thin frame; bottom: regular frame. There is quite a difference.

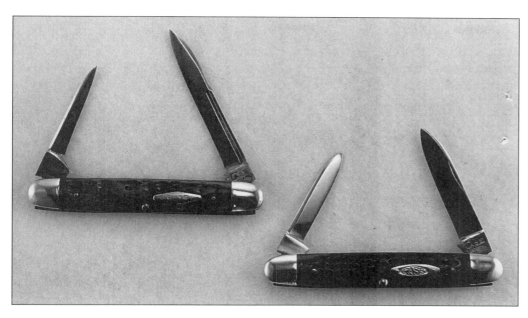

Top: 6253LP, green bone, 3-1/4", Tested XX, $200. Bottom: 6253, green bone, 3-1/4", Tested XX, $200.

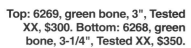

Top: 6269, green bone, 3", Tested XX, $300. Bottom: 6268, green bone, 3-1/4", Tested XX, $350.

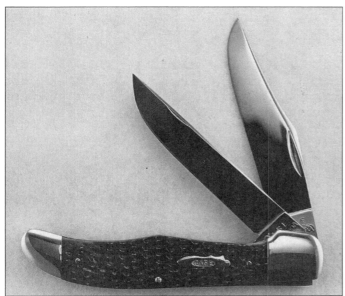

6265Flat, green bone, 5-1/4", thin frame, Tested XX, rare, $750.

6276, green bone, 3-5/8", oval Tested XX, $350.

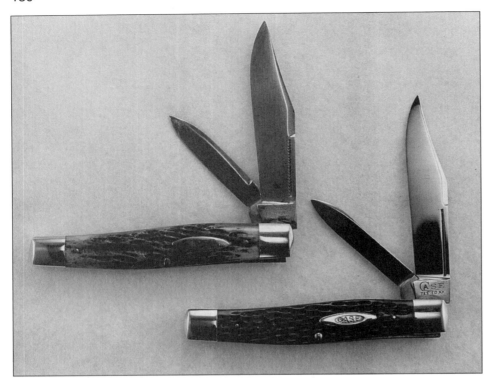

Top: 6275 Pen, tan bone, 4-1/4", W.R. Case & Sons Cutlery Co., $750. Bottom: 6275 Pen, green bone, 4-1/4", Tested XX, $600.

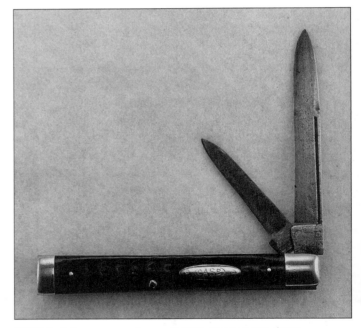

6285 Bolsters, green bone, 3-5/8", Tested XX, $700.

62076, brown bone, 3-3/4", W.R. Case & Sons, contract by Schatt & Morgan, $650.

62079, green bone, 3-1/4", Tested XX, $225.

62089, green bone, 3-3/4", pinched bolsters, Tested XX, rare, $1,500.

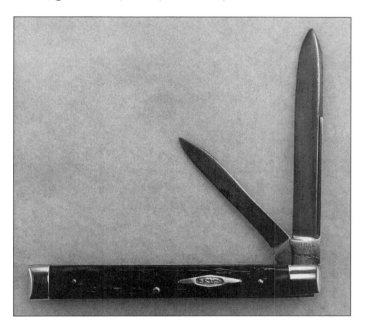

6280, Rogers bone, 3-5/8", W.R. Case & Sons, $700.

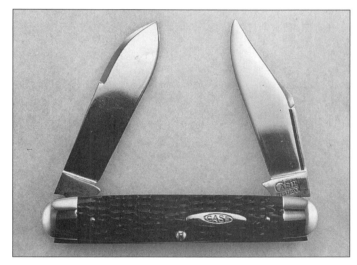

6294J, green bone, 4-1/4", Tested XX, $2,000.

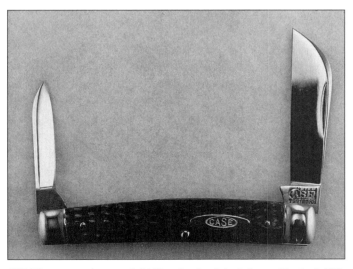

62089, green bone, 3-3/4", pinched bolsters, Tested XX, rare, $1,500.

6294J, green bone, 4-1/4", flat grooved bolsters, Tested XX, $2,000.

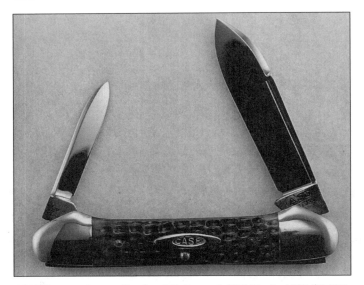

6294X, green bone, Gunboat Pattern, 4-1/4", Tested XX, $2,000.

06294, green bone, 4-1/4V, flat grooved bolsters, Case, Bradford, $800.

6294-1/2, green bone, Cigar Pattern, 4-1/4", Tested XX, $700.

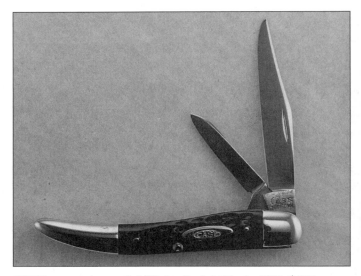

62096, green bone, 3-1/8", toothpick, Tested XX, $450.

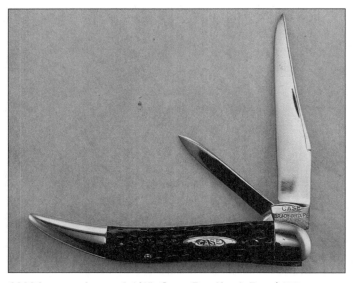

62094, green bone, 4-1/4", Case Bradford, Pa., $450.

6330, green bone, 3-1/4", Tested XX, $450.

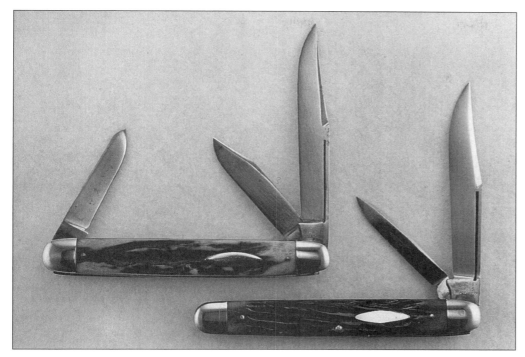

Top: 5395LP, stag, 4-1/4", Case Bradford, Pa., $1,000. Bottom: 6295, Winterbottom bone, 4-1/4", W.R. Case & Sons, $900.

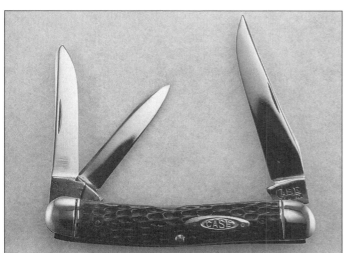

63038, green bone, 3-3/8", Tested XX, $900.

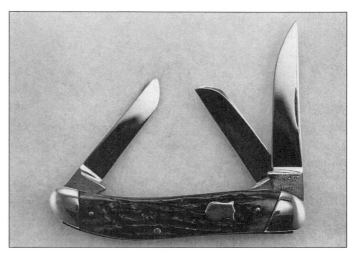

63039, Winterbottom bone, slant bolsters-small sow belly, 3-3/8", W.R. Case & Sons, $800.

63042F, Rogers bone, slant bolsters, 3", W.R. Case & Sons, $350.

6345, Rogers bone, 3-7/8", W.R. Case & Sons, $500.

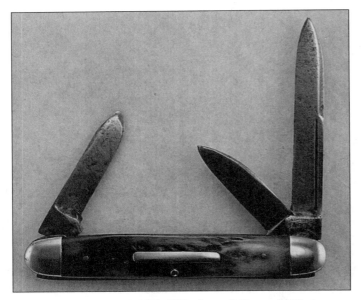

6353, Rogers bone, 3-1/4", W.R. Case & Sons, $250.

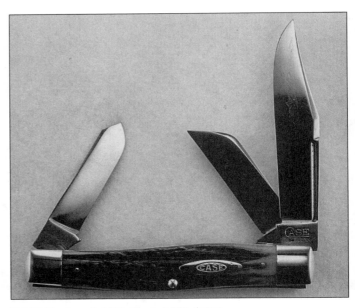

5375LP, stag, 4-1/4", Tested XX, $900.

63046, Rogers bone, 3-7/8", Humpback, W.R. Case & Sons, $650.

6378F, brown bone, 3-1/4", Case Bros., L.V., $500.

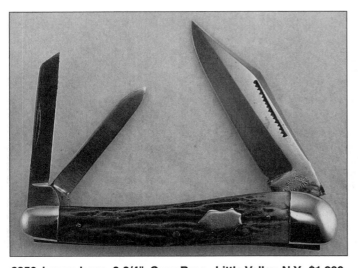

6356, brown bone, 3-3/4", Case Bros., Little Valley, N.Y., $1,200.

6307, brown bone, 3-1/4", W.R. Case & Sons, $450.

6391, green bone, 4-1/2", Tested XX, $3,000.

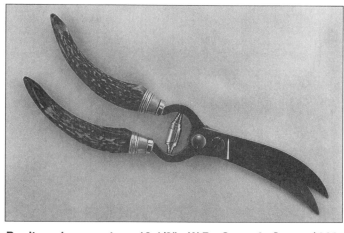

Poultry shears, stag, 10-1/2", W.R. Case & Sons, $200. Photo courtesy Dave Fitzgerald.

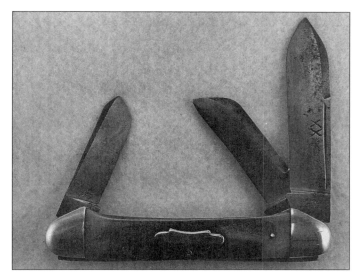

5394, stag, 4-15/16", Case Bros., Springville, N.Y., $3,000.

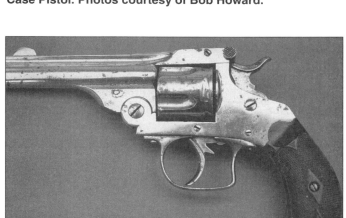

Case Pistol. Photos courtesy of Bob Howard.

Unknown, green swirl, 3-3/8", W.R. Case, Made in U.S.A., $450.

Unknown, metal, one-blade LP, metal end makes a pair of tweezers, back spring is a nail file, very rare, Case Bradford, Pa., $400. Photo courtesy Carl Lindahl.

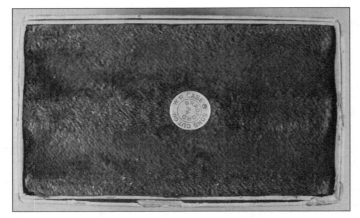

Case Knife Box with W.R. Case Button, $30-$50.

Box with Job Case Button for Sheath Knives, $30-$50.

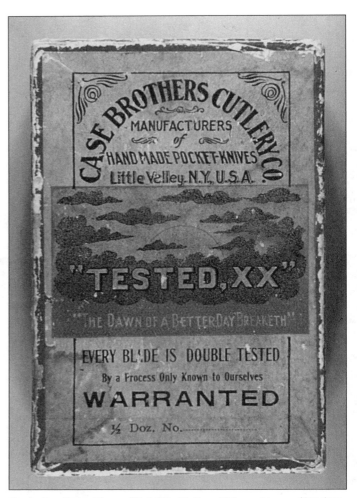

Case Brothers Box with Little Valley, NY markings, $40-$50.

SPECIAL 'LIMITED-EDITION' KNIVES

Due to the large number of Club and limited-edition Case knives, it is difficult to place a market value on them. As a general rule, Club knives, especially those produced by Case, with special handles and the "CC" stamping, will have a higher value because fewer are produced.

Commemorative limited editions have a higher value when they are serial numbered and limited to 500 or less. The majority of special-edition Case knives have appeared in the past few years so it is too early to assess their value as an investment.

Note: All prices listed are for knives in mint condition.

82101 S.S., Case XX Stainless, presented to Case officials, pearl, (6 made) 250

6205R (1981), R.G. Werner Co., light jigged bone Serial numbered (500 made) 60

Not numbered (4,500 made)................................ 30

A6205 SSP RAZ, Appaloosa handle, (5,000 made) 60

GR 6205 SSP RAZ, jigged green bone handle, (5,000 made) 60

SG 6205 SSP RAZ, smooth green bone handle, (5,000 made) 60

SR 6205 SSP RAZ, smooth rose bone handle, (5,000 made) 60

5207 SP SSP, 8 Dot ('80), CC-1982, Three Rivers Knife Club, (150 made)........................ 75

6207 SP SSP, 62109X, Muskrat 10 Dot ('80), "Young Trapper's Dream" Trio set; etched, numbered and boxed, (300 made)..... 150

6207 SSP, 9 Dot ('80), Rebel Knife Club, 1981; etched and serial numbered, (115 made) 50

6207 SP SSP, 8 Dot ('80), CC with stag handles, not numbered, (150 made for Case rep.) 50

6207 SP SSP, polished, jigged red bone, 8 Dot ('80), 1982 Noccalula Knife Club Assoc.: Etched and serial numbered (100 made) 50

No etching or serial numbers (approx. 70 made)... 50

6207 SP SSP, 9 Dot ('80), Forsyth County 150th Anniv., smooth green bone, rare, (380 made) 100

6207 SP SSP, "Tennessee River Boat," with genuine river pearl handles, etched and serial numbered, (100 made) 100

G6207 SP SSP, 9 Dot ('80), 1981, Three Rivers Knife Club, green jigged bone, etched and serial numbered, (155 made)........................... 85

A limited number of 6207 SP SSP in 10, 9 and 8 Dot ('80), contain serrated spay blades. This will add about $5 to the normal price of knife ... 45

Rigid "Pocket Partner" is an '07 "mini trapper" made by Case under contract;

they are stainless steel with hardwood handles(5,000 made), (actually 10 Dot '80)...... 35

6207 SP SSP (1982), Forsyth County K.C., CC stag handles, (400 made) 75

5207 SS (1983), Blue Grass Sportsman's League, stag, (250 made).................................. 60

W207 SP SSP, (1983), West Texas K.C., smooth white bone, CC, (150 made)............................. 60

W107 SS, (1983), Chatham Manufacturing, smooth white bone, (250 made) 60

9107 SS, Smoky Mountain Knife Collectors, midnight pearl, (150 made) 75

8207 SP SSP, 7 Dot ('80), Three Rivers K.C., pearl, (150 made) 100

R207 SP SSP, (CC), West Texas Knife Club, (150 made) 60

6207 SP SSP, polished, 8 Dot ('80), red bone, over-run from trapper trio sets, (approx. 70 made).. 90

6207 SP SSP, 8 Dot ('80), Sharp Top, The Bargain Barn, limited, stag............................... 60

6207 SP SSP, 1984, Black Walnut Festival, West Virginia, (175 made) 50

6107 SSP, Imitation smoked pearl, collectors, 7 Dot ('80), (75 made)...................................... 75

6308 WB, (1982), West Texas K.C., CC, smooth white bone, (150 made) 75

6308, "Words" 85th Year, 1892-1977, (Word's Lumber Co.), limited edition................. 50

6308, 1982, Wood Carvers Club of America, Maryville, Tenn., (82 made)............................... 50

51009 RAZ SS, (1983), Betchler Mint K.C., CC, (150 made) 75

52009 RAZ SSP, 52009-1/2 SSP, 52009 SSP In display case, (5,000 sets made) 200

A62009-1/2, (1982), CC Vulcan Knife, c. stag handles, (150 made) 75

61011, (1979), "Ace Pruner," (500 made) 35

3318 SH PEN, 1980 Webster County Scottish Rite Club, limited... 35

A6220, (Appaloosa)..35

5120 R, Wall Drug 50th Anniv. (182 made),
2 Dot with shield (168 made), 10 Dot ('80),
without shield, either variation 65

SR 6120, Wall Drug 1981 50th Anniv.
(350 made), smooth rose bone........................50

8220, World's Fair 1982, genuine pearl in box,
numbered, (5,000 made) 75

3120 SS, R6120 SS, A6120SS Peanut trio set,
Cash & Carry Stores Inc., 1984, 300 sets
with engraved bolsters...................................250
700 sets with plain bolsters............................175

8220, pearl, (1984), Marilyn Monroe,
limited edition...75

5120 SSP, Greencastle Bicentennial,
(825 made with box) 45

8225-1/2, 9 Dot ('80), "Trip to Heaven"
presentation knives, 1981, pearl handled,
(8 made) 250

2226-1/2, 1 Dot, 75th Anniv. of "Coca Cola,"
slick black handles, (5,000 made) 65

31131, 32131, 33131 (1984) Canoe Set,
Cherokee Heritage Collection, yellow
handles, (1,500 sets made) 250

53131, (1983), CC, Central Kentucky K.C.,
stag canoe, (150 made)..................................125

SW62131, (1982), CC, Northeast Cutlery
C.A., smooth white bone, scrimshawed,
(150 made with box) 100

13031LR, (1977), Swinston Co. National Mines
Service, (3,000 made) 35

12031LHR, (1979), "Ace Pruner Lock,"
(500 made) 35

82033LO, (1980), letter opener made for
American Brand executives, pearl,
(60 made) 275

82033, 9 Dot ('80), "Trip to Heaven,"
presentation knives, pearl, shad, no bolsters,
1981, (7 made) 250

A6235-1/2, "Corvette" Series, 8 different
etchings of various Corvette models,
(limited edition) 40

6235-1/2, "Dixie" with flag, limited.................30

92033B and 92042B Imitation smoked pearl,
first CCC premium knives, 1982, (4,500
sets made) 75

2137, green delrin, (1980), B & H Hardware,
San Angelo, Texas, (150 made) 35

2137, green delrin, (1980), Clayton Cattle
Feeders, (100 made) 35

5137 SS, stag handle, Kentucky Bicentennial,
4 Dot, boxed, (30,000 made) 45

5137 SS, stag handle, Kentucky Bicentennial,
4 Dot "Stainless" on the blade, (approx.
3,000 made)..60

G137 SS, green delrin, Kentucky Bicentennial,
5 Dot, boxed, (35,000 made) 35

G137 SS, green handled, Kentucky
Bicentennial; stamped on the handle:
"Grand Opening South Bradford Plant
April 1975," (100 made) 100

P137 SS, wood handle, Kentucky Bicentennial,
5 Dot, boxed, (30,000 made) 35

2138 SS, Historical Bicentennial Collection for
South Carolina, 56 different blade etchings,
with 200 made for each one, serial
numbered, 4 Dot 35

P138L SS, "Alyeska" Alaskan Pipeline,
etched, (500 made)...175

62040 SP SSP, green bone, 1985 National
Knife Collectors Assoc., limited.......................75

V-42 Stilletto, American Historical Foundation,
American Version, (1,500 made) 200

5143 SSP, (1981), Vulcan Knife Club, CC, stag,
(150 made) 75

5143 SSP, 1 Dot, Case Founder's Knife,
etched and serial numbered, in box,
(2,500 with each prefix C-A-S-E) 85

6143 A62009-1/2, "My Grandad and Me,"
etched, numbered and boxed, (600 sets) 75

9244 SMO, smoked pearl, limited...................35

6246L R SS and 1199 SH R SS "The Old Man
and the Sea" set, (600 sets made) 75

SR63047 and GR63047, 1 Dot Smooth green
(6,000 made) 45
Smooth red (3,000 made)................................50

3347, 6347, 6347 SS 1982 Liberty Bowl,
(1,000 of each made)......................................45

4247FK, Greenskeeper Knife, 1973 Von
Senden Co. (1,300 made) 350

31048 SH R SSP, (1979), "Ace Florist,"
(500 made) 100

21048, (1984), slick black, "We Dig Coal,"
(limited edition) 35

6249, (1983), George Washington, limited 40

5149 SSP, (1983), 2 shields, Bechtler Mint K.C.,
(150 made) 75

3250, (1984), "Yellow Gold," gold-plated blades,
(600 made) 125

C61050L SAB, (1983), National Knife Collectors
Assoc., jigged bone, (7,000 made) 100

C61050 SAB, Case XX USA, 3 Dot, etched
"Best of Show," (50 made as Case awards
at national knife shows) 150

A6250, NKCA, Museum Set (1 of 4 knives in set), 2,600 made with serial numbers; 200 made with no numbers 250

6151 SSP, polished, "Case Collector's Club," 1981 knife with plaque, etched and numbered, (5,500 made) 100

6251 SSP SP, polished, "Case Collector's Club," 1982 knife, etched and numbered, spay blade, (4,825 made) 90

6251FK SS, polished, 7 Dot ('80), Case Collector's Club, "Hobo," limited, (3,900 made) 165

P1051-1/2 L SSP and M279 SS With Mossberg Gun Co. logo imprinted on handles, (limited edition), pair 50

21051L SSP, 1979 Oregon Knife Club Assoc., (200 made) 40

61051L SSP, (1980), Central Knife Exchange, "Horse Racing" set, 11 different etchings, special shield, (100 sets of 11) 500

K1051 SSP L., (1983), whitetail deer, ebony handles, gold and silver decoration, (300 made) 80

K1051L SSP, (1984), John Wayne, with cast-bronze handles, (287 made) 150

K1051L SSP
"Pennsylvania Tricentennial," Shaw-Leibowitz, Cast pewter handles (300 made) 90
Cast silver (300 made) 100

3254, 7 Dot ('70), 1974 NKC & DA, Arlington, Texas show, (50 made) 60

3254, "Carolina Bright Leaf Tobacco," etched and serial numbered: 1976, 4 Dot (150 made) 50
1977, 3 Dot (150 made) 55
1978, 2 Dot (150 made) 50
1979, 1 Dot (250 made) 40
1980, 10 Dot ('80) (150 made) 45

3254, "Caswell County-Home of Carolina Bright Leaf," etched and numbered, 1981 9 Dot ('80), (150 made) 45

1982, 8 Dot ('80), (200 made) 45

3254, 1 and 3 Dot, 1980 Northwest Knife Collectors: Etched and numbered, rare, (40 made) 80
Engraved-filed, rare, (10 made) 100

3254, 9 Dot ('80), "Winchester Yellow Boy," etched and numbered, (150 made) 65

3254, 9 Dot ('80), "Grand Opening NKCA Museum," 1981, serial numbered, (50 made) 100

3254, Indiana Knife Collectors Club, 1981, Indianapolis Show, scrimshawed and serial numbered, (50 made) 50

3254, 8 Dot ('80), Tulsa K.C., 1982, etched and numbered (100 made), "Charter Member" 50

3254, Indiana Knife Collectors Club, scrimshawed and numbered, (100 made) 50

3254, 3 Dot, "Kentucky Trapper," etched and serial numbered, (300 made) 50

3254, 7 Dot ('80), Redskins-Super Bowl Champs, (75 made) 60

3254, 8 Dot ('80), Track Magazine, (100 made) ... 60

3254, 10 Dot ('80), Baker & Sons Anniversary, 1939-1980, (50 made) 60

3254, 9 Dot ('80), Delta Merchantile Season's Greetings, (very few made) 60

3254, 8 Dot ('80), Knife Nook-Season's Greetings, 1982, (12 made) 50

3254, 7 Dot ('80), Bear Bryant, gold-plated blades, limited edition 60

3254, 7 Dot ('80), 1983, Caswell County bright leaf, (150 made) 45

3254, 7 Dot ('80), Legion of Kentucky Sportsman-35th Anniversary, (300 made) 50

3254, 3 Dot, 1977 Mid-South Knife Collectors Club, serial numbered, (125 made) 75

3254-6254-6254 SSP 2 Dot, "Smoky Mountain" Trio Set, etched and numbered, (600 made) .. 125

3254, 6254, 6254 SSP 4 Dots, "Carolina from the Mountain to the Seas" Trio set, etched, numbered and boxed (many without a box), 100 made 150

3254, 8 Dot ('80), Indiana K.C. 1982, serrated spay, etched and numbered 45

3254, 9 Dot ('80), "Glasgow KY," 1981, 1 of 50 40

3254, 8 Dot, Fort Worth, Texas July 1982 Knife Show, (50 made) 50

5154 SSP, NKCA-1979 Club Knife, etched and serial numbered, (12,000 made) 65

2254-4254, 9 Dot ('80), set of white and black handled trappers (pair), serial numbered, (2,500 sets made) 75

2254, 9 Dot ('80), slick black, "Fur Takers of America 1982," etched and numbered, (300 made) 50

2254, 9 Dot ('80), slick black, "Chester County Centennial," 1982, etched and numbered, (150 made) 50

3254, 7 Dot ('80), John Wayne, gold-plated blades, limited edition 65

3254, 7 Dot ('80), Knife Nook Season's Greetings 1983, (12 made) 50

3254, 8 Dot ('80), Black Walnut Festival Spencer, W.V., 1982, (150 made) 50

3254, 7 Dot ('80), T.V.A. 50th Anniversary, gold-plated blades, limited 50

3254, 9 Dot ('80), Liberty Bowl, 1982, (1,000 made) 40

3254, 6 Dot ('80), Elvis Presley, gold-plated blades, limited..................75

3254, 7 Dot ('80), Johnny Reb., limited 45

3254, 6 Dot ('80), Heritage Foundation of Franklin & Williamson County, (100 made).......50

3254, (1984), Johnny Appleseed K.C., gold-plated blades, limited 65

G6154, 8 Dot ('80), Bear Bryant, green jigged bone, (12 made)..................85

R6154, 8 Dot ('80), Bear Bryant, red jigged bone, (12 made) 85

G6254, 8 Dot ('80), Bear Bryant, green jigged bone, (100 made)..................85

R6254, 8 Dot ('80), Bear Bryant, red jigged bone, (100 made)..................85

6257, 7 Dot ('80), Alabama Gun Collectors Club, 1982, walnut handles, (265 made) 75

6254 SSP, polished, 8 Dot ('80), Permian Basin K.C., 1983, CC, imitation black pearl with worked back springs, (200 made) 150

6254 SSP, 8 Dot ('80), yellow handles, CC, Rebel Knife Club, 1982, (150 made) 45

6254 SSP, 8 Dot ('80), Choo Choo K.C., 1982, red jigged bone, CC, (150 made) 50

6254, 9 Dot ('80), Expo 1982, Knoxville, rare, (25 made) 60

6254, 8 Dot ('80), Daniel Boone, (100 made).......50

6254 SSP, polished, 2 Dot, CC, Western Reserve Cutlery Assoc., stag, (150 made).......65

6254 SSP, 2 Dot, Fort City K.C., 1982, stag handles, CC, (220 made)..................55

6254 SSP, blue delrin, 1984, N.C. Wildlife Resources Comm.-Div. of Inland Fisheries, (100 made) 60

6254, 3 Dot, 1977 Western Reserve Cutlery Alliance, etched and serial numbered, (100 made) 75

6254 SSP and 1199 SH R 4 Dot, "Burnt Chimney Anniversary," etched, serial numbered and boxed, (100 sets) 80

6254 SSP, 2 Dot and 3 Dot, 1980, Rebel Knife Collector's Club, etched and serial numbered, (155 made) 60

6254, 2 Dot, Alabama Gun Collector's Assoc. 25th Anniversary, etched, boxed and serial numbered, (264 made) 100

6254 SSP, 1 Dot, 1980, Three Rivers Knife Club, etched and serial numbered, (100 made) 75

6254, 6249, 6275 SP 10 Dot ('80), "Trappers Life" Trio Set, etched, boxed and serial numbered, (500 made) 150

6254, 8 Dot ('80), "Tulsa Locomotion-100th Anniversary," etched and numbered, (50 made) 50

6254, 9 Dot ('80), "Mountain Man," etched and numbered, (150 made) 60

6254, 9 and 10 Dot ('80), "Jedediah Smith" Mountainman, etched, boxed and serial numbered, (200 made) 65

6254, 9 and 10 Dot ('80), "Cabela's," etched and serrated spay blade, (500 made) 60

6254 SSP, Bootheel Knife Collectors Club, 1981, etched and serial numbered, (less than 30 made)..................75

6254 SSP, 1 Dot, Northwest Tennessee Knife Collectors, 1982, etched and serial numbered, (approx. 100 made) 50

6254 SSP, 8 Dot ('80), CC, 1982, Trapper Knife Collectors Club, imitation pearl, polished stainless steel with engraved shield, (251 made) 150

6254 SSP, CC, 8 Dot ('80), 1982, Texas Knife Collectors, polished stainless with stag handles, shield is a circle with Texas map, (255 made) 90

3254, 8 Dot ('80), Bootheel Knife Collectors Club Anniversary Knife, 1982, (25 made).........75

6254 SSP, CC, 9 Dot ('80), Bold City Knife Collectors, 1981, single blade trappers with stag handles, etched and serial numbered, (200 made) 60

6254, 9 Dot ('80), "Texans Choice" Etched and serial numbered (100 made)..................50
With engraved bolsters (10 made)..................100

6254 SSP, Green jigged bone, CC, 2 Dot, Choo Choo Knife Club, etched and serial numbered, (150 made) 60

6254 SSP, 8 Dot ('80), "Forest City Masonic Lodge," etched and serial numbered, (100 made) 60

6254 SSP, 8 Dot ('80), 1982, Sho Me Cutlery Club, jigged red bone, circle shield with mule's head, etched and numbered, (150 made) 50

6254 SSP, 8 Dot ('80), 1982, Hard Hat Knife Collector's Club, etched and numbered, (200 made) 35

B6254 SSP, 9 Dot ('80), 1981, Trapper Knife Collectors Club, polished stainless with slick black handles, etched and serial numbered, (165 made) 150

R6254-G6254, 8 Dot ('80), red and green jigged bone set (pair), serrated spay blade, (1,200 sets made) 75

SR6254, 9 Dot ('80), Alabama Gun Collectors Assoc., 1980 Knife, etched, boxed and numbered, handled in smooth rose bone, (250 made) 100

6254 SSP and 5254 SSP, 8 Dot ('80), Kirkland Sod Company since 1953, etched and numbered, pair, (24 made) 125

6254, 9 Dot ('80), "Jim Bridger," etched and numbered, (200 made) 50

6254 and 6254 SSP, 9 Dot ('80), "Buckeye Trapper," serrated spay, numbered and etched-pair, (100 pairs made) 85

6254, 9 Dot ('80), "Journeyman Wireman," etched and numbered, (1,000 made) 35

6254, 9 Dot ('80), "Jim Bowie" Trapper, numbered and etched, (100 made) 50

6254 SSP, 8 Dot ('80), Flint River K.C., 1982, red jigged bone, CC, (168 made) 50

6254, 7 Dot ('80), Hardeman County K.C., 1983, (50 made) 60

6254, 7 Dot ('80), Smoky Mountain Carvers, 1983, (56 made) 75

6254, 7 Dot ('80), Ft. Worth, Texas 1983 show knife, (102 made) 50

6254, 7 Dot ('80), Rattle & Snap Tool Co., (600 made) 50

6254SR, 9 Dot ('80), smooth rose bone, factory prototype, no etch, (15 made) 125

6154R, 8 Dot ('80), Kentucky Long Rifle, red bone, (600 made) 50

6154G, 8 Dot ('80), Kentucky Long Rifle, green bone, (600 made) 50

6254 SSP, Polished, 7 Dot ('80), Choo Choo K.C., 1983, CC, imitation smoky pearl, (150 made) 90

6254, 8 Dot ('80), Music City K.C., 1983, gold-plated blades, (75 made) 90

6254SB 7 Dot ('80), Blue Ridge Trapper, smooth blue bone, (300 made) 50

6254B, 7 Dot ('80), Blue Ridge Trapper, jigged blue bone, (300 made) 50

6254 SSP, 8 Dot ('80), factory prototype, red jigged bone, no shield, (7 made) 100

6254 SSP, Polished, 7 Dot ('80), Trapper Knife Collectors Club, 1983, CC, smooth appaloosa bone with shield, (203 made) 150

6154R, 7 Dot ('80), Bold City K.C., 1983, red jigged bone, (155 made) 50

6254, 7 Dot ('80), Tennessee Jaycees, 1983, limited edition 45

6254, 7 Dot ('80), Black Walnut Festival, Spencer, W. V., 1983, (200 made) 50

6254 SSP, polished, 7 Dot ('80), smooth appaloosa bone, 3rd anniversary of Knife Nook, (5 made) 150

6254G, 8 Dot ('80), "Delta Queen," jigged green bone, (150 made) 60

5254 SSP, 1985 Fort Myers K.C., with two shields, second club knife, (150 made) 75

6254R, 8 Dot ('80), "Southern Belle," jigged red bone, (150 made) 50

6254, 7 Dot ('80), John Wayne, "Duke," (600 made) 125

6254, 7 Dot ('80), 200th anniversary of Clarksville, (500 made) 50

6254, 9 Dot ('80), Yellow Banks C. Club, 1981, "Charter Member," (100 made) 50

6254 SSP, polished, 7 Dot ('80), Flint River K.C., 1983, CC, smooth white bone, (150 made) 75

6254, 7 Dot ('80), N.C. Wild Turkey Federation, 1983, (300 made) 60

6254, 7 Dot ('80), N.C. Highway Patrol, serial number is badge number, (863 made) 100

6254, 7 Dot ('80), "Pearl Harbor," (500 made) 50

6254, 7 Dot ('80), "Sargent York," (500 made) 50

6254 SSP, 7 Dot ('80), Hardeman County K.C., 1984, (100 made) 50

6254, 7 Dot ('80), "Chief Crazy Horse," (500 made) 60

6254, 7 Dot ('80), "Bear Bryant," second cut bone (not case stag), limited 75

6254, 7 Dot ('80), "Iwo Jima," smooth white bone, (500 made) 60

6254, 7 Dot ('80), Case 80th anniversary, jigged white bone, limited 60

6254, 1984, pair, "Buffalo Bill's and Annie Oakley's Wild West," gun blued blades with gold etching, (1,500 pairs) 100

6254, 7 Dot ('80), "Chief Crazy Horse," smooth white bone, (500 made) 60

6254, 7 Dot ('80), Jackson Gun & Knife Show, bone, (20 made) 60

6254, 9 Dot ('80), Liberty Bowl, 1982, bone, (1,000 made) 40

6254, 6 Dot ('80), Alamo High School, 1983, (200 made) 45

6254, 7 Dot ('80), Rose Bowl, 1984, bone, (1,000 made) 50

6254, 9 Dot ('80), CC, Permian Basin K.C., 1981, etched and numbered, smooth white bone, (150 made) 100

6254SSP, 8 Dot ('80), North Carolina Wild Turkey Federation, etched and numbered, 1981, (300 made) 75

6254, 8 Dot ('80), North Carolina Wild Turkey Federation, etched and numbered, 1982, (300 made) 75

6254, 9 Dot ('80), jigged green bone, 1981, Alabama Gun Collectors, boxed, (224 made) 100

6254, 8 Dot ('80), "Kentucky Coal Miner," etched and numbered, (1,000 made) 40

6254, 8 Dot ('80), "Paradise Steam Plant," etched and numbered, (1,000 made) 40

6254 SSP, 8 Dot ('80), single blade trapper, jigged green bone, Bold City K.C., 1982........... 50

6254 SSP, 8 Dot ('80), 1982, Flint River K.C., polished S.S., jigged red bone, (150 made) 60

6254, 8 Dot ('80), Oklahoma Diamond Jubilee, 1907-1982, etched and numbered, (50 made) 40

6254, 9 Dot ('80), Tulsa K.C., etched "Life Member," (25 made) 75

6254 SSP, 8 Dot ('80), Permian Basin K.C., 1982, CC blonde pakkawood, (200 made) 90

R6154, 8 Dot ('80), red bone and G6154 green bone single-blade trapper, (2,500 pairs made) 90

Rigid "Gaucho" 6254 SSP Made under contract by Case, hardwood handles (actually a 10 Dot 1980), (5,000 made) 40

A number of **6254 and 6254 SSP** trappers have serrated spay blades. They can be found in 3, 2, 1, 10, 9, and 8 Dot stampings. This adds about $5 to the normal price of the knife 50

6254, 7 Dot ('80), 1983 Alabama Gun Collectors, CC, stag handle, (281 made)........................ 100

6254 SSP, 7 Dot ('80), Ft. Meyers K.C., 1984, 2 shields, (100 made) 50

6254, 7 Dot (80), "Adolph Rupp," bone, limited edition 50

6254, 6 Dot ('80), "Buford Pusser," smooth white bone, limited 50

3254, 1984, Knife Nook "Season's Greetings," (18 made) 50

6254, 6 Dot ('80), "Buford Pusser," jigged white bone, limited 50

6254, 7 Dot ('80), "John Wayne," jigged white bone, "A" serial number, limited 60

6254, 7 Dot ('80), "John Wayne," smooth white bone, "W" serial number, limited 60

6254, 6 Dot ('80), "Ulysses S. Grant," jigged white bone, limited 50

6254, 6 Dot ('80), "Robert E. Lee," jigged white bone, limited 50

6254, 7 Dot ('80), Sportsmans Wildlife Club, Greensboro, N.C., bone, (200 made) 50

6154 SSP, 9 Dot ('80), Bold City K.C., 1984, CC, smooth white bone, (155 made) 50

6254, 6 Dot ('80), "44 Magnum," bone, (500 made) 45

6254, 6 Dot ('80), Ft. Worth, Texas Knife Show, 1984, bone, fifth anniversary, (100) made 45

6254 SSP, 1984, "Beaver Creek Cutlery," serial number, (50 made) 45

6254, 1984, blue delrin, "Billy Yank," limited edition 40

6254, 6 Dot ('80), "Marilyn Monroe," jigged blue bone, limited................................. 65

6254, 6 Dot ('80), NKCA Museum Fund, 1984, second cut bone (not case stag), (2,500 made) 75

6254, 6 Dot ('80), "Statue of Liberty"- Enlightening the World," bone, limited 65

6254, 6 Dot ('80), "Statue of Liberty"-"Gateway to Freedom," jigged green bone, limited 65

6254 SSP, 10 Dot (1970), factory prototype, special gut-hoot spay blade, very rare, (only 6 made) 600

6254 SSP, (1976), Dewees Fertilizer Co., composition yellow, (50 made) 45

2254, 9 Dot ('80), Golden Circle K.C., 5th anniversary, slick black, (150) made 40

2254, 9 Dot ('80), "Midnight Santa," slick black, (300 made) 40

B254 SS, 6 Dot ('80), Louisiana World Expo, 1984, blue delrin handles, (500) made 75

2254 SS LWE, 6 Dot ('80), Louisiana World Expo, 1984, slick black, (2,500 made) 40

2254 SS, 6 Dot ('80), Louisiana World Expo, 1984, slick black, limited 40

2254, (1984), slick black, "The Coal Miner," (limited edition) 40

4254, 9 Dot ('80), Golden Circle K.C., 1983, slick white, (300 made) 40

4254, 8 Dot ('80), Battle of Parker's Crossroads, slick white, (50 made).................. 50

4254, 9 Dot ('80), White Knight, slick white, (300 made) 40

5254 SSP, 9 Dot ('80), "Andrew Jackson," stag, (300 made)..................................... 50

5254 SSP 9 Dot ('80), "Davey Crocket," stag, (300 made) 50

5254 SSP, 9 Dot ('80), "Sam Houston," stag, (300 made) 50

5254 SSP, 9 Dot ('80), "Jim Bowie," stag, (300 made) 50

5254 SSP, 9 Dot ('80), "Liberty Bowl 1982," stag, (1,000) made..................................50

5254 SSP, polished, 6 Dot ('80), Trapper Knife Collectors Club, 1984, second cut stag (250 made)..90

5254 SS, 1984, Wolverine K.C., second cut stag, (107 made)...75

5254 SS, (1984), Noccalulu K.C., second cut stag, (100 made)..75

5254 SS, (1984), second cut stag, Northeast Cutlery Collectors Assoc. spring show prize, (10 made)..................................... 100

8254 SS, polished, 6 Dot ('80), Permian Basin K.C., 1984, CC, pearl, (210 made) 150

6254 SSP, polished, Permian Basin K.C., 1985, 5th anniversary, old green bone, (200 made) 75

6254, Virginia Wild Turkey Federation, 1984, (300 made)..50

6254, North Carolina Wild Turkey Federation, 1984, (300 made) 50

3254, Vietnam Commemorative, blued blades deep etched, 1984, (1,500 made).................50

11055, (1975), spay blade, no shield, C.M. Hobbs & Sons Inc. (50 made).........................75

11055, (1976), spay blade, no shield, "Stark Brothers," (144 made) 50

M1056L SSP, "Zem Zem Temple," shrine emblem, (2,000 made).................................30

P158L SSP, (1983), Pennsylvania Game Commission, logo engraved on bolster, (375 made) 50

P158L SSP, U.S. Repeating Arms, Winchester logo, (850 made)......................55

P158L SSP, (1983), O'Dell Hardware Co., special etching, (2,000 made).....................45

2159L SS, "Hiawatha," limited edition 50

2159L SS, "Paul Bear Bryant," 5,000 made 50

5159L SS, "Paul Bear Bryant," (1,000 made).......90

2159L SS, "Liberty Bowl 1982," (1,000 made) 50

P159L SSP and P158L SSP CC, 1982, Chesapeake Bay Knife Club, green bone, (200 made), pair 100

06263 SSP, CC, 8 Dot ('80), Northern Virginia Knife Collectors, 1982, genuine pearl, (150 made) 75

2165 SS, "Black Diamond" folding hunter, (approx. 2,000 made) 75

5165 SS, Heart of Dixie Knife Club, CC, (150 made)..75

5165 and 6165, Flat ground, 1981, Texas K.C., shield with map of Texas, (345 sets made), pair......................................175

6265 SAB, 8 Dot ('80), red jigged bone, 1982, Golden Circle K.C., etched and numbered, (500 made) 45

4165, "Texas Special," etched and numbered, (5,000) made 65

Knife with plaque 90

W165 SSP, "Moby Dick," engraved bolsters with scrimshawed handles, (10,000 made), numbered with 2,500 of each prefix C-A-S-E..... 150

W165 SSP, "Nantucket Sleigh Ride," scrimshawed handles, serial numbered, engraved and in a box, (7,500 made)............ 150

5165 SSP L, (CC), Central Kentucky Knife Club, 1984, stag, (160 made) 75

W165 SSP, (1978), white bone, no engraving or scrimshaw, J.A. Parker Co., (100 made) 75

6265 DR SAB, (1982), Blue Grass Sportsman's League, (CC), stag, (250 made) 65

5165 SSP, "American Spirit" Bicentennial, 4 Dot, serial numbered, engraved and in a box, (10,000 made)................................... 140

6265 SAB, "Oklahoma Diamond Jubilee," 1907-1982, etched and serial numbered, (50 made) 50

P172, (1977), handled in ebony for American Blade Magazine, P172 stamp omitted, (50 made) 200

P172, (1981), Avellino Knives, serial numbered, (1,000 made) 50

6275, (1982), King Coal Knife Club, jigged pakkawood black, (150 made)........................50

6375, (1984), "He-Man Stock Knife" 40

I278, Reagan and Carter limited-edition presidential knives, either knife......................35

I278, "Bradford Centennial," limited edition 15

S278, "Case Diamond Jubilee," imitation tortoiseshell, limited edition............................20

I278, Cincinnati Union Terminal, silk screened, (300 made) 20

I278, World's Fair, 1982, silk screened, unlimited 20

OL278, 1980 Winter Olympics in Lake Placid, N.Y., serial numbered with cast sterling-silver handles, (1,000 made)..............175

I278 SS, "Bradford Pennsylvania" Centennial, limited run with white handles.........................20

I278 SS, Mid-America Advertising knives, Mid-America Transport Inc., Canning Corp. andInsurance Inc., Madisonville, KY, (250 sets made)..50

S278 and S2033, with Shaw-Liebowitz
Cast-pewter handles: Limited edition, pair...... 100
Silver cast handles, pair.................................... 125

I278 SS, "Armadillo" silk screened, "One Tough
Hombre," limited edition 20

I278 SS, "A Celebration of
Friends-Pennsylvania's 300th Birthday,"
silk screened, limited edition 15

I278, 1984 Louisiana Wold Expo., imitation
ivory, limited edition... 25

82079, pearl, Great Smoky Mountain National
Park 50th Anniv., (1,000 made) 65

82079, pearl, 1984 Louisiana World Expo,
limited edition 65

M279 SS, (1976), Owens, Illinois Inc.,
Miracle Edge, (77 made) 25

6279 SS, (1976), Maramec Mining Co. Green
Cross Safety Emblem, (60 made).................... 35

6279 SS, (1977), UNHP Mines General,
(165 made) 25

8179 LO, (1980), pearl letter opener,
Swingline executives, (60 made) 200

M279 SS, (1982), Owens, Illinois, pen blade
has miracle edge, (50 made) 25

82079, World's Fair 1982, genuine pearl with
serial numbers, (5,000 made) 65

6380 SSP and 6488 SSP NKCA set, Museum
Dedication and Reward Fund, both are
etched, serial numbered and have smooth
rose bone handles, (about 1,800 sets) 150

4380, NKCA 1976 Club Knife, 4 Dot white
handles, etched and serial numbered,
(3,000 made) 160

6185 SSP, SR6185 SSP, 5185 SSP "Doctor's
Knife" set, (5,000 made): 500 sets were
boxed and serial numbered 150
Unnumbered sets 125

22087, (1984), slick black, "Coal Miners of
America," limited edition 30

5288 SSP, American Blade Collectors Club,
(5,000 made) 65

6592 SSP, polished, 10th Anniv. NKCA,
(1,600 made) 100

61093, SSP SG, (1981), Gator Cutlery Club,
smooth green bone, (350 made) 75

GB61093 SSP and RB61093 SSP, Set,
jigged bone toothpicks, boxed, (1,250 sets) ... 130

SR61093 SSP NKCA Membership Drive,
NKCA shield with smooth rose bone,
(less than 3,000 made) 90

61093 SSP and 51093 SSP, "Gator Set,"
etched, numbered and boxed,
(2,750 sets made).. 175

1199 SH R SS, three-knife set, etched
"Dixie Special," "General" and "The
Horse Drawn," limited edition-set...................... 85

62109X, pakkawood with a pearl shield, 1982,
"Trip to Heaven" presentations, (7 made) 150

52131 SSP, 53131 SSP, 5394 SSP, Three
Canoe Set, gold plated, engraved,
numbered and boxed, (5,000 sets made) 375

A number of Case patterns in yellow and slick
black handles have been engraved with
advertising such as "Coca Cola," football
terms, clubs and company messages.
These knives generally bring $5 to $20
over the normal cost of the knife. Some
are serial numbered 35

Muskrat G, (1981), jigged green bone,
miracle edge, (1,200 made) 60

Muskrat R, (1981), Hawbaker special,
jigged green bone, (1,200 made)...................... 60

Muskrat G, (1981), Hawbaker special,
jigged green bone, (1,000 made)...................... 90

Muskrat R, (1981), Hawbaker special,
jigged red bone, (1,000 made).......................... 90

Muskrat R, (1982), Hawbaker special,
jigged red bone, (681 made)........................... 100

Muskrat G, (1982), Hawbaker special,
jigged green bone, (1,114 made)...................... 90

Muskrat, red and green jigged bone,
"Hawbaker," (1,200 sets) 150

Muskrat, red and green jigged bone, (600 sets) .. 90

"Texas Lockhorn," genuine pearl handles
with center bolster, special Case
presentations to the NKCA officers, board
members, 1981, Knoxville, (21 made) 500

Texas Lockhorn, with serrated blade made
for "Cabela's," limited edition 125

"Double Eagle," bicentennial stag sheath
knife, etched, numbered and boxed,
(2,500 made) 300

5300, "Apache" sheath knife, stainless with
stag handle, serial numbered, (2,000 made) 65

5400, "Cheyenne" sheath knife, stainless with
stag handle, serial numbered (2,000 made) 65

"Bowie Knife," with stag handle and etched
blade, comes with a wood plaque,
(2,000 made) 250

Case Vietnam Commemorative Boot Knife
A set honoring the Marines, Navy, Army and
Air Force, cast, three-dimensional
handles by Shaw-Liebowitz. Numbered
and in a presentation box (750 sets made):
Set of four 450
Optional gold-plated emblem-add................... 75

Case Bowie stag handles, 50th Anniversary of Smoky Mountain State Park, (1,000 made) 175

Louisiana World Expo 1984 knives. All knives have L.W.E. logo silk-screened on handles. Limited set of 500, with blue delrin handles:
B159L SSP 60
B254 SS 75
B2087 SS 30
B318 HPSS 35
B1048 SS 30

Limited set of black handles, pearl, imitation ivory and metal, silk-screened logo, (approx. 5,000 made of each):
I278 20
82079-1/2 75
21048 SS 30
2318 HPSS 35
22087 SS 45
2254 SS 45
2159L SSP 45
M1090 SS 20

M5 FINN & 5 FINN Stag, 125th anniversary of oil in America, Drakes oil well, Titusville, Pa., with plaque, (1,000 sets made) 200

Kodiak Stag, "Chief Crazy Horse," boxed with medallion, (5,000 made) 325

Kodiak Stag, "Custer's Last Stand," (1984), gun blued blade with gold etching, (1,000 made) 175

Stag Bowie (1984), Mason-Dixon Series, "The Union" and "The Confederacy," three-color etching, (750 made of each knife):
Singles 175
Pair 350

NASA 25th Anniversary (1984) Astronaut's knife on plaque, serial numbered, (1,000) made 175

NASA Original Astronaut knife in special box, numbered, (2,494 made 1970-71) 400

Case Collector's Club 1981 - 6151 SSP, polished, (5,500 made) 100

1982 - 6251 SP SSP, polished, (4,825 made) 90

1983 - 6251 FK SS, polished, (3,900 made) 160

1984 - 64088, green bone, limited 75

1982 CCC 1st Premium Set, 92033B and 92042B, imitation smoked pearl, (4,500 sets made), pair 75

Case Special "Winchester" Contract (pre-1940) 6291, "Winchester"-Case contract, green bone, rare 1,000

3291, "Winchester"-Case contract, rare 900

Special "Limited Edition" Sets

Case Genuine Pearl Set, 1982. File worked back springs, 8254 SS polished, 8207 SP SSP polished, 8249 SS polished, (1,000 sets made) 600

Stag Barlow Set: 52009 SSP, 52009 RAZ SSP, 52009-1/2 SSP, display case, (5,000 sets made) 175

Stag Whittler Set: 5308 SSP, 5380 SSP, 5383 SSP, polished with gold-filled engraved bolsters, display case, (2,500 sets made) 375

Stag Canoe Set: 52131 SSP, 53131 SSP, 5394 SSP, gold plated and engraved, display case, (5,000 sets made) 375

Trapper Trio Set: 6207 SP SSP, 6249 SP SSP and 6254 SSP, polished, red bone in display case, (2,500 sets made) 200

1984 Stag Congress Set: 52052 SS, 53052 SS and 54052 SS: Raised Case shield,
2,000 sets 250
Engraved, 500 sets 350

Cherokee Canoe Set 1984: 31131, 32131 and 33131, (1,000 sets) 225

Case Genuine Stag Sets

1978, 4 Dot Stag Set: 5172 SSP, 5111-1/2 L SSP, 5233 SSP, 52087 SSP, 5347 HP SSP, 5254 SSP, 5265 SAB SSP, approx. 15,000 made of each pattern), set 450

1979, 3 Dot Blue Scroll Stag Set: 5111-1/2L SSP, 52087 SSP, 5347 HP SSP, 52131 SSP, 5233 SSP, 5172 SSP, 5254 SSP, 5265 SAB SSP, (approx. 19,000 made of each pattern), set 525
Engraved bolsters, (1,000 sets) 650

Note: 52033 SSP and 52087 SSP "Blue Scroll" stags can be found in 2 Dot stamping, which is rarer. These patterns in 2 Dot are each 50

1980, 2 Dot Red Etch Stag Set: 5220 SSP, 52087 SSP, 5279 SSP, 52032 SSP, Muskrat, 5347 HP SSP, 5254 SSP, (approx: 14,000 made of each pattern), set 300
Engraved bolsters, (1,000 sets) 400

Note: 5254 SSP Red Etch can be found in 1 Dot stamping which is very rare; 5254 SSP 1 Dot 125

1981, 1 Dot Bradford Centennial Stag Set: 5318 SH SSP, 52027 SSP, 5207 SP SSP, 5275 SSP, 5292 SSP, 5249 SSP, (7,500 sets made) 300
Engraved bolsters, (1,000 sets) 375

1982, 10 Dot 75th Anniversary Stag Set:
Green etch, 5208 SSP, 5235-1/2 SSP,
5207 SP SSP, 5318 HP SSP, 5275 SSP,
5244 SSP, 52109X SSP, (approx.
7,500 sets made), set 325
Engraved bolsters, (1,000 sets) 375

1983, 9 Dot Stag Set: 52027 SSP,
5235-1/2 SSP, 5149 SSP, 5254 SSP,
53131 SSP, Muskrat, limited 250
Engraved bolsters (1,000 sets) 300
52027 SSP (4,200 made) 30
5235-1/2 SSP (4,100 made) 30
5149 SSP (5,000 made) 45
5254 SSP (6,200 made) 50
Muskrat SSP (4,300 made) 45
53131 SSP (5,800 made) 50
1983, 9 Dot 2nd Cut Stag Set: 5383 SS,
Muskrat SS, 52131 SS, 5220 SS, 5254 SS,
(approx. 700 sets made), set 300
Engraved bolsters (400 sets) 425
Open Stock Stags, 1984 (6 Dots) 53033 SS 40
52032 SS 45
53032 SS 50
5254 SS 60

5225-1/2 SS 45
5318 HP SS 45
5158L SSP 65
5197L SSP 75

Note: The 1984 (6 Dot) open stock stags will have a slightly different texture on the shield side. Case has always had difficulty installing the shields on rough textured stag. In 1984, Case smoothed the stag slab to readily accept the shield and then use a special type jigging to return the texture of stag. It is different than second-cut stag and resembles genuine stag texture quite closely.

The first 1,000 knives in open stags have old square grind with polished blades, except for the 5318 HP SS pattern. All the 5318s and all patterns after 1,000 have the new shoulderless grind with the polished finish. Any polished old square grind patterns will be rarer and worth between $20 and $30 more. They will be one of 1,000.

Case started releasing these stag sets in 1978, although the Dots reflect 1976 (4 Dots). For example, in 1980, the 2 Dot (1978) sets were released. All are two years behind.

OTHER CASE KNIVES

The knives listed below are for 1971 through 1984. All prices listed are mint:

Case XX U.S.A. (9 Dot) 1971

One Blade

4100 SS, "Melon Tester" 85
11011, "Hawk Bill" 35
61011, "Hawk Bill," wood handle 30
6111-1/2L, "Lock Back" 125
1116 SP, "Budding Knife" 40
11031 SH 30
2137, "Sod Buster Jr." 22
2137 SS, "Sod Buster Jr." 28
2138, "Sod Buster" 25
2138 L SS, "Sod Buster," blade locks open 75
6143, "Daddy Barlow," Delrin 45
6143, bone 55
31048 30
31048 SP 45
61048, delrin 22
61048 SP, delrin 35
61048 SSP, delrin 20
C61050 SAB, "Big Coke Bottle," wood handle 65
6165 SAB DR, "Folding Hunter," wood handle.....60
P172, "Buffalo" 90
3185, "Doctors Knife" 90
6185, "Doctors Knife" 100
61093, "Texas Toothpick," bone 120
61093, Delrin 85
1199 SH R SS, "Grafting Knife" 30

Two Blade

Muskrat 75
Muskrat "Hawbaker's Special,"
  (9 Dot to 8 Dot) 125
Muskrat "Hawbaker's Special" 150
4200 SS, "Melon Tester" 125
3201 30
6201 30
9201 25
6202-1/2, delrin 22
6205, "RAZ or One Arm Man" 75
6207 40
6208, "Half Whittler" 30
62009, "Barlow," delrin 25
62009, "Barlow," "RAZ or One Arm Man,"
  delrin 40

62009-1/2, "Barlow," delrin 22
6214, delrin 25
6214-1/2, delrin 25
6217, "Half Hawk Bill," laminated wood handle 50
2220, "Peanut" 55
3220, "Peanut" 55
6220, "Peanut," delrin handle 40
6220, "Peanut," bone stag handle 100
6225-1/2, "Coke Bottle" 45
6227, delrin 25
2231-1/2 SAB, Long Pull Standard 30
6231-1/2, Long Pull Standard 40
12031 L R, "Electrician's Knife" 30
6232 30
5232 85
3233 40
6233, delrin 25
8233 70
9233 40
6235-1/2 25
62042 25
92042 30
66244, delrin 25
6244, delrin 25
6246 R SS, "Rigger's Knife" 75
06247 PEN 40
32048 SP 45
62048 SP, delrin 35
62048 SP SSP, delrin 35
6249, "Copperhead or Vietnam" 60
6250, "Sunfish," laminated wood handle 95
62052 45
82053 SR SS 70
3254, "Trapper," rare 125
6254, "Trapper" 75
6254 SSP, "Trapper" 75
6254 SSP, Large Stamp 150
62055 35
8261 70
9261 30
06263 SSP 28
06263 F SSP 30
6265 SAB DR "Folding Hunter," wood handle......50

Mariners Knife Set 75
6269 35
6275 SP, "Moose" 45
6279 SS, delrin 25
82079-1/2 SS, "Sleeve Board" 75
M279 SC SS, stainless-steel handle 35
M279 SS, stainless-steel handle 25
22087 25
62087, delrin 25
6292, "Texas Jack" 30
32095 F SS, "Fisherman's Knife" 60
3299-1/2 45
62109X, "Small Copperhead" 45
62131, "Canoe" 65

Three Blade

6308, "Whittler" 60
3318 SH PEN 40
4318 SH SP 50
+4318 SH SP 100

+This knife (4318 SH SP) is the same as a regular 4318 SHSP 9 Dot, except the handle is inscribed:
Dewey P. Ferguson, Author "ROMANCE OF COLLECTING CASE KNIVES." Quantity made, 280.

6318 SH SP 30
6318 SP P 35
6318 SH PEN 30
6318 SH SP SSP, edge of blade polished 35
6327 SH SP, delrin 30
9327 SH SP 35
13031 L R "Electrician's Knife" 40
5332 (Collectors Set) 85
6332 35
6333, delrin 25
9333 30
6344 SH PEN, delrin handle 30
6344 SH PEN, bone stag handle 40
6344 SH SP, delrin 30
33044, SH SP, "Birdseye" 50
3347 SH SP 40
5347 SH SP SSP, (Collectors Set) 90
6347 SH SP 45
6347 SP P 50
6347 SH SP SSP 45
63047 50
8364 SC SS 110
6375 60
6380, "Whittler" 100
6383, "Whittler" 85

23087 SH PEN 30
53087 SH PEN, (Collectors Set) 75
63087 SP PEN, Delrin 30
6392 50
33092, "Birdseye" 60
M3102 R SS 35

Four Blade

Case's SS, "Fly Fisherman" 250
6445 R, "Scout's Knife" 45
640045 R, "Scout's Knife" 25
64047P 90
64052 90

Case XX U.S.A. (8 Dot) 1972

One Blade

4100 SS, "Melon Tester" 85
11011, "Hawk Bill" 35
61011, "Hawk Bill," laminated wood handle 30
5111-1/2 L SSP, "Cheetah," large
  pattern number 350
5111-1/2 L SS, "Cheetah," small pattern
  number 350
6111-1/2 L, "Lock Back" 100
11031 SH 25
2137, "Sod Buster Jr." 20
2137 SS, "Sod Buster Jr." 25
2138, "Sod Buster" 25
2138 SS, "Sod Buster" 25
2138 L SS, "Sod Buster," blade locks open 75
6143, bone 55
6143, "Daddy Barlow," delrin 40
31048 30
61048, delrin 20
61048 SSP, delrin 22
C61050 SAB, "Big Coke Bottle," wood handle 50
6165 SAB DR, "Folding Hunter," wood handle 50
P172, "Buffalo" 90
3185, "Doctor's Knife" 90
6185, "Doctor's Knife" 100
61093, "Texas Toothpick," bone 120
61093, delrin 85
7197 L SSP, "Shark Tooth," pakkawood 95
7197 L SSP, curly maple 125
P197 L SSP, pakkawood 50
1199 SH R SS, "Grafting Knife" 30

Two Blade

Muskrat 65
Muskrat "Hawbaker's Special" (8 Dot to
  7 Dot) 125

4200 SS, "Melon Tester" 125
3201 30
6201 25
9201 30
6202-1/2, delrin 20
6205, "RAZ or One Arm Man" 65
6207 40
6208, "Half Whittler" 30
62009, "Barlow," delrin 30
62009, "Barlow," "RAZ or One Arm Man,"
   delrin 40
62009-1/2, "Barlow," delrin 20
6214, delrin 25
6214-1/2, delrin 25
6217, "Half Hawk Bill," wood handle 50
2220, "Peanut" 45
3220, "Peanut" 45
6220, "Peanut," delrin 40
6225-1/2, "Coke Bottle" 45
6227, Delrin 25
2231-1/2 SAB, Long Pull Standard 40
6231-1/2, Long Pull Standard 40
12031 L R, "Electrician's Knife" 30
62048 SP SSP, delrin 35
6232 30
3233 35
6233, delrin 25
8233 70
9233 35
6235-1/2 25
62042 25
92042 30
06244, delrin 25
6244, delrin 25
6246 R SS, "Rigger's Knife" 75
06247 PEN 40
32048 SP 45
62048 SP, delrin 35
62048 SP SSP 35
6249, "Copperhead or Vietnam" 50
6250, "Sunfish," laminated wood handle ... 95
62052 40
82053 SR SS 70
3254, "Trapper" 55
6254, "Trapper" 55
6254 SSP, "Trapper" 65
6254 SSP, large stamp 150
62055 35

8261 70
9261 30
06263 F SSP 30
06263 SSP 25
6265 SAB DR "Folding Hunter," wood handle 50
6265 SAB DR SSP "Folding Hunter,"
   wood handle 60
Mariners Knife Set 75
Mariners Knife Set SSP 75
6269 35
6275 SP, "Moose" 45
6279 SS, Delrin 25
6279 SS, bone 40
82079-1/2 SS, "Sleeve Board" 75
M279 SC SS, stainless-steel handle 35
M279 F SS, stainless-steel handle 28
M279 SS, stainless-steel handle 25
22087 25
62087, delrin 25
6292, "Texas Jack" 30
32095 F SS, "Fisherman's Knife" 60
3299-1/2 40
62109X, "Small Copperhead" 45
62131, "Canoe," bone 55

Three Blade

6308, "Whittler" 60
3318 SH PEN 40
4318 SH SP 50
6318 SH SP 35
6318 SP P 40
6318 SH PEN 30
6318 SH SP SSP 35
6327 SH SP, delrin 30
9327 SH SP 35
13031 L R "Electrician's Knife" 40
6332 35
6333, delrin 30
9333 35
6344 SH PEN, delrin 30
6344 SH SP, delrin 30
33044, SH SP, "Birdseye" 50
3347 SH SP 40
5347 SH SP SSP, (Collectors Set) 90
6347 SH SP 40
6347 SP P 50
6347 SP PEN 50
6347 SH SP SSP 45
63047 50

8364 SC SS	110
6375	60
6380, "Whittler"	100
6383, "Whittler"	85
23087 SH PEN	30
63087 SP PEN, delrin	30
6392	50
33092, "Birdseye"	60
M3102 R SS	35

Four Blade

Case's SS, "Fly Fisherman"	250
6445 R, "Scout's Knife"	45
640045 R, "Scout's Knife"	25
64047 P	90
64052	90
6488	125

Case XX U.S.A. (7 Dot) 1973

One Blade

4100 SS, "Melon Tester"	85
4100, "Melon Tester," polished blade	100
11011, "Hawk Bill"	35
61011, "Hawk Bill," laminated wood handle	30
6111-1/2L, "Lock Back," bone stag handle	100
6111-1/2L, "Lock Back," Delrin handle	125

(6111-1/2L, 7 Dot, Delrin, was made only in 7 Dots, 1973).

11031 SH	25
2137, "Sod Buster Jr."	20
2137 SS, "Sod Buster Jr."	20
2138, "Sod Buster"	25
2138 SS, "Sod Buster"	25
2138 L SS, "Sod Buster," blade locks open	75
6143, "Daddy Barlow," Delrin	40
31048	30
61048, Delrin	20
61048 SSP, Delrin	22
C61050 SAB, "Big Coke Bottle," wood handle	50
6165 SAB DR, "Folding Hunter," wood handle	50
P172, "Buffalo"	90
3185, "Doctor's Knife," with shield	90
3185, "Doctor's Knife," no shield	100
6185, "Doctor's Knife"	100
61093, "Texas Toothpick," delrin, rare	150
7197 L SSP, "Shark Tooth," Pakkawood	95
7197 L SSP, curly maple	125

(Caution: Many of these originally handled in pakkawood have been rehandled in curly maple.)

P197 L SSP, pakkawood	50
1199 SH R SS, "Grafting Knife"	30

Two Blade

Muskrat	60
Muskrat, "Hawbaker," bone	400
Muskrat "Hawbaker's Special," delrin	100
4200 SS, "Melon Tester"	125
3201	30
6201	25
9201	30
6202-1/2, delrin	20
6205 RAZ, delrin	45
6205, "RAZ or One Arm Man"	65
6207, bone	40
6207, delrin	30
6208, "Half Whittler"	30
62009, "Barlow," delrin	30
62009, "Barlow RAZ or One Arm Man," delrin	30
62009-1/2, "Barlow," delrin	20
6214, delrin	25
6214-1/2, delrin	25
6217, "Half Hawk Bill," wood handle	50
2220, "Peanut"	100
3220, "Peanut"	100
6220, "Peanut," delrin	40
6225-1/2, "Coke Bottle"	45
6227, delrin	25
2231-1/2 SAB, Long Pull Standard	30
6231-1/2, Long Pull Standard	40
12031 L R, "Electrician's Knife"	30
6232	30
3233, rare	65
6233, delrin	25
8233	70
9233	30
6235-1/2	25
62042	30
92042	30
06244, delrin	25
6244, delrin	25
6246 R SS, "Rigger's Knife"	65
06247 PEN	35
4247 FK, Greenskeeper, (1,300 made)	350
32048 SP	40
62048 SP, delrin	30
62048 SP SSP, delrin	30
6249, "Copperhead or Vietnam"	45
6250, "Sunfish," laminated wood handle	95

62052	35
82053 SR SS	70
3254, "Trapper"	50
6254, "Trapper"	50
6254 SSP, "Trapper," bone	45
6254 SSP, "Trapper," delrin	50
62055	30
8261	70
9261	30
06263 SSP	25
06263 F SSP	30
6265 SAB DR "Folding Hunter," wood handle	50
6265 SAB DR SSP, "Folding Hunter," wood handle	50
Mariners Knife Set	75
Mariners Knife Set SSP	75
6269	30
6275 SP, "Moose"	40
6279 SS, delrin	35
M279 SC SS, stainless-steel handle	30
M279 F SS, stainless-steel handle	25
M279 SS, stainless-steel handle	25
82079-1/2 SS, "Sleeve Board"	75
22087	25
62087, delrin	25
6292, "Texas Jack"	30
32095 F SS, "Fisherman's Knife"	55
3299-1/2	40
62109X, "Small Copperhead"	45
62131, "Canoe," bone	40
62131, "Canoe," delrin handle, rare	100

Three Blade

6308, "Whittler"	60
3318 SH PEN	35
4318 SH SP	50
6318 SH SP	30
6318 SP P	40
6318 SH PEN	30
6318 SH SP SSP	35
6327 SH SP, delrin	30
9327 SH SP	35
13031 L R "Electrician's Knife"	40
6332	35
6333, delrin	30
9333	35
6344 SH PEN, delrin	30
6344 SH SP, delrin	30
33044, SH SP, "Birdseye"	50

3347 SH SP	40
6347 SH SP	45
6347 SP P	50
6347 SP PEN	50
6347 SH SP SSP	45
63047	50
8364 SC SS	110
6375	50
6380, "Whittler"	80
6383, "Whittler"	75
23087 SH PEN	30
63087 SP PEN, delrin	25
6392	45
33092, "Birdseye"	60
M3102 R SS	35

Four Blade

Case's SS, "Fly Fisherman"	250
6445 R, "Scout's Knife"	45
640045 R, "Scout's Knife"	25
64047 P	90
64052	80
6488	125

Case XX U.S.A. (6 Dot) 1974

One Blade

4100 SS, "Melon Tester," brushed	85
11011, "Hawk Bill"	35
11011, "Hawk Bill," pakkawood handle, rare	55
61011, "Hawk Bill," laminated wood handle	30
6111-1/2L, "Lock Back"	100
11031 SH	25
2137, "Sod Buster Jr."	20
2137 SS, "Sod Buster Jr."	20
2138, "Sod Buster"	25
2138 SS, "Sod Buster"	25
2138 L SS, "Sod Buster," blade locks open	75
6143, "Daddy Barlow," delrin	35
31048	25
61048, delrin	20
61048 SSP, delrin	20
C61050 SAB, "Big Coke Bottle," wood handle	50
6165 SAB DR, "Folding Hunter," wood handle	50
P172, "Buffalo," scarce	90
3185, "Doctor's Knife," with shield	90
3185, "Doctor's Knife," no shield	100
6185, "Doctor's Knife," Delrin	65
61093, "Texas Toothpick," Delrin	65
P197 L SSP, "Shark Tooth," "Lock Back"	50

7197 L SSP, "Shark Tooth," "Lock Back" 125
1199 SH R SS, "Grafting Knife" 30

Two Blade

Muskrat 50
3201 30
6201 25
9201 30
6202-1/2, delrin 20
6205 RAZ, delrin 45
6205, "RAZ or One Arm Man," delrin 45
6205, "RAZ or One Arm Man," bone 65
6207, bone 35
6207, delrin 25
6208, "Half Whittler" 30
62009, "Barlow," delrin 30
62009, "RAZ or One Arm Man," "Barlow,"
   delrin 30
62009-1/2, "Barlow," delrin 20
6214, delrin 25
6214-1/2, delrin 25
6217, "Half Hawk Bill," wood handle 50
2220, "Peanut" 40
3220, "Peanut" 40
6220, "Peanut," delrin 40
6225-1/2, "Coke Bottle" 40
6227, delrin 25
2231-1/2 SAB 30
6231-1/2 40
12031 L R, "Electrician's Knife" 30
6232 30
3233 35
6233, delrin 25
8233 70
9233 30
6235-1/2 25
62042 25
92042 30
06244, delrin 25
6244, delrin 25
6246 R SS, "Rigger's Knife" 60
06247 PEN 35
32048 SP 40
62048 SP, delrin 30
62048 SP SSP, delrin 30
6249, "Copperhead or Vietnam" 45
6250, "Sunfish," laminated wood handle 95
6250, "Sunfish," blade etched 95
62052 30

82053 S R SS 70
3254, "Trapper" 50
6254, "Trapper" 45
6254 SSP, "Trapper," bone 45
6254 SSP, "Trapper," delrin 55
62055 30
8261 70
9261 30
06263 SSP 25
06263 F SSP 30
6265 SAB DR "Folding Hunter," wood handle 50
6265 SAB DR SSP, "Folding Hunter," wood
   handle 50
Mariners Knife Set 75
Mariners Knife Set SSP 75
6269 30
6275 SP, "Moose" 40
6279 SS, delrin 35
M279 SS, stainless-steel handle 30
M279SC SS, stainless-steel handle 25
M279F SS, stainless-steel handle 25
82079-1/2 SS, "Sleeve Board" 75
22087 25
62087, delrin 25
6292, "Texas Jack" 30
32095 F SS, "Fisherman's Knife" 55
3299-1/2 40
62109X, "Small Copperhead" 40
62131, "Canoe," blade etched 40

Three Blade

6308, "Whittler" 60
3318 SH PEN 35
6318 SH SP 30
6318 SH PEN 30
6318 SP P 40
6318 SH SP SSP 35
6327 SH SP, delrin 30
9327 SH SP 35
13031 L R "Electrician's Knife" 35
6332 35
6333, delrin 30
6344 SH PEN, delrin 30
6344 SH SP, delrin 30
33044 SH SP, "Small Birdseye" 50
3347 SH SP 40
6347 SH SP 45
6347 SH SP SSP 40
6347 SP PEN 45

63047	50
8364 SC SS	110
6375	50
6380, "Whittler"	80
6383, "Whittler," bone stag handle	75
23087 SH PEN	30
63087 SP PEN, delrin	25
33092, "Birdseye"	50
6392	45
M3102 R SS	35

Four Blade

6445R, "Scout's Knife"	40
640045R, "Scout's Knife," brown plastic handle	25
64047P	90
64052	65
6488	110
Case's SS, "Fly Fisherman"	225

Case XX U.S.A. (5 Dot) 1975

One Blade

11011, "Hawk Bill"	35
61011, "Hawk Bill," laminated wood handle	30
6111-1/2L, "Lock Back"	85
11031 SH	25
2137, "Sod Buster Jr."	20
2137 SS, "Sod Buster Jr."	20
2138, "Sod Buster"	25
2138 SS, "Sod Buster"	25
2138 L SS, "Sod Buster," blade locks open	65
P138 L SS, "Alyeska Sod Buster," (500 made)	175
6143, "Daddy Barlow," delrin	35
31048	25
61048, delrin	20
61048 SSP, delrin	20
C61050 SAB, "Big Coke Bottle," wood handle	50
11055, (no shield), C. Hobbs, (50 made)	75
6165 SAB DR, "Folding Hunter," wood handle	50
P172, "Buffalo"	90
P197 L SSP, "Shark Tooth," "Lock Back"	50
1199 SH R SS, "Grafting Knife"	30

Two Blade

Muskrat	45
6202-1/2, delrin	20
6205, "RAZ or One Arm Man," delrin	40
6205, "RAZ," bone handle	60
6207, bone	40

6207, delrin	30
6208, "Half Whittler"	30
62009, "Barlow," RAZ or One Arm Man, delrin	30
62009-1/2, "Barlow," delrin handle	20
62009-1/2, "Barlow," bone stag handle, 1975 only	55
6217, "Half Hawk Bill," wood handle	45
6220, "Peanut," delrin	35
6225-1/2, "Coke Bottle"	40
6227, delrin	25
2231-1/2 SAB, Long Pull Standard	30
6231-1/2, Long Pull Standard	35
12031 L R, "Electrician's Knife"	30
6232	30
6233, delrin	25
9233	30
6235-1/2, delrin	25
62042	25
92042	30
06244, delrin	25
6244, delrin	25
6246 R SS, "Rigger's Knife"	50
06247 PEN	35
32048 SP	40
62048 SP, delrin	30
62048 SP SSP, delrin	30
6249, "Copperhead or Vietnam"	45
6250, "Sunfish," wood handle, blade etched	90
62052	30
3254, "Trapper"	40
6254, "Trapper"	45
6254 SSP, "Trapper"	45
6254 SSP, "Trapper," delrin	55
62055, delrin	25
62055, bone	35
06263 SSP	25
06263 F SSP	30
6265 SAB DR "Folding Hunter," wood handle	45
6265 SAB DR SSP, "Folding Hunter," wood handle	45
Mariners Knife Set	65
Mariners Knife Set SSP	65
6269	30
6275 SP, "Moose"	40
6279 SS, delrin	25
M279 F SS, brushed stainless-steel handle	25
M279 SS, brushed stainless-steel handle	30
22087	25

62087, delrin 25
6292, "Texas Jack"........................30
32095 F SS, "Fisherman's Knife".....................55
3299-1/2 35
62109X, "Small Copperhead" 35
62131, "Canoe," blade etched 40

Three Blade

6308, "Whittler" 50
3318 SH PEN 30
6318 SH PEN 30
6318 SP P 35
6318 SH SP 30
6318 SH SP SSP 30
6327 SH SP, delrin 30
9327 SH SP 35
13031 L R "Electrician's Knife" 35
6332 35
6333, delrin 30
6344 SH PEN, delrin 25
6344 SH SP, delrin 25
33044, SH SP, "Birdseye" 45
3347 SH SP 35
6347 SH SP SSP 40
6347 SP PEN 45
63047 45
6375 45
6380, "Whittler" 75
6383, "Whittler" 65
23087 SH PEN 25
63087 SP PEN, delrin 25
33092, "Birdseye" 45
6392 45

Four Blade

640045 R, "Scout's Knife"........................25
6445 R, "Scout's Knife" 40
64047 P 80
64052 60
6488 100

Case XX—USA—4 Dot (1976)

One Blade

5111-1/2 L SSP, DISC. 100
6111-1/2L 75
61011, wood handle........................25
11031 SH, DISC. 25
2137 20
2137 SS 20
2138 25

2138 SS 25
2138 L SS 65
6143, delrin 30
31048 25
61048, delrin 20
61048 SSP, delrin 20
C61050 SAB DISC. 50
21051 L SSP 30
61051 L SSP, DISC. 30
11055, spay (no shield), Stark B., (144 made) 60
6165 SAB DR, wood handle........................50
5165, "American Spirit," (10,000 made)..........150
P172 90
5172 SSP, (no box), DISC. 90
P197 L SSP 50
1199 SH R SS........................30

Two Blade

Muskrat 40
6202-1/2, DISC. 20
6205, razor bone DISC. 50
6205, razor, delrin DISC. 40
6207, bone 35
6207, delrin 30
6208, bone 30
62009-1/2, delrin, DISC. 20
6217, wood handle, DISC. 45
6220, delrin, DISC. 30
6225-1/2, DISC. 30
6227, DISC. 25
2231-1/2 SAB,-Long Pull DISC. 30
6231-1/2, Long Pull-Delrin 30
12031 L R 25
6232, delrin 25
6233, DISC. 25
62033, delrin, DISC. 25
9233, DISC. 30
5233 SSP, DISC. 50
6235-1/2, delrin, DISC. 20
62042, DISC. 20
92042, DISC. 25
06244, delrin, DISC. 25
3244, (Special Order), 1,500 made 60
6244, delrin, DISC. 25
03244 25
6246 R SS, DISC. 50
06247 PEN 30
32048 SP 35
62048 SP, delrin........................25

62048 SP SSP, delrin 25
6249 40
6250, wood handle, etched 90
62052, DISC. 30
3254 35
5254 SSP, DISC. 65
6254, bone 40
6254, delrin 75
6254 SSP, bone 40
6254 SSP, delrin 60
62055, DISC. 30
06263 SSP 25
5265 SSP, DISC. 80
6265 SAB DR, wood handle.............................. 45
6265 SAB DR SSP, wood handle 45
6265 SAB, "Bill Boatman," (588 made) 200
Mariners Set 60
Mariners Set SSP 60
6269, DISC. 25
6275 SP 40
M279 SS 25
M279 F SS 25
M279 SS, bark handle, (250 made) 40
M279 F SS, bark handle, (250 made) 40
M279 SS, jeweler's handle, (250 made) 40
M279 F SS, jeweler's handle, (250 made).......... 40
6279 SS, delrin 25
22087 25
52087 SSP, DISC. 50
62087, Delrin 25
6292 30
32095 F SS 50
3299-1/2, DISC. 35
62109X 35
62131, blade etched 40

Three Blade
6308 50
3318 SH PEN 30
6318 SH PEN 30
6318 SH SP SSP 30
6318 SH PEN 30
6318 SP P 35
6327 SH SP, delrin, DISC. 30
6332 30
6333, delrin, DISC. 30
6344 SH PEN, delrin 25
6344 SH SP, delrin, DISC. 25
33044, SH SP, DISC. 40

3347 SH SP 35
5347 SH SP SSP, DISC...................................... 60
6347 SH SP SSP 35
6347 SH SP 35
63047, DISC. 45
6375 40
6380 70
4380 WH. N.K.C. & D.A., (3,000 made) 160
6383 65
23087 SH PEN 25
63087 SP PEN, delrin 25
33092 45
6392 45

Four Blade
640045R 25
6445 R, DISC. 40
64047 P, DISC. 75
64052 55
6488, DISC. 90

Case XX USA 3 Dot (1977)
One Blade
61011, "Hawk Bill," wood handle 25
6111-1/2L 75
5111-1/2L SSP, DISC.. 100
11031 SH, DISC. 25
2137 SS, "Sod Buster Jr." 20
2137, "Sod Buster Jr." 20
2138, "Sod Buster".. 25
2138 SS, "Sod Buster" 25
2138 L SS, "Sod Buster" 65
6143, "Daddy Barlow," delrin 30
31048 25
61048, delrin 20
61048 SSP, delrin 20
C61050 SAB, "Big Coke Bottle," DISC. 50
M1051 L SSP, "Hornet" 25
21051 L SSP, "Hornet" 30
61051 L SSP, "Hornet," DISC. 30
6165 SAB DR, L SSP, "Folding Hunter" 40
W165 SAB SSP, "Moby Dick" 150
6165 SAB DR 45
5172 SSP, "Bulldog," DISC. 90
P172, "Buffalo" 90
P197 L SSP, "Shark Tooth" 50
1199 SH RSS, "Grafting Knife" 30

Two Blade
Muskrat 35

Muskrat, "Hawbaker's Special," (3 to 7 Dot) 100
Muskrat, "Hawbaker's Special," (3 to 9 Dot) 100
6202-1/2, delrin, DISC. 20
6205, RAZ, "One Arm Man," Delrin, DISC. 40
6207, bone 35
6207, delrin 30
6208, "Half Whittler," DISC. 30
62009-1/2, "Barlow," DISC., Delrin 20
6217, "Half Hawk Bill," DISC. 45
6220, "Peanut," delrin, DISC. 30
6225-1/2, "Coke Bottle," DISC. 30
6227, DISC., delrin 25
62027, delrin, DISC. 25
12031 L H R, "Electrician's Knife" 30
12031 LR, "Electrician's Knife," DISC. 20
2231-1/2 SAB, Long Pull, DISC. 30
6231-1/2, Long Pull, delrin, DISC. 30
6232, delrin 25
5233 SSP, DISC. 50
52033, SSP, DISC. 50
62033, delrin, DISC. 25
9233, DISC. 30
92033, cracked ice, DISC. 30
6235-1/2, delrin, DISC. 20
62042, DISC. 20
92042, DISC. 25
6244, delrin, DISC. 25
06244, delrin, DISC. 25
6246 R SS, "Rigger's Knife," DISC. 45
06247 PEN 30
32048 SP 35
62048 SP, delrin 25
62048 SP SSP, delrin 25
6249, "Copperhead" 40
6250, "Sunfish," blade etched 90
62052, DISC. 30
3254, "Trapper" 30
5254 SSP, "Trapper," DISC. 65
6254, "Trapper" 35
6254 SSP, "Trapper" 35
62055, DISC. 30
06263 SSP 25
5265 SAB SSP, "Folding Hunter," DISC. 75
6265 SAB DR, "Folding Hunter" 45
6265 SAB DR SSP, "Folding Hunter" 45
6265 SAB, "Bill Boatman," (300 made) 200
Mariners Knife Set 55
Mariners Knife Set SSP 55

6269, DISC. 25
6275 SP, "Moose" 35
M279 SS, stainless-steel handle 20
M279 F SS, stainless-steel handle 20
6279 SS, delrin 20
22087 25
62087, delrin 20
6292, "Texas Jack" 30
32095 F SS, "Fisherman's Knife" 45
3299-1/2, DISC. 30
62109 X, "Small Copperhead" 35
52131 SSP, DISC. 75
62131, "Canoe," blade etched 35

Three Blade

6308, "Whittler" 45
3318 SH PEN 30
6318 SH PEN 30
6318 SP P 35
6318 SH SP SSP 30
6318 SH SP 30
63027 SH SP 25
6327 SH SP, DISC. 25
6332 30
63032 30
6333, delrin, DISC. 25
6344 SH PEN, delrin 25
6344 SH SP, delrin, DISC. 25
3347 SH SP 35
5347 SH SP SSP, DISC. 65
6347 SH SP, DISC. 35
6347 SH SP SSP 35
63047, DISC. 45
6375 40
6380, "Whittler," DISC. 70
6383, "Whittler" 60
23087 SH PEN 25
63087 SP PEN, delrin 25
33092, "Birdseye" 45
6392 45

Four Blade

6445 R, "Scout's Knife" 40
640045 R, "Scout's Knife" 25
64047 P, DISC. 65
64052 55
6488, DISC. 90
1977, Stag Set with blue-scroll etching and engraved bolsters, 8 knives in the set, only 1,000 sets produced, all knives serial numbered; per set 650

Case XX USA 2 Dot (1978)

One Blade

61011, "Hawk Bill," wood handle 25
6111-1/2L 75
5120R SSP, (no shield) 40
5120R SSP, (shield) 40
2137 SS, "Sod Buster Jr." 20
2137, "Sod Buster Jr." 20
2138, "Sod Buster" 25
2138 SS, "Sod Buster" 22
2138 L SS, "Sod Buster" 60
6143, "Daddy Barlow," delrin 30
31048 25
61048, delrin 20
61048 SSP, delrin 20
M1051 L SSP, "Hornet" 25
21051 L SSP, "Hornet" 30
61051 L SSP, "Hornet," DISC. 30
P158 L SSP, "Mako" 45
P159 L SSP, "Hammerhead" 50
6165 SAB DR, L SSP, wood handle 40
W165 SAB SSP, "Moby Dick" 150
6165 SAB DR, wood handle 40
P172, "Buffalo" 90
P197 L SSP, "Shark Tooth" 50
1199 SH R SS, "Grafting Knife" 30

Two Blade

Muskrat SSP, stag, DISC. 65
Muskrat 35
Muskrat, "Hawbaker's Special," (2 to 3 Dot),
    (1,000 made) 90
6207, bone 30
6208, "Half Whittler," DISC. 30
62009-1/2, "Barlow," DISC., delrin 20
6217, wood handle, DISC. 45
6220, "Peanut," DISC. 30
5220 SSP, DISC. 60
6225-1/2, "Coke Bottle," DISC. 30
6227, DISC., delrin 25
62027, delrin, DISC. 25
12031 L H R, "Electrician's Knife" 30
12031 LR, DISC. 30
2231-1/2 SAB, Long Pull, DISC. 27
6231-1/2, Long Pull, DISC. 30
6232 30
52032 SSP, DISC. 55
62033, delrin, DISC. 25
92033, cracked ice, DISC. 30

6235-1/2, delrin, DISC. 20
62042, DISC. 20
92042, DISC. 25
6244, delrin, DISC. 25
06244, delrin, DISC. 25
6246 R SS, "Rigger's Knife," DISC. 45
06247 PEN 30
32048 SP 35
62048 SP, delrin 25
62048 SP SSP, delrin 25
6249, "Copperhead" 40
6250, "Sunfish," etched blade 90
3254, "Trapper" 30
5254 SSP, red etching, DISC. 65
6254, "Trapper" 35
6254 SSP, "Trapper" 35
62055, DISC. 30
06263 SSP 25
6265 SAB DR "Folding Hunter" 40
6265 SAB DR SSP 40
Mariners Knife Set SSP 50
Mariners Knife Set 50
6269, DISC. 25
6275 SP, "Moose" 35
M279 SS, stainless-steel handle 20
M279F SS, stainless-steel handle 20
5279 SSP, DISC. 45
6279 SS, delrin 20
22087 25
52087 SSP, DISC., red etched 50
52087 SSP, blue scroll, (rare) 65
62087, delrin 20
6292, "Texas Jack" 30
32095 F SS, "Fisherman's Knife" 45
62109 X, "Small Copperhead" 35
62131, "Canoe," blade etched 35

Three Blade

6308, "Whittler" 45
3318 SH PEN 30
6318 SH PEN 30
6318 SP P 35
6318 SH SP SSP 30
6318 SH SP 30
63027 SH SP, delrin 25
6332 30
63032 30
63033, delrin 25
6344 SH PEN 25

6344 SH SP, delrin, DISC. 25
3347 SH SP 30
5347 SSP, DISC. 65
6347 SH SP, DISC. 35
6347 SH SP SSP 32
63047, DISC. 40
6375 40
6380, "Whittler," DISC. 70
6383, "Whittler" 60
23087 SH PEN 25
63087 SP PEN, delrin 25
33092, "Birdseye" 45
6392 40

Four Blade

640045 R, "Scout's Knife" 20
64047 P, DISC. 60
64052 55
6488, delrin, DISC. 75
1978 Case Stag Set, with engraved bolsters
 and red etching, 7 knives in the set, serial
 numbered, 1,000 sets; per set 400

Case XX USA 1 Dot (1979)
(Listed by pattern numbers)

6207, bone..30
6208, DISC. 30
6308 40
62009-1/2 20
6111-1/2L 65
61011 25
6217, DISC. 40
3318 SH PEN 30
6318 SH SP 30
6318 SH SP SSP 30
6318 SH PEN 30
6318 SP P 35
6220 DISC. 25
SR6220, smooth rose 35
6225-1/2, DISC. 30
62027, DISC. 25
2231-1/2 SAB, DISC. 25
6231-1/2 30
12031 LR DISC. 30
6232 30
6332 30
62033, DISC. 25
92033, DISC. 30
63033 30
6235-1/2, DISC. 20

2137 20
2137 SS 20
2138 25
2138 SS 25
2138 L SS 75
62042, DISC. 20
92042, DISC. 25
5143 SSP, Case Founders-2,500
 of each letter C-A-S-E 80
6143..30
6244, DISC. 25
6344 SH PEN 25
6344 SH SP, DISC. 25
06244, DISC. 25
640045R 20
6246 R SS, DISC. 45
3347 SH SP 30
6347 SH SP, DISC. 35
6347 SH SP SSP 35
63047, DISC. 35
64047 P, DISC. 60
06247 PEN 30
63047 SR, (3,000 smooth red) 55
63047 GR, (6,000 smooth green) 50
31048 25
61048 20
61048 SSP 20
32048 SP 30
62048 SP 25
62048 SP SSP 25
6249 35
6250, Bradford Bonanza 100
21051 L SSP 25
61051 L SSP, DISC. 30
M1051 L SSP 20
64052, 1 Dot to 10 Dot (Trans.) 65
64052...55
3254 30
6254 35
5254 SSP, red etch, (1 Dot), (rare) 125
6254 SSP 35
M1057L SSP 20
P158 L SSP 45
5158 L-SSP, (2,400 made) 100
P159 L SSP 50
06263 SSP...25
6165 SAB DR 40
6265 SAB DR 40

6265 SAB DR SSP	40
6265 SAB, "Bill Boatman," (144 made)	200
P172	90
6275 SP	35
M279 SS	20
M279 F SS	20
5279 SSP, DISC.	45
6279 SS	20
82079	75
6380, DISC.	75
6383	55
22087	25
62087	20
23087 SH PEN	25
63087 SP PEN	25
6488, DISC.	75
6292	30
33092	45
32095 F SS	45
P197 L SSP	50
5197 L SSP, (7,000 made)	100
1199 SH R SS	30
HA 199-1/2 SSP (7,500 made), serial numbered	60
62109 X	35
62131	35
Mariner's Set	50
Mariner's Set SS	50
Muskrat	35

1 Dot Starter Kit, released in mid-1979, contains 7 serial numbered knives in a collector's case. Set contains: 6344 SH SP delrin, 63027 SH SP delrin, 2138, 6250, 06247 Pen bone, 6165 SAB SR, SR 6225-1/2 smooth rose bone. A total of 1,500 sets were produced; per set 175

1879-1979 Bradford Centennial Stag Set With collector's case. Only 7,500 sets were produced that contained: 5207 SP SSP, 52027 SSP, 52092 SSP, 5249 SSP, 5275 SP SSP, 53 18 H P SSP; price per set 300

1879-1979 Bradford Centennial Stag Set With engraved bolsters and serial numbered. Only 1,000 sets produced, which contained the same knife patterns as above stag set. Per set 375

Case XX USA—10 and 9 Dot (1980-81)
(Lightning "S")

On the majority of Case knives produced between 1980-1984, I have given the list price. Many of these knives can be purchased below the mint prices listed.

One Blade

61011, DISC.	20
11011, DISC.	30
6111-1/2, DISC.	65
5120R SSP, without shield	35
5120R SSP, with shield	40
11031 SH, DISC.	20
2137	20
2137 SS	20
2138	22
2138 SS	22
2138 L SS	75
6143, DISC.	25
31048	20
61048	20
61048 SSP	20
051051-1/2L SSP, 10 Dot, rare	65
21051 L SSP	30
061051 L SSP, DISC.	35
61051 L SSP, DISC.	35
M1051 L SSP	25
051051L SSP, 10 Dot, (1,200 made)	50
051051L SSP, 9 Dot, (6,685 made)	40
M1056L SSP	20
M1057 L SSP	20
5158 L SSP	70
P158 SSP	45
5159 L SSP	75
P159 L SSP	50
6165 SAB DR DISC.	40
6165 DR L SSP SAB	40
P172 DISC.	90
P172 L SSP, Boss	75
P197 L SSP	50
5197 L SSP	80
1199 SH R SS	22
Sidewinder	200

Two Blade

6201 R SS	20
9201 R SS	25
Texas Lockhorn	100
6202-1/2, DISC.	20
6205, RAZ DISC.	35
6207 SP SSP	25
5207 SSP, 75th Anniv.	55
5207 SSP, 75th Anniv. (engraved)	85

A6208 35

6208, DISC. 22

A62009-1/2 40

62009-1/2, DISC. 20

6217, DISC. 40

SR 6220 30

6220, DISC. 20

SR 6225-1/2 40

6225-1/2, DISC. 30

SR 62027 30

62027, DISC. 20

2231-1/2 SAB, DISC. 22

6231-1/2 25

12031 L H R 25

12031 LR 25

6232 25

52033 R SSP 45

A62033 35

62033, DISC. 20

92033 25

A6235-1/2 35

52042 R SSP 45

92042 R SSP 30

62042, DISC. 20

92042 25

03244 25

6244, DISC. 20

06244, DISC. 35

03244R 25

6246 R SS, DISC. 40

6246 R L SS 45

06247 PEN 30

32048 SP 30

62048 SP 25

62048 SP SSP 25

6249 35

6250, Bradford Bon 95

6250, DISC. 85

3254 30

6254 30

6254 SSP, (no 10 Dots made) 45

5254 SSP, 9 Dot polished, rare 150

5254 SSP, 9 Dot 50

62055, DISC. 22

06263 SSP 20

05263 R SSP 40

6265 SAB DR 40

6265 SAB DR SSP 40

6269, DISC. 22

6275 SP 35

E278 SS 20

I278 SS 16

IS278 SS 25

S278 SS 20

M279 R SS 20

M279 FR SS 20

M279 SS 20

M279 F SS 20

6279 SS 20

22087 20

62087 20

6292 30

32095 F SS 20

3299-1/2, DISC. 35

62109X 35

62131 35

Mariner's Knife Set 45

Mariner's Knife Set SS 50

Muskrat 30

Three Blade

6308 40

3318 SH PEN 30

6318 SH SP 30

6318 SH SP SSP 30

6318 SH PEN 30

6318 SP P 35

63027 SH SP 22

6332 30

63033 22

6344 SH PEN 25

6344 SH SP DISC. 25

3347 SH SP 32

6347 SH SP 32

6347 SH SP SSP 32

SR6347-1/2, 10 Dot (80) 50

6375 35

6380, "Whittler," DISC. 70

6383 55

23087 SH PEN 25

63087 SP PEN 25

6392 35

33092 40

Four Blade

6445 R DISC. 45

640045R 20

64052 50

Case XX USA-8 Dot (1982)

(Lightning "S")

One Blade

61011	20
6111-1/2 L	75
5120 R SSP	40
2137	20
2137 SS	20
2138	22
2138 SS	22
6143	25
31048	22
61048	20
61048 SSP	20
M1051L SSP	25
P10051L SSP	30
P1051-1/2 L SSP	30
M1057L SSP	30
P158L SSP	45
P159L SSP, DISC.	50
6165 SAB DR, DISC.	40
6165 SAB DRL SSP	40
P172, DISC.	90
P172L SSP, Boss	75
P197L SSP	50
1199 SH R SS	22
Sidewinder	200

Two Blade

6201R SS, Disc.	20
9201R SS, Disc.	25
6702 SP SSP, "Mini Trapper"	25
A6208, Disc.	35
A62009-1/2, Disc.	40
SR 6220, Disc.	30
SR 6225-1/2, Disc.	40
SR 62027	30
12031 LR	25
12031 LHR, Disc.	25
6231-1/2	25
62032	25
52033 R SSP	40
A62033 SS, Disc.	35
92033	25
A6235-1/2 SS, Disc.	35
A62042 SS, Disc.	35
92042	25
52042 R SSP, Disc.	40
SR6244 SS, Disc.	35

03244	25
03244 R, Disc.	25
6246 LR SS, Disc.	40
06247, PEN Disc.	30
32048 SP, Disc.	30
62048 SP	25
62048 SP SSP	25
6249	35
6250, "Bradford Bonanza," Disc.	95
3254	30
6254	30
6254 SSP	45
5254 SSP, 8 Dot, rare	150
05263 R SSP	40
06263 SSP	20
6265 SAB DR	40
6265 SAB DR SSP	40
6275 SP	35
E278 SS, Disc.	20
I278 SS	16
IS278SS, Disc.	25
S278 SS	20
M279 SS	20
M279 R SS, Disc.	20
M279 F SS, Disc.	20
M279 FR SS, Disc.	20
6279 SS	20
22087 SS	22
62087 SS	20
6292	30
32095 F SS	45
62109 X	35
62131	35
Mariner's Knife Set	45
Mariner's Knife Set SS	50
Muskrat	30
Texas Lockhorn	125

Three Blade

6308	40
3318 SH PEN, Disc.	30
6318 SH SP	30
6318 SH SP SSP	30
6318 SH PEN	30
6318 SP P	35
63027 SH SP	22
63032	22
63033	22
6344 SH PEN	25

3347 SH SP, Disc. 32
6347 SH SP 32
6347 SH SP SSP 32
SR6347-1/2, with shield, Disc. 50
6375 35
6383 55
63087 SH PEN 25
63087 SP PEN SS 25
23087 SH PEN, Disc. 25
6392 35
33092 40

Four Blade

640045R 20
64052 50
Stag Barlow Set, 8 Dot ('80), 52009RAZ SSP, 52009-1/2 SSP and 52009 SSP in a display case,(5,000 sets made) 180
Genuine Pearl Set, 8 Dot ('80), 8207 SP SS, 8249 SS and 8254 SS, all with worked back springs and in a display case, (1,000 sets made) 650
Case Sidewinder, 1980-10 Dot. First type stamped on back of blade, "Case XX U.S.A. PAT. PEND. 10 Dot." About 5,000 made. Second type stamp on back, "PAT. PEND," Front side stamped, "Case XX USA 9 Dot." Third type stamped on front, "Case XX USA with Dots." Stamped on back, "Pat. No. 4274200." The first type is more rare and will bring about $25 more than other types 200

(Lightning "S")

It is possible to find Case patterns with new or old grinds, as well as some with inter-mixed blades. Any stainless patterns with the new style grind are more rare, as Case has returned to the old style grind on stainless blades. In 1983, Case eliminated the etching, "For Flesh Only," from the spay blades of the 6318 SH SP.

1 Blade

5210 SSP 45
2137 20
2138 SS 25
2138L SS 60
61048 SS 20
5149 SSP 50
21051L SSP 30
P10051L SSP 30
P1051L SSP 30
M1056L SSP 22

M1057L SSP 20
P158L SSP 45
5158L SSP 75
2159L SSP 40
6165L SSP 35
P172L SSP, Boss 75
P197L SSP 50
5197L SSP 80
1199 SH R SS 22
Sidewinder 200
Case Pro-locks, laminated wood
073 35
074 35
***075** 40
***076** 40
Case Dura-Locks
062 20
063 20
***064** 25
***065** 25
(*Patterns include nylon sheaths)

2 Blade

8201 SS 50
6207 SP SSP 25
6208 SS, delrin 25
62009-1/2, delrin 20
6220 SS, delrin 20
8220 SS 65
6225-1/2 SS, delrin 20
5225-1/2 SS 45
52027 SSP 40
52032 SS 40
62032 30
62033 SS, delrin 20
92033 SS 25
52033 SS 50
6235-1/2 SS, delrin 20
5235-1/2 SS 50
92042 SS 25
62042 SS, delrin 20
03244 25
6244 SS, delrin 25
62048 SP 25
6249 30
3254 30
6254 30
6254 SSP, (old grind) 30
6254 SSP, (new grind), 7 Dot, (4,000 made) 50

5254 SSP, (old grind), rare, polished, 6 Dot, (1,000 made) 75

5254 SSP, (new grind), polished 40

05263 SSP 45

06263 SSP 20

6265 SAB 40

6275 SP 35

S278 SS 20

I278 SS 16

M279 SS 20

82079-1/2 75

22087 SS 22

62087 SS 20

6292 30

62109 X 35

62131 35

Muskrat 30

Muskrat SSP, stag 75

Texas Lockhorn 125

3 Blade

6308 40

3318 HP 30

6318 HP 30

5318 HP SSP 65

53032 SS 65

63032 30

53033 SSP 45

63033 SS 20

6344 SS 25

6347-1/2 SS, delrin 45

6347 HP 30

6375 35

63087 SS 25

6392 35

53131 SSP 85

4 Blade

60045R 20

CASE OLDER KNIVES

Note: Many of the Case knives will have the same pattern number, but be totally different styles. Several of the older knives and numbers are retired— only to have the retired number show up again on a new but different style.

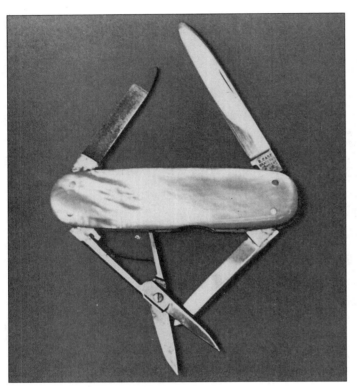

Unnumbered lobster, pearl, rare, 2-7/8", R. Case Bradford-Germany; $300.

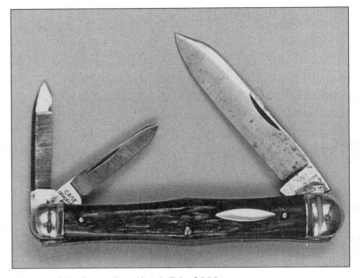

File, 4-1/2", Case Bradford, PA; $900.

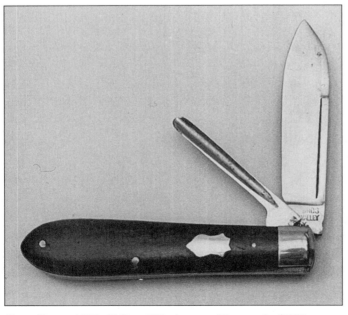

Case Bros., Little Valley, NY, ebony with punch; $200.

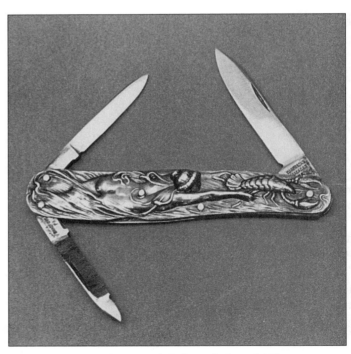

Figural, sterling silver, 3-3/4", Case & Son; $400.

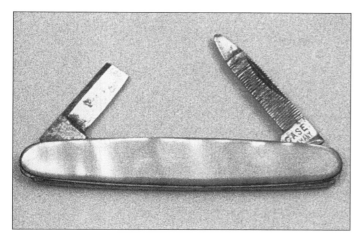

Unknown, 2-blade miniature, abalone pearl-rare, 1-7/8", Case, Germany; $225.

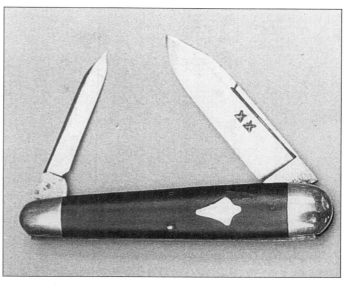

Unknown, composition (odd shield), 3-3/8", Case Bros., Little Valley NY; $300. Unknown, genuine stag; $400.

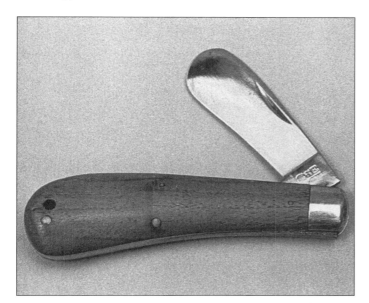

Maize, walnut handle, 1 blade, 4", Case Tested XX; $225.

Knife and razor combination, Case Brothers, Little Valley, NY, 9-1/4" overall, solid steel piece, rare.

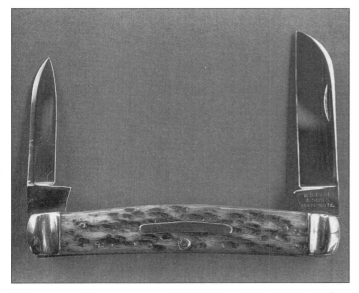

Unknown pattern, recessed bolsters, green bone, 3-3/4", W.R. Case & Sons, Bradford, Pa.; $500.

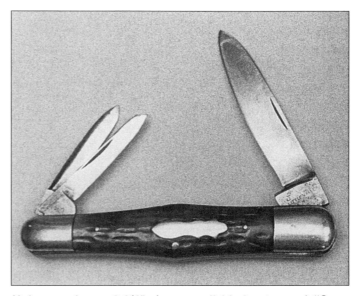

Unknown, bone, 3-3/4", (one small blade stamped "Case Brothers," the other small blade stamped "Case Bros."), Case Bros. & Co., LV, NY; $550.

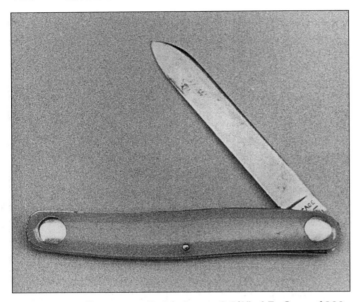

Unknown, yellow pyremite birdseye, 3-5/8", J.D. Case; $200.

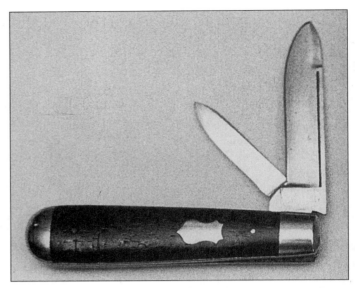

Unknown, wood, 3-3/8", R. Case & Son, Little Valley, NY; $200.

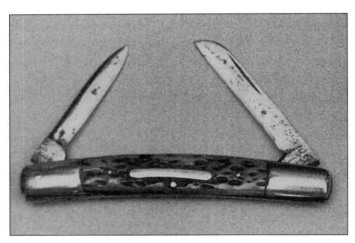

Unknown, bone, 3-5/16", J.D.C., Kane PA; $250.

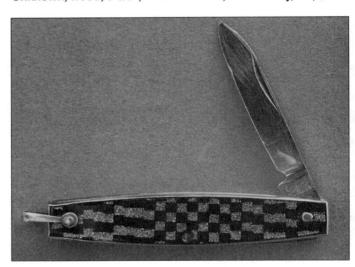

Unknown pattern, Case black and gold stone, checkered handles, Tested XX, miniature 2-1/4", rare; $300.

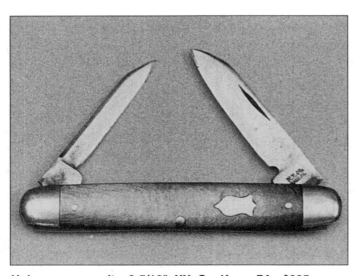

Unknown, pyremite, 3-5/16", XX, Co. Kane, PA.; $225.

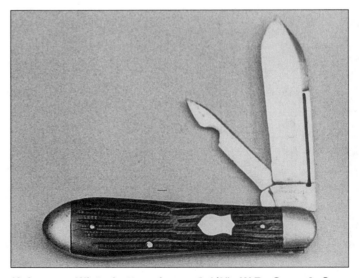

Unknown, Winterbottom bone, 3-1/2", W.R. Case & Son, Bradford, PA.; $300.

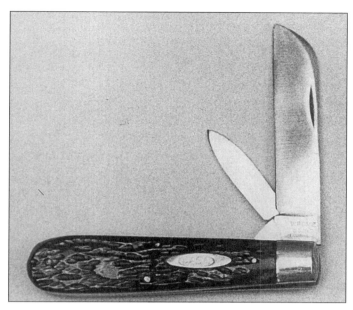

Unknown, bone, 3-3/8", W.R. Case & Son, Bradford, PA.; $250.

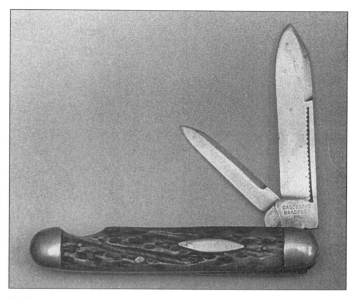

Unknown, bone, 3-1/2", Case & Sons, Bradford, PA.; $250.

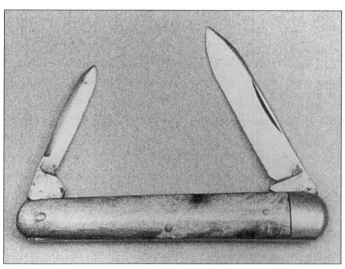

Unknown, plastic, 2-13/16", Crandall Cut. Co., Bradford, PA.; $150.

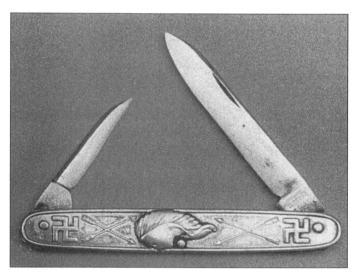

Unknown, metal (figural), made for "Royal Order of Red Men," W.R. Case & Sons, 3-1/4"; $300.

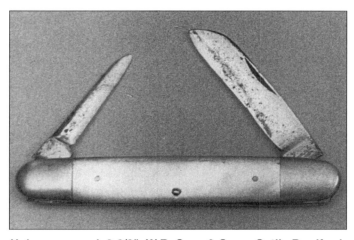

Unknown, pearl, 3-3/8", W.R. Case & Sons, Cut'l., Bradford, PA.; $225.

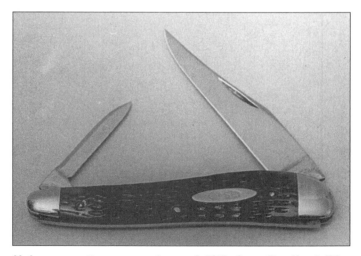

Unknown pattern, green bone, 3-3/4", Case Bradford, PA.; $400.

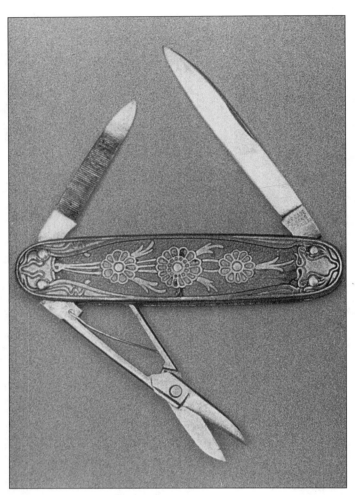

Unknown, cloisonne, 2-13/16", (back of blade reads "German Factory"), W.R. Case & Sons, Bradford, PA.; $300.

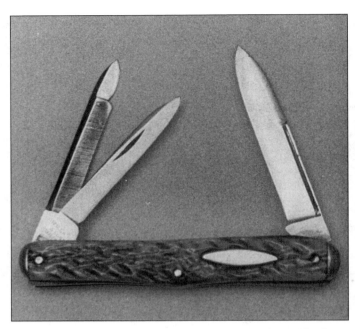

Unknown, bone, (whittler with 3 springs), 3-3/8", W.R. Case & Sons, Bradford, PA.; $500.

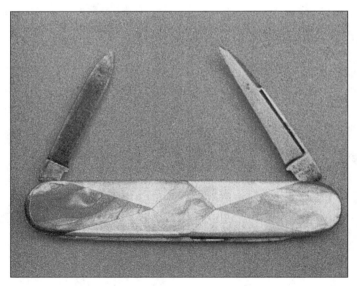

Unknown, pearl and abalone, 3", R. Case, Bradford, Germany, rare; $200.

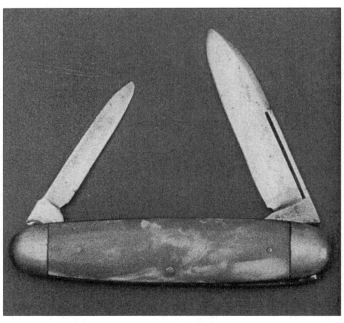

Unknown, cracked ice, 3", Case's Bradford, PA.; $300.

Unknown, Christmas tree, rare stamp and handles, 3-1/16",
Case (in script); $300.

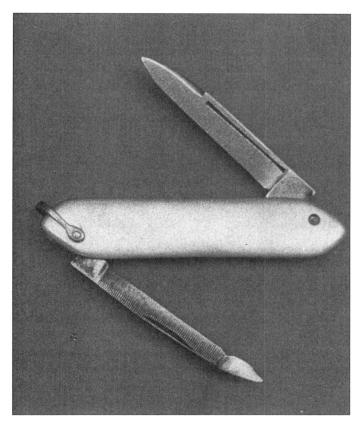

Unknown, pearl, bail, 2-1/2", Circle Case; $150.

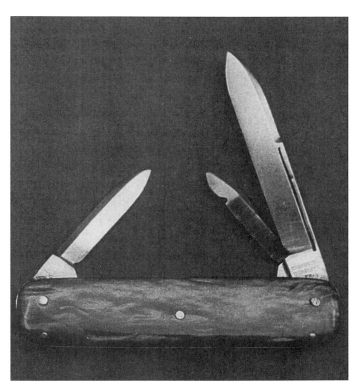

Unknown, pyremite, (covered backspring), 3-1/16", Case &
Sons, Bradford PA.; $400.

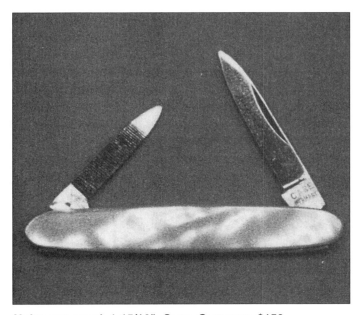

Unknown, pearl, 1-15/16", Case, Germany; $150.

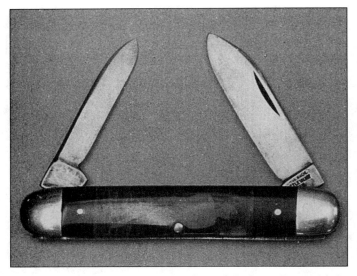

Unknown, Hi Art, (naughty lady), 3-3/8", Case Bros., Little Valley, NY; $400.

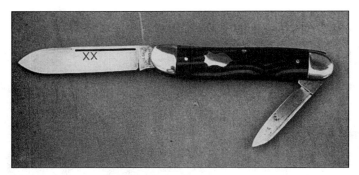

Unknown pattern, yellow and brown waterfall-type stripes on handle, 3-1/2", both blades stamped, Case Bros., Springfield, NY; $500. Photo courtesy Wayne Robertson.

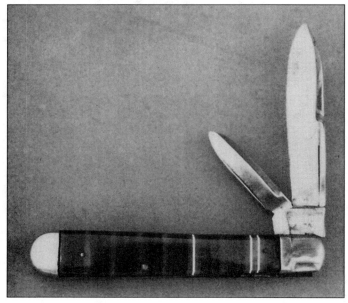

Unknown pattern, candy stripe, fancy bolsters, 3-3/8", both blades stamped, Case & Sons, Bradford, PA.; $300. Photo courtesy Wayne Robertson.

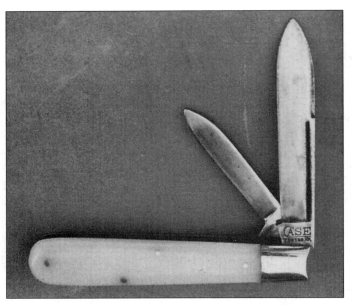

Unknown pattern, yellow celluloid, 3-3/4", Tested XX; $350. Photo courtesy Wayne Robertson.

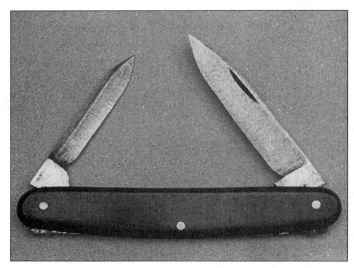

Unknown, red plastic, 3", Case Mfg. Co., Warren, PA., rare stamp; $250.

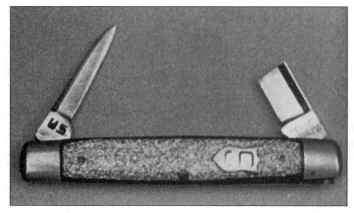

Unknown, gold stone, broken spear blade-rare stamp, 3", Case Tested XX (US Stamp); $200.

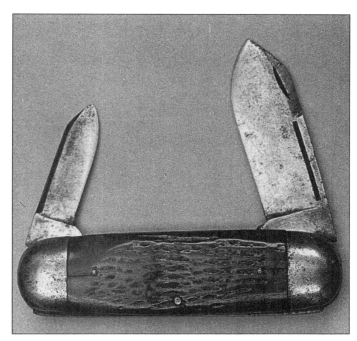

Sunfish, bone, (two pulls), 4-1/4", Crandall Cutlery Co.; $600.

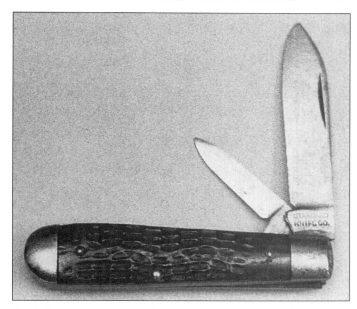

Jack, bone, 1920-23, 3-1/2", Standard Knife Co.; $150.

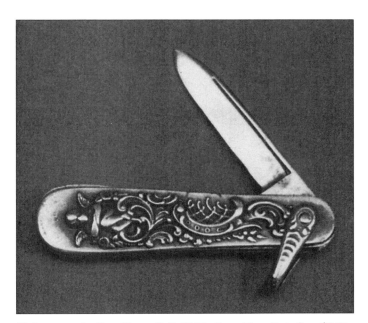

Unknown, sterling (figural), 2-1/16", Case Bro. Cut. Co.; $250.

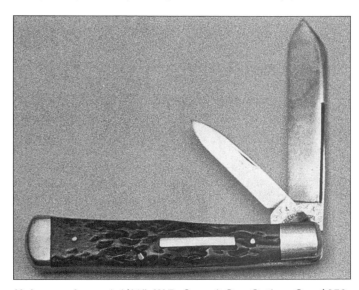

Unknown, bone, 3-1/16", W.R. Case & Son Cutlery Co.; $350.

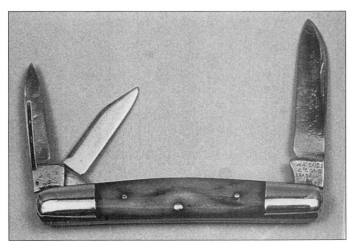

Unknown, stag, Congress, whittler, 3", W.R. Case & Sons, Bradford, PA.; $450.

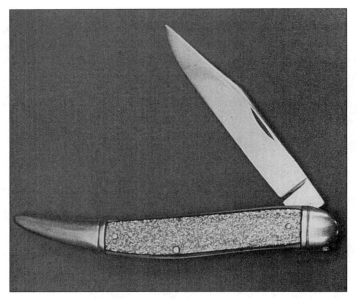

Unknown, gold stone, 4-3/8", Case Mfg. Co., Warren, PA.; $500.

Very rare stamp-L.V. Knife Association, Little Valley, NY, stag, 3-3/4"; $275.

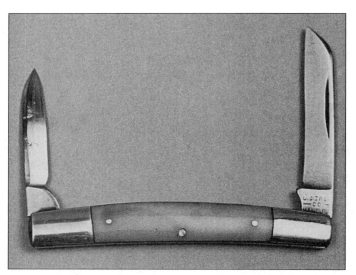

Waterfall, 3-1/4", J.D. Case Co., Kane, PA.; $300.

Y4062K, amber celluloid, 3-1/4", all blades stamped W.R. Case & Sons; $300.

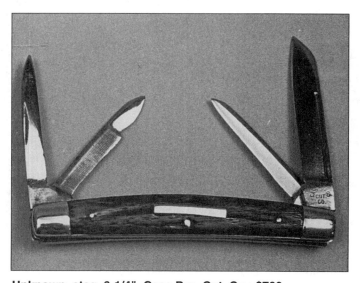

Unknown, stag, 3-1/4", Case Bro. Cut. Co.; $700.

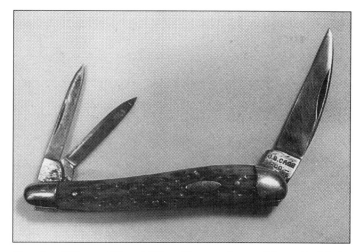

Dog-leg Wharncliffe whittler, Rogers bone, 3", main blade stamped J.D. Case Co., Kane, PA; small blades stamped Case Kane, PA.; $600.

Rogers bone, 3-5/16", all blades stamped, Case & Sons, Bradford, PA.; $250.

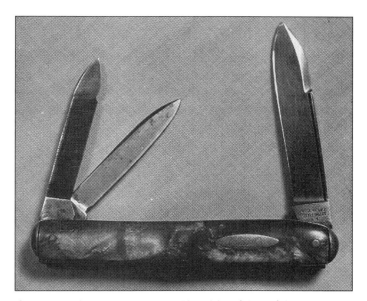

Case Mfg. Co., Little Valley, NY, gold swirl, 3-3/8", all blades stamped, shield engraved "Chas Our"; $650.

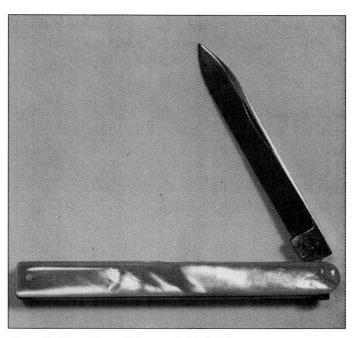

Kane Cutlery, Kane, PA., pearl, 3"; $300.

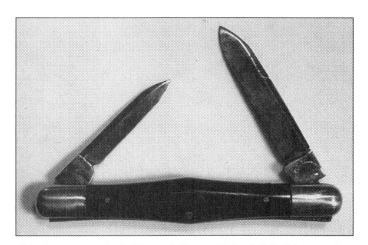

(Similar to 2258): C. Platts & Sons, Eldred, PA., black celluloid, 2-7/8", both blades stamped; $225.

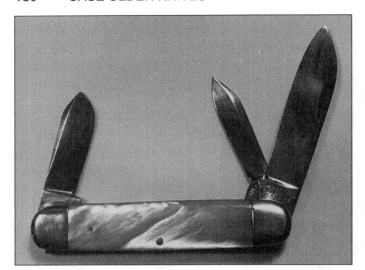

Kane Cutlery, Kane, PA., pearl, 3-5/8", all blades stamped; $550.

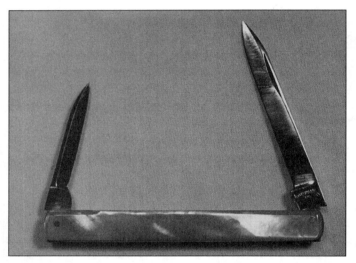

Pearl, 3", Kane Cutlery Co., both stamped; $250.

Unknown, horn scales, 3-1/4", Case Bros., Little Valley, NY.; $400.

Unknown, brown bone, (rare "Son" stamp), 3-1/2", W.R. Case & Son Cutlery Co.; $400.

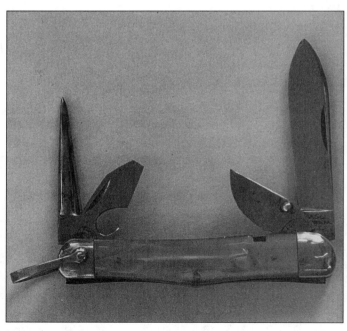

Unknown, French pearl scales, 3-3/8", Case, Brad. Pa.; $600.

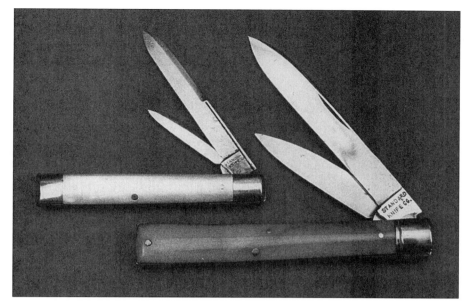

Top: Unknown, pearl, Dr.'s knife, 2-7/8", Standard Knife Co., (made by Case 1920-23); $600. Bottom: Unknown, waterfall, 3-5/8", Standard Knife Co., (made by Case 1920-23); $600.

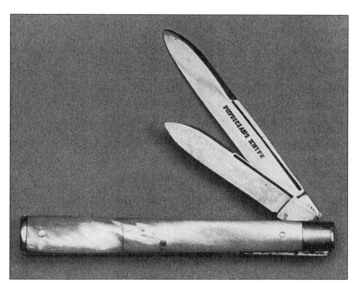

Unknown, pearl, Dr.'s knife, 3-3/4", Tested XX; $900.

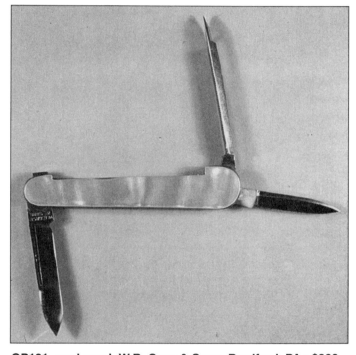

OP101, opal pearl, W.R. Case & Sons, Bradford, PA.; $300.

Unknown, gold stone, Dr.'s knife, 3-3/4", Tested XX; $900.

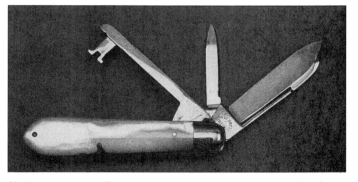

Unknown, pearl, (3 backsprings), skeleton key, 3-1/2", Case Bros., Little Valley, NY; $900.

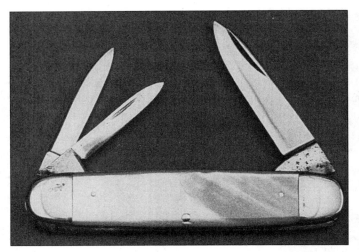

Unknown, pearl, 3-1/4", Case Bros. Cut. Co., Little Valley, NY; $600.

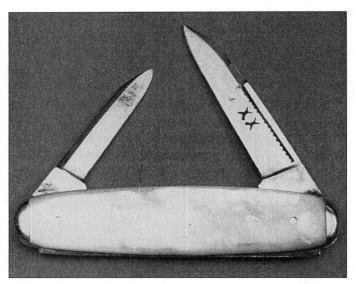

Unknown, pearl, 3", Case Bros., Springville, NY; $300.

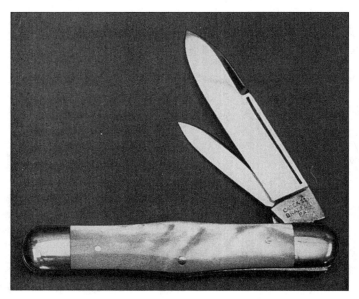

Unknown, 3-3/8", Case & Sons, Brad., PA.; $300.

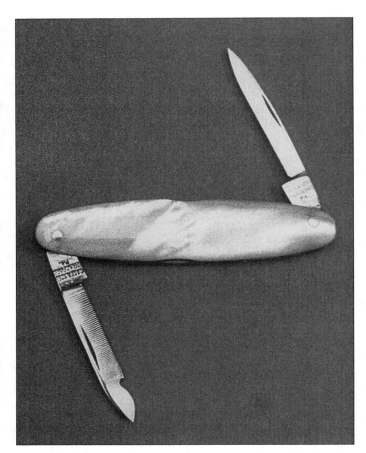

Unknown, pearl, 2-3/8", Case & Sons, Brad., PA.; $175.

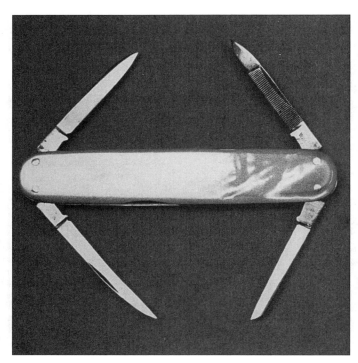

Unknown, pearl, 3-1/4", W.R. Case & Son; $300.

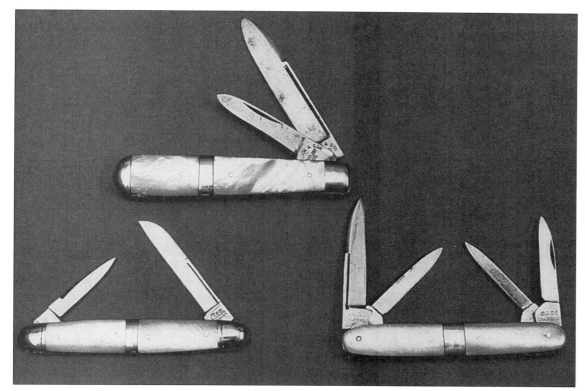

Top: Unknown, pearl (nickel silver), 3-1/4", W.R. Case & Sons Cutlery Co., $275. Bottom left: Unknown, pearl, 3-1/8", Tested XX, $250. Bottom right: Unknown, pearl (nickel silver), 3", Case Brad. PA.; $450.

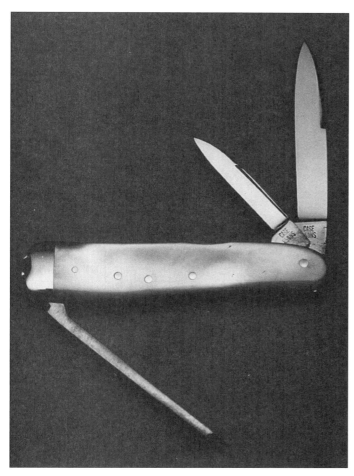

Unknown, pearl, fingernail clipper in backspring-super rare, 2-7/8", Case & Sons; $750.

M281, butter and molasses, 3-3/4", W.R. Case & Sons, Brad PA, super rare; $1,000.

Cigar pattern, brown bone, 4-1/8", Crandall, Brad. PA.; $450.

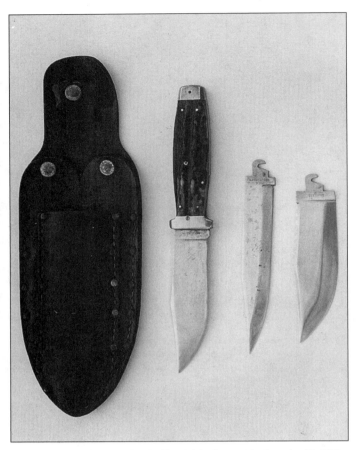

W.R. Case & Son, hobo knife, 3 blades and sheath; $2,500.

Hobo-type handle with spoon; Case Camp Set (?).

Same set, except it shows how to take apart.

6208, sheep's foot, Rogers bone, 3-7/8"; $500.

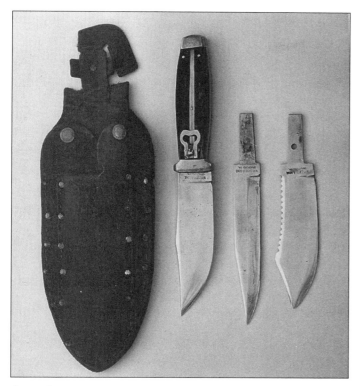

Case Sportsman, W.R. Case & Son, 3 blades and sheath; $2,500.

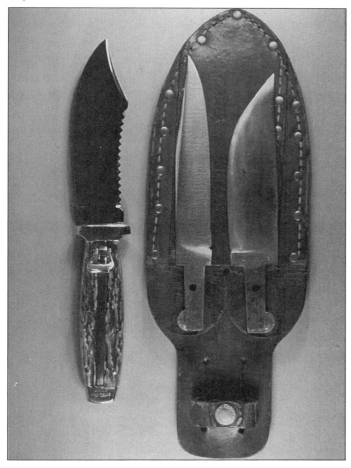

Case Sportsman Set, 3 blades and sheath, handle marked Case Bradford, PA.; $2,500.

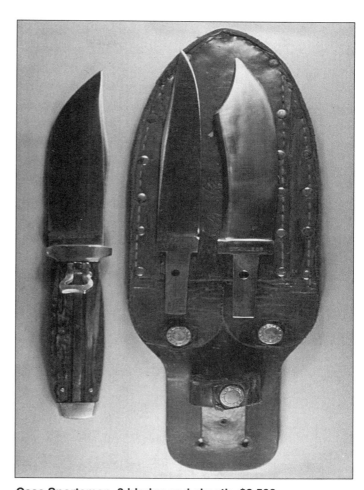

Case Sportsman, 3 blades and sheath; $2,500.

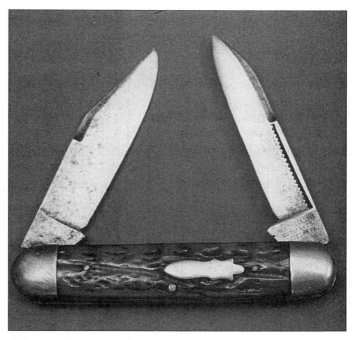

J Pattern, bone, 3-11/16", W.R. Case & Sons Cut. Co., Bradford, PA.; $1,200.

6100SAB, saddle horn, green bone, Case Tested XX; $800.

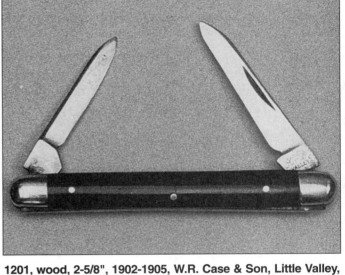

1201, wood, 2-5/8", 1902-1905, W.R. Case & Son, Little Valley, NY; $200.

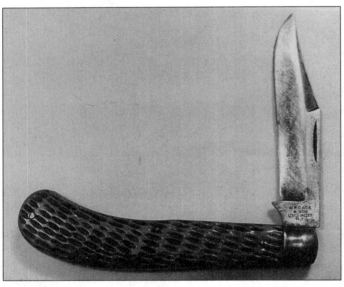

6100SAB, saddle horn, pick bone, W.R. Case & Son, Little Valley, NY, 1902-1903 (rare stamp); $1,000.

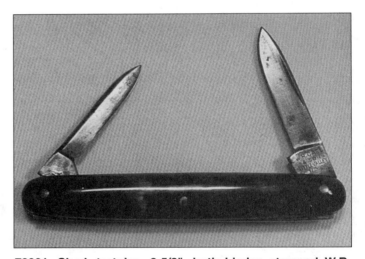

72001, Shad, tortoise, 2-5/8", both blades stamped W.R. Case & Son, Little Valley, NY; $200.

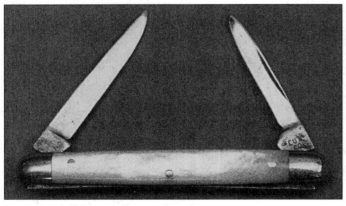

8201 (shown), pearl, 2-11/16", Case Bros. Cut. Co.; $200. Not shown: R201, candy stripe, 2-11/16", Case Bros. Cut. Co.; $225.

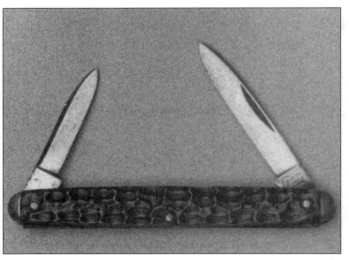

62001, bone, 2-11/16", Case Tested with no writing below line, (Case is written in script); $225.

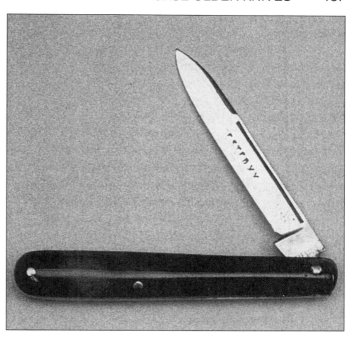

71006, tortoise, (shadow-no bolsters), 2-1/2", Case Bros., Little Valley, NY; $250.

6202EO, SH, FR, Rogers bone, 3-1/4". Both blades stamped W.R. Case & Sons, Bradford, PA; main blade also stamped Made in USA (inside circle.). This was a military stamp used in WW I; $250.

72006, tortoise-rare, 2-5/8", Case Brad., PA.; $300.

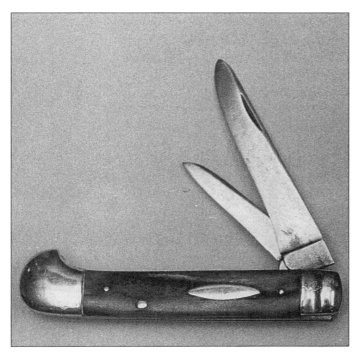

5203SP, stag, budding knife, 3-5/8", W.R. Case & Sons; $400.

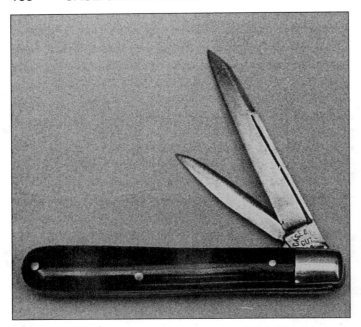

7206, tortoise, 2-5/8", Case Bro. Cut. Co., $300. Also in pearl, 8206; $250.

6106, green bone, 2-9/16", Case 25 cent, rare; $400.

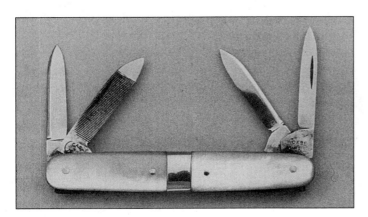

8407F, pearl, 4 blade, 3", Case, Brad., PA.; $750.

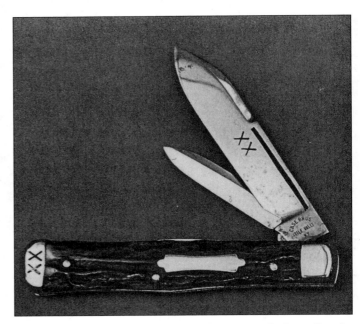

5208LP, genuine stag (note "Coffin" bolster), Case Brothers, Little Valley, NY; $600.

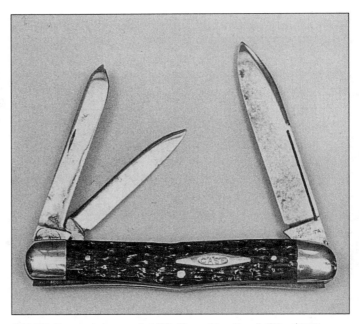

63109LP, green bone, 3-1/2", Case Bradford, PA.; $800.

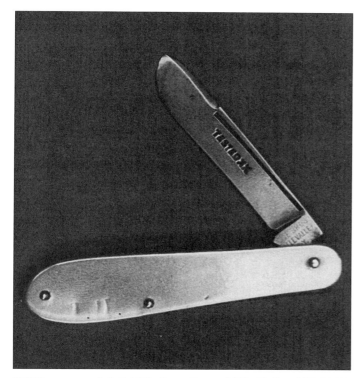

M110, spay metal, 3-1/8", Case Bros., Little Valley, NY; $200.

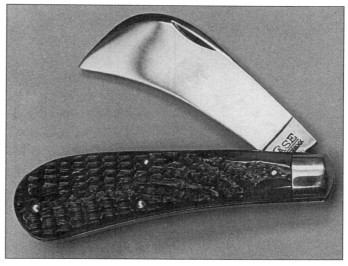

61011, Hawkbill, Rogers bone, Case Tested XX; $250.

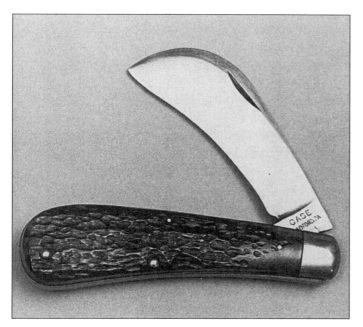

61011, Hawkbill, early Rogers bone, 4", Case Bradford, PA.; $300.

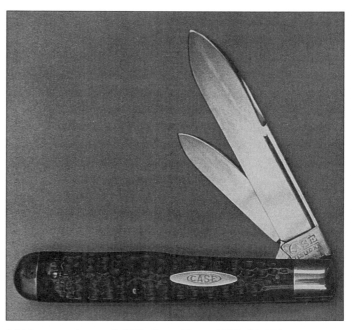

6211, green bone, 4-1/2", Case Tested XX; $1,000.

6213LP, Rogers bone, 3-15/16", W.R. Case & Sons; $900.

8216F, pearl, 2-1/2", Case Bros. Cut. Co., Tested XX; $250.

6214, bone, 3-3/8", Case Bros., L.V., NY, (Cline Hardware Co. warranted), rare; $400.

6116, green bone, 3-1/2", Case, Tested XX; $175.

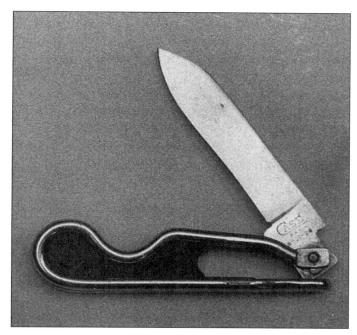

W1216, metal wire, 3-1/4", Case Tested, Pat. 9-21-26; $150.

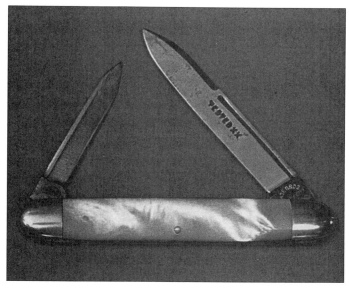

8220LP, pearl, 3-3/8", (not a peanut), Case Brothers Little Valley, NY; $350.

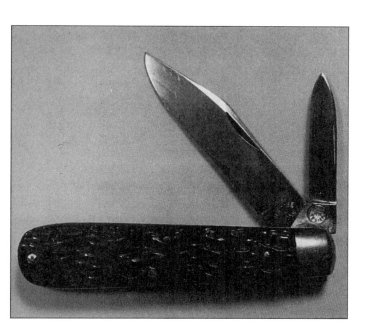

6216-1/2, Rogers bone, 3-1/2" main blade, W.R. Case & Sons, Made in USA, also Tested XX; secondary blade Case XX Tested (in circle); $250.

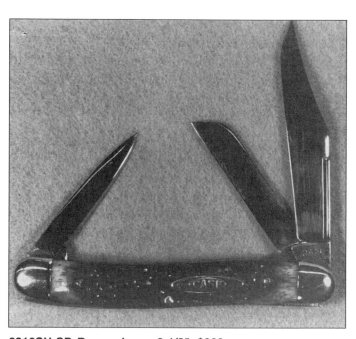

6318SH-SP, Rogers bone, 3-1/2"; $300.

Case Bros., Little Valley, NY, genuine pearl, whittler, 3-3/8"; $750.

62020-1/2, Rogers bone, 3-1/4", Case XX Tested; $350.

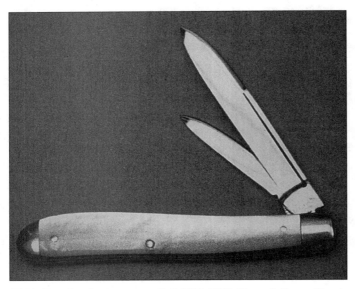

8220, Dog leg (not a peanut), 2-3/4", W.R. Case & Sons, Brad. PA.; $350.

6221LP, Rogers bone, tip bolsters, 3-1/4", W.R. Case & Sons; $500.

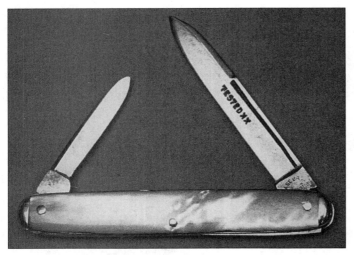

8220 (shown), pearl (tip bolsters), 3-3/8", Case Bros., LVNY; $350. Not shown: 4220, peanut, 2-7/8", W.R. Case & Sons; $300.

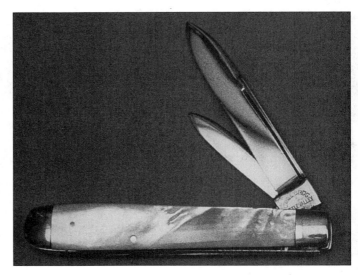

8222, pearl, 3-1/4", Case Bros., Little Valley, NY; $275.

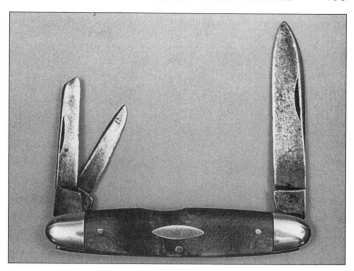

P3024, green celluloid, rare, 3-1/4", Case Bradford, PA.; $500.

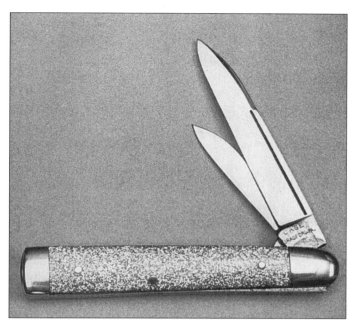

GS222, doctor's knife, gold stone LP, Case, Brad. PA.; $650.

8224, pearl, 3-1/16", main blade stamped Case's Bradford; small blade stamped Case XX Tested; $300.

P2026LP, doctor's knife, greenish gray swirl pinch bolsters, 2-7/8", W.R. Case & Sons, Bradford, PA.; $700.

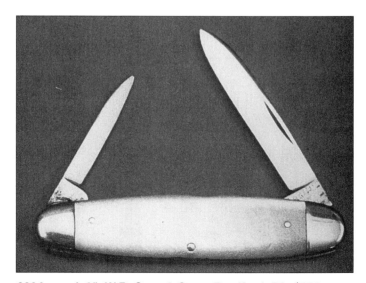

8224, pearl, 3", W.R. Case & Sons, Bradford, PA; $250.

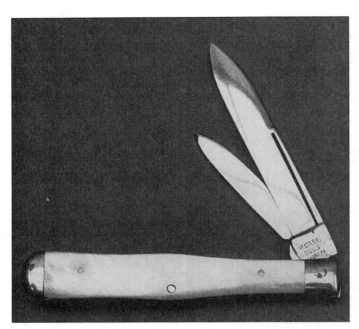

8225LP, pearl, 3", W.R. Case & Sons, Bradford, PA.; $350.

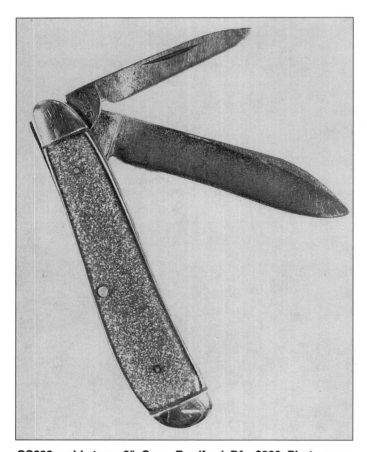

GS226, gold stone, 3", Case, Bradford, PA.; $300. Photo courtesy Carlton Montoya.

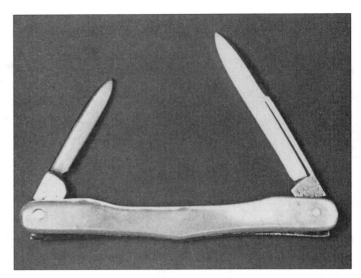

8227LP, pearl, 3", W.R. Case & Sons; $350.

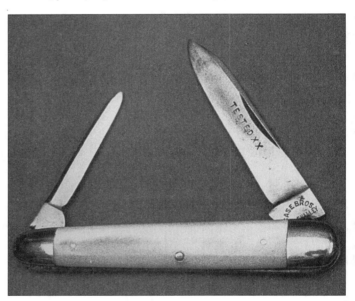

82027, pearl, 2-7/8", Case Bros., Little Valley, NY; $300.

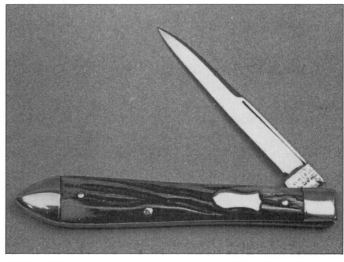

61028, Winterbottom, 1 blade, 2-7/8", W.R. Case & Sons, Bradford, PA.; rare; $275.

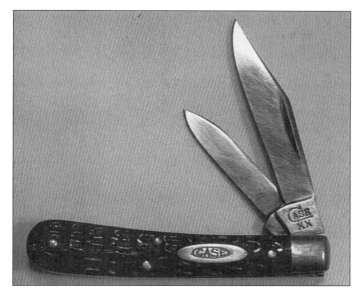

6229-1/2, green bone, 2-1/2", main blade, Case XX; $200.

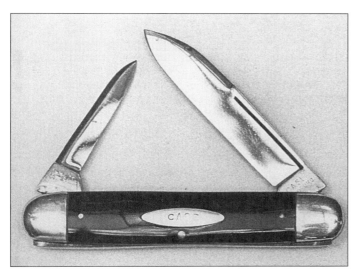

02230 (shown), slick black, 3-1/4", Case, Bradford, PA.; $200. Not shown: 06230, bone 1902-1905, 3-1/4", W.R. Case & Son; $250.

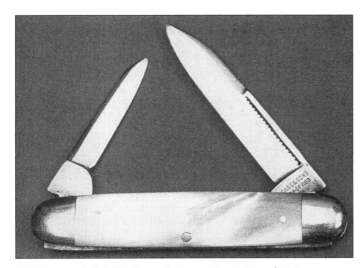

08230, pearl, 3-1/4", Case & Sons, Brad. PA.; $300.

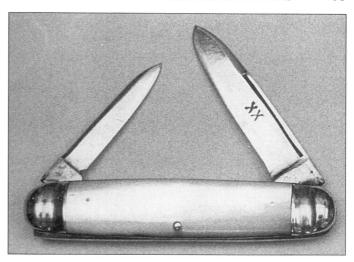

08230, pearl, (also in bone), (recessed bolsters), 3-1/4", Case Bros. Little Valley, NY; $350.

06230, bone, 3-1/4", W.R. Case & Son, Little Valley, NY; $350.

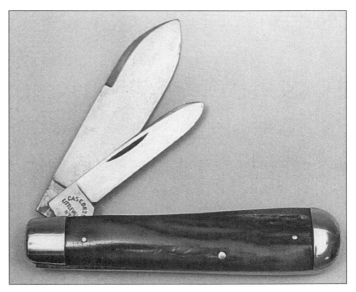

5231, stag, 3-3/4", Case Brothers, Little Valley, NY; $325.

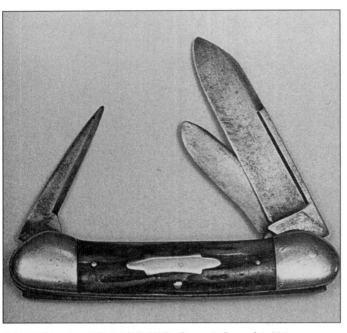

53131PU, stag LP, 3-5/8", W.R. Case & Son; $1,400.

6213, 2-blade, jack, imitation jig bone, iron bolsters, no emblem (stamp not in any previous book.) Case, Tested XX. The author believes this to be a WW I military contract knife, rare, approx. 1917; $300.

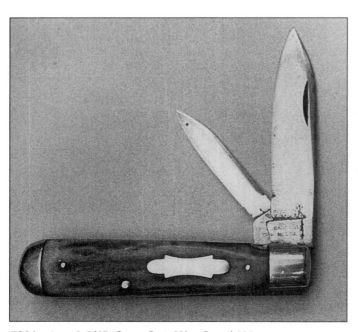

5231, stag, 3-3/4", Case Cut. Mfg. Co.; $400.

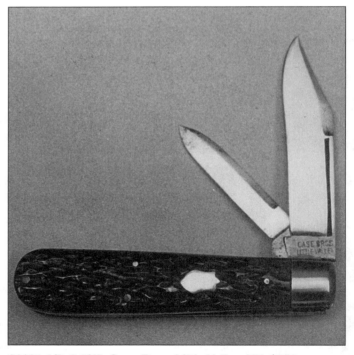

62031-1/2, 3-3/4", Case Bros. Little Valley, NY; $250.

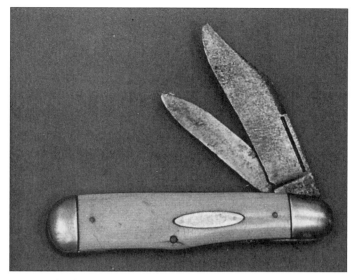

42035-1/2 (shown), white composition, LP, 3-1/4", Case, Bradford, PA.; $250. Not shown: 62035-1/2, bone, LP clip, 3-1/4", bomb shield, Tested XX; $300.

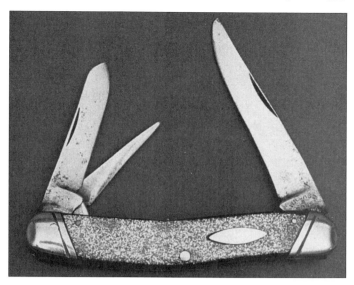

GS3038, gold stone, slant bolsters, 3-1/2", W.R. Case & Son; $450.

G2039, green-swirl celluloid (sow belly), 3-5/8", W.R. Case & Sons, Bradford, PA.; $300.

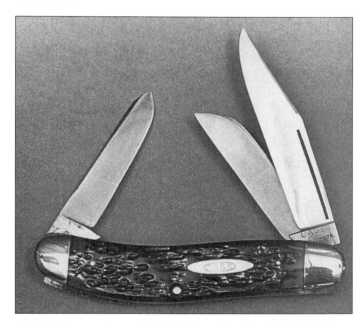

6339LP, Rogers bone, 3-3/4", Case, Bradford, PA.; $750.

6237LP, green bone, 3-1/2", Case ,Bradford, PA.; $700.

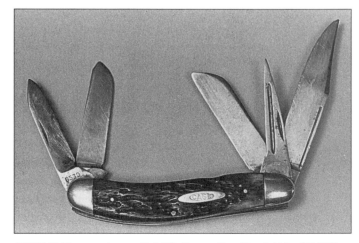

6539LP, Rogers bone, 3-3/4", Case, Bradford, PA.; $5,000

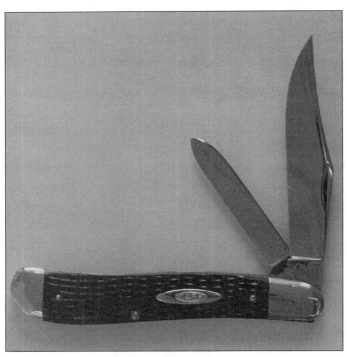

6240, pen, green bone, 4-1/2", Case Tested XX; $1,000.

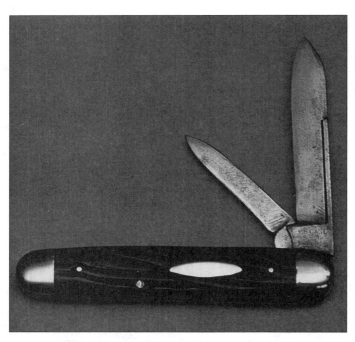

6241, red Winterbottom, bone, 3-1/2", W.R. Case & Son, 1902-1905, rare; $250.

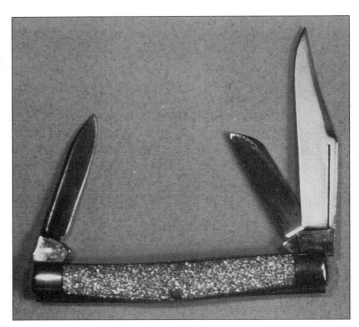

GS344, gold stone, small blades have Case Tested XX; $350.

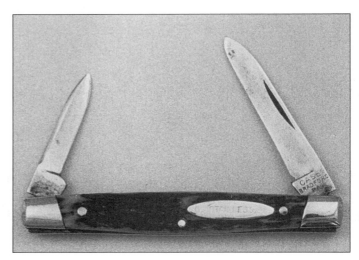

62042, slant bolsters, stainless emblem, small blade stamped Case's Stainless, Rogers bone, 3", Case, Brad., PA.; $300.

63042, 3", Case, Bradford, PA.; $400.

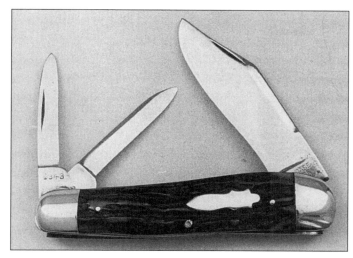

5343, whittler, 3-3/4", W.R. Case & Son, Brad., PA.; $1,200.

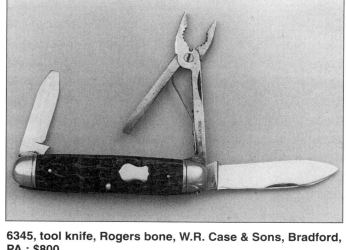

6345, tool knife, Rogers bone, W.R. Case & Sons, Bradford, PA.; $800.

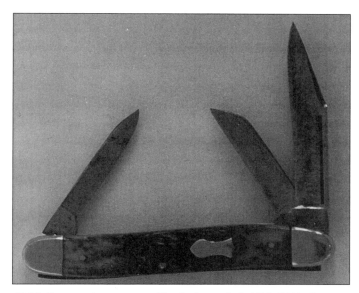

6344, Rogers bone-rare, (flat bolsters), 3-1/2", W.R. Case & Sons; $250.

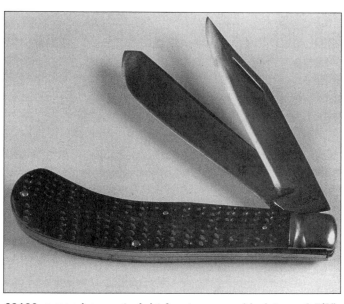

62100, green bone, straight front, grooved bolsters, 4-5/8", W.R. Case and Sons; $1,100.

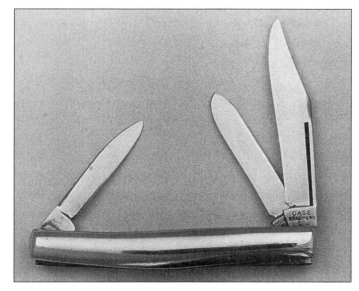

M344LP, all metal, 3-1/4", Case, Brad., PA.; $225.

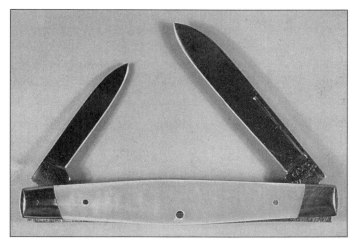

82042LP, genuine pearl, 3", Stainless, small blade stamped in oval; $300.

M445, camp pattern, 3-3/4", Case, Bradford, PA. Nickel scales with Boy Scout scene on both sides, very rare; $800.

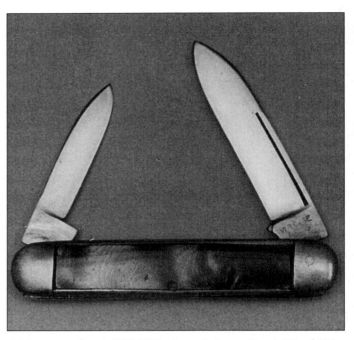

G245, pyremite, 3-5/8", W.R. Case & Sons, Brad. PA.; $350.

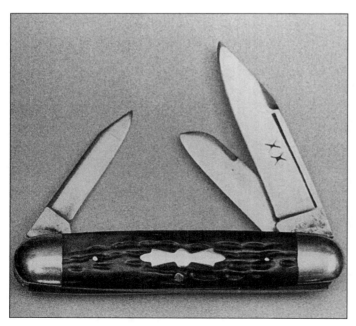

6345LP, bone, 3-5/8", Case Bros. Springville, (rare stamp); $900.

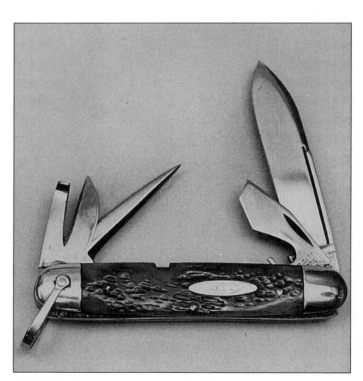

6445RLP, Rogers bone, 3-3/4", W.R. Case & Sons, Bradford, PA.; $600.

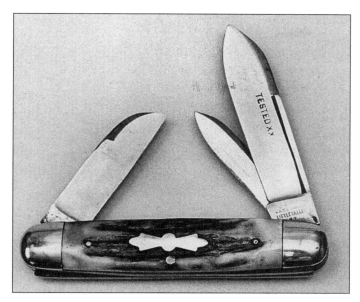

5345LP, stag, 2-3/4", Case Brothers, Little Valley, NY; $700.

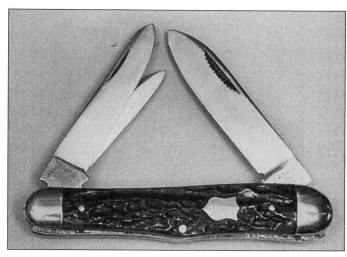

6346, Rogers bone, 3 backsprings, 3-5/8", W.R. Case & Sons; $1,200.

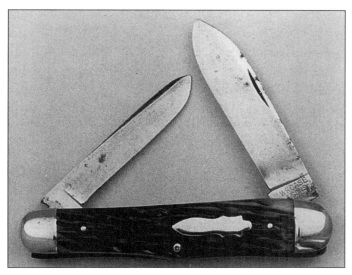

6246, bone, 3-5/8", W.R. Case & Sons, Brad, PA.; $450.

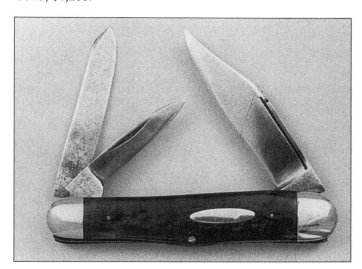

6346-1/2 LP, 3 backsprings, 3-5/8", W.R. Case & Sons, Brad., PA.; $1,200.

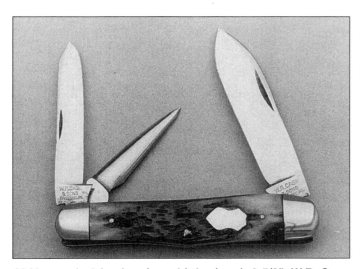

6346, punch, 3-backspring whittler (rare), 3-5/8", W.R .Case & Sons, Brad., PA.; $900.

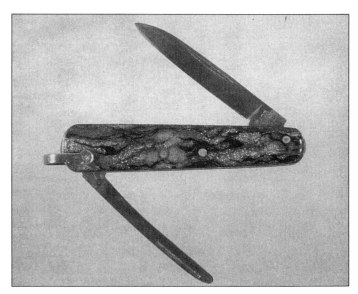

RM2101R, Christmas tree, pen, 2-1/4", Case, Bradford, PA.; 1915, $250.

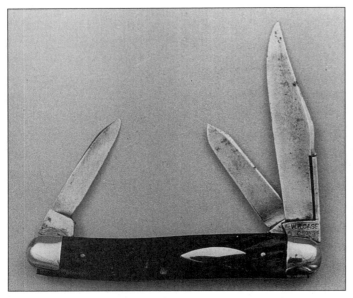

6347, Rogers bone, LP, W.R. Case & Sons; $700.

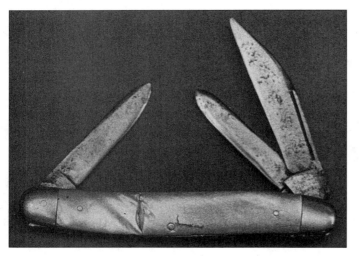

8347LP, pearl, 3-15/16", Case & Sons, Bradford, PA.; $1,000. Not shown: B347LP, waterfall, 3-15/16", 1910-15, W.R. Case & Sons; $700.

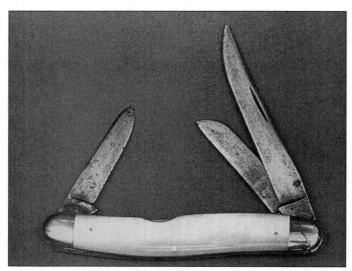

83047, pearl, 4", W.R. Case & Sons; $1,000.

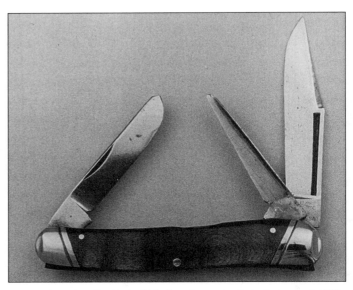

P348LP, swirl, Made in U.S.A., slant pinch bolsters, 3-1/4", W. R. Case & Sons; $600.

R201, candy stripe, 2-3/4", Case Brothers Cutlery Co.; $250.

6250LP, Sunfish (toenail), 4", Case Brothers, Little Valley, NY; $1,500.

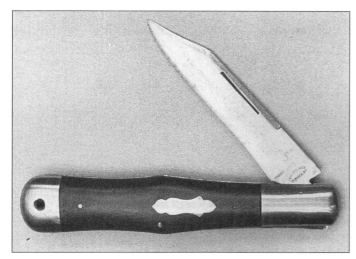

C21050, ebony (rare stamp), 5-5/16", Case Bros. & Co., Gowanda, NY; $2,000.

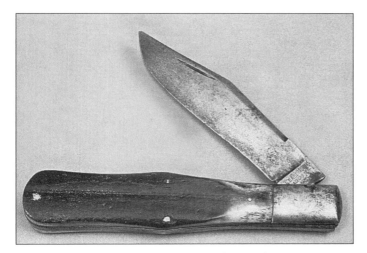

61050, slab stag, 1 blade, 5-3/8", W.R. Case & Sons, Brad., PA.; $550.

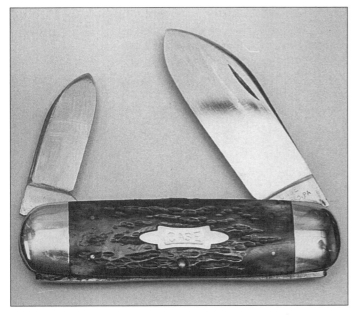

6250, Rogers bone, 4-3/8", Case, Bradford, PA.; $1,500.

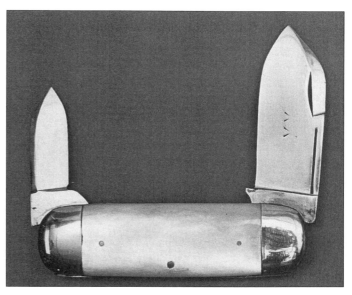

8250LP, genuine pearl, 4", Case Bros., Case Brothers, Bradford, PA.; $2,500.

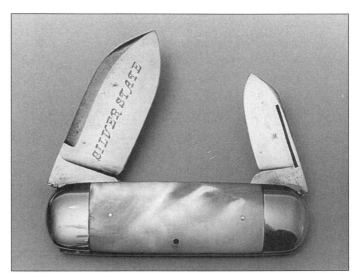

8250, toenail, genuine pearl handle, 4", back of blade shows silver states etched, Case Brothers, Little Valley, NY, rare; $3,000.

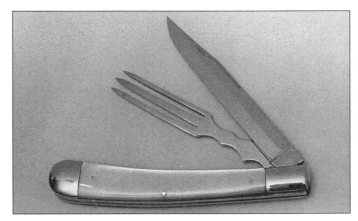

8251, pearl handles, hobo, 5-3/8", W.R. Case & Sons, Bradford, PA.; $2,500.

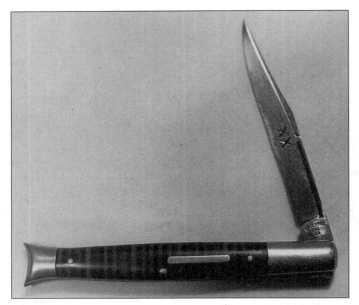

B1051?, fishtail stripe celluloid, 3-7/8", (arc) Case Bros. Cut. Co., (rare stamp); $550.

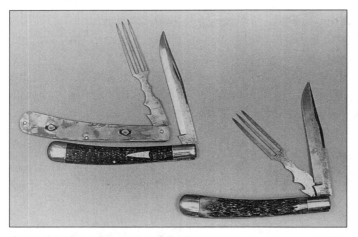

Case, Bradford, PA., hobo knife: Top: 6251, green bone, 5-1/4", $600. Bottom: 6251, Rogers bone, 5-1/4", $650.

82063, abalone, W.R. Case & Sons, Brad., PA.; $250.

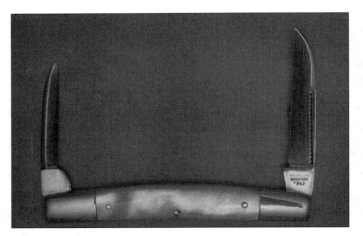

8268, pearl, 3-1/4", Case & Sons, Bradford, PA., both blades stamped; $500.

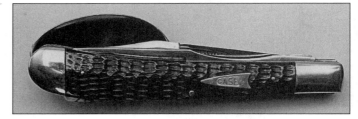

Case Bros. Springville, NY, hobo: 6351SP, green bone, 5-1/4", knife, fork and spoon come apart; $2,500.

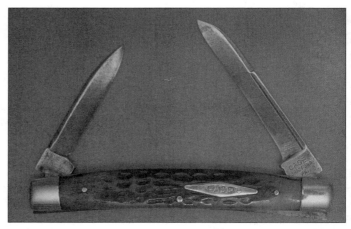

6268LP, green bone, 3-1/4", Case, Bradford, PA-Pen stamped oval stamp; $400.

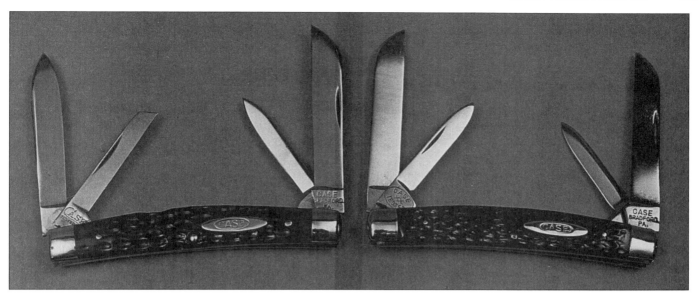

Left: 64052, green bone, transition, master blade, Case, Brad. Pa., other 3-Tested XX; $2,000. Right: 64052, green bone, Tested oval stamp, Case, Brad. PA., recessed bolsters, 3-1/2"; $2,000.

G2069, amber swirl congress, 2-3/4", W.R. Case & Sons, Bradford, PA.; $350.

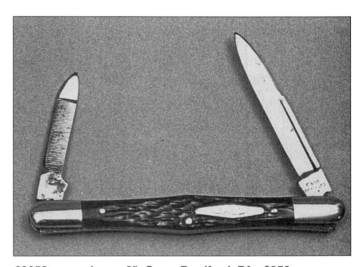

62056, green bone, 3", Case, Bradford, PA.; $250.

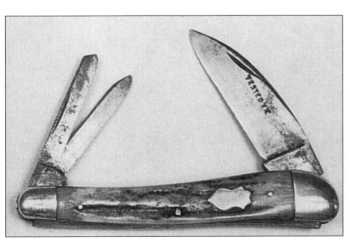

5355, stag, 3-3/4", with Wharncliffe blade, Case Bros., Little Valley, NY; $1,000.

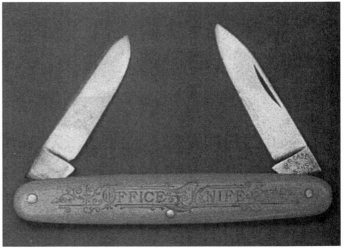

42057, 3-5/16", W.R. Case & Sons, Made in USA (used around 1900), scarce; $150.

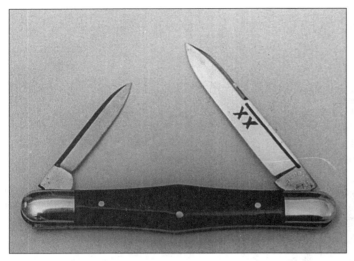

72056, tortoise-shell handle, 3", Case Brothers, Little Valley, NY; $400.

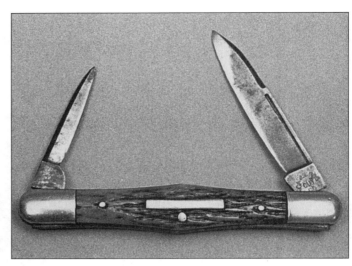

62056, brown bone, 3", Case Bros. Cut. Co., rare stamp; $350.

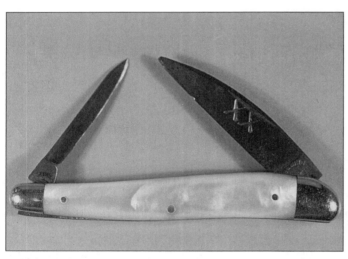

8254, genuine pearl, 3-1/4", Case Brothers, Little Valley, NY; $700.

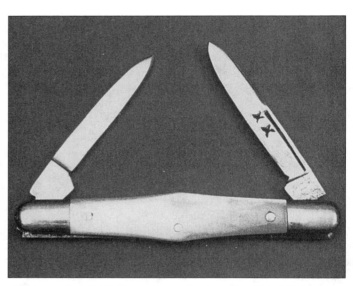

8258, pearl, 2-7/8", Case Bros., Springville, NY; $400.

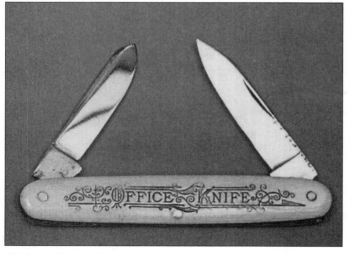

42057, office knife, composition, 3-3/8", W.R. Case & Son; $150.

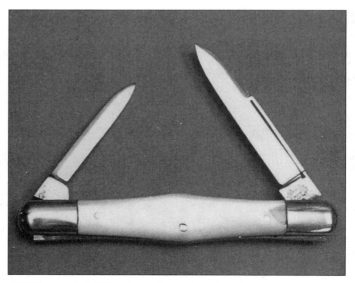

82058, pearl, 2-7/8", Case Bros. Cut Co.; $400.

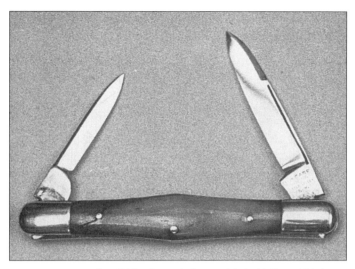

6258, bone, 2-7/8", W.R. Case & Sons, Little Valley, NY, (rare stamp, most are Brad. PA.); $400.

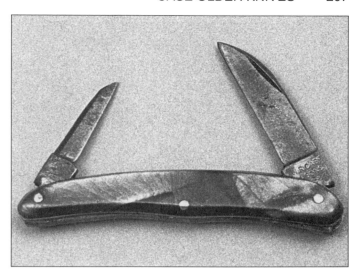

P259, greenish swirl-rare, 2-1/4", W. R. Case & Sons, Bradford, PA.; $350.

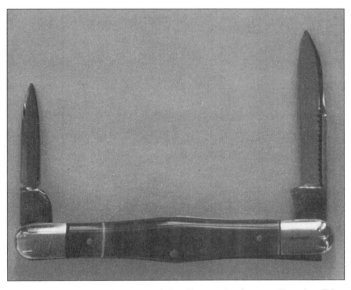

R258F, candy stripe, 2-7/8", Case & Sons, Brad., PA., (match striker pull), rare; $350.

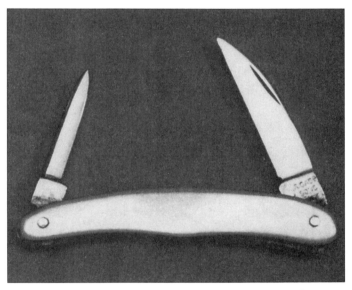

8259, pearl, Wharncliffe, 2-1/4", W.R. Case & Sons; $350.

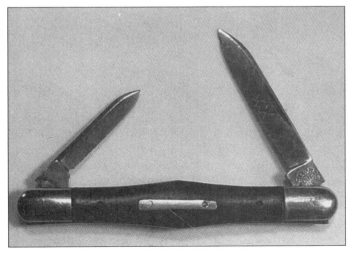

2258, ebony, 2-7/8", both blades Case Bros. Cut. Co., main blade also XX; $250.

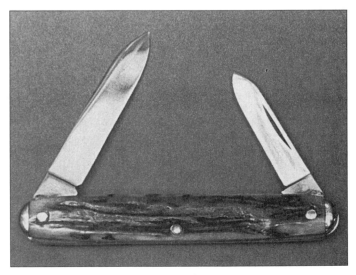

5260T, stag, W.R. Case & Sons; $300.

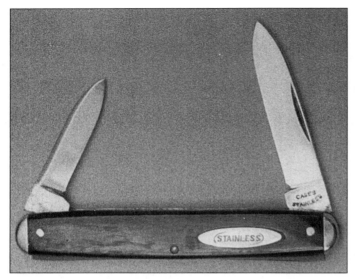

7260T, red plastic, 3-1/16", Case's Stainless (stainless shield), $300.

8460, pearl (1902-1905), 3-7/16", all blades stamped W.R. Case & Son, Bradford, PA.; $450.

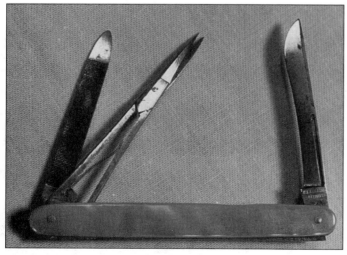

8361SC, gold pearl, 2-7/8", W.R. Case & Sons, Germany (rare), $400.

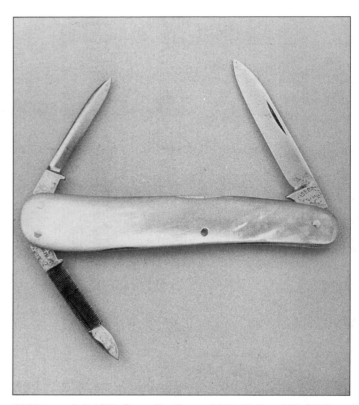

8363, pearl, 3-1/4", Case Brothers, Little Valley, NY; $350.

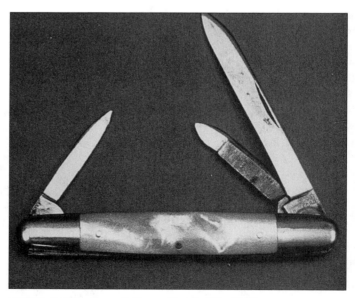

83063, 3-1/4", Case & Sons, Brad., PA.; $300.

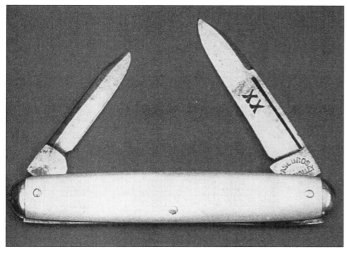

8264, pearl, 3-1/8", Case Bros., Little Valley, NY; $300.

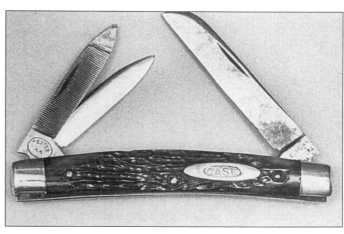

6368F, Congress whittler, green bone, 3-1/4", Case, Bradford, PA.; $1,200.

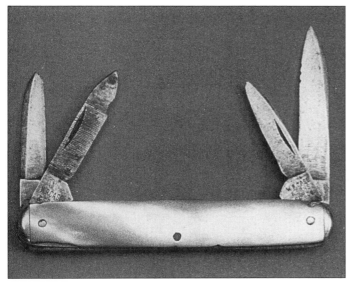

8464F (shown), pearl, 3-1/8", Case & Sons, Bradford, Pa.; $450. Not shown: 9464F, imitation pearl, C.I., Tested XXD-oval file; $350.

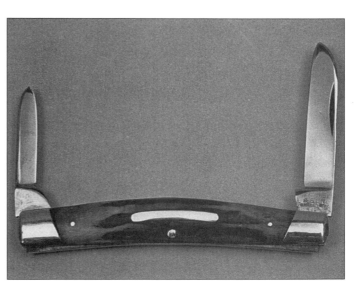

52068, stag, 3-11/16", W.R. Case & Son., c.1902-05; $350.

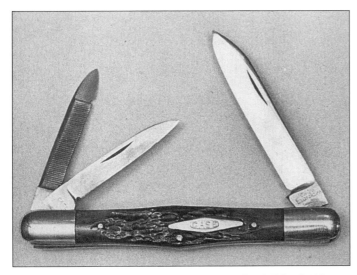

63067F, Rogers bone, 3-7/8", Case, Bradford, PA.; $500.

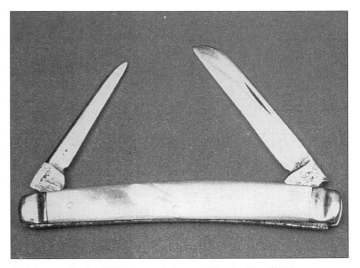

8269, pearl, 3", W.R. Case & Sons, Brad. PA.; $300.

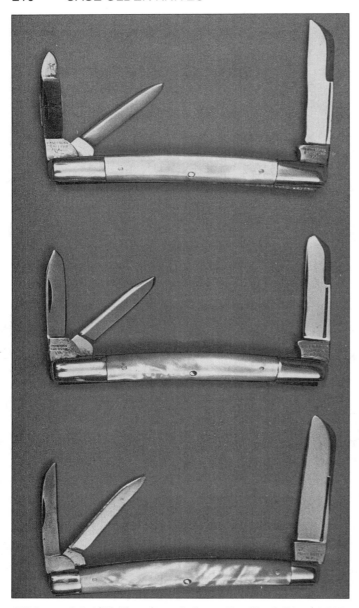

8368, pearl, 3-1/4": Top: Case & Sons, Bradford, PA.; $1,000. Center: Case & Sons, Bradford, PA.; $1,000. Bottom: Case Bro. Little Valley, NY; $1,000.

62079-1/2, Rogers bone, flat bolsters, 3-5/8", W.R. Case and Sons, Bradford, PA; $300.

6370, ebony, c.1896, 3-5/8", Tested XX, Case Bros. & Co., Gowanda, NY; $1,500.

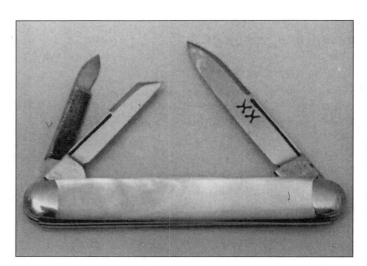

8371, genuine pearl, 3-1/2", Case Bros., Little Valley, NY; $900.

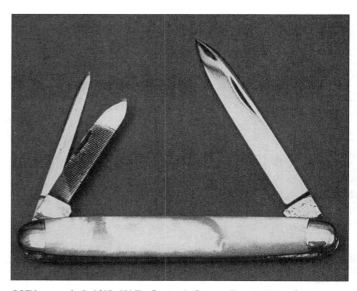

8371, pearl, 3-1/4", W.R. Case & Sons, Brad., PA.; $900.

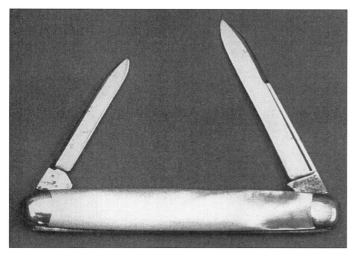

8271LP, pearl, 3-1/4", W.R. Case & Sons, Brad., PA.; $500.

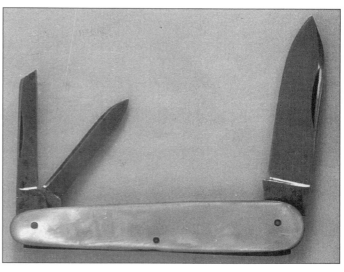

8377, pearl shadow, 3-3/8", Case Bros., Little Valley, NY; $500.

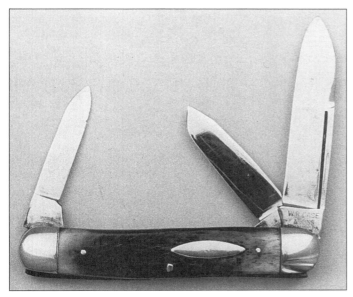

63074 LP, Rogers bone, 3-1/2", W.R. Case & Sons, Brad., PA.; $750.

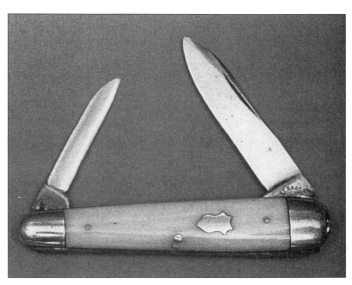

6287, white bone, 3-1/2", Case Bro., Little Valley, NY, sleeveboard; $300.

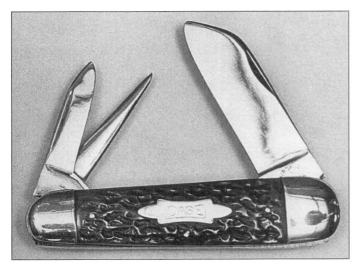

63076PU, green bone, rare, 4", W.R. Case & Sons, Bradford, PA.; $1,800.

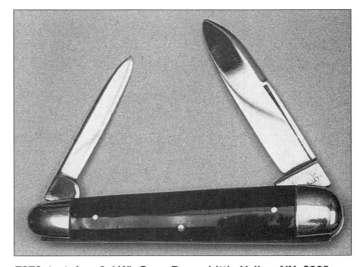

7278, tortoise, 3-1/4", Case Bros., Little Valley, NY: $300.

M279, sterling, 3-1/8", Case's Stainless; $250.

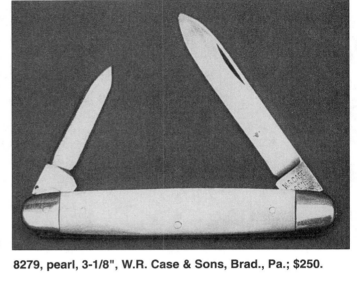

8279, pearl, 3-1/8", W.R. Case & Sons, Brad., Pa.; $250.

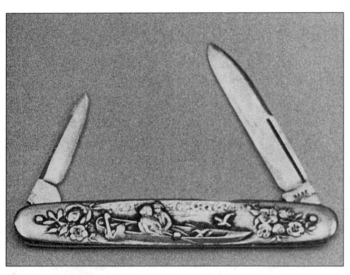

M279, metal (figural), 3-1/8", Case Bradford, Pa.; $250.

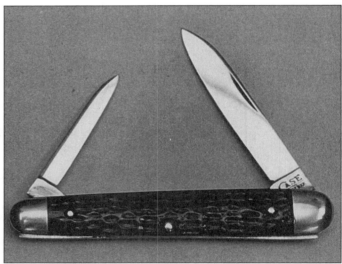

62079, green bone, SP, 3-1/4", Case Tested XX; $200.

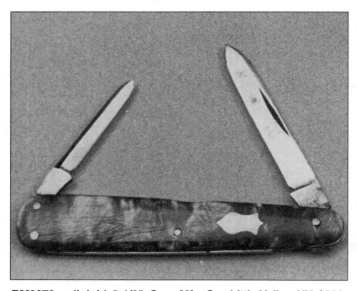

RM3079, celluloid, 3-1/8", Case Mfg. Co., Little Valley, NY; $300.

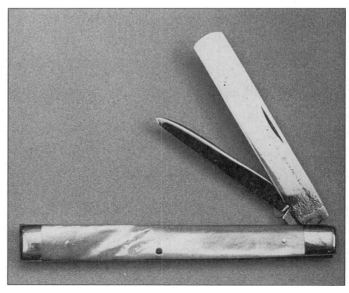

8280, Dr.'s knife, pearl, 3-5/8", W.R. Case & Son, Brad., Pa.; $1,000.

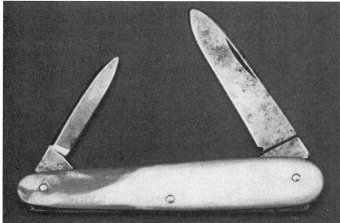

82079 and 62079, pearl and bone (salesman's sample), 3-1/4", Case Bros., Little Valley, NY; $300.

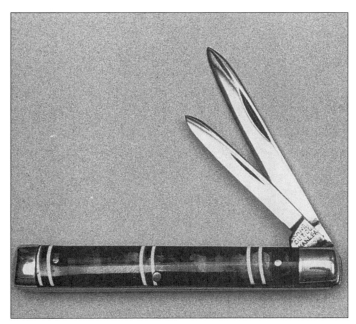

R2082, Dr.'s knife, candy stripe, 2-7/8", Kane Cutlery Co., Kane, Pa.; $600.

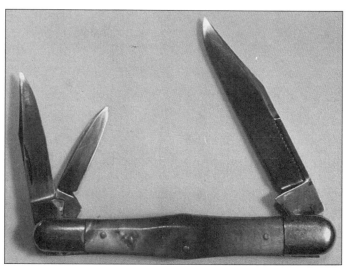

RM383, gold swirl, 3-1/2", all blades stamped Case & Sons, Bradford, PA; $600.

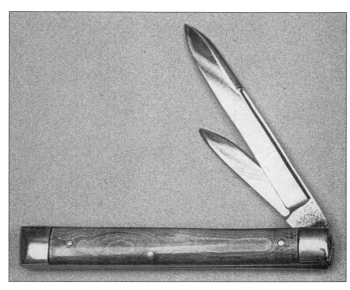

BC283, doctor's knife, green swirl, 2-7/8", W.R. Case & Sons, Brad., Pa.; $600.

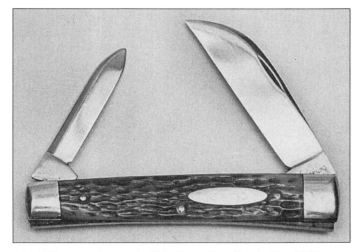

6284SH, green bone, 3-1/8", Case, Bradford, PA.; $600.

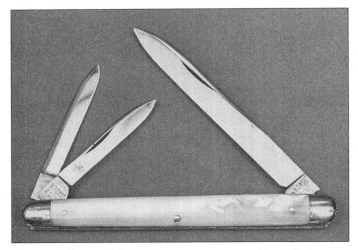

8385, pearl, 3-5/8", W.R. Case & Sons, Bradford, PA.; $600.

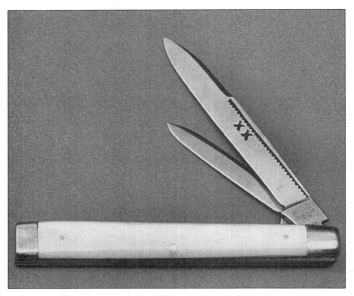

8285LP, doctor's knife, pearl, 3-3/4", Case Bros. Cutler Co., Little Valley; $1,000.

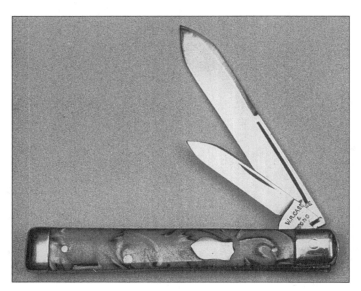

BM2086, pyralin, 3-1/4", W.R. Case & Sons; $750.

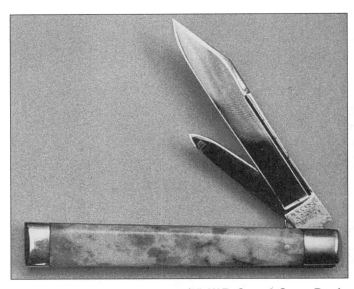

M2086, Dr.'s knife, linoleum, 3-1/8", W.R. Case & Sons, Brad., Pa.; $750.

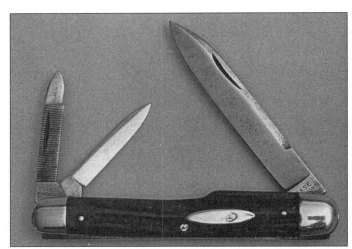

5387F, Gunstock whittler, stag, 3-1/2", Case, Bradford, PA.; $1,000.

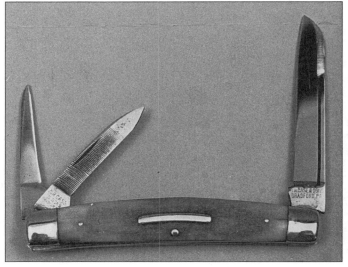

5388FLP, stag, bar shield, Congress whittler, recessed bolsters, 4-1/8", W.R. Case & Sons, Brad., Pa.; $1,500.

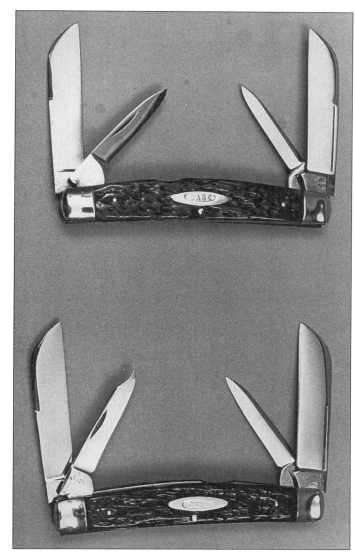

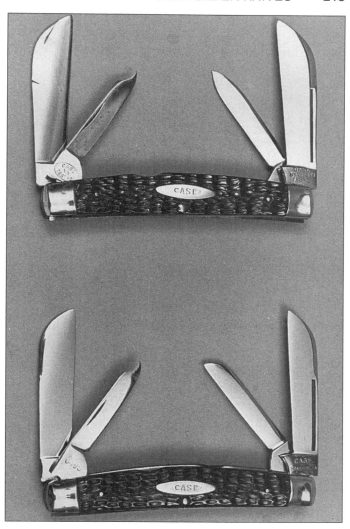

Top: 6488LP, Rogers bone, recessed bolster, center shield, 4-1/8", Case, Bradford, PA.; $3,000. Bottom: 6488LP, Rogers bone, recessed bolster, center shield, W.R. Case & Sons, Brad., PA. (cuticle blade); $3,000.

Top: 6488LP, green bone, recessed bolsters, center shield, Case, Bradford, PA. (cuticle blade) oval stamp on cuticle blade; $3,000. Bottom: 6488LP, green bone, recessed bolsters, center shield, Case Bradford, PA., Pat. No. stamped on cuticle blade; $3,000.

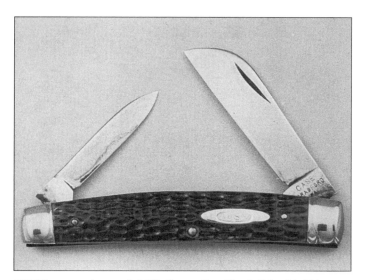

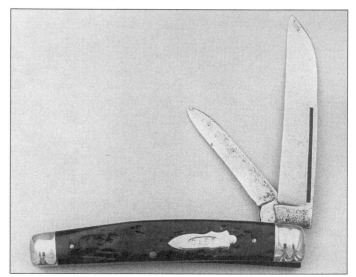

62089, green bone, 3-3/4", Case, Bradford, PA.; $1,400.

6289, Semi-Wharncliffe Congress, rare, 3-3/4", W.R. Case & Sons, Brad., PA.; $750.

Whittler, Wharncliffe, Rogers bone, 3", Case-Kane, PA; $400.

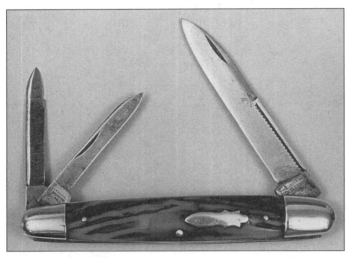

5391FLP, stag, rare-2 pulls, 4-1/2", W.R. Case & Sons, Bradford, PA.; $3,000.

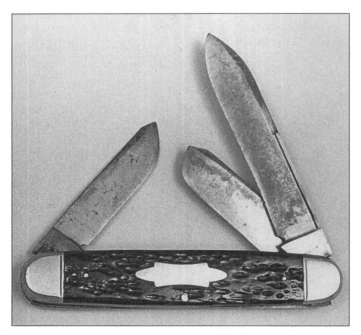

6394LP, Rogers bone, flat bolsters, 4-1/4", Case, Bradford, PA.; $3,000.

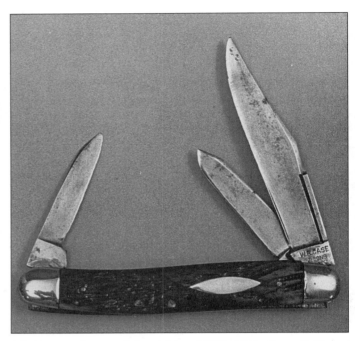

LP, Rogers bone, plain shield, 3-7/8", W.R. Case & Sons, Brad., PA; $650.

G347LP, stainless, green swirl pyremite, 3-7/8", W.R. Case and Sons, Made in U.S.A.-U.S., Supreme Shield (rare); $700.

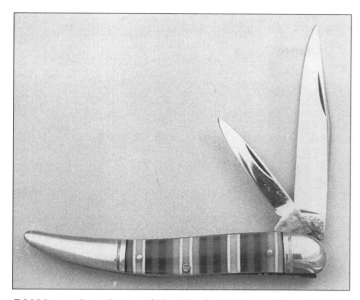

R2096, candy stripe, 3-1/4", W.R. Case & Sons; $450.

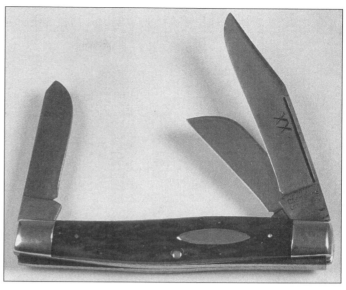

6375, Rogers bone, 4-1/4", Case Brothers, Little Valley, NY; $1,000.

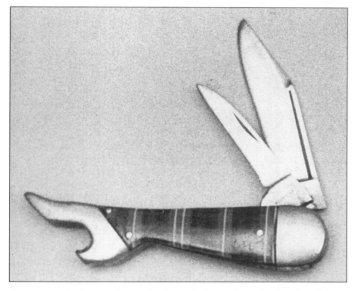

R2097, red plastic, 1920-23, 3-1/4", Standard Knife Co.; $400.

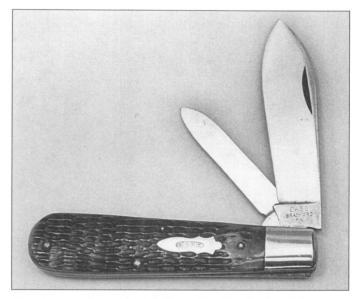

62099, green bone, 4-1/8", Case, Bradford, PA; $450.

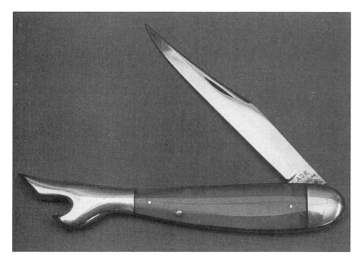

B1097SAB, leg knife, waterfall, 5", Case, Bradford, Pa.; $450.

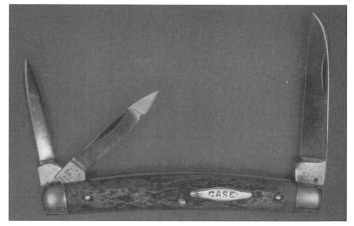

6369, Rogers bone, 3", file blade stamped W.R. Case & Sons, Brad., PA, pen blade stamped with pattern No.; $800.

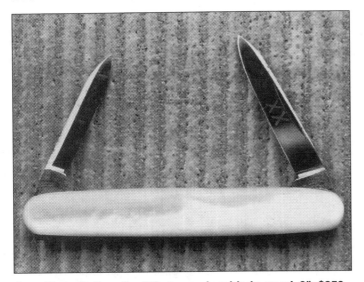

Case Bros. Cutlery Co. XX stamped on blade, pearl, 3"; $250.

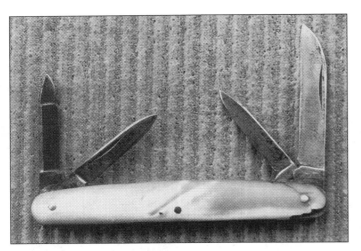

Pearl (rare), 3-5/8", W.R. Case & Sons; $700.

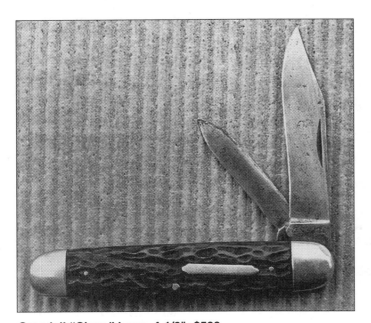

Crandall "Cigar," bone, 4-1/8"; $500.

Official Barnum & Bailey Circus throwing knife, black micarta, 1940 era, Case XX, 12" overall, 8" blade; $150. Photo courtesy J. Merrigan.

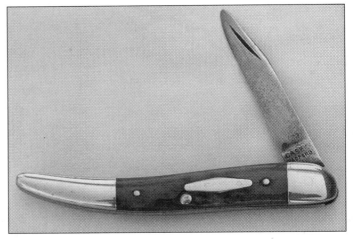

61096, pointed shield, 3-1/8", Case, Bradford, PA., 1 blade mini toothpick, green bone; $400.

W.R. Case & Son Cutlery Co., (rare stamp), waterfall, 1902-1905; $350.

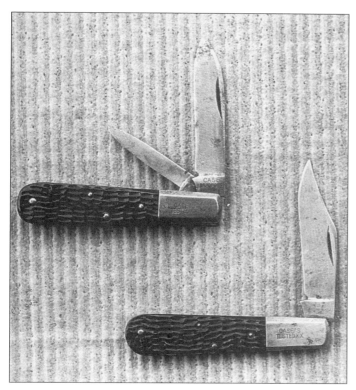

Top: 62005, green bone Barlow, 3-3/8", Case, Brad. Pa.; $450.
Bottom: 61005-1/2, green bone Barlow, 3-3/8", Case, Brad. Pa.; $450.

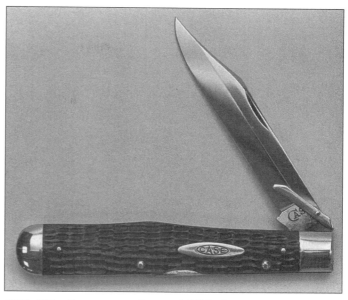

6111-1/2L, Case green bone, 4-3/8", Case (rare), 1920-40; $1,200.

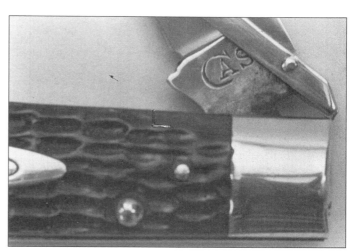

A close up of the Case stamp found on 6111-1/2L.

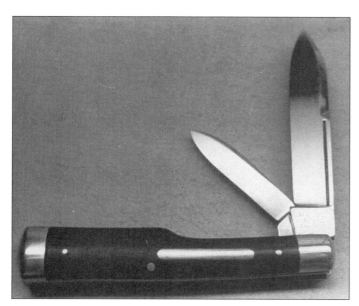

1215, Gunstock, walnut, 3", W.R. Case & Sons, Bradford, PA.; $750. Photo courtesy Armand Micciuli.

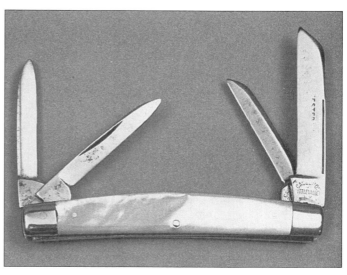

84052, pearl, 3-3/4", Case Bros., Little Valley, NY; $1,500.

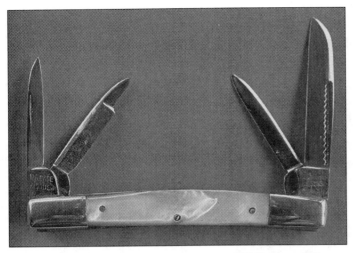

8468LP, pearl, 3-1/4", all blades stamped, W.R. Case & Sons, Bradford, PA.; $1,500. Photo courtesy Herbert Aycock.

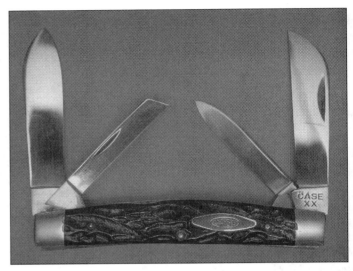

6488RP, rough black, tested shield, 4-1/8", Case XX; $900. Photo courtesy Herbert Aycock.

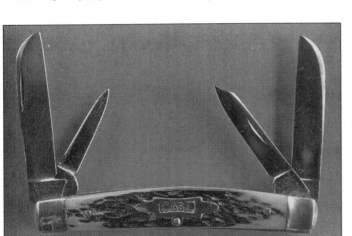

6488RP, W.R. Case & Sons, Roger bone, 4-1/8", recessed bolsters, bow-tie shield, all blades stamped 6488. Note that large blades are left-hand blades the opposite of other 88s; $3,000. Photo courtesy Herbert Aycock.

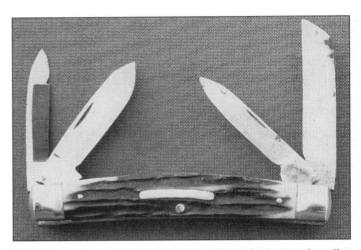

5488LP, master sheep foot blade, all marked, stag handle, 4-1/16", large spay as secondary blade, W.R. Case & Son, Brad., Pa., very rare; $12,000.

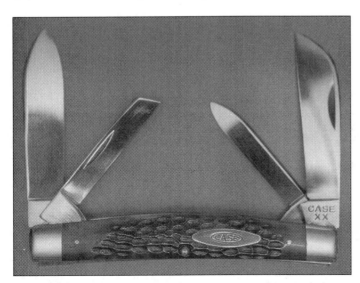

6488, red bone, 4-1/8", Case XX to USA transition; $600. Photo courtesy Herbert Aycock.

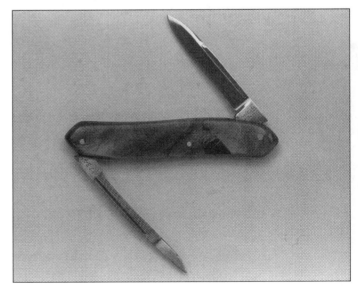

P254, pyramite, very rare, 3", W.R. Case & Sons, Brad., Pa.; $300.

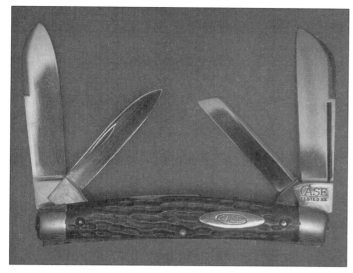

6488LP, red bone, 4-1/8", Case Tested XX, has XX shield; $2,000. Photo courtesy Herbert Aycock.

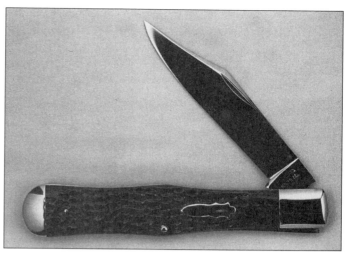

C610050, green bone, 5-1/4", slick bomb shield, Standard Knife Co.; $400. Photo courtesy G. Witcher.

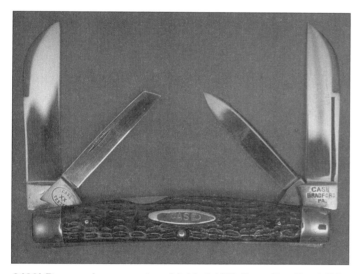

6488LP, green bone, center shield, 4-1/8", Case Bradford, PA., oval stamp small blades, Case Bradford large blade, 6488 on back of Master; $3,000. Photo courtesy Herbert Aycock.

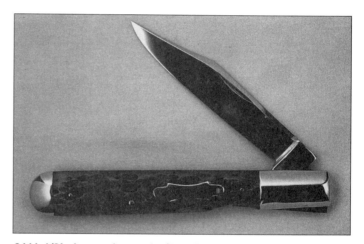

6111-1/2L, brown bone, 4-7/16", flat blade, Case Bros., Little Valley; $800. Photo courtesy G. Witcher.

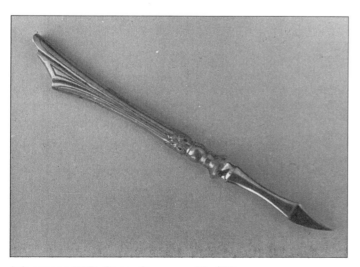

Ink eraser, W.R. Case, Germany, 5"; $25.

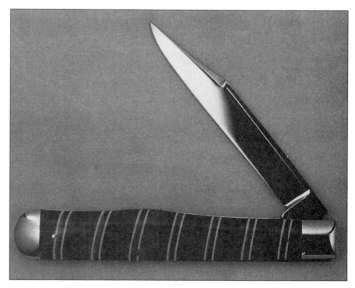

R111-1/2 LP, candy stripe, 4-7/16", W.R. Case & Sons, Bradford, PA, number stamped on back of blade; $800. Photo courtesy G. Witcher.

6111-1/2L, green bone, Tested, 4-7/16", flat blade, no guard; $1,000. Photo courtesy G. Witcher.

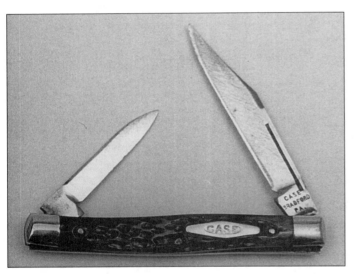

6233LP, 2-5/8", 2 blades, Rogers bone, Case, Brad., PA; $250.

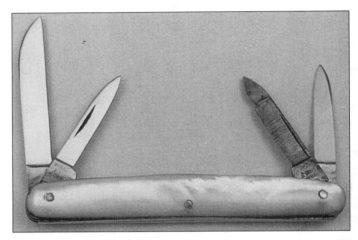

8438, 3-5/8", 4 blades, Congress, genuine pearl shadow, W.R. Case & Sons, Brad., PA; $800. Photo courtesy Joe Chance.

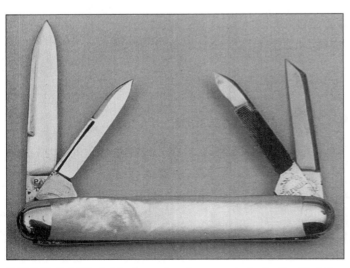

8471LP, 3-3/8", 4 blades, genuine pearl, (pat. Applied for Case Bros., Little Valley, NY); $1,500.

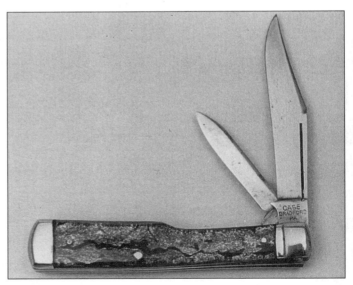

RM215, 3", 2 blades, gunstock, Christmas tree, Case, Bradford, Pa.; $550. Photo courtesy Joe Chance.

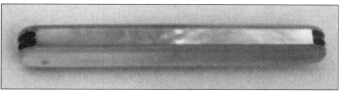

3-3/8", 4 blades, genuine pearl handle, pearl-covered back springs, shadow; $1,500. Photo courtesy Joe Chance.

B3109LP, green swirl, tip bolsters, 3 blades, whittler, Case Mfg. Co., Little Valley, NY; $700. Photo courtesy Joe Chance.

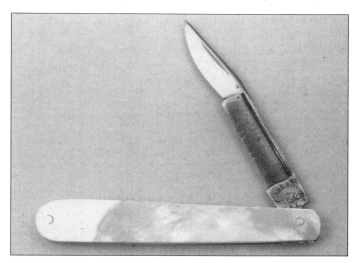

Pattern unknown, 2-5/8", 1 blade, genuine pearl, Case Bros., Little Valley, NY; $200. Photo courtesy Joe Chance.

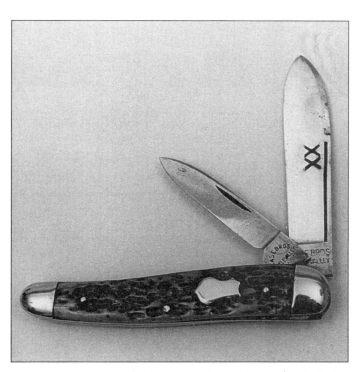

Pattern unknown, 3-3/8", 2 blades, brown bone; $350. Photo courtesy Joe Chance.

P3092 XX, 3-7/8", 3 blades, stockman, greenish-pink swirl celluloid, birdseye rivets, Case, Bradford, PA; $750.

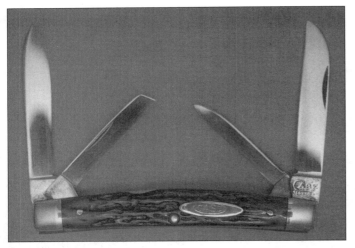

64052, green bone, (rare), 3-1/2", Case tested XX; $1,500. Photo courtesy Herbert Aycock.

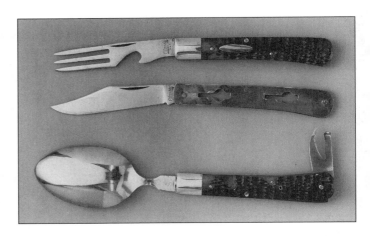

Game shears, stag handle, 11-1/2", Case Tested XX; $125.

6452, Hobo, 1920-35, 3-3/4", Clauss, Fremont, Ohio, U.S.A., green bone, Case contract knife; $600. Photo courtesy Herbert Aycock.

6100, honey comb. 700

3100, yellow comb. 650

P200, celluloid 700

5200 700

6200, green bone 700

9200, cracked ice 600

1201, ebony wood 200

M201, metal 100

R201T, candy stripe 200

2201 100

3201 90

3201R 100

6001, green bone 800

GS001, gold stone 800

6201, green bone 125

62001, green bone 110

8201 150

72001, tortoiseshell 200

82001 150

9201 85

9201R 100

P202 150

R202, candy stripe 200

1202, D&B 500

1502, Scout 350

B3102, Christmas tree 200

5202 200

5202, RAZ 400

5202-1/2 250

6202, green bone 150

6202 SH R, Rogers bone, WW I 250

6202-1/2, green bone 150

63102, green bone 175

83102 200

1203CP, cocoa 3-1/2", Case Bros. 350

1503, Jr. Scout 400

2203CP, ebony 3-1/2", Case Bros. 400

5203LPCP, Case Bros. 400

5203SP, budding, W.R. Case 400

6103, B&G 150

6203 400

6203LPCP, Case Bros. 400

M204, metal 140

1204, cocoa, 3-5/8", Case Bros. 150

5204CPSP 600

6104B 250

6204, bone, 3-5/8", Case Bros. 550

6204-1/2 300

1205, spear, Case Bros. 250

2205, spear, Case Bros. 300

3205, pyralin, 3-3/8", Case Bros. 325

5205, spear, Case Bros. 350

5205 325

5205RAZ 500

6205 400

6205RAZ 500

6205, spear, Case Bros. 500

6205-1/2 325

7205, pyralin, 3-3/8", Case Bros. 500

65206, gold stone 250

B206, Christmas tree 500

5206, physician's, Case Bros. 600

5206-1/2 200

6106 150

6106, 25 cents 400

6106, 50 cents 400

6206 225

6206-1/2 200

62006-1/2 200

72006 300

7206, tortoise 250

7106, tortoise 250

8106, pearl 275

8206 300

8206, physician's, Case Bros. 650

1207, cocoa, 3-5/8", Case Bros. 200

1207LP, Case Bros. 250

3207, yellow celluloid 350

5207LP, Case Bros. 400

5207 350

5307, whittler 600

6207, green bone 325

6207, Rogers bone 350

6207LP, Case Bros. 300

6207, Case Bros., congress 400

8207, Case Bros., congress 400

8407 750

2208, ebony, 3-3/8", Case Bros. 300

2308 400

3308 400

5208, Case Bros. 450

5308 500

6308 500

6208, bone, 3-3/8", Case Bros. 300

6208 150

8308 600

6209 200

62009 200

62009RAZ 250

62009, sheep foot 250

62009, spay 200

62009-1/2 200

B3109, Wh. Christmas tree 700

63109, Wh., 3 backsprings 600

83109, Wh., 3 backsprings 700

92009, onyx, bolster stamped 250

92009-1/2, onyx 250

2210, ebony, 3-3/8", Case Bros. 225

3210-1/2 200

5210, genuine stag 3-3/8", Case Bros. 300

5210-1/2 225

6210 210

62105 225

62010 200

6210-1/2 200

7210, pyralin, 3-3/8", Case Bros. 350

8210, pearl, 3-3/8", Case Bros. 250

R111-1/2, candy stripe 700

R211, candy stripe 700

R211-1/2, candy stripe 750

B1011, Christmas tree 300

3111-1/2 600

5111L, CP, Case Bros. 1,000

6111, bone, Case Bros. 900

6111-1/2, red Winterbottom,
W.R. Case & Sons, 4-3/8" 1,200

6111-1/2 750

6111-1/2L, W.R. Case & Sons 1,000

R111-1/2LP, W.R. Case & Sons, 4-7/16" 800

6211 700

6211-1/2 700

61011, Rogers 300

11011, walnut 150

61011, green bone 150

1212, cocoa, 3-1/4", Case Bros. 200

1212L 200

2212, ebony 3-1/4", Case Bros. 225

6212, bone 3-1/4", Case Bros. 250

62012, bone, 3-1/8" L.P., spear-pen 225

7212, pyralin, 3-1/4", Case Bros. 275

8212, spear, Case Bros. 275

1213, clip-Case Bros. 300

2213, clip-Case Bros. 225

61013, green bone 300

61013, Rogers bone 350

6213, Rogers bone 700

6213, green bone 600

6213, clip-Case Bros. 600

5214 300

5214-1/2 300

6214 300

6214-1/2 250

6214LP, spay, Case Bros. 225

7214LP, spay, Case Bros. 250

P215, gunstock 550

6215, gunstock 550

8215, gunstock 650

1215 550

8315F, pearl 3-1/4", Case Bros. 600

8315NP, pearl 3-1/4", Case Bros. 600

8415, shad, Case Bros. 700

22016 200

22016-1/2 200

6116 200

6116-1/2 200

61016-1/2 175

6216 300

6216EO 300

62016 200

6216, spear, Case Bros. 275

62016-1/2 200

620165 200

6216-1/2 200

7216, spear ,Case Bros. 300

8116, pearl, 2-1/2", Case Bros. 250

8116F, pearl, 2-1/2", Case Bros. 250

8216, spear, Case Bros. 250

2217 250

6217 300

B318SHSP, Christmas tree 400

1118, Case Bros. 150

3318SHSP 300

3318SHPEN 300

5318SHSP 500

6318SHSP 300

6318SPP 300

6318SHPEN 400

8318SHSP 550

9318SHPEN, onyx 450

9318SHSP, onyx 450

1119, Cotton Sampler, Case Bros. 500

6219 500

62019	500
Y220	350
B220, Christmas tree	400
2220, Case Mfg. Co.	300
3220	300
4220	300
5220	400
5320, Whittler, Case Bros.	500
6220	350
6220SAB, long pull	450
62020	300
620205	300
62020-1/2	300
2320	400
P320, pyremite, Peanut	300
6320, bone, 3-3/8", Case Bros.	400
7220, shell, 3-3/8", Case Bros.	350
7320, Whittler, Case Bros.	450
8220, pearl, 3-3/8", Case Bros.	400
8220, (not Peanut pattern)	350
8220, pearl, Peanut	400
8320, Whittler, Case Bros.	500
9220SABLP, Case Bros., Bradford, PA	400
9220	250
B221, waterfall	400
B221, Christmas tree	400
5421, Case Bros.	450
6221, Rogers bone	300
06221	300
06221-1/2	300
6321	400
7421, Case Bros.	500
08221	400
8221, pearl, 3-3/8", Case Bros.	250
8221NP, pearl, 3-3/8", Case Bros.	250
8321, pearl, 3-3/8", Case Bros.	400
8321NP, pearl, 3-3/8", Case Bros.	400
8421, Case Bros.	500
GS222, gold stone, phy.	600
2222, ebony, 3-1/4", Case Bros.	225
22122, ebony, 2-5/8", Case Bros.	250
5222, genuine stag, 3-1/4", Case, Bros.	350
6222	200
6222, bone, 3-1/4", Case Bros.	250
62122SH, bone, 2-5/8", Case Bros.	300
62122, bone, 2-5/8", Case Bros.	275
7222, shell, 3-1/4", Case Bros.	600
8222, Dr.'s knife	800

P223	500
2223, ebony, 3-5/8", Case Bros.	400
5223LP, spear, Case Bros.	800
6223LP, spear, Case Bros.	600
6223	450
8223LP, spear, Case Bros.	800
9223	450
B224, Christmas tree	400
P3024, Wh., rare, gold swirl	500
3124	175
3124-1/2	175
3224	200
3224-1/2	200
5224	250
52024	250
5224-1/2	250
52024-1/2	250
5424, Case Bros.	400
6124	175
6124-1/2	175
6224	175
62024	175
62024RAZ	250
62024, sheep foot	250
62024-1/2	175
8224	300
8424, Case Bros.	450
32025-1/2	225
5225-1/2	250
6225	250
6225-1/2	225
62025-1/2	200
8225	300
B226, Christmas tree	450
4226, spear, smooth white	350
6226	300
62026	250
6226-1/2	250
82026	400
62027	200
62027-1/2	125
7327, Whittler, Case Bros.	450
8227	250
82027	200
B2027, Christmas tree	350
8327, Whittler, Case Bros.	450
92027	200
92027-1/2	200

P228EO	250
1228EO, walnut	200
2228	175
2228EO	300
2228PU	200
61028, W.R. Case	275
6228	225
6228EO	250
6228PU	30
62028	250
82028, oval Case Bros., Bradford, PA	300
820028	350
1229, spear-punch, Case Bros.	225
5229-1/2	30
6229, spear-punch, Case Bros.	250
6229-1/2	225
7229-1/2, tortoise	300
9229-1/2	200
P0230	200
02230	250
022301/2	250
05230-1/2	300
06230	300
06230-1/2	275
08230	40
09230	300
09230-1/2	300
6230SH	200
12130, cocoa, 3-3/8", Case Bros.	225
22130, ebony, 3-3/8", Case Bros.	225
62130	225
82130, Case Bros.	275
1131SH	125
1231CP, cocoa, 3-3/4", Case Bro.	175
2231SAB, spear-Case Bros.	350
2231-1/2, Case Bros.	250
2231	250
22031	200
2231-1/2, Case Bros.	250
2231-1/2SAB, Case Bros.	350
22031-1/2	200
52031	350
52031-1/2	300
52031-1/2SAB	450
52131LP	1,100
53131	1,000
53131, punch	1,200
5231, Case Bros.	325
6231	250
62031	250
6231-1/2	250
62031-1/2	250
62031-1/2SAB	250
G232	250
3232	225
5332	300
6232	200
6332	250
B233LP, Christmas tree	300
GS233LP, gold stone	300
2233	300
3233	200
6233, Case Bros.	450
6233	250
62033	200
6333	225
6333LP	250
8233	250
9233LP	200
9333	200
9333LP	225
G234, Dr. knife	600
5234, Dr. Knife	700
6234SH	400
G2035	300
3235-1/2	250
42035-1/2LP	300
5235-1/2	300
6235	200
6235EO	225
62035	200
6235-1/2	200
62035-1/2, green bone	200
62035-1/2, Rogers bone	300
8236, gunstock	550
6236, gunstock, Case Bros.	500
2237	500
2237-1/2	500
6237LP, Case Bros., Bradford, PA	500
6237-1/2	450
5238	300
GS3038, Case Brad.	650
5438	800
8438	1,000
B239, waterfall, sow belly	450
G2039, gold swirl	450

B339, onyx, sow belly	450
62039, Rogers bone, Case Brad, Pa	350
G3039, gold swirl	450
1139	250
6239	300
6339	600
63039	300
6539, 5 blade	5,000
11040	200
3240SP	550
6240	650
6240SP	650
9240SP	600
6241, Winterbottom	250
6241, Rogers bone	250
B242, Christmas tree	350
B3042, F. Wh. Christmas tree	450
3342, Case Bros.	300
5342, Case Bros.	400
52042	250
05242	250
6242	200
62042, Rogers bone	200
6342, Case Bros.	300
63042, Wh. green bone	300
82042	250
63042, Case Brad., Pa	350
83042, Wh. pearl	450
93042, Wh. onyx	375
92042	150
5343	1,000
6143	250
M144	200
GS344, Case Bros., Bradford, PA	250
B244, Christmas tree	300
B344SHSP	300
M344SHSP, metal	200
3244	150
3344SHSP	200
5244	225
05244	225
5344SHSP	300
6244	175
06244	175
62044	170
62044F	200
6344SHSP	225
6344SHPEN	225

8244	300
82044	300
82044F	300
08244	300
8344	375
9144EO, Case Bros.	200
9244	200
9344SHPEN	200
S445R, sterling silver figural	700
02245	250
02245-1/2	50
02245, ebony, Case Bros.	225
2345, ebony, Case Bros.	300
2345-1/2	325
04245B&G	300
05245	300
05245-1/2	300
5345	400
5345PU	400
5345-1/2	350
06245	250
08245, Case & Sons	300
06245-1/2, W.R. Case, Rogers bone	250
06245, bone, Case Bros.	250
6345SH, Case Bros.	325
6345	300
6345, pliers	800
6345PU	325
6345-1/2	300
6345-1/2PU	325
6445R	250
640045R	200
6445R, Scout Shield	350
G2046	300
B346PU, onyx	500
2246, ebony, 3-5/8", Case Bro.	300
G3046	450
3246	200
6246, Case Bros.	350
6246, W. R. Case & Sons, Brad, Pa	350
6246-1/2	325
62046	250
6346, Whittler	800
6346, punch, Rogers bone	700
6346-1/2, W. R. Case, whittler	700
63046	300
P347SHSP	400
B3047, Christmas tree	500

P3047 400

G347LP, green swirl, rare, W.R. Case & Sons,
Made in U.S.A, U.S. back tang 600

3247J 500

3347SHSPLP 400

3347SHPEN 400

04247SP 300

43047 300

5247J 700

05247SP 500

5347SHPEN 300

53047 450

5447SHSP 500

5447SPPU 450

6247J 500

06247PEN 250

06247SP 250

6347SHPEN 400

6347SHPU 400

6347PUPEN 400

6347LP, W.R. Case, Rogers bone 600

6347PUJ 600

6347SHSP 400

63047 500

630047 400

630047PU 400

64047PU 500

64047PU, Rogers bone 600

8347SHSP 1,000

83047 1,000

9347SHSPCI 400

9347SHSP, onyx 400

9347PJ 700

93047 400

94047PU 600

P348, green swirl 600

B1048, Christmas tree 350

G1048 300

R1048 300

B1048, onyx 300

B2048, Christmas tree 400

B2048SP, Christmas tree 400

G2048 300

G2048S 300

R2048 400

R2048SP, candy stripe 400

61048 250

62048SP 300

B249, onyx 400

BM249, mottled 400

R1049L, candy stripe 700

R2049, candy stripe 400

61049 300

61049L 600

6249 600

62049 400

B10050, flat blade, Christmas tree 900

CB1050SAB, Christmas tree 900

C31050SAB 650

C51050SAB 900

610050, flat 650

61050, flat 550

C61050, flat blade, switch blade, "zipper"
release 3,000

C61050, flat 650

C61050SAB 550

C61050SAB, lock blade 2,500

C91050SAB 650

M250, nickel silver 900

5250, Case Bros. 2,000

6250, bone, Case Bros. 1,500

6250 1,500

7250, Case Bros. 2,000

8250 3,000

R251, candy stripe 800

B1051, Christmas tree 400

G1051 300

R1051, candy stripe 400

R1051, lock-back candy stripe 500

2251, Sunfish, ebony, Case Bros. 1,500

31051L 600

5251, Sunfish, Case Bros. 2,000

6151 700

6151, lock back 750

61051 350

61051, Rogers bone 400

61051, lock back 450

6251 700

6351, Springville 3,000

8151L 2,500

81051 400

8251, knife-fork comb., (pearl) 2,500

9151, onyx 650

8152 300

P2052 400

3252, knife-fork comb. 500

32052	300
3452	500
52052	400
6252, knife-fork comb.	400
62052	400
63052, Wh.	1,200
6452	600
64052	1,200
84052, Case Bros.	1,500
G253, shad.	200
HA253	400
5253	250
6253	200
62053	200
6353	300
6353PU	300
8253	300
82053, bolsters	300
82053SR	250
9253	200
2254	400
5254, genuine stag, 3", Case Bros.	1,000
5354, genuine stag, 3", Case Bros.	400
6254, bone, 3", Case Bros.	3,000
6254, Wharncliffe, (not trapper)	350
6354, bone, 3", Case Bros.	400
8254, pearl, round, 3", Case Bros.	300
P254, round	300
82054, lobster	225
P254, lobster, W.R. Case	225
8354, pearl, lobster, 3", Case Bros.	400
22055	300
23055	450
23055PU	450
32055	300
5355, Whittler-Wharncliffe, Case Bros.	900
6255, bone, 3-3/4", Case Bro.	400
62055	250
6355, Whittler-Wharncliffe, Case Bros.	600
63055	450
64055PU	800
82055	400
8355, Whittler-Wharncliffe, Case Bros.	900
92055	300
62056, swell center	300
62056, swell center, Rogers bone	250
2356	600
6356SAB, Whittler, Case Bros.	700
63056, Whittler	600
8256, pearl 3-3/4 Case Bros.	400
82056	300
8356SAB, Whittler, Case Bros.	700
83056	400
4257	150
42057	150
5257LP, Case Bros.	225
6257LP, Case Bros.	225
7257, pyralin, 3", Case Bros.	250
8257	250
92057	150
2258, Case Bros. Cut. Co.	250
32058	200
5358, genuine stag, 2-7/8", Case Bros.	400
6258, Case Mfg.	275
6358, bone, 2-7/8", Case Bros.	350
7258, shell, 2-7/8", Case Bros.	250
7358, shell, 2-7/8", Case Bros.	400
8258	250
8358, Whittler, Case Bros.	400
92058	200
P259	300
62059	200
62059SP	200
8259	300
5260	300
5260, red stag	350
8460, W. R. Case & Son	600
3361, K Case Bros.	250
5161L, Springer	1,600
5161L, flat blade	1,600
5361K, Case Bros.	250
6161L, Springer	1,600
8261	200
8361K, Case Bros.	400
1162LP, Case Bros.	150
Y4062K, shad.	400
82062K	300
8362, lobster, Case Bros.	225
83062K	300
84062K	400
94062K	350
P263	225
B2063, Christmas tree	300
B3063, Christmas tree	350
05263, non stainless	200
62063, non stainless	200

06263, non stainless	200
62063-1/2, non stainless	200
63063	400
08263	300
8363	300
82063-1/2	250
83063	400
92063-1/2	200
3264, pyralin, 3", Case Bros.	200
6264	200
6264F	250
62064	200
8264, lobster, Case Bros.	200
8264T	300
8264T, file	300
82064	250
9264T, file	250
8464F	500
G265	600
3165SAB	500
3165, flat	500
3265SAB	450
5165SAB	325
5165, flat	400
5265SAB	450
5265, flat	500
6165SAB	400
6165, flat	500
6265SAB	450
6265, flat	500
9165SAB	500
9165, flat	500
9265SAB	500
9265, flat	500
6166L, switchblade	4,000
6366	300
6366PEN	300
8366PEN, pearl	400
B3067, Christmas tree	400
62067	200
06267	250
6367	400
63067F, Wh.	500
82067	300
08267	300
8367	450
63067, file, Case Bradford, PA	450
83067, Case Bradford, PA	450
9367	400
52068, slant bolsters, congress	600
6268, slant bolsters, congress	600
6368, Wh., congress	1,200
8268, slant bolsters, congress	600
8368, Whittler-pearl	1,200
84068, Case Bros.	1,200
54068, W.R. Case	1,200
G2069	225
6269	225
6369	400
8269	400
8369	600
9269	200
2370, ebony, 3-1/2", Case Bros.	1,200
5370, sleeveboard, Whittler	1,500
6370, Rogers bone	1,500
6370F	500
6470F	500
8370F	500
5171L, Springer	2,500
8271	300
8371, Wh.	700
5172L, "zipper" switchblade	4,500
6172L, "zipper" switchblade	6,000
5172L, red stag	6,500
5172, Case, Brad. Pa.	1,500
6172, clasp	1,600
6272, bone, 2-7/8", Case Bros.	200
8272, Case Bros.	250
6273, Case Bros.	250
8273, Case Bros.	250
22074-1/2PU	300
B3074, Christmas tree	400
B3074-1/2, Christmas tree	400
B3074-1/2PU, Christmas tree	400
5374	350
62074-1/2	250
63074, Rogers bone	550
63074-1/2	325
63074-1/2PU	325
83074	400
G375	400
5275SP, stag	600
5375	600
6275SP, Rogers	600
06275-1/2	300
6375	600

2376-1/2 500

5376-1/2 600

6276-1/2 300

06276, oval Tested XX 250

06276-1/2 225

6376 500

6376-1/2 500

63076, Whittler (rare), large sleeveboard 1,800

4277 200

7277, shell, 3-1/4", Case Bros. 250

8277 250

8377, pearl, 3-1/4", Case Bros. 350

1278, cocoa, 3-1/4", Case Bros. 200

2278, Case Bros. 250

2378, ebony, 3-1/4", Case Bros. 275

5278, Case Bros. 225

5378, genuine stag, 3-1/4", Case Bros. 325

6278T 200

6278, Case Bros. 250

7278, Case Bros., tortoiseshell 300

7378, shell, 3-1/4", Case Bros. 325

8278, Case Bros. 250

8378, pearl, 3-1/4", Case Bros. 325

2279 225

GM279 200

M279R 150

B3079, Wh., Christmas tree 550

RM3079, Case Mfg. Co. 550

3279 200

3279R 200

5279 200

6279, green bone 200

6279, Rogers bone 200

62079 200

62079-1/2 200

63079, Wh. W.R. Case & Sons, 3-3/8" 400

63079-1/2F, Wh. 400

7279, pyralin, 3-1/4", Case Bros. 250

8279, pearl, 3-1/4", Case Bros. 250

8279 200

82795 200

82079 200

82079-1/2 200

83079, Wh. 400

92079-1/2 200

P280, physician's knife 600

2280, Case Bros., physician's 600

3280, Case Bros., physician's 600

4280, Wh. pyralin, 3-3/4", Case Bros. 600

6280, physician 600

7280, shell, pyralin, 3-3/4", Case Bros. 850

8280, physician 800

G281, physician 600

6281, physician 600

64081, lobster, gunstock, file 400

8281, lobster, Case Bros. 200

83081, lobster 200

84081, lobster 250

9281, physician 600

6282, (physician), green bone 600

8282, lobster, Case Bros. 200

8282, (physician), pearl 700

BC283, physician 600

P383, Whittler 450

2383, Whittler 400

5383, Whittler 500

6383, Whittler 500

6383SAB, Whittler 600

63083, lobster 200

8383, Whittler 800

83083, lobster 200

9383, Whittler 600

B285, physician's, waterfall, spatula blade 800

B285, Christmas tree 800

G285, (physician's) 700

R285, candy stripe, physician's 700

B385, Whittler 700

3185, (physician's) 400

3285, (physician's) 600

3385, pyralin, 3-1/2", Case Bros. 450

5385, Whittler 700

6185, (physician's) 400

6285, (physician's) 700

6385, Whittler 500

8285, (physician's) 700

8385, Whittler 700

B2086, Christmas tree 500

G2086, gold stone 500

B2086, Christmas tree, physician's 600

G2086, gold stone, physician's 400

M2086, physician's 500

52086, (physician's) 500

62086, (physician's) 600

82086, (physician's) 500

5287, gunstock 500

5387, gunstock Whittler 800

8387, gunstock-pearl	1,000
5488F, Case Bros.	10,000
5488	7,500
6288, Congress	1,200
6288, bone, 3-3/8", Case Bros.	1,200
6388, bone, 3-3/8", Case Bros.	1,500
6388, Whittler	2,000
5388	2,000
6488LP	2,000
7488F, Case Bros.	7,500
83088, lobster	300
8488F, Case Bros.	7,500
6289, Wharncliffe, Congress	650
62089, W.R. Case & Sons, Congress	400
83089	300
8389, covered backsprings	350
84089SCISF, (Bradford, Germany)	350
B490R, Christmas tree	500
M2090R	200
2290, ebony, 3-1/4", Case Bros.	225
6290, bone, 3-1/4", Case Bros.	250
6390, bone, 3-1/4", Case Bros.	350
63090, Whittler	500
6490R	300
640090R	300
8290, genuine stag, 3-3/4", Case Bros.	300
8390	400
83090SCIS	225
Y3091F	225
GM3091	175
GM3091R	175
5391, Whittler	3,000
5391, Whittler, (2 pulls), file	3,300
82091F	250
83091	250
2392, ebony, 3-3/4", Case Bros.	400
3292	350
33092	350
5292	400
5392, genuine stag, 3-3/4", Case Bros.	600
6292	300
6592, (5 blade)	3,000
5292, Case Bros., 1/2 Whittler	400
6292, Case Bros., 1/2 Whittler	400
2292, Case Bros., 1/2 Whittler	350
6392, bone, 3-3/4", Case Bros.	450
6392	400
6392PU	450
630092	400
630092PU	400
6392-1/2, Whittler	1,200
B1093, Christmas tree	450
B1093, barn-door hinge	600
G1093	400
R1093, candy stripe	400
HA1093, high art	600
61093	400
32093F	300
5293LP	400
6293	250
62093F	250
B393, Christmas tree	600
H393, mottled	500
4393	400
5393	600
6393	600
6393R	600
6393PEN	600
9393	600
93093	450
05294	400
GS1094, gold stone	400
61094T/P, Rogers bone	400
R1094T/P, candy stripe	400
6294LP	450
6294LP, Rogers bone	700
6294LP, flat bolsters, Rogers bone	1,500
6294J	900
5394, gun boat	2,000
6394, gun boat	2,000
6394, Rogers bone	2,000
B1095, Christmas tree	450
B1095, waterfall	450
GS1095SAB	450
G1095	400
HA1095, high art	600
R1095, candy stripe	450
31095	350
61095	350
61095, Rogers bone	400
B2095F	300
32095F	300
5395	650
R2096, candy stripe	400
6296	400
B396, Whittler, 3 blade	400

CASE SHEATH KNIVES

This sheath section is made possible by the following collector:

Elmer Kirkland is an avid knife collector living in Florida. He is a member of NKCA and FKCA. Elmer specializes in collecting Case knives and memorabilia.

Elmer Kirkland

Top: 5FINN, second-cut stag, around 1965, 7-7/8", very scarce, Case XX, U.S.A.; $125. Bottom: 516-5, second-cut stag, 9", 1965-66, very scarce, Case XX, U.S.A.; $125.

Stag, Kodiak Hunter, chrome, 11", Case XX, U.S.A; $125.

Top: 5361, Scout on back tang, split stag round butt, 8-1/2", Case Tested XX; $150. Middle: 5324-4-1/2, Cody stamped back tang, split stag, heavy saber, round butt, black and red spacers, Case tested XX; $200. Bottom: Leather washer, iron butt, military case, M3, 11-1/4"; $75.

From the top: 561, stag, flat blade, 7-1/2", Case XX; $90. 516-5, stag, Case, Big C, disc. early '40s, 9"; $65. 564, stag slabs, saber blade, 8", Case XX; $150. Green bone, back tang stamped King Fisher, 8-3/4", Case Stainless; $150.

Top: 600, green bone, fish scaler, 8-3/8", disc. mid-40s, Case stainless script; $125. Middle: Green bone, stainless back tang, 8-7/8", Case Tested XX; $125. Bottom: Green bone, fish scaler, 8-7/8", Case Stainless; $125.

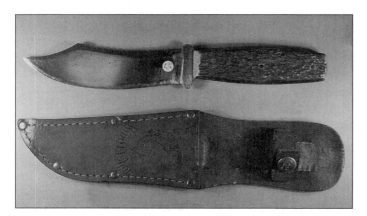

700, Rogers bone, fish knife, note sheath marked king-fisher; $150.

Bowie Hunters, Case, 8-3/4": Top: Green bone, "Boone" on back tang; $250. Bottom: Mottled green with brown; $250. Small long tail C Stamp. Photo courtesy Wayne Robertson.

From the top: 600, green bone, fish scaler, 8-3/8", Case XX, disc. '40s; $125. Kinfolks, U.S.A., same as Case 700, fish knife, wood, 8-7/8"; $35. 700, wood, fish knife, disc. late '50s, 8-3/8", Case XX; $65. Rogers bone, Case's Stainless, fish knife, 8-5/8", Case's Tested XX; $150.

Top: Rogers bone, small Bowie style, 8-3/4", Case, Brad., PA., Case's Tested XX; $200. Bottom: Rogers bone, med. Bowie, back tang, 10", Case Tested XX, W.R. Case & Sons, Brad., PA; $250.

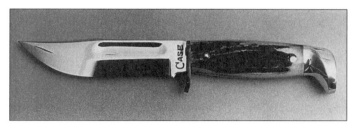

557, saber, Case Big C, stag, 8"; $90.

From the top: M5F, stag, disc. 1964, Case XX; $55. M5F, stag, scarce stamp, 6-1/8", Case XX, Stainless; $65. 557, flat blade, split N.S. bolsters, grooved stag, Case Tested XX; $125. 657, green bone, tapered butt, 6-3/4", Case Tested XX; $150.

Top: 13F, walnut, has been on board, (rare), 6-1/2", Case Big C on stamp; $60. Middle: One-arm man knife and fork combo., pakkawood, Case XX, (made for war veterans who lost an arm); $100. Bottom: 18, Hawkbill carpet-cutting tool, wood, 7-1/2", Case XX; $40.

From the top: RM57, green pearl celluloid, round butt, 6-7/8", Case XX; $125. Kinfolks, U.S.A., same as Case 652-5, Rogers bone; $65. 208-5, flat blade, hard rubber, no logo, 9-1/2", Case XX; $60. E23-5, mottled pearl and greenish-gray handle, round butt, 9-1/4", Case XX; $225.

From the top: 661, green bone, 7-1/2", Case Tested XX; $75. 652-5, green bone, flat blade, Guard; $125. 652-5, green bone, N.S. bolsters, stamped Case Tested XX; $125. 652-5, green bone, N.S. bolsters, stamped saber blade, Tested XX; $125.

557, round butt, stag, 7-7/8", Case XX; $90.

557, stag, disc. 1966, 7-7/8", Case XX, USA; $90.

5361, round reg. butt, stag, disc. about 1950, Case XX, stag, 8-1/2"; $90

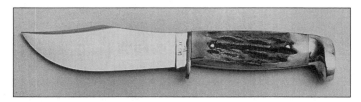

5361, reg. butt, disc. 1966, stag, 8-1/2", Case XX, U.S.A.; $90.

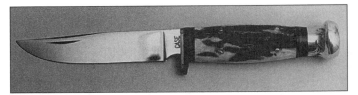

515-4, very early, split stag with spacers, round butt, 1940, (rare), 7-1/2", Case XX; $150.

5325-6, split stag, spacers, round butt, possibly 1935 era, 10-1/2", Tested XX, W.R. Case & Sons, Brad., PA; $400.

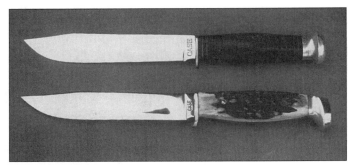

Top: Case, 10-1/4" OA, black, red, brass spacers 3352-6; $100. Bottom: Case 10-3/8" stag, 5325-6; $135. Photo courtesy Wayne Robertson.

From the top: Unknown, cracked ice, black spacers, N.S. bolsters, round butt, 7-1/2", Case's Tested XX; $125. 352-5, yellow celluloid, 9", Case XX; $125. Kinfolks, U.S.A., same as Case 661-4", number 6161, Rogers bone, 7-5/8"; $65. RM52-5, blue mottled pearl, celluloid, 9", Case XX; $200.

6025-5, second-cut groove bone, pinned, round butt, around 1940, 9-1/4", Case XX; $175.

Slab, 8-1/8" OA, imitation pearl handles; $125. Photo courtesy Wayne Robertson.

523-5, stag, Case XX, disc. 1964, 9-1/4"; $75.

523-5, stag, Case XX, U.S.A., disc. 1973, 9-1/4"; $75.

523-5, thin stag, slabs, light etched stamp, square butt, Case XX, disc. about 1950, rare, 9-1/8"; $90.

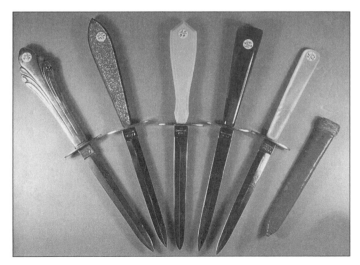

Case ladies dirks; ladies double-edge garter knives; five different handle materials; ruby red celluloid out of John O'Kain Collection. Three different stamps: Case Bradford, W.R. Case, and Tested.

From the top: Double edge garter knife, mingled celluloid handle, rare, Case, Brad., PA; $400. Double edge garter knife, genuine pearl handle, W.R. Case & Sons, Brad., PA; $400. Double edge garter knife, stag handle, silver ferrel, rare, W.R. Case & Sons, Brad., PA; $350. Double edge garter knife, ivory handle, rare, 7-1/2", Case Brad., PA; $350. Ladies gartner knife, double edge gold stone handles, (rare), 7-3/8", Case Brad., PA; $400. Double edge ladies of the night gartner knife, 7-5/8", yellow celluloid handles, Case's Brad., PA, (rare); $400.

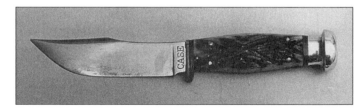

5362, split, second-cut stag, round butt, disc. about 1940, 8-5/8", Case XX; $175.

5300, stainless, (lighting S), round stag, 1981 only, 9-3/4", Case XX, U.S.A., 2,000 made; $65.

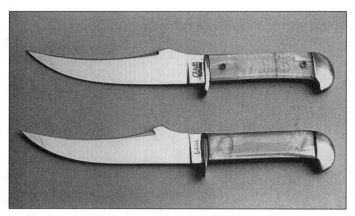

Top: Midget, cracked-ice handle, rare, 5-1/4", Case Tested XX; $175. Bottom: Case midget, imitation pearl celluloid, rare, blade 2-7/8", 5"; $175.

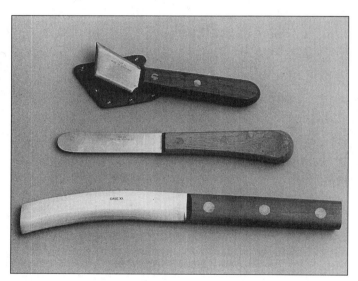

Top: 775, fish knife and sheath, disc. 1950, Case XX, Stainless; $45, Middle: 233-6, black composition, disc. 1988, 10-1/4", Case XX, U.S.A.; $45. Bottom: Unknown, wood, birds-eye rivets, 10-1/2", Case XX; $45.

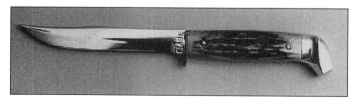

Stag, square butt, Case, Big C, 5 Finn, 7-3/4",1940 era; $95.

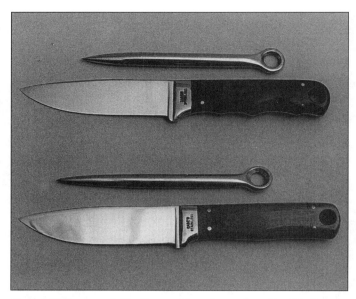

Top: 147, Lanyard, Marling spike, ebony handle, 8", Case's Stainless; $75. Bottom: 147, walnut handle, Lanyard hole, Marlin spike, 8", Case's Stainless; $65.

Stag, square butt, 5 Finn, Case XX, disc. about 1950, 7-7/8"; $60.

From the top: 661, green bone, 7-1/4", script Case stainless; $90. Unknown, Rogers bone, 8", Case's Tested XX; $225. 208-5, flat blade, hard rubber checkered handle, 9-1/2", Case XX; $60. Unknown, Rogers bone, 8-1/4", Case Brad., PA, back tang, Case's Tested XX; $300.

Bowie, Backside Pheasant etched. Value? Ralph Scruton Collection.

From the top: Kinfolks, Inc., like Case 67-5 pattern, greenish swirl handle, 7-5/8"; $60. RM361, mottled pearl and brown swirl handles, round butt, 9-3/4", Case XX; $225. Amber handle with guard, red, black, brass and bone spacers, brass butt, 9-1/8", Jean Case Cut. Co., Little Valley, NY; $200. B325-5, waterfall handles, round butt, 9-1/2", Case XX; $300.

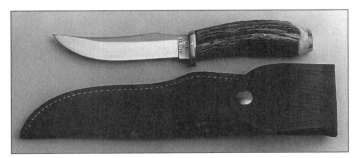

5400, Stainless (lighting S), round stag, 1981 only, 9-1/2", Case XX, USA., 2,000 made; $65.

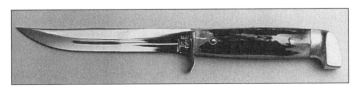

Stag, Stainless, 5 Finn, Case XX, mid-'40s, 7-7/8", rare; $95.

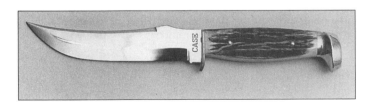

523-6, stag, Case XX, disc. 1964, 10-1/4"; $80.

523-6, stag, Case XX, U.S.A., disc. 1970, 10-1/4"; $80.

From the top: 361-4-1/2, walnut handle, round butt, 8-3/4", Case XX; $125. 3361-4-1/2, leather, round butt, 8-3/4", Case (script); $75. 67, green bone, disc. about 1950, blade 4", Case XX, 7-3/4"; $110. Stag, saber blade, butt cap, unknown pattern, 9-1/4", Case XX; $225.

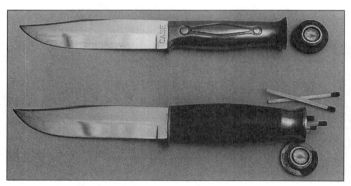

Top: 709, aluminum handle, hollow with match container and compass in cap, 9", Case XX; $150. Bottom: 365, hollow leather handle, match container with compass in cap, 9-1/2", Case XX; $150.

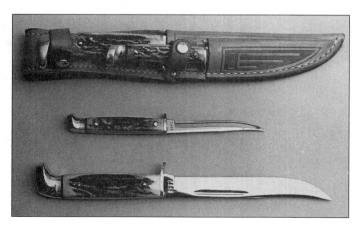

Top: R503SSP, pakkawood handle, no etch, Arapaho or Indian, Case, 8-1/4"; $50. Middle: Desert Prince, pakka-wood handle, 10-1/2", Case XX, U.S.A., 1980s; $50. Bottom: Caribou skinner, pakkawood handle, disc. about 1985, Case XX, U.S.A; $125.

Stag, piggy-back leather, sheath, Twin Finn Set, Case XX, disc. 1964; 516-5 is 9" and M5F, 1964, is 6-1/4". The set; $150.

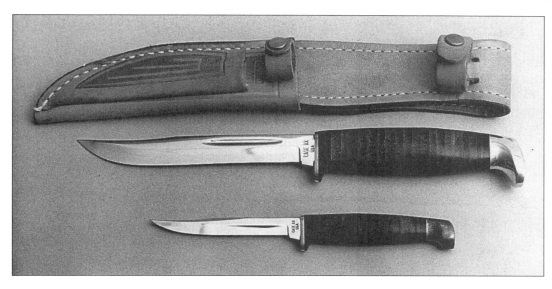

316-5 & M3F, 3 Twin Finn Piggy Back Set, leather handles, double sheath, disc. 1973, Case XX, U.S.A.; $90.

From the top: Unknown, mingled celluloid, black, green, and pink, 5-3/8", Case XX; $100. M3FSSP, leather, scalloped edge, 1982 (miracle edge), Case XX, U.S.A.; $90. Leather, same as Case No. 315, 7-3/4", Jean Case Cut. Co., Little Valley, NY; $45. 3 Finn, leather, 7-3/4", Case Big C; $55.

5325-6, stag, Case XX, U.S.A., reg. butt, disc. 1965, 10-1/2"; $150.

516-5, stag, square butt, Case XX, disc. about 1950, 9"; $65.

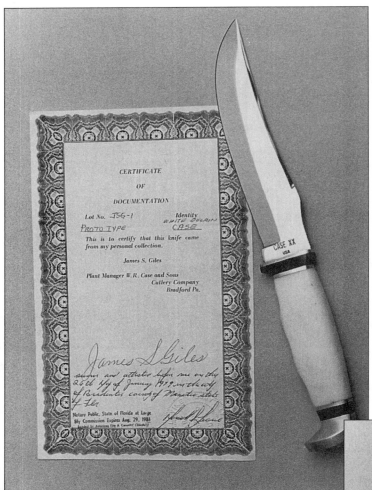

JSG-1, prototype, white delrin, Case XX, U.S.A. (same blade as 233-6), one of a kind, 10-1/4". Jim Sargent Collection.

JSG-2, prototype, white delrin, Case XX, U.S.A., one of a kind, 10-1/4". Jim Sargent Collection.

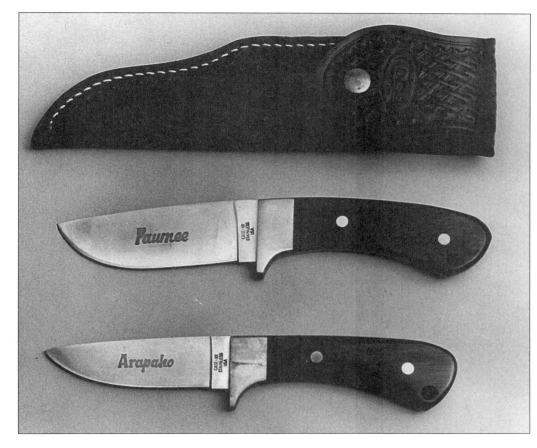

Top: R603SSP, Pawnee, brown pakkawood, fold-over sheath, disc. 1984, Case, 9"; $50. **Bottom:** R503SSP, Arapaho, brown pakkawood, fold-over sheath, disc. 1984, Case, 8-1/2"; $50.

516-5, stag, reg. butt, disc. 1973, Case XX, U.S.A.; $65.

Two Finn, black composition, disc. 1988, 8-1/2", Case XX, U.S.A.; $40.

M5F, stag, (bird knife), disc. 1973, Case XX, U.S.A., 6-1/4"; $50.

223-5, black composition, disc. 1988, 9-1/2", Case XX, U.S.A.; $50.

523-3-1/4, stag, small game, disc. 1964, Case XX, 6-1/4"; $65.

1300-3-1/2", Stainless, wood, discontinued, Case XX; $45.

523-3-1/4, stag, small game, disc. 1969, 6-1/4", Case XX, U.S.A.; $65.

516-5, leather, square butt, disc. 1964, 9", Case XX; $40.

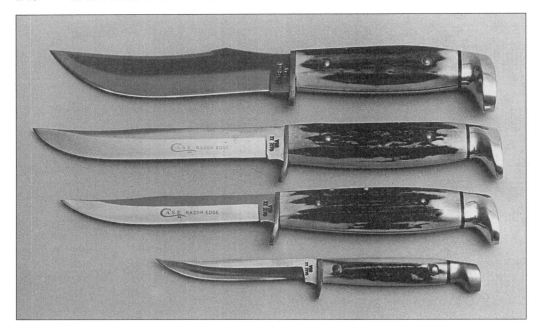

Case Stainless, 4 dot, 1976, stag set 523-5SSP, 516-5SSP, 5 Finn SSP, M5F SSP, gray etch, made 1976 only, (the four); $200. A. Same set of 4 in blue scroll, 1977 only; $200. B. Same set of 4 in red etch, 1978 only; $200. C. Same set of 4 in Bradford, Cent., 1979 only; $200.

3362, leather, round butt, disc. about 1950, 8-3/4", Case XX; $60.

325-6 (3325-6), leather, disc. about 1966, 10-1/2", Case XX, U.S.A.; $90.

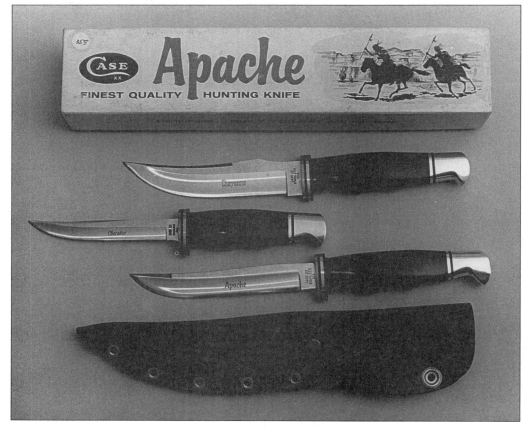

Top: Cheyenne, black composition, disc. 1979, 9-3/4", Case XX, U.S.A.; $50. Middle: Apache, black composition, disc. 1979, 10", Case XX, U.S.A.; $50. Bottom: Cherokee, black composition, disc. 1979, 8-3/8", Case XX, U.S.A.; $50.

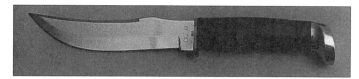

323-5, leather, disc. 1988, 9", Case XX, U.S.A.; $45.

(3323-5), leather, disc. about 1966, 9", Case XX, U.S.A.; $60.

323-6, leather, disc. about 1975, 10-1/2", Case XX, U.S.A. (note the difference between 3325-6); $45.

315-4, leather, round butt, disc. about 1950, 7-3/4", Case XX; $35.

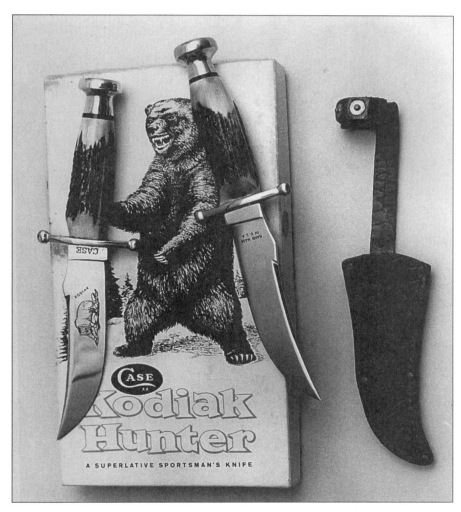

Kodiak Hunter, stag, brass guard and butt, 10-3/4", alligator sheath, Case XX; $150.

315-4-3/4", leather round butt, 9", disc. about 1950, Case XX; $40.

Leather, color spacers, round butt, disc. 1940, 7-3/4", Case Tested XX; $75.

523-3-1/4", brushed stainless, stag, etched blade, disc. in colorful small game box, 1988, 7", Case; $65. Current model 523-3-1/4SSP; $45.

(3323-5), 323-5, leather, round butt, disc. 1950, 9", Case XX; $60.

365SAB, leather, round butt, 9", disc. about 1950, Case XX; $55.

366, leather, disc. 1967, (handle 4-1/4"), 8-1/4", Case XX, U.S.A.; $30.

366, leather, disc. 1967, (handle 4-1/4"), 8-1/4", Case XX, U.S.A.; $30.

3, Finn, leather, square butt, disc. about 1950, Case XX; $30.

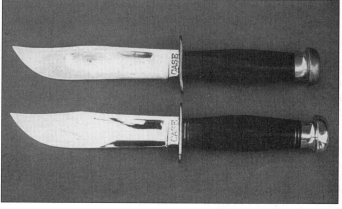

Top: Case 9-1/8", black and red spacers; $75. Bottom: Case 9-1/4", black, red and brass spacers, patterns unknown; $75. Photo courtesy Wayne Robertson.

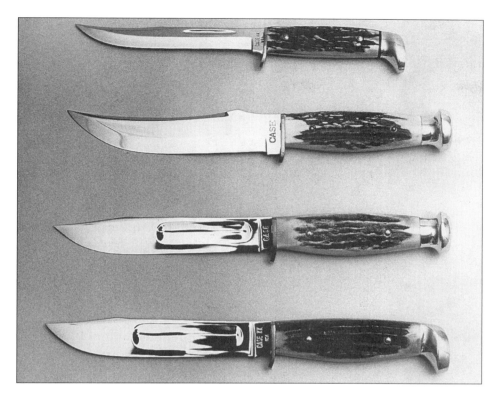

From the top: 516-5, stag, 9", Case XX, U.S.A.;$60. 523-6, stag, round butt, 10-1/4", Case XX; $80. 5325-6, stag, round butt, disc. about 1950, 10-1/2", Case XX; $135. 5325-6, stag, blood groove, 10-1/4", Case XX, U.S.A.; $135.

5 Finn, stainless, leather, square butt, made about 1945-46, polished stainless, 8", Case XX; $65.

366, leather, round butt, (handle 3-5/8"), disc. about 1950, 7-3/4", Case XX; $35.

M3F, leather, stainless, (scarce), polished stainless, 6-1/4", Case XX; $45.

M3F, leather, disc. 1964, 6-1/4", Case XX; $35.

M3FSSP, leather, current, 6-1/4", Case XX, U.S.A.; $30.

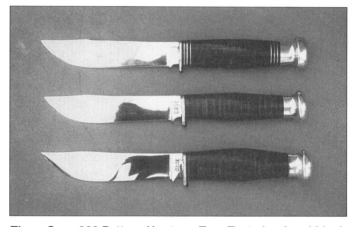

Three Case 366 Pattern Hunters: Top: Tested red and black and MSL spacers; $75. Middle: Case Large Stamp, red and black; $45. Bottom: Case Small Stamp, red and black; $45. Photo courtesy Wayne Robertson.

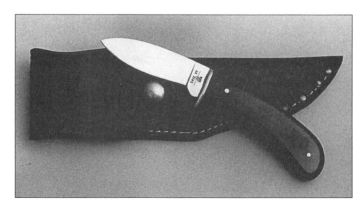

P51SSP, Li'l Devil, dark pakkawood, fold-over sheath, disc. 1982, 6-1/4", Case; $45.

From the top: 652-5, green bone, saber blade, disc. early '50s, 8-3/4", Case XX; $125. 652-6, green bone, saber blade, Case, Brad., PA (bolsters stamp); $150. Green bone, sticker, double-edge, 10-1/2", Case XX; $300. 652, Rogers bone, 9-1/4", Case's Tested XX, Case, Brad., Pa.; $200.

652-5, one green bone, one Rogers bone, Cento stamped back tang on both, Case Tested XX; $125.

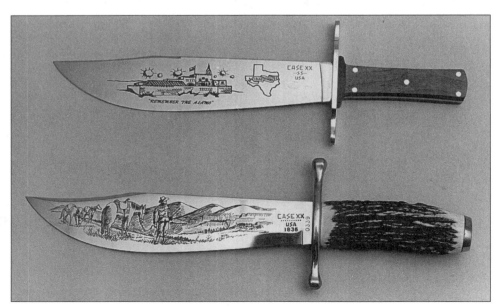

Wood, Hardwood box: Top: Case Alamo Bowie, 13-7/8", mint; $150. Bottom: Stag, Case Wildwest and Plaque (Cowboy), Bowie, 14-1/2"; $200.

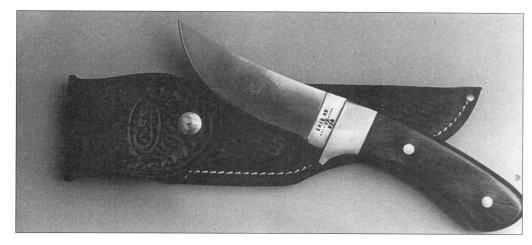

703SSP, Kiowa, brown pakka-wood, fold-over sheath, disc. 1984, Case, 9-1/4"; $50.

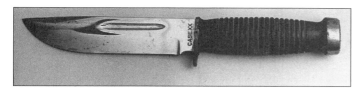

337-6Q, leather, round-checked iron butt, military, 11"; $100.

Rogers bone, Bowie, 7" blade, 11" overall, very rare, W.R. Case & Sons, Bradford, PA, Case's Tested XX; $500.

Stag, Case Mason & Dixon Series, Bowies and Plaque, 14-1/4"; $200.

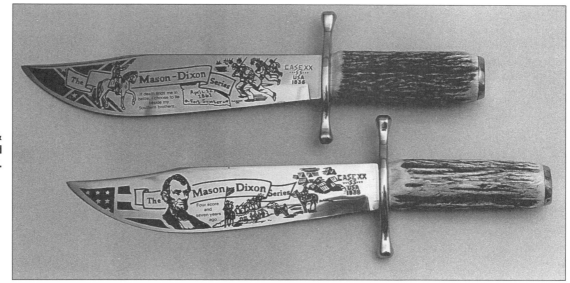

652-5, red bone, sabler blade, disc. about 1960, 8-3/4", Case XX; $125.

3325-6, leather with black plastic butt, WW II, military N.S. Guard, Case Big C; $300.

278-2-3/4, chromium-finished blade, bone stag, disc., rare, Case XX; $125.

362-5, round butt, red with red, black and brass spacers, disc. in '20s, Case, Brad., PA, Case Tested XX; $150.

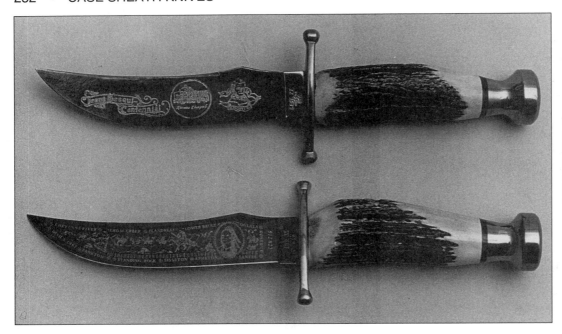

Top: Texas Sesquicentennial, proto, stag, Kodiak, hunter, etched, 10-3/4"; $250. Bottom: Chief Crazy Horse, Kodiak, stag, blue blade, gold etched, Case, 10-7/8"; $350.

362-4-1/2, leather with aluminum spacers, round butt, disc. about 1940, Case Tested XX; $125.

BM57SAB, mottled celluloid, round butt, rare, 7", Case; $150.

3325-6, Carson (back tang), leather with red, black and brass spacers, round butt; $125.

557, flat, stag slabs, round two-piece N.S. butt, rare, disc. about 1945, 7"; $150.

964, greenish imitation pearl celluloid, early '30s, 8", Case Tested XX; $150.

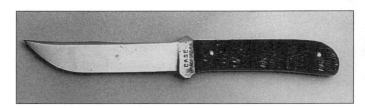

161, green bone, 7-1/2", Case Bradford, PA, Case's Tested XX; $100.

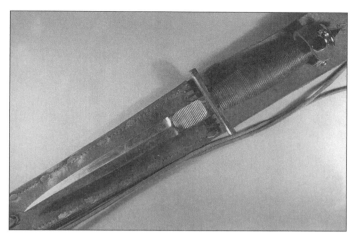

V-42, Case original with sheath, U.S. Gov. would not accept, early 1940s, Chromed Plated; $2,200.

666-4, early brown Rogers bone, 7-1/2", Case Tested XX; $125.

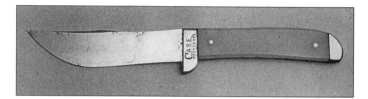

366-4, early yellow celluloid, 7-1/2", Case Tested XX; $125.

V-42, American and Canadian, comm., 1 blue blade, 1 polished finish, leather handles, thumb rest, 12-3/8"; $200.

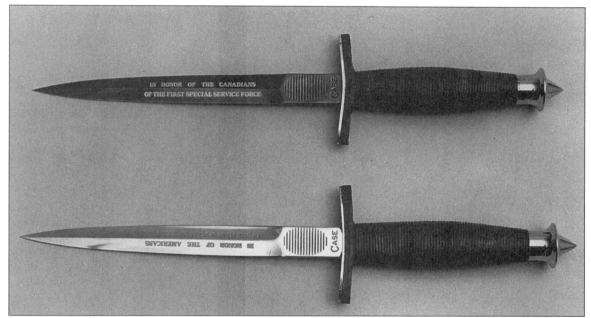

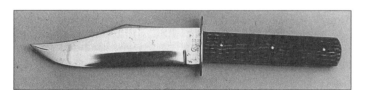

Green bone, small Bowie-type saber, 9", Case Tested XX; $250.

Case Kodiak with experimental handle, purchased from John Osborne Jr. Value? Ralph Scruton Collection.

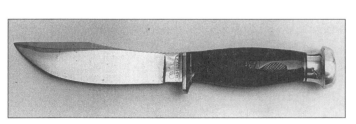

262-5, hard black composition, checkered with logo, round butt, 1940, Case Tested XX; $150.

Case XX, double edge blade, 10-1/2" overall, walnut handle; $200. Photo courtesy Wayne Robertson.

Top: 303, throwing knife, red micarti, 7-7/8", disc. about 1980, Case XX; $30. Bottom: 303, throwing knife, red miscarti, disc. about 1950, Case XX, Curly XXs; $45.

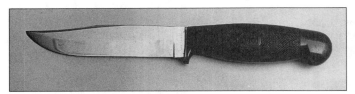

208-5SAB, hard rubber checkered handle with logo imprint, Case XX; $50.

208-6, flat, hard rubber checkered handle, 1940, back tang stamped Expert, Case Tested XX; $65.

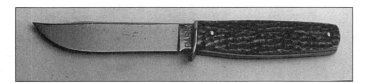

64, green bone, 8", disc. 1950, Case XX; $80.

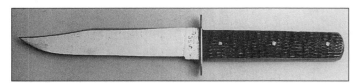

662, green bone, flat blade, 9", Case Brad., PA, Case' Tested XX; $125.

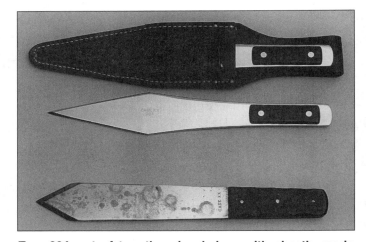

Top: 304, set of two throwing knives with sheath, made 1980 to around 1983, 12", Case XX; $150. Bottom: Barnum & Bailey Circus throwing knife, heavy professional type, 12", very scarce, Case XX; $150.

552SAB, stag slabs, scarce, Case XX; $150.

326-7, leather handle, with black plastic butt cap, polished blade, double edge, WW II very rare, mint in sheath; $800.

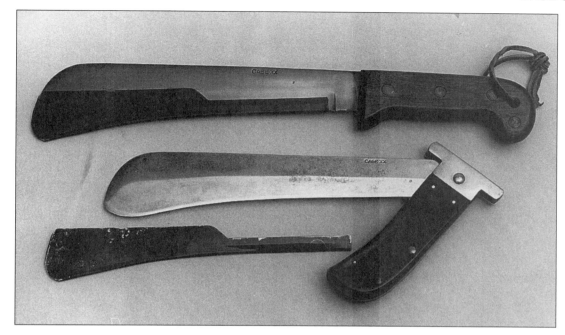

Top: WW II fixed machette with guard, wood, military specs., 15-1/2"; $125. Bottom: WW II machette, folding type with guard, black handle, military specs., 15-1/2", Case XX; $100.

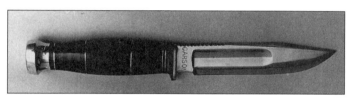

3325-5, Carson back tang, leather, red, black and brass spacers, round butt; $150.

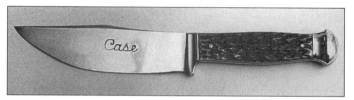

6361-5, Rogers bone, round N.S. split bolsters, Case script, (rare); $400.

663-5SAB, Rogers bone, tan, Case, Bradford, PA (stamp lower bolsters); $150.

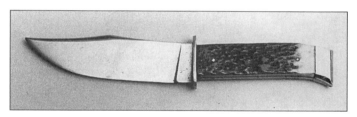

661, Rogers bone, flat N.S. bolsters, 8-1/4", W.R. Case & Sons, Brad., PA, Case Tested XX, (rare); $400.

663-5SAB, green bone, Case tested stamp back tang, 9-1/4", W.R. Case & Sons, Brad., PA; $125.

361-4-1/2, leather, round butt Case (stamped on aluminum guard only), 8-1/2"; $125.

3025-4-1/2, flat blade, leather, black, red and brass spacers, round butt, disc. 1920s, Brad., PA; $150.

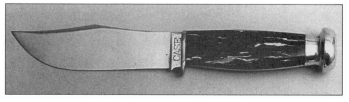

M361-4-1/2, mottled celluloid, round butt, 8-1/2", Case (rare); $200.

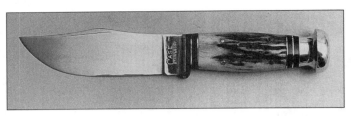

5361-4-1/2, stag slabs, red, black & brass spacers, round butt, 8-1/2", $200

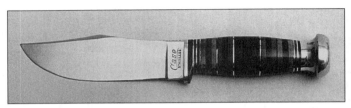

361-4-1/2, leather, black, red and brass spacers, round butt, 8-1/2", Case Tested stainless; $150.

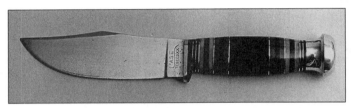

361-4-1/2, leather, black, red and brass and bone spacers, round butt, 8-1/2", back tang stamped Scout, Case Tested XX; $150.

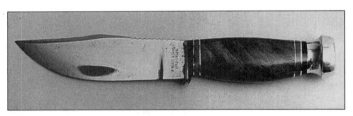

1361-4-1/2, walnut handle, round butt, 8-1/2", Tested Stamp Back Tang, W.R. Case & Sons, Brad., PA, oval; $150.

5361-4-1/2, split stag, round butt, 8-1/2", Case, Brad., PA, Case's Tested XX; $200.

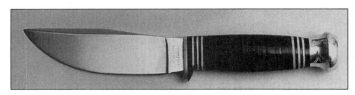

Leather, white and black spacers, 8-3/4", Jean Case Cut. Co., Little Valley, NY; $60.

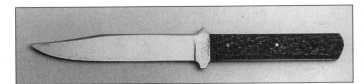

663-5, Rogers bone, same as Case, 9-1/4", Jean Case Cut. Co., Little Valley, NY; $75.

Leather, red, white, black and brass spacers, black plastic butt, Jean Case Cut. Co., Little Valley, NY; $85.

Yellow celluloid handles, flat blade, 9-1/4", Jean Case Cut. Co., Little Valley, NY; $60.

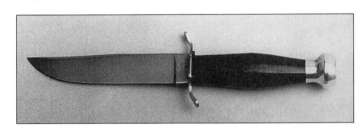

Leather, guard, round butt, 7-3/4", Jean Case Cut. Co., Little Valley, NY; $75.

Hard rubber, same as Case 208-5 with guard, 9-1/2", Jean Case Cut. Co., Little Valley, NY; $45.

Leather, black, red, white and brass spacers, round butt, 10", Jean Case Cut. Co., Little Valley, NY; $65.

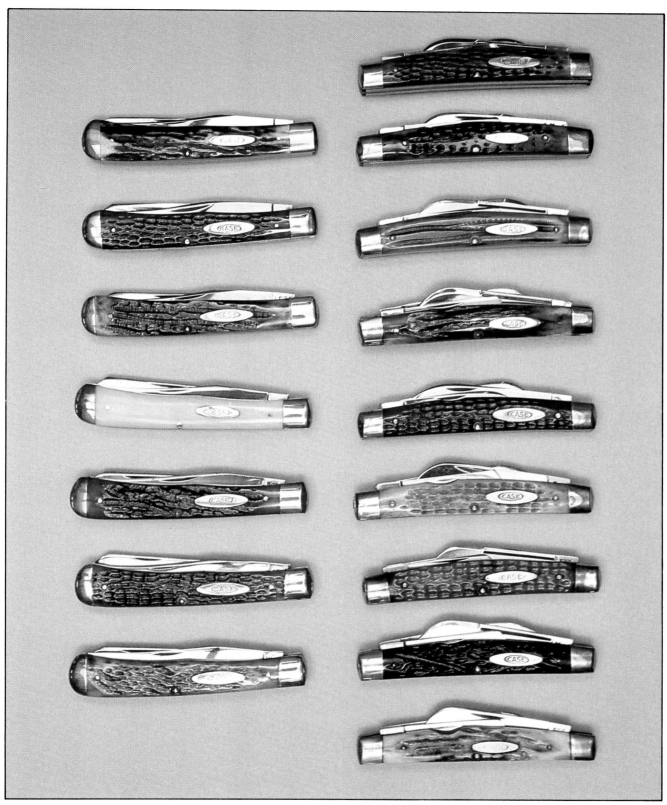

(left, top to botton)
CASE
#54 patterns Trappers...Genuine Stag, Red Bone, 2nd Cut Stag, Yellow Composition, Red Stag, Green Bone, Rogers Bone.

(right, top to bottom)
CASE
#88 patterns Congress...Green Bone, Bone, Winterbottom Bone, Genuine Stag, Red Bone, 2nd Cut Stag, Green Bone, Rough Black, Genuine White Stag.
Courtesy Joe Chance & Barney Hightower

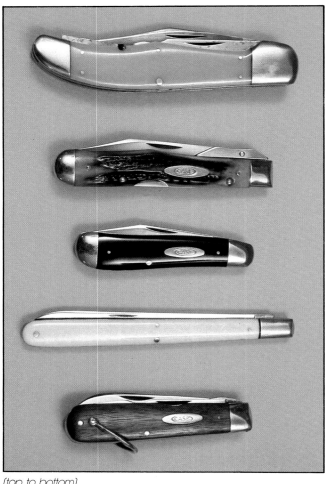

CASE
#A6250 Museum Founders Knife, Elephant
Toenail with Appaloosa handle. Shown is 1 of
set of 4.
Jim Sargent Collection

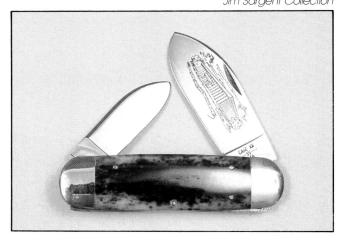

(top to bottom)
CASE
#3465 4 blade Folding Hunter (flat blade) with Yellow
Composition handle, #5111½ L Cheetah with Genuine
Stag handle, #22028 Dog Leg Jack with Black
Composition handle, #4100SS Citrus Knife with White
Composition handle, #12031LR Electrician's Knife with
Walnut handle.
Jim Sargent Collection

(top to bottom)
QUEEN
NKCA 10th Anniversary (1972-1982) with
emblem with Genuine Stag handle (1200
made), #58 Cokebottle with Red Imitation
Winterbottom Bone handle, #11 (knife shown
is upside down) Winterbottom Bone handle,
Serpentine Jack with Imitation Red
Winterbottom Bone handle.
Jim Sargent Collection

(top to bottom)
CASE
#6254SSP Trapper with Delrin handle,
#61011 Hawlbill with Pakkawood handle,
#6488 Congress with Bone handle.
Jim Sargent Collection

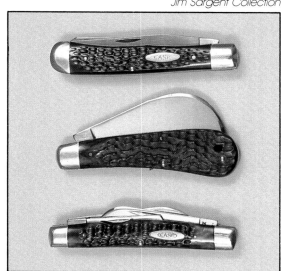

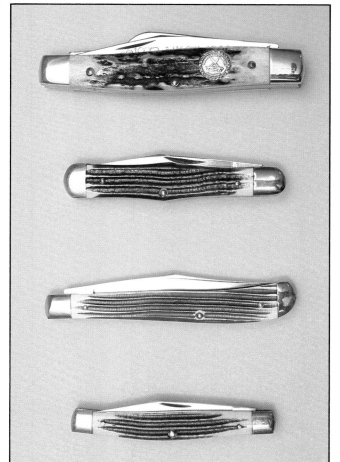

CASE
75th Anniversary of Case Cutlery Co. Canoe Set. #5394SSP, #53131SSP, #52131SSP...each one has the blade etched with one of Case's three factories and the factory date, engraved brass bolsters, Genuine Stag handles.

CASE
1976 Bi-Centennial Set...#523-7SS Double Eagle Hunting Knife with Genuine Stag handle (2500 made), #5165SSP Pocket Knife with Genuine Stag handle.

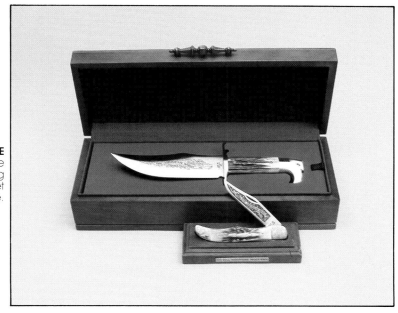

CASE
#W165 SAB SSP Moby Dick with Genuine Natural Bone scrimshawed with whaling scene, has brass liners and engraved nickel silver bolsters.

(top to bottom)
QUEEN
These Queens exhibit older handle materials. #35 small Serpentine with Rough Black handle, rare Q Stainless stamp, #15 Congress with Brown Rogers Bone, rare Q Stainless stamp, #20 Folding Outdoors Knife with Green Rogers Bone, rare Q Stainless stamp.

WINCHESTER
#1920 Folding Hunter (Cokebottle) with bone handle.
Jim Sargent Collection

(top to bottom)
REMINGTON
Teardrop Easy Opener Jack with Brass handle, Equal End Jack with Candy Stripe handle, Pruner with Imitation Ivory handle, Serpentine with Christmas Tree handle, Serpentine with Nickel Silver handle, Jack with Multi-Color handle, Serpentine Jack with Candy Stripe handle.
Jim Sargent Collection

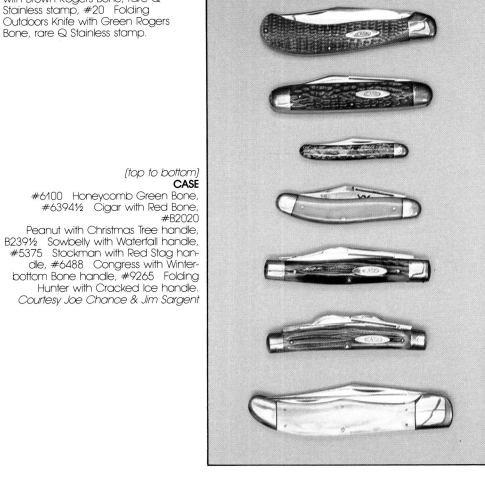
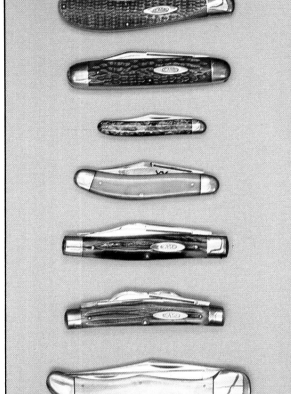
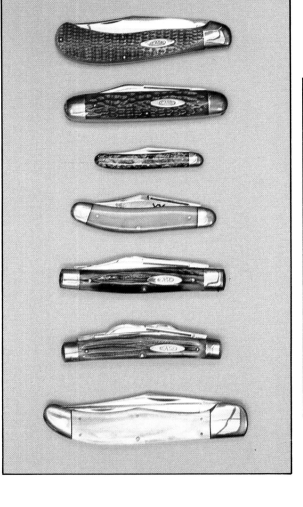

(top to bottom)
CASE
#6100 Honeycomb Green Bone, #6394½ Cigar with Red Bone, #B2020 Peanut with Christmas Tree handle, B239½ Sowbelly with Waterfall handle, #5375 Stockman with Red Stag handle, #6488 Congress with Winterbottom Bone handle, #9265 Folding Hunter with Cracked Ice handle.
Courtesy Joe Chance & Jim Sargent

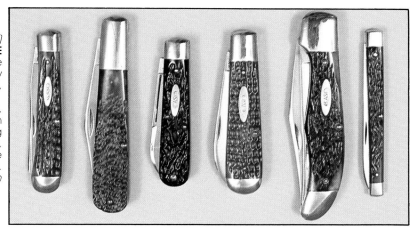

(left to right)
CASE
#6254 Trapper with 2nd Cut Bone handle, #6143 Prototype Daddy Barlow with Jigged Bone handle, #62031LP Jack with Rough Black, #6299 Teardrop Jack with Green Bone handle, #6265SAB Folding Hunter with Rogers Bone handle, #6296X Citrus Knife with Red Bone Handle.
Jim Sargent Collection

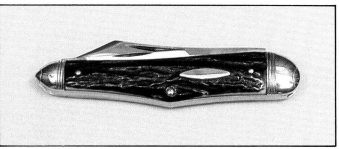

REMINGTON
#R6836 Humpback Whittler, Genuine Stag handle.
Jim Sargent Collection

WINCHESTER
Improved Muskrat with Bone handle.
Courtesy Joe Chance

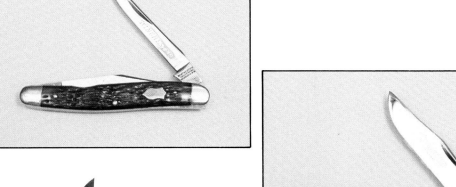

REMINGTON
#R4283 5 blade Sowbelly with Bone handle.
Jim Sargent Collection

(top to bottom)
QUEEN
These Queens exhibit older handle material. #9 Stockman's with Green Winterbottom Bone, rare Q Stainless stamp, #19 Heavy Duty Trapper with White & Brown Winterbottom Bone, rare satin finished blades, Q Steel stamp, #46 Folding Fishing Knife with rare, light brown winterbottom bone, blade etched (no tang stamp).

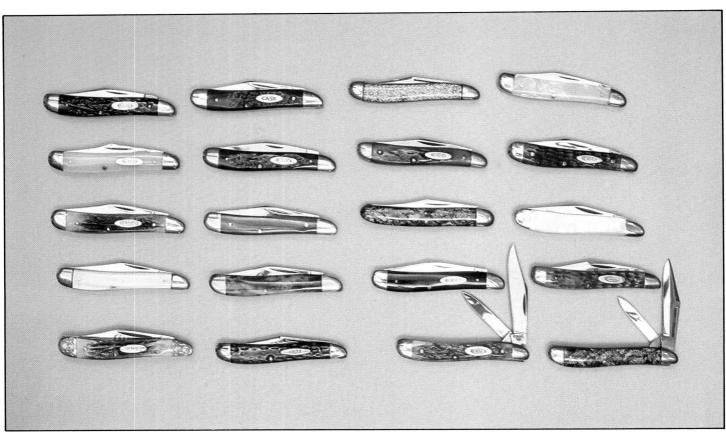

CASE
This particular display of Case Peanuts shows 20 variations of handle
materials, stampings and pulls.
Courtesy Joe Chance

REMINGTON
Handsomely boxed assortment of Scout Knives which were introduced in the
late 20's to early 30's.

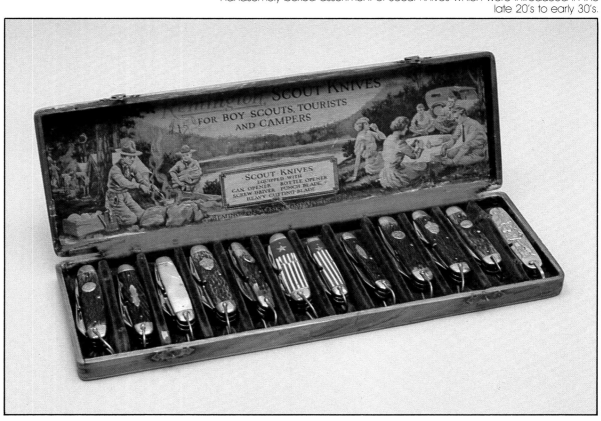

The above colorful assortment includes
Case, Case Tested, W.R. Case and Jean Case.

(Top to Bottom)
Leather and brass spacer, brown marbled pyremite, blue agate pyremite, amber celluloid,
cream and black pyremite, waterfall (rare).

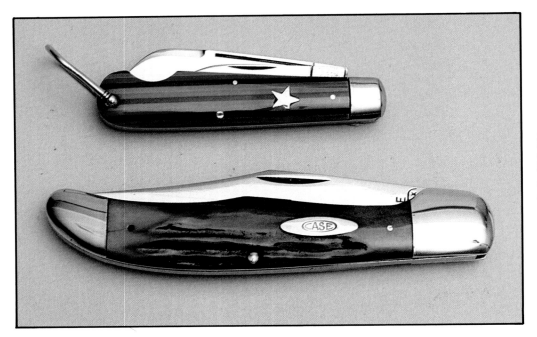

(top to bottom)
Remington, UMC, 3 3/4" Easy Opener with blue and red striped handle, star emblem, bail.

Case Tested XX, Folding Hunter, 5 1/4", red stag handle.

(top to bottm)
Remington Dr.s Knife with spatula, UMC, pearl, 3 3/4"

Case Tested XX, Christmas tree with barn door hinge bolsters, 5".

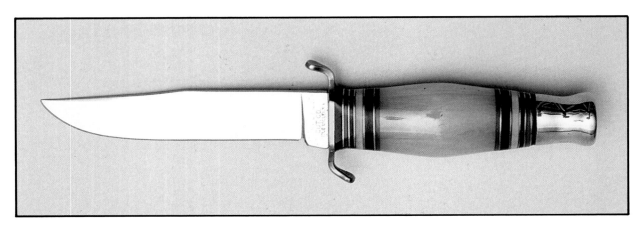

Jean Case Sheath Knife, amber handle, red black and brass spacers, brass butt and guard. Courtesy Elmer Kirkland.

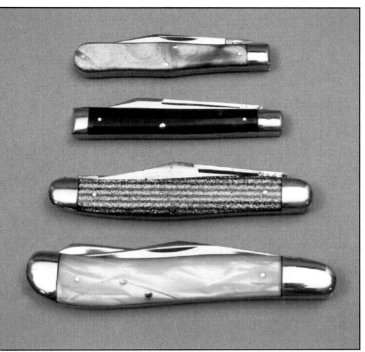

(From the top)
Case Tested XX, B2025-1/2, 2 blade, Coke Bottle, 3", green swirl, rare, $300. W.R. Case & Sons, Bradford, Pa., M72086, 2 blade physician's knife, 3-1/8", tortoise, rare, $600. Standard Knife Co., 3-7/8", 3 blade, green and gold stripe, rare, $350. Case Tested XX, 9240SP, 2 blade Trapper, 4-1/2", French pearl, $650.

(From the top)
Case Tested XX, GS172 clasp knife, 5-1/2"; Case Tested XX, RM172 clasp; and Case Tested XX, 3172 clasp.

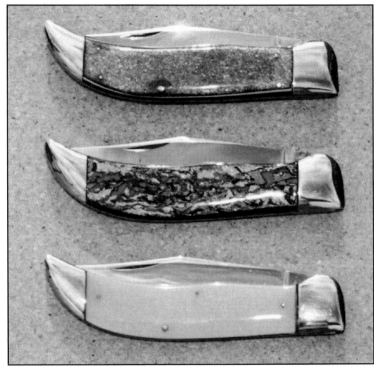

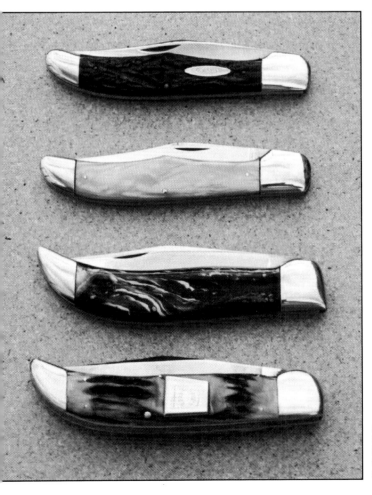

(From the top)
Case XX, 6265SAB, 5-1/4", rough-black handle; Case tested XX, 9265 flat blade, C.I. French-pearl handle; Case Tested XX, GYP172 clasp, 5-1/2", celluloid handle; and Case, Bradford, Pa., 5172L, Zipper, 5-1/2", switchblade, genuine stag handle.

Right: 5325-5, stag, 9-1/8" overall, Case XX, mint value is $125.

Left: 5325-5, red stag, 9-1/8" overall, Case XX, mint value is $175.

5165 Flat, red stag, 5-1/4", Case XX, mint value is $500. Photos courtesy of J.L. Johnson III.

Right: 5362, split stag, 8-3/4" overall, Case XX, mint value is $75.

Left: 9362, cracked ice with black spacers, 8-3/4" overall, Case XX, mint value is $175.

6265SAB, red bone, 5-1/4", Case XX, mint value is $400.

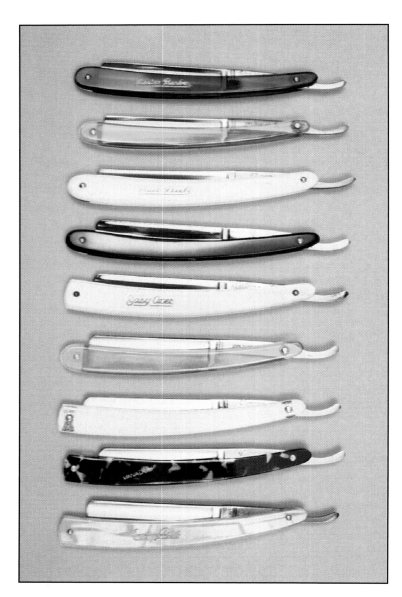

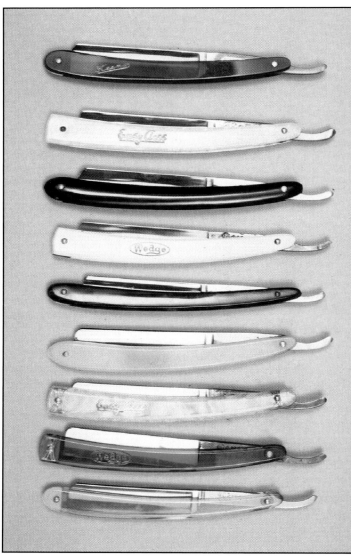

The Case razors shown here and in the photos on the following page exhibit a wide range of exotic and fanciful handle materials and designs that has made razor collecting so popular throughout the years.

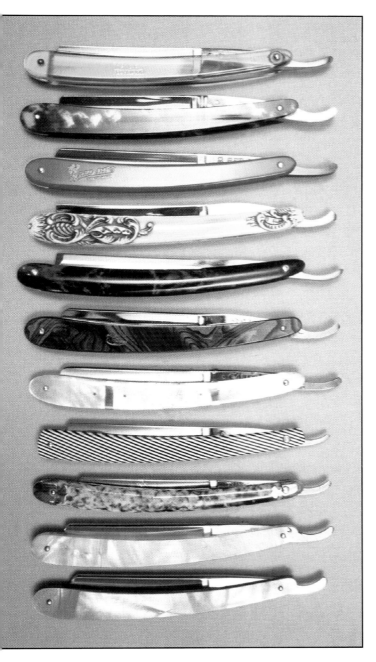
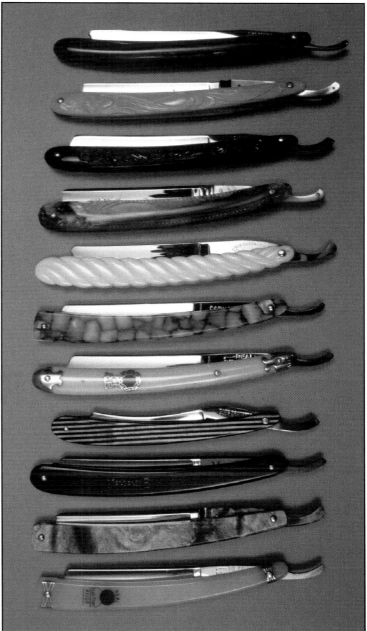

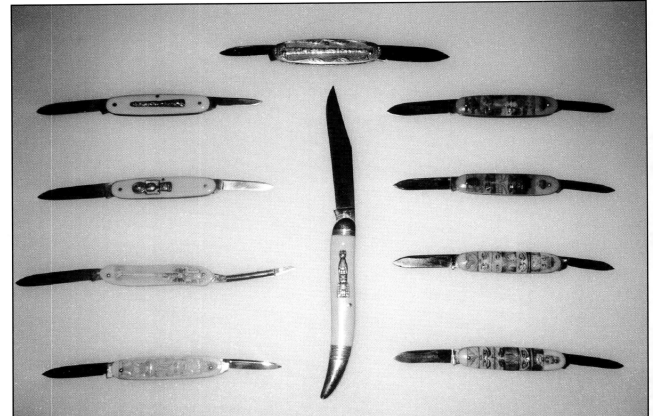

This collection of 10 different Remington Totem Pole knives, from 1917-1940, is the largest collection the author knows of. These knives are quite rare. Photo courtesy of G.A. Miller.

Top: Case Tested XX, 3465 flat blade, 5-1/4", four-blade folding hunter. **Top left:** Case XX, 6265 Flat, green bone, folding hunter. **Top right:** Case Tested XX, RM172 clasp knife, Christmas-tree handle. **Center:** Case Bradford, Pa., 5172L, Zipper (switchblade), 5-1/2", stag. **Bottom left:** Case XX proto, 6365SAB, three-blade, three-backspring folding hunter (saw blade). **Bottom right:** Case Tested XX, 6465, flat blade, 5-1/4", four-blade folding hunter.

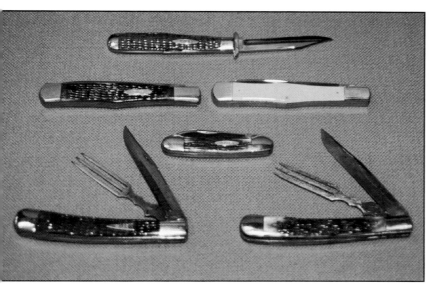

Top: Tested XX, 6111-1/2L, green bone. **Top left:** Tested XX, 62213, swell center, green bone. **Top right:** Tested XX, 32213, yellow celluloid. **Center:** Tested XX, 53131, three-blade stag canoe. **Bottom left:** Case Bradford, Pa., 6251F, Hobo, knife and fork, green bone, arrow shield. **Bottom right:** W.R. Case & Sons, Bradford, Pa., 6251F, Hobo, old Rogers bone.

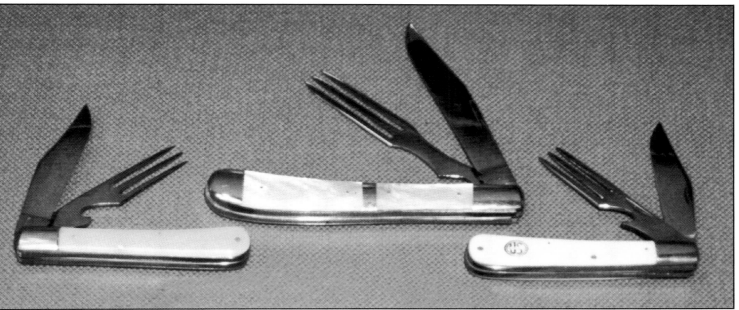

Hobo knives. All knives slide apart into two pieces to use as a knife and fork.

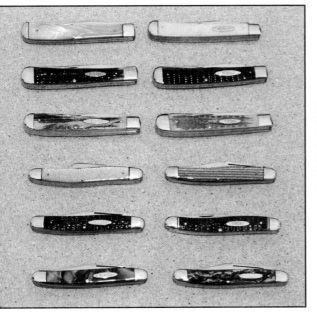

Knives pictured **on the left, from top to bottom,** are: Case Tested XX, 9254, French pearl (C.I.), small frame; 6254 USA, second cut; 5254 XX, first model; GS3047, Case, Bradford, Pa.; 6347LP, Case, Bradford, Pa.; and GPY347LP, W.R. Case & Sons. Pictured **at right, from top to bottom,** are: Case Tested XX, 3254, first model; Case Tested XX, 6254, 5254 USA, second-cut stag; Standard Knife Co., 47 Pattern; 64047PU, Tested XX, groove bolsters; and RM347LP, Tested XX, Christmas-tree handle.

R. Case, Bradford, Germany, 1-7/8", abalone; early 1900s.

Remington knives, showing eight different colorful handles. Remington used the term "pyremite" for this handle material.

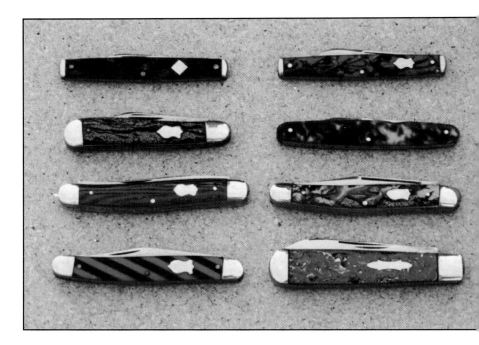

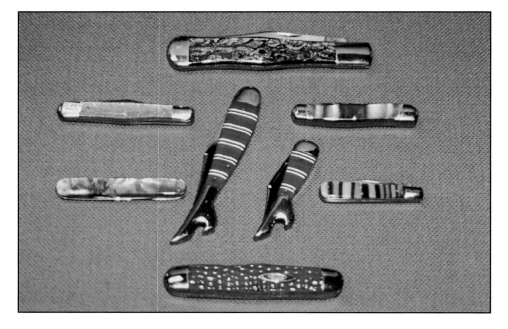

Eight Case knives, showing colorful handle materials used from early 1900 to around 1940.

Blue blade trimmed in gold, stag, 3,000 made, comes with sheath and plaque, 14", Case Bowie, 80th Anniversary; $200.

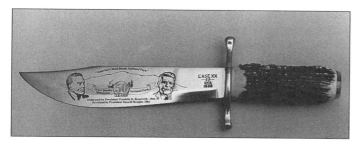

Case President's Bowie, stag, etched Reagan, Roosevelt, Plaque, 14-1/2"; $200.

5325-6, stag, round butt, flat blade, 10-3/8", Case XX; $135.

5325-6, stag, round butt, blood groove, 10-3/8", Case XX; $135.

5325-5, stag, round butt, flat blade, 9-1/8", Case XX; $125.

5325-5, stag, round butt, Case XX; $135.

3361-4-1/2, leather, red, black and brass spacers, round butt, Scout stamped back tang, Case Tested XX, scarce; $125.

3325-6, leather, round butt, 10-3/4", Case XX; $90.

315-4-3/4, leather, 8-7/8", Case XX, U.S.A.; $40.

365-5, leather, flat blade, 9-1/4", Case XX; $40.

RE66, mottled pearl, gray and black, round butt, 8", Case long tail C; $125.

364-4SAB, leather, 8", Case XX ,U.S.A.; $40.

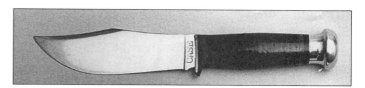

361-4, leather, round butt, 8",Case Big C; $150.

3361-4-1/2, leather, round butt, 8-3/4", Case XX; $75.

362-5, leather, round butt, 9-1/4", Case Tested XX; $90.

365-5, leather, red, brass and bone spacers, round butt, 9", Case XX; $65.

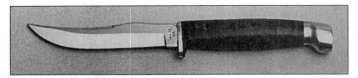

323-4-1/4, leather, Case XX, U.S.A., 6-1/2"; $40.

3325-5, leather, disc. 1966, 9-3/8", Case XX, U.S.A.; $65.

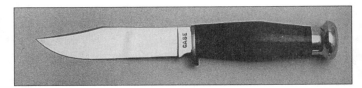

357, leather, round butt, 3-3/4", Case XX; $45.

3 Finn, leather, 8-3/4", Case XX, U.S.A; $30.

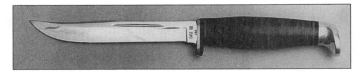

316-5, leather, 9-3/8", Case XX, U.S.A.; $30.

Case Bradford, PA, pattern unknown, 5" blade, 9-7/8" OA; $90.

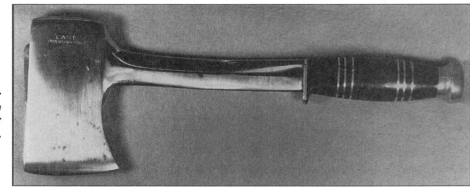

Hatchet Indestructible, Pat'd. Feb. 23-26, 12-1/2", folding guard over blade edge. Leather and aluminum spacer handle, very rare; $500.

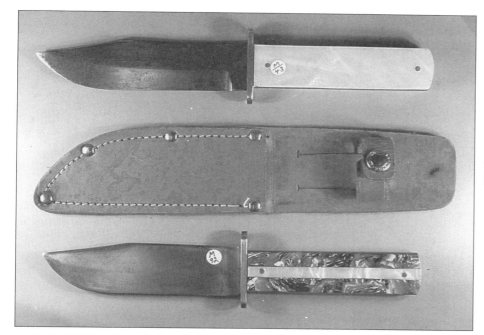

Contract knife, Fred Hook & Son examples, W.R. Case & Sons; $60-$75.

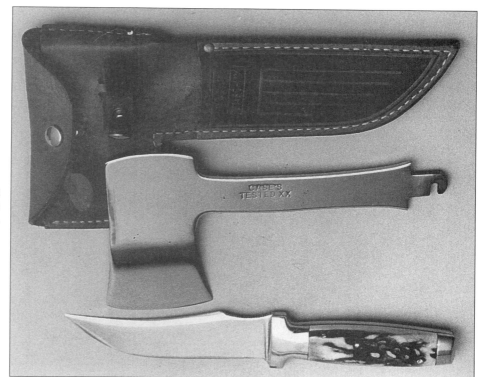

561, leather sheath, deluxe knife-ax combo., genuine stag, Case XX, U.S.A.; $425.

Hooker & Son examples, contact knife by Case; $60-$75.

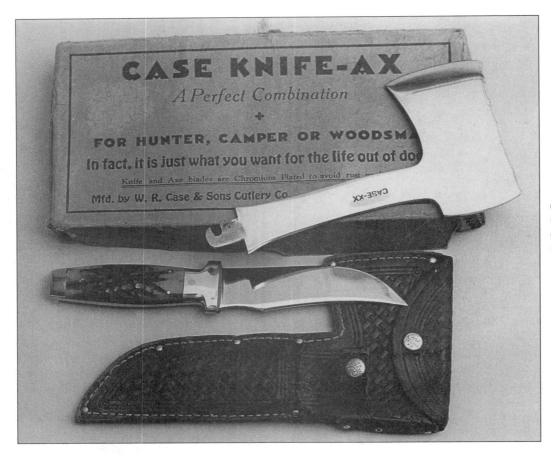

661, second-cut green bone, Case Tested XX, knife-ax combo., basket weave sheath; $425.

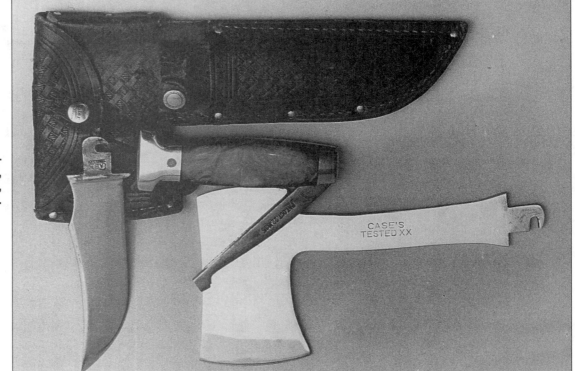

961, imitation onyx celluloid, Case Tested XX, regular knife-ax combo., (note thin ax); $400.

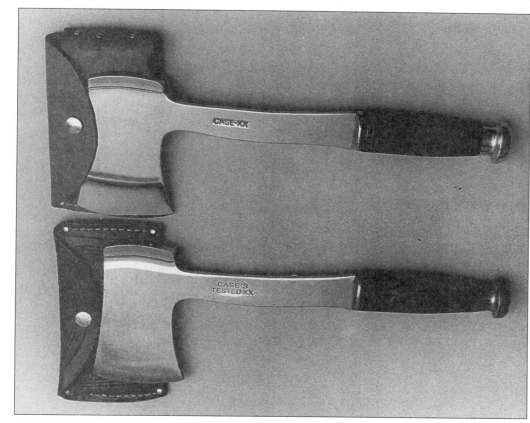

380AXE, leather, Case XX, 11", $75; 380AXE, Case XX, USA, with sheath, $75; 380AXE, leather, Case's Tested XX, deluxe head, tested basket weave sheath; $95.

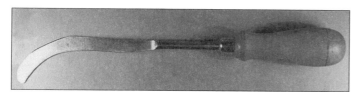

Banana knife, wood handle, 11-1/4" overall, 7" blade, Tested XX, rare; value? Ralph Scruton Collection.

223-6, black composition, 10-1/4", disc. 1988, Case XX, U.S.A.; $50.

364SAB, leather, round butt, 8-1/4", disc. about 1950, Case XX; $45.

Case long trench knife, WW I; $250. Photos courtesy Lee Anthony.

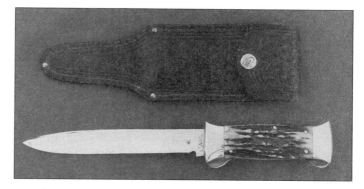

551-Case, genuine stag, early '40s, 5-3/4" folding lock blade, 10-5/8" OA, mint; $1,000.

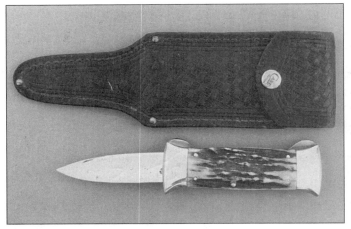

651-Case, green bone, early '40s, 10-5/8" OA, 5-3/4" folding lock blade, mint; $1,000.

Clauss Fremount O. (Case contract), green bone, 8-7/8", "Stainless Made in U.S.A." on back of blade; $75. Photo courtesy Wayne Robertson.

Green bone, medium Bowie type sabler, 10", Case Bradford, PA, Case's Tested XX; $400.

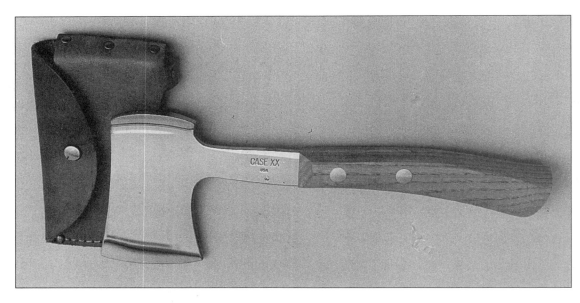

580AXE, oak, 10", 1965-19--, Case XX, USA, $90; 580AXE, Case's Tested XX; $100.

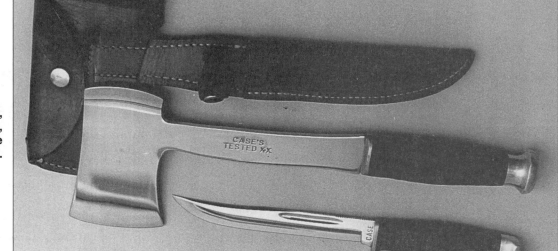

380AXE, combo., leather, deluxe head, sheath, Case's Tested XX, Case transition; $125.

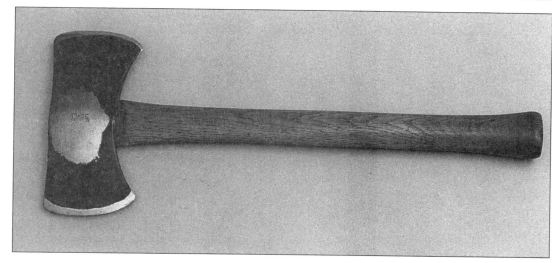

Cruiser ax, double bit, (rare), disc. mid-940s, 6-1/4", handle length 15", Case Tested XX; $300.

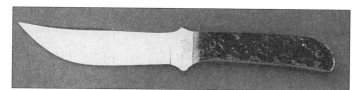

Kinfolks Outers Mode, 7-3/8", brown pick bone; $45. Photo courtesy Wayne Robertson.

Kinfolks throwing knife, 7-3/8" OA, red fiber handles, no blade etch., lighter made than Case thrower; $30. Photo courtesy Wayne Robertson.

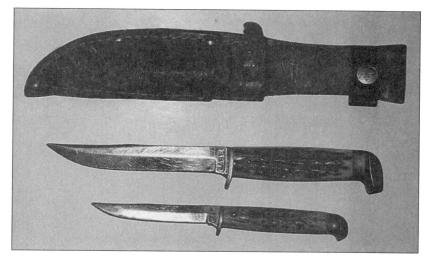

516-5-M5-F, twin Finn, piggy-back set, stag handle, sabor, no blood groove, disc. early '40s, Case Long Tail C, (Tested XX stamp); $150. Photo courtesy Dave Springer.

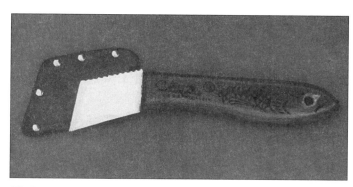

Kinfolks "fish knife," wood, 6-3/8", U.S.A. Stainless; $40. Photo courtesy Wayne Robertson.

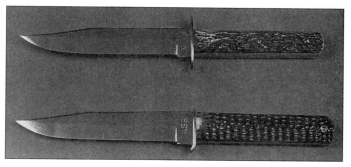

Top: No number, slab Rogers bone, 9" overall., Kinfolks U.S.A.; $100. Bottom: 652-5, slab greenbone, 7-1/2" O.A., Case XX; $125. Photo courtesy J.L. Johnson III.

Top: 957 Flat, cracked ice, 7" overall, Case's Tested Guard XX; $150. Middle: 915-4, cracked ice, 9" overall, Case Tested XX; $150. Bottom: 957SAB, cracked ice, 7" overall, Case's Tested Guard XX; $150. Photo courtesy J.L. Johnson III.

Left: No number, leather washer, 10" overall, Kinfolks USA; $100. Right: No number, leather washer, 9" overall, Kinfolks USA, round plastic knob, WW II military; $125. Photo courtesy J.L. Johnson III.

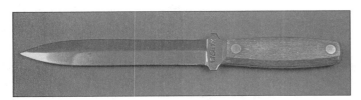

Case Double-Edge Pig Sticker; 162, beechwood, 10-1/2" overall, Case XX; $125.

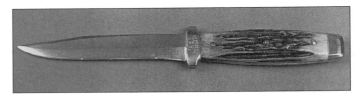

563SAB, stag, 8-1/2", Case Texted XX; $150. Photo courtesy J.L. Johnson III.

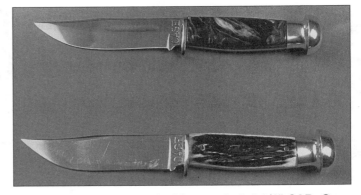

Top: 957SAB, brown and white mottled, 3-3/4" SAB, Case XX; $125. Bottom: 557 Flat, stag, 3-3/4" Flat, Case XX; $110.

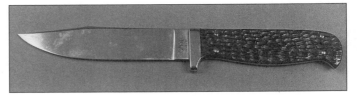

Number unknown, green bone, 8-1/4", Case Tested XX (arch), piston-grip handle, flat blade, guard, rare; $150.

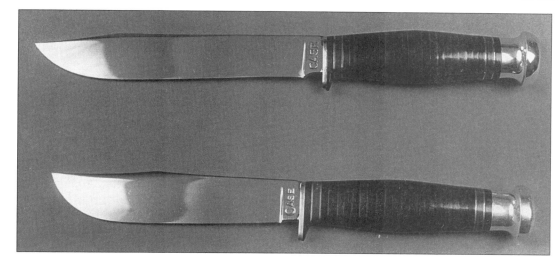

Top: 3025-6, black and red brass spacers, 10-1/4", Case XX, round butt; $75. Bottom: 366, black and red brass spacers, 5" blade, Big C; $75. Photo courtesy J.L. Johnson III.

Top: 964, green pearl pyremite, 8", Tested XX; $150. Middle: 644, green bone, 8", Tested XX; $150. Bottom: 964, cracked ice, 8V, Tested XX; $150. Photo courtesy J.L. Johnson III.

Outlander, black no-slip, 10-1/2", 1986 4 Dot; $65. Sheath contains a honing stone, whistle, match, disc. Photo courtesy J.L. Johnson III.

CASE RAZORS

Rich Kupillas

The information contained in this section is the end result of more than four years of meticulous research. I have endeavored to make this the most accurate and up to date information available. Although sometimes very frustrating, it was a labor of love.

With the exception of "Knifemakers Who Went West" (Platts) and Case related catalogs and literature, I have researched and evaluated all information from scratch. Available published dates and information was not relied upon.

Where precise dating was not possible, circa or approximate are used. In most instances, exact day and month were not available and dates are given in whole years.

A great debt of gratitude is owed to those who let us photograph their collections: Jim Branch, Steve Cary, Steve Froehlich and Joe Kranz, with a special thanks to Larry Robertson for letting us photograph his extensive collection accumulated over a 14-year period.

I also wish to thank the following people, who, without their information and advice, I could not have completed this project: Robert Crandall, Jerry Hnot, Fred and Carol Marziotto, H. Platts, Cindy Rabb, Bob Richardson, Jim Sargent, W.R. Case and Sons Bradford, Pa., Dept. of Patents and Tradesmark, Washington, D.C., librarians, historians, chambers of commerce and the nice people of the following cities and towns: Bradford, Pa.; Kane, Pa.; Little Valley, NY; New York, NY; Philadelphia, Pa.; Smethport, Pa.; Springville, NY; and Warren, Pa.

Collecting Case razors

As the price of older Case knives rose to astronomical figures, so has the popularity of Case razors. Buying a Case Brothers, W.R. Case and Son, or an old Bradford knife is just out of the reach of most collector's budgets. Razors enable a collector of modest means to add rare marks and handle materials to their collection. While some Case razors are expensive, all are far below equal knives of the same rarity, and with razors rapidly rising, they are an excellent financial investment. Razors with older marks, inlaid tangs, ornate handles and blade etchings seem to be the most sought after and consequently, have the highest rate of gain.

As a word of caution, please remember to use extreme care when handling and storing your razors! Razors, unlike knives, do not have backsprings; therefore, they can be opened by even the smallest hand.

Grading a 'mint' razor

Due to the decline of straight razor use and their relative modern production, W.R. Case and Sons (1920-1955) razors in "mint" condition are still available. Razors manufactured by Case Cutlers between 1900-1920 graded as "true mint" are extremely rare. Razors for the most part were stropped, not ground like a knife edge. A man competent with a strop could keep a keen edge on his razor for years and the blade would show minimal wear. Razor blades were of higher temper than knife blades of the period and were stropped on leather, not stone.

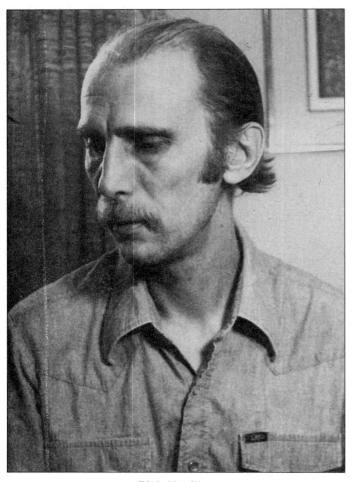

Rich Kupillas

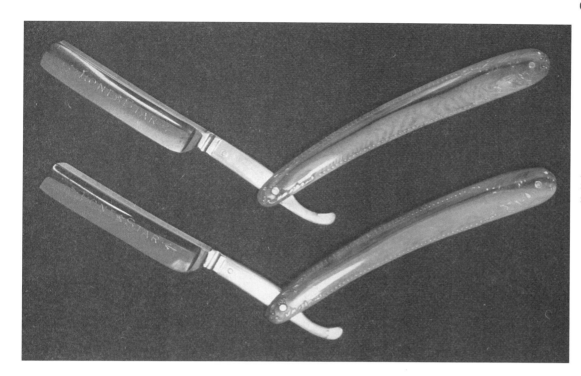

A rare pair of W.R. Case & Sons (1905-1920) "Lone Star" razors.

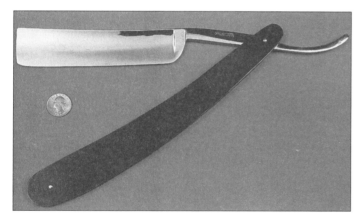

Case Brothers Cutlery Co., Little Valley, N.Y. Display razor, 14" closed, imitation tortoise-shell handles. (This razor also came in slick black handles.) Value in mint condition: $1,000.

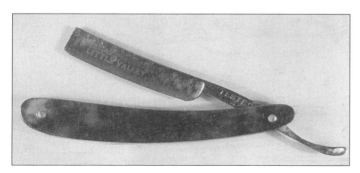

Saleman's sample, imitation tortoise-shell handle, Case Bros., Little Valley, N.Y., very rare; $550.

Larry Robertson was kind enough to pack up his whole collection of razors and travel to Nashville for an intensive photo session; the results are featured throughout this section. Larry is shown, above, with an oversized display razor. After being sold to Jim Sargent and resold to Elmer Kirkland of Florida, the collection was then sold at an auction in August 1996 and went into several collections across the country.

A mint "Genco, Bradford, Pa., Easy Aces," (1930-55).

Look at the blade carefully, especially along the top of the blade and the cutting edge where the strop rides. The point of the blade usually shows slight rounding, and the heel of the blade will show some wearing into the shoulderline due to the lapping of the strop. Case razors of this period did not have cut or ground edges; the edge was finely polished. When a blade is in true "mint" condition, there is simply no edge to see, just an even mirror-polished blade.

Cleaning

As with any collectible, you want to have as much of the original finish as you can. Buffing, polishing and reshaping only "destroys," not adds to, the value of a razor.

The proper ways to clean razors is with soap, water, a soft toothbrush and a few Q-tips. Rust and most stuck-on substances can be removed by soaking the blade in oil overnight. Light stains on both blades and handles can be removed with semi-chrome polish. (DO NOT use on painted handles—it will remove the paint.) This is the only abrasive product I would recommend using on either knives or razors.

Counterfeits

Unfortunately, the rise in price and popularity of Case razors has also increased the likelihood of counterfeits. The simplest form of deceiving the buyer is to switch handles to a more ornate or rarer material. More complex methods are used as the value of the piece rises, ranging from false stampings and welded blades, to making complete razors. The best way to avoid most counterfeit razors is to gather as much information as you can and make use of it. Knowledge is the best defense against counterfeiters.

Prices that are just too good to be true are usually just that. You can still find a bargain, but you can get stung just as easily. With the wide availability of pricing guides, there are very few dealers who do not know the value of the "Case" mark.

The original blade for the razor on the next page must have been in such poor shape, it was cut off at the tang and replaced. You can clearly see the remaining weld marks where the new blade was attached. Although it does not show up well in photographs, the metal of the blade is of slightly different color than the tang. If it were a Case Brothers of the

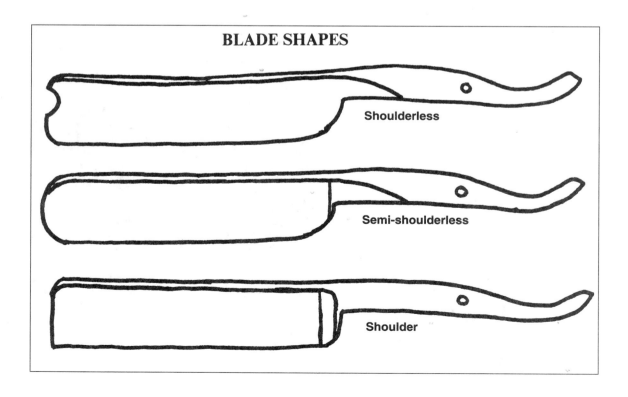

BLADE SHAPES

Shoulderless

Semi-shoulderless

Shoulder

BLADE POINT

SQUARE POINT	For decorative beards such as mutton chops and goatees. This point style was notorious for cutting ear lobes and noses.
HOLLOW POINT	For mustaches, to lift the ends up out of the way of the blade edge. Also just decorative in later years.
DISH POINT	For larger handle-bar type mustaches.
ROUND POINT	General use, for the "clean shaving man," also called "safety point."

Larger, heavier blades were for men with heavy beards; smaller blades were for men with light beards or those who shaved more frequently. Women who shaved used "ladies" or "travel" razors or (I'm sure without permission) their husband's razors.

same period as the marking indicated, it should have a shoulder ground into the blade. The handles are genuine Case Brothers and belong with the tang.

The four razor photos on the following page here show a good example of a re-stamped tang. The razor is German circa 1940. Case Brothers razors (1900-1915) were all handforged and then ground to shape by hand. All surfaces of the Case Brothers blade have beautiful luster to them, even the underside of the tang. If you compare them to most razors of the period—American, German, even W.R. Case and Sons Bradford (1905-20) —you would see they are all made from stamped blanks with the tangs shaped in the stamping process, leaving the underside of the tang blackened. The number 176 is original, but the "XX" was added at the same time as the Case mark. If you look carefully, you can see that the scratches made by the handle opening are lower than the raised

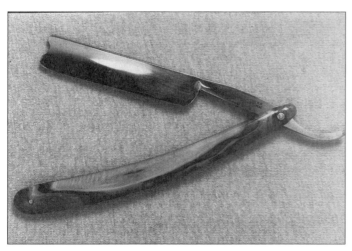 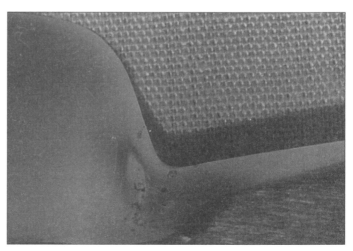

Counterfeit Case Brothers, Little Valley, N.Y.

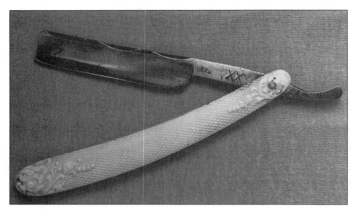

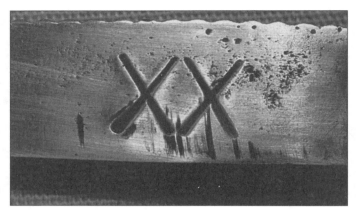

Counterfeit Case Brothers, Springville, N.Y.

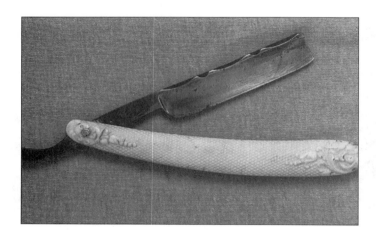

edges of the "XX." The Case Brothers Springville mark is incorrectly spelled as "SRRINGVILLE," and you can see where someone tried to pick out the leg of the first "R." The style of stamps used were both for knives and not razors, so I would think that this was just a test piece and I would check all your Case Brothers' Springville knives very carefully.

Handle facts

Molded handles were used by Case Brothers, W.R. Case and Son, and W.R. Case and Sons (until approx. 1915-1920), with the exception of the "Classic" pattern, which was used only on W.R. Case and Son (Napanoch) and on W.R. Case and Sons German imports (1905-1914).

These handles were not used on Case razors after 1920 and were available in the following colors:

Flowing Hair	Imitation ivory
	Black
Bamboo (both	
full-size and travel)	Imitation tortoise
	Cream
Twisted Rope	Cream
	Cream and rust (marble)
	Imitation ivory
Beaded Border	Various colored celluloid
Classic	Various colored celluloid

Case Brothers and W.R. Case and Son used these handles indiscriminately. Therefore, blade style cannot be used as a judge.

For W.R. Case and Sons (1905-20), the vast majority of molded handles were used on razors with inlaid tangs and/or blade etching. This doesn't mean you wouldn't find a plain blade with molded handles, but it should alert you to check the razor more carefully. Both Case Brothers and W.R. Case and Sons used the same handle supplier and are identical pattern for pattern. The "Classic" handles used by W.R. Case and Son (Naponoch) are larger than those used on W.R. Case and Sons German imports.

Rare cream bamboo handles are virtually identical to their less rare tortoise handles and should be used for verification.

Modern handles used by Case Companies

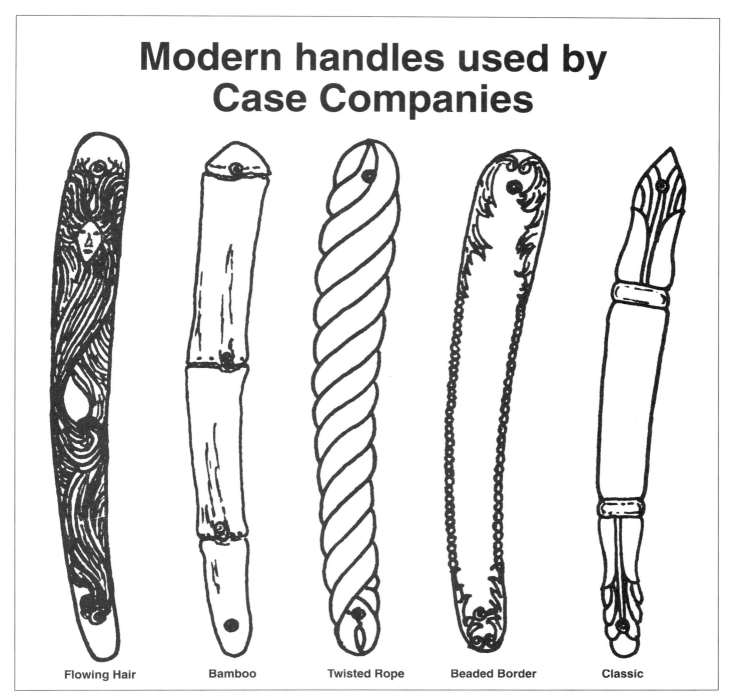

| Flowing Hair | Bamboo | Twisted Rope | Beaded Border | Classic |

Case Brothers, W.R. Case and Son, and W.R. Case and Sons used these handles only between 1900-1920. Not only are they rare, but add both beauty and value to razors of this period. Because of this, many people switch handles of imported or lesser American razors. Fortunately, there are some defenses against this practice.

All handles were made both with and without handle pins and with and without handle pin collars.

Observation

First try to be objective; looking at a piece through "starry eyes" will not help you in any way. Try to think of yourself as an appraiser, advising someone else whether to buy or not. Enjoy the razor after you buy it, not before.

Tang pins

While it's true that tang pins were routinely replaced in barber shops up until the 1940s, this should in no way be used as an excuse for a replaced pin on a razor graded excellent to "mint." Razor pins were replaced normally on well-used razors of the period. Even if the pin was replaced in the 1940s, it should have a gray pewter-like look.

Look closely at the finish on the pin. The hammering and grinding of the pin should match the other razors of the same mark.

Blades

Look where the handle rides (rubs) against the tang. There should be rubmarks on the inside of the handles to match those on the tang.

The front of the blade sometimes will show a slight discoloration (graying) right where the blade hits the handle. If this mark is higher or lower the razor should be checked carefully. This could, of course, be from warping of the handle due to heat, but that should be obvious.

There is no way to be 100 percent sure all of the time. By using the information above, you should at least have a fighting chance against razor collecting's most common fraud—handle switching.

Case-Related Boxes and Paper

Boxes	Range
Case Brothers, Little Valley, N.Y. (red, green, tan, blue and black)	$5 to $25 (depends on cond.)
W.R. Case and Son, Little Valley, N.Y.	10 to $35 (depends on cond.)
W.R. Case and Sons, Bradford, PA (1905-1920) (black, tan, gray and marble all with a "star" on theshort end) (depends on cond.)	$5 to $25
W.R. Case and Sons, Bradford, PA (1920-1955) (black only, "CASE TESTED XX" on the short end) (depends on cond.)	$5 to $15
W.R. Case and Sons, Bradford, PA (1955-1962) (gray, red, etc.) (depends on cond.)	$1 to $10

Catalogs

Case Brothers, Little Valley, N.Y.; complete in good condition	$100 to $200
W.R. Case and Sons, Bradford, PA (1905-20); complete in good condition	$100 to $200

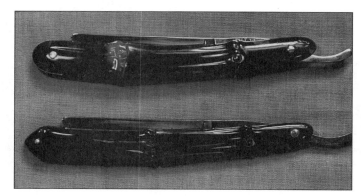

Little Valley Knife Association, Little Valley N.Y. (1900-1905); Case Brothers, Little Valley, N.Y. (1900-1905). Look at the handles carefully. The handle on the Case Brothers razor, (bottom), was manufactured just for use on travel razors, while the other one is a cut-down handle for a full-size razor. This was correct for travel razors manufactured by Napanoch, but it should not be correct on a Case Brothers travel razor.

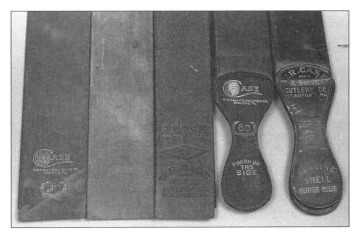

The above strops were all made by W.R. Case and Sons before 1920. As you can see, there were many styles of strops available. Strops of this period in good condition are worth $45 to $65. "Mint," with the original box; $100-$125.

W.R. Case and Sons "Tested XX"
(1920-40);
    complete in good condition $75 to $150
W.R. Case and Sons XX (1940-60)
    complete in good condition $25 to $75

Note: Salesmen's or full-line catalogs and those with a complete line price list command the highest price.

Strops and Hones

Razor strops or hones enhance any collection and come in many various shapes and styles.

Contract (Jobber) razors

All Case companies made "Contract Razors" for many different hardware stores, barber supply companies and jobbing house. They are identical to razors having a "Case" mark, except they bear a private linemark.

Contract razors usually sell for 40% to 50% less than equal razors having a "Case" mark.

Razor hones having the "W.R. Case & Sons" mark are very rare, especially with their original box. One is marked "extra choice #232," the other "NON FILLING MALGMIT #32." They are valued at $125 each.

Rare "W.R. Case & Sons" common sense razor strop and hone, with its own razor storage compartment. This one is complete with original box and papers and is worth $165.

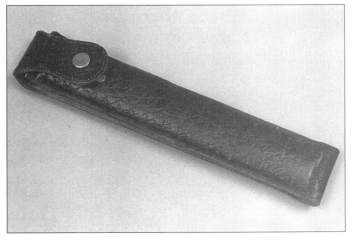

Extremely rare folding (travel) razor strop, stamped Case Brothers Little Valley, N.Y. Brass button carries patent date July 11, 1901; &175.

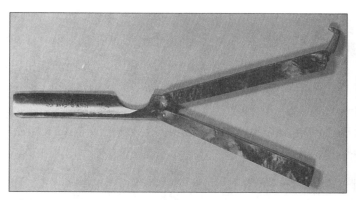

JOHN D. CASE CO., Little Valley, N.Y. (etched on blade), butterfly razor, imitation green pearl scales. Extremely rare; $625.

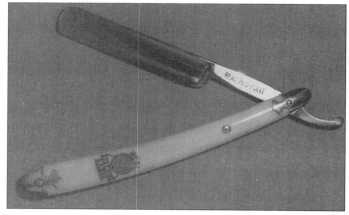

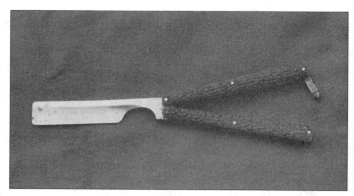

Butterfly-travel razor, John D. Case & Sons, Kane, PA. Etched patent applied for, brown pic bone, extremely rare; $650.

"Real Red Point," H. Geo. Henk, Columbia, Pa. While this razor is virtually identical to its W.R. Case and Sons brother, it does not bear the "Case" name and is worth $45.

Case Brothers and related companies

Note: Due to the rarity of razors in "true-mint" condition, the prices in this section are based on razors in excellent condition.

John D. Case Co. Little Valley, N.Y.

While not as famous as Job or W.R. Case (who were real people but fictional cutlers), John D. Case was making razors around 1880 and in fact held a patent for his butterfly razor dated Feb. 8, 1881—a full 20 years before his future company Case Brothers was credited with being the first Case Cutlery Manufacturing Co. This John D. Case Co. mark is the oldest Case mark known, and is more than 100 years old.

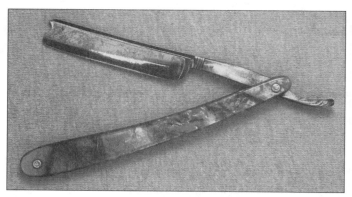

JOHN D. CASE CO., Little Valley, N.Y. (etched on blade), travel razor, hollow point blade, etched "CASHIER," green pearl handles with matching tang. Extremely rare; $500.

John D. Case Kane, PA (1909-1914)	John D. Case Sons Co. Kane, PA (1909-1914)	John D. Case Little Valley, N.Y. (1909-1914)

After Case Brothers divested itself of Case Brothers, Kane, Pa. (reorganized under the name Kane Cutlery Company in 1909), John D. Case retained some interest in the company, and it manufactured his own private line marked John D. Case, Kane, Pa., John D. Case, Little Valley, N.Y. and J.D. Case Sons Co.

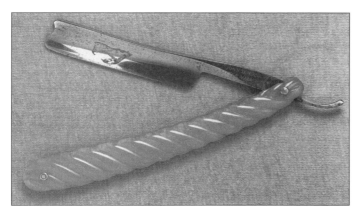

JOHN D. CASE, LITTLE VALLEY, N.Y., hollow point, cream and rust, twisted rope handles, rare; $150.

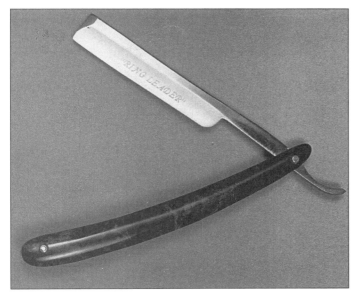

JOHN D. CASE SONS CO., KANE, P.A., ax point, blade etched "RINGLEADER," brown and red mottled handles, rare; $200.

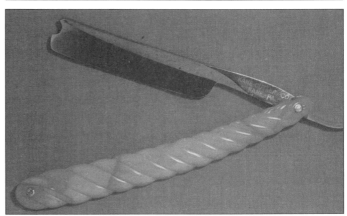

KANE CUTLERY CO., KANE, PA., hollow point, cream and rust twisted rope handles; $75.

Kane Cutlery Company

Sometime in 1909, Case Brothers Cutlery Company, Kane, Pa., was reorganized under the name Kane Cutlery Company. It manufactured razors under the name Kane Cut. Co., John D. Case, Kane, Pa., and John D, Case Sons Co., Kane, Pa.

J.B.F. Champlin & Son Little Valley, N.Y. (1882-1886)	Cattaraugus Cut Co. Little Valley, N.Y. (1887-1963)

J.B.F. Champlin married Thersa Case in the late 1860s. They had a son named Tint, who, with his father, formed "J.B.F. Champlin and Son in 1882. In 1886, they were joined by John, Jean and Andrew Case and the company's name was changed to "Cattaraugus Cutlery Co." Their association lasted for only a short period of time and the Case Brothers left sometime in 1887.

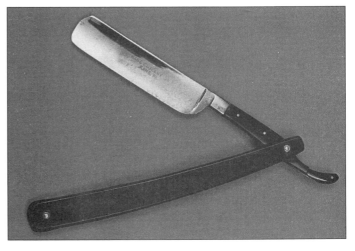

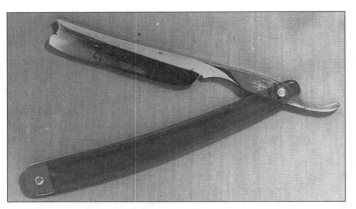

KANE CUTLERY, hollow point, worked tang with transparent red handles; $50

The Standard Knife Co.
Little Valley, N.Y.
(1901-1903)

In 1901, Dean and Elliot Case, sons of Jean Case, started a jobbing house in Little Valley, N.Y. under the name "The Standard Knife Co." Their knives carried an unusual promise from the two brothers, "If you die with a Standard Knife in your pocket, we'll pay the funeral expenses."

Although the new company did well, Elliot Case's untimely death in 1903 forced the closing of the company.

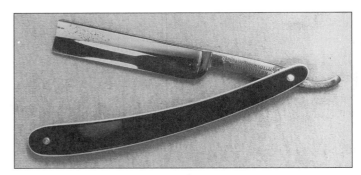

CATTARAUGUS CUT. CO., LITTLE VALLEY, N.Y. square point, blue handles with white liners; $25.

Note: In the late 1920s, W.R. Case & Sons marketed a line of razors under the name of "Standard Knife Co." The words "Little Valley, N.Y." do not appear in these tang stamps. Prices of Standard Knife razors are comparable to those of Kinfolks razors of the period.

Union Cutlery Company
Olean, N.Y.
A.J. Case
Shoo-fly
(circa 1912)

When Andrew Case left Case Brothers in 1909, he joined his nephew, W.R. Brown, at Union Cutlery

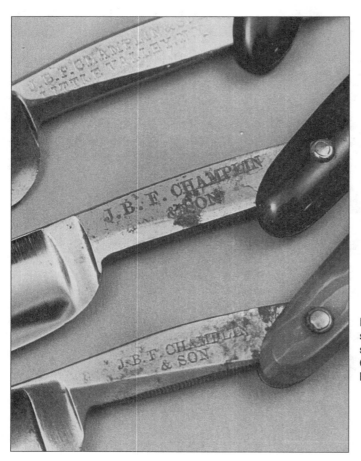

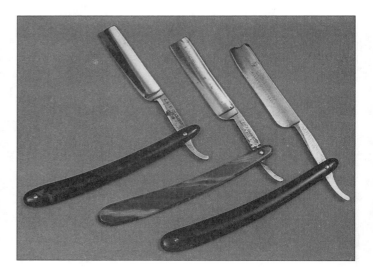

From left: J.B.F. Champlin & Son, square point, brown streaked celluloid handles, $85.; J.B.F. Champlin & Son, square point, red streaked celluloid handles, $85.; J.B.F. Champlin & Son, Little Valley, N.Y., hollow point, slick black handles, blade etched "Warranted hollow ground"; $105.

Manufactured by: NAPANOCH.

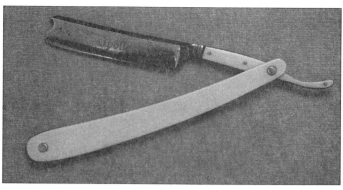

CASE BROS. CUTLERY CO., LITTLE VALLEY, N.Y., (jobber), (c. 1896-1900) travel razor, hollow-point blade, etched "APOLLO" on front; Case Bros. Cutlery Co., Little Valley, N.Y. on the back, imitation ivory tang with matching handles, extremely rare; $425.

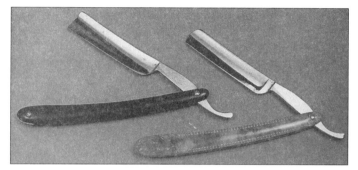

THE STANDARD KNIFE CO., LITTLE VALLEY, N.Y. (arc mark). Left: Square point, slick black handles; $100. Right: Round point, yellow mottled beaded boarded handles; $145.

Company in Tidioute, Pa., later moving to Olean, N.Y. in 1912. It is not known if he was involved with the workings of the company, or was a sales representative/jobber with his own private line.

house in Spring Green, Nebraska as a sideline to their livestock-breeding business.

In 1896, John D. Case, together with his brothers Jean and Andrew, formed Case Brothers Cutlery Co. in Little Valley, N.Y. jobbing for C. Platt's Sons Co. and other manufacturers of the period. Case Bros. & Co. is a shortened form of the company name (Platts). Some razors of this period have Case Bros. Cutlery Co., Little Valley, N.Y. etched in two lines on the back of the blade. These razors do not have the trademark "TESTED XX" and are identical to John D. Case Co. razors of this period.

Case Bros. Wholesalers of Cutlery Spring Green, Nebraska (c. 1890-1900)	Case Brothers Cutlery Co. Little Valley, N.Y. (1896-1900)

Several years after the Case brothers left Cattaraugus Cutlery, they operated a cutlery wholesale

Case Brothers Cutlery Company Little Valley, N.Y. (1900-1912) Kane, Pa. (1907-1909)	Case Manufacturing Company Little Valley, N.Y. (1910) Warren, Pa. (1911-1912?)

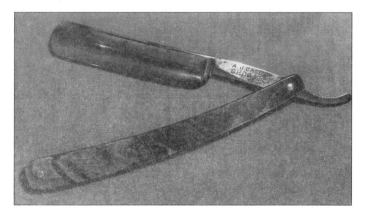

A.J. CASE'S SHOO-FLY UNION CUT. CO., OLEAN, N.Y. Round point, tiger-eye handle with shoo-fly pressed into it, rare; $150.

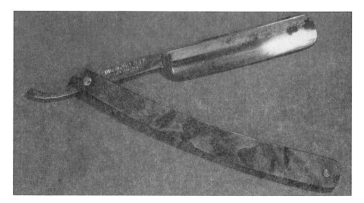

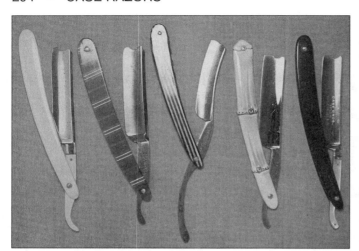

The five razors shown here are rare Case Brothers razors.

Case Brothers Cutlery Company
Springville, N.Y.
(1912-1915)

In February 1900, Case Brothers Cutlery Company was incorporated in Little Valley, N.Y. Razor production played a large part in the early success of the company. It is interesting to note the reason for the company's famous "hand-forged cutlery" logo was simply that it had to employ so many hand forgers for razor production it was financially prudent to hand forge all blades, rather than use the new technology of the day—drop hammers.

Razors made by Case Brothers were extremely fine, well-balanced razors, with the largest variety of tang stampings. They are very sought after by collectors. The majority of razors manufactured by Case Brothers are of plain design with smooth handles, but retain a refined beauty unique to the mark. Case Brothers, Little Valley, manufactured some razors with inlaid tangs and etched blades, but they are a very rare find and command high prices.

Another rare razor manufactured at Little Valley, N.Y. was the "Ladies" or travel razor. These are perfect half scale razors used for small hands or small spaces. Travel razors were produced from 1900-1912. Most have tortoise bamboo handles. Some early ones have slick black handles. Case Brothers was the only major Case related company to actually make this style of razor.

Case Brothers operated a second factory in Kane, Pa. from 1907-1909, when it was reorganized under the name Kane Cutlery Co. It was also about the same time that Andrew Case left Case Brothers to join Union Cutlery Co.

In January of 1910, Case Brothers purchased Smethport Cutlery Co. in Smethport, Pa., reportedly marking their razors Case Mfg. Co. Little Valley, N.Y.

After only a short period of operation, the factory burned down in June 1910. After receiving many incentives from the Board of Trade and Commerce, Case decided to rebuild in the town of Warren, Pa. under the name Case Manufacturing Company, Warren, Pa. This factory was most likely completed in early 1911 and remained in operation for only a short period. This mark may be the rarest of all Case Brothers marks.

On March 27, 1912, Case Brothers, Little Valley, N.Y., burned to the ground. It rebuilt in Springville, N.Y. in 1913, but was never able to recover from two devastating fires and went out of business late in 1914. On Oct. 21, 1914, Case Brothers sold its rights to the "Tested XX" trademark to W.R. Case and Sons, ending the 18-year history of the Case Brothers Cutlery Company.

Arc etching with full spelling, (c. 1900-1907).

Line etching with "TESTED XX," (c. 1900-1907).

Arc etching with "TESTED XX," (c. 1900-1907).

Little Valley Stamping, (c. 1907-1912).

Line etching, c. 1900-1907.

Springville stamping (1912-1915).

KANE, PA., LITTLE VALLEY, N.Y., 1907-1909; extremely rare.

LITTLE VALLEY, N.Y. & KANE, PA.; extremely rare.

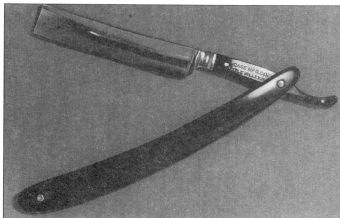

CASE MFG. CO., LITTLE VALLEY, N.Y. square point, inlaid black tang with matching handles. Rare; $260.

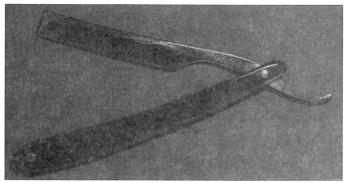

CASE MFG. CO., WARREN, PA. (etched), travel razor, square-point blade, etched "RINGLEADER," transparent gold handles. Extremely rare mark; $400.

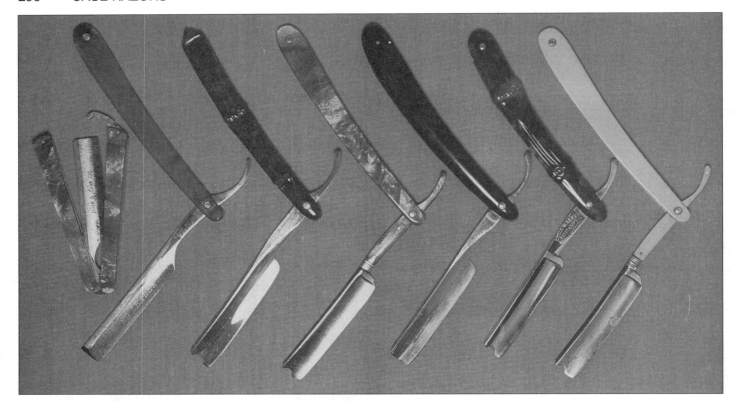

Travel rarities, from left: John D. Case Co., Butterfly; Case Mfg. Co., Warren, Pa.; Case Brothers Cutlery Co., Little Valley, N.Y. (rare arc etching); John D. Case Co. Little Valley N.Y.; Case Brothers, Cutlery Co., Little Valley, N.Y. (arc etching, rare slick black handles); Little Valley Knife Association, Little Valley, N.Y.; Case Bros. Cutlery Co., Little Valley, N.Y. (1896-1900).

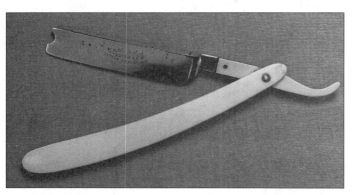

CASE BROS. "TESTED XX," LITTLE VALLEY, N.Y. (arc etching), hollow-point blade, etched "MFG FOR JONES & CO" on rear of blade, with extremely rare style of inlaid tang, imitation ivory with matching handles (note the blade stops at the pivot pin, the entire finger loop is celluloid); $375.

Near right: CASE BROTHERS CUTLERY CO., LITTLE VALLEY, N.Y. (arc etch), hollow-point blade, butter and molasses handles; $125. Far right: CASE BROTHERS, LITTLE VALLEY, N.Y. (arc etch), square-point blade with worked tang, cream-colored beaded border handles; $150.

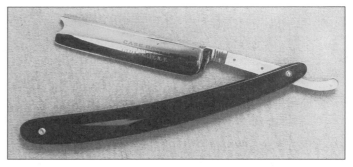

CASE BROS., TESTED XX, LITTLE VALLEY, N.Y. (line etching), hollow-point blade, slick black handles, with rare mother of pearl inlaid tang; $400.

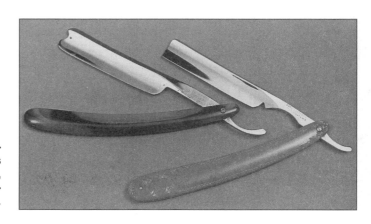

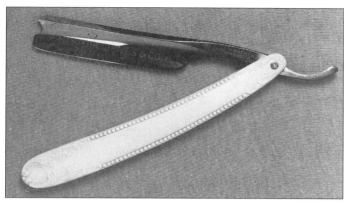

CASE BROTHERS CUTLERY CO., LITTLE VALLEY, N.Y. (arc etching), hollow-point blade, etched "MFG FOR JONES & CO." with worked tang, imitation ivory handles in the beaded border pattern; $165.

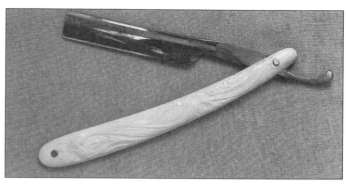

CASE BROTHERS CUTLERY CO., LITTLE VALLEY, N.Y. (arc etch), square-point, imitation ivory flowing hair handles; $100

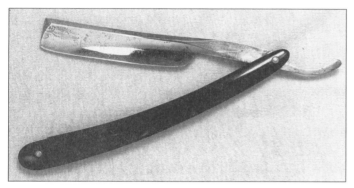

CASE BROTHERS CUTLERY CO. (arc etch), ax-point blade, etched "SHARON HDW," slick black handles; $135.

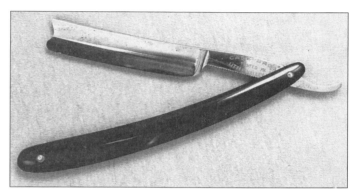

CASE BROTHERS, TESTED XX, LITTLE VALLEY, N.Y. (arc etch), hollow point, slick black handles, rare mark; $150.

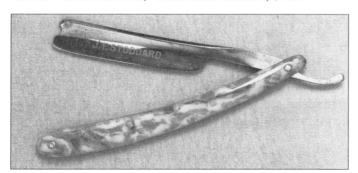

CASE BROTHERS CUTLERY CO. (arc etch), hollow-point blade, etched "J.F. Stoddard," cream, rust and green handles; $150.

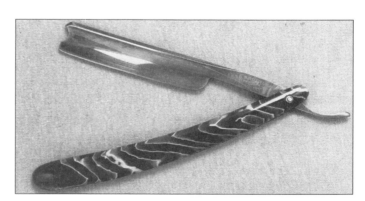

CASE BROTHERS, TESTED XX, LITTLE VALLEY, N.Y. (arc etch), hollow point, imitation horn handles, rare mark; $165.

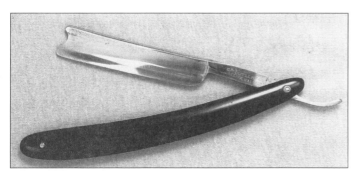

CASE BROTHERS CUTLERY CO. (arc etch), hollow-point blade, slick black handles; $100.

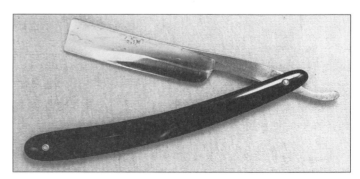

CASE BROTHERS, TESTED XX, LITTLE VALLEY, N.Y. (arc etch), square point, slick black handles, rare mark; $150.

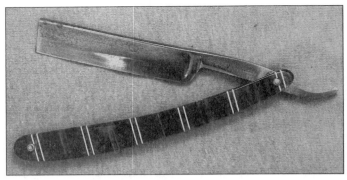

CASE BROS., TESTED XX, LITTLE VALLEY, N.Y. (arc etch), square point, candy-stripe handles, rare mark; $225.

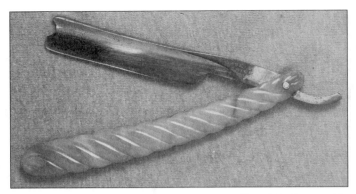

CASE BROS., "Tested XX," LITTLE VALLEY, N.Y. (line etch), hollow point, cream and rust twisted rope handles, rare mark; $160.

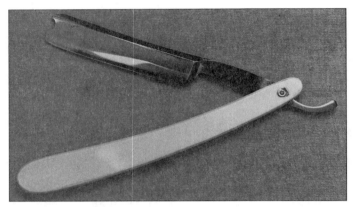

CASE BROTHERS CUTLERY CO., LITTLE VALLEY, N.Y. (arc etch), hollow point, imitation ivory handles, rare mark; $150.

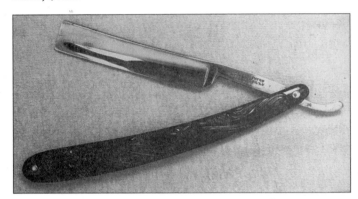

CASE BROTHERS, LITTLE VALLEY, N.Y. (stamp), square point, black flowing hair handles; $135.

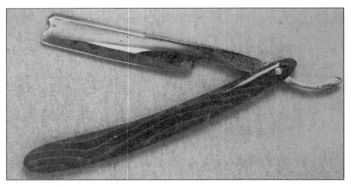

CASE BROTHERS, LITTLE VALLEY, N.Y. (fine etch), hollow point, imitation horn handles, rare mark; $160.

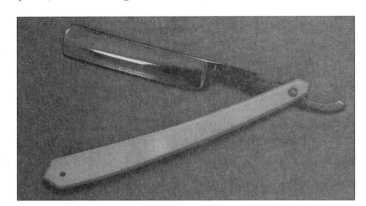

CASE BROTHERS, LITTLE VALLEY, N.Y. (stamp), round point, imitation ivory coffin handles; $125.

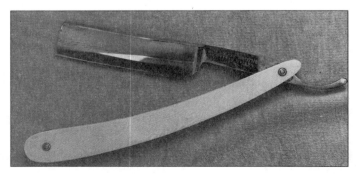

CASE BROTHERS, LITTLE VALLEY, N.Y. (line etch), square point, blade has an extremely thick tang, imitation ivory handles, rare; $185.

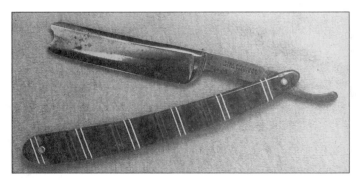

CASE BROTHERS, LITTLE VALLEY, N.Y. (stamp), hollow point, candy-stripe handles; $200.

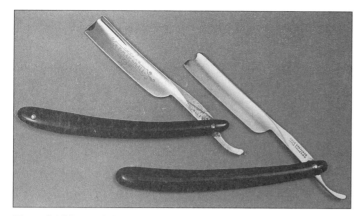

Top: CASE BROS. TESTED XX, LITTLE VALLEY, N.Y. (arc etch), square point, blade etched "A.E. MARSHALL" red and brown streaked handles; $160. Bottom: CASE BROTHERS, LITTLE VALLEY, N.Y.. (stamp), hollow point, red and brown streaked handles; $125.

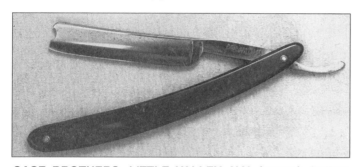

CASE BROTHERS, LITTLE VALLEY, N.Y. (stamp), hollow point, slick black handles; $100

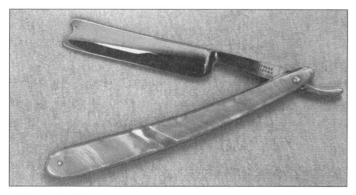

CASE BROTHERS, LITTLE VALLEY, N.Y. (stamp), hollow point, green pearl handles; $125.

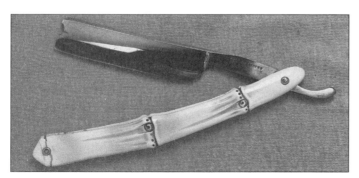

CASE BROTHERS, LITTLE VALLEY, N.Y. (stamp), hollow point, rare imitation-ivory bamboo handles; $150.

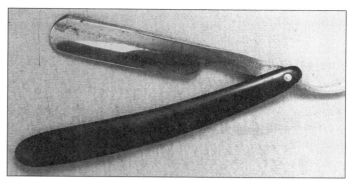

CASE BROTHERS, LITTLE VALLEY, N.Y. (stamp), round point, slick black handles, very large blade; $100.

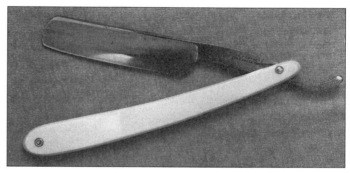

CASE BROTHERS, LITTLE VALLEY, N.Y. (stamp), round point, imitation ivory handles; $100.

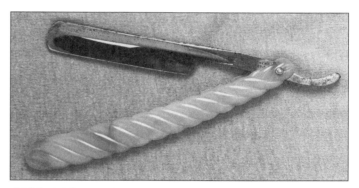

CASE BROTHERS, LITTLE VALLEY, N.Y. (stamp), cream and rust twisted rope handle; $125.

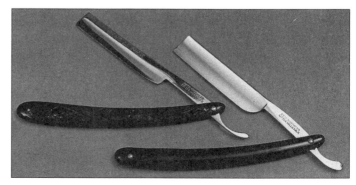

Top: CASE BROTHERS, LITTLE VALLEY, N.Y. (stamp), square-point blade, etched "RINGLEADER," black flowing hair handles, rare; $175. Bottom: CASE BROTHERS, LITTLE VALLEY, N.Y. (stamp), square point, slick black; $100.

Case Brothers Travel Razors

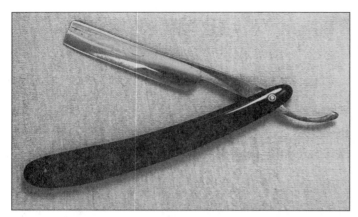

CASE BROTHERS CUTLERY CO., LITTLE VALLEY, N.Y. (arc etch), travel razor, square point, rare slick black handles, rare mark; $300.

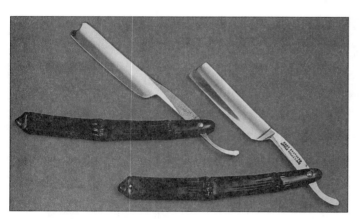

Top: CASE BROTHERS CUTLERY CO., LITTLE VALLEY, N.Y. (arc etch), hollow point, tortoise bamboo handles, rare mark; $175. Bottom: CASE BROTHERS, LITTLE VALLEY, N.Y. (stamp), square point tortoise bamboo handles; $150.

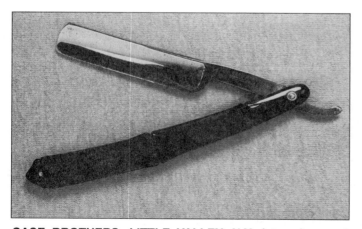

CASE BROTHERS, LITTLE VALLEY, N.Y. (stamp), round point, tortoise bamboo handles; $150.

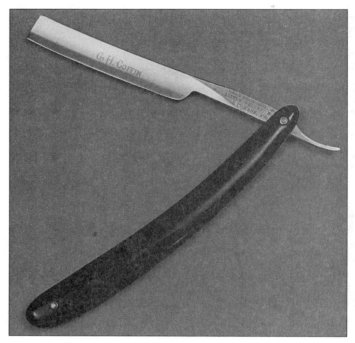

CASE BROS. CUT CO., LITTLE VALLEY, N.Y. and KANE, PA (etch), square-point blade etched "G.H. COFFIN," red and brown mottled handles, extremely rare mark; $225.

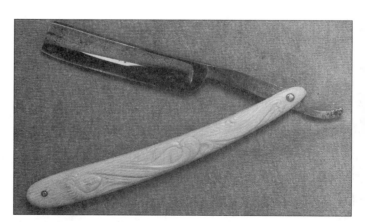

CASE BROS. KANE, PA, LITTLE VALLEY, N.Y. (etch), square point imitation ivory handles in the flowing-hair pattern, extremely rare mark; $225.

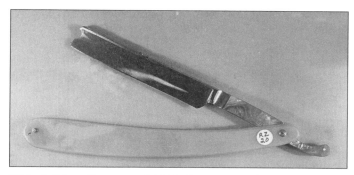

Waterfall handle, around 1912, Case Bros., Springville, N.Y.; $175.

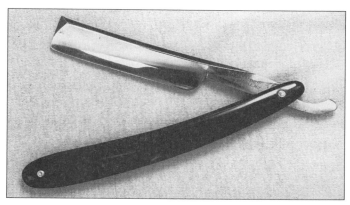

CASE BROTHERS, SPRINGVILLE, N.Y. (stamp), ax point, very heavy blade, slick black handles; $140.

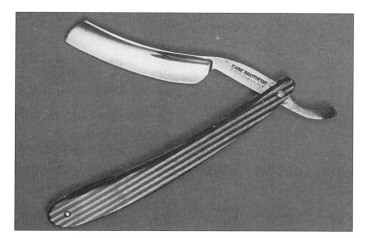

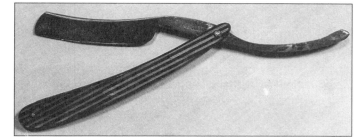

CASE BROTHERS, SPRINGVILLE, N.Y. (stamp), rare curved blade, silver and black handles: regular tang, $195; monkey tail (rare), $375.

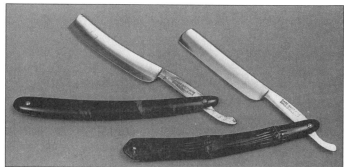

Left: CASE BROTHERS, SPRINGVILLE, N.Y. (stamp), square point, red and brown mottled handles; $125. Right: CASE BROTHERS, SPRINGVILLE, N.Y. (stamp), round point, tortoise bamboo handles; $160.

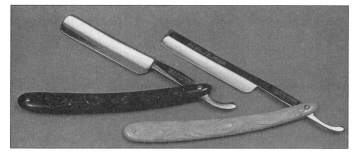

Left: CASE BROTHERS, SPRINGVILLE, N.Y. (stamp), round point, black handles molded in a leaf pattern; $175. Right: CASE BROTHERS, SPRINGVILLE, N.Y. (stamp), square point, blade etched "RINGLEADER," imitation ivory flowing hair handles; $225.

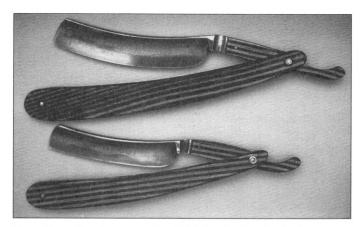

Top: Case Brothers, Springfield, N.Y.; standard-size razor, silver and black celluloid handles, covered tang; $195. Bottom: Case Brothers, Springfield, N.Y.; travel razor, 4-3/4" handle, 5-3/8" overall; silver and black celluloid handles, covered tang; $275. Photo courtesy Marlyn Kepner.

W.R. Case & Sons and related companies

Note: Due to the rarity of razors in "true-mint" condition, the prices in this section are based on razors in excellent condition.

Little Valley Knife Ass'n Little Valley, N.Y. (1900-1905)

Crandall Cutlery Bradford, PA (1905-1912)

Herbert E. Crandall (husband of Theresa Case) operated a jobbing house under the name Little Valley Knife Ass'n., later moving to Bradford, Pa., as a manufacturer under the name "Crandall Cutlery Company."

Crandall Cutlery Company was absorbed by W. R. Case and Sons in 1912. Herbert Crandall remained as an executive at Case.

Kinfolks Incorporated Little Valley, N.Y. (1926-1958)

Dean J., J. Russell, J. Elliott Case and Tint Champlin formed Kinfolks Incorporated in Little Valley, N.Y. in 1926, later to be joined by Jean Case in 1928.

While Kinfolks was a manufacturing company, most razors sold under the Kinfolks mark were made by W.R. Case and Sons. Kinfolks Incorporated went out of business sometime around 1958.

Robson Cutlery obtained the Kinfolks trademark and manufactured a line of pocket knives into the 1960s under the Kinfolks mark.

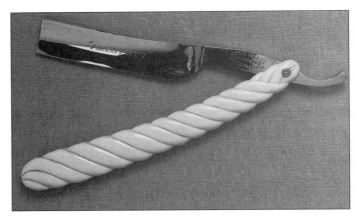

Manufactured by Napanoch: LITTLE VALLEY KNIFE ASS'N., LITTLE VALLEY, N.Y., square-point blade, etched "I MUST KUT," imitation ivory, twisted rope handle; $125.

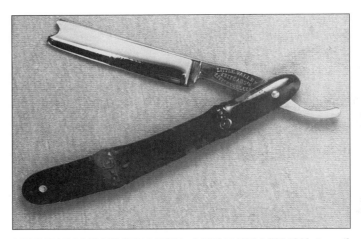

LITTLE VALLEY KNIFE ASS'N., LITTLE VALLEY, N.Y., travel razor, hollow-point blade, etched "I MUST KUT"; $140.

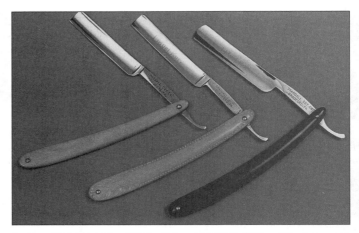

Left: CRANDALL CUT. CO., BRADFORD, PA (stamp), square point, rear of tang stamped "GUILT EDGE," smooth bone handles; $65. Middle: square point, blade etched "I MUST KUT," cream-colored beaded border handles; $65. Right: square point, blade etched "I MUST KUT," slick black handles; $65.

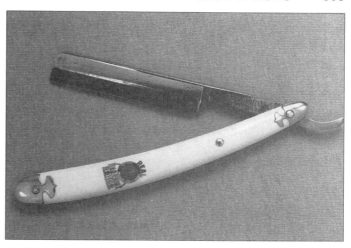

KINFOLKS INC., square point, "real red point," imitation ivory with silver endcaps; $75.

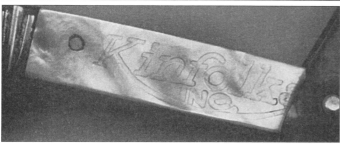

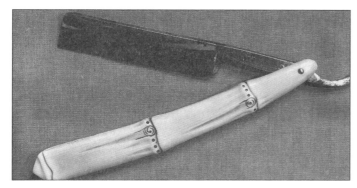

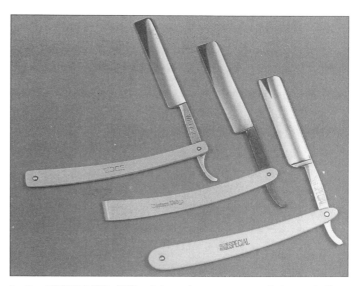

Left: KINFOLKS INC. (stamp), square point, mutation ivory handles with "WEDGE" stamped on them; $40. Middle: Square point, imitation ivory handles with "WESTERN WEDGE" stamped on them; $50. Right: square point, white Celluloid handles with "BLUE STEEL SPECIAL" on them; $35.

KINFOLKS INC., square point, ivory bamboo handles; $55.

Genco Company
Bradford, PA

In 1936, W.R. Case and Sons bought out the razor division of Geneva Cutlery Company in Geneva, N.Y. Only razors marked "GENCO" Bradford, Pa. were made at the Case factory and were marketed until about 1955.

W.R. Case and Sons used various pattern names on the markside and the "GENCO" tang stamp was on the fireside of its Genco line, just as it did on its own line of razors during this period.

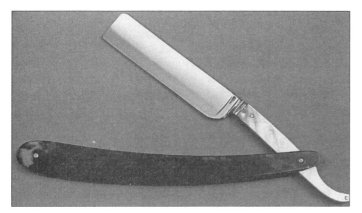

KINFOLKS INC. (etch), square point, mother of pearl inlaid tang, with tortoise-shell handles; $125.

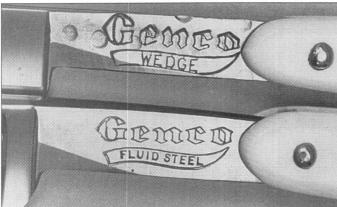

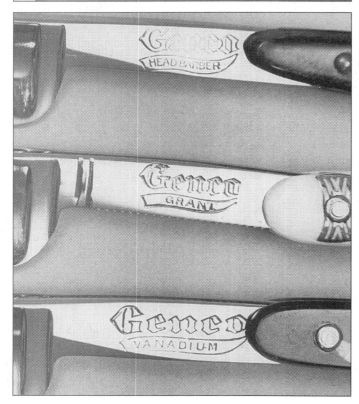

Mint "GENCO," Bradford, Pa. razors sell for between $35 to $65.

THE GENCO CO. BRADFORD, PA (1935-1955), gun blue tang marked "EASY ACES" (the GENCO version of the "CASE ACE," square point, cracked ice handles with inlaid silver logo; $65.

W.R. Case and Son
Little Valley, N.Y.
(1902-1905)

J. Russell Case broke away from his uncles at Case Brothers to form his jobbing company, incorporated in Little Valley, N.Y. in 1902 under the name of W.R. Case and Son Cutlery Company. Although Case and Son never manufactured cutlery, it was jobbing for Napanoch and other cutlery manufacturers of the day. This company went on to merge with N.H. Platts in late 1904, and later to form W. R. Case and Sons, Bradford, Pa. in 1905. This became the cornerstone of W. R. Case and Sons that we know today. Razors with these stampings are extremely rare and valuable, as well as historically interesting to the collector.

Manufactured by Napanoch.

Manufactured by George W. Korn.

Manufactured by C. Platt's Sons Co.

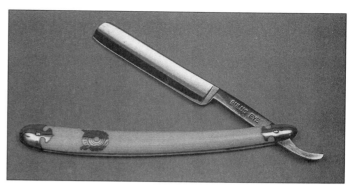

W.R. CASE & SON, LITTLE VALLEY, N.Y. (fireside), "BULLS EYE" on markside, imitation ivory handles with silver end-caps and inlaid logo; $280.

CASE'S GOLD SEAL, LITTLE VALLEY, N.Y. (mfg. by Platts), square point, blade etched "CASE'S GOLD SEAL," gold-wash, genuine mother of pearl tang, with tortoise bamboo handles. Extremely rare; $425.

W.R. CASE & SON CUTLERY CO., LITTLE VALLEY, N.Y. (mfg. by G.W. Korn), square point, mottled yellow celluloid handles, rare; $175.

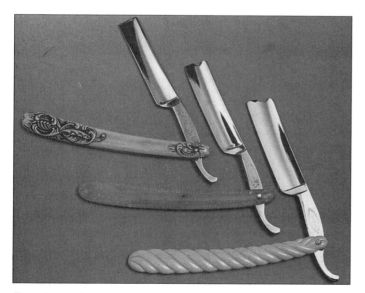

Top: W.R. CASE & SON CUTLERY CO., LITTLE VALLEY, N.Y. (arc mark), square point, cream handles with wine-colored scroll; $180. Middle: hollow point, cream beaded border handles; $195. Bottom: hollow point, imitation ivory twisted rope handles; $195.

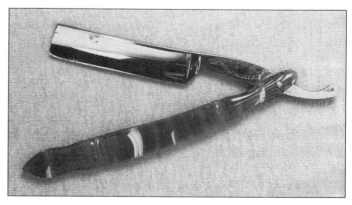

W.R. CASE & SON CUTLERY CO., LITTLE VALLEY, N.Y. (mfg. by Napanoch), candy stripe, classic pattern, very rare; $275.

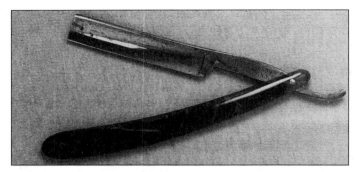

W.R. CASE & SON, LITTLE VALLEY, N.Y. (mfg. by Platts), square point, imitation horn handles; $175.

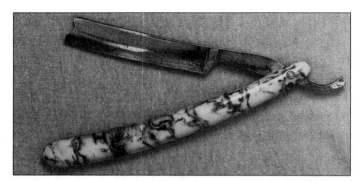

W.R. CASE & SON CUTLERY CO., LITTLE VALLEY, N.Y. (mfg. by Napanoch), mottled cream and brown celluloid handles; $160.

W.R. Case and Sons
Bradford, PA
(1905-1920)

These razors were the first razors actually manufactured by the merger of W.R. Case and Son and Platts Brothers, Eldrid, Pa., forming W.R. Case and Sons. All of these razors have the stamping on the mark side only. A few of these razors have pattern numbers on the finger loop. No information is available on the meaning of these markings, but they only appear on razors of this period.

Razors made during this period are the most beautiful of W.R. Case and Sons gender, having the widest selection of handles—some with very ornate molded designs—many having inlaid tangs of pearl, tortoise shell, imitation ivory, etc. Blades were more ornate too, with gimping or firework, and some with etching ranging from fancy "W.R. Case & Sons," to having a blade completely etched with a Damascus rosette pattern. While most razors made during this period were of plain design for the average man, many more ornate razors were made by W.R. Case and Sons in this time span than any other period in its history. It was the only period W.R. Case and Sons etched its blades, with the few exceptions such as the "No Cussing" and the "Hand-Forged" (1920-1955) or used inlaid tangs. This was indeed a classic period for W.R. Case and Sons razor production.

Known W.R. CASE & SONS, BRADFORD, PA. markings (markside 1905-1920).

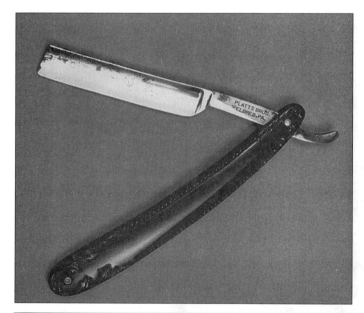

PLATTS BROS., ELDRED PA., square point, brown beaded border handles; $65.

Note: W. R. Case (1905 to date) was a product of a merger with Platts Brothers Company. It was Platts' equipment, workers and expertise that made W. R. Case and Sons Cutlery. J. Russell Case was the office and sales end of the company. Therefore, W. R. Case Cutlery (1905-1920) and that of C. Platts Sons (1895-1905) and Western States (1915-1925) look very much alike, and in fact were manufactured by the same man—N.H. Platts.

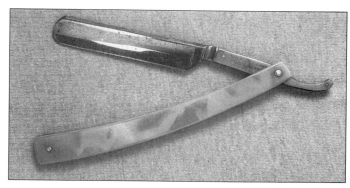

W.R. CASE & SONS, BRADFORD, PA., round point, waterfall tang with waterfall handles. Extremely rare; $425.

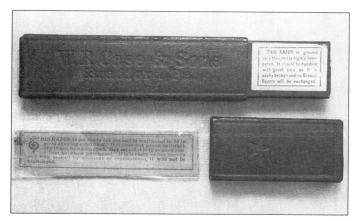

W.R. CASE & SONS, BRADFORD, PA., razor box with hard-to-find original papers.

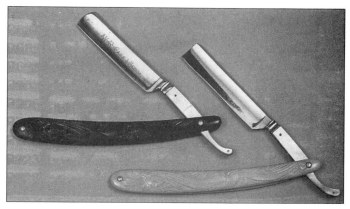

Left: W.R. CASE, BRADFORD, PA. Round point, blade etched "W.R. CASE & SONS" inlaid mother of pearl tang, black flowing hair handles; $250. Right: Square point, inlaid mother of pearl tang with imitation ivory flowing hair handles; $225.

Tortoise bamboo handle, pearl tang, W.R. Case & Sons, Inc.; $250.

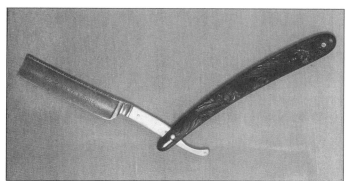

W.R. CASE & SONS, BRADFORD, PA., square point, blade fully etched to look like Damascus rosettes with "W.R. CASE & SONS" across it, top of blade fully gimped, genuine mother-of-pearl tang with black flowing hair handles. Extremely rare; $750.

W.R. CASE & SONS, BRADFORD, PA., round point, blade etched "W.R. CASE & SONS," black tang with black flowing hair handles; $225.

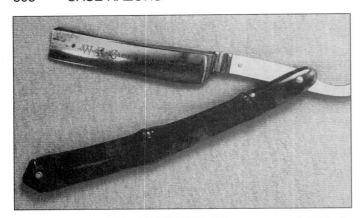

W.R. CASE & SONS, BRADFORD, PA., square point, blade etched "W.R. Case & Sons," genuine mother of pearl tang, tortoise bamboo handles; $250.

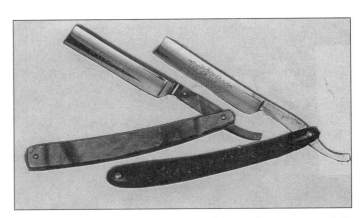

Left: W.R. CASE & SONS, BRADFORD, PA., square-point, blade etched "W.R. Case & Sons," silver swirl inlaid tang with matching handles; $300. Right: Square point, blade with rare tang etching. Blade etched "The Bradford," black molded leaf handles; $175.

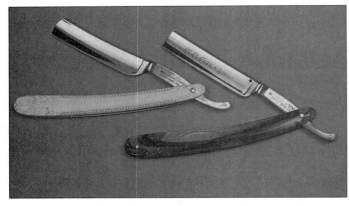

Left: W.R. CASE & SONS, BRADFORD, P.A. (script), round point, inlaid mother of pearl tang, imitation ivory beaded border handles; $275. Right: Square-point blade, etched "W.R. Case & Sons," inlaid mother of pearl tang with butter and molasses beaded border handles; $250.

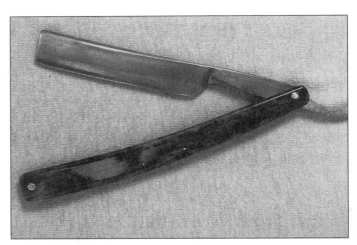

W.R. CASE & SONS, BRADFORD, PA. (rare etching), square point, imitation bone handles; $155.

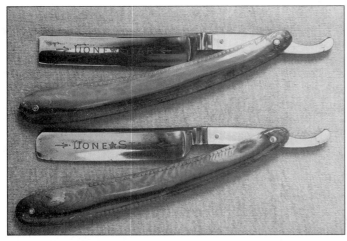

W.R. CASE & SONS, BRADFORD, PA., round point, blade etched "LONE STAR" with goldwash, genuine mother of pearl tang with butter and molasses beaded border; $275. Square point; $275.

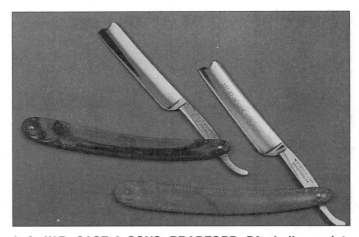

Left: W.R. CASE & SONS, BRADFORD, PA., hollow point, butter and molasses beaded border handles; $160. Right: Hollow point, blade etched "W.R. Case & Sons," cream streaked beaded border handles; $180.

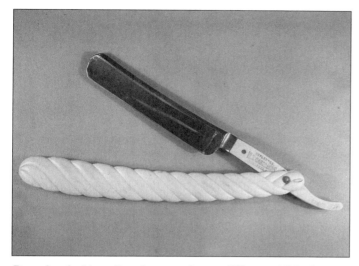

Rope ivoriod handle, stamp and tang different, W.R. Case & Sons Cutlery Co.; $200.

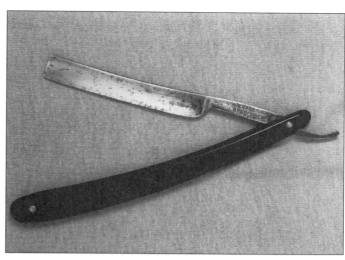

W.R. CASE & SONS, BRADFORD, square point blade ground extremely thin, slick black handles; $140.

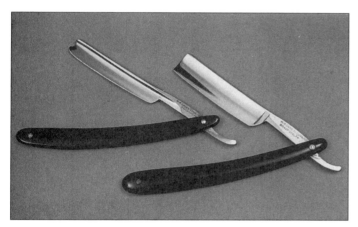

Left: W.R. CASE & SONS, BRADFORD, PA., hollow point with unusual shape blade, slick black handles; $150. Right: Square point, slick black handles; $125.

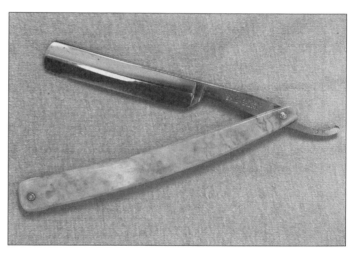

W.R. CASE & SONS, BRADFORD, PA., round point, mottled yellow celluloid handles; $125.

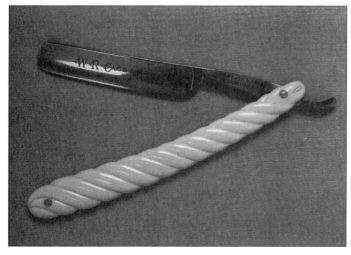

W.R. CASE & SONS, BRADFORD, PA., round point, blade etched "W.R. CASE & SONS," imitation ivory twisted rope handles; $175.

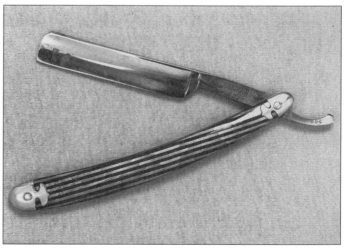

W.R. CASE & SONS, BRADFORD, PA., No. 354, square point, silver and black handles with silver end caps; $225.

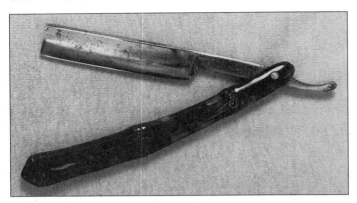

W.R. CASE & SONS, BRADFORD, PA., square point, tortoise bamboo handles; $140.

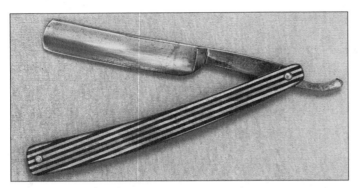

W.R. CASE & SONS, BRADFORD, PA., No. 334, round point, silver and black stripe handles; $135.

W.R. Case and Sons
(made in Germany)
(1905-1915)

Razors having this German stamp were imported for a short period of time somewhere between 1905 and the start of World War I. All have the backs of the blades worked in a floral pattern, with W.R. Case and Sons etched on them. Handles are of various colored celluloids, molded in the "Classic" pattern. As the war grew more and more imminent with Germany, many of these razors were imported without "Germany" stamped on the tang, and some have no marking at all except the blade etching.

This stamp is on the file side.

W.R. CASE & SONS, BRADFORD, PA., "Made in Germany" on file side, worked back, blade etched "W.R. CASE & SONS," goldstone classic handles, rare; $225.

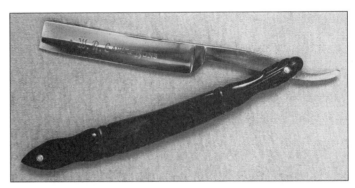

"W.R. CASE & SONS" etched on blade only; this tang escaped marking in Germany, worked back blade, black classic handles; $150.

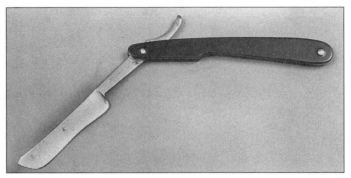

"W.R. CASE AND SONS," "Corn Razor." Although not actually manufactured by W.R. Case and Sons, the company marketed a corn razor for a very short period of time between 1905 to 1920. They are very rare; $250.

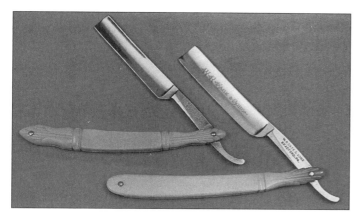

Left: W.R. CASE & SONS, BRADFORD, PA., square point, imitation-ivory classic handles; $135. Right: Square point, blade etched "W.R. CASE & SONS," bone handles with the top carved in the classic pattern; $200.

W.R. Case and Sons
Bradford, PA.
(1920-1955)

All razors of this period have a pattern name such as "Adoration," Gold Nuggett, etc. on the mark side and the Case stamping appears on the fileside. Both style stamps seems to appear throughout the entire time span; therefore, it cannot be used to date earlier razors. As a general rule, razors that are more ornate with silver inlays and endcaps on the handles, etc. are of the older gender.

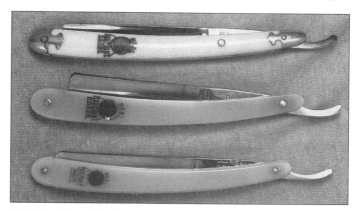

"REAL RED POINT," silver endcaps and in-laid logo; $125. Inlaid logo, $90. Painted logo, $45.

Let's take, for example, the real "Red Point" razor. The "Red Point," c. 1920, had silver endcaps, imitation ivory handles, inlaid silver logo with red enamel center. The "Red Point," c. 1930, continued with the inlaid silver logo with the red enamel dot; however, the handle material was changed to cream-colored celluloid and no longer had the silver endcaps. "Red Point" razors of the 1940s had cream-colored celluloid handles with a painted red-dot logo. As you can see, as the years passed, less and less extra work went into razor production.

With very few exceptions, razor patterns of this period always had the same handle material. For example, "Gold Nuggett" razors always had gold-colored handles and the "Bull's Eye" razor used tortoise shell for its handles. There were no handles with molded designs such as beaded borders, or flowing hair. Except for rare decorations such as inlays or endcaps, all razors were smooth handles.

Blades of this period, with a few exceptions, are identical in style, having either square or round point. A rare example of a hollow-point razor of this period is the "Cornhusker." All razors had fully polished blades and were available in either 9/16" or 5/8" width, some with gun blue or goldwash tangs. The "Bulls Eye" and the "No Cussing" (c. 1920-1955) razors are some of the rare examples of etch-

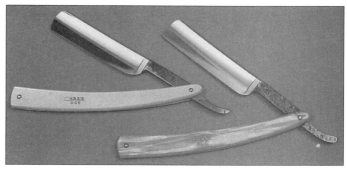

Left: "CASE'S ACE," imitation white pearl, stamped logo; $75. Right: Cracked ice, inlaid silver logo; $95.

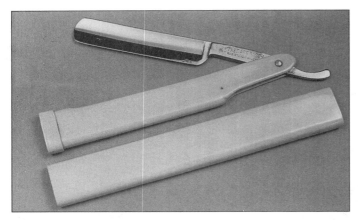

"THE CASE RAZOR," Reg. No. 1915, imitation ivory handles with matching case; $125.

ing during this period. Some are a combination of etching and goldwash, the "Bulls Eye" having a hand-hammered tang.

Most of these razors were discontinued before 1940, but since there were large stocks of many of these razors, they were listed in catalogs and sold throughout the 1940s and into the early 1950s. Case still sold several of these patterns up until 1955.

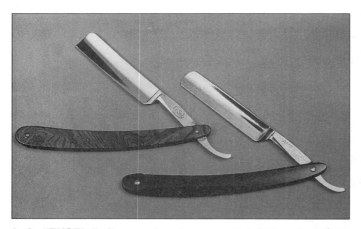

Left: "EKSEL," silver and molasses celluloid handles; $75. Right: "AMERICAN BARBER," slick black handles; $60.

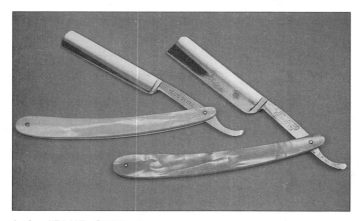

Left: "BLUE STEEL," cracked-ice handles; $65. Right: "HONOR ROLL," cracked-ice handles; $65.

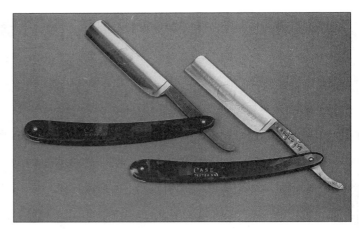

"BULL'S EYE," hammered tang, imitation tortoise handles, blade etched "HAND FORGED," round point; $100. Square point; $100.

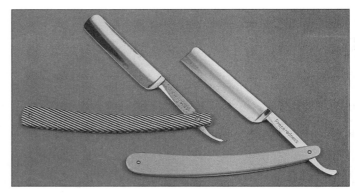

"PREPAREDNESS," black and white stripe; $75. Imitation ivory; $60.

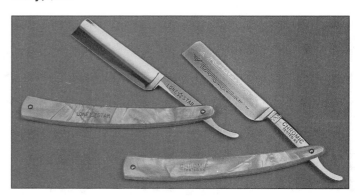

Left: "LONE STAR," cracked ice handles; $70. Right: "CHROMATIC TESTED XX," blade etched "OUR BEST RAZOR"; $125.

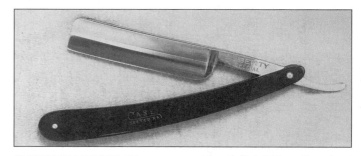

"LIBERTY SPECIAL," transparent blue celluloid handles; $65.

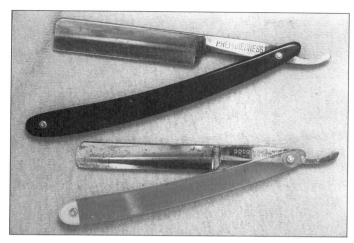

"PREPAREDNESS," slick black; $50. Clear yellow; $55.

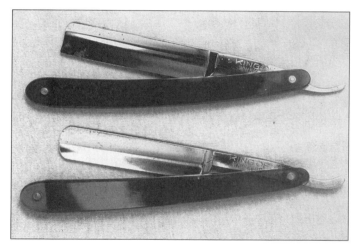

"KING OF WHISKERS," transparent red celluloid handles: Square point; $55. Round point; $55.

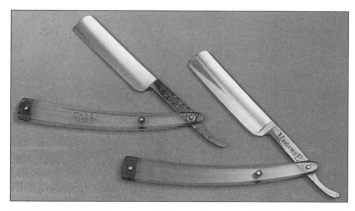

Left: "WEDGE," hammered tang, clear smoke handles; $65. Right: "MANANESE," clear smoke handles; $65.

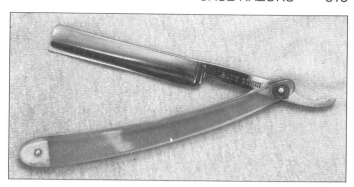

"BLUE STEEL," transparent yellow handles; $50.

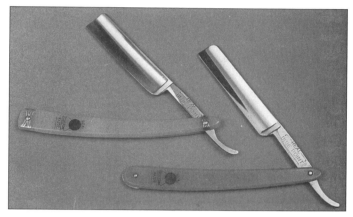

"REAL BLUE POINT": Inlaid bowties; $75. Painted logo; $45.

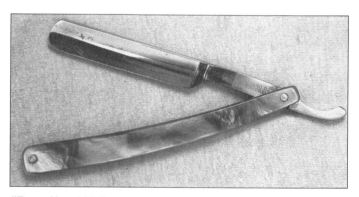

"Reg. No. 023," "WARRANTED FOR LIFE," green pearl handles; $80.

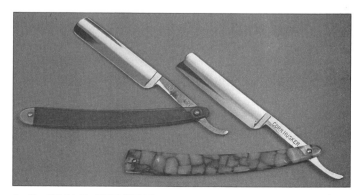

Left: "GOLD NUGGET," transparent gold handles; $40. Right: "CORN HUSKER," cracked marble handles; $125.

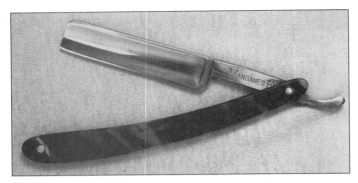

"MANGANESE," imitation tortoise handles; $60.

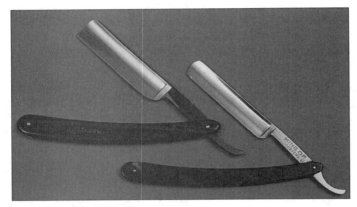

Left: "MANGANESE," streaked oak handles, $75. Right: "KING OF WHISKERS," imitation tortoise handles; $65.

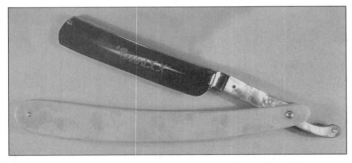

Abalone pearl tang, Tested XX, waterfall handle; $250.

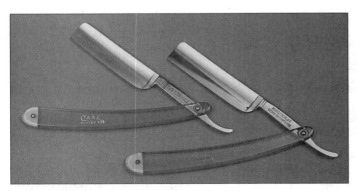

Left: "GOLD NUGGET," gold wash tang, transparent gold handles; $80. Right: "KUNSTSCHIFF VOLTAGE TEMPER," transparent gold handles; $65.

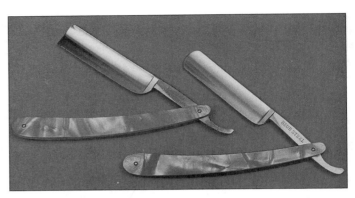

Left: "KUNSTSCHIFF VOLTAGE TEMPER," goldwash tang, gold pearl handles; $90. Right: "BLUE STEEL," green pearl handles; $75. Warning! The handle material used on these razors is extremely corrosive to metal surfaces.

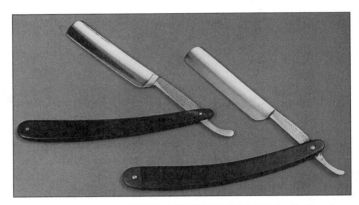

Left: "Reg. No. 023, WARRANTED FOR LIFE," imitation tortoise handles; $75. Right: "KING OF WHISKERS," transparent red celluloid handles; $55.

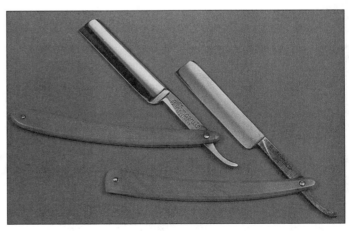

Right: "ADORATION," yellow-swirl handles with logo, any type; $45. Far right: "TEMPERITE," yellow-swirl handles, any type; $45.

W. R. CASE & SONS CUTLERY CO.
BRADFORD, PENNSYLVANIA

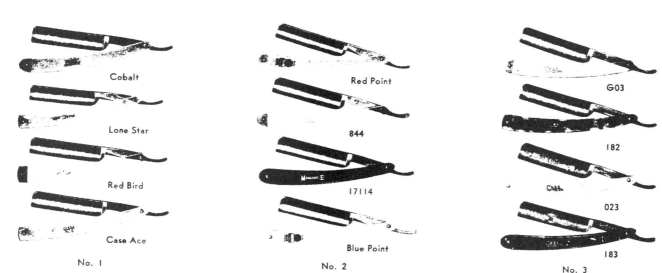

ILLUSTRATION NO. 1

COBALT Full concave ground blade of the finest barber quality. Gun-metal tang. Handle stamped "COBALT". Blade made in ⅝" width with hone point.

LONE STAR This is one of our finest full concave blades perfectly ground and finished. Tang is mirror polished and branded "LONE STAR". Blade is made in ⁹⁄₁₆ or ⅝ inches in width, hone point. Handle is made of beautiful imitation pearl with "LONE STAR" stamped in gold.

RED BIRD One of the most popular barber razors that is also used by self shavers. Blade is full concave perfectly ground and finished. Tang is mirror finished, branded "RED BIRD". Blade is made in ⅝ inch width in hone point only. Handle is transparent celluloid. Red Bird stamped in red on handle.

CASE ACE Full concave blade for barber or self shaver, finish and grind are of our finest quality. Tang is hand hammered and blue finish, branded "CASE ACE". Made in ⁹⁄₁₆ or ⅝ inch width blade with round and hone point. Handle of beautiful imitation pearl celluloid. Name in metal inlay on handle.

ILLUSTRATION NO. 2

RED POINT Full concave ground blade of the highest quality, fine glaze finish. Mirror finish tang branded "REAL RED POINT". Made in ⁹⁄₁₆ or ⅝ inch width blade with hone or round point. Cream color celluloid handle with red stamping.

No. 844 Full concave ground blade the same as the finest barber's razor, beautiful finish. Gold plated tang branded "KUNSTSCHLIFF VOLTAGE TEMPER". Made in ⅝ inch width with hone point. Handle is amber celluloid.

No. 17114 Full concave ground highly finished blade. Gun-metal tang branded "MANGANESE". Blade made in ⅝ inch width blade in hone point. Handle of oak colored celluloid. "MANGANESE" stamped on handle in silver.

BLUE POINT Full concave ground blade that is preferred by barbers. No finer razor for quality and workmanship has ever been made anywhere. Tang is mirror finished and branded "REAL BLUE POINT". Blade is made in ⅝ inch width with hone point. Handle is cream colored celluloid with name stamped in blue.

ILLUSTRATION NO. 3

No. G03 Full concave ground blade highly polished. Tang, gold plated, branded "GOLD NUGGET." Made in ⁹⁄₁₆, ⅝ or 6⁄8 inch width blade with hone or round point. Handle is amber colored celluloid, with our trade mark stamped in handle in silver. loid, with our trade mark stamped on handle in silver.

No. 182 Full concave ground blade, highly polished mirror finish tang branded "CORN HUSKER". Made in ⅝ inch width blade and hollow hone point. Handle mottled cream and black celluloid, our trade mark stamped on handle in gold.

No. 023 Full concave ground blade. Highly finished gold etching on blade, tang mirror finished. Made in ⅝ inch width in hone point. Handle cream colored celluloid with trade marks in red.

No. 183 Full concave ground blade. Etched "HAND FORGED" with gold plated center. Tang gun-metal finish, and hand hammered. Made in ⅝ inch blade in hone point. Handle is imitation tortoise shell celluloid, our trade mark stamped in silver on the handle.

CASE XX catalog, dated 1946.

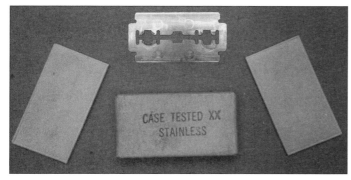

Case Tested XX, stainless (box top); three individually wrapped safety razor blades per box. (Blades unmarked).

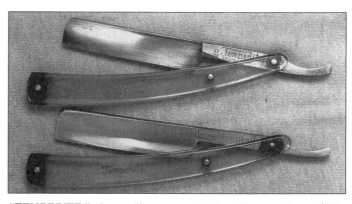

"TEMPERITE," clear yellow or smoke handles, any type; $45.

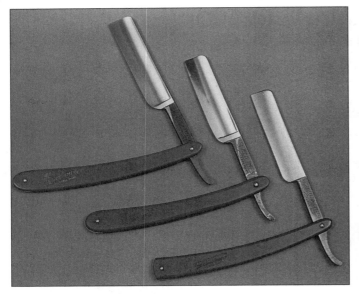

"RED IMP," red handles, any type; $25.

W.R. Case and Sons
Germany
(1920-1940)

These razors were made to look just like Case razors of the period. The tang reads "Made by Soligin Germany Experts" (on the markside). This is the second German invasion, which came sometime between 1920 and the start of World War II. Though they are not quite as rare as the early German razor, they are still very hard to find.

Made in USA
By Case
(1955-1962)

In the early 1950s, W.R. Case started to exhaust its existing stock of straight razors. There was still a

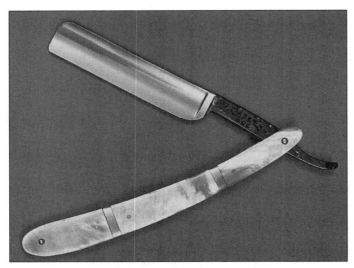

"CASE ACE," genuine mother of pearl handles, gun blue hammered tang; $500.

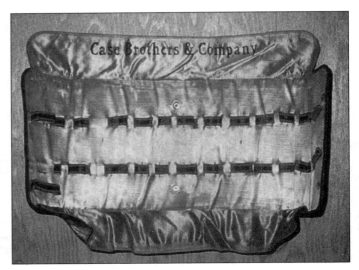

Case Razor Roll, owners initials on front, J.R.C.; $75.

Razor Roll, embossed, Case Brothers & Co.; $75.

small demand for razors in the United States, but there was even a greater market in South America. In 1955, Case introduced a line of lesser-quality razors mainly for the export market, marked "MADE IN USA BY CASE." Razors made during this period were of plain design and the blades were non-polished. In 1962, W.R. Case and Sons discontinued its production of straight razors, thus ending 57 years of razor production.

Approximately 100 genuine mother-of-pearl "CASE ACE" razors were made in 1962, when W.R. Case and Sons ended razor production—62 of the best were given to Case executives, salesmen and employees.

Facts on the 'Hawbaker Special' Knife

Ralph H. Scruton, Jr.

Hawbaker Special.

I am writing this article to try and clear up the myths and mysteries about the fabled "Hawbaker Special" knife. We would also like to commemorate the man who is its father, S. Stanley Hawbaker, and the man (a friend of Hawbaker's) who started this pen on its mission, Glenn N. Helmuth. Unfortunately, Hawbaker and Helmuth have both passed on to that place where all good trappers, hunters, fishermen and knife collectors go.

S. Stanley Hawbaker started the S. Stanley Hawbaker & Sons, General Trapping and Supply Co., Fort Loudon, PA, in 1938 and put out his first catalog in 1940. The first knives made for his trade were sheath knives, a 5-inch blade and a 7-inch blade, with maple handles and three copper rivets. These were made by a prisoner in State College, PA, and the only markings on them were the prisoner's name and State College, PA. The company also had a folding knife it sold, which was a Schrade "Improved Muskrat," pattern number 7817S, with a jigged bone handle. This knife was etched "Improved Muskrat Knife" on the front blade and no etching on the back blade. How many of these knives he sold from 1938 into the early '50s is anyone's guess.

Hawbaker wanted to put a personal touch into his business, so he contacted York Cutlery Co., 552 West Market Street, York, PA. Julius Guteman took an order for 50 dozen (600), 4416 1/4, "German Hawbaker

Trappers Knives," thus the "Hawbaker Special" was conceived in 1955. These knives have a jigged bone handle, are stamped York Cutlery Company, Soligen Germany and the blades are etched, "Improved Muskrat Knife" on the front blade, with "Hawbaker Special" on the back blade. From 1955 through August 1958, it purchased 1728 of these knives. But as we all know, a trapper's knife must take a lot of abuse and punishment, and these proved weak at the knick and the blade would break off there. Unfortunately, this made a lot of trappers unhappy, so Hawbaker started looking for another manufacturer.

He contacted W.R. Case & Sons, Bradford, PA, in February 1960, and became a Case dealer on Oct. 3, 1960. Case agreed to make the "Hawbaker Special" on Oct. 12, 1960, if Hawbaker would purchase a blanking die to make the sheep-foot blade. They stated the knife would be in their Muskrat pattern, with the sheep-foot blade substituted for their current blade and the blanking die would be held there for the Hawbaker's exclusive use. This is still true today. Hawbaker had to order 50 dozen (600) knives at a time.

Mr. S. Stanley Hawbaker.

This order could be broken into separate orders, as long as the total was used within a one-year period.

The first order for the "Hawbaker Special" was written on Sept. 11, 1961 and they received the "Proto-Type" knife on Sept. 18, 1961, which was approved at this time. The first shipment of knives, 180, was received in November 1961. To keep track of the rest of the knives received over the years, please refer to the information below, where I have stated facts as per order dates, dates shipped and quantity shipped. As to the blade markings, I can only guess to what markings were in each shipment and thus it is only conjecture on the part of the author as to what information is listed.

With Case's production schedule set on 600 knives, there had to be over-runs; therefore, we have many transition knives in the "Hawbaker Specials," sometimes even more than the regular stampings. Also keep in mind some of these knives were ordered and made one year, but some of them would be shipped the following year. Remember another thing: the "Hawbaker Special" is identical to the standard Case Muskrat, except the back handle and the back blade. The Hawbaker does not have a nail groove in the back handle and of course the sheep-foot back blade. Case never used regular Muskrat handles on the 4% handled in bone, in 1973. But some quick-thinking counterfeiter has already changed some of these from delrin to bone, so BEWARE. In May 1971, Case informed them they had enough parts left over from previous (600) knife runs, to make approximately 180 knives. They shipped 182 knives, probably all transitions of some sort.

Contradictory to some thinking, I don't believe there were any USA-XX transitions, as neither order in this period was shipped in full (595-591); therefore, no over-runs on the XX blades. In 1982, 603 of the green handled and 181 red-handled knives were sent back to the factory because of the colors. (So the reorder June 1982.)

Case made the "Hawbaker Specials" for the Hawbakers from 1961 through 1982, but in 1974 Hawbaker placed his order too late for Case to put them in a production run and get them to him for that trapping season. Hawbaker contacted Queen Cutlery Company, Titusville, PA and placed an order with that company for 600 knives. These knives had the same etching as the Case knife, but were stamped Queen Steel on the tang, and had imitation Winterbottom plastic handles. The company had sold this knife prior to this and after, but there were no etchings on the blades; therefore, it was not a true "Hawbaker Special."

As of this time, I have, or have seen, 29 different "Hawbaker Specials," starting with the Schrade and continuing through the 1982 Case. At this time, I have 23 different ones in my collection. There are other collections in this area with 22-23 different knives in them also, but none of us have the exact same variations, so therefore, there are 29 different variations. These knives were shipped all over the United States, including Alaska and Canada. They were bought and used by trappers. You must note the small quantities spread out over the years. With these things in mind, you can imagine the sheer exuberance of finding one of these fine knives at a show or for sale anywhere.

It seems that some other facts about the fabled "Hawbaker Special Knife" need some help.

First, you might have either a Schrade Cut (straight line 1930-1948) or a Schrade Walden (1948-1973) or both in peach-seed bone handles in your collection. They are both correct and should be considered correct in this collection. Let's go back one step and take a look at the same knife, with different markings. Up in Ogdensburg, NY, was the famous Adirondack's trapper and lure maker, Mr. E.J. Dailey. He and Mr. Hawbaker were very good friends, even though they were competitors. Mr. Dailey had been in business long before Mr. Hawbaker and Mr. Hawbaker used quite a few of his ideas in marketing his own products, such as catalogs and even eventually his name on a knife. Therefore, if you should run across a Schrade Cut, peach-seed bone handled, with "Dailey's Skinning Knife" etched on the master blade, you'll know what it is. These are very, very rare and the mint price is $550.

Moving on, to the order of 182 knives shipped in 1971, I said there were no two nail grooved bone handled knives included in this order—this information came from Mr. Hawbaker's son. But since very closely examining 4 or 5 of these knives, we can find no flaws or anything to base this on, so we believe there were some of those knives made, but a very limited quantity. As in any transition or variation, be extremely careful in examining it before purchasing it. It seems there are other transitions showing up that have been made up by switching parts, so be very careful and know who you are buying these knives from.

S. Stanley Hawbaker & Sons, 358 Hawbaker Drive South, Fort Loudon, PA, still operates today under his son, Edwin M. Hawbaker—without whose help, along with that of Mrs. S. Stanley Hawbaker, this article could not have been written, so many, many thanks from me and all the knife collectors and enthusiasts out there.

S. Stanley Hawbaker passed away on Oct. 27, 1983, following a timber-cutting accident. His and my personal friend, Glenn N. Helmuth, died unexpectedly on March 1, 1986.

The interest in these knives has been growing so fast and the values have increased accordingly, especially the early and uncommon transitions—so buy with pride and care.

Date	Maker	Handle	# ordered	# shipped	Date shipped	Blade variations	Hawbaker variations	Value
1938-48	Schrade Cut	peach-seed bone	Unknown	Unknown	Unknown	Improved Muskrat	Not Etched	$650
1948-73	Schrade Walden	peach-seed bone	Unknown	Unknown	Unknown	Improved Muskrat	Not Etched	$600
1955	York Deep-Etch	jigged bone	600	600	Dec. '55	Improved Muskrat	Hawbaker Special	$650
Oct. '56	York #1 & #2	jigged bone	600	600	March '57	Improved Muskrat	Hawbaker Special	$650
1958	York #2	jigged bone	600	538	Aug. '58	Improved Muskrat	Hawbaker Special	$650
Sept. '61	Case	jigged bone	600	180 180 235	Nov. '61 Dec. '61 Feb. '62	Case XX Case XX Case XX	Case XX Case XX Case XX	$650 $650 $650
Sept. '63	Case	jigged bone	600	180 411	Oct. '63 Oct. '64	Case XX Case XX	Case XX Case XX	$650 $650
Sept. '66	Case	jigged bone	600	180 420	Oct. '66 Oct. '67	Case XX, USA Case XX, USA	Case XX, USA Case XX, USA	$550 $550
July '69	Case	jigged bone	600	180 144 282	Aug. '69 Oct. '69 July '70	Case XX, USA Case XX, USA Case XX, USA 10 Dots	Case XX, USA Case XX, USA 10 Dots 10 Dots	$550 $550 $500 $650
May '71	Case	jigged bone	180	182	May '71	10 Dots 10 Dots 9 Dots 9 Dots	Case XX, USA 9 Dots Case XX, USA 10 Dots	$600 $550 $550 $500
Nov. '71	Case	jigged bone	600	300 311	Jan. '72 Oct. '72	9 Dots 8 Dots	9 Dots 7 Dots	$250 $150
Apr. '73	Case	delrin	600	180 462	June '73 Sept. '73	7 Dots 7 Dots	7 Dots 7 Dots	$250 $200
Nov. '73	Case	delrin jigged bone jigged bone	600 Approx. 4% Approx. 4%	600	March '74	7 Dots 7 Dots 7 Dots	7 Dots 7 Dots 1 Nail Gr. 7 Dots 2 Nail Gr.	$200 $600 $600
Sept. '74	Queen	imitation Winterbottom			Oct. '74	Improved Muskrat	Hawbaker Special	$350
Mar. '78	Case	jigged bone	1,000	1,000	Apr. '78	3 Dots 3 Dots 3 Dots 2 Dots 2 Dots 2 Dots	9 Dots 7 Dots 2 Dots 9 Dots 7 Dots 2 Dots	$150 $150 $150 $150 $150 $150
Oct. '81	Case	jigged green bone	1,000	1,000	1982	S 9 Dots S 9 Dots	8 Dots 1 Nail Gr. 8 Dots 2 Nail Gr.	$100 $100
Nov. '81	Case	jigged red bone	1,000	1,000	1982	S 9 Dots S 9 Dots	8 Dots 1 Nail Gr. 8 Dots 2 Nail Gr.	$100 $100
June '82	Case	jigged green bone	1,000	1,114	1982	S 8 Dots S 8 Dots	8 Dots 1 Nail Gr. 8 Dots 2 Nail Gr.	$100 $100
June '82	Case	jigged red bone	1,000	681	1982	S 8 Dots S 8 Dots	8 Dots 1 Nail Gr. 8 Dots 2 Nail Gr.	$100 $100
Apr. '87	Case	stag 50th Anniv.	1,000	1,000	June '87	SS 3 Dots	Stag Hawbaker Spl.	$300

Queen

Titusville, PA

Back in 1918, nine men with a dream left their jobs, secured space in a garage in Titusville, Pa. and founded their own company.

All former employees of Schatt & Morgan Cutlery Co., they did what they knew best—produce knives. For the first four years, the company didn't have a name. It didn't need one because its entire production was under contract for other companies.

The company continues contract work to this day. Some of the production is private-label work and some is very special. In the latter category is the National Knife Collectors Association 1981 club knife.

In 1922, just four years after starting up, the partners realized there was a place for a new name in the cutlery industry and named their organization Queen City Cutlery Co., Inc.

Genza Revitsky became the first president; Jess Baker, E. Clarence Erickson, and Frank Foresther were all vice presidents; Harry L. Matthews was secretary of treasury.

The name was derived from Titusville, which was called Queen City because the petroleum industry was started when Col. Edwin L. Drake drilled the first oil well there in 1859.

Soon after adopting a name, the company had to find larger quarters as it began to market its own knives under the Queen City stamp.

In 1930, Schatt & Morgan went broke and in 1932, Queen bought all property and equipment of the company which had originally employed Queen's founders. The property included the building still occupied by Queen. It was built in 1895 by the City of Titusville to entice Schatt & Morgan to move from Gowanga, NY, where it had been organized in 1890.

During the early 1940s, two of Queen's founders (Erickson & Matthews) began to experiment with stainless steel for blades and springs, and by 1945, had switched from carbon steel to 440C Stainless for blades and other type stainless for springs.

Other cutlers were also switching to stainless steel, but were using other grades that proved unsuitable for blades because they wouldn't hold an edge.

As a result, many knife makers returned to the use of carbon steel. Queen's founders, having found the right grade of stainless and convinced of its high quality and serviceability, continued with the 440C.

To avoid the stigma attached by the public to stainless steel, Queen stopped using the word "stainless" on its knives. The company registered the name "Queen Steel" for use on the 440C blades and continues to use it. Queen was purchased by Servotronics, Inc. of Buffalo, NY in 1969.

(The above information is courtesy of *The Outdoor News*; Grove City, PA.)

John M. Lussier
Central Falls, Rhode Island
(Queen contributor)

"I became interested in Queen pocket knives many years ago because of three reasons: 1) Their designs; 2.) Queen was the first to use all stainless steel and 3.) They were the only pocket knives to use Winterbottom bone, a material not used by any other manufacturer with the exception of W.R. Case & Sons, which occasionally used it on a few patterns. It is a real challenge to acquire all the patterns and tang stamps from 1946 to the present, especially the 'Q Stainless' and smoked pearls."

Key figures associated with Queen throughout the years

Walter W. Bell became associated with Queen Cutlery in 1953. In 1958, he was elected to the Board of Directors and vice president. In 1961, he was elected president upon the death of his father-in-law, E. Clarence Erickson. Although the company was sold to Servotronics, Inc. in October 1969, he remained as president until his retirement in 1972.

Louis P. Foresther joined Queen Cutlery Company at the time of his father's (Frank Foresther) death in October of 1939. At this time, he bought his father's interest in the company. He became 1st vice president, officer and director and was also very active in the building and maintenance of machinery and tools until the time of his death on Oct. 17, 1956.

Fred R. Sampson became associated with Queen Cutlery Company in August 1948. Working in all departments, he was appointed foreman of the Cover Room in 1952 and Assembly Room in 1955. He remained in these departments until 1976 when he was appointed Master Cutler and Designer.

Gerald J. Matthews, son of Adell Matthews and the late Harry Matthews became associated with

QUEEN CITY

ca. 1922-1932

QUEEN CITY
TITUSVILLE PA.

ca. 1925-1932

ca. 1930-1932

ca. 1925-1945

QUEEN CUT. CO.

ca. 1932-1949

ca. 1932-1955

QUEENCUTLERYCO TITUSVILLE, PA.

ca. 1932-1950

ca. 1935-1955

ca. 1946-1950

STAINLESS

ca. 1946-1948

ca. 1946-1950

ca. 1946-1948

ca. 1946-1948

ca. 1946-1949

ca. 1949-1958

ca. 1958-1960

1972 Only

ca. 1973-1975

1976 Only

1976 Only

USA
1977 Only

USA
1978 Only

USA
1979 Only

USA
1980 Only

USA
1981 Only

USA
1982 Only

USA
1983 Only

USA

Starting in 1984

Queen Cutlery Company in 1947. In 1958, he was elected to the board of directors and secretary/treasurer. He remained with the company until 1972.

John H. Erickson, son of the late E. Clarence and Rebecca Erickson, became associated with Queen Cutlery Company in March 1946. He worked in the grinding room, later transferred to the hafting room and then to display work.

Carl C. Eldred joined Queen Cutlery in 1973 as supervisor. In 1974, he was promoted to his present position as plant manager.

Robert E. Matthews, son of Adell Matthews and the late Harry Matthews became associated with Queen Cutlery in 1949. In 1958, he was elected vice president and to the board of directors. He remained with the company until 1972.

Robert L. Stamp joined Queen Cutlery Company in July 1972 as materials manager. He was promoted to plant manager in 1973. In 1974, he was promoted to general manager. He remained in this position until October 1983.

William J. Hunter was elected president in October 1983. He had previously held the position of vice president of sales and marketing for Ontario Knife Company, sister company to Queen Cutlery. Along with the position of president of Queen Cutlery Company, he was also promoted to executive vice president and general manager of Ontario Knife Company.

John Wyllie is the current general manager of Queen. His title is vice president-general manager and he is responsible for both Queen and Ontario. He joined Ontario in 1978 as materials manager and was promoted to vice president-general manager in 1987.

Type of handle material used by Queen, 1922-1986

Rogers bone, Winterbottom bone, celluloid, metal, ebony, rosewood, genuine stag, pearl, imitation pearl, amber, yellow delrin, red, black, black micarta, smoked pearl, (burnt orange and red imitation Winterbottom bone) and imitation brown and black Winterbottom bone.

Special Note: Burnt orange—This Winterbottom bone was used in 1959-1960 as a substitute for Winterbottom bone. The handles were attached and the

Mr. and Mrs. Fred Fisher of Ohio are Queen knife collectors and contributors.

knives were then dipped in a vat of red dye. It was found that the colors were not uniform as they streaked and colors ranged from a dark red to pink red and even a purple red. It was decided to discontinue this material with all the problems Queen was having.

Genuine stag—Queen used stag in its early Queen City Knives, but reintroduced stag in 1981 on a limited basis for a few patterns until 1986. At the present time, stag is being used only on a limited basis for club knives, etc.

Second-cut stag—used for one club knife, the Wolverine Knife Collectors 1986 Trapper.

Glazed finish stainless steel blades—used only on a very few patterns for market test. Six patterns known, possibly a few others. The six patterns are numbers 11 E.O., 24, 19, 49, 52 and 6280. They were made for a few months around 1960.

Winterbottom knives produced 1970-1986—very few patterns, produced with later tang marks. Some will be found with 1922-1972 tang stamps, others with Queen, Q76, etc. One Club Canoe produced in 1985. All are extremely scarce, with very few made. Desirable in any condition.

Note: All patterns will not be found with all tang stamps, as some were introduced later and will be found in only one or two tang stamps.

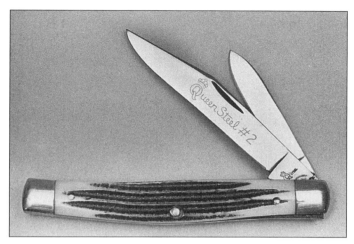

#2, serpentine jack, Queen Steel, imitation burnt orange, 3-1/4"; $40.

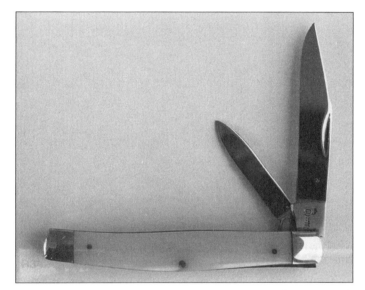

#2A, amber handle, 2 blades with tang stamp, Queen steel, 3-14"; $35.

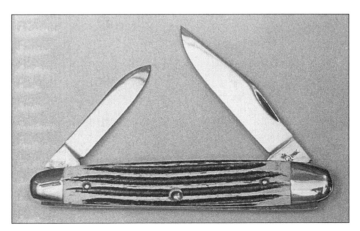

#3, sleeveboard, Queen Steel, Winterbottom bone, 3-5/16"; $35.

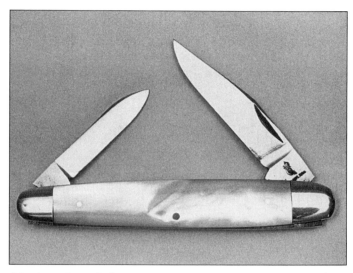

#4, sleeveboard, Queen, pearl, stainless stamp, 3-3/8"; $50.

#4, smoke-pearl handle, 2 blades with no tang stamp, 3-5/16", Queen Steel No. 4. etched on blade; $160.

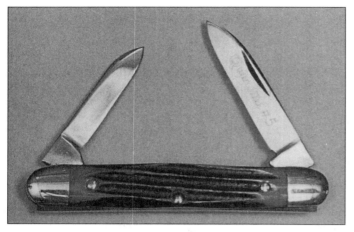

#5, senator, Queen Steel, Winterbottom bone, 2-1/2"; $20.

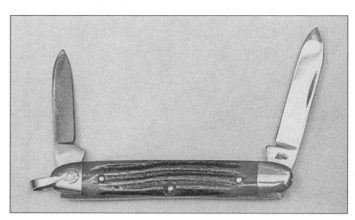

#7, senator, Big Q, Winterbottom bone, 2-1/2"; $35.

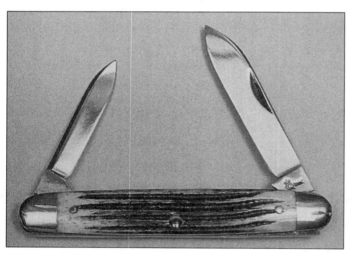

#6, senator, Queen, Winterbottom bone, 2-1/2"; $30.

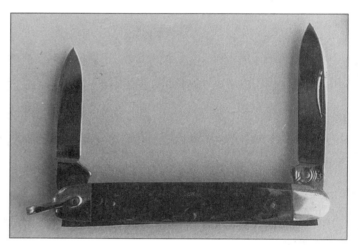

#7, Rogers bone handle, 2 blades with tang stamp Q., 2-1/2", with bale, no etch; $45.

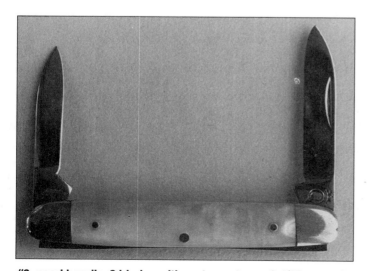

#6, pearl handle, 2 blades with no tang stamp, 2-1/2", no etch; $45.

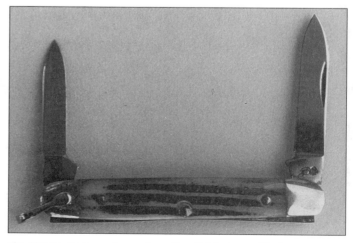

#7, Winterbottom bone handle, 2 blades with tang stamp Q., 2-1/2", with bale, Queen Steel No. 7, etch on blade; $40.

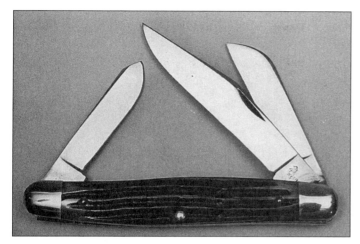

#9, Stockman, Queen, Winterbottom bone, 4"; $35.

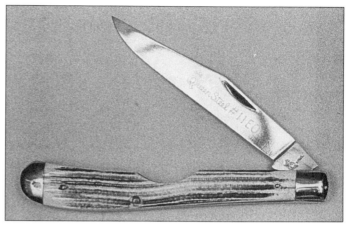

#11EO, easy opener, Queen Steel, Winterbottom bone, 4"; $35.

#9, amber handle, 3 blades with tang stamp, Queen steel, 4", no etch; $60.

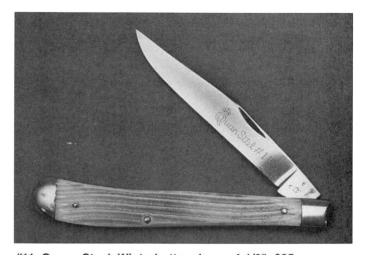

#11, Queen Steel, Winterbottom bone, 4-1/8"; $35.

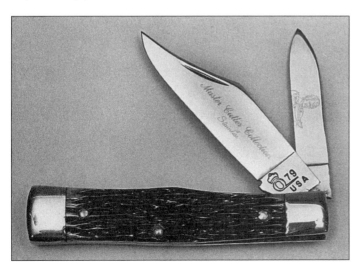

Gunstock, Queen USA, 1979 (Master Cutler Collection), Rogers bone, 3-1/2"; $40.

#12, simulated pearl handle, 1 blade, with tang stamp Q-Stainless, 4-1/8", no etch; $65.

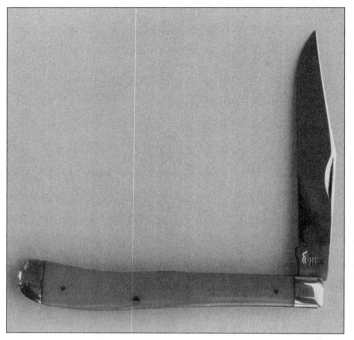

#13, amber handle, 1 blade with tang stamp, Queen Steel, 4-1/8", no etch; $50. Not shown: #13, Queen Steel, flat yellow, 4-1/8"; $30.

#14-P, smoke-pearl handle, 2 blades with no tang stamp, 2-3/4", Queen Steel No. 14P, etch on blade; $200.

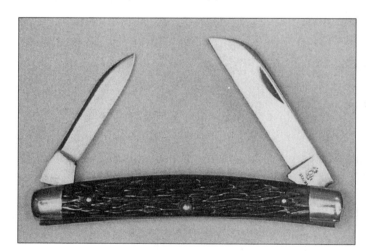

#15, Congress, Queen, Rogers bone, 3-1/2"; $60.

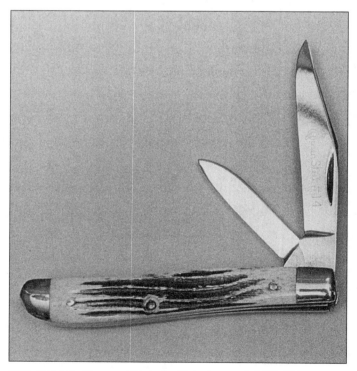

#14, peanut, Queen, Winterbottom bone, 2-3/4"; $30.

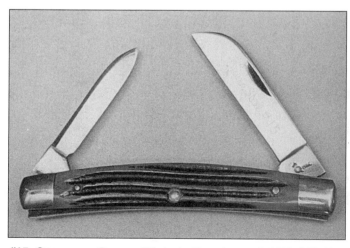

#15, Congress, Queen, Winterbottom bone, 3-1/2"; $40. Not shown: #15, Congress, Queen Stainless, Rogers bone, $65; and #15, Medium Congress, Queen Steel, $30.

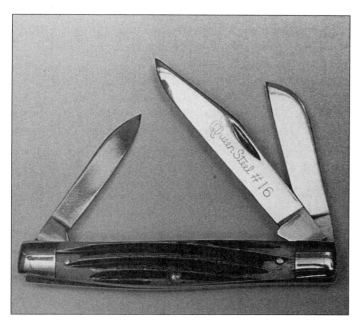

#16, Queen Steel, Winterbottom bone, 3-1/4"; $40.

#16A, amber handle, 3 blades with tang stamp, Queen steel, 3-1/4", no etch; $40.

#16, Stockman, Queen, Rogers bone (Crown & Queen Stamp), 3-1/4"; $85.

#17, amber handle, 2 blades with tang stamp, Q Stainless, 2-3/4", no etch; $40.

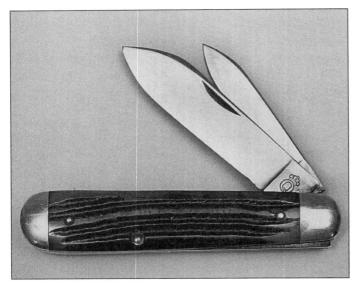

#18, jack, Big Q, Winterbottom bone, 3-11/16"; $50.

#19A, amber handle, 2 satin blades with tang stamp Q. Steel, 4-1/8", Queen Steel 19A, etch on blade; $150.

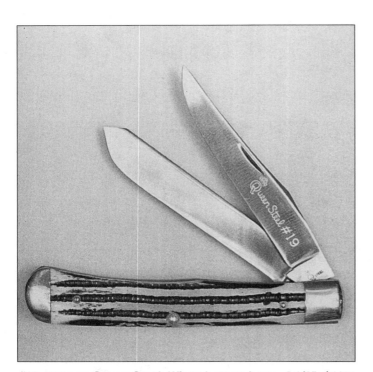

#19, trapper, Queen Steel, Winterbottom bone, 4-1/8"; $125. Not shown: 19, Queen Steel, glazed finish; $150.

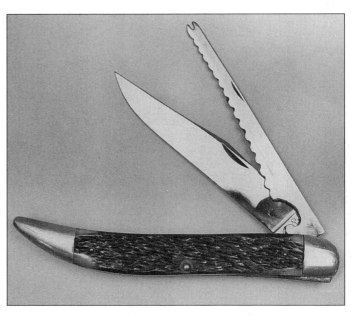

#19, fisherman's, Big Q, Rogers bone, 5"; $125.

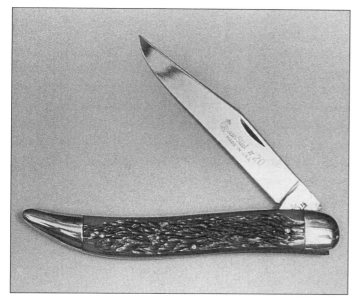

#20, Texas toothpick, Queen Steel, Rogers bone (1,200 made) 5"; $65. Not shown: $20, Texas toothpick, Queen Stainless, Rogers bone, Big Q, 1940; $125.

#22, sawn bone handle, 2 blades with tang stamp, Pat. No., 3-1/2", Queen Steel No. 22 etch on blade, aluminum frame; $60.

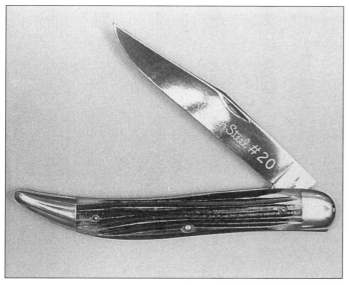

#20, Texas toothpick, Queen Steel, Winterbottom bone, 5"; $100. Not shown: #21, sleeveboard, Queen Steel; $40.

#23, sawn bone handle, 2 blades with tang stamp Pat. No., 3-1/2", Queen Steel No. 23 etch on blade, aluminum frame; $60.

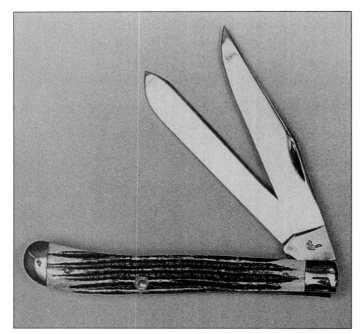

#24, Slimline Trapper, Queen Steel, Winterbottom bone, 4";
$55.

#25, sawn bone handle, 2 blades with tang stamp Pat. No.,
3-1/2", Queen Steel No. 25 etch on blade, aluminum frame;
$65.

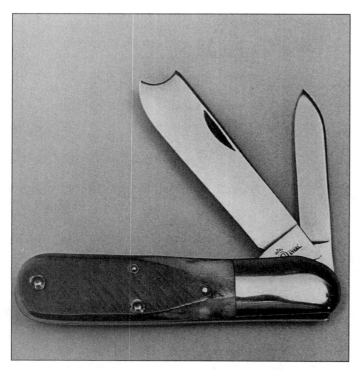

#25, Barlow, Queen Steel, brown bone, 3-1/2"; $65.

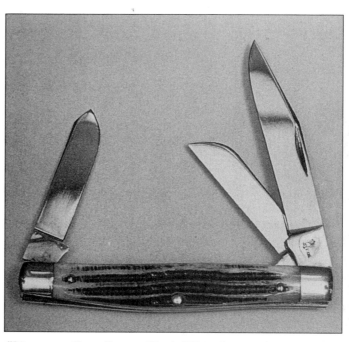

#26, serpentine, Queen Steel, Winterbottom bone, 3-1/4";
$40. Also burnt orange imitation bone; $35.

#26A, amber handle, 3 blades with tang stamp, Queen steel, 3-1/4", no etch; $65.

#27, sawn bone handle, 2 blades with tang stamp Q-Steel, 3-1/2", Queen steel No. 27, etch on blade, aluminum frame; $65.

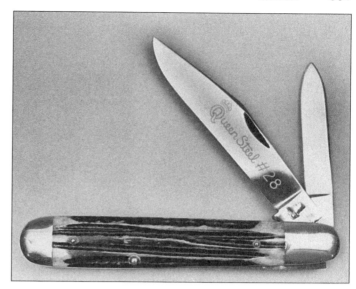

#28, jack, Queen Steel, Winterbottom bone, 4-1/2"; $75.

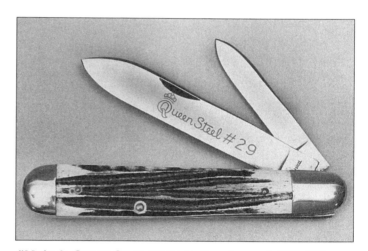

#29, jack, Queen Steel, Winterbottom bone, 4-1/2"; $75.

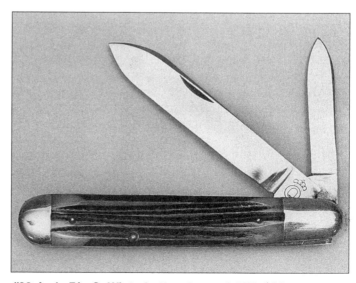

#29, jack, Big Q, Winterbottom bone, 4-1/2"; $90.

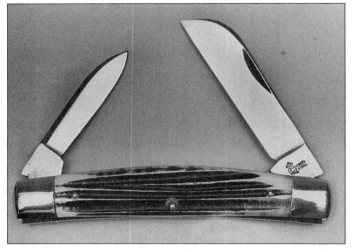

#31, Congress, Queen Steel, Winterbottom bone, 4"; $40.

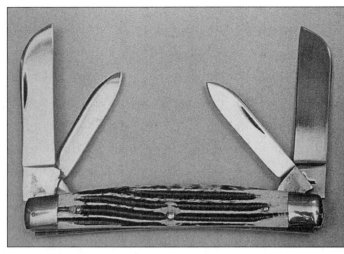

#33, Congress, Queen, Winterbottom bone, 3-1/2"; $90.

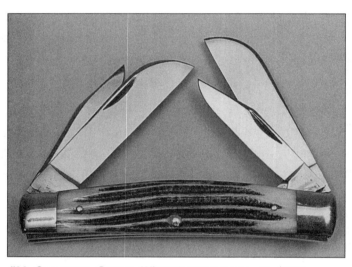

#32, Congress, Queen, Winterbottom bone, 4"; $100.

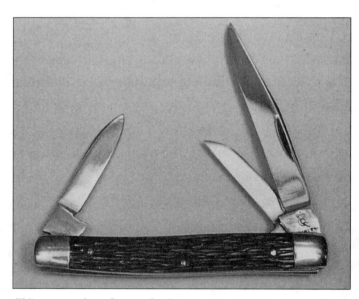

#35, serpentine, Queen Stainless, rough black, 2-5/8"; $30.

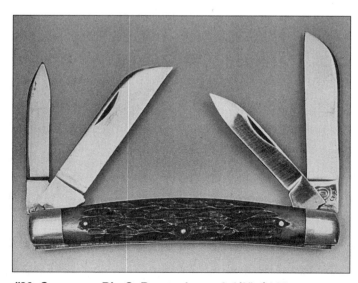

#33, Congress, Big Q, Rogers bone, 3-1/2"; $140.

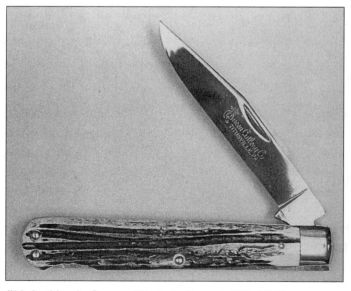

#36, lockback, Queen, Winterbottom, 4-1/2"; $125.

#36, lockback, Queen, Rogers bone, 4-1/2"; $125.

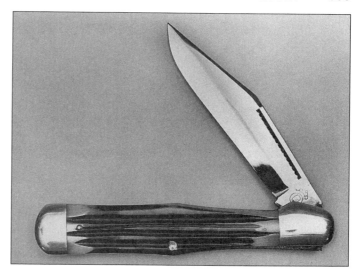

#38, swell-center jumbo, Big Q, Winterbottom bone, 5-1/4"; $200.

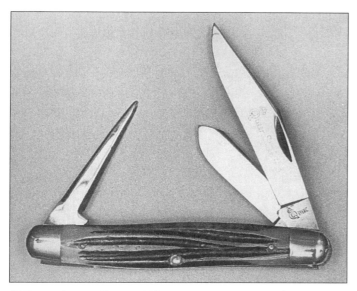

#37, stockman, Queen, Winterbottom bone, 4"; $75.

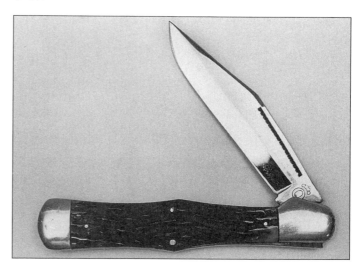

#38, swell-center jumbo, Big Q, jigged bone, 5-1/4"; $200.

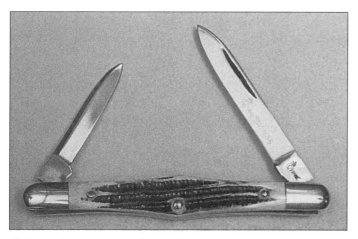

#38, swell-center pen, Queen Steel, Winterbottom bone, 3"; $70.

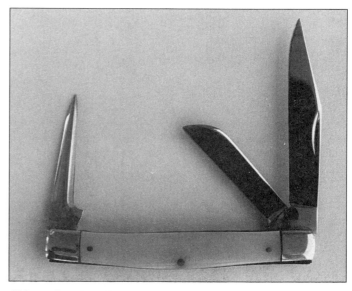

#38, amber handle, 3 blades with no tang stamp, 3-1/4", Queen Steel No. 38, etch on blade, leather punch; $40.

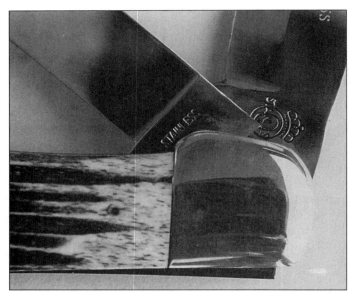

#39, Winterbottom bone handle, 2 blades with tang stamp stainless, 5-1/4", Queen Steel etch on blade; $150.

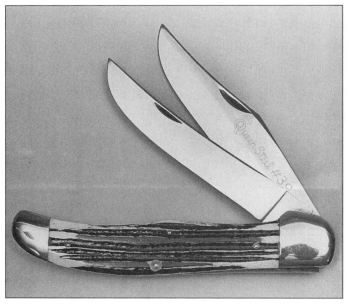

#39, folding hunter, Queen Steel, Winterbottom bone, 5-1/4"; $125.

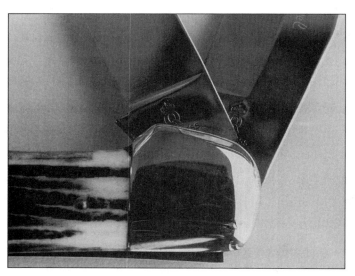

#39, Winterbottom bone handle, 2 blades with tang stamp stainless, 5-1/4", finest stainless etch on blade; $150.

#41, red handle, 1 blade with tang stamp Q-Stainless, 4-1/8", no etch; $65.

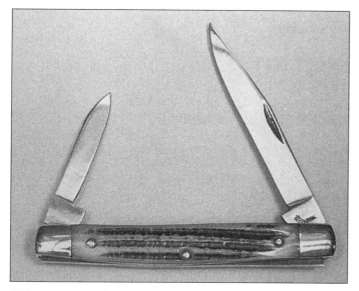

#43, serpentine, Queen Steel, Winterbottom bone, 2-5/8"; $30.

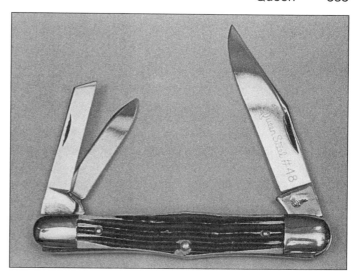

#48, whittler, Queen Steel, Winterbottom bone, 3-1/2"; $75.

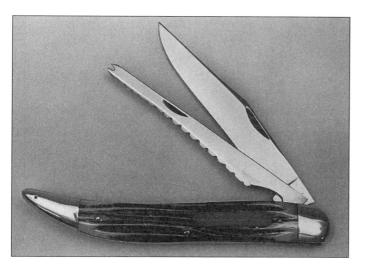

#46, fisherman's, Queen Steel, Winterbottom bone, 5"; $75.

#49, stockman, Queen Steel, Winterbottom bone, 4-1/4", $75

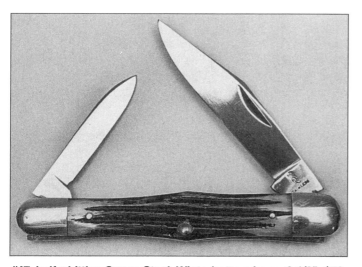

#47, half whittler, Queen Steel, Winterbottom bone, 3-1/2"; $50.

#50, celluloid handle, 2-blade, with no tang stamp, 3-1/4", no etch, salesman sample; $40.

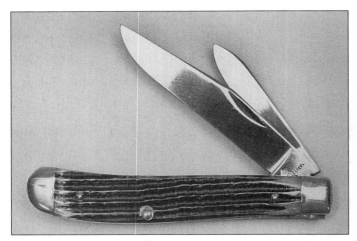

#51, dog-leg jack, Queen Steel, Winterbottom bone, 3-1/2"; $45.

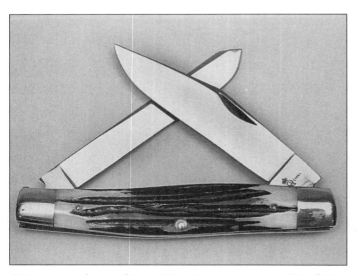

#52, moose, Queen Steel, Winterbottom bone, 4-1/2"; $65.

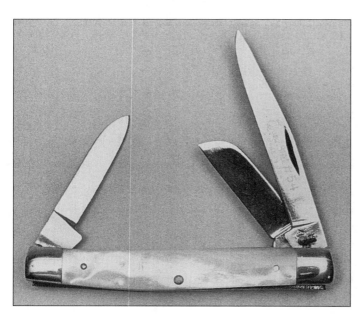

#54, Queen Steel, pearl, 2-5/8"; $45.

#55, cracked ice handle, 2 blades with tang stamp Queen, 3-5/16", Queen Steel No. 55, etch on blade, advertiser; $35.

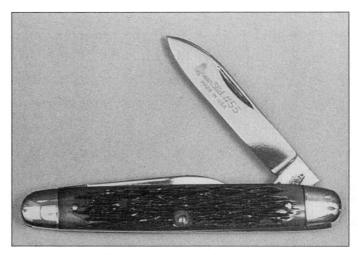

#55, pen, Queen Steel, green Rogers bone, 200 made, 3-5/16"; $35.

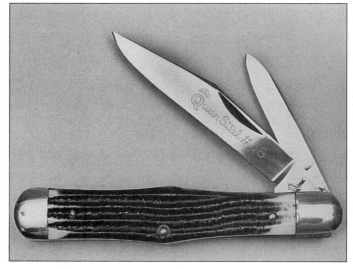

#56, swell center, Queen Steel, burnt orange imitation bone, 3-1/2"; $40.

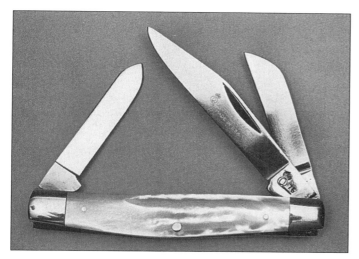

#57, Queen, pearl, 3-3/8"; $65.

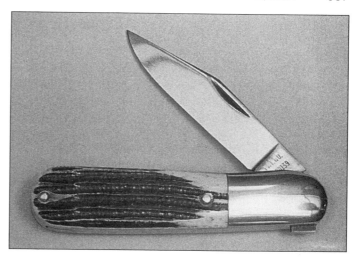

#60, Barlow, Queen, Winterbottom bone, 3-1/2", aluminum lightweight enclosed backspring; $35.

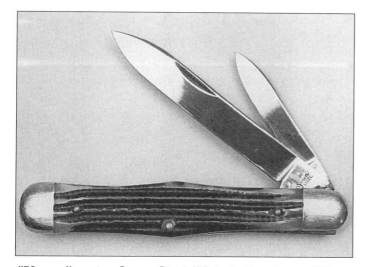

#58, swell center, Queen Steel, Winterbottom bone; $75.

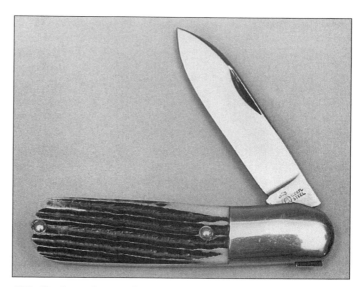

#60, Barlow, Queen Steel, Winterbottom bone, 3-1/2", aluminum lightweight enclosed backspring; $35.

#59, smoke-pearl handle, 2 blades with no tang stamp, 2-5/8", Queen Steel No. 59, etch on blade; $150.

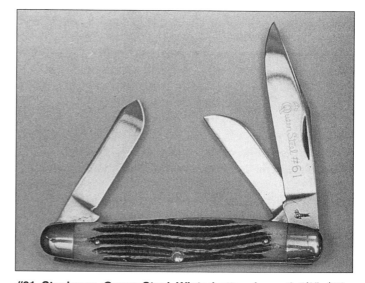

#61, Stockman, Queen Steel, Winterbottom bone, 3-5/8"; $50.

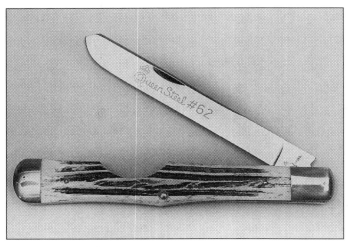

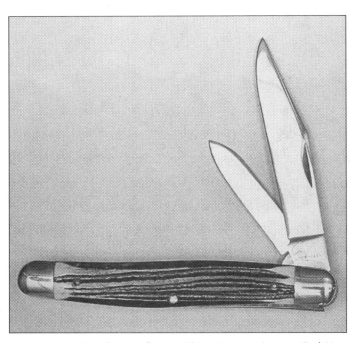

#63, serpentine, Queen Steel, Winterbottom bone, 4"; $40.

**#62, easy opener, Queen Steel, Winterbottom bone, 5-3/8";
$50.**

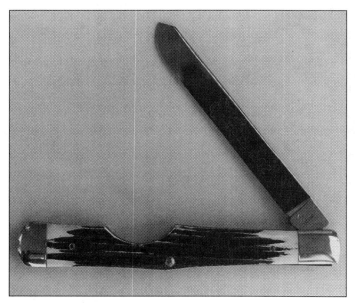

**#64P, pearl handle, 1 blade, 1 nail file with tang stamp Q-
Steel, 3-5/16", Queen Steel No. 64P, etch on blade; $65.**

**#62, Winterbottom bone handle, 1 blade with tang stamp Q-
Steel, 4-1/8", Queen Steel No. 62, etch on blade, first series,
no nail nick; $90.**

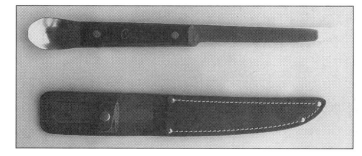

**#71, rosewood handle, "coho," 12-7/8" overall with 6-1/4"
blade and 2" spoon, no etch; $30.**

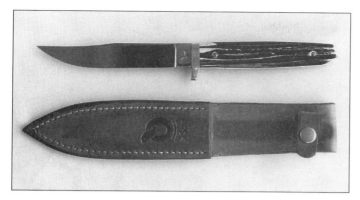

#73, Winterbottom bone with tang stamp Q-Steel, blade length 4", no etch; $50. Not shown: #73, Winterbottom bone, with Q Stainless stamp, 4", no etch, $65; and #73, imitation Winterbottom bone, 8" x 4", Q Steel etch, $30.

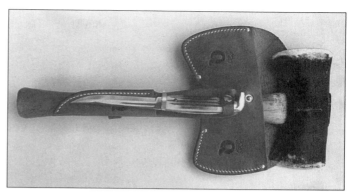

#KA79, knife-ax combo, 1 lb. double-bit ax, 4" saber, ground knife blade; $350.

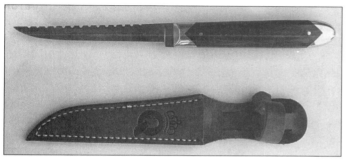

#76, Formica handle, no tang stamp, blade length 4" and 8-1/2" overall, Queen Steel No. 76, etch on blade; $30.

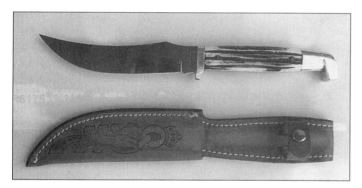

#77, Winterbottom bone handle, tang stamp Q-Stainless, 9-1/2" overall with 5" scimitar blade; $65.

#39, stag handle, 2 blades with tang stamp Q80, 5-1/4", show special, shot show, 1 of 50; $100.

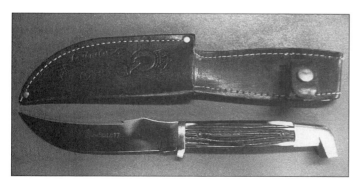

#77, imitation Winterbottom, 9-1/2" x 5" blade, Q Steel blade etch; $40.

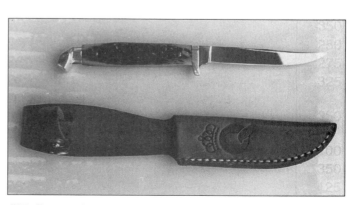

#85, Rogers bone handle with tang stamp stainless, blade length is 3" and 6-1/4" overall, no etch; $45.

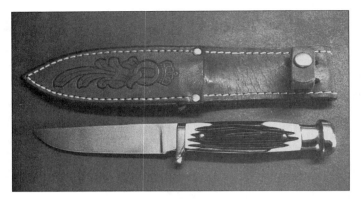

#89, imitation winterbottom, 7-3/4" x 4" blade, Q steel blade etch; $35.

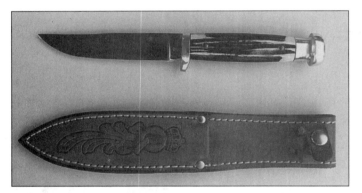

#89, Winterbottom bone handle with tang stamp Q-Steel, blade length 3-7/8" and 7-7/8" overall, no etch; $50.

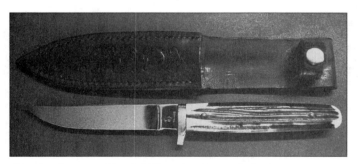

#90, leather handle, 8-3/8" x 4" blade, Q Stainless stamp, round butt; $50.

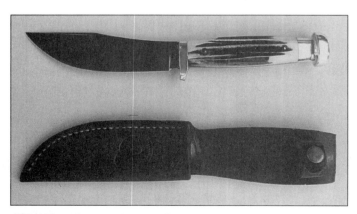

#98, Winterbottom bone with tang stamp stainless, blade length 4" and 7-7/8" overall; $60.

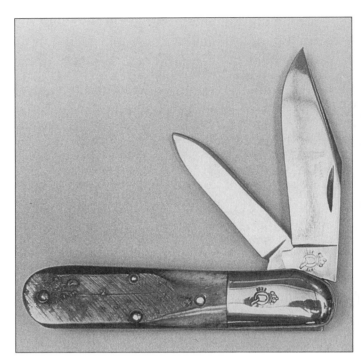

#139, Barlow, Queen, brown bone, 3-1/2"; $45.

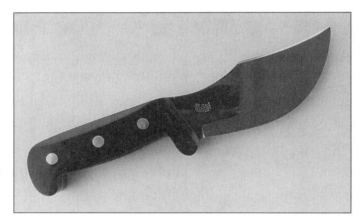

#399, black micarta handle with tang stamp Q, blade length 5-3/4" and 11" overall, Moose Skinner etch on blade; $100.

#1450, Daddy Barlow, Bicentennial Edition, Queen, black delrin, flag emblem, 5"; $40.

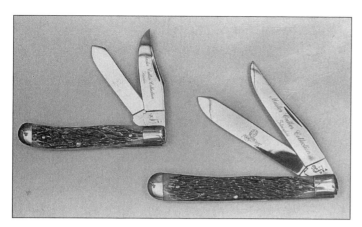

#1490, Queen, Rogers bone, 1st edition, Trapper Set; $75 for the set.

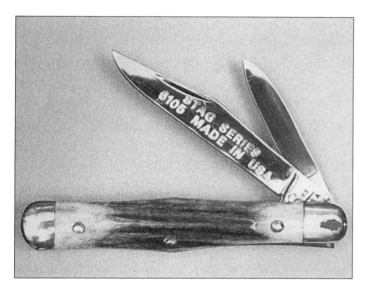

#6105, swell center, Queen, stag, 3-1/2"; $45.

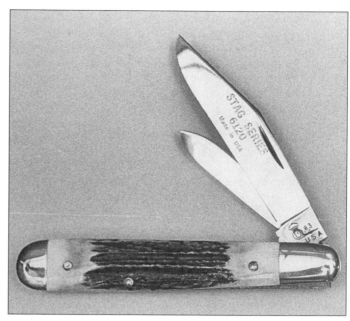

#6120, jack, Queen, stag, 4-1/2"; $60.

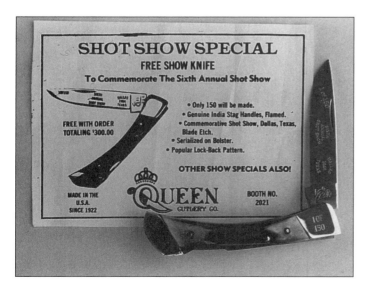

#6115, burnt stag handle, 1 blade with tang stamp Q, 4-1/8", Shot Show Special engraved on blade; $60.

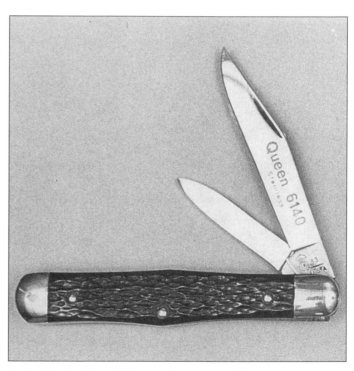

#6140, swell center, Queen, bone, 3-1/2"; $40.

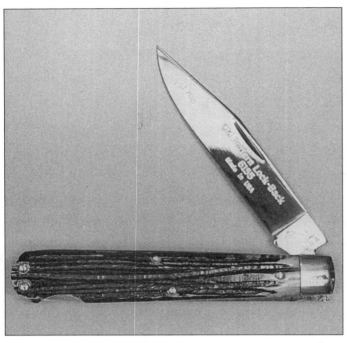

#6155, lockback, Queen, Winterbottom bone, 1 of 700; $75.

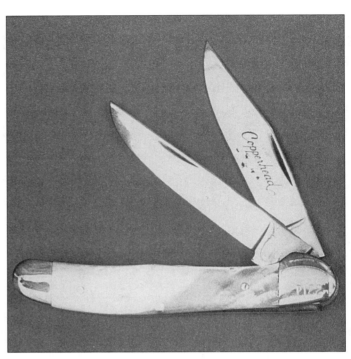

#8145, Copperhead, Queen (set consists of pearl and stag set of two), 3-1/2"; $150.

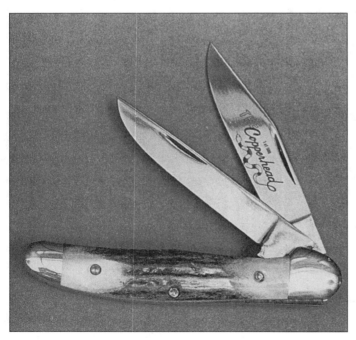

Copperheads: #8145, Queen, pearl and stag, two-knife set, $150 set; #8145, Queen, stag copper-head, $75.

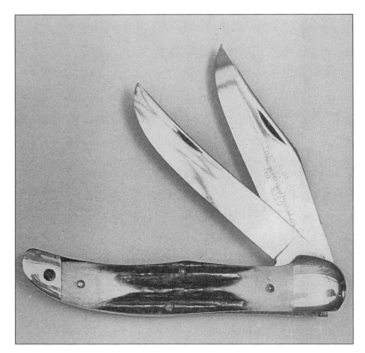

#8150, folding hunter, Queen, genuine stag (800 made), 5-1/4"; $75.

Stockman, Queen USA, 1982 NKCA 10th Anniversary, genuine stag, blade is deep etched in gold, (1,200 made), 4-1/4"; $90.

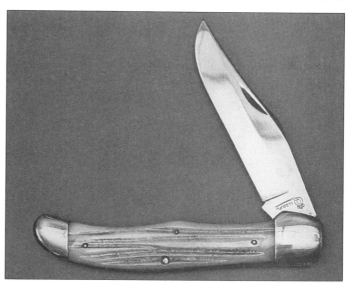

Folding hunter, Queen Stamp upside down, Winterbottom bone; $125.

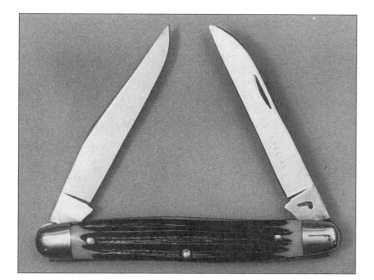

Improved Muskrat, 1974, Queen Steel, imitation Winterbottom, 600 made, bone, Hawbaker's Special, rare, 4"; $300.

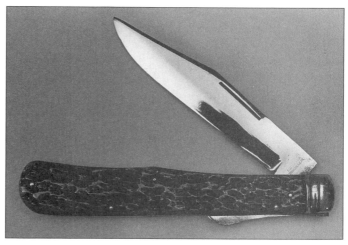

Lockback, Schatt & Morgan (Queen forerunner), heavy bone scales, 5-1/2"; $300.

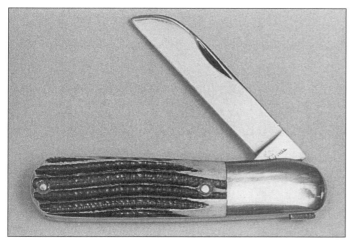

Barlow, Queen Steel, Winterbottom bone, 3-1/2", aluminum lightweight enclosed backspring; $60.

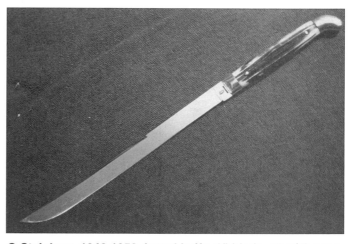

Q Stainless, 1946-1950, bread knife, 9" blade, 13-3/4" overall, Winterbottom bone; $25. Photo courtesy Bill Hudock.

Additional Queens

#5, Rogers bone, 2-1/2", Big Q; $35.

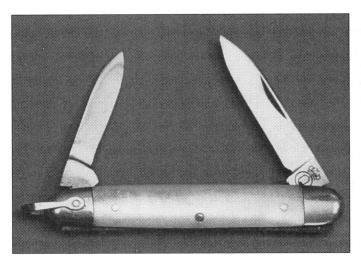

#7, Queen Big Q Carbon, 2-1/2", genuine pearl; $45.

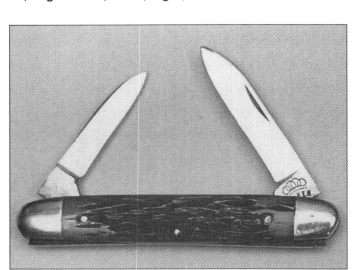

#5, Rogers bone, 2-1/2", Crown & Dots, rare; $45.

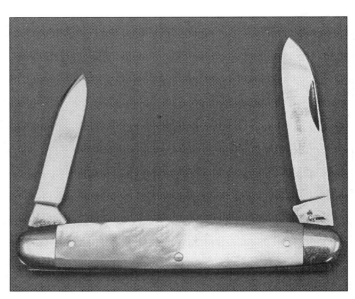

Genuine pearl, 3-1/4"; $50.

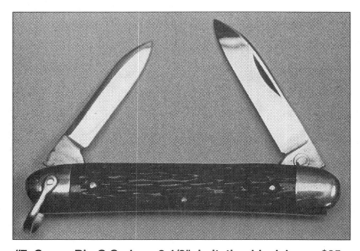

#7, Queen Big Q Carbon, 2-1/2", imitation black bone; $35.

Queen City, 3-3/4", 2 blades, congress, Rogers bone; $150.

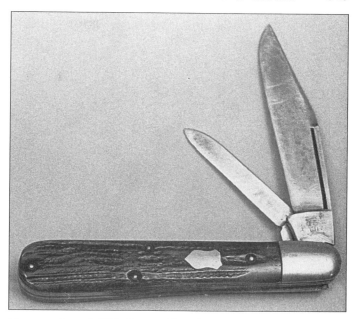

Rogers stag, 4-1/2", Queen City; $125.

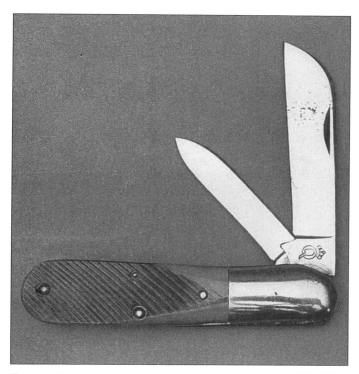

Barlow, brown bone, sheep foot, carbon steel, 3-1/2"; $65.

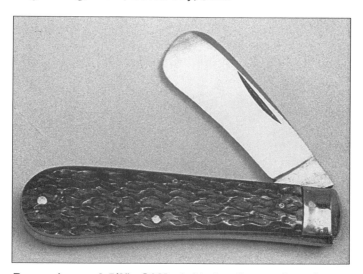

Brown bone, 3-5/8", S&M, 1 blade, Cotton Sampler or Maize, Schatt & Morgan; $300.

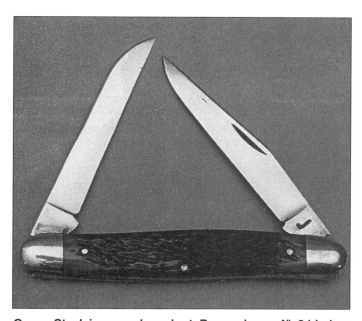

Queen Steel, improved muskrat, Rogers bone, 4", 2 blades, made as prototype around 1975, never sold on market, rare; $250.

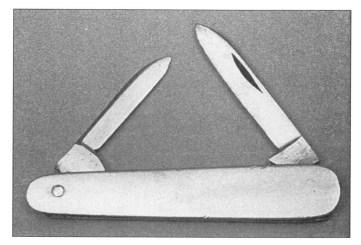

Two blades, stainless scales, 2-1/4", "Queen" Stainless, very rare; $100.

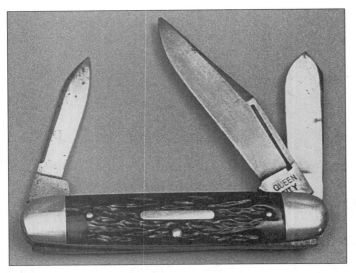

Green bone, 2-1/2", Queen City, 3 blades, small cattle pattern; $125.

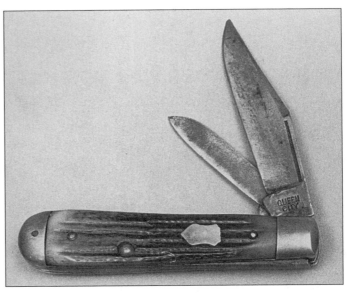

Two-blade jack, Winterbottom, 3-7/8", Queen City; $125.

#13, Rogers bone, 1 blade, 4-1/8", Queen Big Q; $55.

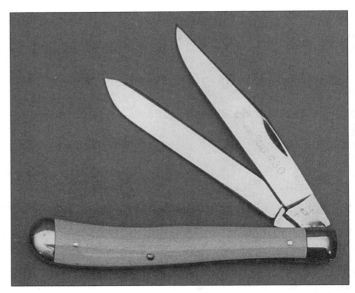

#30, Queen Steel semi-trapper, yellow scales, 4-1/8", 2 blades; $50.

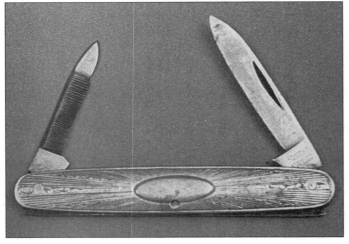

Silver scales, 2 blades, 2-5/8", "Queen" Stainless, very rare stamp; $125.

#42, yellow scales, 2-3/4"; $30.

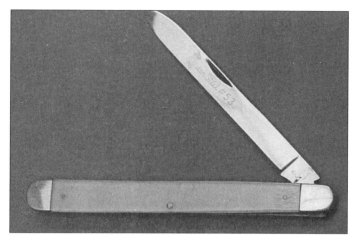

#53, citrus knife, imitation onyx celluoid, 4-3/4"; $45.

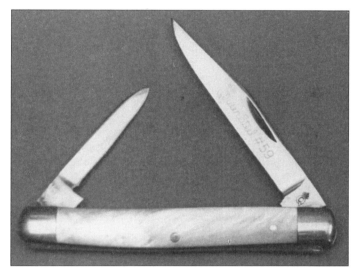

#59, genuine pearl, 2-3/4"; $45. Not shown: #59, smoked pearl, 2-3/4"; $100.

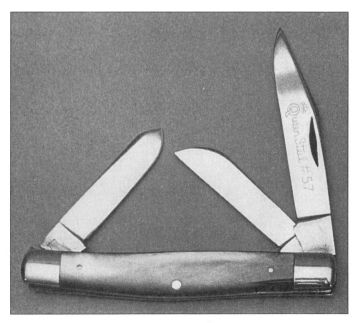

#57, Queen, smoked pearl, 3-3/8"; $150.

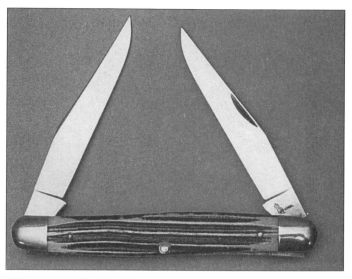

#66, Queen Steel Muskrat, Winterbottom bone, 2 blades, mint; $150.

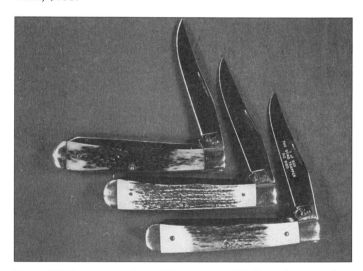

Top: #Q77, overrun from Trapper, no blade etch, very few made. Middle: Q78, stag prototype for 1981, stag trapper, no blade etch. Bottom: Q81, stag 8160, (1 of 800); $60 each.

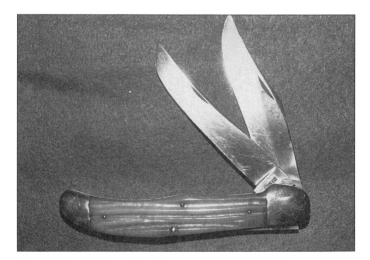

Two-blade folding hunter marked Q Stainless, 5-1/4" closed, Winterbottom bone, excellent, mint; $125.

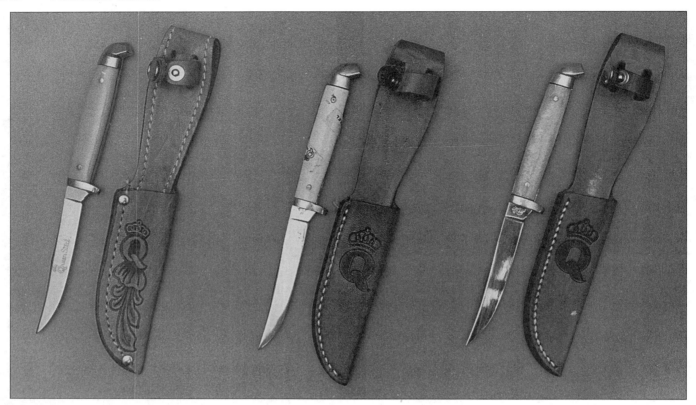

Left: #85, Queen Steel, yellow scales, bird knife, 6-1/8" overall, 3" blade; $40. Middle: #85, Queen Steel, imitation ivory, bird knife, 6-1/8", 3" blade; $40. Right: Queen Steel, imitation onyx scales, bird knife, 6-1/8", 3" blade; $40. Not shown: #85, Queen Steel, red celluloid, bird knife, 6-1/8", 3" blade; $40.

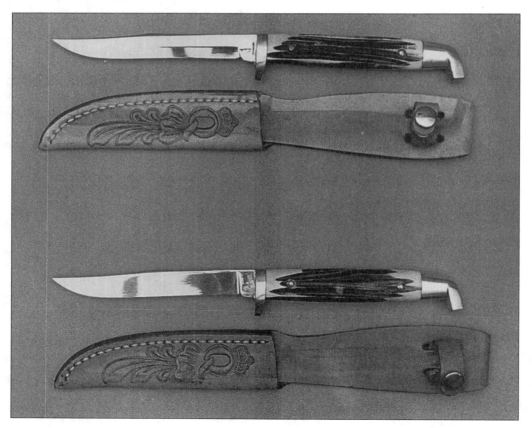

Top: #85, Queen Stainless, Winterbottom, 7-1/4"-3-5/8" blade, intermediate size, scarce-saber blade; $65. Bottom: #85, same as the knife shown above, except with a flat blade; $50.

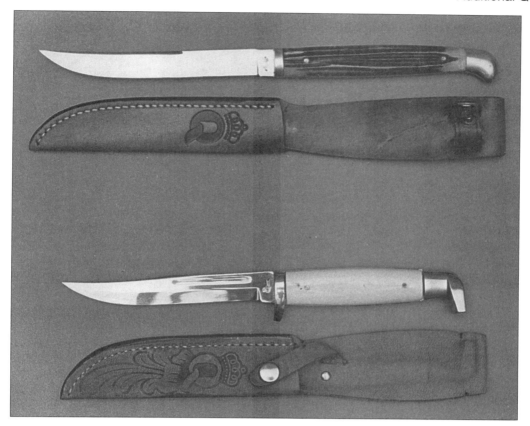

Top: Queen Steel, Winterbottom, 9-1/4"-4-3/4" blade, very scarce; $50. Queen Steel, imitation ivory, 8"-4-1/4" blade, saber, blood groove, very scarce; $60.

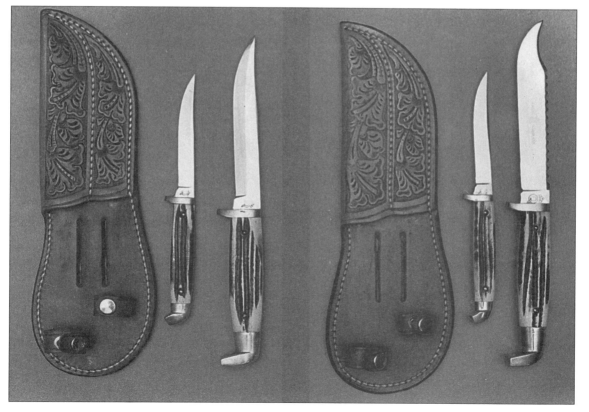

Left: Queen Steel Twin Pak, Winterbottom bone, stainless, Big Q's, 8"-4-1/4" blade and 6-1/8"-3" blade; $75. Right: Same as above, except larger knife has fish scaler back; $95.

Top: #75, Queen Steel sheath knife, Winterbottom bone, 10-1/2"-6" blade, double edge, very scarce; $90. Bottom: Queen Steel sheath knife, genuine stag handles with red and white spacers, 11-1/2"-7" blade, 1" edge top of blade, very scarce; $150.

Top: #84, Queen Steel sheath knife, leather washer with white spacers, 9-1/4"-4-1/4" blade, rare; $40. Bottom: Queen Stainless, leather washer with red, white and black spacers, 8-3/4"-4" blade, flat ground; $50.

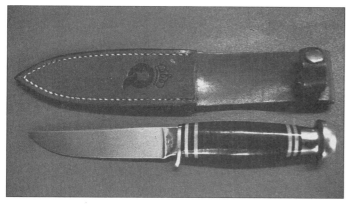

#90, leather handle, 8-3/4"-4" blade, Queen Stainless stamp, misplaced spacers on one end; $50.

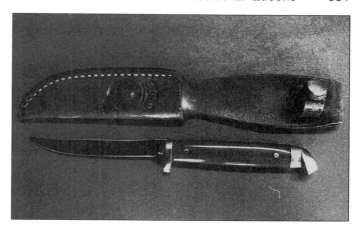

#85, bird knife, red scales, 6"-3" blade, Queen Steel stamp; $50.

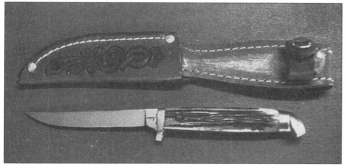

#85, brown winterbottom (scarce), 6"-3" blade, Queen Stainless stamp; $45.

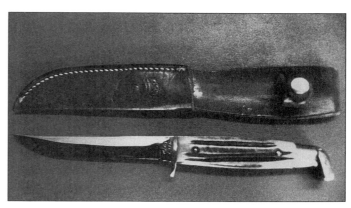

#82, brown Winterbottom (scarce), 8"-4" blade, saber grind, crown and dot stamp; $55.

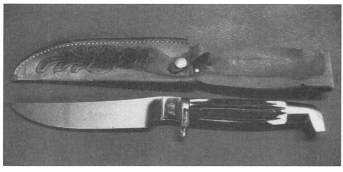

#75, imitation winterbottom, 10-1/2"-6" blade, flat grind, Big Queen stamp, Queen steel blade etch; $45.

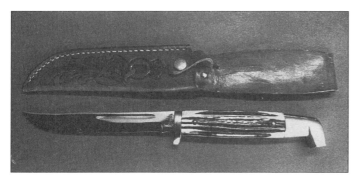

#95, Winterbottom bone, 9-1/2"-5" blade, Queen Steel stamp; $50.

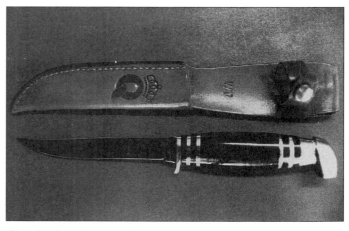

#84, leather handle with aluminum spacers, 8"-4" blade, Queen Stainless stamp (scarce); $45.

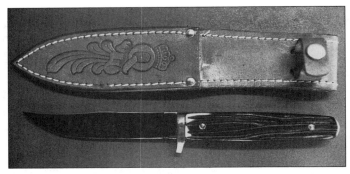

#73, imitation Winterbottom, 8"-4" blade, Queen Steel blade etch; $30.

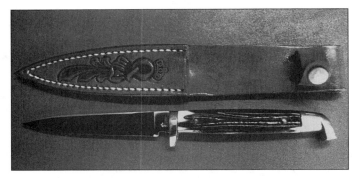

#79, imitation Winterbottom, 7-1/2"-3-1/2" blade, Queen Cutlery etch, Queen Steel stamp (very rare); $45.

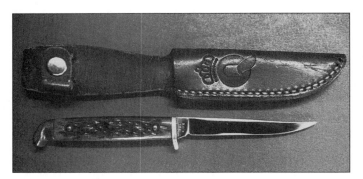

#85, bird knife, Rogers bone, 6"-3" blade, Queen City stamp; $55.

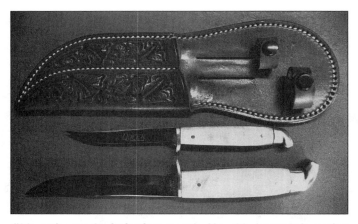

#80, twin pack, imitation pearl; No. 82 stamped, script Queen City, 8"-4" blade; No. 85 blade etched script Queen, 6"-3" blade; $100.

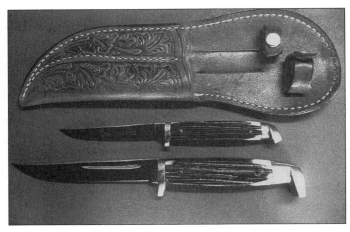

#80, twin pack, imitation Winterbottom bone; both the No. 82 and No. 85 are blade etched Queen steel; #82 is 8"-4" blade and #85, 6"-3" blade; $85.

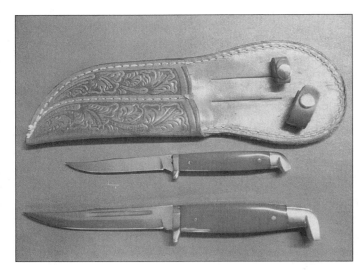

#80, twin pack, red handles, both #82 and #85 are blade etched Queen steel; #82, 8"-4" blade; #85, 6"-3" blade (rare); $100.

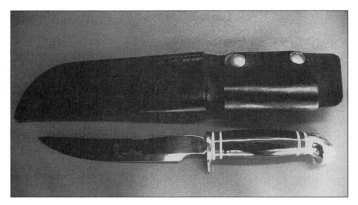

#78, rosewood handle with red and white spacers, 12"-7" blade, saber grind, Queen Steel stamp (very rare); $125.

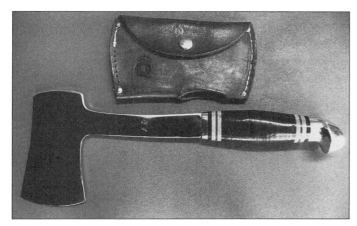

SBA80, archer's ax, leather handle with red, black and white spacers, one peace shank and head, Big Queen stamp (scarce); $200.

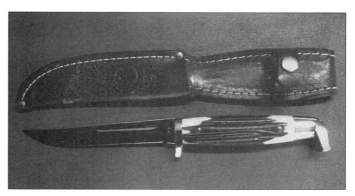

#82, imitation Winterbottom, 8"-4" blade, Queen Steel etch and small Queen stamp; $30.

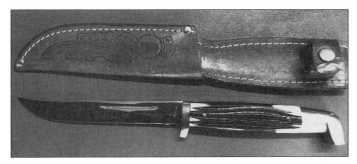

#95, imitation Winterbottom, 9-1/2"-5" blade, Queen Steel etch and stamp; $35.

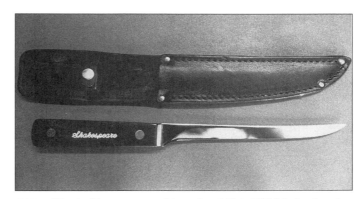

#417, fillet knife, rosewood handle, 11"-6-1/4" blade, (prototype), made for Shakespeare; $45.

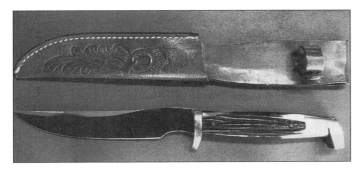

#75, imitation Winterbottom, 10-1/2"-6" blade, saber grind, Queen Steel blade etch (scarce); $50.

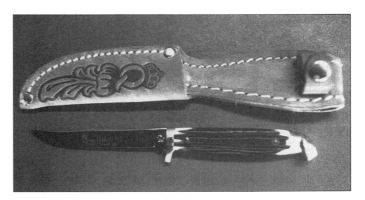

#85, bird knife, imitation Winterbottom bone, 6"-3" blade, Queen Steel etch and small Queen stamp; $30.

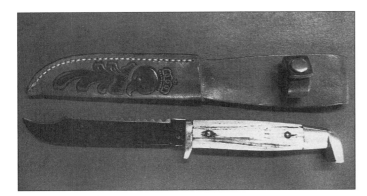

Hunting and fishing knife, Winterbottom bone, 8-1/2"-4-1/2" blade, Big Queen stamp with Finest Stainless etch (rare); $60.

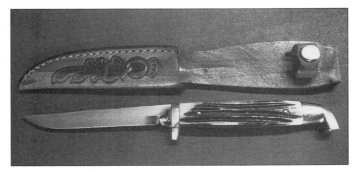

#74, brown Winterbottom (scarce), 7-1/2"-3-1/2" blade, saber grind, small Queen stainless stamp; $45.

Boy Scout knife, imitation jigged bone, 2-5/8" blade, 3-3/4" closed, Queen stamped on handle; $50.

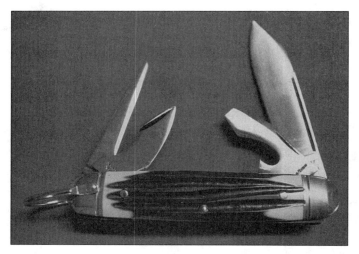

Boy Scout knife, imitation Winterbottom bone, 2-5/8" blade, 3-3/4" closed, stamped Queen Steel (one of four); $150.

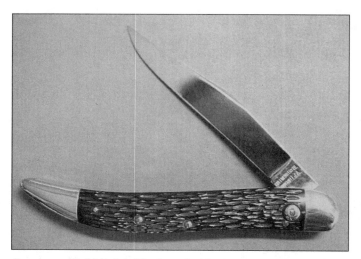

Queen switchblade, 5" closed, 4" blade, imitation jigged bone. This knife has no lock and is the forerunner of the locking one. Stamped Queen Cutlery Co. in block lettering (very rare); $400.

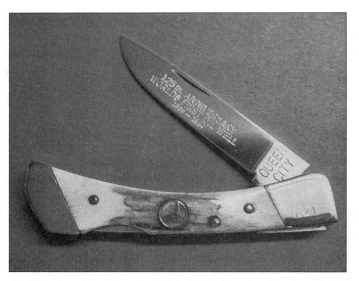

#6115, stag handle, single-blade lockback, 4" closed, 3" blade. Stamped Queen City and blade etched with 125th Anniversary, World's First Oil Well, 1859-1984, 1,700 made; $60.

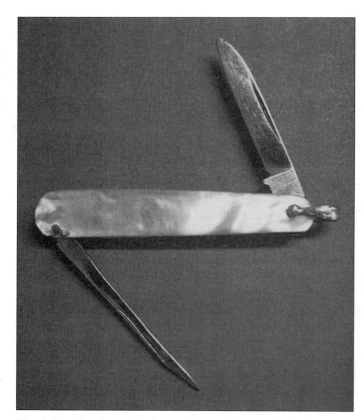

Pearl handle (one blade and one fingernail file), 2-1/4" closed, stamped Queen Stainless in blocked lettering; $75.

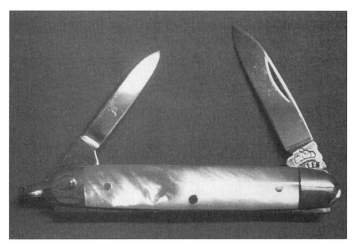

#7, pearl handle, two blades, 2-1/2" closed, stamped Crown & Dot; $50.

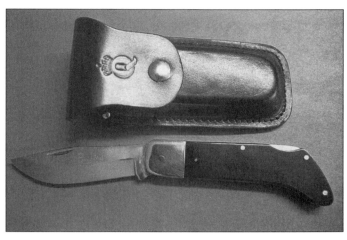

#390, folding gamekeeper, black micarta handle, 5" closed, 4" blade, blade locks, blade stamped Queen Steel and serial number; $100.

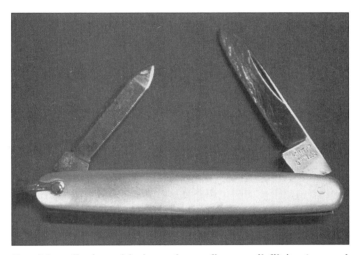

Pearl handle (one blade and one fingernail file), stamped Queen Stainless in block lettering, 2-5/8" closed; $55.

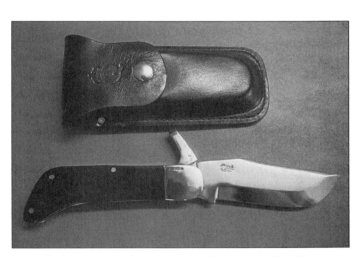

#396, folding gamekeeper, black micarta handle, 5" closed, 4" blade, blade locks, blade stamped Queen Steel. This is a proto to #390; $100.

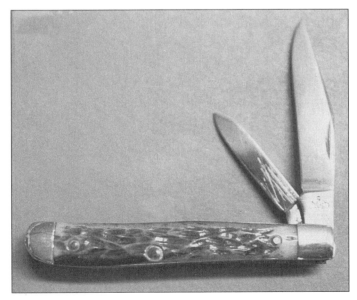

#14, peanut, green Rogers bone, two blades, 2-3/4" closed, stamped Crown & Dot; $45.

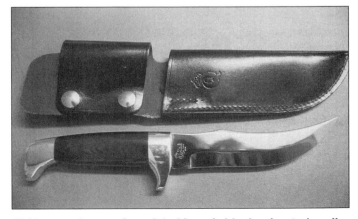

#393, gamekeeper (special skinner), black micarta handle, 10-1/2"-5-3/4" blade, blade stamped Queen Steel and serial number; $100.

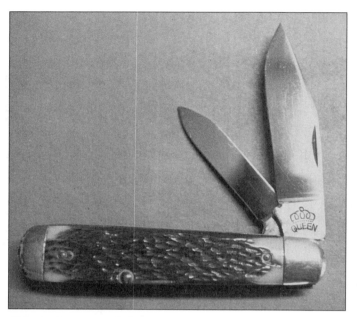

#10, jack, green Rogers bone, 3-1/2" closed, stamped Crown & Dot; $65.

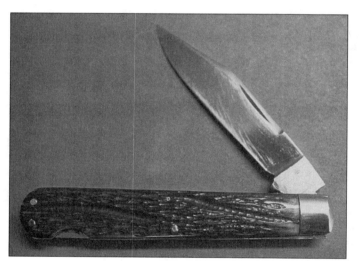

#106, Schatt & Morgan, jigged bone, 4-1/2"-3-9/16 blade, lockback, stamped S & M, Titusville, Pa., made before 1930; $200.

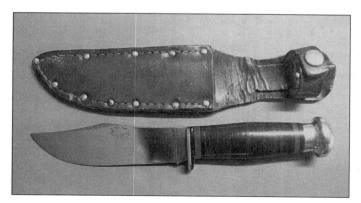

Hunting knife, leather handle with red and black spacers, 8-1/2"-4-1/2" blade, stamped Queen City in block lettering; $75.

Early Stainless Queen (rare stamp), 5"; $125.

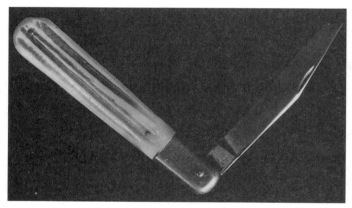

Prototype, extremely rare Queen Daddy Barlow (only a few made), lightweight aluminum bolsters, 5"; $250.

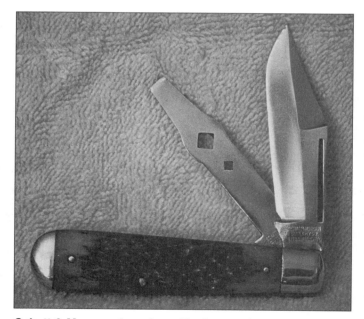

Schatt & Morgan sleeveboard jack, greenish brown Rogers bone or jigged bone handle, 3-1/2", similar to Queen City 1146-1/2; $150. Photo courtesy David Huff.

THE SATURDAY EVENING POST

December 9, 1922

18 K Solid Gold; inlaid platinum center. Hand engraved. Ring for attaching to watch chain. $3.00

"How did you know I wanted a Remington Pocket Knife?"

IT doesn't take a mind-reader to know *that!* Fifty times during the past year you've asked him for his penknife.

And he always answered—"Sure—take it. But it won't *cut* anything."

And because every man he knew had the same trouble with his own knife, it didn't seem worth while to buy a new one.

* * *

But about a year ago, the *Remington Pocket Knives* came out.

People said—"Remington, eh! Must be pretty good."

Men everywhere bought the knives. Tried them. Found them *more* than "pretty good" —*the very finest pocket knives in America today.*

* * *

So this year at least *his* gift is the easiest part of your Christmas shopping.

He expects a *Remington Pocket Knife.* Don't disappoint him!

There are more than 700 patterns of Remington Knives to choose from. A knife for every purpose—in all combinations of blades and handles, ranging in price from 50 cents to $50.

Remington

THE AUTHORITY IN FIRE ARMS, AMMUNITION AND CUTLERY

REMINGTON ARMS COMPANY, Inc.—New York City.

REMINGTON

When Eliphalet Remington started his arms manufacturing plant in 1816, he had no idea this new venture would lead to the eventual production of some of the most highly prized and sought after knives in the world.

Upon his death, the arms company passed to his sons, who soon sold to Marcellus Hartley of Union Metallic Cartridge Company. When Hartley died, his grandson Marcellus Dodge took over both the Remington Union Metallic Cartridge Company. Since the Remington name was better known, the Union Metallic Cartridge name was dropped; however, most of the knives will have the UMC stamped within the Remington circle on the tang.

It took more than a century and World War I to spur the company into manufacturing these highly prized knives.

Remington was a major manufacturer of bayonets for WW I and upon the war's end, the company found itself with a tremendous production capability but no contracts; hence, the decision to enter the pocket-knife market, which it did in February 1920.

From this beginning, things progressed well within an ever-increasing number of patterns. In 1929, Remington felt the crunch of the Depression and sold controlling interest to the DuPont Company in 1933.

With the war looming ever larger in Europe, the US Government began gearing up, and increasing arms contracts pushed the pocket knives aside.

Pal Cutlery Company bought the cutlery equipment in approximately 1940.

(Thanks to G.A. Miller of Wisconsin for helping furnish information and photos on Remington. Bill Wright of Indiana also furnished photos and information on Remington Sheath Knives.)

Remington pattern numbers

The Remington pattern number was stamped on the reverse side of the tang, with either the circle stamp or the straight line. The "circle" was reserved for the higher-quality knives. Some stamps were inked on.

The "R" preceding a number denotes that it is a pocket knife and the last digit reveals the handle material.

1. Redwood
2. Black composition
3. Bone
4. Pearl
5. Pyremite
6. Genuine stag
7. Ivory or white bone
8. Cocobolo wood
9. Metal—stainless, nickel, brass, etc.
0. Horn—buffalo, cow
CH.—designates knife with chain.

Author's note: Remington manufactured advertising knives for many companies. The author has seen very few Remington advertising knives with a pattern number.

Tips for Remington collectors

Since Remington only made pocket knives for about 20 years (1920-1940), and Pal Cutlery Com-

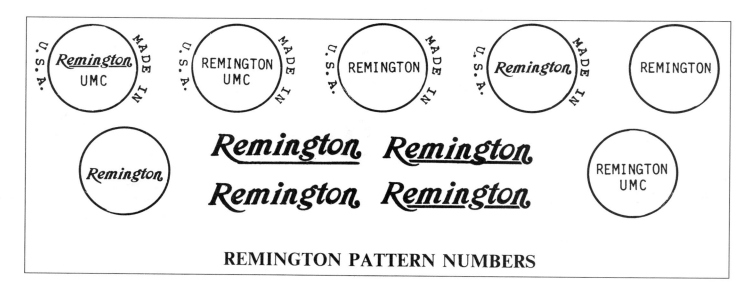

REMINGTON PATTERN NUMBERS

pany purchased them in approximately 1940, and continued to use parts in inventory to make transition knives after the purchase, there are very few authentic Remington parts available to use in counterfeited knives. As a result, you mainly will find very poor quality imported copies of Remington patterns and junk knives made from worn authentic parts.

Generally speaking, most counterfeiting of Remington knives occurs with the smaller, less-common patterns, rather than the famous bullet patterns. However, I have seen some counterfeited bullets as well.

As with all knife manufacturers, Remington had a few inconsistencies in various patterns, which causes confusion. The following are tips all serious Remington collectors and dealers should know:

Bullet patterns

There were thirteen bullet patterns produced by Remington. They are:

R293   This is a H.T.T. (Hunter, Trader, Trapper) pattern with two long blades, clip and spay, both with long pulls. The length is 5-1/4". It should have a bullet shield and brown bone handles.

R1123   This is a thick trapper pattern with two long blades with regular pulls. The length is 4-1/2". It has a bullet shield, brown bone handles and a lanyard hole. It also has grooved bolsters.

R1128   This pattern is identical to the R1123, except it has cocobolo handle material instead of brown bone.

R1173   This pattern is referred to as the baby bullet. It looks like the R1123, except its length is 3-1/2" (1" shorter). It also has bone handles.

R1253L   This is a long hobo pattern, which is a lockback. The length is 5-1/4". It has a bullet shield and brown bone handles. This pattern has one clip blade with a long pull. It sometimes can be found with a bail.

R1263   This pattern has a hobo frame. The length is 5-3/8". It has two blades. The front one is a short pen blade with a regular pull. The back one is a long clip blade with a long pull. It has brown bone handles, a bullet shield and grooved bolsters.

R1273   This pattern is identical to the R1263, except the long blade in the back is a spear blade instead of a clip blade. This long slender blade also has a long pull.

R1303   The frame of this pattern is the same size and shape as the R1123 (4-1/2"). However, this is a single blade lockback knife. The blade has a regular pull. It also has a bullet shield, brown bone handles and a lanyard hole.

R1306   This pattern is the same as the R1303, except it has stag handles instead of bone. Some R1306s have a thumb groove on the top of the blade. If the knife has two handle rivets near the bolster, it will have the groove on top of the blade. If there is only one rivet, it will not have the thumb groove.

R1613BL   This is a toothpick pattern. The length is 5". It has a bullet shield, brown bone handles and grooved bolsters. Remington also made this knife with a cartridge shield instead of a bullet shield. The pattern number is the same, except it does not have "BL" at the end of the number.

R4243   This is a big camp knife pattern. The length is 4-3/4". It has flat grooved bolsters, a bullet shield, brown bone handles and a bail. This pattern has four blades. A can opener and a punch blade are on one end. The other end has a short sheep-foot blade with a long pull in the front and a long clip blade, with a long pull in the back.

R4353   This pattern is referred to as the big muskrat. The length is 4-1/2". It has a blade at each end with regular pulls. The handles are brown bone and it has a Bullet shield.

R4466   This pattern is referred to as the baby muskrat. The length is 3-3/4". It has stag handles, a bullet shield and grooved bolsters. One blade is at each end and they have regular pulls. Blades are clip and spay.

If you count the stamp variations on the thirteen patterns and pin placements on the R1306, there are probably 25-30 different bullet combinations; however, the above thirteen patterns constitute a complete set. In the past couple of years, a complete set of near-mint bullets sold for approximately $30,000. You can see how the high price of these knives are attractive to counterfeiters.

Here are some additional things to know about bullet patterns:

On almost all of the R1128 cocobolo-handled bullets, the "8" in the pattern number looks like it has been stamped over a "3." This is not unusual and should not cause you to be alarmed. Apparently, the factory must have restamped existing R1123 blades for this knife.

There were a few authentic Pal bullets made. The master blade was made by Pal, and stamped Pal Blade Co. Because the examples found were used, it is uncertain whether there was an original blade etch.

On the R4353 big muskrat, the master blade is supposed to be a plain unmarked blade. However, a few did have a Remington blade etching. Normally, two-bladed bullets had a Remington etch on the big spay blade.

Here are some tips on Remington patterns, which were not bullets:

The R3943 sleeveboard pattern normally only has a blade etch and no tang stamp. However, a few were made with both a tang stamp and blade etch.

If you find a knife with this tang stamp, you have a Remington contract pattern. This stands for Southwestern Paper Company. Remington also made another advertising knife, with a special stamp on the front tang. It was made for Quickpoint in St. Louis, Mo.

All Remington patterns with a punch blade should have an acorn shield, except for the five-blade sowbelly pattern (R4283). This knife has a heavy pen blade, which some people consider to be a punch blade. It does not have an acorn shield.

Remington made three patterns with five blades. They are the R3143 stockman, R4283 sowbelly and R3843 Scout. Remington did not make a knife with more than five blades.

Remington actually made a knife with smoked pearl handles about 1920, before Queen Cutlery, which is often credited with first using smoked pearl handle material.

There were three types of dog-groomer knives produced by Remington. The R4733 was made with and without an Airedale dog-head shield. There was also a thinner version made, which had no pattern number or shield. All three of these knives had two dog-groomer blades, one at each end.

Other than the bullet patterns, Remington made very few folding knives with stag handles. They are all considered to be rare and very collectible.

For about four years, Remington inked on pattern numbers and blade markings. This was not just on cheaper patterns. This process was used from about 1936-1940 (Remington was bought by Pal Cutlery Co. in 1940).

Remington produced many various advertising knives. Most of these did not have pattern numbers on them. Roughly 5 percent of these knives did have a number on the blade. This probably occurred because some blades in inventory already had numbers on them and they were pulled out of inventory to complete an order or finish a production run of a certain advertising knife.

Here are examples of Remington tang stamps:

Remington used about a dozen different tang stamps in its 20 years of pocket-knife production. These were all variations of either the circle stamp or the straight line stamp. For example, these are the more frequently used stamps, and the years used.

Other facts about Remington knives:

Knives with REMINGTON UMC within a circle were made from 1921-1924.

Knives with MADE IN USA outside of the circle were made from 1924-1933.

Knives with REMINGTON in the circle and MADE IN USA outside the circle were made from 1933-35.

Same as above, but REMINGTON is in script instead of block, and these were made from 1935-1940.

Note: All prices given are mint value.

R1, redwood, 3-3/8" 125
R2, black, 3-3/8" 125
R3, bone, 3-3/8" 125
RC5, pyremite 100
RC6, genuine stag 100
RC7, ivory 100
RC8, cocobolo 100
RC9, metal 100

RA1, 3-3/8", redwood; $125.

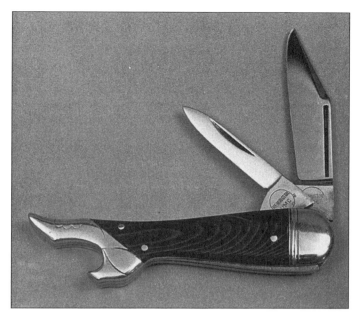

R15, 3-1/4", 2 blade, small leg, gray swirl pyremite, 3-1/4", Remington Circle UMC; $300.

R23CH, imitation black bone, 3-3/8", 2 blade with chain, Remington, UMC; $150.

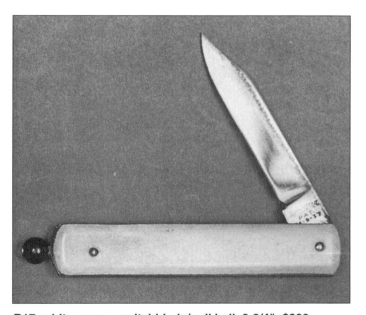

R17, white comp., switchblade/pull ball, 2-3/4"; $200.

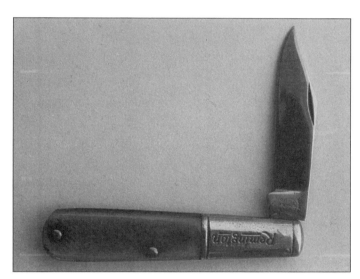

RB041, Barlow, 3-3/8", bone; $125.

R015, pyremite 100
R21CH, redwood bl., Jack, chain, 3-3/8" 150
R23CH, bone, 2-blade Jack, 3-3/8" 150
RLO24, letter opener, ... 125
R25, white pyremite, 2-blade Jack, 3-3/8" 125
R31, redwood, 3-3/8" 125
R32, black, 2-blade Jack, 3-3/8" 125
R35, pyremite, 3-3/8" 125
RLO35, letter opener 90
RB040, brown bone, spear blade, Barlow,
    3-3/8" 125

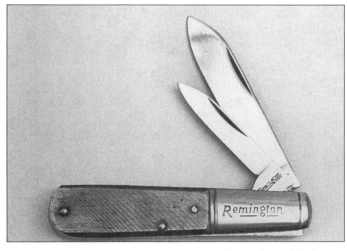

RB041, Barlow spear, brown bone, regular pull, 3-3/8"; $150.

RB43, 2-blade Barlow, LP, 3-3/8", Remington Circle UMC; $150.

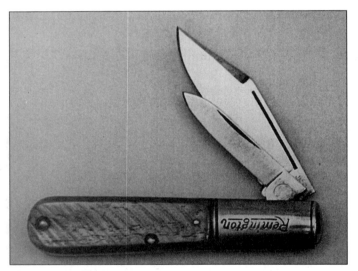

RB44, Barlow (clip), brown bone, 3-3/8", $150.

RB45, Barlow (spay), brown bone, 3-3/8"; $175.

R473, 3-1/4", Bone, slant Bols; $250.

RB46, Barlow (sheep foot), brown bone, 3-3/8"; $200.

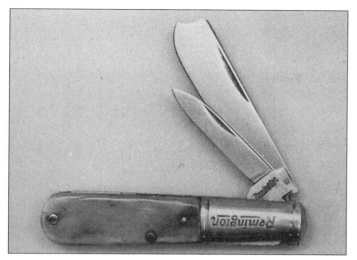

RB47, Barlow, brown bone, 3-3/8"; $200.

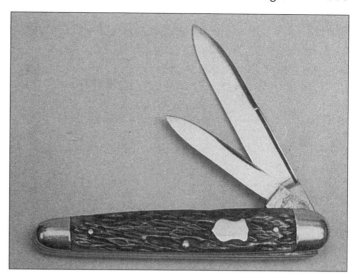

R73, 2-blade jack, brown bone, 3-1/8"; $140.

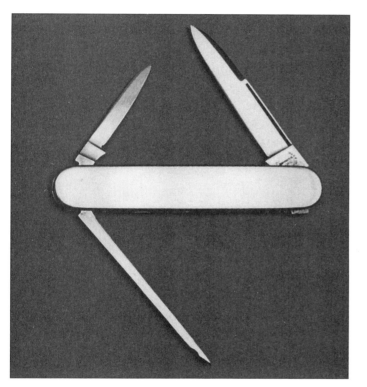

R64, lobster, metal; $100.

RB041, brown bone, clip blade, Barlow,
3-3/8" 125

RB43, brown bone LP, 3-3/8" 150

RB44W, white, 3-3/8".. 150

R51, redwood 90

R52, black.. 160

R53, bone 180

R55, pyremite 170

R63, bone 170

R65, pyremite 100

RLO70, fancy letter opener 150

R81, 3-1/2", redwood; $110.

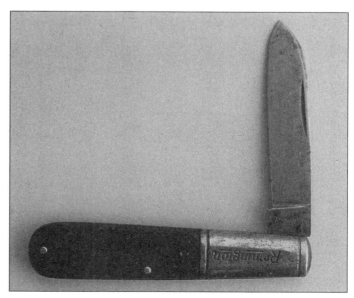

RC090, Barlow, 3-3/8", horn handle; $125.

RC091, Barlow, 3-3/8", horn; $125.

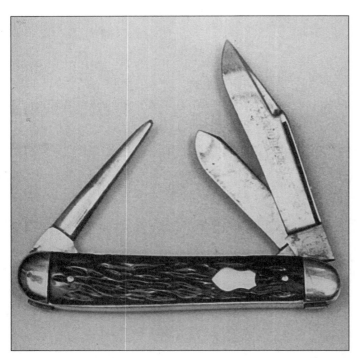

R100R, brown bone, long pull, punch blade, enclosed back spring, 3-3/8; $300.

R71, redwood, 3-1/8" 100
R72, black, 3-1/8" 100
R75, pyremite, 3-1/8" 125
R82, black, 3-1/2" 115
R83, bone, 3-1/2" 150
R85, pyremite, 3-1/2" 125
R91, redwood 130
R92, black 140
R93, bone 165
R95, pyremite 130
R100, bone back springs not covered,
   3-1/4" 160
R102CH, black, 3-1/2" 140
R102A, black composition, 3-1/8" 200
R103CH, bone, 3-1/2" 150
R105B, pyremite, punch blade, 3-3/8" 150
R108CH, cocobolo 100
R111, redwood 100
R112, black 100
R113, bone 145
R115, pyremite 115
R122, black, 3-1/2" 135
R123, bone, 3-1/2" 150
R125, pyremite, 3-1/2" 135
R131, redwood 135
R132, black 135
R133, bone 160
R135, pyremite 150
R141, redwood, 3-1/4" 125

R143, 3-1/4", bone, recess bolsters; $150.

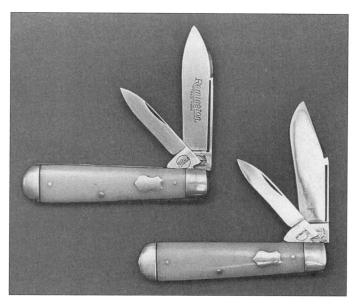

R165, jack, yellow scale, 3-1/2"; $140.

R142, black, 3-1/4"	125
R145, pyremite, 3-1/4"	150
R151, redwood, 3-1/2"	140
R152, black, 3-1/2"	140
R153, bone, 3-1/2"	160
R155, pyremite, 3-1/2"	140
R161, redwood, 2-blade Jack, 3-1/2"	140
R162, black, 2-blade Jack, 3-1/2"	140
R163, bone, 2-blade Jack, 3-1/2"	160
R171, redwood, 3-3/4"	150
R172, black, 3-3/4"	150
R175, pyremite, 3-3/4"	175
R181, redwood, 3-5/8"	150
R183, bone, 3-5/8"	180
R185, pyremite, 3-5/8"	155
R191, redwood	140
R192, black	140
R193, bone	180

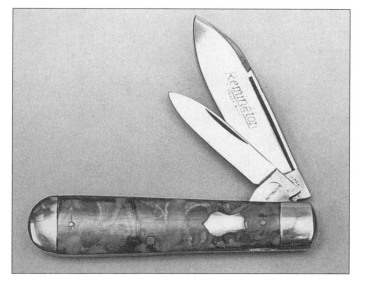

R165, jack, pyremite, 3-1/2"; $140.

R203, jack/easy opener, brown bone, 3-5/8"; $200.

R173, jack, brown bone, teardrop, 3-3/4; $200.

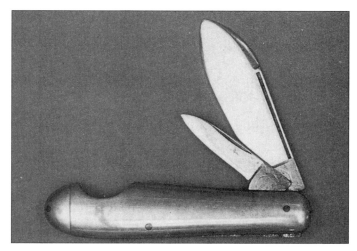

R219, Remington, solid brass, long pull, 3 5/8"; $175.

R273, Texas jack, brown bone, acorn shield, 4"; $250.

R195, pyremite	160
R201, redwood, Easy Opener Jack, 3-5/8"	150
R202, black, Easy Opener Jack, 3-5/8"	150
R205, pyremite, Easy Opener Jack, 3-5/8"	200
R211, redwood,	150
R212, black, Easy Opener Jack, 3-5/8"	150
R213, bone, Easy Opener Jack, 3-5/8"	180
R222, black	130
R223, bone	180
R225, pyremite	150
R228, cocobolo	140
R232, black	140
R233, bone	180
R235, pyremite	160
R238, cocobolo	130
R242, black	180

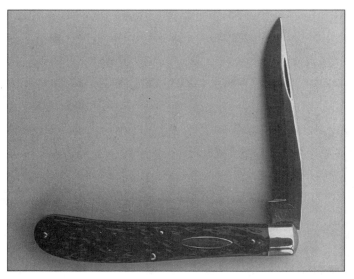

R303, 3-3/4", bone; $250.

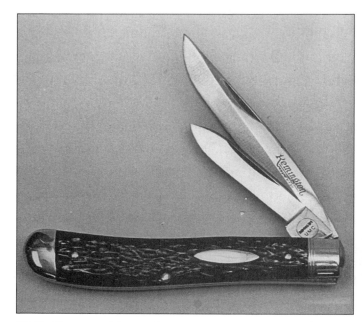

R313, Trapper with pen, brown bone, saber, 3-7/8"; $600.

R243, bone	200
R245, pyremite	180
R248, cocobolo	160
R252, black	150
R253, bone	180
R255, pyremite	170
R258, cocobolo	150
R262, black, 4"	140
R263, bone, 2-blade jack, 4"	225
R272, pyremite, candy stripe, jack, 4"	200
R272, black	170
R275, pyremite, 4"	225
R282, black	170

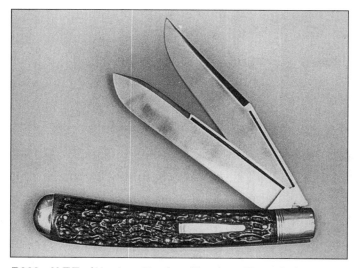

R293, H.T.T. (*Hunter, Trader, Trapper Magazine*), brown bone, long pull, bullet shield, 5-1/4"; $3,500.

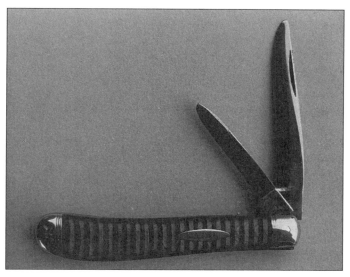

R315, 3-7/8", pyremite; $400.

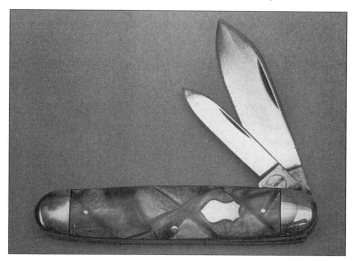

R365, jack, gold swirl pyremite, 3-3/4"; $200.

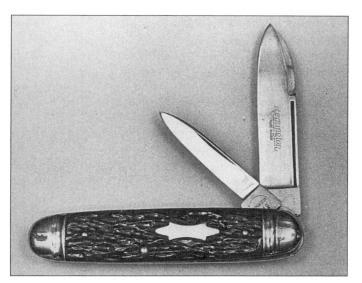

R333, equal end, brown bone, 3-3/4"; $175.

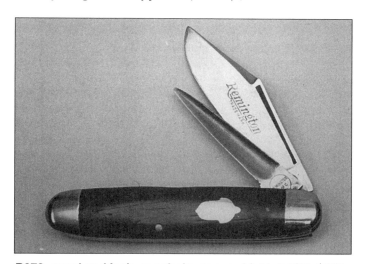

R378, equal end jack, cocobolo, acorn shield, 3-3/4"; $200.

R283, bone		200
R305, pyremite, 3-3/4"		250
R322, black		160
R323, bone		180
R325, pyremite		170
R328, cocobolo		160
R341, redwood		170
R342, black		170
R343, bone		170
R352, black, 2-blade equal-end jack, 3-3/4"		150
R353, bone, 2-blade equal end jack, 3-3/4"		200
R355, pyremite, 2-blade equal jack, 3-3/4"		200
R358, cocobolo, 3-3/4"		160
R372, black, equal-end jack, 3-3/4"		160
R373, bone, equal-end jack, 3-3/4"		200
R375, pyremite, equal-end jack, 3-3/4"		170
R391, redwood, tear-drop jack, 3-3/8"		160
R392, black, tear-drop jack, 3-3/8"		160

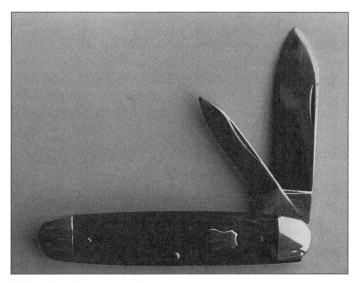

R363, 3-3/4", bone; $200.

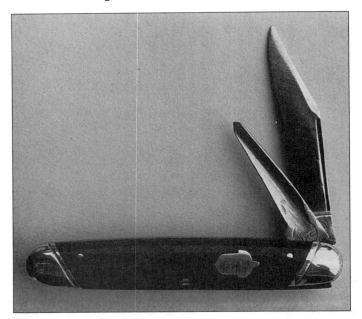

R465, 3-1/4", pyremite, slant bolsters; $150.

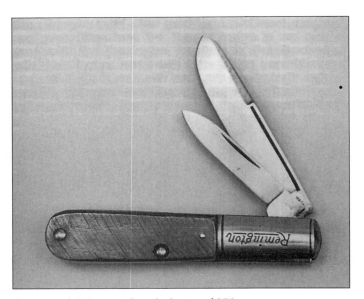

R473, 3-1/4", bone, slant bolsters; $250.

R475, 3-1/4", pyremite, slant bolsters; $250.

R485, 3-1/2", pyremite; $150.

R393, bone, 2 blade-spear, tear-drop jack,
3-3/8" 200

R402, black 150

R403, bone 185

R405, pyremite 170

R410, buffalo horn 150

R412, black 150

R415, pyremite 170

R423, bone 170

R432, black, 3-1/2" 250

R435, pyremite, 3-1/2" 250

R443, bond 450

R444, pearl, Dr.'s knife, spatula blade 500

R453, bone 360

R455, pyremite 300

R463, bone, equal-end jack, 3-1/4" 170

R482, black, 3-1/2" 150

R483, bone, 3-1/2" 180

R488, cocobolo, 2-blade spear, equal end,
3-1/2" 150

R493, bone 180

R495, pyremite 150

R503, bone 180

R505, pyremite 150

R512, black, equal-end jack, 3-1/2" 200

R513, bone, equal-end jack, 3-1/2" 225

R523, bone 200

R525, pyremite 200

R551, redwood, 3-1/4" 150

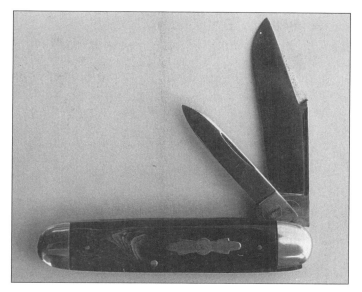

R515, 3-1/2", pyremite; $225.

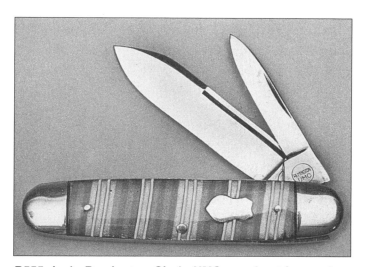

R555, jack, Remington Circle UMC, candy-stripe scales, 3-1/4"; $225.

R563, brown bone, acorn shield, 3-1/4"; $150.

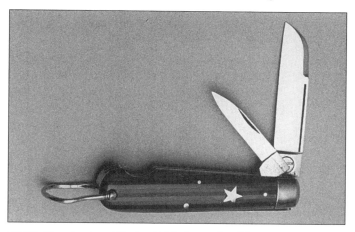

R565, Remington Circle, 2 blade, red, white and blue with star, 3-1/2"; $350.

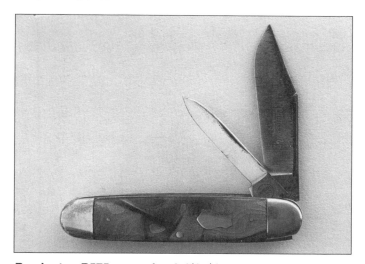

Remington R575, pyremite, 3-1/4; $200.

R552, black, 3-1/4"		150
R572, black		150
R583, bone		170
R585, pyremite		150
R590, Buffalo horn, slant bols., 2 blades, 3-1/4"		250
R593, Bone, 2 blades, slant bols., jack, 3-1/4"		250
R595, Pyremite, 2 blades, slant bols., jack, 3-1/4"		250
R609, metal, 3-3/8"		140
R613, bone		185
R615, pyremite		150
R622, black, 4"		160
R623, bone, 4"		275
R625, pyremite, 4"		275
R633, bone		180
R635, pyremite		150
R643, bone		250
R645, pyremite		220

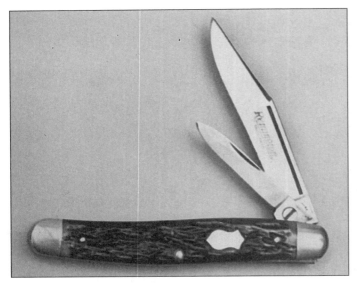

R603, small serpentine jack, bone, 3-3/8"; $125.

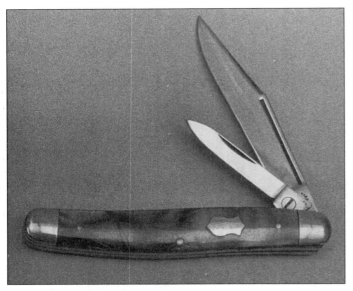

R605, jack, gold-swirl pyremite, 3-3/8"; $150.

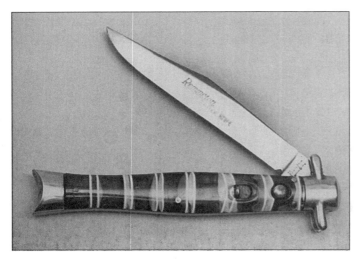

R645, switchblade, candy stripe, 4"; $750.

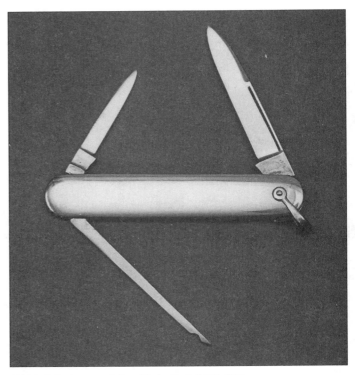

R629, lobster, metal, with bail, 2-3/4"; $90.

R655, pyremite, bow tie, 3-7/8"...........................450
R663, bone 300
R668, cocobolo..275
R672, black, 2-blade dog-leg jack, 3" 150
R674, pearl, 2-blade dog-leg jack, 3"................225
R675, pyremite, 2-blade, dog-leg jack, 3"..........175
R677, ivory, 2-blade dog-leg jack, 3" 200
R682, black, gunstock, 3" 350

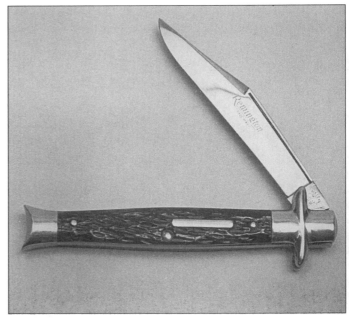

R653, bowtie, bone, 3-7/8"; $400.

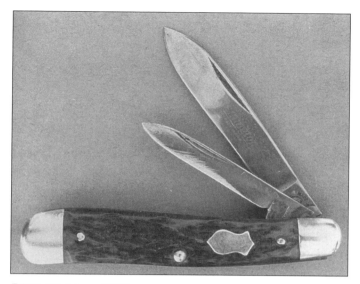

R673, 3", bone; $150.

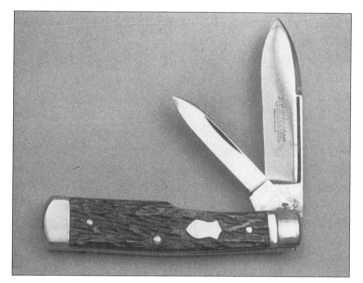

R683, gunstock, Remington, brown bone, long pull, 3"; $450.

R698, hawkbill, cocobolo, 4"; $125.

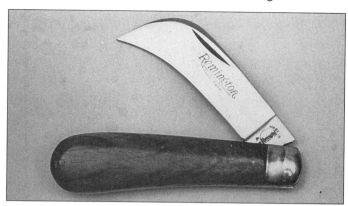

R708, hawkbill, cocobolo, 3-5/8"; $125.

R684, pearl, gunstock, 3"....................................500
R685, pyremite, gunstock, 3"............................400
R693, bone, hawkbill, 4" 175
R703, bone, small hawkbill, 3-5/8".....................150
R706, genuine stag, small hawkbill, 3-5/8".........175
R713, bone, 3-3/4"..170
R718, cocobolo, 2-blade hawkbill, 3-3/4"............200
R723, bone, large 1-blade hawkbill, 4-1/2".........250
R728, cocobolo, large 1-blade hawkbill, 4-1/2"...175

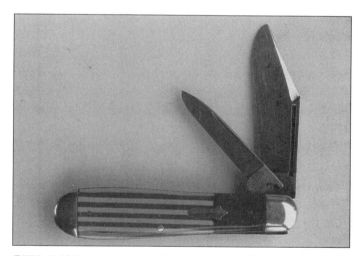

R775, 3-1/2", pyremite, red/white/blue; $400.

R933, 5", bone, saber blade; $450.

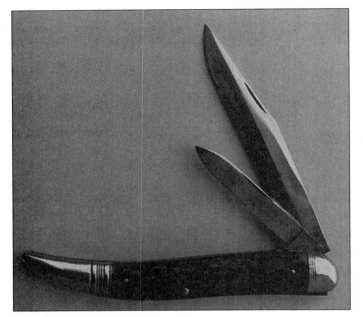

R943, 5", bone; $500.

R732, black	120
R733, bone	160
R735, pyremite	140
R738, cocobolo	120
R743, bone	160
R745, pyremite	135
R753, bone, 3-1/2	200
R755, pyremite, red, white and blue, 3-1/2"	350
R756, genuine stag, 3-1/2"	250
R763, bone	150
R772, black	150
R773, bone	175
R783, bone	190
R793, bone	230
R803, bone, 3"	100
RC803, bone, 3"	50
R805, pyremite	100
R813, bone	220
R823, bone	170

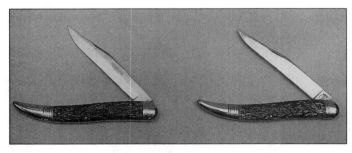

Toothpick: Left: R953, brown bone, grooved bolster, saber blade, 5"; $500. Right: R953, brown bone, grooved bolster, flat blade, no shield, 5"; $300.

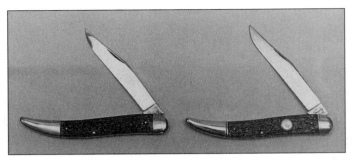

Left: R953, brown bone, 5"; $225. Right: R953, Remington UMC, brown bone, round bullet shield, 5"; $700.

R825, pyremite	135
R833, bone, 2-blade serpentine long spay, 3-5/8"	225
R835, pyremite, 2-blade serpentine long spay, 3-5/8"	225
R843, bone	170
R845, pyremite	140
R853, bone	175
R855, pyremite	150
R863, bone	210
R865, pyremite	150
R873, bone, 2-blade sleeve board jack, 3-1/8"	110
R874, pearl, 2-blade sleeve board jack, 3-1/8"	125
R875, pyremite, 2-blade sleeve board jack, 3-1/8"	110
R881, redwood	120
R882, black	125
R883, bone	160
R892, black	140
R893, bone	200
R895, pyremite	170

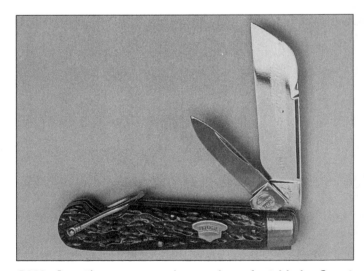

R963, Scout/easy opener, bone, sheep-foot blade, Scout hat shield, bail; $700.

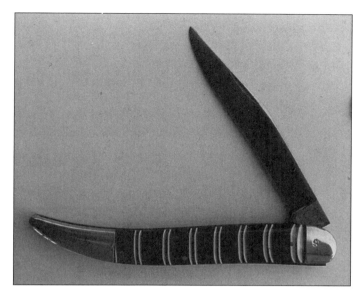

R955, 5", pyremite candy stripe; $300.

R973, jack, imitation bone, 4-1/4"; $450.

R901, redwood 140

R913, bone, # front tang 200

R921, redwood, 1-blade maize, 4-1/8" 200

R932, black 200

R935, pyremite, 2-blade toothpick, 5" 285

R942, black, 2-blade toothpick, 5" 450

R945, pyremite, 5" 500

R962, black, 4-1/4" 130

R965, pyremite, 4-1/4" 150

R982SAB, black, 2 dog-leg jack, 2-7/8" 150

R983, bone, SAB, 2-blade, dog-leg jack,
2-7/8" 300

R985, pyremite, SAB, 2-blade, dog-leg jack,
2-7/8" 300

R992, black, 3-1/4" 115

R993, bone, 3-1/4" 130

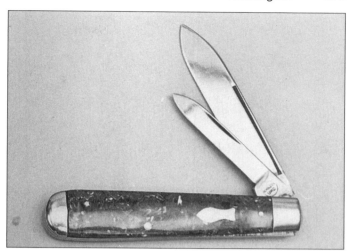

R995, jack, blue and white composition, 3-1/4"; $125.

R1002, black, 2-blade jack, front bols.,
grooved, 3-5/8" 200

R1003, bone, 2-blade jack, front bols.,
grooved, 3-3/8" 225

R1005, pyremite, 2-blade jack, front bols.,
grooved, 3-5/8" 225

R1012, black, 2-blade jack, 3-5/8" 150

R1013, bone, 2-blade jack, 3-5/8" 200

R1022, black, large English-style jack, 4-1/4" 500

R1023, bone, large English-style jack, 4-1/4" 500

R1032, black, 2-blade tear-drop jack, 3-3/8" 100

R1033, bone, 2-blade tear-drop jack, 3-3/8" 115

R1035, pyremite, 2-blade tear-drop jack,
3-3/8" 100

R1042, black, 2-blade jack, 3-3/8" 150

R1043, bone, 2-blade jack, 3-3/8" 200

R1045, pyremite, 2-blade jack, 3-3/8" 175

R1051, redwood, 1-blade budding knife,
3-1/2" 125

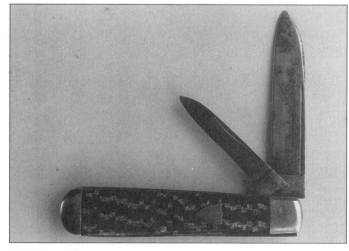

R1065, 3-3/8", pyremite; $125,

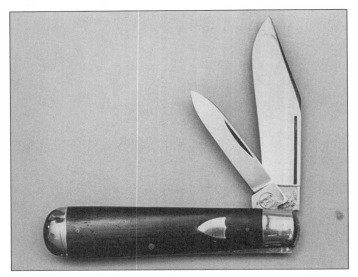

R1071, cocobolo (shows 2 blade styles), 3-3/8"; $125.

R1073, Remington, bone, 3-3/8"; $150.

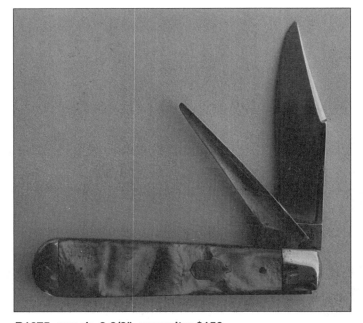

R1075, punch, 3-3/8", pyremite; $150.

R1103, brown bone, 3-3/8"; $135.

R1053, bone, 2-blade jack knife, 3-1/2" 125
R1055, pyremite, 2-blade jack, punch, 3-3/8" 150
R1061, redwood, 2-blade jack, 3-3/8" 90
R1063, bone, 2-blade jack, 3-3/8" 130
R1072, black, 2-blade jack, 3-3/8" 125
R1082, black, 1-blade sheep-foot LP, 3-3/8" 80
R1083, bone, 1-blade sheep-foot LP, 3-3/8 100
R1085, pyremite, 1-blade sheep-foot LP,
3-3/8" 80
R1092, black 75
R1093, bone 90
R1102, black, 2-blade bear-head jack,
3-3/8" 95
R1112, black 95

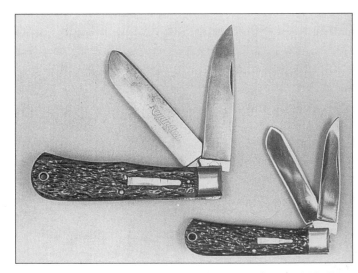

Top: R1123, brown bone, bullet shield, 4-1/2"; $2,000. Bottom: R1173, brown bone, baby bullet, 3-1/2"; $6,000.

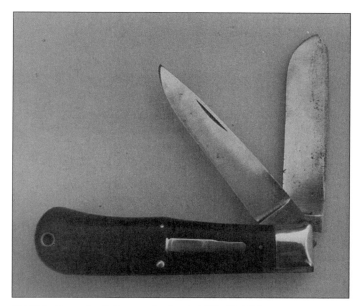

R1128, Rem. bullet, cocobolo, 4-1/2"; $3,500.

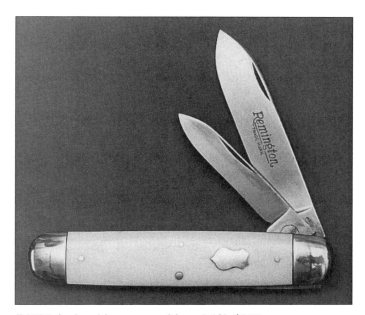

R1225, jack, white composition, 4-1/4; $275.

R1113, bone, 3-3/8"		125
R1133, bone		160
R1143, bone, 4-3/8"		160
R1182, black		125
R1192, black		100
R1193, bone		125
R1202, black		140
R1203, bone		150
R1212, black		235
R1213, bone		300
R1222, black, 4-1/4"		250
R1223, bone, 4-1/4"		300
R1232, black		150

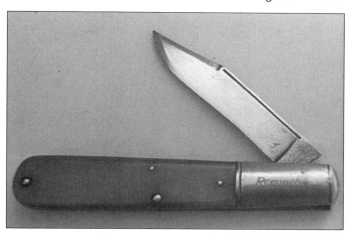

R1240, Rem. Daddy B., bone, 5"; $300.

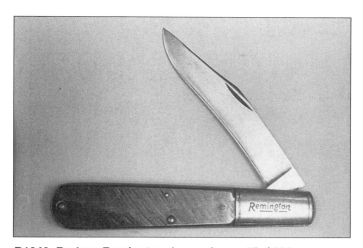

R1240, Barlow, Remington, brown bone, 5"; $300.

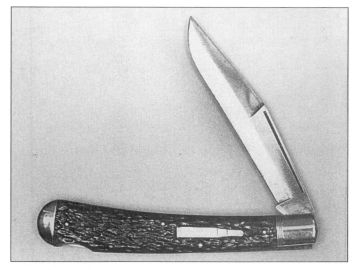

R1253L, Remington, brown bone, long pull, lockback, bullet shield (bail), 5-1/4"; $2,500.

R1241, redwood, Daddy Barlow, 5"		285
R1242, black, Daddy Barlow, 5"		300
R1243, bone, Daddy Barlow, 5"		300

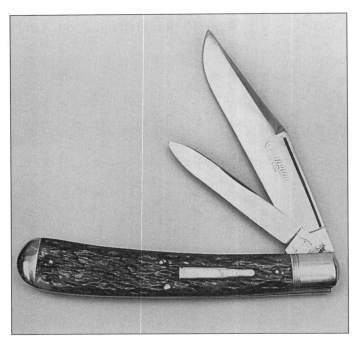

R1263, Remington bullet, brown bone, 5-3/8"; $3,000.

R1273, bullet, brown bone, 5-3/8"; $3,500.

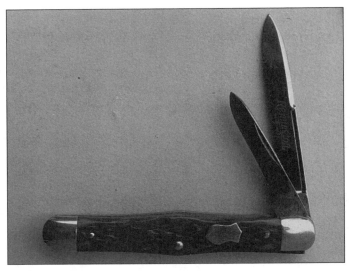

R1283, 3", bone, swell center; $200.

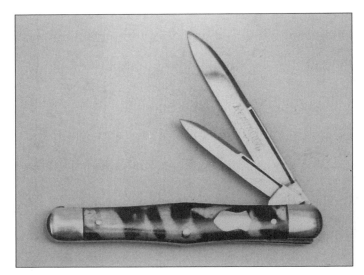

R1285, swell center, tortoise shell, 3"; $200.

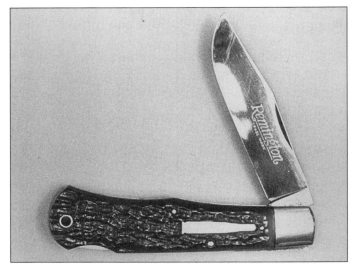

R1303, Remington bullet, brown bone, lockback, bullet shield, 4-1/2"; $2,500.

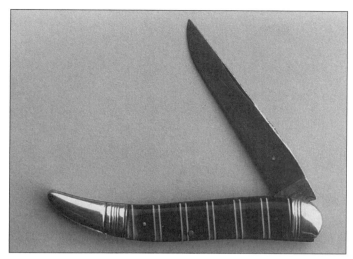

R1255, 4-1/4", pyremite, candy stripe; $400.

R1284, pearl, 3"	240
R1295, pyremite	215
R1315, bone, 2-blade, dog-leg jack, 3"	160
R1323, bone, 2-blade dogleg	150
R1324, pearl, 2-blade dog-leg jack, 3"	200
R1325, pyremite, 3"	130
R1333, bone	90
R1343, bone, 4-1/4"	285
R1353, bone	215
R1363, bone	215
R1373, bone, lock back, 4-1/4"	300
R1379, metal, 4-1/4"	250
R1389, metal	200
R1399, metal, 3-1/2"	100
R1409, metal	100
R1413, bone	115
R1423, bone	115
R1437, ivory	140
R1447, ivory	140
R1457, ivory	160
R1483, bone	140
R1485, pyremite	115
R1493, bone	140
R1495, pyremite	140
R1568, cocobolo	120
R1572, black, 3"	100
R1573, bone, 3"	100
R1593, bone, 3-1/8"	150

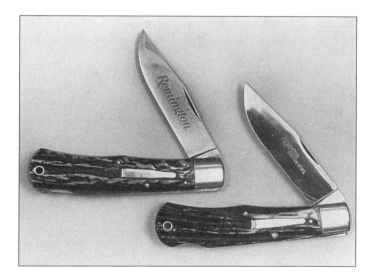

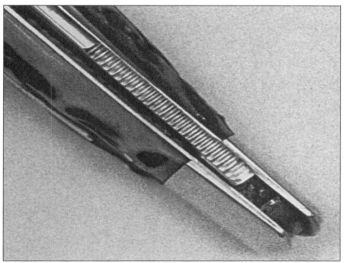

The author has observed many R1303 and R1306 Bullets and has found that the knives with two handle rivets at the front bolster have the thumb groove on the blade. The knives with one rivet do not have the thumb groove. R1306, Remington bullet, stag, thumb groove on top of blade (bottom), 4-5/8"; $2,000.

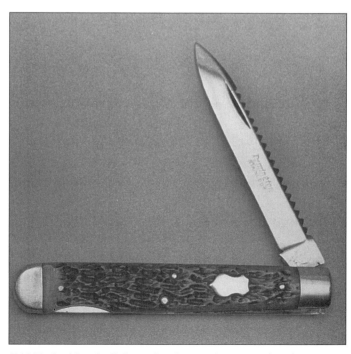

R1383, lockback, fish scaler, brown bone, 4-1/4"; $450.

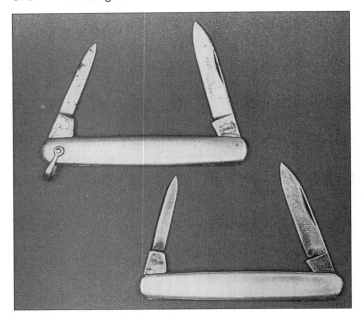

R1339, Remington, all metal, 3"; $65.

R1595, pyremite, 3-1/8" 150
R1608, cocobolo 75
R1615, pyremite, 5" 300
R1622, black, 2-blade jack, 3" 100
R1623, bone, 2-blade jack, 3" 115
R1623CH, imitation bone 125

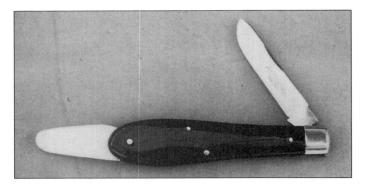

R1465, 3-5/8, pyremite, $225. Photo courtesy Wayne Robertson.

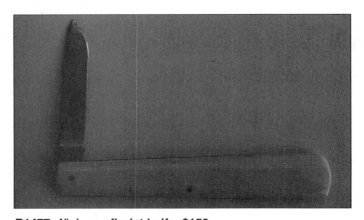

R1477, 4", ivory, florist knife; $150.

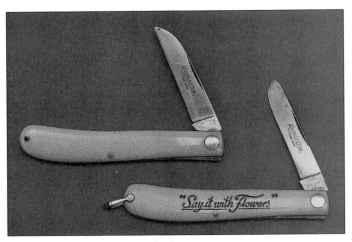

Top: R1535, florist knife, imitation ivory, 3-3/4"; $100. Bottom: R1545, florist knife, imitation ivory, with bail, 3-3/4"; $100.

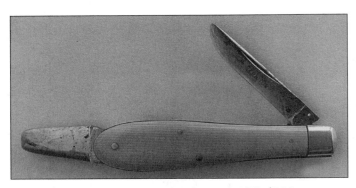

R1555, budding knife, imitation ivory, 3-1/2"; $200.

R1630, buffalo horn 400
R1644, pearl, 2-7/8" 200
R1645, pyremite, 2-7/8" 140
R1668, cocobolo 160

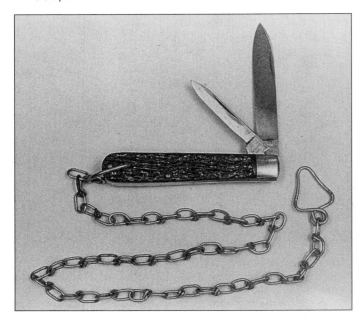

R1537CH, Remington, imitation bone, reg. pull, with chain, 3"; $150.

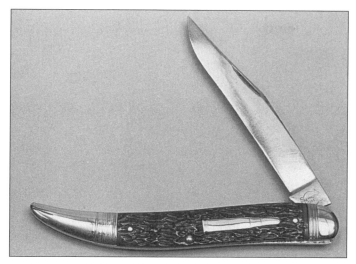

R1613BL, Toothpick bullet, brown bone, bullet shield, grooved bolsters; $3,500.

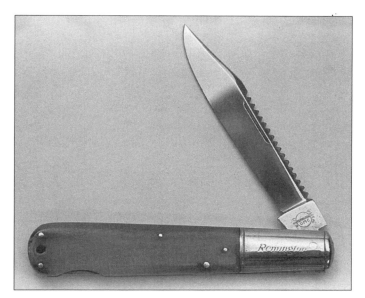

R1630, fish scaler, Daddy Barlow, brown bone, 5", lock back, Remington Circle, UMC, rare; $600.

R1671, redwood, 3-3/8"	100
R1685, pyremite, budding-feathered, 3-3/4"	125
R1687, ivory, feathered budding knife	150
R1688, cocobolo, feathered budding knife	125
R1707, ivory	100
R1715, Pyremite, feathered budding knife, 4-1/4"	125
R1717, Ivory, feathered budding knife, 4-1/4"	125
R1723, bone, 2-blade jack sheep foot, 3-1/2"	150
R1751, redwood, 3-1/2"	80
R1752, black, 3-1/2"	80
R1753, bone, 3-1/2"	100
R1755, pyremite, 3-1/2"	80
R1763, bone	115

R1772, black	115
R1782, black, 3-1/2"	150
R1785, pyremite, 3-1/2"	150
R1803, bone	100
R1833, bone	150
R1853, bone, 2-blade equal-end jack, 3-3/8"	150
R1855, pyremite, 2-blade equal-end jack, 3-3/8"	150
R1882, black, 2-blade jack, razor blade, 3"	150
R1903, bone	100
R1905, pyremite	80
R1913, bone, 3-3/8"	140

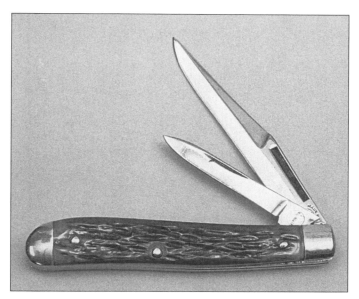

R1653, peanut, brown bone, 2-7/8"; $150.

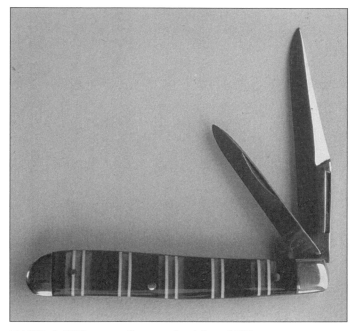

R1655, 2-7/8", pyremite, candy stripe; $150.

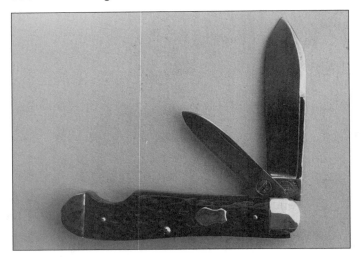

R1773, 3-1/2", bone, easy opener; $175.

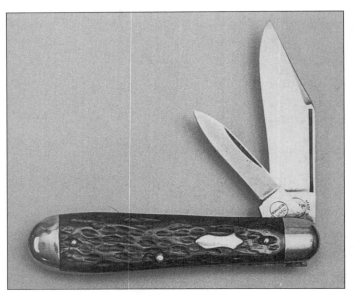

R1783, jack teardrop, brown bone, 3-1/2"; $150.

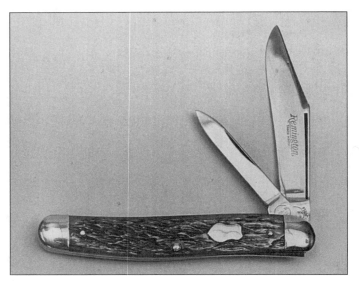

R1823, brown bone, long pull, 3-5/8"; $125.

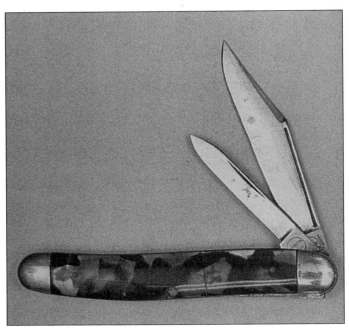

R1825, Remington, imitation tortoise, long pull, 3-5/8"; $125.

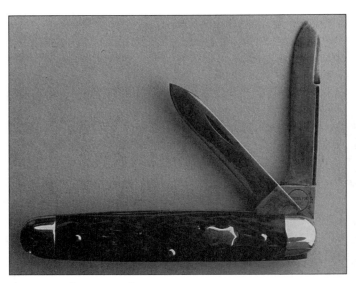

R1863, 3-3/8", bone; $200.

R1873, 3-5/8", bone; $150.

R1962, black	100
R1973, bone	185
R1995, pyremite, feathered budding knife, 4-1/4"	125
R2043, bone, 3-1/4"	85
R2045, pyremite, 3-1/4"	85
R2053, bone, 3-1/4"	125
R2065, pyremite, 2-blade tear-drop jack, 3-1/8"	100
R2075, pyremite, 2-blade tear-drop jack, 3-1/8"	85
R2083, bone, 3-1/4"	85
R2085, pyremite	85
R2093, bone, 3-1/8"	90
R2103, bone, 2-blade jack, 3-1/8"	110
R2111, redwood	120
R2203, bone, 3-3/8"	125

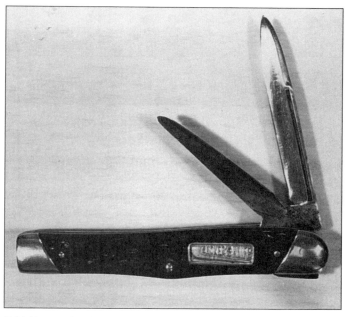

R2013, smoker's knife, brown bone, slant bolsters; $300.

R2055, 3-1/4", waterfall pyremite; $150.

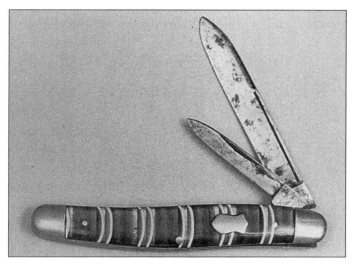

R1915, Remington, candy stripe, long pull, 3-3/8"; $150.

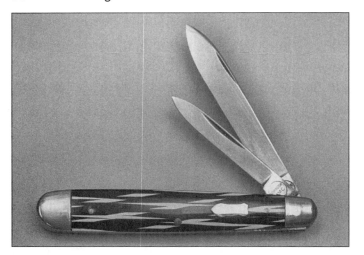

R2095, black and white composition, 3-1/8"; $90.

R2223, bone, 3-3/8"	75
R2503, bone	75
R2505B, pyremite	75
2505M, pyremite	75
2505R, pyremite	75

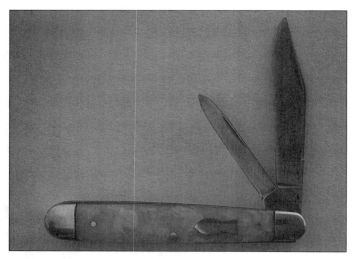

R2105, 3-1/8", pyremite; $110.

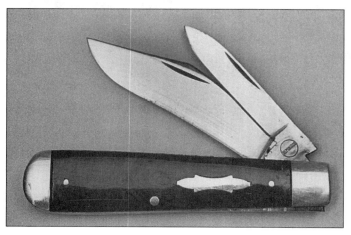

R2215, jack, red and black pyremite, 3-3/8"; $125.

Top: R2403, 1 blade, brown bone, straight-line (stamp), 5"; $800. Bottom: R2303, brown bone, straight-line (stamp), 1 blade, 4-1/8"; $700.

R2605, jack, red scale, 3-3/8"; $110.

R2603, bone, serpentine jack, 3-3/8"	125
R3003, bone	285
R3005, pyremite	250
R3013, bone	285
R3015, pyremite	250
R3033, bone	330

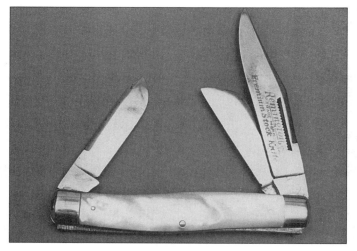

R3054, stockman, genuine pearl, 4"; $700.

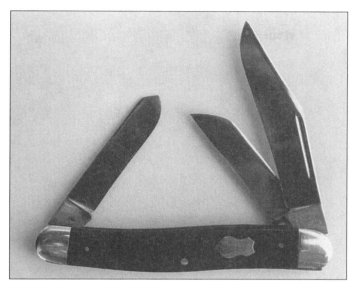

R3055, 4", pyremite; $400.

R3035, pyremite 300
R3050, buffalo horn, 4" 400
R3056, genuine stag, 4" 450
R3062, black, 4" 250
R3064, pearl, 4" 400
R3070, buffalo horn 600
R3073, bone, Stockman Whittler, 4" 800
R3075, pyremite 700
R3083LP, bone 400
R3085, pyremite 330
R3093, bone 250
R3095, pyremite 185
R3103, bone 285

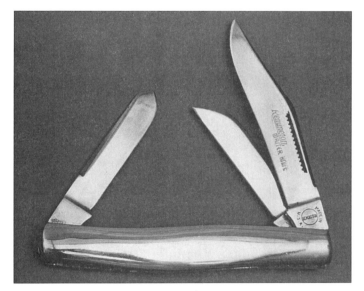

R3059, stockman, all metal, 4"; $350.

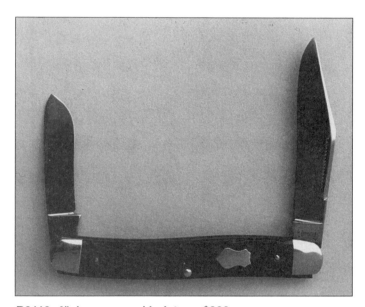

R3113, 4", bone, round bolsters; $300.

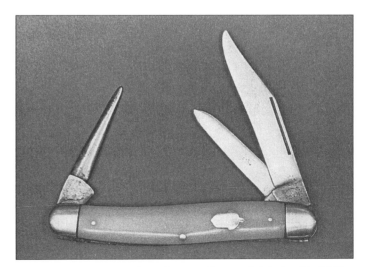

R3065, stockman, yellow, long pull, punch blade, 4"; $250.

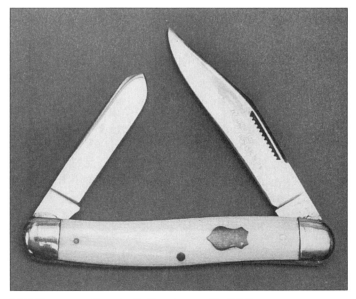

R3115, serpentine, imitation ivory, 4"; $250.

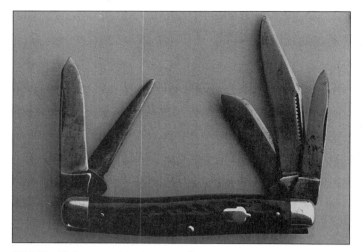

R3143, 4", bone, 5 blade, rare; $5,000.

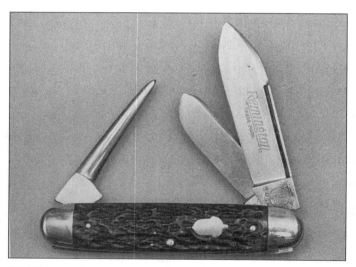

R3153, equal end, brown bone, acorn shield, 3-1/2"; $250.

R3273, cattle, brown bone, equal end, 3-3/4"; $400.

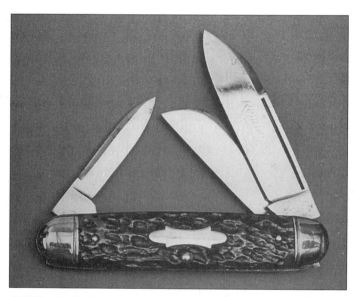

R3273, cattle, brown bone, long pull, equal end, grooved bolster, 3-3/4"; $400.

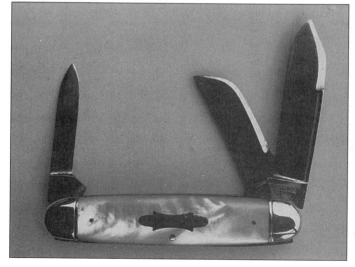

R3274, 3-3/4", genuine pearl, cattle knife; $600.

R3105, pyremite	235
R3115G, pyremite, 4"	250
R3115W, pyremite, 4"	250
R3123, bone, moose 2-blade, 3-7/8"	300
R3133, bone, 4"	300
R3155, pyremite	250
R3155B, pyremite	250
R3163, bone, 3-blade cattle pattern, 3-1/2"	285
R3165, pyremite, 3-blade cattle pattern, 3-1/2"	250
R3183, bone, acorn-punch, 3-blade cattle, 3-1/2"	400
R3185, pyremite, acorn-punch, cattle, 3-1/2"	400
R3193, bone	265
R3202, black	260
R3203, bone, 3-1/2"	265
R3212, black	300
R3213, bone	300

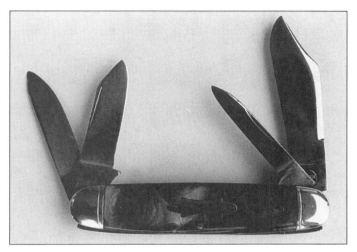

R3305, 3-3/4", pyremite, $600.

R3215, pyremite		260
R3222, black		190
R3223, bone		250
R3225, pyremite		225
R3232, black		190
R3233, bone		260
R3235, pyremite		260
R3242, black, 3-3/4"		260
R3243W, pyremite, 3-3/4"		240
R3253, bone		300
R3255, pyremite		260
R3263, bone		300
R3265, pyremite		260
R3275, pyremite, 3-3/4"		500
R3283, bone		275
R3285, pyremite		250
R3293, bone		275
R3295, pyremite		250
R3302, black, 4-blade equal end, 3-3/4"		500
R3303, bone, 4-blade equal end, 3-3/4"		600

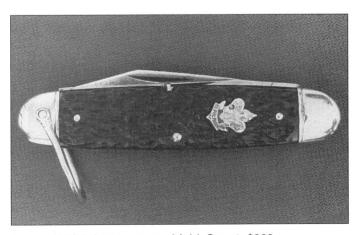

R3333, 3-3/4", bone, trans. shield, Scout; $300.

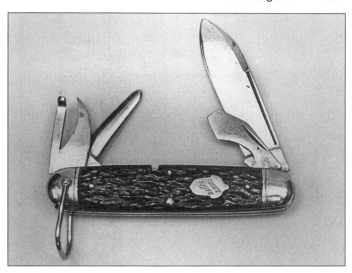

R3333, Scout knife, brown bone, official Scout, acorn shield, bail, 3-3/4"; $400.

RS3333, brown bone, with bail, official Scout shield, "Be Prepared," 3-3/4"; $250.

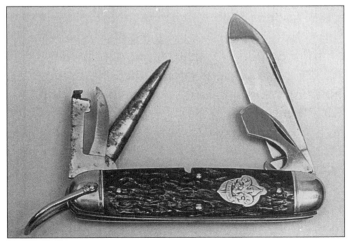

RS3333, Scout knife, brown bone, Scout shield, acorn shape, 3-3/4"; $250.

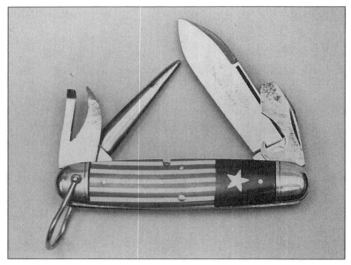

R3335, Scout knife, red, white, and blue, 3-3/4"; $400.

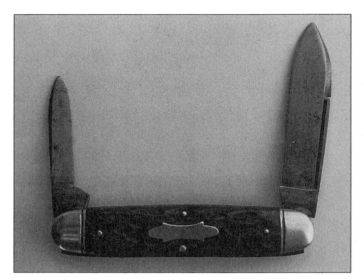

R3373, 3-3/4", bone; $175.

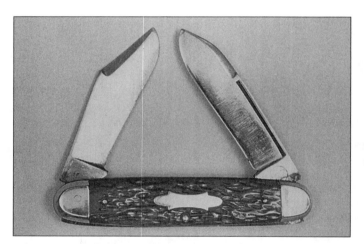

R3363, Remington, brown bone, long pull, J pattern, 3-3/4"; $400.

R3312, black, 3-3/4"	300
R3313, bone, 3-3/4"	385
R3315B, pyremite	360
R3322, black	200
3352, black, 3-3/4"	300
3353, bone, 2-blade equal-end J pattern, 3-3/4"	400
R3372, black, 2-blade equal end, 3-3/4"	170
R3375, pyremite, 2-blade equal end, 3-3/4"	200
R3382, black	200
R3383, bone	215
R3385S, pyremite	200
R3393, bone, 2-blade equal end, 3-3/4"	200
R3395T, 2-blade birdseye rivet, 3-3/4"	200
R3403, bone	250
R3405J, pyremite	215
R3414, pearl	290
3415H, pyremite, 3-3/8"	200

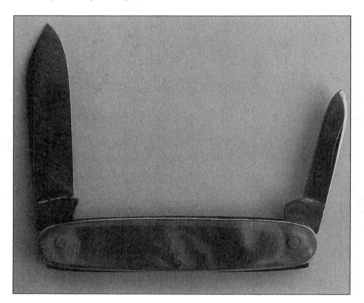

R3395, 3-3/4", pyremite; $200.

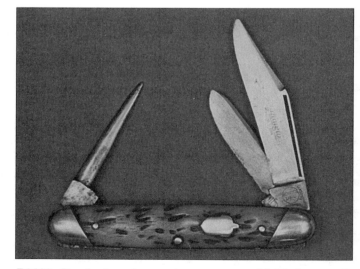

R3413, Remington, brown bone, acorn shield, long pull, slant bolsters, 3-3/8"; $185.

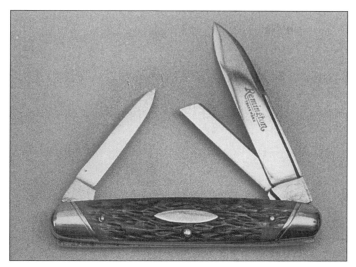

R3423, equal end, slant bolsters, bone, 3-1/4"; $300.

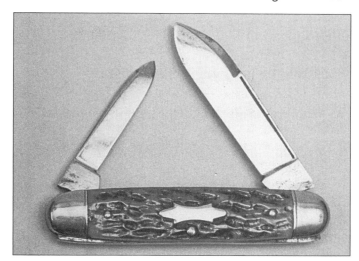

R3443, 2 blades, brown bone, 3-1/4"; $225.

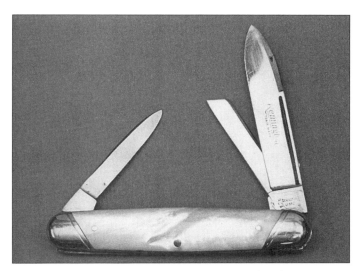

R3424, equal end, pearl, slant bolsters, 3-3/8"; $450.

R3455, 3-1/4", pyremite, slant bolsters, saber blade; $500.

R3425P, pyremite, 3-3/8"		300
R3432, black		170
R3433, bone		190
R3435, pyremite		170
R3442, black, 3-1/4"		170
R3453, bone, Whittler, 3-1/4"		500
R3463, bone, Whittler		350
R3475K, pyremite, 3-1/4"		250
R3475J, pyremite, 3-1/4"		250
R3480, buffalo horn, small stockman, 3-3/8"		200
R3483, bone, small stockman, 3-3/8"		225
R3484, pearl, small stockman, 3-3/8"		300
R3489, metal		175
R3494, pearl, 3-3/8"		300
R3495M, pyremite, 3-3/8"		250
R3500BU, buffalo horn		200
R3503, bone		215

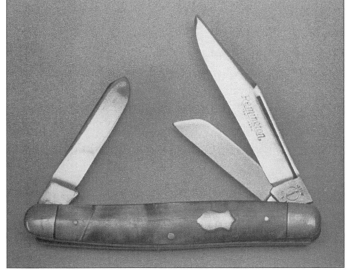

R3485, equal end, gold-swirl pyremite, 3-3/8"; $200.

R3504, pearl 300
R3514, pearl, 3-3/8" 225
R3515, pyremite, 3-3/8" 200
R3520BU, buffalo horn, 3-blade whittler,
   3-3/8" 400
R3523, bone, 3-blade whittler, 3-3/8" 300
R3524, pearl, 3-blade whittler, 3-3/8" 350
R3525, pyremite, 3-blade whittler, 3-3/8" 300
R3545, pyremite 150
R3554, pearl, square bolsters, Stockman, 4" 500
R3555G, pyremite, 3-7/8" 350
R3565D, pyremite, 3-7/8" 350
R3573, bone 240
R3575, pyremite 200
R3583, bone, Whittler, 4" 400
R3585, pyremite, 4" 350

R3553, brown bone, square bolsters, 4"; $450.

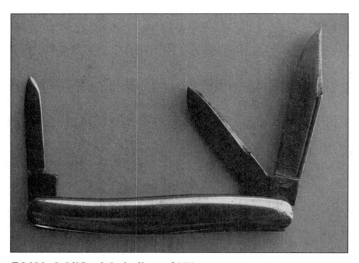

R3499, 3-3/8", nickel-silver; $250.

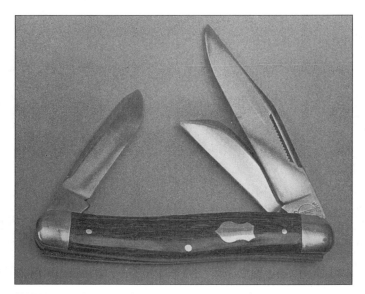

R3555, stockman, mingled red scale, 4"; $400.

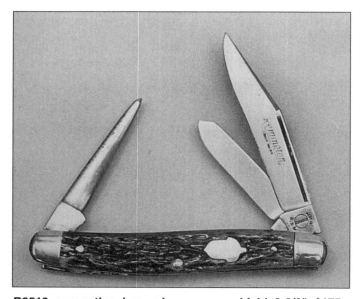

R3513, serpentine, brown bone, acorn shield, 3-3/8"; $175.

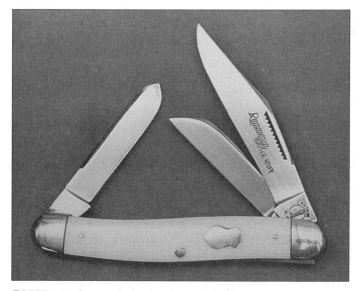

R3557, stockman, imitation ivory, 4"; $350.

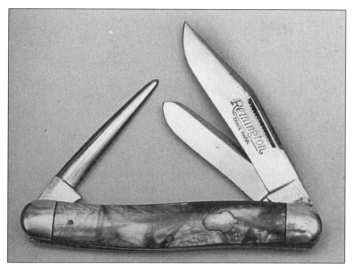

R3565, stockman, brown swirl pyremite, acorn shield, 4"; $350.

R3563, bone, acorn shield, 4"; $400.

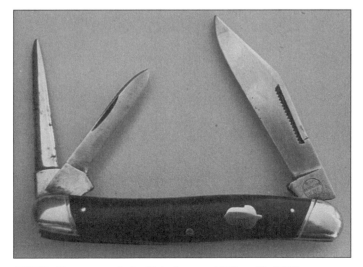

R3580, Rem. punch, buffalo horn whittler, 4"; $400.

R3593, bone	300
R3595, pyremite	300
R3596, genuine stag	350
R3600, buffalo horn	200
R3603, bone	215
R3604, pearl	300
R3605, pyremite	215
R3613, bone	200
R3615, pyremite	200
R3620BU, buffalo horn	140
R3623, bone	150
R3625, pyremite	140
R3633, bone	150
R3635, pyremite	140
R3643, bone, stockman slant bols., 4"	400
R3645, pyremite, 4"	400
R3653, bone, punch, long spar, 3-7/8"	400
R3655, pyremite, long spay	400
R3665, pyremite	300
R3675, pyremite	300
R3685C, pyremite, whittler, 3-1/2"	500
R3700BU, buffalo horn, 4"	230
R3703, bone, 4"	250
R3704, pearl, 4"	350
R3705, pyremite, 4"	225
R3710BU, buffalo horn	225
R3713, bone, 3-7/8"	300
R3714, pearl, 3-7/8"	400
R3715, pyremite, 3-7/8"	300
R3722, black comp.	750
R3723, bone, whittler, big sleeve board	900
R3725, pyremite	750
R3732, black	330
R3733, bone	385
R3735, pyremite	330

R3644, stockman, pearl scale, slant bolster, 4"; $600.

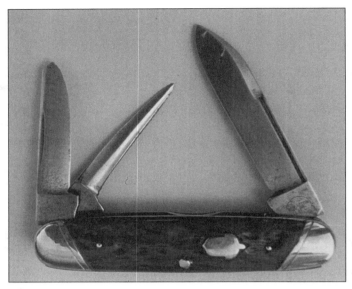

R3683, Rem., 3 backsprings, bone, 3-1/2"; $400.

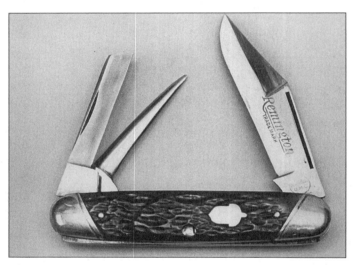

R3693, whittler, brown bone, acorn shield, saber blade, slant bolsters, 3-1/2"; $450.

R3853, bone, 4"..350
R3858, cocobolo, 4"..300
R3870BU, buffalo horn, 3-blade stockman, 4"...350
R3873, bone, 3-blade stockman, 4"....................350
R3874, pearl, 3-blade stockman, 4"....................450
R3875A, pyremite, 3-blade stockman, 4"..........300
R3885, pyremite, 4"...500
R3893, bone, 3-7/8"...150
R3895, pyremite...150
R3903, bone, 2-blade J pattern, 3-7/8"..............300
R3923, bone, 3-blade stockman........................400
R3926, genuine stag...400
R3932, black..350
R3933, stag...400
R3935, pyremite..350

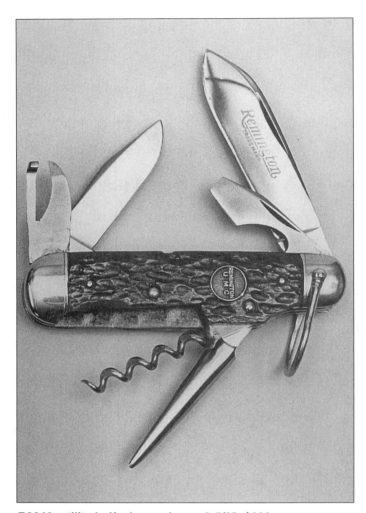

R3843, utility knife, brown bone, 3-5/8"; $600.

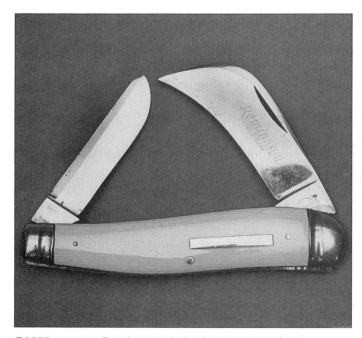

R3855, pruner, Remington, imitation ivory, 4"; $350.

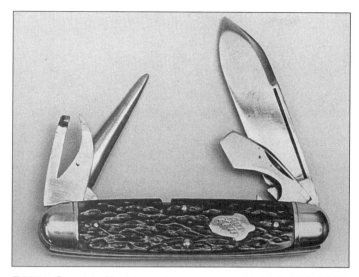

R3863, Scout knife, brown bone, acorn shield, 3-3/4"; $300.

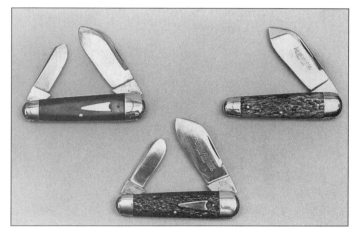

Top left: R3942, large sleeveboard, ebony, 3-5/8"; $500. Top right: R3943, sleeveboard, Rogers bone, 3-5/8"; $600. Bottom: R3943, sleeveboard, brown bone, 3-5/8"; $600.

R4073, serpentine, brown bone, saber blade, acorn shield, slant bolsters, 4"; $350.

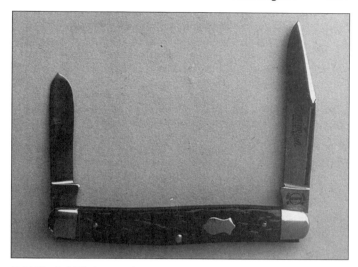

R4103, 3-3/8", bone; $250.

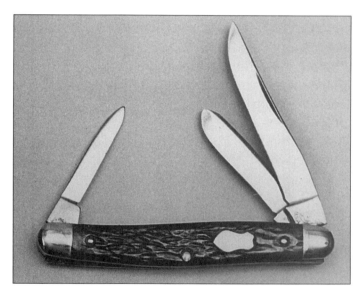

R4133, stockman, bone, 3-3/8"; $225.

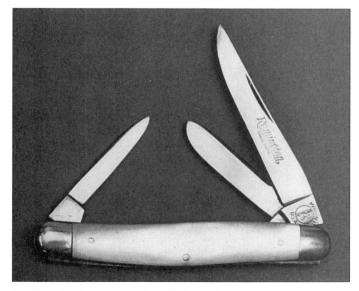

R4134, stockman, pearl, 3-3/8"; $400.

R3953, bone, 3-3/4" 200
R3955, pyremite, 3-3/4" 190
R3962, black, 3-3/4" 190
R3963, bone 215
R3965, pyremite 190
R3973, bone, 3-blade stockman, 3-3/5" 225
R3983, bone 200
R3985, pyremite 150
R3993, bone, 3-blade stockman, 3-5/8" 200
R3995, pyremite, 3-blade stockman 200
R4003, bone, 2-blade serpentine 150
R4005, pyremite, 2-blade serpentine, 3-3/8" 125
R4013, bone 150
R4015, pyremite 150
R4023, bone 240
R4025, pyremite 200
R4033, bone, 3-blade serpentine, 3-5/8" 350
R4035, pyremite, 3-blade serpentine, 3-5/8" 225
R4045, pyremite, stockman, 3-5/8" 300
R4053, bone 215
R4055, pyremite 200
R4063, bone 200
R4065, pyremite 200
R4075, pyremite, 4 300
R4083, bone, 3-7/8" 240
R4085, pyremite, 3-7/8" 240
R4093, bone 225
R4095, pyremite 225
R4105, pyremite, 3-3/8" 225
R4113, bone, 3-7/8" 225
R4114, pearl, 3-7/8" 325
R4123, bone 300
R4124, pearl 325
R4135, pyremite, 3-3/8" 200
R4143, bone, 2-blade tip bols., 3-3/8" 175
R4144, pearl, 2-blade tip bols., 3-3/8" 200
R4145, pyremite, 2-blade tip bols., 3-3/8" 175
R4163, bone 215
R4173, bone 200
R4175, pyremite 200
R4200, buffalo horn 215
R4203, bone 240
R4113, bone 240
R4223, bone, 3-blade equal-end cattle,
   3-1/4" 240
R4225, pyremite, 3-blade equal-end cattle 225
R4233, bone 200
R4234, pearl, 3-3/8" 400

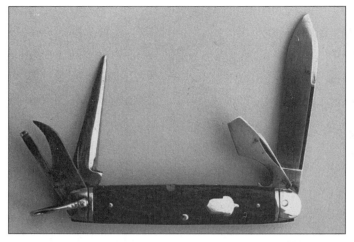

RS4233, 3-3/8", bone, note different acorn shield; $300.

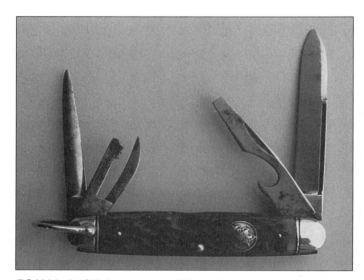

RS4233, 3-3/8", bone, note different long screwdriver blade and bolsters smooth; $300.

RS4233, little Scout knife, brown bone, Scout shield, pinched bolsters, 3-3/8"; $300.

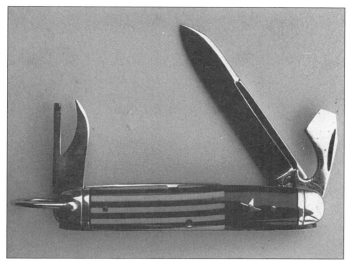

R4235, 3-3/8", red/white/blue, star emblem; $300.

R4235, 3-3/8", red/white/blue handle, plain shield; $300.

R4243, camp bullet, Remington, brown bone, long pull, bullet shield, 4-3/4"; $2,800.

R4253, bone 235
R4274, sowbelly, 3-blade, 3- 3/4",
    genuine pearl 700
R4293, bone 215
R4303, bone 215
R4313, bone, 3-7/8"...215
R4343, bone, 4-1/4"...325
R4363, bone 285
R4365, pyremite 285
R4375, pyremite, 3-3/8" 275
R4383, bone, 3-3/8"..225
R4384, pearl, 3-3/8"...300

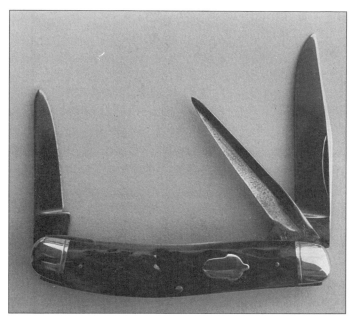

R4263, 3-3/4", bone, punch, sowbelly; $700.

R4273, sowbelly, 3 blades, 3-3/4" brown bone; $1,200.

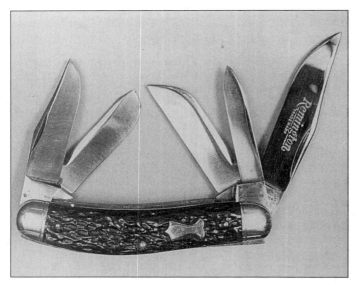

R4283, sowbelly, Remington, brown bone, 3-3/4"; $6,500.

R4336, bartender's knife, stag, 3-1/2"; $400.

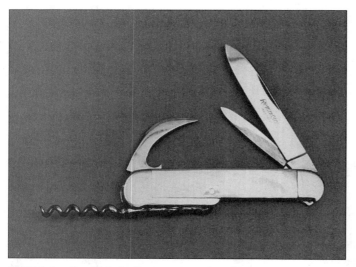

R4334, bartender's knife, pearl, 3-1/2"; $400.

R4345, 4-1/4", imitation ivory; $300.

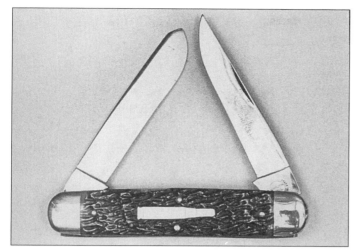

R4353, bullet/big muskrat, Remington, brown bone, bullet shield, 4-1/4"; $2,200.

R4373, Girl Scout knife, bone, 3-3/8"; $300.

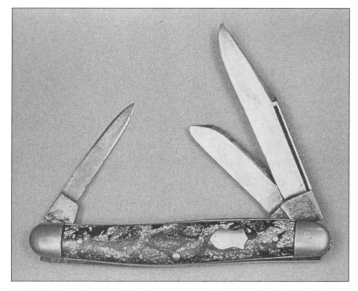

R4405, Remington, Christmas tree, long pull, 3-3/8"; $250.

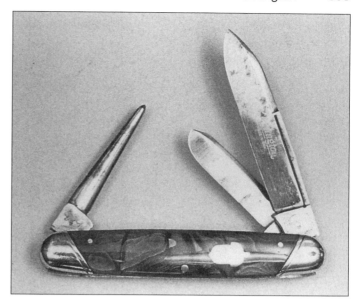

R4425, Remington, pyremite, long pull, acorn shield, slant bolsters, 3-3/8"; $275.

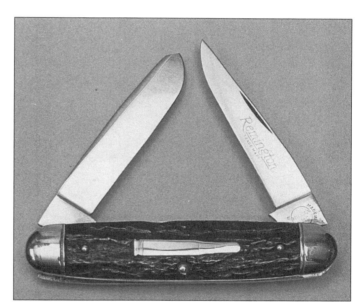

R4466, baby muskrat, stag, shield, 3-3/4"; $7,500.

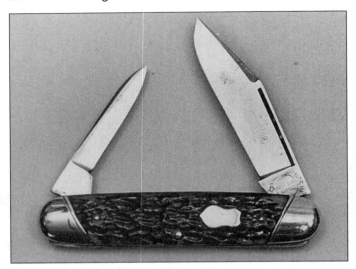

R4473, slant bolsters, 3-1/4"; $225.

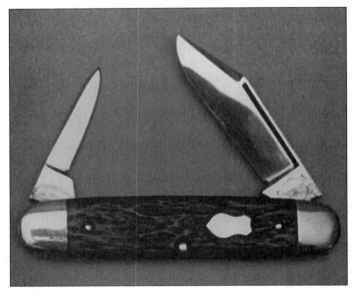

R4473, brown bone, 2 blades, LP, 3-1/4", Remington, straight bolsters; $175.

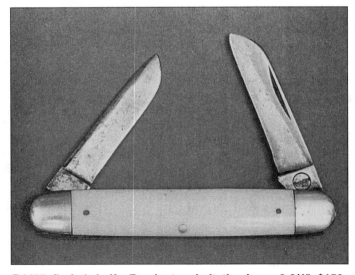

R4497, florist's knife, Remington, imitation ivory, 3-3/4"; $150.

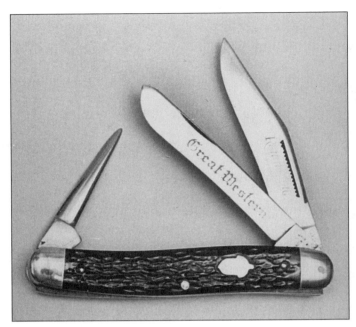

R4513, brown bone, acorn shield, etched "Great Western," 4"; $600.

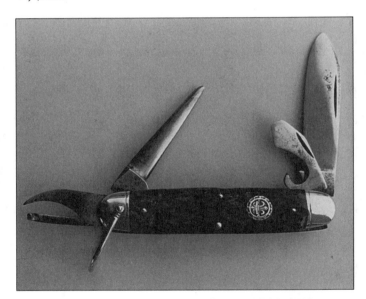

R4523, 3-3/4", bone, Spanish Boy Scout shield; $300.

R4563, bone, 3 blade stockman, 4-1/4"..............400
R4573, bone 250
R4583, bone 160
R4605, pyremite, 3-1/4".....................................225
R4613, bone, 3 175
R4615, pyremite, dog-leg jack, 3 200
R4625, pyremite, 3-3/8".....................................160
R4633, bone, 3-blade equal end, 3-3/8" 150
R4635, pyremite, 3-blade equal end, 3-3/8" 150
R4643, bone, 3-blade serpentine, 3-3/8"............145
R4685, pyremite, 3-blade equal end, punch, 3-1/4" 200

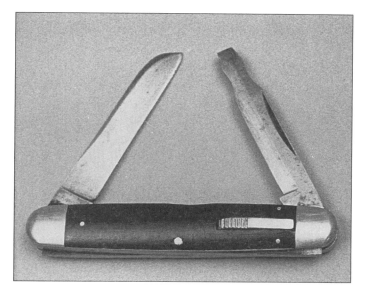

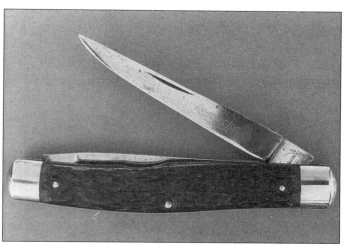

R4593, muskrat, 4", bone, etch blade, rare; $300.

R4548, Remington Circle, U.M.C., 3-3/4", 2 blades, electrician knife with lock-blade, release in handle, rare, cocobolo wood; $300.

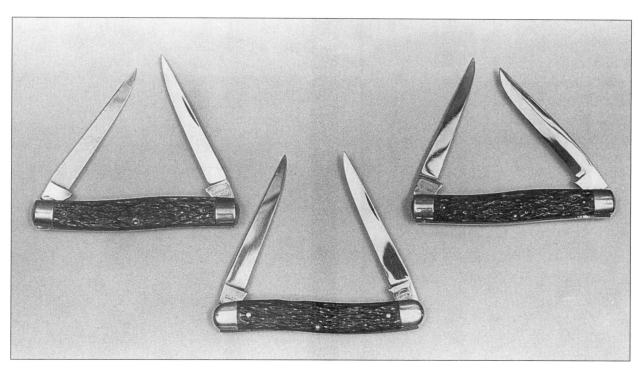

Top left: R4593, Muskrat, Remington, brown bone, square bolsters, 4"; $250. Middle: R4593, Muskrat, Remington, brown bone, round bolsters, 4"; $275. Top right: R4593, Muskrat, Remington, brown bone, square bolster, saber blade, 4"; $300.

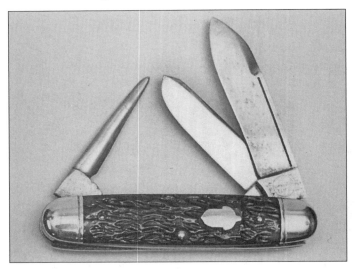

R4603, equal end, brown bone, acorn shield, 3-1/4"; $250.

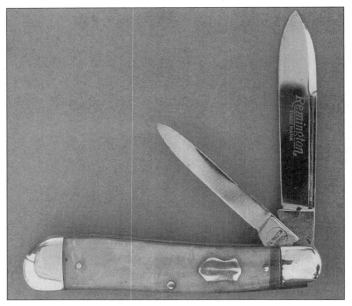

R4615, 3", gold swirl; $200.

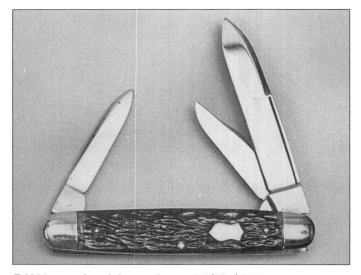

R4623, equal end, brown bone, 3-3/8"; $175.

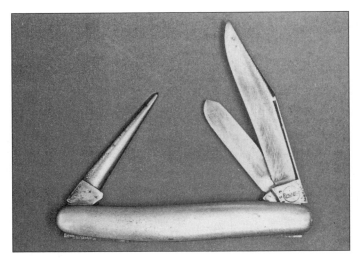

R4679, Remington, all metal, long pull, 3-3/8"; $150.

R4683PU, brown bone, acorn shield, 3-1/4"; $200.

R4695, pyremite 165
R4713, bone 150
R4813, bone 125
R4815, pyremite 115
R4823, bone 100
R4825, pyremite 100
R4833, bone 150
R4835, pyremite 150
R4853, bone 100
R4855, pyremite 95
R4863, bone 95
R4565, pyremite 90
R6015, pyremite, fluted bolsters, 3-1/4"............. 350
R6023, bone 235
R6024, pearl 300

R4723, Girl Scout, brown bone, bail, 3-3/4"; $400.

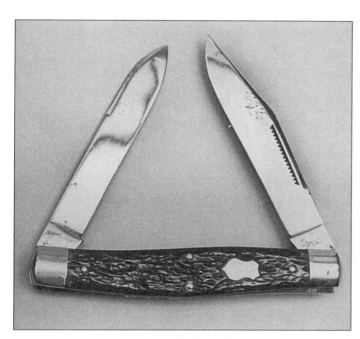

R4703, brown bone, moose, 4-1/4"; $400.

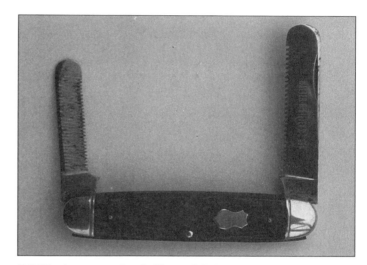

R4733, dog-grooming knife, 3-3/4", bone, reg. shield, etched; $350.

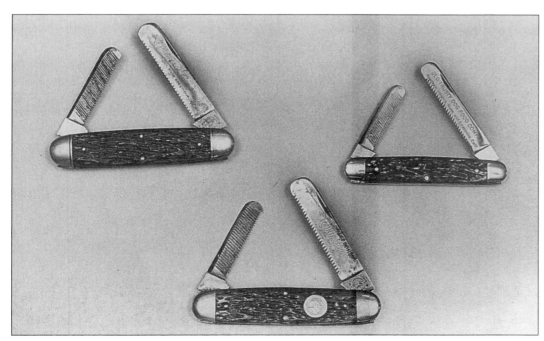

Top left: R4733, Dog Grooming Knife, Remington, brown bone, no shield, 3-3/4"; $300. Bottom: R4733, Dog Grooming Knife, brown bone, Airdale doghead shield, 3-3/4"; $350. Top right: No number, Dog Grooming Knife, Remington, brown bone, no shield, 3-3/8"; $300.

R4733, dog-grooming knife, 3-3/4", bone, plain round emblem; $350.

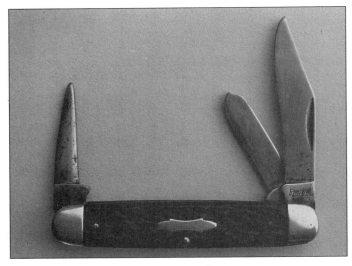

R4832, 3-3/8", black composition; $150.

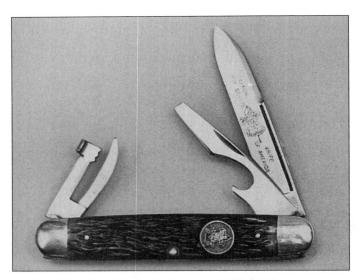

RS4773, Scout knife, brown bone, 3-3/8"; $250.

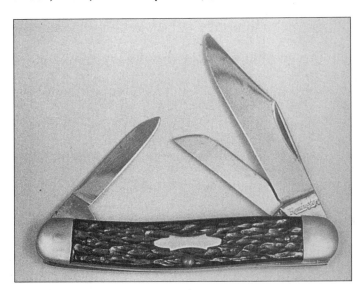

R4843, imitation bone, 3-3/8"; $110.

RS4783, Scout knife, brown bone, with emblem, 3-1/2"; $300.

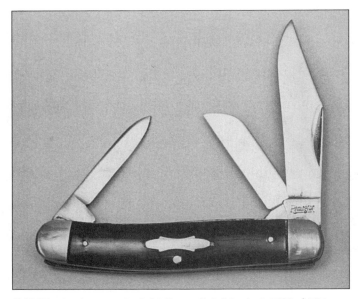

R4845, stockman, straight line, slick black, 3-3/8"; $125.

R6013, brown bone, fluted bolsters, 3-1/4"; $450.

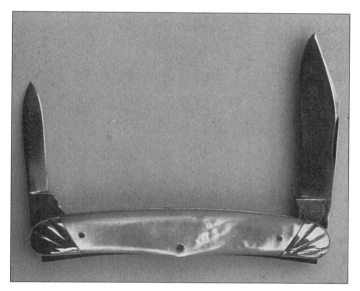

R6014, 3-1/4", genuine pearl, slant fluted bolsters, rare; $500.

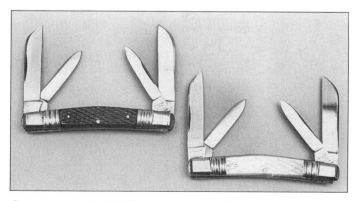

Congress: Left: R6032, black composition, scale, extended grooved bolsters, 3-1/2"; $500. Right: R6034, pearl, extended grooved bolsters, 3-1/2"; $550.

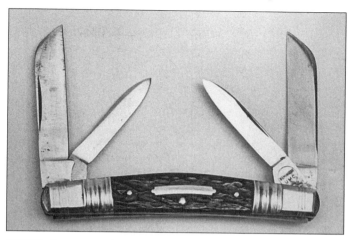

R6033, Congress, brown bone, extended grooved bolsters, 3-1/2"; $400.

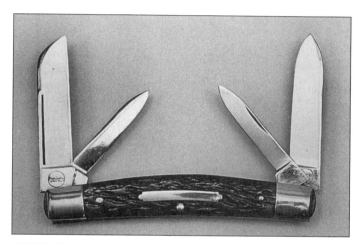

R6043, Congress, brown bone, 4-1/8"; $800.

R6025, pyremite	200
R6053, bone, 4-1/8"	500
R6103, bone, 3"	160
R6105, pyremite, 3	125
R6113, bone	260

R6063, Congress, brown bone, 4-1/4"; $300.

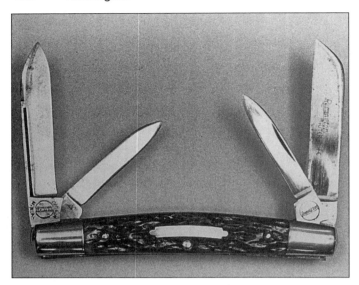

R6073, brown bone, long pull, 3-3/4"; $450.

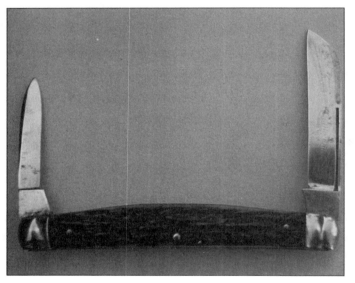

R6093, Rem. Congress, 3-3/4"; $200.

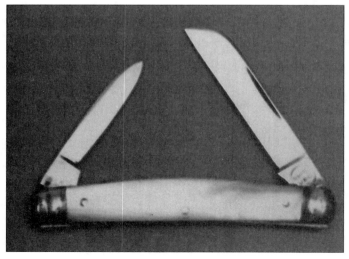

R6104, Congress, pearl, 3"; $200.

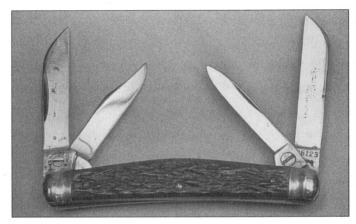

R6123, Congress, brown bone, grooved bolsters, 3-1/2"; $350.

R6133, whittler, Remington, brown bone, threaded bolsters, 3-1/2"; $450.

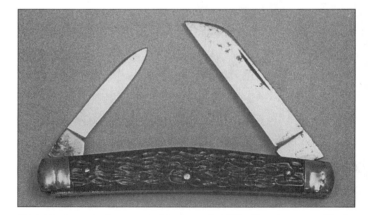

R6143, brown bone, 2 blades, 3-1/2", Remington Circle Congress, UMC; $200.

R6145, pyremite, 2-blade congress, 3-1/2" 225
R6153, bone 150
R6155, pyremite 150
R6182, black, 2-blade shadow, 3-1/4" 75
R6183, bone, 2-blade shadow, 3-1/4"................100
R6184, pearl, 2-blade shadow, 3-1/4"................150

R6163, Congress, bone, 4"; $300.

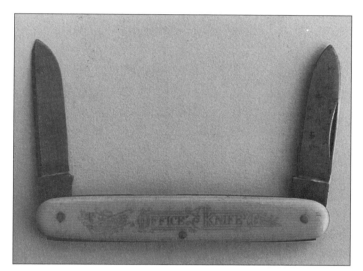

R6175, 3-3/4", pyremite, office knife; $150.

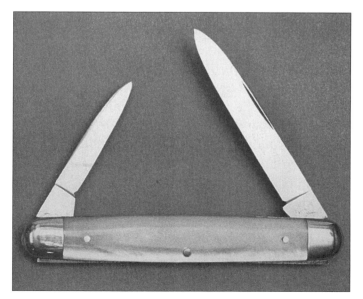

R6194, equal end, pearl, 3-3/8"; $175.

R6195, equal end, brown mottled, 3-1/4"; $140.

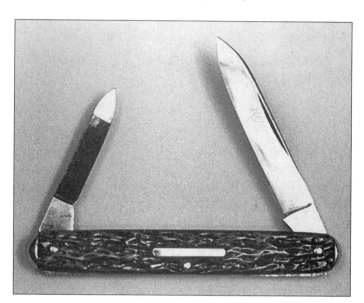

R6203, Remington, bone, file blade, 3-1/4"; $125.

R6185, pyremite, 2-blade shadow, 3-1/4"...........125
R6192, black, 3-3/8" 100
R6193, bone, 3-3/8" 130
R6204, pearl 150
R6205, pyremite 125
R6214, pearl, whittler, 3-1/4"..............................350
R6215, pyremite, 3-1/4" 250
R6223, bone, 3-blade whittler, 3-1/4"..................275
R6224, pearl, 3-blade whittler............................325
R6233, bone, 3-blade whittler equal end,
    3-1/4" 350
R6234, pearl, 3-blade Whittler Equal End,
    3-1/4" 400
R6235, pyremite, 3-blade Whittler, 3-1/4"...........350
R6243, bone, lobster 125
R6249, metal, 3" 90
R6255, pyremite 70

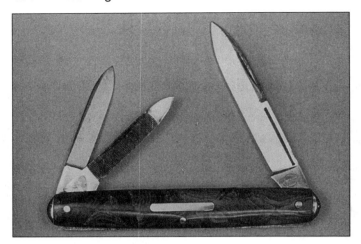

R6225, whittler, Remington, green-swirl pyremite, long pull and reg. pull, 3-1/4"; $300.

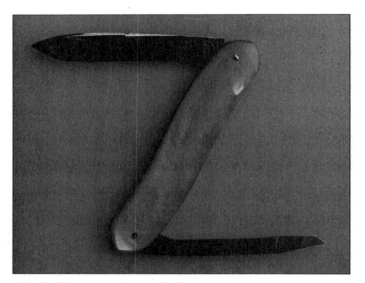

R6244, 3", pearl, lobster; $125.

R6295, 3-1/4", pyremite, scalloped bolsters, whittler, rare; $800.

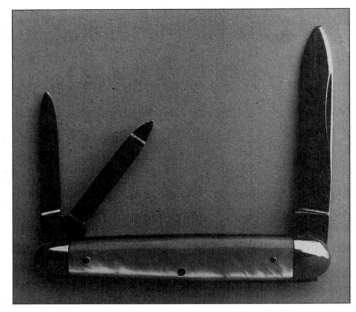

R6334, 3-1/8", genuine pearl, whittler; $350.

R6259, metal, lobster blade and file 100
R6265, pyremite 150
R6275, pyremite 335
R6285, pyremite 335
R6303, bone 150
R6313, bone 225
R6323, bone 240
R6325, pyremite 200
R6330, buffalo horn 175
R6333, bone, 3-1/8" 300
R6334, pearl, 3-1/8" 350
R6335, pyremite, 3-1/8" 300
R6340, buffalo horn whittler, 3-1/2" 350
R6343, bone, 3-blade whittler, 3-1/2" 400
R6344, pearl, 3-blade whittler, 3-1/2" 450
R6345, pyremite, 3-blade whittler, 3-1/2" 300
R6350, buffalo horn 200
R6353, bone 250
R6355G, pyremite... 250
R6362, black, 2-blade half whittler, 3-1/2" 125
R6363, bone, 2-blade half whittler, 3-1/2" 150
R6365, pyremite, 2-blade half whittler, 3-1/2" 150
R6390, buffalo horn whittler, 3-3/8".................... 400
R6395, pyremite, whittler, blood groove,
   3-3/8" 500
R6400, buffalo horn 130
R6403, bone 130
R6404, pearl 200
R6405, pyremite 175
R6423, bone 125

R6393, whittler, brown bone, blood groove, 3-3/8"; $600.

R6429, metal	85
R6433, bone, lobster	100
R6439, metal, lobster, 2-3/4"	150
R6443, bone, 3-blade lobster, 2-11/16"	125
R6444, pearl, 3-blade lobster, 2-11/16"	150
R6445, Pyremite, 3-blade lobster, 2-11/16"	125
R6448, cocobolo, 3-blade lobster, 2-11/16"	100
R6463, bone, 3"	75
R6464, pearl, 3"	100
R6473, bone	100
R6474, pearl	125

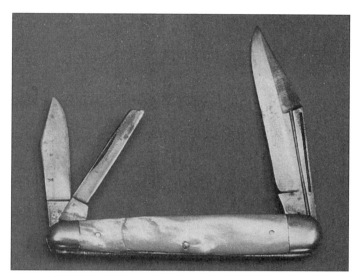

R6394, pearl whittler, blood groove, 3-1/2", rare, Remington, Circle, UMC; $800.

R6434, 2-3/4", pearl, lobster; $150.

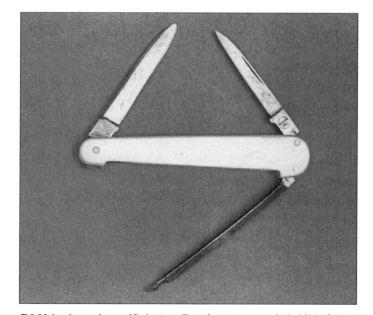

R6424, sleeveboard/lobster, Remington, pearl, 2-3/4"; $125.

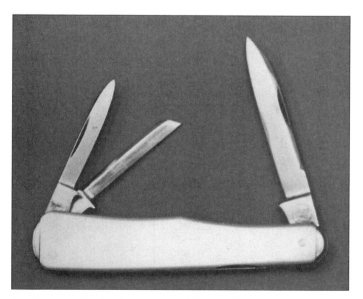

R6454, gunstock whittler, pearl, 3"; $500.

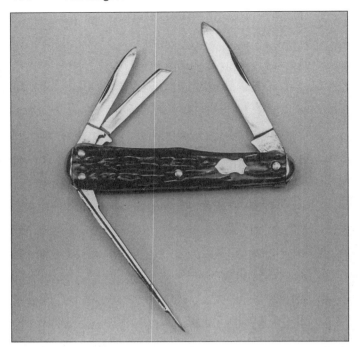

R6456, gunstock lobster, genuine stag, shows grooved file, 3"; $450.

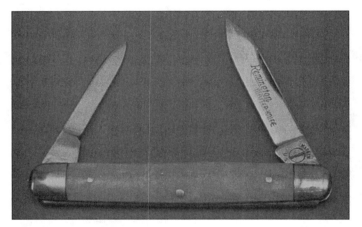

R6465, onyx, 3"; $90.

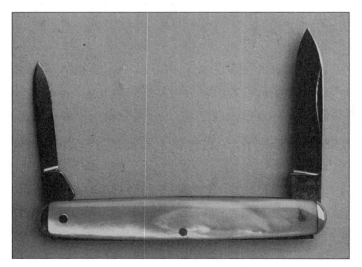

R6484, 3", genuine pearl, tip bolsters; $200.

R6483, bone, senator pen, tip bols., 3"...............125
R6494, pearl, 3"..100
R6495, pyremite, 3" 80
R6505, pyremite 100
R6519, metal, lobster, 3 blade 125
R6520, buffalo horn, equal-end whittler, 3".........250
R6524, pearl, equal-end whittler, 3"....................350

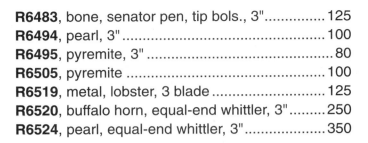
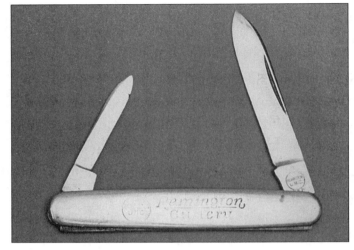

R6499, Remington, all metal, 3"; $75.

R6504, file, pearl, tip bolsters, with bail, 3"; $125.

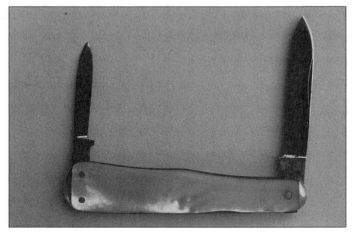

R6514, 3-1/8", pearl, gunstock; $250.

R6533, whittler, Remington, brown bone, 3"; $300.

R6534, pearl, whittler, 3" 350
R6543, bone 200
R6545, pyremite 175
R6559, metal, 3-blade lobster............................100
R6565, pyremite, 3-5/8" 150
R6575, pyremite 125
R6585, pyremite, 3-1/2" 125
R6593, bone 135
R6595, pyremite 125
R6603, bone, whittler, 3-1/2" 300
R6605, pyremite, whittler, 3-1/2".......................300
R6613, bone 140
R6615, pyremite 130
R6623, bone, 3-1/8"...200
R6624, pearl, alum. bols. and liner, 3-1/8"..........225

R6573, sleeveboard, brown bone, tip bolsters, 3-1/2"; $125.

R6583, sleeveboard, bone, 3-1/2"; $150.

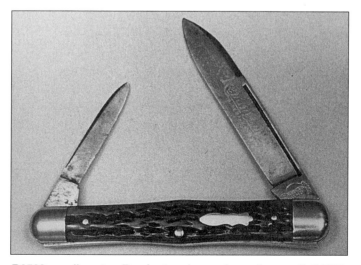

R6563, swell center, Remington, brown bone, long pull, 3-5/8"; $150.

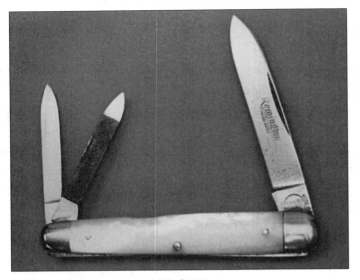

R6604, whittler, pearl, 3-1/2"; $350.

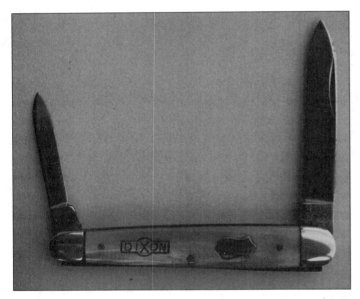

R6625, 3-1/2", celluloid, advertising, aluminum bolsters; $150.

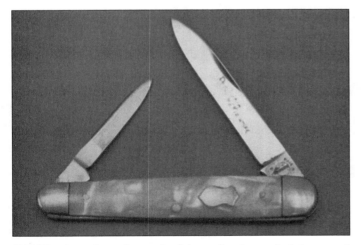

R6625, sleeveboard, cracked ice, aluminum bolsters and liners, 3-1/8; $200.

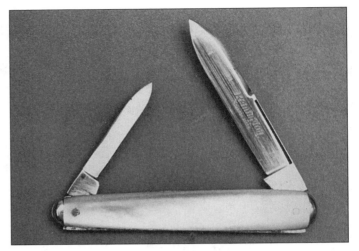

R6644, sleeveboard, pearl, 3-1/8"; $150.

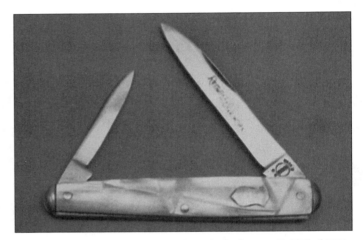

R6645, sleeveboard, cracked ice, tip bolsters, 3-1/8"; $125.

R6633, bone, 3-1/8"	150
R6634, pearl, 3-1/8"	175
R6654, pearl, whittler, 3-1/8"	350
R6663, bone	140
R6664, pearl	185
R6673, bone, 4-blade congress, 3-1/8"	250
R6683, bone	175
R6695, pyremite, 3-1/8"	500
R6703, bone, 4-blade equal end, 3"	250
R6704, pearl, equal end congress, 3"	300
R6705Q, pyremite, 4-blade equal-end congress, 3"	250
R6714, pearl, 4-blade tip bolsters, 3"	300
R6724, pearl, whittler, 3-1/8"	350
R6725, pyremite, whittler, 3-1/8"	300
R6733, bone, 2-blade tip bolsters, 3-1/4"	125
R6735, pyremite, 2-blade tip bolsters, 3-1/4"	100
R6745F, pyremite, 3-1/8"	125
R6754, pearl	200

R6653, whittler, brown bone, 3-1/8"; $300.

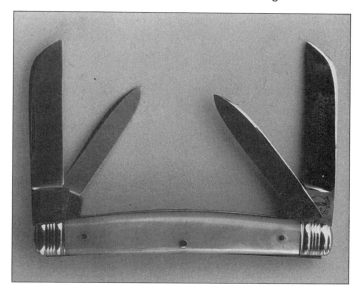

R6694, 3-1/8", genuine pearl, Congress; $600.

R6674, 3-1/8", pearl, Congress; $500.

R6713, equal end, Remington, brown bone, 3"; $250.

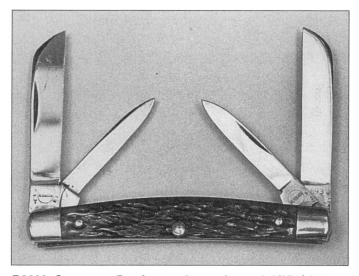

R6693, Congress, Remington, brown bone, 3-1/8"; $400.

R6755A, pyremite 160
R6763, bone 225
R6764, pearl 275
R6765A, pyremite 150
R6773, bone 235
R6775, pyremite 175
R6781, redwood, 3-1/4" 100
R6793, bone 125
R6795, pyremite 100
R6803, bone, whittler, 3-3/8" 250
R6825, pyremite, whittler, 3-3/8" 750
R6834, pearl, whittler, 3-1/8" 600
R6835, pyremite, whittler, 3-1/8" 500
R6843, bone, 2-blade pen, tip bolsters, 2-7/8" ... 100
R6845, pyremite, 2-7/8" 75

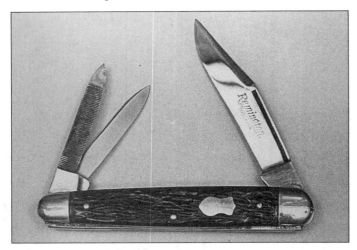

**R6723, whittler, Remington, brown bone, long pull, 3-1/8";
$300.**

R6805, Remington, waterfall, whittler, 3-3/8"; $250.

R6744, 3-1/8", pearl; $150.

**R6816, 3-5/8", genuine stag, humpback, lock-blade whittler,
rare; $7,500.**

R6785, 3-3/8", pyremite; $125.

R6854, pearl, 2-blade shadow, 2-7/8"................. 125

R6859, metal, 2-blade shadow, 2-7/8".................. 75

R6863, bone, 2-blade sleeveboard tip bolster,
  2-5/8" 75

R6872, jack, 2-blade equal-end tip bolsters,
  3-1/8" 125

R6875, pyremite, 3-1/8" 125

R6883, bone, 2-blade Wharncliffe blade, 3" 225

R6885, pyremite, 2-blade Wharncliffe blade,
  3" 150

R6893, bone, 3-blade Wharncliffe whittler,
  3-1/8" 400

R6894, pearl, 3-blade, Wharncliffe whittler,
  3-1/8" 450

R6895, pyremite, 3-blade Wharncliffe whittler,
  3-1/8" 400

R6823, humpback whittler, grooved bolsters, 3-5/8"; $1,000

R6864, 2-5/8", pearl; $100.

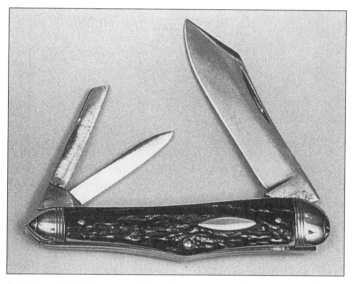

R6836 , humpback whittler, Remington, stag, grooved bolsters, 3-1/8"; $600.

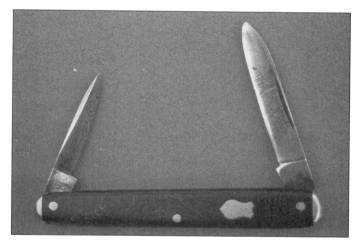

R6865, pyremite, 2-5/8"; $90.

R6903, bone, 2-blade equal end, tip bolsters, 2-1/2" 100
R6923, bone, congress, grooved bolsters, 3".....150
R6924, pearl, congress, grooved bolsters, 3".....175
R6933, bone 175

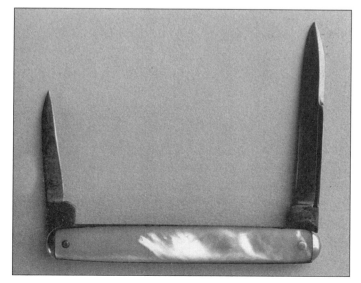

R6844, 2-7/8", pearl; $100.

R6874, 3-1/8", split pearl; $175.

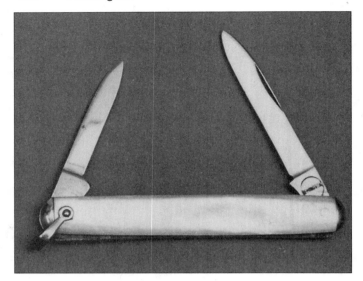

R6904, pen, pearl, with bail, 2-1/2"; $100.

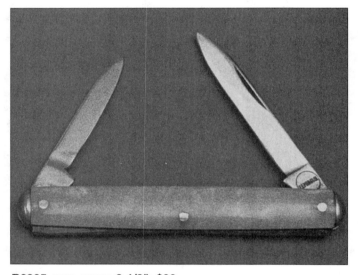

R6905, pen, onyx, 2-1/2"; $90.

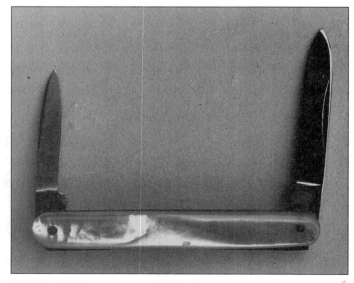

R6914, 2-1/2", pearl pen; $125.

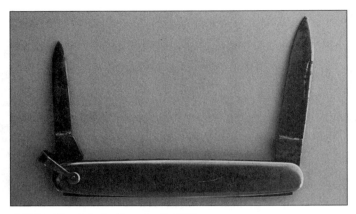

R6919, 3", nickel silver, bail; $75.

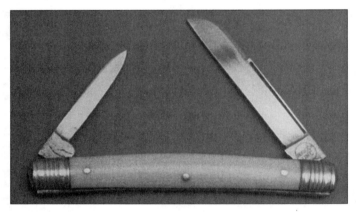

R6925, Congress, imitation ivory, threaded bolsters, 3"; $150.

R6934, pearl		225
R6949, metal		50
R6954, pearl		325
R6956, genuine stag		325
R6964, pearl, long slim sleeveboard		325
R6973, bone		185
R6974, pearl		375
R6993, bone		175
R6994, pearl		250

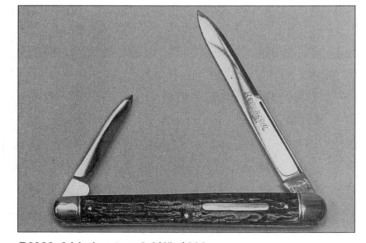

R6966, 2 blade, stag, 3-3/4"; $300.

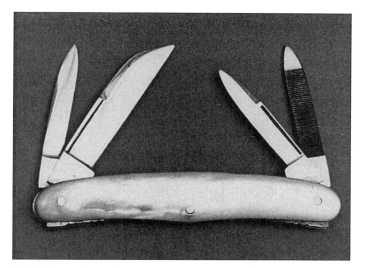

R6984, pearl, worked backspring, 3-1/4"; $800.

R6995, pyremite, sway-back congress 225
R7003, bone 250
R7004, pearl 285
R7005, pyremite 200
R7023, bone, 3-1/4" 250
R7026, genuine stag, 3-1/4" 250
R7034, pearl 75
R7045, pyremite 70
R7039/5, metal 75
R7039/6, metal 75
R7039/7, metal 75
R7039/8, metal 75
R7044, pearl 75
RG7049/21, metal 75
RG7049/22, metal 75
RG7049/23, metal 75
RG7049/24, metal 75
RG7054, pearl 75
RG7059/17, metal 75
RG7059/18, metal 75
RG7059/19, metal 75
RG7059/20, metal 75
RG7064, pearl 75
R7069/25, metal 75
R7069/26, metal 75
R7069/27, metal 75
R7069/, metal 75
R7073, whittler 400
R7074, pearl 75
RG7079/10, metal 75
RG7079/11, metal 75
RG7079/12, metal 75
RG7079/35, metal 75

RG7079/36, metal 75
RG7079/37, metal 75
R7084, pearl 100
RG7084, gold metal 170
RG7089/13, metal 75
RG7089/14, metal 75
RG7089/15, metal 75
RG7089/16, metal 75
RG7089/32, metal 75
RG7089/33, metal 75
RG7089/34, metal 75
R7090, buffalo horn 100
R7091, redwood 200
R7094, lobster, pearl, 3 blade, bail 125
RG7099/1, metal 100
RG7099/2, metal 100
RG7099/3, metal 100
RG7099/4, metal 100
RG7099/29, metal 100
RG7099/30, metal 100
RG7099/31, metal 100
RT7099, metal 70
R7103, bone 70
R7104, pearl 100
R7114, pearl 115
R7116, genuine stag 75
R7126, genuine stag, 4-blade sleeveboard,
    3-1/4" 350
R7134, pearl 150
R7144, pearl 250
R7146, genuine stag 200
R7153, bone 150
R7163, bone 135
R7176, genuine stag 175
R7183, bone 250
R7196, genuine stag 230
R7203, bone 270
R7223, bone, 2-blade swell center, 3 125
R7224, pearl 150
R7233, bone, 2-blade swell center, tip
    bolsters, 3 130
R7236, genuine stag, 2-blade swell center,
    tip bolsters, 3 150
R7243, bone swell-center whittler, 3 250
R7246, genuine stag, swell-center whittler, 3 300
R7254, pearl 90
R7264, pearl 90
R7274, pearl 90
R7309, metal 90

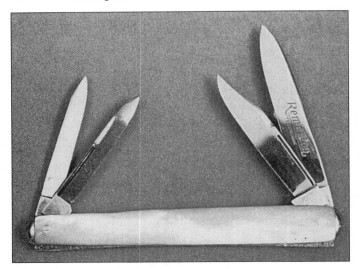

R7124, sleeveboard, Circle UMN, pearl, long pull, 3-1/4"; $400.

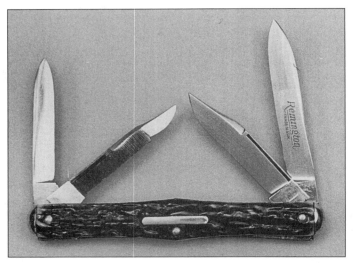

R7216, swell center, genuine stag, tip bolsters, 3-1/2"; $300.

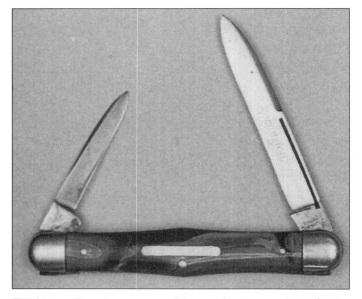

R7225, swell center, green swirl pyremite, long pull, 3"; $150.

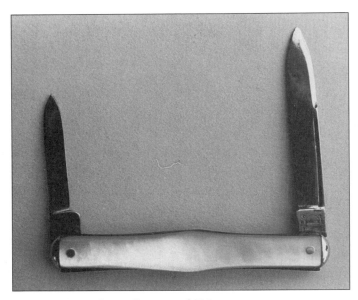

R7234, 3", pearl, swell center; $200.

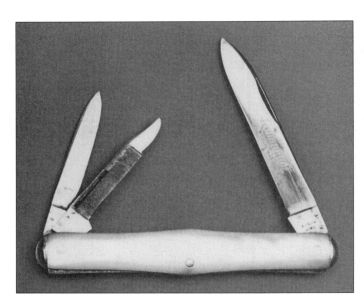

R7244, swell center whittler, genuine pearl, 3"; $300.

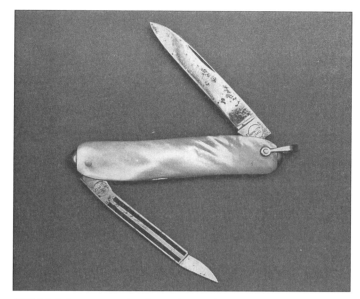

R7284, lobster, pearl, with bail, 3"; $100.

R7293, whittler, brown bone, long pull, grooved saber blade, 3-3/8"; $600.

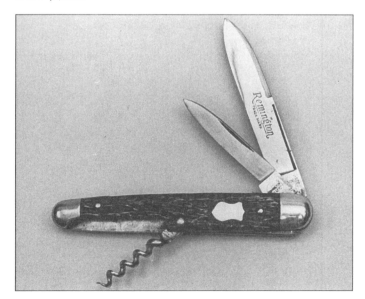

R7343, corkscrew, brown bone, 3-1/8"; $200.

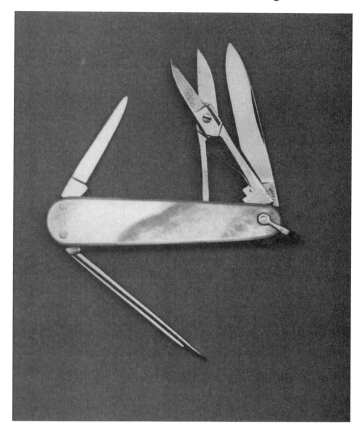

R7343, corkscrew, brown bone, 3-1/8"; $200.

R7396, genuine stag, 2-5/8" 125
R7404, pearl, 3-3/8" 250
R7414, pearl, scissors 250
R7433, bone 150
R7443, bone 110

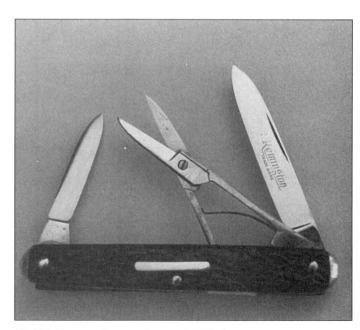

R7403, Rem. scissors, bone, 3-3/8"; $250.

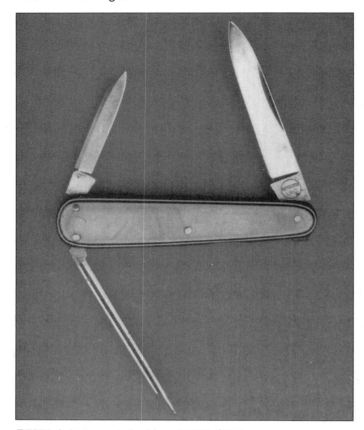

R7375, lobster, cracked ice, 2-5/8"; $150.

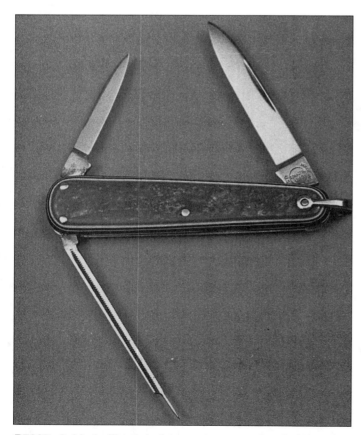

R7385, 2 blade-file, lobster, green pyremite, bail, 2-5/8", Remington Circle UMC; $130.

R7394, 2-5/8", pearl; $100.

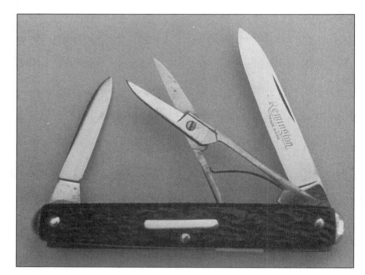

R7403, Rem. scissors, bone, 3-3/8"; $250.

R7423, 2 blades, blade etched Pal Fine Cutlery, 3-1/8", $150.

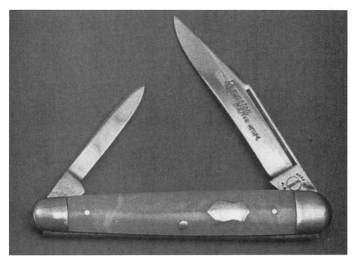

R7425, sleeveboard, onyx, 3-1/8"; $125.

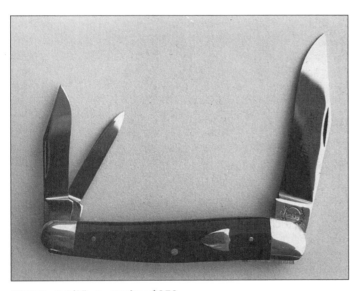

R7495, 3-3/8", pyremite; $350.

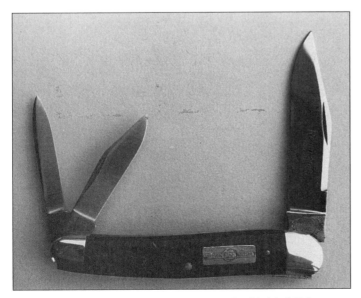

R7495, 3-3/8", pyremite, Isaacson, Nash shield; $500.

R7500, whittler, horn, 3-3/8"; $350.

R7453, bone 110
R7463, bone 110
R7465, pyremite 100
R7473, bone 110
R7475, pyremite 100
R7483, bone 200
R7485, pyremite 200
R7493, bone, whittler, 3-3/8"..............................350
R7503, bone, whittler, 3-3/8"..............................250
R7513, bone 235
R7526, genuine stag...150
R7536, genuine stag...150
R7544, pearl 125
R7546, genuine stag...125
R7554, pearl 100
R7564, pearl, 2-blade Wharncliffe, 3-3/8"...........125
R7566, genuine stag, 2-blade Wharncliffe,
 3-3/8" 125
R7573, bone, Wharncliffe, tip bolsters 150
R7576, genuine stag, Wharncliffe......................200
R7584, pearl whittler, 3-3/8"..............................250
R7586, genuine stag, barshield whittler, 3-3/8" ..250
R7593, bone, 3-1/4" 115
R7594, pearl, 3-1/4".. 175
R7596, genuine stag, 3-1/4" 175
R7604, pearl, 3-1/4"..300
R7606, genuine stag, 3-1/4" 350
R7613, bone 75
R7614, pearl 75
R7624, pearl, 3" 150
R7633, bone, 3-1/8" 150
R7643, bone 90
R7645, pyremite 75

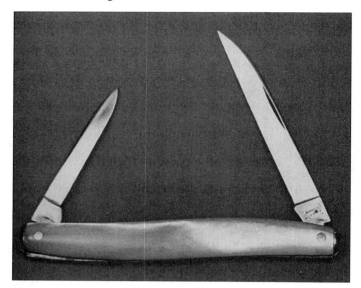

R7574, Wharncliffe, pearl, tip bolsters, 3-1/4"; $150.

R7603, serpentine, bone, tip bolsters, 3-1/4"; $300.

R7604, 3-1/4", pearl; $300.

R7654, 3-1/8", pearl, whittler; $400.

R7653, bone		175
R7663, bone, whittler, 3 blades, 3"		225
R7664, bone, pearl, whittler, 3 blades, 3"		250
R7674, pearl		75
R7683, bone		90
R7684, pearl		125
R7706, genuine stag		200
R7725, pyremite		100
R7744, pearl		100
R7756, genuine stag, whittler, 4-1/2"		1,800
R7772, black, 3-1/8"		50
R7773, bone, 3-1/8"		65
R7775, pyremite, 3-1/8"		65
R7783, bone		100
R7785, pyremite		125
R7793, bone		75
R7795, pyremite		75
R7805, pyremite, whittler, 3-1/8"		225
R7813, bone, 3-3/8"		150

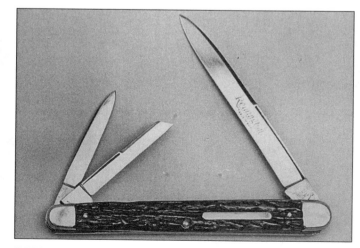

R7696, whittler, stag, flat bolsters, 3-5/8"; $600.

R7713, bone, with bail, 2-1/2"; $90.

R7803, Rem. Wh. pyremite, 3-1/8"; $250.

R7814, pearl, 3-3/8"		150
R7853, bone, 3"		125
RC7853, bone, 3"		100
R7857, ivory, 3"		100
R7863, bone		75
R7873, bone		75
R7895, pyremite		50
R7925, pyremite, 2-13/16"		65
R7993, bone, bartender knife, 3-3/8"		200
R8004, pearl, 3"		175
R8013, bone		50

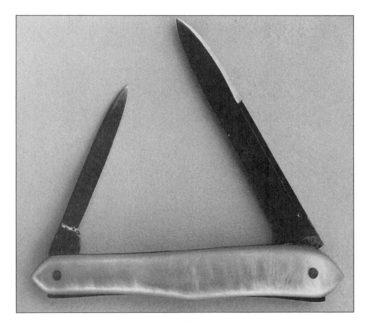

R7734, 2-3/4", genuine pearl; $150.

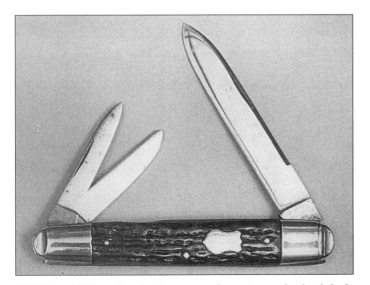

R7766, whittler, Remington, genuine stag, pinched bolsters, 4-1/2"; $1,800.

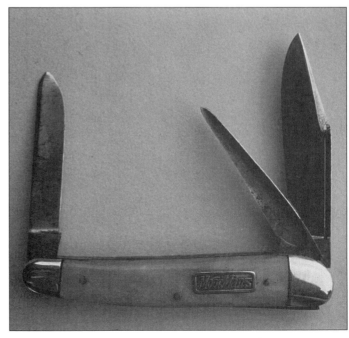

R7825, 3-3/8", pyremite, Moor Mans shield; $200.

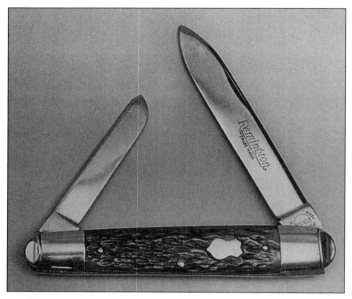

R7833, brown bone, pinched bolsters, 4-1/2"; $900.

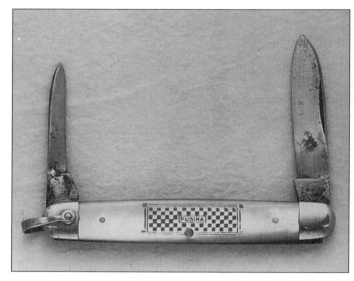

R7854, pearl with bail Purina checkerboard engraved, very rare, 3", mint price; $450. Photo courtesy John Petzl.

R8023, bone, 3-3/8"	175
R8053, bone, switchblade, 3-3/8"	450
R8069, metal sterling	450
R8623, brown bone, 3-1/8"	100
R9003SS, bone	150

R7945, Rem. pyremite, bail, 2-7/8"; $90.

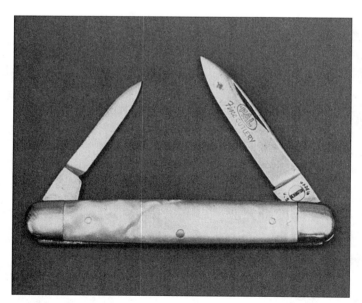

R7854, equal end, pearl, blade etched "Pal Fine Cutlery," 3"; $150.

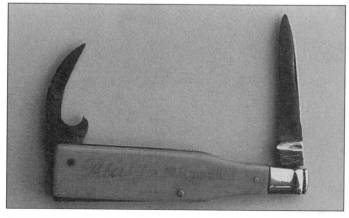

R7985, 3-1/8", imitation ivory, bartender knife; $250.

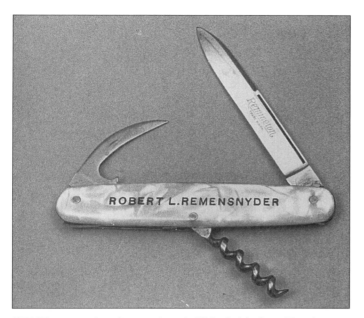

R7995, pyremite, bartender, 3-3/8", 3 blades, Remington Circle UMC; $150.

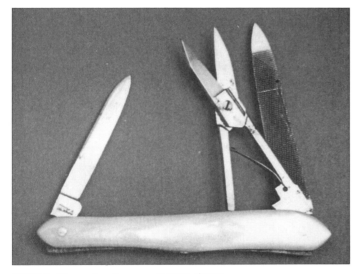

R8044, file and scissors, 2-3/4"; $250.

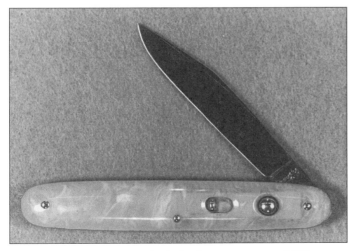

R8055, switch blade, 3-3/8, imitation onyx, rare; $450.

R8059, 3-1/2", metal bartender; $250.

R8065, double switchblade, pyremite, 3-1/2"; $550.

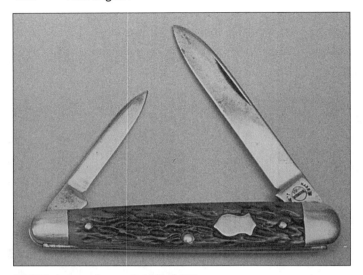

R8623, brown bone, 3-1/8"; $100.

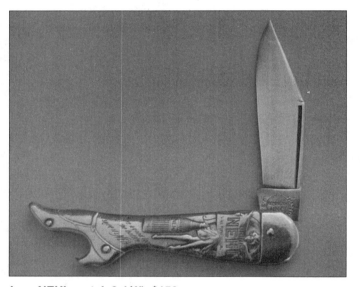

Leg, NEHI, metal, 3-1/4"; $150.

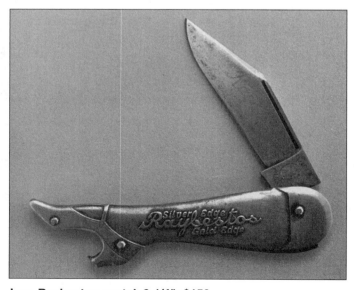

Leg, Raybestos, metal, 3-1/4"; $150.

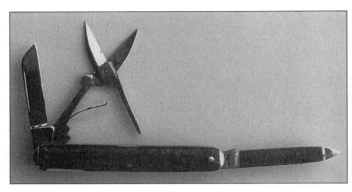

Unknown, 2-1/2", pyremite; $250.

Unknown, 2-3/4", pyremite, gargoyle shield; $150.

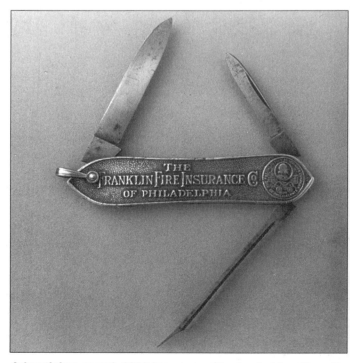

Advertising, metal, 1929 Insurance (the backside of handle reads: The Franklin Fire, Philadelphia, 1829-1929), 3"; $125.

Pipe knife, metal, punch, 3-1/8"; $150.

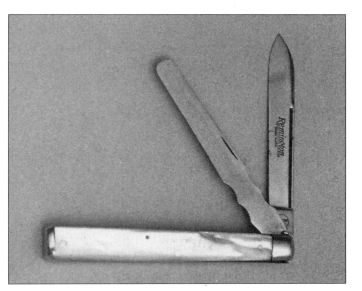

Phy. unknown, spatula, genuine pearl, Circle UMC, 3-5/8", embossed mentholatum; $700.

R7854: Only one feature makes this a super rare knife. Please note the Purina checkerboard engraved in the pearl. With good eyes or a high-powered glass, you might be able to see Purina spelled out in the center of the checkerboard. You will see a lot of Remington Purina red checkerboard knives under clear pyremite handles, but not in pearl. This is indeed a little jewel; $400. Photo courtesy J. Paul Turner.

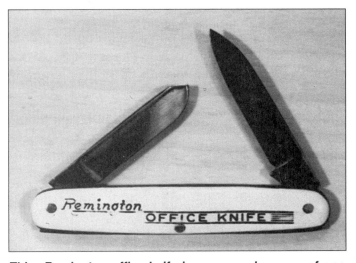

This Remington office knife is very rare because of one feature: The spear blade is marked Circle Remington and the spay blade is marked straight line Remington, which would be called a transition knife. I have never seen this marking before. You will see quite a few transitions marked Remington Circle UMC and Remington Circle; $150. Photo courtesy J. Paul Turner.

This is a super rare Camp Fire Girls Remington Knife and, in my estimation, should be rated very high in value. The triangular WO HE LO emblem shield stands for Camp Fire Girls and is etched on the master blade. The two-part can opener is marked straight line Remington with Pat. No. 1635649. The two cutting blades are marked Remington Circle UMC. The screwdriver cap lifter blade is not marked. Please note the smaller blade is a very unusual shape. As far as I know, this knife has not been cataloged and does not have a number. The knife is mint and is a real prize in a Remington collection; $1,000. Photo courtesy Paul J. Turner.

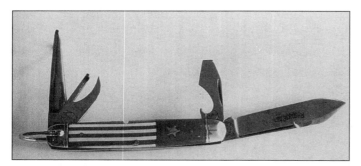

Rem. Patriotic Scout Pattern, 3-3/4", rare, pyremite handle; $400.

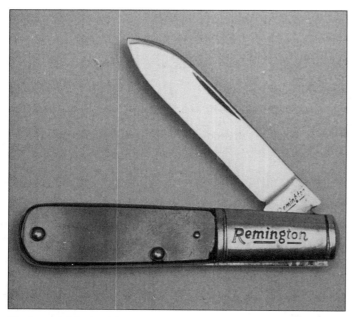

Barlow, 1 blade, black bone, straighted lined, no number, 3-3/8"; $125.

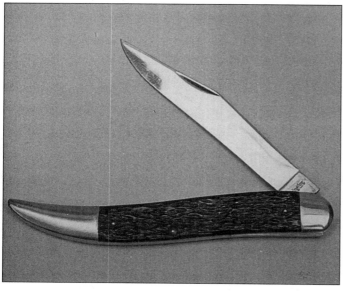

One blade, straight lined, no number, imitation bone; $200.

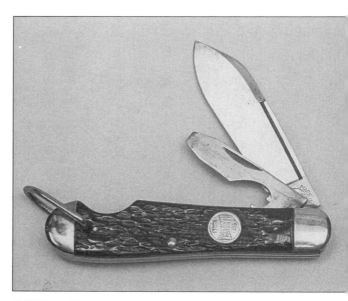

R1773, 2 blades, imitation bone, Hanover Shoe Emblem 3-1/2"; $175.

Easy opener, brown bone, chain, 3-1/2"; $175.

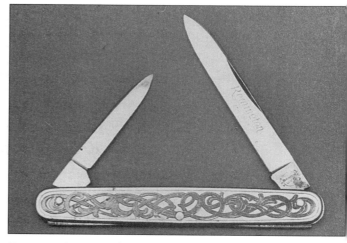

Pen, metal, 3-1/8"; $125.

Easy opener, Remington, imitation bone, round Endicott Johnson Emblem, screw driver/cap lifter, 3-1/2", $150.

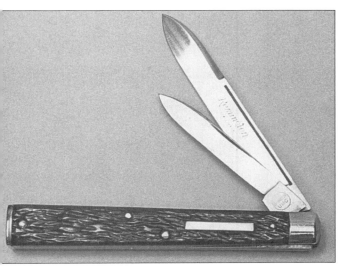

Dr.'s knife, Rem., brown bone, 2 blades, 3-1/2"; $600.

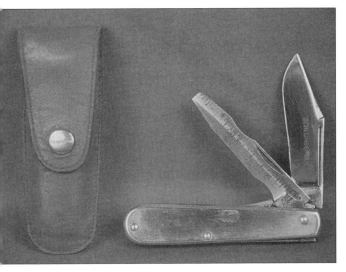

R43, electrician's knife, aluminum handle, both blades stamped circle Remington (rare); $250. Photo courtesy Ron Burton.

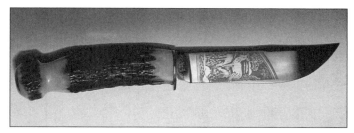

Rem. stag handle, blade etched with wildlife scene; $200.

R233, Remington, 7.65MM cartridge case, custom made; price varies.

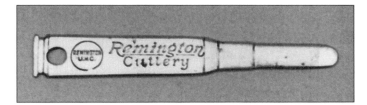

R234, Remington knife opener; $25.

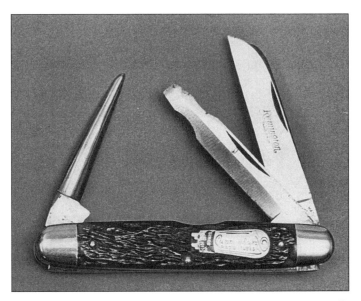

Cunningham radio tube, Remington, brown bone, reg. pull, radio tube shield, electrician's blade and punch; $800.

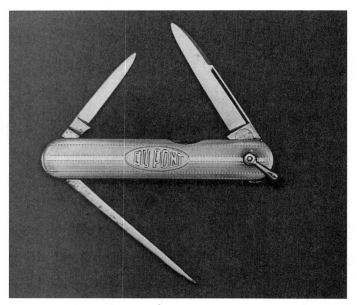

Lobster, advertising display knife, gold scale, with bail, 2-3/4"; $150.

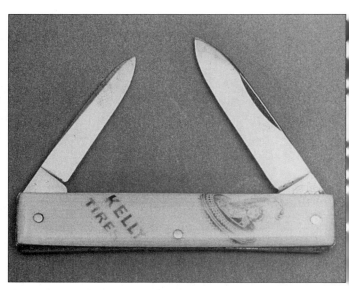

Advertising, imitation ivory, 2-7/8"; $100.

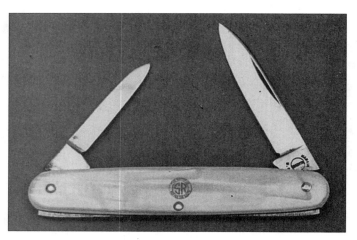

Pen, imitation pearl, (Southern Railroad Emblem), 3-1/4"; $100.

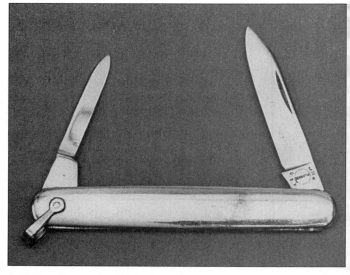

R6919, all metal, with bail, 3"; $75.

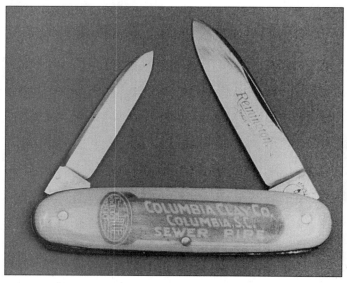

Advertising, imitation ivory, 2-7/8"; $100.

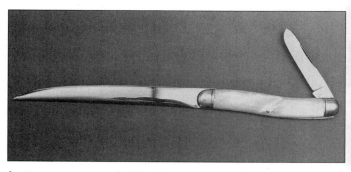

Letter opener, pearl, 4" knife handle, 9"; $350.

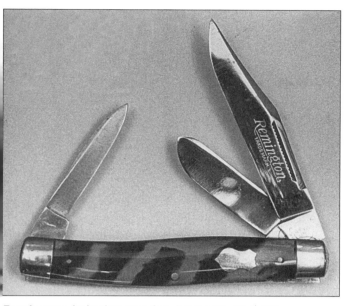

Remington, imitation tortoise, long pull, 4"; $400.

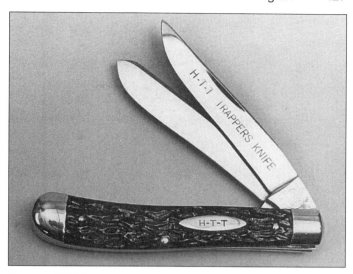

Trapper HTT, brown bone, reg. pull, HTT shield, 3-3/4"; $1,000.

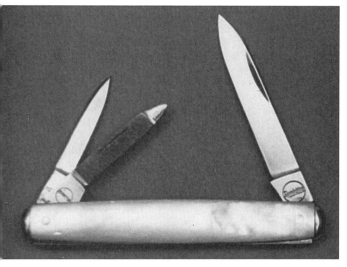

Whittler, pearl, 3"; $250.

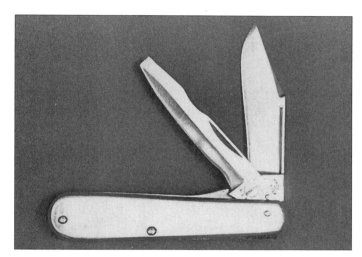

Electrician's knife, all metal, long pull, screwdriver blade, with lock, 3-1/2"; $250.

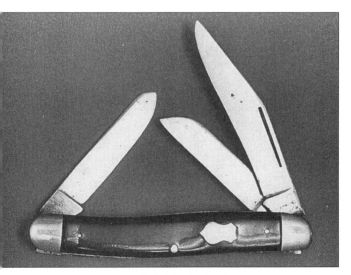

Stockman, Remington, slick black, 4"; $250.

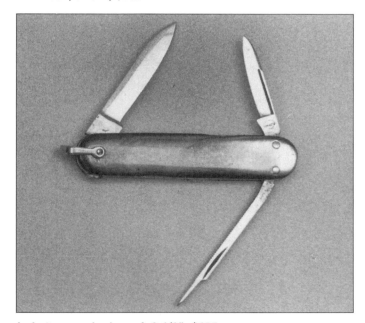

Lobster, smoked pearl, 2-1/8"; $125.

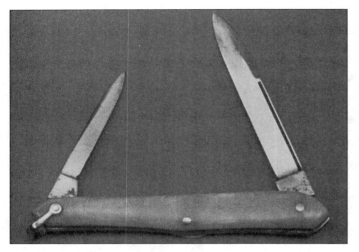

Swell center, imitation pearl, 2-7/8"; $90.

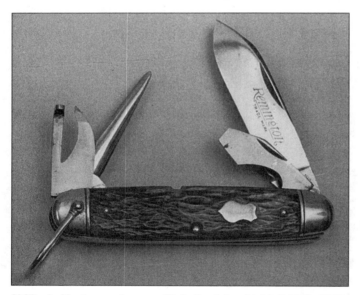

Utility knife, brown bone, with bail, plain shield, 3-3/4"; $300.

Wharncliffe equal end, round Wayne Feed emblem, 3-1/4"; $275.

Jack, Rogers bone, straight line; $140.

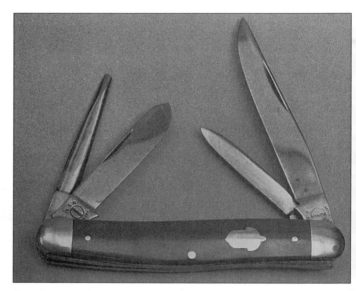

Stockman, red composition; $400.

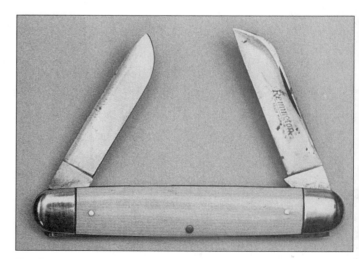

Florist or drafting knife, imitation ivory, 3-7/8"; $150.

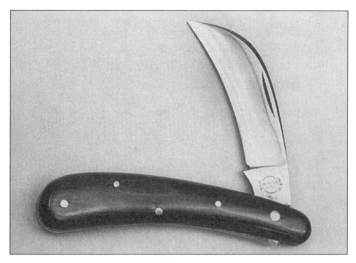

Hawkbill, rosewood, 4"; $125.

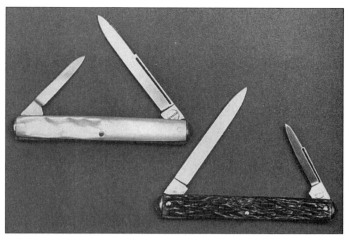

Salesman's knife showing a different handle for each side, pearl and bone (same knife), 2-7/8"; $400.

Imitation ivory, totem pole, 2-7/8"; $800.

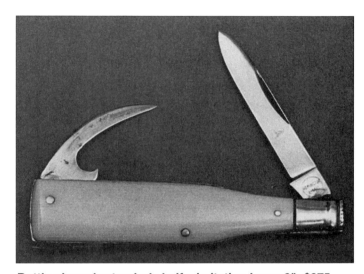

Bottle-shape bartender's knife, imitation ivory, 3"; $275.

Jack: Left: brown bone, 4-1/2"; $600. Right: Brown bone, Pal shield, 4-1/2"; $600.

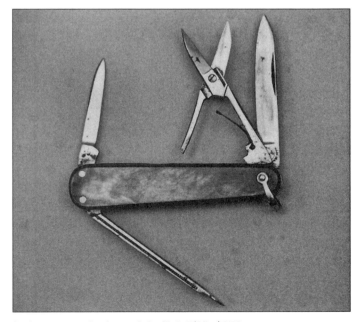

Lobster, smoked pearl, bail, 2-5/8"; $250.

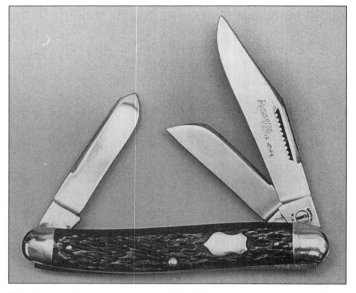

Stockman, brown bone, 3-3/4"; $300.

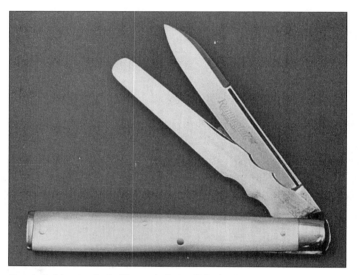

Spatula/doctor's knife, pearl, 3-1/2"; $750.

Purina advertising knife, checkerboard, 3-3/8"; $350.

Jack, brown bone, Axton shield, 3-1/2"; $350.

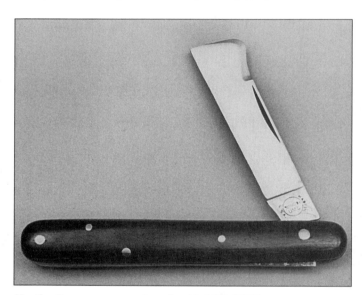

Horticulture, rosewood scales, 4-1/8"; $150.

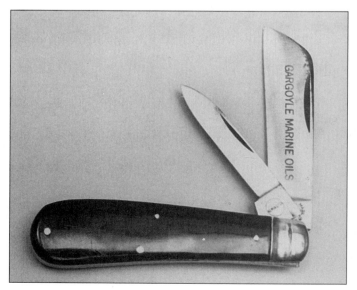

Half hawkbill, Rem., slick black scales, 3-3/4"; $150.

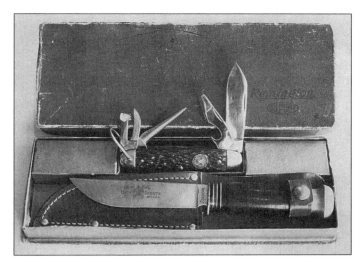

Boy Scout Set: RH51, Boy Scout pocket knife; R333, Boy Scout sheath knife. Mint in original box; $700. Photo courtesy Gurney Davis.

Remington Totem Pole, Mastadon ivory scale handles, rare; $700.

No number, 3 blades, black composition, scalloped handles, whittler, 3-1/4", Rem. Circle, rare handle; $350.

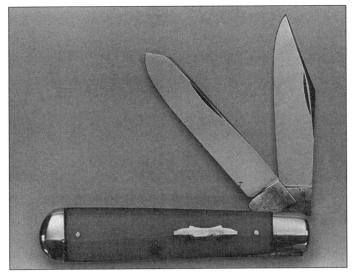

Two-blade jack, long spay blade, yellow scales w/sh., no number, 3-3/8", Remington, Circle, UMC; $200.

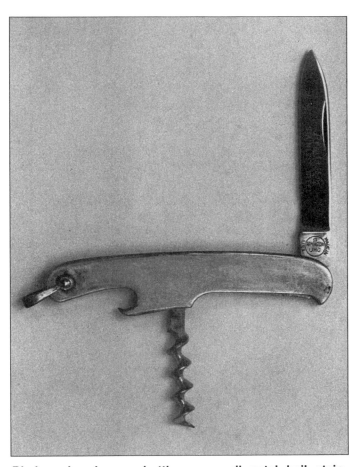

Blade and corkscrew, bottle opener, all metal, bail, stainless, no number, 3-1/8", Remington, Circle UMC; $125.

This Remington Dupont Cutlery counter mat serves well for the R1123 Remington bullet knife. The Remington Model 1875 44-cal. single-action revolver is not out of place, even though it is about 50 years older. The serial number of this revolver 579 was probably made in the first year of production (1875). It is well known that most of the Texas Rangers used the Colt single-action revolver and the Winchester rifle. It is also a well-known fact some of the Rangers used other good brands of hand guns and long guns. Therefore, the Ranger badge is not out of place with the Remington revolver or the Remington knife. This badge was made from a five peso Mexican coin, and it fits in well with most any gun or knife collection. All is super rare. Photo courtesy J. Paul Turner. Author's note: Mr. Turner passed away last year. He was an avid Remington and Winchester collector. We'll miss you, J. Paul.

Unknown, 3-3/8", Purina advertising; $250.

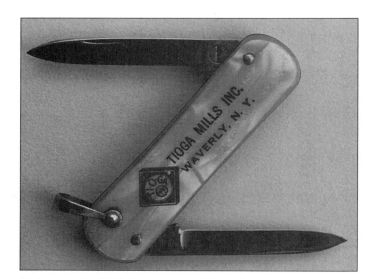

Unknown, 2-1/4", lobster, advertising; $75.

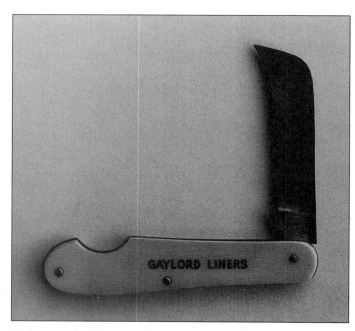

Unknown, 3-1/2", pyremite, advertising; $125.

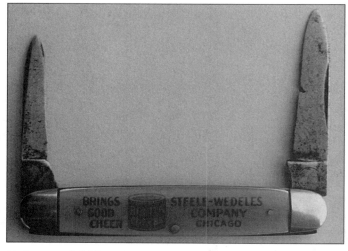

Unknown, 3-3/8", celluloid, advertising knife; $125.

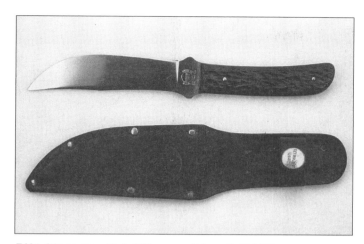

RH4, blade length 4-1/2", overall length 7-1/2".
VG	Exc	Mint
$50	$75	$125

RH22, blade length 2", overall length 6-1/4".
VG	Exc	Mint
$75	$100	$150

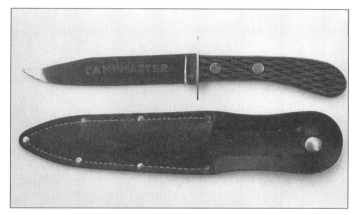

RH 6, blade length 5-1/4", overall length 9-1/4".
VG	Exc	Mint
$50	$85	$125

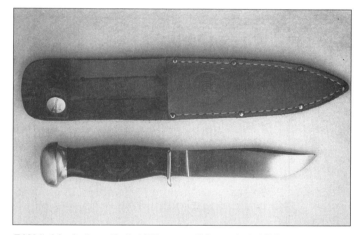

RH28, blade length 4-1/2", overall length 8-1/2".
VG	Exc	Mint
$75	$125	$200

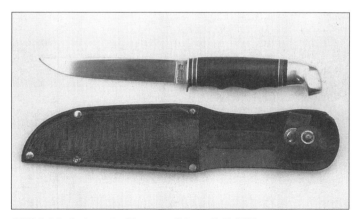

RH14, blade length 4", overall length 7-3/4".
VG	Exc	Mint
$75	$125	$175

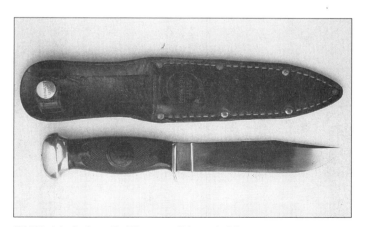

RH29, blade length 5", overall length 9".
VG	Exc	Mint
$100	$150	$225

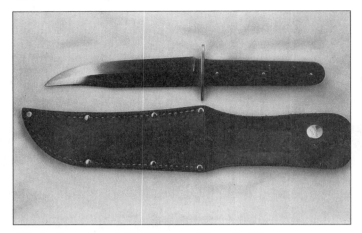

RH30, blade length 5-3/4", overall length 10".
VG   Exc   Mint
$225 $450 $700

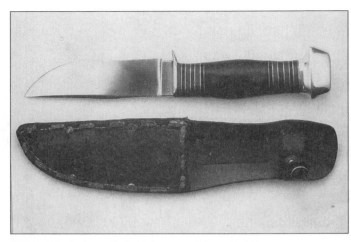

RH33, blade length 4-1/2", overall length 9".
VG   Exc   Mint
$150 $250 $375

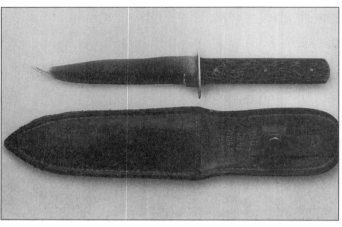

Remington RH30, made by Dupont (Remington sold out to Dupont). This is a contract knife marked and sold by LL Bean; $250.

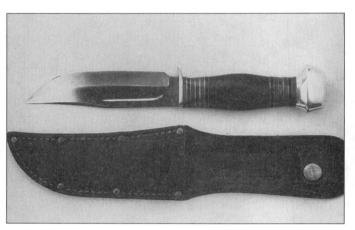

RH34, blade length 5", overall length 9-3/8".
VG   Exc   Mint
$100 $175 $350

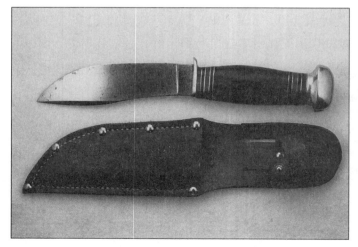

RH32, blade length 4-1/2", overall length 8-1/2".
VG   Exc   Mint
$75 $135 $200

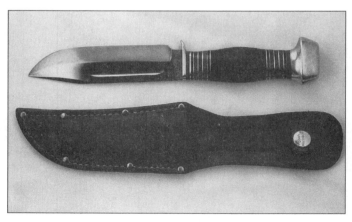

RH35, blade length 5-1/4", overall length 9-3/4".
VG   Exc   Mint
$125 $250 $400

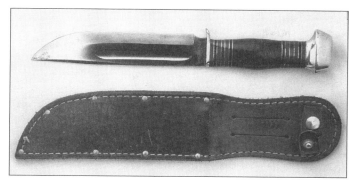

RH36, blade length 6-1/4", overall length 10-1/2".
VG	Exc	Mint
$150	$325	$500

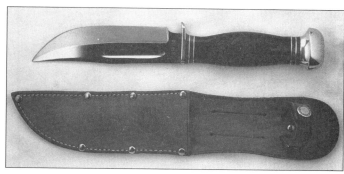

RH44, blade length 5", overall length 9-3/8".
VG	Exc	Mint
$400	$600	$850

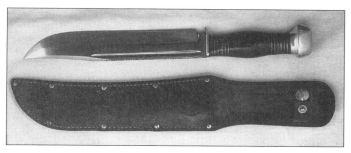

RH38, blade length 8", overall length 12-1/2".
VG	Exc	Mint
$500	$850	$1,200

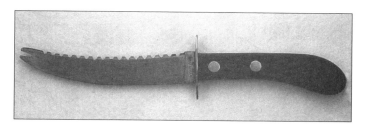

RH45, blade length 5-1/4", overall length 9-3/4".
VG	Exc	Mint
$100	$125	$175

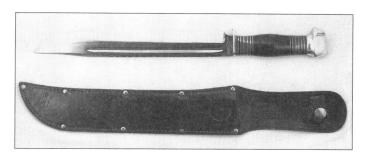

RH40, blade length 10", overall length 14-1/2".
VG	Exc	Mint
$1,200	$1,800	$2,500

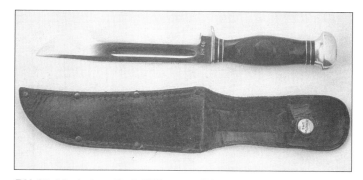

RH 46, blade length 6-1/4", overall length 10-1/2".
VG	Exc	Mint
$500	$750	$1,000

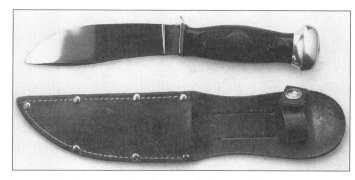

RH42, blade length 4-1/2", overall length 8-1/2".
VG	Exc	Mint
$150	$275	$400

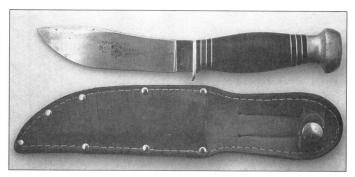

RH50, blade length 4-1/2", overall length 8-1/2". **Blade etched with Boy Scout logo.**
VG	Exc	Mint
$125	$200	$350

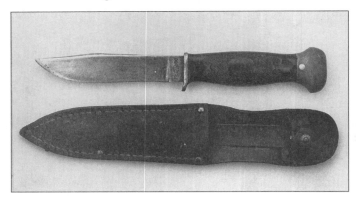

PAL RH50, rare. This knife is just like Remington RH28, with black hard rubber handle; $250.

RH65, blade length 4-1/2", overall length 8".
VG   Exc   Mint
$75 $150 $200

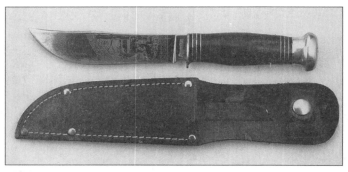

RH71, blade length 4-1/2", overall length 8". Blade etched with deer scene.
VG   Exc   Mint
$85 $200 $250

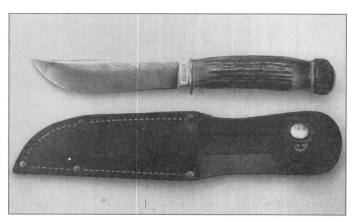

RH73, blade length 4-1/2", overall length 8". Blade etched with deer scene.
VG   Exc   Mint
$85 $175 $300

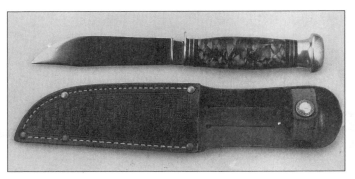

RH74P, blade length 4", overall length 8".
VG   Exc   Mint
$75 $100 $150

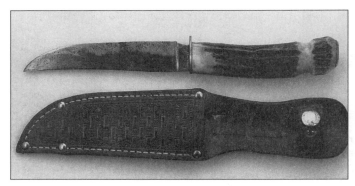

RH75, blade length 4", overall length 8".
VG   Exc   Mint
$100 $150 $250

RH84, blade length 4", overall length 8".
VG   Exc   Mint
$100 $150 $225

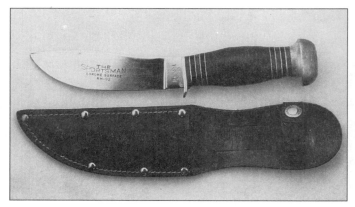

RH92, blade length 4-1/2", overall length 8-1/2". Blade chrome plated and etched "The Sportsman Chrome Surface RH92."
VG   Exc   Mint
$150 $300 $400

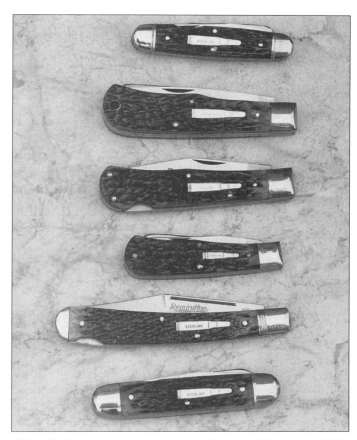

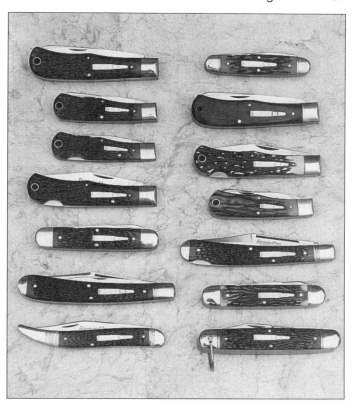

Silver Bullets: From the top: '88, '89, '90, '91, '92 and '93. Started in 1988—only 5,000 serialized knives produced for each year. Made exclusively for Smoky Mountain. They have genuine bone handles, with sterling-silver bullet.

At left, from the top, are 1982, '83, '84, '84, '85, '86 and '87. At the right, from the top, are 1988, '89, '90, '91, '92, '93 and '94. Started in 1982. All have Delron handles, except '89, which is cocobolo wood.

1988 Engraved Silver Bullet; only 500 produced. Each has bone handles, with sterling-silver bullet.

Rare bullet knife, 1920s-'30s vintage bone handles, blades are marked, 1123 bullet appears to be a pistol cartridge instead of the normal 30-cal. rifle cartridge. This could have been a special production for one of the pistol manufacturers? Maybe a lunch-box knife?

REMINGTON YEAR KNIVES & POSTERS

YEAR KNIVES

This information Courtesy of Steve Koonce, Smoky Mountain Knife Works

1982-R1123 TRAPPER.........$625
1983-R1173 BABY BULLET....$275
1984-R1173L LOCKBACK.....$175
1984-R1303 LOCKBACK.......$225
1985-R4353 WOODSMAN......$225
1986-R1263 HUNTER.........$275
1987-R1613 FISHERMAN......$175
1988-R4466 MUSKRAT........$125
1989-R1128 TRAPPER.........$95
1990-R1306 TRACKER.........$45
1991-R1178 BABY BULLET.....$55
1992-R1253 GUIDE LB.........$55
1993-R4356 BUSH PILOT.......$65
1994-R4243 CAMP KNIFE......$65

YEAR KNIFE POSTERS

1982 POSTER...............$375
1983 POSTER . $1000 (VERY RARE)
1984 POSTER................$250
1985 POSTER................$195
1986 POSTER................$125
1987 POSTER................$125
1988 POSTER.................$55
1989 POSTER.................$55
1990 POSTER.................$30
1991 POSTER.................$30
1992 POSTER.................$25
1993 POSTER.................$25
1994 POSTER.................$25

SPECIAL EDITIONS

10th Anniv. Bullet........$250
Lost Poster Knife.........$250

SILVER BULLETS

R4466SB - 1988.........$225
R1128SB - 1989.........$175
R1306SB - 1990.........$125
R1178SB - 1991.........$125
R1253SB - 1992.........$100
R4256SB - 1993..........$75

} Only 5000 Made

ENGRAVED SILVER BULLETS

R4466SBE - 1988........$275
R1128SBE - 1989........$225
R1306SBE - 1990........$175
R1178SBE - 1991........$150
R1253SBE - 1992........$150
R4256SBE - 1993........$125

} Only 5000 Made

THE ROBESON CUTLERY COMPANY

by Charlie Noyes

The history of the Robeson Cutlery Company has been related in several publications by others, including Dewey P. and Lavona Ferguson, James Parker, Bruce Voyles, Houston Price, and Bernard Levine. A few of the pertinent facts surrounding the founding of the Robeson Cutlery Co. and its developmental stages will be related here, plus some information gleaned from examining hundreds of Robeson pocket knives.

Millard F. Robeson was a salesman from Elmira, N.Y. It is not known what manufacturers he might have represented; it is known, however, that he began to sell pocket cutlery as a sideline to his regular sales items probably as early as 1879. Sometime before 1890, he was having knives made with his name on them. The earliest knives and razors I have seen from that period are marked:

MILLARD F. ROBESON
(1)

These knives were probably being made by various manufacturers, both in America and Germany. The majority I have seen were made in Germany after 1891, as they are identified with that country of origin. Knives dating from 1891 to 1894 are marked as:

M. F. ROBESON **GERMANY** **(2)**	**ROBESON** **CUTLERY Co.** **(3)**	**ROBESON** **CUTLERY Co.** **GERMANY** **(4)**

Probably due to the increased cost of imported knives after 1891, Millard Robeson sought an American manufacturer. He contracted with Charles E. Sherwood and Denton E. Bingham, immigrant Sheffield cutlers, who had started a small cutlery business in Camillus, N.Y. They made knives on contract for Robeson until about 1896, when they became financially insolvent. Millard Robeson reportedly assumed management of that business, but retained the original owners as officers. This particular arrangement continued until 1898, when business interests in Rochester, N.Y., enticed Robeson to establish his cutlery business there. The knives that had been made for Robeson in Camillus by the Sherwood-Bingham cutlers are marked on the front of the tang:

ROBESON
CUTLERY Co.
(5)

The back of the tang is marked **PREMIER** or **WARRANTED**. Most of the knives I have seen are much like Sheffield knives of that time. Most are ebony handled and are either large whittler patterns, heavy jacks or smaller, more delicate knives, such as Wharncliffe whittlers.

Robeson established his business in Rochester, but it is doubted by some that a cutlery factory ever operated there. A factory was established in Perry, N.Y., up the Genesee River from Rochester. The facilities in Rochester may have been administrative only. According to a billhead from 1901, the offices were located at 12 Saratoga Ave. in Rochester. The factory is shown on the billhead as being in Perry. M. F. Robeson is listed as president, I. S. Robeson as vice president, G. W. Robeson as treasurer, and C. W. Silcox as secretary.

Early knives marketed out of Rochester, but probably made in Perry, are marked:

ROBESON **CUTLERY** **CO.** **(6)**	or	**ROBESON** **CUTLERY** **ROCHESTER** **(7)**

Knives are known that are simply marked:

ROBESON
GENESEE
(8)

The Genesee River flows near Perry and through Rochester. The age and origin of knives with this mark are unknown, but I suspect they are from the earliest days in Rochester. Knives are later marked:

ROBESON (arched) **CO.** **CUTLERY** **(9)**	**ROBESON** **(arched)** **U.S.A.** **CUTLERY** **(10)**
ROBESON **ShurEdge** **ROCHESTER** **11)**	**ROBESON** **ShurEdge** **ROCHESTER, N.Y.** **(12)**

ROBESON
ShurEdge
U.S.A.
(13)

ROBESON
DEMONSTRATOR
(14)

A rather rare mark, probably dating from around 1901, most likely represents the earliest use of the *ShurEdge* logo:

ROBESON (arched from 9 o'clock to 12 o'clock)
ShurEdge (slanted from lower left—
upper right, but larger)
ROCHESTER, N.Y.
(15)

Earlier, pre-World War II knives are generally marked on all blades. Early knives have marks 9 or 10 on all blades. Premium knives were later marked with one of the full "Rochester" marks on all blades. The secondary blades of most other knives were usually marked with marks numbered 9 or 10, above, while the master blade was marked with a "Rochester" or "Rochester, *ShurEdge*" mark.

Small knives, especially small pearl-handled knives, are marked with a simple:

R.C.
Co.
(16)

Each of these marks was apparently used from about 1900 until 1948, although the precise periods that any one marking might have been utilized has, I think, not been determined.

At some time, Robeson Cutlery Co. merged with the Rochester Stamping Co., manufacturers of chafing dishes, casseroles, silent butlers (or crumb trays), and other pressed metal household items. I suppose it is possible that Millard Robeson might have represented this company earlier.

The exact date of the merger is questionable. *Goin's Encyclopedia of Cutlery Markings* states that Robeson Cutlery Co. merged with Rochester Stamping Co. in 1922 to form Robeson-Rochester Corp. However, I have a postcard from a salesman representing both the Rochester Stamping Co. and the Robeson Cutlery Co. The card shows various Rochester points of interest and states that the salesman (Frank) will arrive "...about *20 November, 1907*, with a supply of seasonable goods." Evidently, Robeson Cutlery and Rochester Stamping Co. were connected, in some fashion, at least as early as 1907.

Millard F. Robeson died in 1903, but the company continued and struggled over the next four decades or so. However, the finest knives date from that time period. During the 1920s and 1930s, Robeson arguably made some of the finest American-made knives available.

According to Bernard Levine in *Pocket Knives*, a second factory was added in Mount Morris, N.Y., during World War I. Mount Morris is down the Genesee River from Perry, and located on the banks of Lake Morris.

Robeson Cutlery Co. produced several lines of fine pocket cutlery during this time period. Of course, it produced the *ShurEdge* line of knives; however, lesser-quality knives, without the *ShurEdge* mark exist. They generally have iron liners and bolsters.

PocketEze, **MasterCraft**, and **No-Rustain** knives were also quality lines. PocketEze knives were introduced about 1914, and MasterCraft knives were introduced about 1929. PocketEze knives are made with blade-backs sunk flush with the liners to reduce wear on pocket linings. MasterCraft knives have "oiless" bronze bearings inletted onto the end of the tang, which reduced the friction between the tang and the backspring. The knives open and close easily. The bronze bearings, however, did come off occasionally, leaving the dovetail indentations on the end of the tang. This caused the blade to "stop" in several positions between fully closed and fully opened, as the indentations engaged the backspring. Any MasterCraft knife with a blade that stops in several positions is missing its bronze bearings. No-Rustain knives were a line of knives incorporating stainless-steel blades and liners. All these knives had distinctive shields. However, many Robeson knives can be found with sunken joints, but without a PocketEze shield.

Early Robeson knives have green bone handles, later replaced by brown bone. Rogers bone was used extensively, as well as a very pretty brown bone with "worm-groove" jigging used to simulate stag. Genuine stag was used, but is not frequently encountered. Pearl was also used and many nice patterns can be found with pearl and abalone handles. Various patterns of celluloid and solid compositions such as yellow, black and, rarely, white were used. Several patterned celluloids were used prior to World War II.

In 1940, the company was purchased by Saul Frankel, a Rochester businessman. He hired Emerson Case to manage the company, which flourished and enjoyed its greatest financial success, although in order to do so, the quality of the knives was somewhat compromised.

Emerson Case became president of the company in 1948. At that time, the tang marking was changed. The *ShurEdge* logo was replaced by a block lettering, and knives made from 1948-1965 are marked:

ROBESON
SHUREDGE
U.S.A.
(17)

The earlier post-1948 knives have regular machined nail pulls. The later knives have a "punched" semi-long nail pull that is often referred to as a "long pull." I disagree. I think they are, quite simply, cheaply manufactured regular pulls. Genuine long nail pulls extending to the tang on a Robeson knife indicate *early*, *premium* prices, and are not common. They are most frequently encountered on high-quality, pearl-handled multi-blades.

During Case's tenure, several knife manufacturing innovations were implemented. A special cold-quenching tempering process was developed. Knives treated with this process are etched, "FROZEN HEAT."

Another process involving the "detonation" of heated or molten tungsten carbide onto the edge of a knife blade was developed. These knives are etched "FLAME EDGE," and have a 1/8"-wide layer of tungsten carbide along the edge of the master blade on the front side only.

Sometime after 1948, the bronze bearings on the MasterCraft knives were moved from the end of the tang to the inside of the backspring. The MasterCraft line name was discontinued, and the **PermaLube** line began. PermaLube knives have a distinctive bronze shield indicating they have the "oiless" bronze bearing. Knives can be found with a bronze PocketEze shield, indicating sunken joints *and* "oiless" bronze bearings.

Bone was not readily available during and immediately following World War II, and rough black composition was used instead. Knives with a pattern number indicating bone handles, but having rough black composition instead, are generally thought to date from World War II or shortly afterward. The word "ROBESON" was impressed into the composition material in place of a metallic shield and filled with white paint on some of the knives from that period.

From about 1948 until 1959 or 1960, a beautiful red bone was used. Collectors now call this bone "strawberry" and the finest examples do truly look like a deep red strawberry. About 1960, the strawberry bone was replaced with strawberry-colored delrin, and was used until sometime after 1965 and possibly as late as 1971.

Emerson Case retired in 1965 and the Robeson Cutlery Co. was sold to Cutler Federal Corp. Pocket knife production at Perry, N.Y. was discontinued by Cutler Federal and the knives were made on contract by Camillus Cutlery Co. The tang marking was changed, in that the pattern number was moved from the back of the tang to the front, and the word "ShurEdge" was dropped. The marking from 1965-1977 is:

ROBESON
000000
U.S.A.
(18)

In 1971, the rights to the Robeson name were purchased by the Ontario Knife Co. and the manufacturing of knives was moved to Franklin, N.Y. The tang marking remained the same, but all the knives I've seen that appear to be from that period have a brown jigged delrin handle. The handle slabs are thin, and the knives appear cheaply made.

Ontario Knife dropped the Robeson name altogether in 1977, and the manufacturing of Robeson-marked knives ceased. It's just as well because the quality was, by that time, completely gone. Purists do not consider *any* knife made after 1965 to be a true Robeson.

Pattern numbers

Beginning about 1901, Robeson utilized one of the finest, and easiest to learn, pattern-numbering systems of any knife manufacturer.

The pattern number generally consists of six digits. The first three digits denote certain materials and composition of the knife, and the last three digits denote the handle-die shape.

The first digit represents the handle material:

1	Ebony or smooth black composition
2	Rosewood
3	Smooth black composition
4	White composition or ivoroid
5	Genuine stag or a Barlow
6	Bone
7	Pearl or abalone
8	Patterned celluloid or colored celluloid
9	Gun metal

The second digit represents the number of blades:

1	One
2	Two
3	Three
4	Four
5	Five

The third digit represents the liner and bolster composition:

1	Steel liners and steel bolsters
2	Brass liners and nickel-silver bolsters
3	Nickel-silver liners and nickel-silver bolsters
6	Brass liners and nickel-silver bolsters (same as for No. 2)

8   Life-long liners (materials unknown, but usually seen on an inter-frame knife)

9   Stainless steel or chrome plated

The final three digits represent the handle-die shape.

Handle-die numbers that begin with 0, i.e. 056, can be found with the 0 dropped, especially on smaller knives when space is at a premium. Thus, five-digit pattern numbers are found often; for example, 62256 instead of 622056.

Occasionally a "50," "85," "125," or "250" notation will follow a pattern number on a second line. I have no idea what they signified. Pattern numbers can be found in one line or two, such as 636594 or:

636

594

Thus, a bone-handled, three-blade stockman, with brass liners and nickel-silver bolsters, built upon a number 594 handle die, would have been numbered 632594 or 636594.

It is easier to express Robeson pattern numbers in sets of three: 636-594 or 622-056.

Terrier knives, made and marketed by Robeson from 1910-1916, have the pattern number series reversed: the first three digits denote the handle-die shape, and the last three digits denote the materials and composition of the knife. Thus, a Terrier stockman, as described above, would have been marked 594636. Not all Terrier knives are marked with a pattern number, and those that are marked are often done so on a secondary blade.

Continental knives with a New York stamp were made and marketed by Robeson between 1914-1920. I have a letter on Robeson stationery, dated March 26, 1914, concerning a shipment of Continental pocket knives to an upstate New York hardware dealer. The Continental Cutlery Co., N.Y. knives I have seen are not marked with pattern numbers. However, many are familiar Robeson patterns. I recently acquired a near-mint Robeson pearl-handled Wharncliffe pen knife, with a Robeson-marked master Wharncliffe blade and a Continental-marked secondary pen blade.

The Robeson Cutlery Co. has a rich and well-documented history. It made high-quality knives throughout most of its existence. The company's knives can be dated with reasonable accuracy within limited time periods. It made many interesting patterns and some very interesting variations. Robeson essentially ceased to exist in 1965. Collecting the company's knives has been a great adventure for me and I hope others will join me in preserving them for future generations.

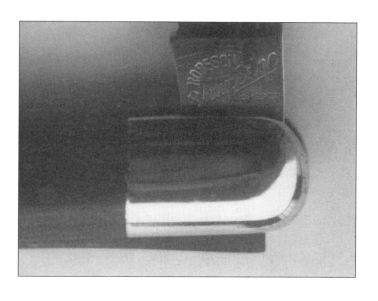

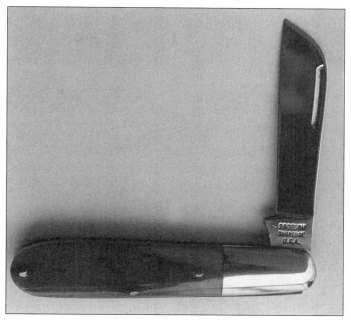

511178, ROBESON/SHUREDGE (block)/U.S.A.; 3-3/8", strawberry bone Barlow/sheep foot; 1948-1965; $100.

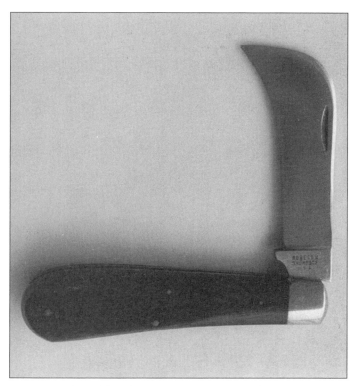

211007, ROBESON/SHUREDGE (block)/U.S.A.; 4", wood pruner/hawkbill; 1948-1965; $75.

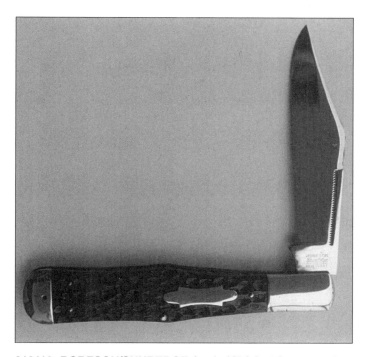

612118, ROBESON/SHUREDGE (script)/ROCHESTER; 5-1/4", brown bone Coke bottle/hunter; 1900-1940; $500.

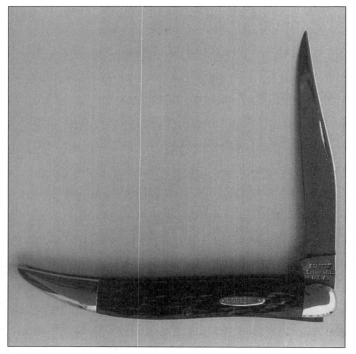

612407, ROBESON/SHUREDGE (block)/U.S.A.; 5", straw-berry bone, toothpick; 1948-1965; $250.

816407, ROBESON/SHUREDGE (script)/ROCHESTER; 5", red-swirl celluloid toothpick; 1900-1948; $200.

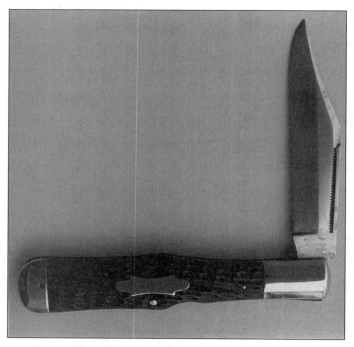

612246, ROBESON/SHUREDGE (script)/ROCHESTER; 5-1/4", brown bone, Coke bottle/lockback; 1900-1940; $600.

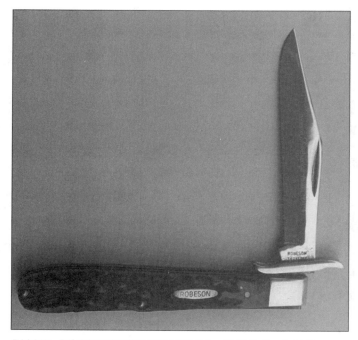

512872, ROBESON/SHUREDGE (block)/U.S.A.; 4-3/8", gen-uine stag, swing-guard hunter; 1948-1965; $250.

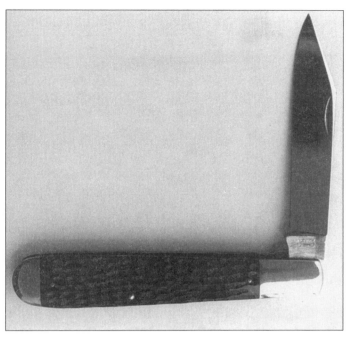

612610, ROBESON/SHUREDGE (script)/ROCHESTER; 5", brown bone, lockback hunter; 1900-1940; $450.

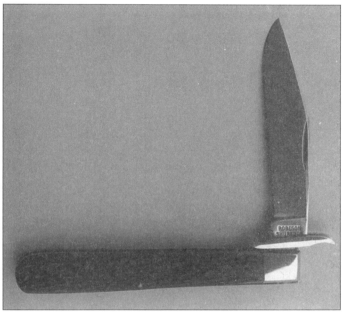

513872, ROBESON/SHUREDGE (block)/U.S.A.; 4-3/8", genuine stag, swing-guard hunter; 1948-1965; $250.

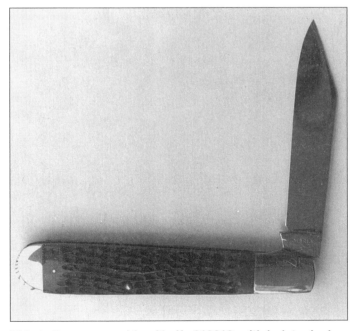

This is the reverse side of knife 612610, with bolster lock.

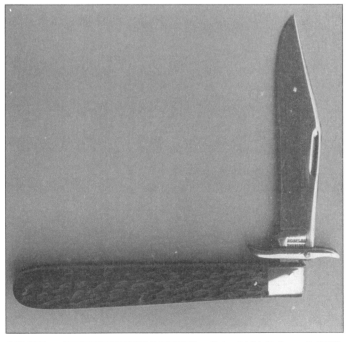

612872, ROBESON/SHUREDGE (block)/U.S.A.; 4-3/8", strawberry bone, swing-guard hunter; 1948-1965; $175.

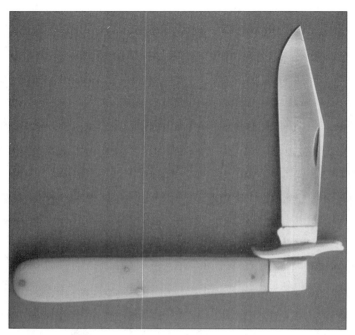

812872, ROBESON/SHUREDGE (block)/U.S.A.; 4-3/8", yellow comp., swing-guard hunter; 1948-1965; $150.

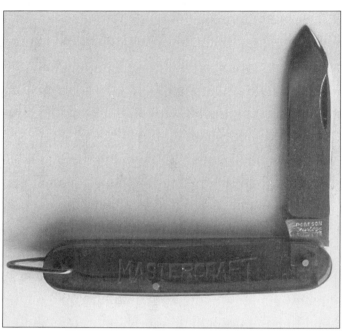

No #; ROBESON/SHUREDGE (script)/ROCHESTER; 3-5/8", clear/green celluloid, salesman's sample; 1929-1948; $500.

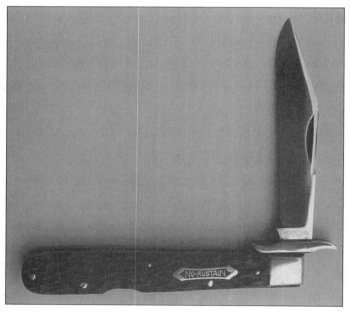

619872, ROBESON/SHUREDGE (script)/ROCHESTER; 4-3/8", brown bone, lockback hunter (No-Rustain); 1900-1940; $500.

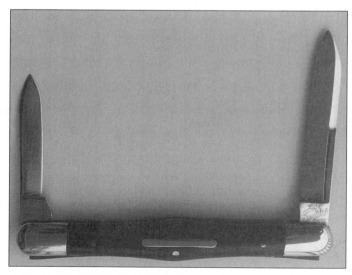

122001, ROBESON/SHUREDGE (script)/ROCHESTER; 3-3/8," ebony, swell-center pen; (#15); c. 1903; $150.

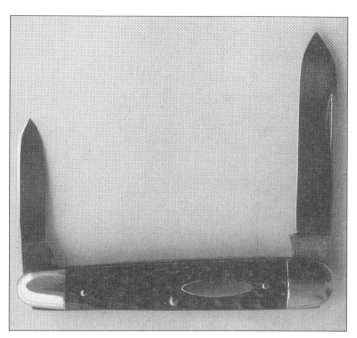

**622022, ROBESON/SHUREDGE (script)/ROCHESTER; 3-1/4",
brown bone, sleeveboard pen; 1900-1940; $150.**

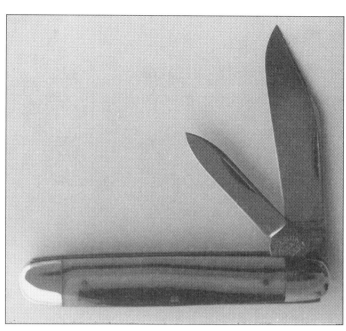

**822023, ROBESON/SHUREDGE (script)/ROCHESTER; 3-1/4",
butter and molasses, equal-end jack; 1900-1948; $100.**

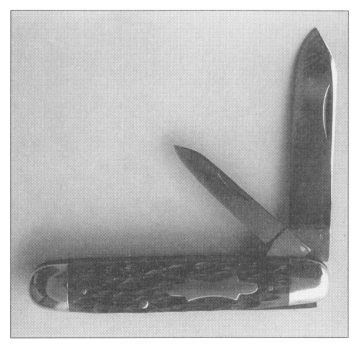

**622013, ROBESON/SHUREDGE (script)/ROCHESTER; 3-1/2",
brown bone, equal-end jack; 1900-1940; $200.**

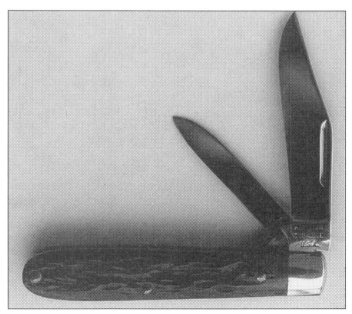

**622026, ROBESON/SHUREDGE (block)/U.S.A.; 3", straw-
berry bone, regular jack; 1948-1965; $75.**

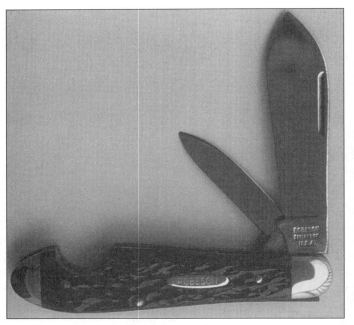

622027, ROBESON/SHUREDGE (block)/U.S.A.; 3-5/8", strawberry bone, E-O, swell-end jack; 1948-1965; $150.

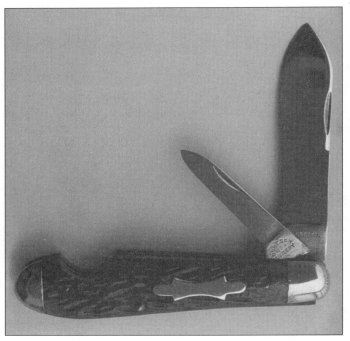

626027, ROBESON/SHUREDGE (script)/ROCHESTER; 3-5/8", green bone, E-O, swell-end jack; 1900-1940; $250.

622026, ROBESON/SHUREDGE (script)/ROCHESTER; 3", brown bone, Clauss, regular jack; 1900-1940; $100.

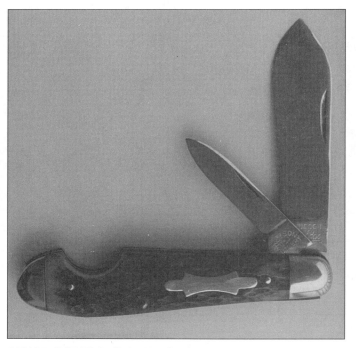

622027, ROBESON/SHUREDGE (script)/ROCHESTER; 3-5/8", brown bone, E-O, swell-end jack; 1900-1940; $250.

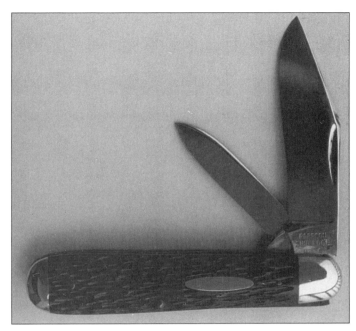

622056, ROBESON/SHUREDGE (block)/U.S.A.; 3-3/4", rough black, swell-end jack; 1948-1965; $75.

622062, ROBESON/SHUREDGE (script)/ROCHESTER; 4", brown bone, regular jack; 1900-1940; $300.

622056, ROBESON/SHUREDGE (block)/U.S.A.; 3-3/4", strawberry bone, swell-end jack; 1948-1965; $175.

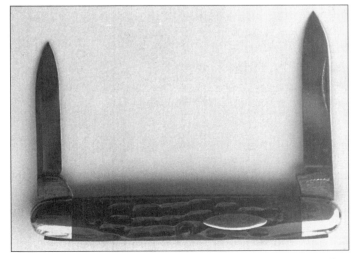

622064, ROBESON/SHUREDGE (script)/ROCHESTER; 2-3/4", green bone, equal-end pen; 1900-1940; $125.

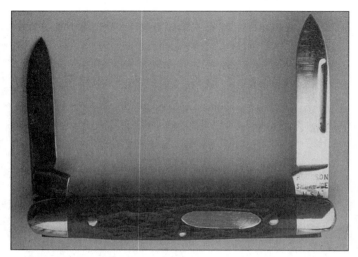

622064, ROBESON/SHUREDGE (block)/U.S.A.; 2-3/4", strawberry bone, equal-end pen; 1948-1965; $100.

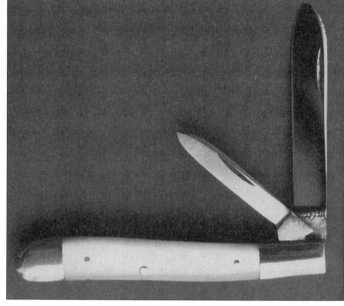

722083, ROBESON/SHUREDGE (script)/ROCHESTER; 2-3/4", genuine pearl, dog-leg jack; 1900-1948; $200.

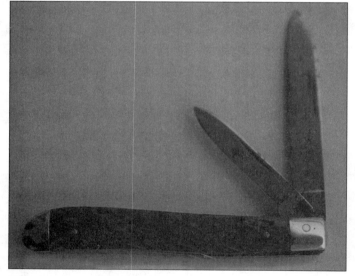

622083, ROBESON/SHUREDGE (script)/ROCHESTER; 2-3/4", brown bone, dog-leg jack; 1900-1940; $175.

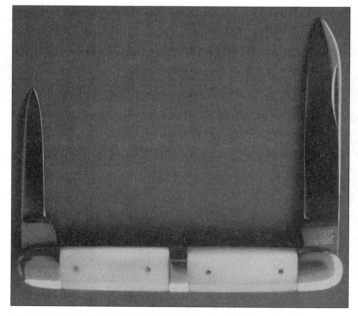

722073, ROBESON/SHUREDGE (script)/ROCHESTER; 3-1/4", genuine pearl, equal-end pen; 1900-1948; $200.

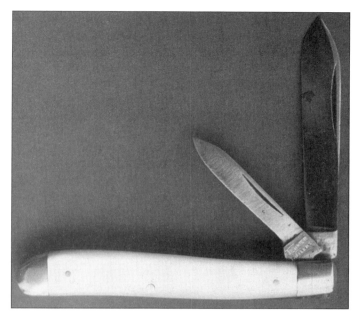

083722, TERRIER CUTLERY; 2-3/4", genuine pearl, dog-leg jack; 1910-1916; $250.

622100, ROBESON/SHUREDGE (script)/ROCHESTER; 3-1/4", brown bone, Official Jimmie Allen Knife; c. 1930s; $250.

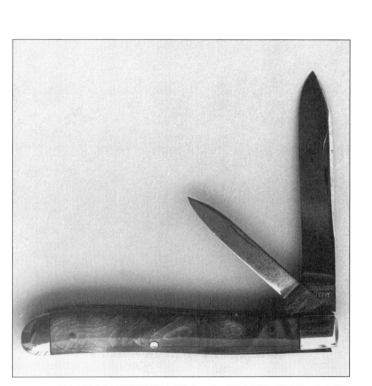

822083, ROBESON/SHUREDGE (script)/ROCHESTER; 2-3/4", brown onyx celluloid, dog-leg jack; 1900-1948; $175.

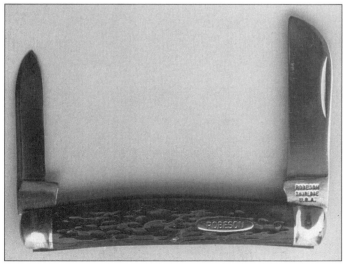

622088, ROBESON/SHUREDGE (block)/U.S.A.; 3-3/4", strawberry bone, Congress, 1948-1965; $150.

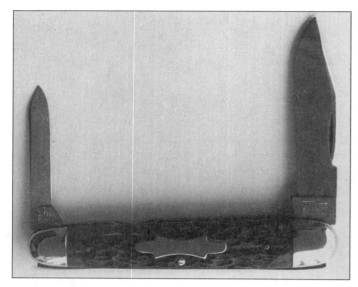

102622, TERRIER CUTLERY/ROCHESTER, N.Y.; 3-5/8", brown bone, sleeveboard pen; 1910-1916; $300.

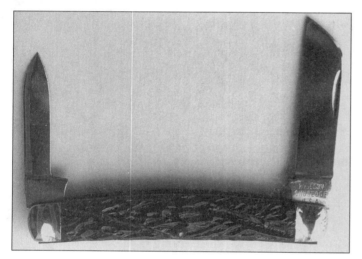

622088, ROBESON/SHUREDGE (block)/U.S.A.; 3-3/4", rough black, Congress, 1948-1965; $100.

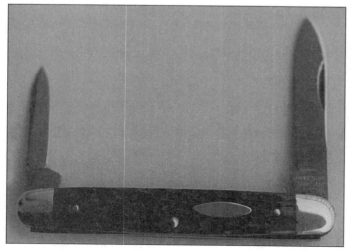

622105, ROBESON/SHUREDGE (script)/ROCHESTER; 3", brown bone, equal-end pen; 1900-1940; $150.

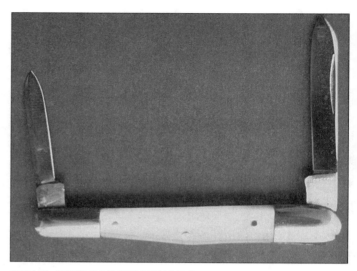

722110, ROBESON/SHUREDGE (script)/ROCHESTER; 2-5/8", genuine pearl, swell-center pen; 1900-1948; $100.

622151, ROBESON/SHUREDGE (block)/U.S.A.; 4-1/2", strawberry bone, English jack; 1948-1965; $250.

622119, ROBESON/SHUREDGE (block)/U.S.A.; 4-1/2", strawberry bone, English jack; 1948-1965; $250.

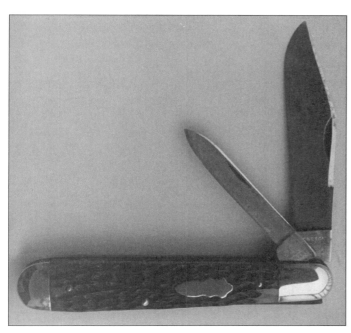

622119, ROBESON/SHUREDGE (script)/ROCHESTER; 4-1/2", brown bone, English jack; 1900-1940; $300.

622167, ROBESON/SHUREDGE (script)/ROCHESTER; 3", brown bone, equal-end pen; 1900-1940; $150.

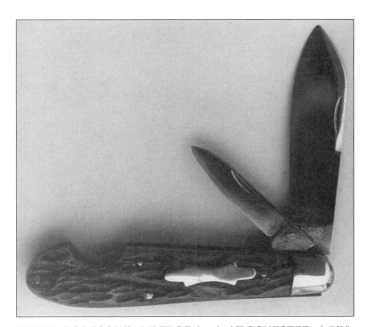

622155, ROBESON/SHUREDGE (script)/ROCHESTER; 3-5/8", brown bone, E-O, boy's knife (bail missing); 1900-1940; $250.

**521168, ROBESON/SHUREDGE (script)/ROCHESTER; 3-3/8",
saw-cut brown bone, Barlow; 1900-1940; $250.**

**623177, ROBESON/SHUREDGE (block)/U.S.A.; 3", straw-
berry bone, Congress; 1948-1965; $125.**

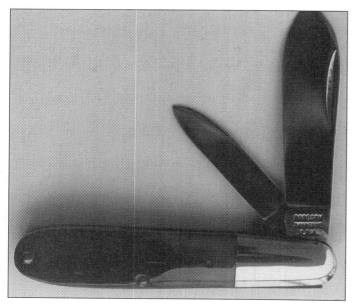

**521168, ROBESON/SHUREDGE (block)/U.S.A.; 3-3/8",
strawberry bone, Barlow; 1948-1965; $150.**

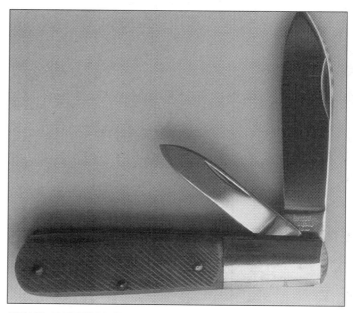

**521168, ROBESON/SHUREDGE (block)/U.S.A. (small); 3-3/8",
saw-cut brown bone, Barlow; 1948-1965; $200.**

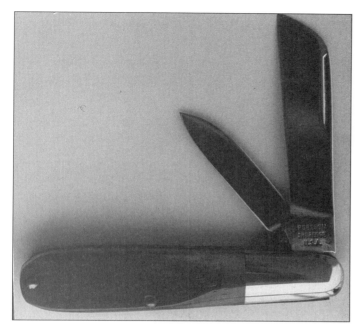

521178, ROBESON/SHUREDGE (block)/U.S.A.; 3-3/8", straw-berry bone, Barlow; 1948-1965; $150.

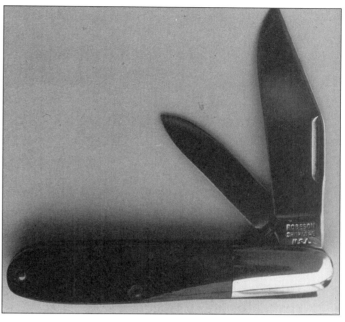

521179, ROBESON/SHUREDGE (block)/U.S.A.; 3-3/8", strawberry bone, sleeveboard, Barlow; 1948-1965; $150.

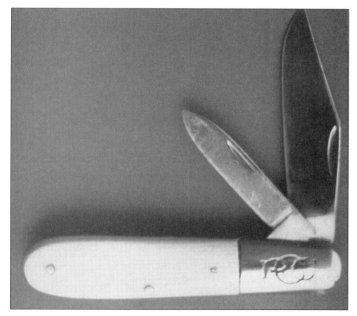

421179, ROBESON/SHUREDGE (script)/U.S.A.; 3-3/8", ivory celluloid, sleeveboard, Barlow; 1900-1948; $175.

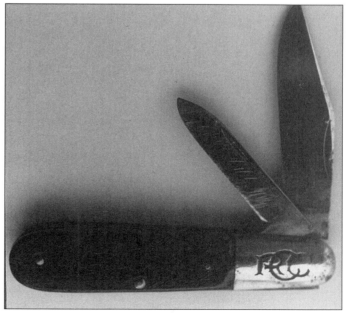

521175, ROBESON/SHUREDGE (script)/ROCHESTER; 3-3/8", saw-cut brown bone, Barlow; 1900-1940; $250.

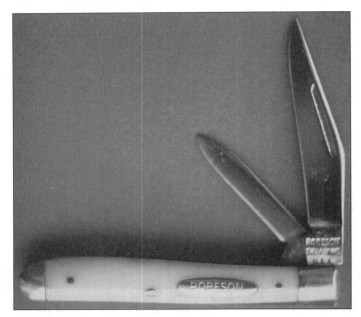

822183, ROBESON/SHUREDGE (block)/U.S.A.; 2-7/8", yellow composition, dog-leg jack; 1948-1965; $75.

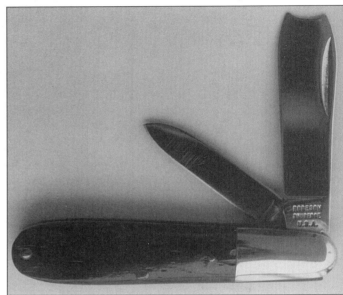

521199, ROBESON/SHUREDGE (block)/U.S.A.; 3-3/8", strawberry bone, one-armed Barlow; 1948-1965; $150.

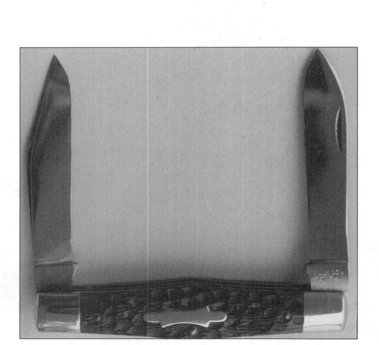

622187, ROBESON/SHUREDGE (script)/U.S.A.; 4", brown bone, bull-head jack (moose); 1900-1940; $350.

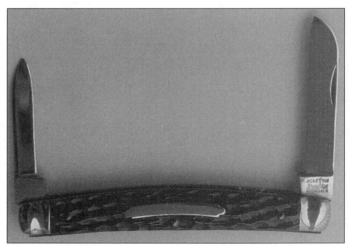

622193, ROBESON/SHUREDGE (script)/ROCHESTER; 3-3/4", brown bone, Congress; 1900-1940; $250.

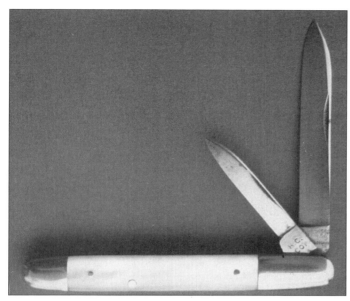

722220, ROBESON/SHUREDGE (script)/ROCHESTER; 2-3/4", genuine pearl, equal-end jack; 1900-1948; $175.

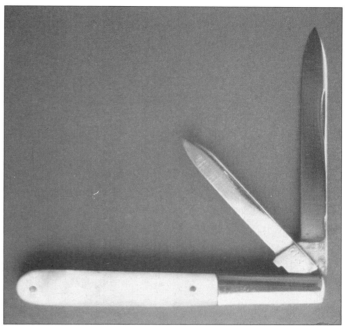

722236, ROBESON/SHUREDGE (script)/ROCHESTER; 2-1/2", genuine pearl, slim Barlow; 1900-1948; $100.

622195, ROBESON/SHUREDGE (block)/U.S.A.; 3", strawberry bone, physician's knife; 1948-1965; $150.

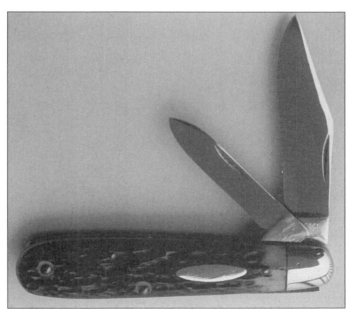

622240, ROBESON/SHUREDGE (script)/ROCHESTER; 3-3/8", green bone, regular jack; 1900-1940; $175.

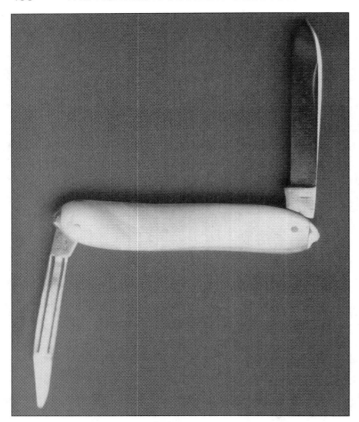

722273, ROBESON/SHUREDGE (script)/ROCHESTER; 3",
genuine pearl, candle-end lobster; 1900-1948; $150.

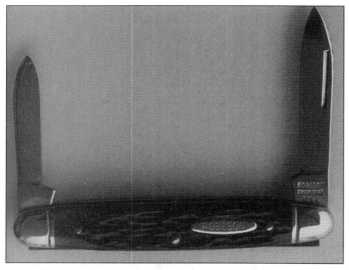

622253, ROBESON/SHUREDGE (block)/U.S.A.; 3-3/8",
strawberry bone, Senator, 1948-1965; $100.

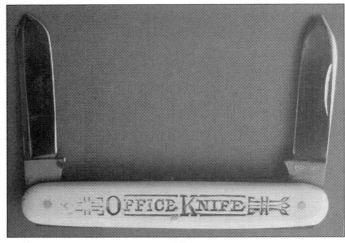

422274, ROBESON/SHUREDGE (script)/ROCHESTER; 3-1/4",
ivory celluloid, office knife; 1900-1948; $100.

622255, ROBESON/SHUREDGE (script)/ROCHESTER; 3-1/4",
brown bone, equal-end pen; 1900-1940; $150.

626285, ROBESON/SHUREDGE (script)/ROCHESTER; 3-1/2",
brown bone, swell-center jack; 1900-1940; $175.

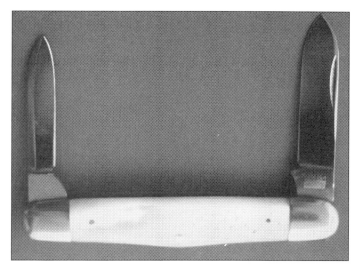

722305, ROBESON/SHUREDGE (script)/ROCHESTER; 3-1/8", genuine pearl, swell-center pen; 1900-1948; $200.

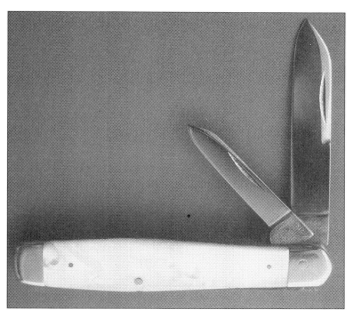

722308, ROBESON/SHUREDGE (script)/ROCHESTER; 3-1/4", genuine pearl, Coke bottle jack, 1900-1948; $250.

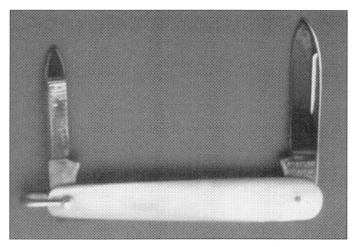

723317, ROBESON/SHUREDGE (script)/ROCHESTER; 3", genuine pearl, sleeveboard pen, 1948-1965; $75.

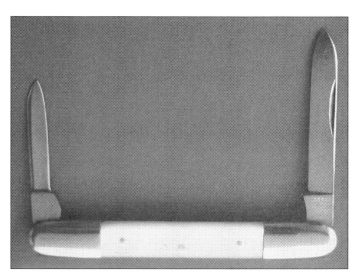

722320, ROBESON/SHUREDGE (script)/ROCHESTER; 3", genuine pearl, equal-end pen, 1900-1948; $100.

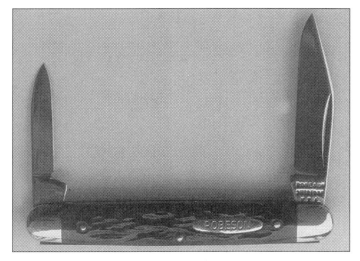

622319, ROBESON/SHUREDGE (block)/U.S.A.; 3", strawberry bone, equal-end pen; 1948-1965; $75.

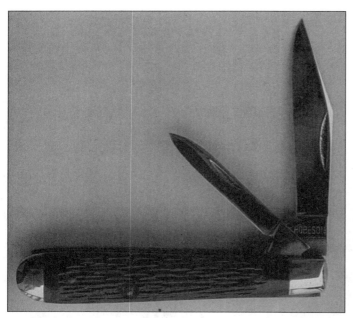

622331, ROBESON/SHUREDGE (block)/U.S.A.; 2-5/8", rough black, small regular jack, 1948-1965; $50.

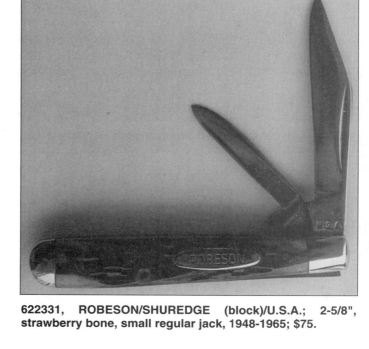

622331, ROBESON/SHUREDGE (block)/U.S.A.; 2-5/8", strawberry bone, small regular jack, 1948-1965; $75.

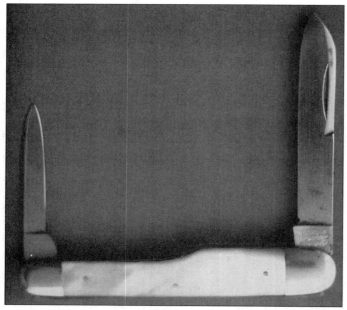

722362, ROBESON/SHUREDGE (script)/ROCHESTER; 3-1/8", genuine pearl, gunstock (seen in bone whittler also); 1900-1948; $200.

622358, ROBESON/SHUREDGE (script)/ROCHESTER; 3-1/2", brown bone, swell-center coffin bolsters; 1900-1940; $250.

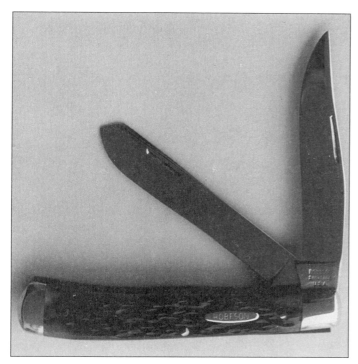

622382, ROBESON/SHUREDGE (block)/U.S.A.; 4-1/8", straw-berry bone, trapper, 1948-1965; $400.

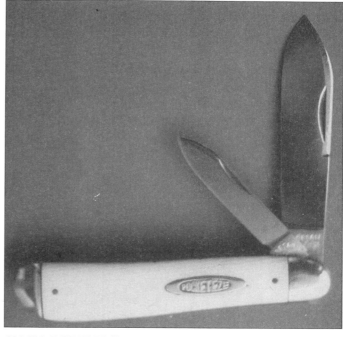

422414, ROBESON/SHUREDGE (script)/ROCHESTER; 3-1/4", ivory celluloid, dog-leg jack; 1900-1948; $175.

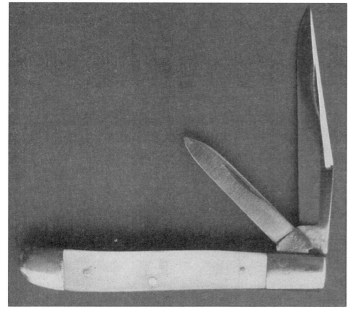

722392, ROBESON/SHUREDGE (script)/ROCHESTER; 2-3/4", genuine pearl, peanut, 1900-1948; $175.

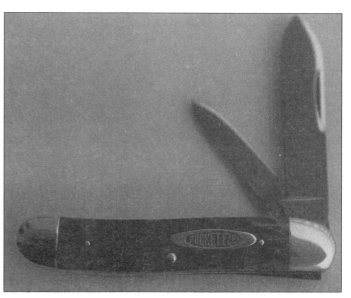

623400, ROBESON/SHUREDGE (script)/ROCHESTER; 3", brown bone, peanut (serpentine); 1900-1940; $150.

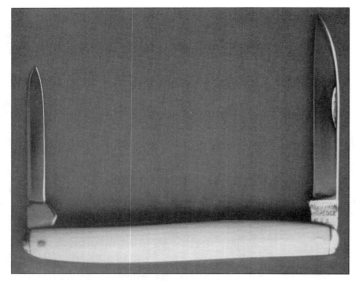

423405, ROBESON/SHUREDGE (block)/U.S.A.; 3-1/4", ivory celluloid, serpentine pen, 1948-1965; $75.

123478, ROBESON/SHUREDGE (script)/ROCHESTER; 3-3/8", smooth black, equal-end jack, 1900-1948; $175.

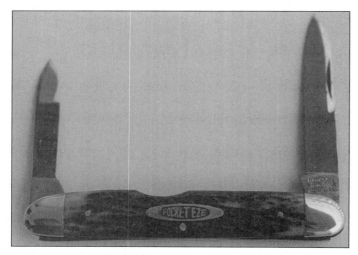

622416, 85 ROBESON/SHUREDGE (script)/ROCHESTER; 3-1/4", brown bone, pen knife; 1900-1940; $175.

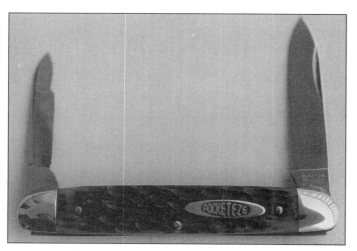

622416, ROBESON/SHUREDGE (script)/ROCHESTER; 3-1/4", brown bone, pen knife, 1900-1940; $175.

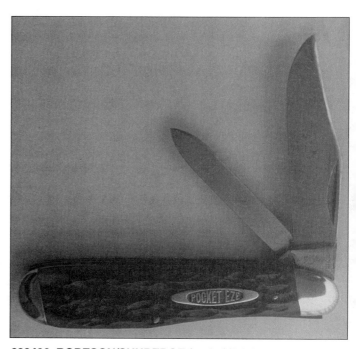

622426, ROBESON/SHUREDGE (script)/ROCHESTER; 3-3/4", brown bone, swell-center jack; 1900-1940; $250.

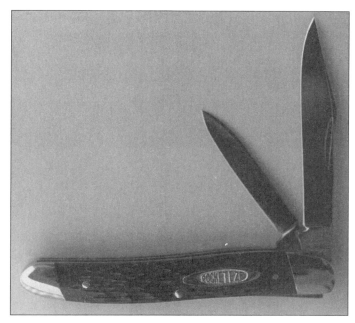

623480, ROBESON/SHUREDGE (block)/U.S.A.; 3-3/8", rough black, serpentine jack, 1948-1965; $75.

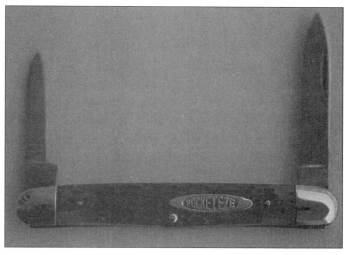

623501, ROBESON/SHUREDGE (script)/ROCHESTER; 3", brown bone, swell-center pen, 1900-1940; $175.

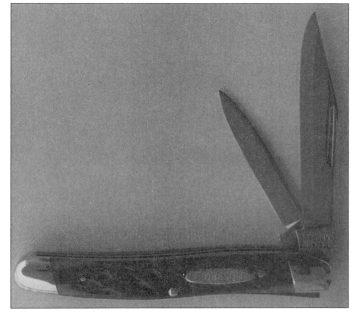

623480, ROBESON/SHUREDGE (block)/U.S.A.; 3-3/8", strawberry bone, serpentine jack ("Flame-Edge"), 1948-1965; $250.

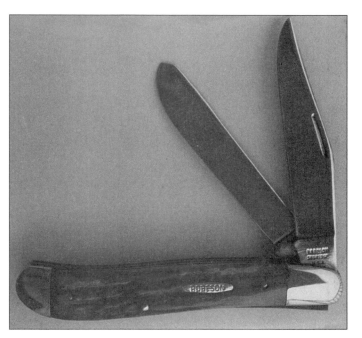

522482, ROBESON/SHUREDGE (block)/U.S.A.; 4-1/2", genuine stag, trapper, 1948-1965; $350.

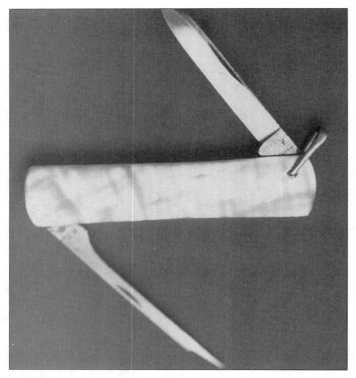

722550, ROBESON/SHUREDGE (script)/ROCHESTER; 2-1/2", genuine pearl, lobster (watch fob knife); 1900-1948; $100.

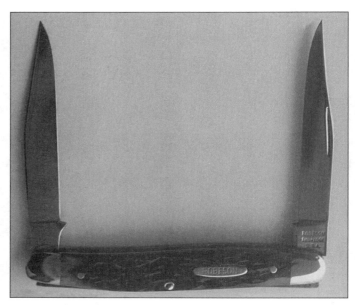

623595, ROBESON/SHUREDGE (block)/U.S.A.; 3-7/8", strawberry bone, serpentine Muskrat, 1948-1965; $350.

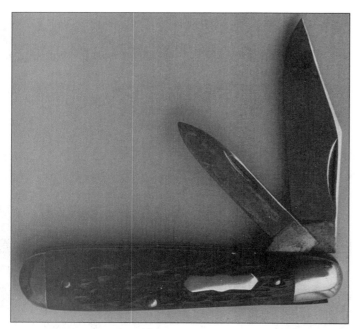

626636, ROBESON/SHUREDGE (script)/ROCHESTER; 3-3/8", green bone, regular jack; 1900-1940; $150.

622636, ROBESON/SHUREDGE (block)/U.S.A.; 3-3/8", strawberry bone, regular jack, 1948-1965; $150.

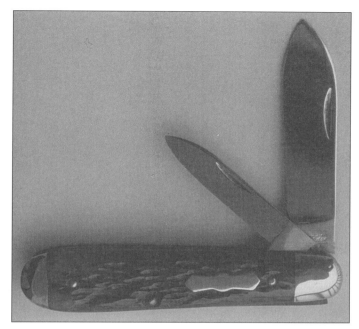

626639, ROBESON/SHUREDGE (script)/ROCHESTER; 3-3/8", green bone, regular jack, 1900-1940; $175.

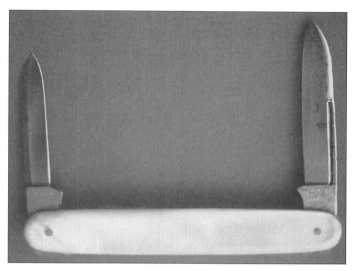

723641, ROBESON/SHUREDGE (script)/ROCHESTER; 3-1/4", genuine pearl, equal-end pen, 1900-1948; $100.

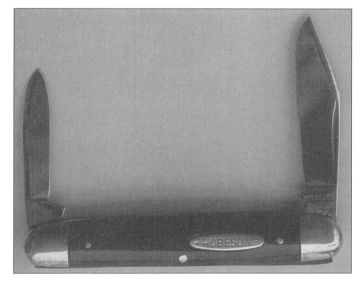

323675, ROBESON/SHUREDGE (block)/U.S.A.; 3", slick black, equal-end pen, 1948-1965; $50.

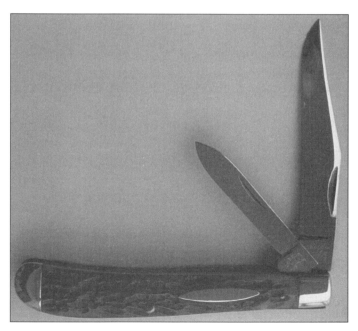

622721, ROBESON/SHUREDGE (script)/ROCHESTER; 3-3/4", brown Rogers bone, half-trapper, 1900-1940; $300.

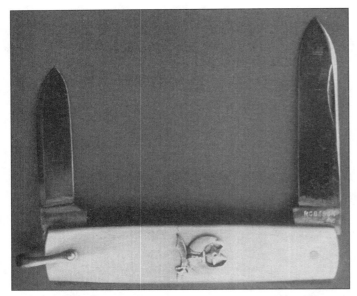

723747, ROBESON/SHUREDGE (script)/ROCHESTER; 2-1/2", genuine pearl, crown pen (Shriners), 1900-1948; $150.

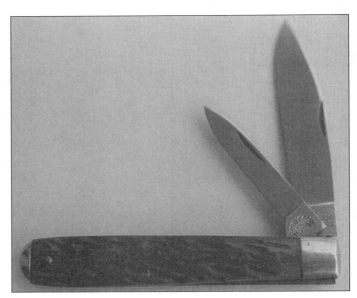

626765, ROBESON/SHUREDGE (script)/ROCHESTER; 3-1/4", green bone, regular jack, 1900-1940; $75.

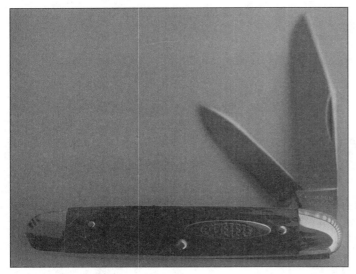

623757, ROBESON/SHUREDGE (script)/ROCHESTER; 3", brown Rogers bone, equal-end, 1900-1940; $175.

622787, ROBESON/SHUREDGE (script)/ROCHESTER; 3-3/4", brown bone, regular jack (PocketEze), 1900-1940; $300. Saber-cut spear blade. Etched, "Indianapolis Paint and Color".

623777, ROBESON/SHUREDGE (script)/ROCHESTER; 3-3/8", brown bone, Congress (PocketEze), 1900-1940; $200.

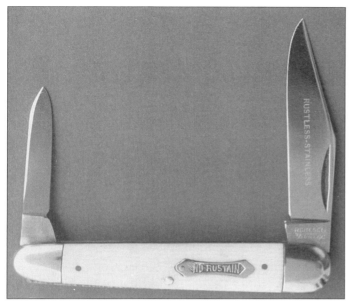

429841, ROBESON/SHUREDGE (script)/ROCHESTER; 3-3/8", ivoroid, sleeveboard (No-Rustain), 1900-1948; $150.

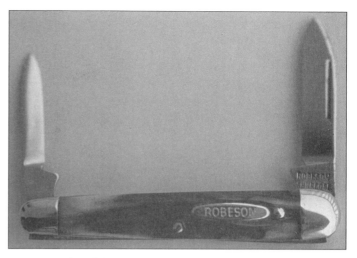

523858, ROBESON/SHUREDGE (block)/U.S.A.; 2-7/8", genuine stag, sleeveboard pen, 1948-1965; $75.

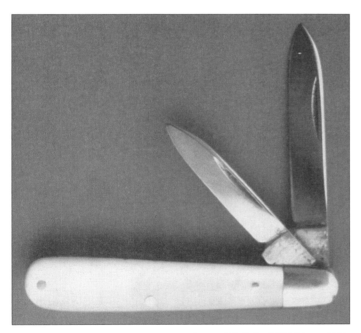

722775, ROBESON/SHUREDGE (script)/ROCHESTER; 2-1/4", genuine pearl, small regular jack, 1900-1948; $100.

822850, ROBESON/SHUREDGE (script)/ROCHESTER; 2-3/4", onyx swirl celluloid, serpentine jack, 1900-1948; $100.

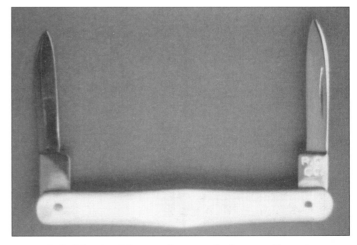

No #, R.C.CO.; 1-7/8", genuine pearl, tiny swell-center pen, 1900-1948; $90.

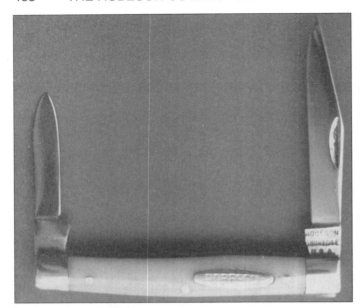

823851, ROBESON/SHUREDGE (block)/U.S.A.; 2-5/8", yellow composition, serpentine pen, 1948-1965; $50.

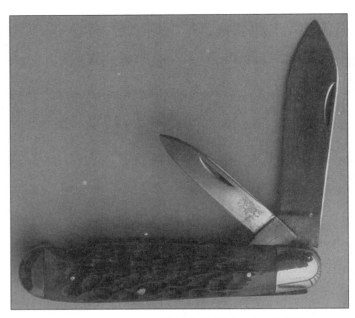

No #; ROBESON (arched)/CUTLERY/U.S.A.; 3-3/8", green bone, E-O regular jack, c. 1900; $100.

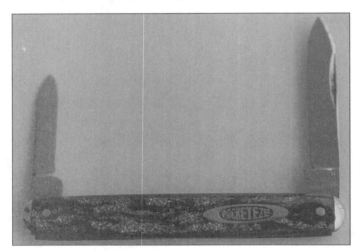

No #; ROBESON/SHUREDGE (script)/ROCHESTER; 3", Christmas tree, equal-end pen, 1900-1948; $100.

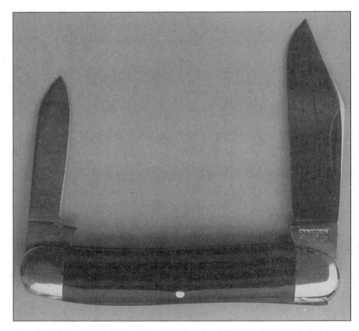

No #; ROBESON/SHUREDGE (script)/ROCHESTER; 3", butter and molasses, serpentine pen, 1900-1948; $75.

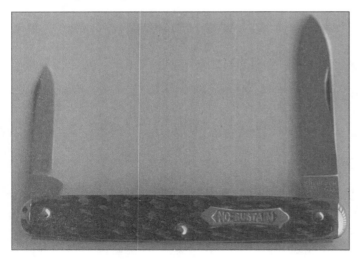

No #; ROBESON/SHUREDGE (script)/ROCHESTER; 3", brown bone, equal-end pen (No-Rustain), 1900-1940; $125.

No #; ROBESON/SHUREDGE (script)/ROCHESTER; 3-3/8",
brown bone, regular jack, 1900-1940; $100.

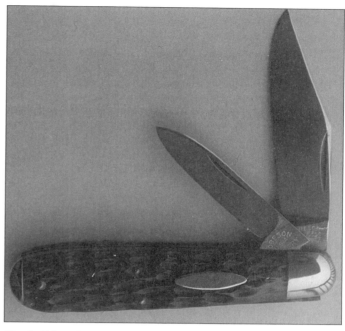

No #; ROBESON/SHUREDGE (script)/ROCHESTER; 3-3/8",
green bone, regular jack, 1900-1940; $150.

No #; ROBESON/SHUREDGE (script)/ROCHESTER; 2-5/8",
rough black, small regular jack, 1900-1948; $50.

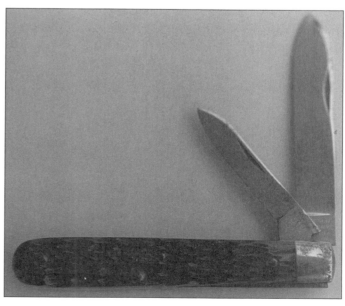

No #; ROBESON/CUTLERY/ROCHESTER (#7); 3-3/8", green
bone, regular jack, 1900-1940; $75.

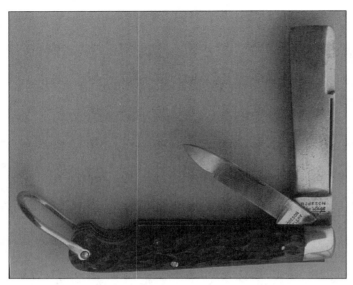

No #; ROBESON/SHUREDGE (script)/ROCHESTER; 3-5/8", brown bone, sailor's knife, c. World War I; $150.

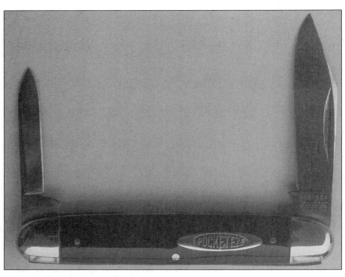

323825, ROBESON/SHUREDGE (script)/ROCHESTER; 3", slick black, equal-end pen; 1900-1948; $50.

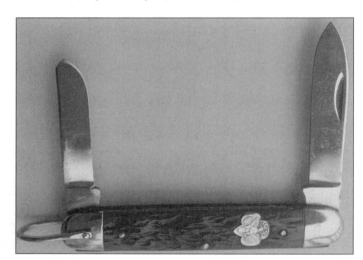

No #; ROBESON/SHUREDGE (script)/ROCHESTER; 3-1/4", brown bone, (GSA) Official Girl Scout (prototype), c. 1930s; $750.

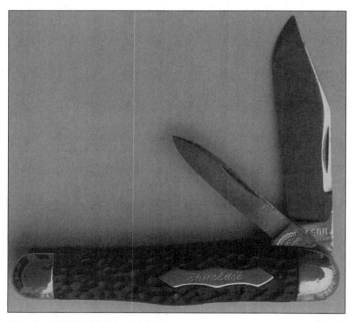

No #; ROBESON/DEMONSTRATOR (#14); 3-5/8", rough black, Eureka jack, 1900-1948; $175.

002832, TERRIER CUTLERY; 3-1/4", tortoiseshell, equal-end whittler, 1910-1916; $250.

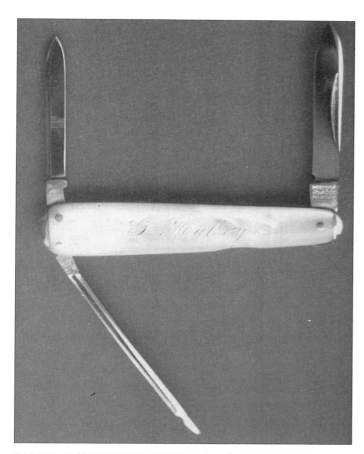

733077, ROBESON/SHUREDGE (script)/ROCHESTER; 3", genuine pearl, sleeveboard lobster, 1900-1948; $150.

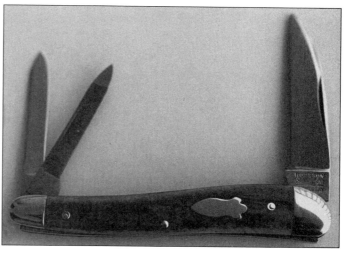

532008, ROBESON/SHUREDGE (script)/ROCHESTER N.Y.; 3-3/8", genuine stag, Wharcliffe whittler, 1900-1940; $300.

632105, ROBESON/SHUREDGE (script)/ROCHESTER; 3", brown bone, equal-end whittler, 1900-1940; $150.

632102, ROBESON/SHUREDGE (script)/ROCHESTER; 3-5/8", brown bone, sleeveboard whittler, 1900-1940; $250.

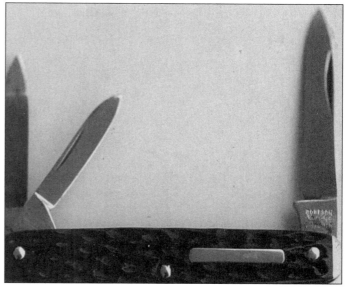

632111, ROBESON/SHUREDGE (script)/ROCHESTER; 3-1/4", rough black, serpentine stock (milled liners), 1900-1948; $125.

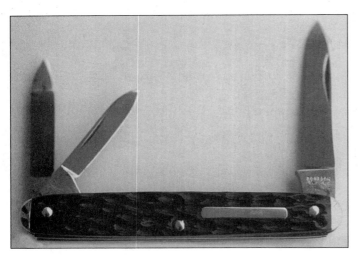

632167, ROBESON/SHUREDGE (script)/ROCHESTER; 3", brown bone, equal-end whittler, 1900-1940; $150.

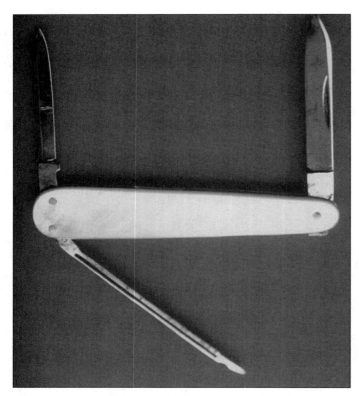

733135, ROBESON/SHUREDGE (script)/ROCHESTER; 3", genuine pearl, sleeveboard lobster, 1900-1948; $150.

632167, ROBESON/SHUREDGE (script)/ROCHESTER; 3", brown bone, equal-end whittler, 1900-1940; 150.

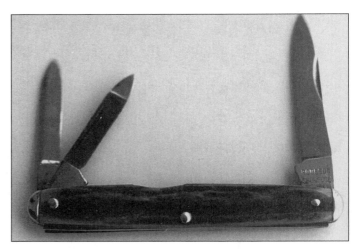

533167, ROBESON/SHUREDGE (block)/U.S.A.; 3", genuine stag, equal-end whittler, 1948-1965; $125.

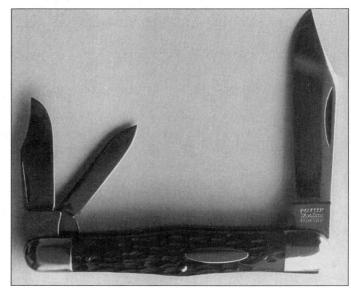

632225, ROBESON/SHUREDGE (script)/ROCHESTER; 3-5/8", brown bone, swell-center whittler, 1900-1940; $300.

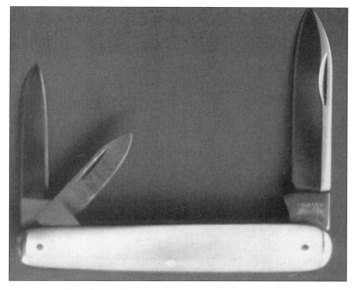

732275, ROBESON/SHUREDGE (script)/ROCHESTER; 3-1/8", genuine pearl, sleeveboard whittler, 1900-1948; $250.

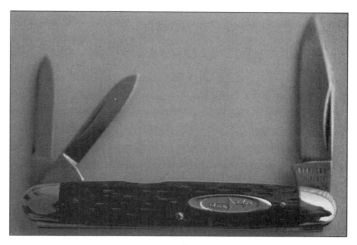

632319, ROBESON/SHUREDGE (block)/U.S.A.; 3", rough black, (ShurEdge shield), equal-end whittler, c. 1950-1960s; $125.

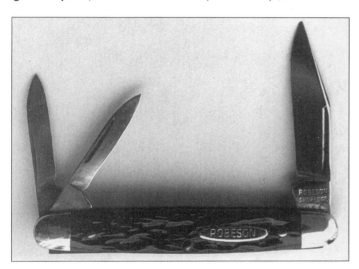

632319, ROBESON/SHUREDGE (block)/U.S.A.; 3", strawberry bone, equal-end whittler, 1948-1965; $150.

632319, ROBESON/SHUREDGE (block)/U.S.A.; 3", rough black, equal-end whittler, 1948-1965; $125.

632319, ROBESON/SHUREDGE (script)/ROCHESTER; 3", brown bone, equal-end whittler, 1900-1940; $175.

733353, ROBESON (arched)/CUTLERY/CO. (#9); 3", genuine pearl, equal-end swell-center, c. 1900; $250.

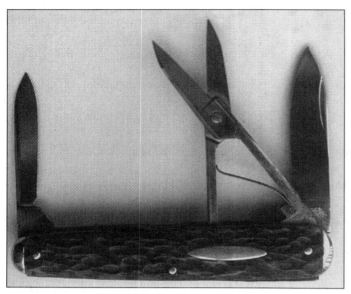

632405, ROBESON/SHUREDGE (script)/ROCHESTER; 3-1/8",
brown Rogers bone, sleeveboard (blade 1/2" short), 1900-
1940; $200.

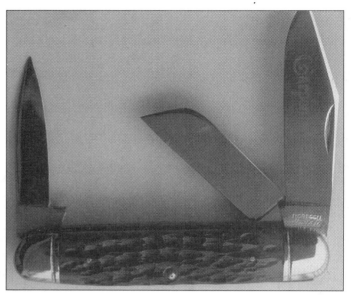

632433, ROBESON/SHUREDGE (script)/U.S.A. (#13); 3-5/8",
brown bone, equal-end, 1900-1940; $300.

632492, ROBESON/SHUREDGE (script)/ROCHESTER N.Y.;
2-7/8", brown Rogers bone, equal-end oval whittler, 1900-
1940; $175.

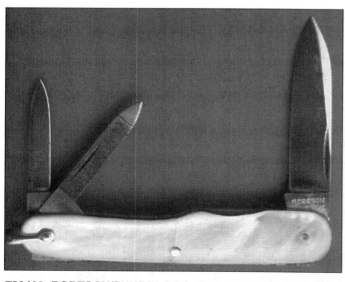

733466, ROBESON/SHUREDGE (script)/ROCHESTER; 2-1/2",
genuine pearl, gunstock whittler, 1900-1948; $150.

733463, ROBESON/SHUREDGE (script)/U.S.A. (#13); 3", genuine pearl, serpentine-sleeveboard whittler, 1900-1948; $175.

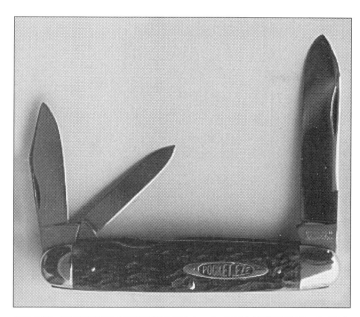

633499, ROBESON/SHUREDGE (script)/ROCHESTER; 3-5/8", brown bone, equal-end whittler, 1900-1940; $300.

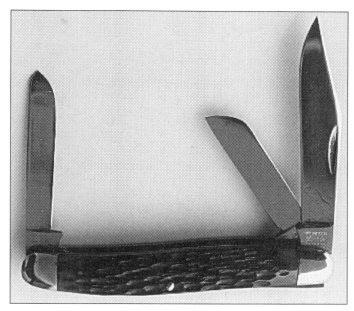

633594, ROBESON/SHUREDGE (script)/U.S.A.; 4", green bone, serpentine stockman, 1900-1940; $200.

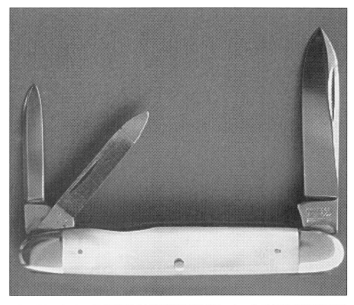

732522 250, ROBESON/SHUREDGE (script)/ROCHESTER N.Y.; 3-1/4", genuine pearl, equal-end whittler, 1900-1948; $200.

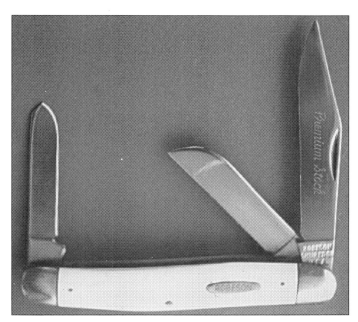

432594, ROBESON/SHUREDGE (block)/U.S.A.; 4", white composition, serpentine stockman, 1948-1965; $100.

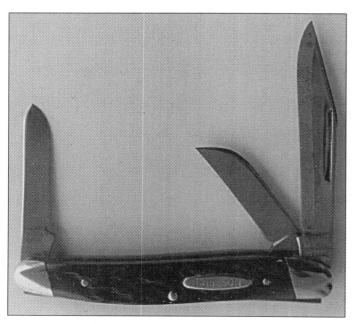

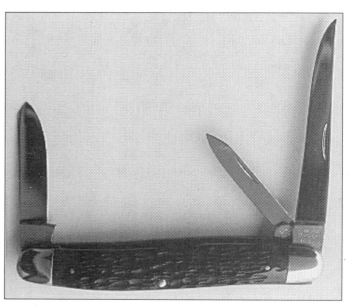

633596, ROBESON/SHUREDGE (script)/U.S.A.; 4", green bone, serpentine stock (Turkish clip), 1900-1940; $200.

633728, ROBESON/SHUREDGE (block)/U.S.A.; 3-1/4", strawberry bone, serpentine stock ("Flame-Edge"), 1948-1965; $250.

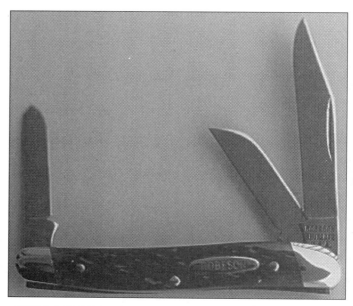

633728, ROBESON/SHUREDGE (block)/U.S.A.; 3-1/4", strawberry bone, serpentine stock, 1948-1965; $150.

633728, ROBESON/SHUREDGE (script)/ROCHESTER; 3-1/4", brown bone, serpentine stockman (PocketEze), 1900-1940; $175.

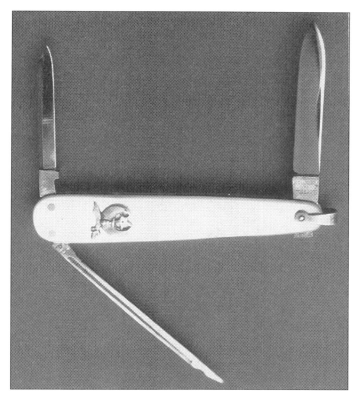

733745, ROBESON/SHUREDGE (script)/U.S.A.; 3", genuine pearl, sleeveboard lobster, 1900-1948; $150.

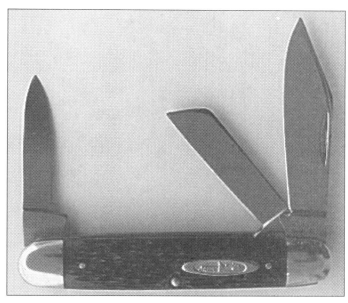

633865, ROBESON/SHUREDGE (block)/U.S.A.; 3-1/4", black, equal-end cattle (Shur-Edge shield), c. 1950-60s; $125.

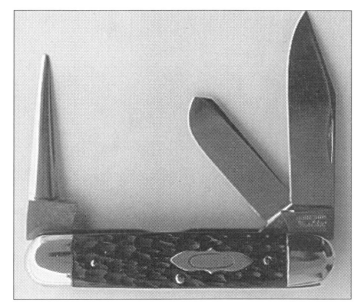

632846, ROBESON/SHUREDGE (script)/ROCHESTER; 3-1/4", brown bone, equal-end cattle knife, 1900-1940; $200.

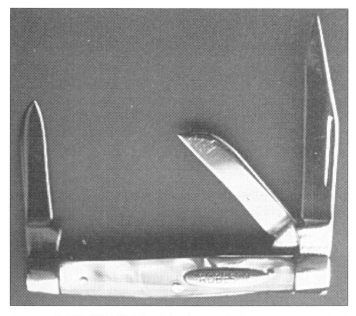

833850, ROBESON/SHUREDGE (block)/U.S.A.; 2-5/8", cracked ice, serpentine stockman, 1948-1965; $50.

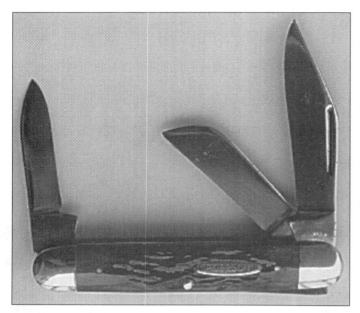

633865, ROBESON/SHUREDGE (block)/U.S.A.; 3-1/4", straw-berry bone, equal-end cattle, 1948-1965; $150.

633885, ROBESON/SHUREDGE (script)/U.S.A.; 3-5/8", brown bone, serpentine (etched "WOODCRAFT"), 1900-1940; $300.

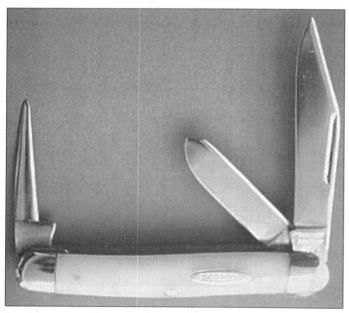

833881, ROBESON/SHUREDGE (block)/U.S.A.; 3-5/8", yel-low composition, serpentine stockman, 1948-1965; $100.

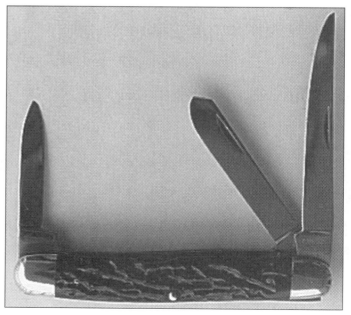

633884, ROBESON/SHUREDGE (block)/U.S.A.; 3-5/8", rough black, serpentine stockman, 1948-1965; $100.

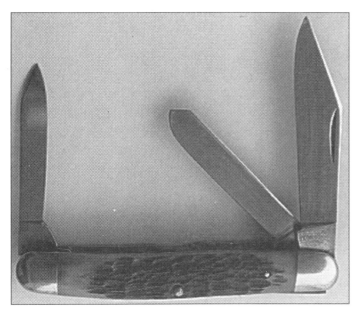

No #; ROBESON/SHUREDGE (script)/U.S.A.; 3-5/8", brown bone, serpentine stockman, 1900-1940; $150.

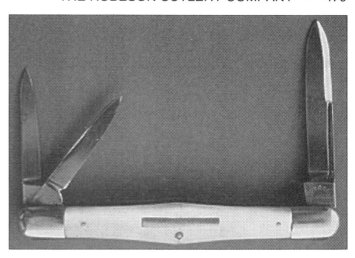

No #; ROBESON (arched)/CUTLERY/U.S.A. (#10); 3", genuine pearl, swell-center whittler, c. 1900; $150.

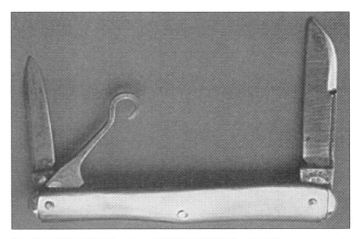

No #; ROBESON (arched)/CUTLERY/CO.; 2-5/8", rose pearl, swell-center whittler, c. 1900; $125.

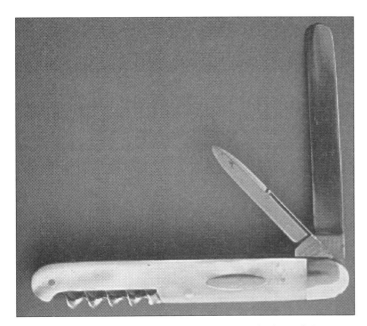

No #; ROBESON/CUTLERY/CO./GERMANY (#4); 3-3/8", genuine pearl, equal-end physician/pharmacist, flexible spatula blade, 1891-1894; $350.

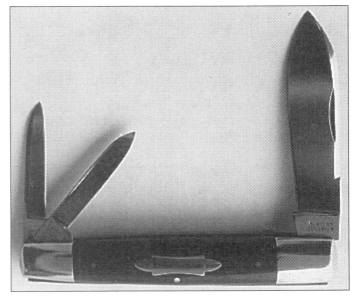

No #; ROBESON/CUTLERY/CO./PREMIER (#5); 4-1/4", ebony, sleeveboard-Crown whittler, c. 1892-1898; $750.

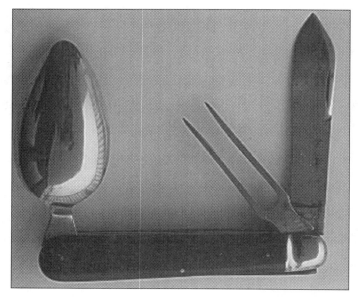

No #; ROBESON/SHUREDGE (script)/ROCHESTER; 4-1/2", wood, take-apart hobo, c. World War I; $250.

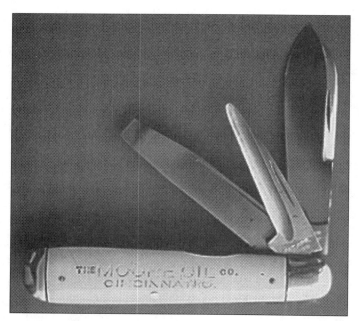

No #; ROBESON/SHUREDGE (script)/ROCHESTER; 3-1/2", ivory celluloid, (Moore Oil Co.) jack, 1900-1948; $200.

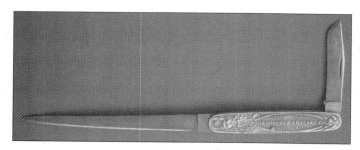

No #; ROBESON/SHUREDGE (script)/ROCHESTER N.Y.; 7-1/2", aluminum, letter opener/pen knife, 1900-1948; $75.

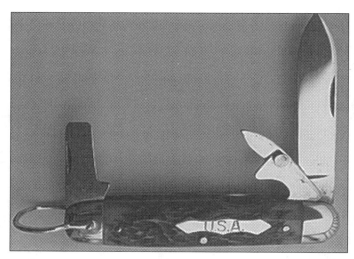

No #; ROBESON/SHUREDGE (script)/ROCHESTER; 3-5/8", green bone, (U.S. Army shield), three- blade utility, c. World War II; $200.

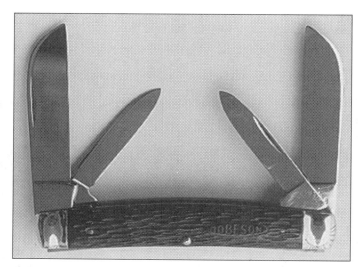

642088, ROBESON/SHUREDGE (block)/U.S.A.; 3-3/4", rough black, (impressed shield) Congress, c. World War II; $150.

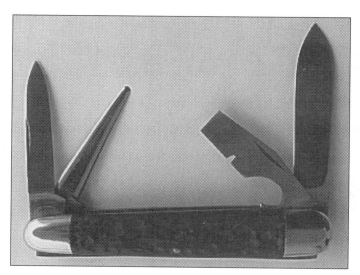

No #; ROBESON/SHUREDGE (script)/ROCHESTER; 3-3/8", rough black, sleeveboard utility, 1900-1948; $120.

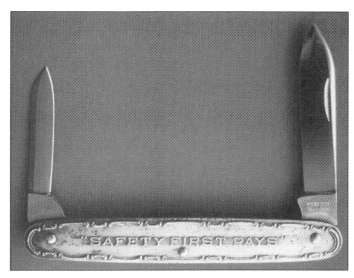

No #; ROBESON/SHUREDGE (script)/ROCHESTER; 3-1/2", nickel-silver, ("Safety First") equal-pen, 1900-1948; $50.

652361, ROBESON/SHUREDGE (script)/U.S.A.; 3-1/2", brown bone, five-blade Senator (very rare), 1900-1940; $1,000.

Small metal knife advertising Robeson w/ flowers, scrolls, etc. This is the reverse side of the knife at right.

No #; ROBESON/SHUREDGE (script)/U.S.A.; 1-1/2" d, nickel-silver, coin fob, 1900-1948; $100.

No #; ROBESON/SHUREDGE (script)/ROCHESTER N.Y.; 3", nickel-silver, equal-end, 1900-1948; $75.

Reverse side of the knife above.

The knives featured on this page are courtesy of Helen and Frank Peppiatt of Kansas.

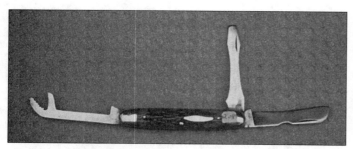

632800 ROBESON/SHUREDGE (script); 3-3/8", brown bone, radio knife, 1900-1940, $500.

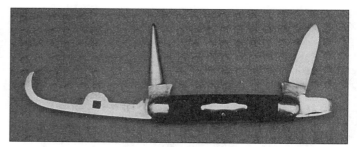

646440, ROBESON/SHUREDGE (script)/ROCHESTER; 3-1/2", brown bone, carriage knife, 1900-1940; $1,000.

No #; ROBESON/SHUREDGE (script)/ROCHESTER; ivory celluloid, (PocketEze) knife opener, 1900-1948; $150.

WINCHESTER

Because of declining governmental contracts after World War I, Winchester made a decision to enter the pocket-knife market. In order to do this, it bought two companies: The Eagle Knife Company and Napanoch Knife Company. With combined knowledge from both companies, Winchester began producing large numbers of pocket knives.

In the early '20s, Associated Simmons Hardware, owners of Walden Knife Company, merged with Winchester and at that time, production of Walden knives was terminated. As with Remington, World War II halted the manufacturing of Winchester pocket knives.

Although a few German-made knives marked with the Winchester name appeared on the market during the late 1970s and early 1980s, however, Winchester licensed the manufacturer and distribution of a quality line of reproduction knives to Blue Grass Cutlery.

The pattern numbers used by Winchester can be used to identify knives as follows:

The first digit signifies the number of blades.
The second digit signifies the handle material.
The third digit signifies the factory pattern.

0	celluloid
1	fancy celluloid
2	nickel silver
3	genuine pearl
6	Cocobolo or other wood
7	bone
8	bone stag
9	sometimes used for bone or stag

Note: All prices given are for knives in mint condition.

1050, toothpick, asst. celluloid, 5" 325
1051, Texas jack, celluloid, 4-1/4" 325
1060, Texas jack, celluloid, 4-1/8" 300
1201, jack, nickel silver, 1 sheep-foot blade, easy opener, 3-3/8" 190
1068, cocobolo, 3-3/8" 90
1610, pruner, cocobolo, hawkbill, 4-1/8" 125
1611, mariner's knife, cocobolo, 3-1/4" 95
1613, maize, cocobolo, 1 blade, 3-3/8" 140
1614, maize, cocobolo, 1 blade, 4-1/8" 140
1621, budding, ebony, 4-3/4" 150
1624, maize, 4" 125
1632, cocobolo, 3-3/8" 100
1633, pruner, cocobolo hawkbill, 3-3/8" 125

1701, barlow, bone, 3-1/2" 200
1703, barlow, smooth bone, 5" 450
1704, barlow, bone stag, EO, 5" 500
1785, barlow, bone, 3-1/2" 225
1905, jack, stag, 1 blade, 4-1/2" 300
1921, stag, 3-3/8" 150
1922, stag, 3-3/8" 150
1923, stag, 1 blade, 4-1/8" 250
1924, powder horn, stag, 1 blade, 4-1/4" 350
1925, jack, stag, 3-1/2" 300
1937, stag, 1 blade, 3-7/8" 200
2028, jack, shell celluloid, 3-3/8" 180
2037, jack, celluloid, 3" 125
2038, jack, pearl celluloid, 3" 170

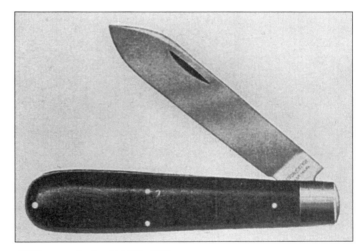

1605, cocobolo, 3-1/2"; $90.

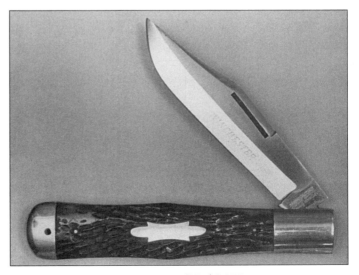

1920, folding hunter, bone, 5-3/8"; $1,250.

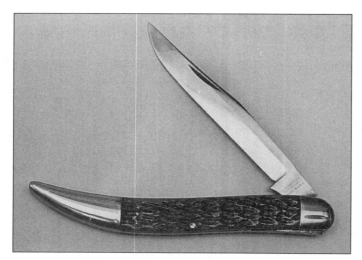

1936, toothpick, brown bone, 5"; $350.

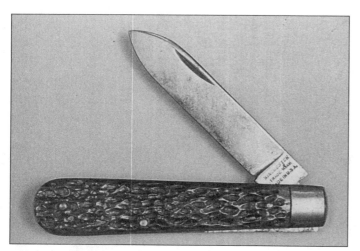

1938, brown bone, 3-3/8"; $125.

2039, jack, celluloid, 3" 100
2047, equal-end jack, white celluloid, 4-1/4"....... 300
2051, senator, white celluloid, 2-5/8" 150
2052, senator, pearl celluloid tip bolsters,
2-5/8" 100
2053, senator, celluloid, 2-5/8" 120
2054, senator, celluloid, 3-1/4" 90
2055, senator, celluloid shadow, 3-1/4" 90
2057, senator, variegated celluloid, 3-3/8".......... 125
2058, senator, blue abalone celluloid, 3-1/4"...... 125
2059, senator, celluloid, 3-1/4" 115
2067, serpentine pen, pearl celluloid, 3"............. 150
2068, sleeveboard, celluloid, 3-3/8".................... 200
2069, jack, blue celluloid, 3-3/8" 225
2070, jack, celluloid, 2 blade, 3-1/2" 175
2078, serpentine pen, black celluloid, 3-3/8" 175
2079, office knife, white celluloid, 3-3/8"............. 150
2082, sleeveboard, pearl celluloid, 3" 175
2083, jack, green celluloid, 3-1/8"...................... 175

2084, sleeveboard, blue celluloid, 3-3/8" 200
2085, serpentine jack, celluloid, 3" 175
2086, dog leg, celluloid, 2 blade, 2-3/4".............. 150
2087, serpentine jack, shell celluloid, 3" 175
2088, serpentine knife, gray celluloid, 3-3/8"...... 150
2089, office knife, white celluloid, 3-3/4"............. 175
2090, serpentine pen, celluloid, 3".................... 150
2094, jack, celluloid, 2-blade easy opener,
3-3/8" 250
2098, jack, celluloid, 3-3/8"............................... 225
2106, jack, blue abalone celluloid, 3-3/8" 160
2107, dog leg, gold celluloid, 2-3/4" 160
2109, sleeveboard, gold celluloid, 2-7/8" 110
2110, jack, celluloid tear drop, 3-1/2" 150
2111, jack, celluloid, 3-1/2" 150
2112, jack, celluloid, 3-1/2" 150
2113, peanut, celluloid, 2 blade, 2-3/4"............... 125
2114, candle end, celluloid, 3" 150
2115, sleeveboard, pearl celluloid, 2-7/8"........... 160
2116, sleeveboard, celluloid, 3-3/8" 150
2117, serpentine jack, black celluloid, 3-1/8"...... 175
2201, senator, nickel silver, 3-1/4" 100
2202, serpentine Jack, smooth, 3"........................ 80
2204, senator, nickel silver, 3-1/8" 100
2207, easy-opening jack,
nickel silver, 3-3/8" 160
2208, jack, nickel silver, 3-3/8"........................... 160
2215, jack, nickel silver, 3-1/2".............................. 80
2301, senator, pearl without bail, 2-1/4".............. 125
2302, senator, pearl with bail, 2-1/4".................. 150
2306, senator, pearl, 2-5/8"............................... 150
2307, senator, pearl, 2-7/8"............................... 150
2308, senator, pearl, 2-7/8"............................... 150

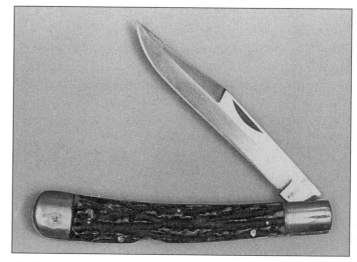

1950, lockback, stag, 5-1/4"; $1,500.

2099, jack, pink celluloid, 3-3/8"; $180.

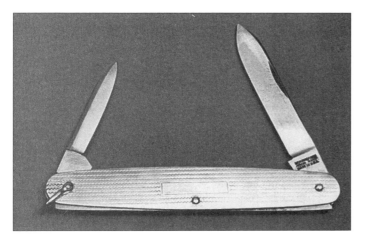

2205, pen, metal, 3-1/4"; $125.

2303, small senator, pearl, 2-5/8"; $165.

2309, senator, pearl, 3".. 175
2314, serpentine jack, pearl, 3" 225
2316, serpentine jack, pearl, 3" 225
2317, serpentine jack, pearl, 3" 200
2320, sleeveboard, pearl, 2-7/8".......................... 125
2331, congress, pearl, 3-1/4"............................... 275
2335, congress, pearl, 3-1/4"............................... 300

2337, senator, pearl, 3-1/4"................................. 225
2338, senator, pearl, 3-1/4"................................. 200
2344, senator, pearl, 3-1/4"................................. 200
2345, senator, pearl, 3-1/4"................................. 200
2346, lobster, pearl, 3" 200
2352, jack, pearl, 3-1/8" 180
2356, lobster, pearl, 3" 250
2361, dog leg, pearl, 2-3/4"................................. 175
2363, congress, pearl, 3" 225
2366, sleeveboard, pearl, 3-3/8"......................... 300
2367, sleeveboard, pearl, 3" 200
2368, sleeveboard, pearl, 3" 200
2369, senator, pearl, 2-5/8"................................. 200
2374, senator, pearl, 2-7/8"................................. 150
2375, senator, pearl, 2-5/8"................................. 150
2376, senator, pearl, 3".......................................150
2377, senator, pearl, 2-5/8"................................. 200
2603, jack, cocobolo, 3-3/8"............................... 160
2604, jack, cocobolo, 3-1/2"................................ 175
2605, jack, cocobolo, 3-3/8"................................ 200
2606, jack, cocobolo, 3-3/8"................................ 200

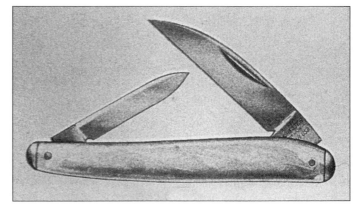

2312, wharncliffe, pearl, 2-7/8"; $225.

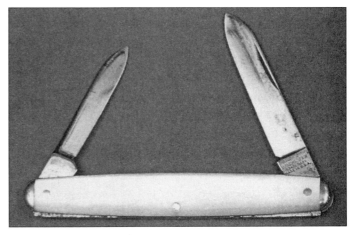

2324, pen, pearl, 3"; $175.

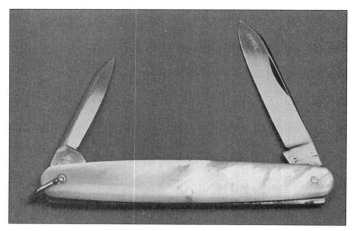

2330, pen, pearl, 3-1/4"; $175.

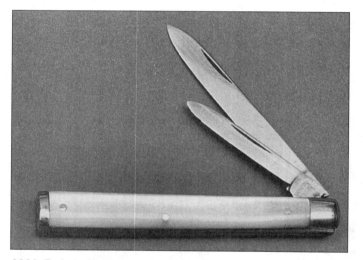

2380, Dr.'s knife, pearl, 3-1/4"; $600.

2610, jack, cocobolo, 3-3/8" 175
2611, serpentine jack, cocobolo, 3" 150
2612, jack, cocobolo, 3-5/8" 225
2613, jack, cocobolo, 3-5/8" 200
2614, jack, cocobolo, 3-3/8" 200
2629, jack, ebony, 3-1/2" 200
2630, jack, ebony, 3-3/8" 200
2633, premium stockman, ebony, 3-1/4" 175
2635, jack, cocobolo, 3-1/2" 150
2636, jack, ebony, 3-1/2" 175
2638, serpentine jack, cocobolo, 3-1/2".............. 200
2641, trapper, cocobolo, 3-7/8"............................ 400
2649, jack, ebony, 3-3/4" 225
2660, jack, ebony, 3-1/2" 200
2661, jack, ebony, 3-1/2" 200
2662, jack, ebony, 3-1/2" 200
2665, jack, ebony, 3-3/8" 180
2666, jack, ebony, 3-3/8" 150
2681, electrician's, ebony, 3-3/4" 175

2701, barlow, bone, 5 spear and pen, 3-1/2" 275
2702, barlow, bone, spay and pen, 3-1/2" 325
2703, barlow, bone, clip and pen, 3-1/2".............300
2820, jack, bone, 3-3/8" 200
2830, senator, stag, 3-1/4" 150
2840, stag, 2" 175
2841, stag, 3" 175
2842, senator, stag, 3-1/4" 200
2843, stag, 3-3/8" 200
2844, jack, stag, 3-3/4" 275
2845, jack, stag, 3-3/4" 250
2846, premium stockman, stag........................... 200
2848, jack, stag with chain, 3-1/2" 200

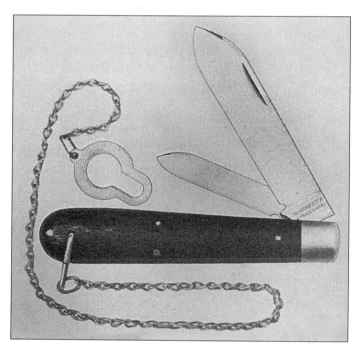

2608, stabber, cocobolo, 3-5/8"; $175.

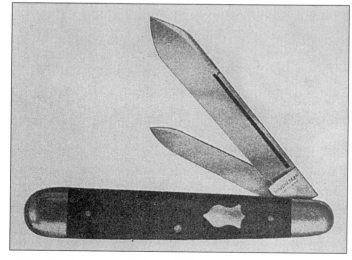

2627, slim jack, cocobolo, 3-1/4"; $175.

2613, sleeveboard, ebony, 3-3/8"; $125.

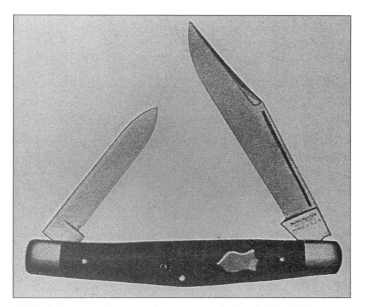

2632, light premium stockman, cocobolo, 3-3/8; $175.

2849, jack, stag, 3-3/8"	....	250
2850, jack, stag, 2-blade coke pattern, 3-3/4"	....	450
2851, gunstock jack, stag, 3"	....	450
2851, serpentine cattle, stag, 3"	....	300
2853, jack, stag, 3-3/8"	....	250
2854, jack, stag, 3-3/8"	....	200
2855, jack, stag, 3-3/8"	....	225
2856, dog leg, stag, 2-3/4"	....	225
2857, serpentine jack, stag, 3-1/8"	....	250
2858, serpentine jack, stag, 3"	....	175
2859, serpentine jack, stag, 3-1/8"	....	250
2860, sleeveboard, stag, 3-1/4"	....	250
2861, sleeveboard, stag, 3-1/4"	....	250
2862, sleeveboard, stag, 3-3/8"	....	225
2863, congress, stag, 3-1/4"	....	300
2864, swell center, stag, 3-3/8"	....	300
2865, swell center, stag, 3-1/2"	....	325

2866, senator, stag, 2-7/8"	....	175
2867, senator, stag, 3-3/8"	....	175
2868, equal-end pen, stag, 3-3/8"	....	175
2869, gunstock, stag, 3-3/4"	....	400
2870, gunstock, stag, 3-3/4"	....	400
2871, gunstock, stag, 3-3/4"	....	400
2872, gunstock, stag, 3-3/4"	....	400
2874, jack, stag, 3-1/2"	....	250
2875, premium stockman, stag, 3-1/4"	....	300
2878, Texas jack, stag, 4-1/4"	....	450
2879, sleeveboard, stag, 4-1/2"	....	900
2880, half whittler, stag, 4-1/2"	....	500
2881, English jack, stag, 4-1/2"	....	500
2901, stag, 3-1/2"	....	200

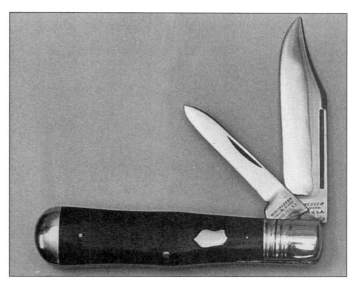

2640, Coke bottle, ebony, 3-3/4"; $325.

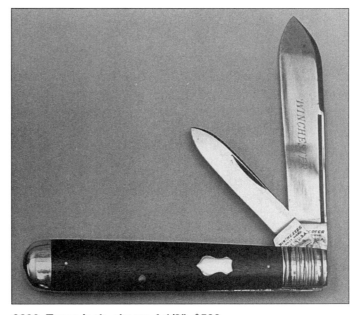

2690, Texas jack, ebony, 4-1/2"; $500.

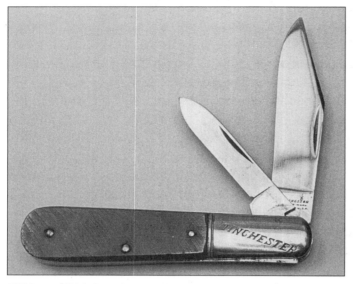

2703, small barlow, bone, clip and pen, 3-1/2"; $300.

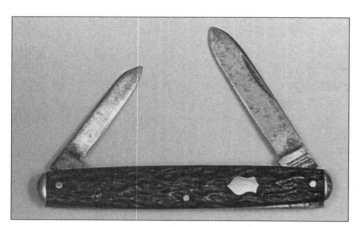

2847, pen, brown bone, 3-1/4"; $175.

2853, gunstock, brown bone, 3-1/2"; $400.

2876, small muskrat, brown bone, 3-1/4"; $350.

2903, swell center, stag, 3-1/2"	275
2904, stag, 2 blade trapper, 3-7/8"	600
2905, stag, English jack, 4-1/2"	600
2907, stag, English jack, 4-1/2"	600
2908, swell center, stag, 3-5/8"	275
2910, lobster, stag, 3"	150
2911, jack, stag, 3-1/2"	200
2914, sleeveboard, stag, 3-3/8"	200
2917, serpentine jack, stag, 3"	250
2918, serpentine pen, stag, 3-3/8"	225
2921, coffin bolsters, bone, 3-1/2"	450
2923, premium stockman, stag, 4"	250
2924, congress, stag, 3"	250
2925, jack, stag, 3-1/8"	200
2928, Texas jack, stag, 4"	300
2930, jack, stag, 3-5/8"	300
2931, jack, stag, 3-3/8"	200
2932, congress, stag, 3-1/4"	250
2933, sleeveboard, stag, 3"	175
2934, senator, stag, 3-3/8"	150
2938, sleeveboard, stag, 3"	200
2940, jack, stag, 3-5/8"	250
2943, sleeveboard, stag, 3-3/8"	200
2948, senator, stag, 3-3/8"	200
2949, jack, stag, 3-1/2"	250
2950, stag, 3-1/2"	200
2951, jack, stag, 3-1/2"	225
2952, jack, stag, 3-1/2"	225
2954, jack, stag, 3-1/2"	250
2956, serpentine jack, stag, 3-1/2"	250
2958, jack, stag, 3-3/8"	250
2959, jack, stag, 3-3/8"	300

2961, jack, stag, 3-3/8" 200
2962, dog leg, stag, 2-3/4" 175
2963, senator, stag, 3" 175
2964, jack, stag, 3-5/8" 250
2966, jack, stag, 3-5/8" 250
2967, swell center, stag, 3-7/8" 500
2973, jack, stag, 3-5/8" 250
2974, serpentine jack, stag, 3-1/2" 250
2976, Texas jack, stag, 4" 150
2978, Dr.'s knife, stag, 2 blade, 3-3/8" 600
2980, cattle, stag, 3-5/8" 250
2982, Texas jack, stag, 4" 320
2983, jack, stag, with chain, 3-3/8" 200
2988, Texas Jack, stag, 4" 325
2990, dog leg, stag, 2-3/4" 225
2992, stag, 3-5/8" 250
2993, stag, trapper pen blade, 3-7/8" 500
2994, jack, stag, 3-5/8" 250
2995, jack, stag, 3-5/8" 250
2996, congress, stag, 3-3/4" 300
2997, serpentine pen, stag, 3-3/8" 225
2998, jack, stag, 3-3/8" 225

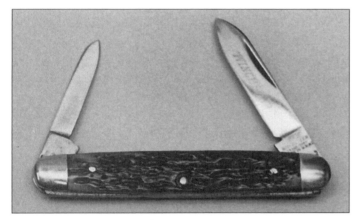
2902, pen, bone, 2-5/8"; $110.

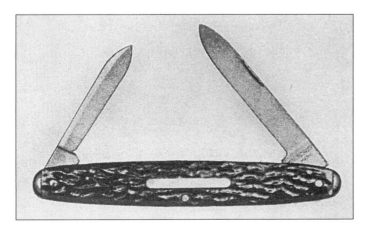
2945, senator, bone, 3-3/8"; $150.

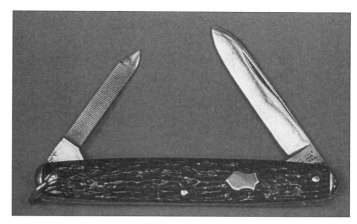
2981, pen, brown bone, 3-1/4"; $175.

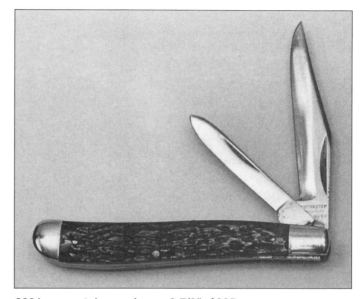
2991, peanut, brown bone, 2-7/8"; $225.

2999, serpentine jack, stag, 3-1/8" 275
3001, swell center cattle, pearl celluloid, 3-1/2" 400
3003, premium stockman, celluloid, 3-1/2" 350
3005, swell center, black celluloid, 3-5/8" 400
3006, serpentine pen, black celluloid, 3-3/8" 400
3007, premium stockman, black celluloid, 4" 400
3008, cattle, white celluloid, 3-5/8" 450
3009, cattle, white celluloid, 3-5/8" 450
3010, swell center cattle, blue abalone celluloid, 3-5/8" 500
3014, premium stockman, pearl celluloid, 4" 500
3015, swell center, gold celluloid, 3-5/8" 400
3017, premium stockman, variegated celluloid, 4" 450
3018, premium stockman, celluloid, 4" 450
3019, whittler, red celluloid, 4" 450
3020, whittler, celluloid, 3-1/2" 400

3023, whittler, red celluloid, 3-5/8" 400

3024, whittler, celluloid, 3-5/8" 400

3025, premium stockman, blue abalone celluloid, 3-1/2" 350

3026, premium stockman, variegated celluloid, 3-1/4" 350

3027, premium stockman, red celluloid, 3-1/4" 250

3028, premium stockman, celluloid, 3-1/4" 325

3029, premium stockman, celluloid, 3-1/4" 300

3030, senator, blue abalone celluloid, 3-3/8" 300

3031, senator, gray celluloid, 3-3/8" 350

3033, serpentine, gold celluloid, 3" 300

3034, serpentine cattle, blue abalone celluloid, 3" 300

3035, gold celluloid, 3-3/8" 300

3036, cattle, celluloid, 3-3/8" 300

3040, whittler, celluloid, 3" 300

3041, senator, celluloid, 3" 300

3042, senator, celluloid, 3-3/8" 275

3043, senator, celluloid, 3-3/8" 275

3044, senator, celluloid, 3-3/8" 275

3045, whittler, celluloid, 3-1/4" 300

3046, whittler, celluloid, 3-1/4" 300

3047, premium stockman, celluloid, 3-1/2" 275

3048, premium stockman, celluloid, 4" 400

3331, lobster, pearl, 3" 175

3338, sleeveboard, pearl, 3" 175

3341, cattle, pearl, 3-3/8" 500

3347, whittler, pearl, 3-1/4" 400

3348, premium stockman, pearl, 3-1/4" 400

3349, sleeveboard, pearl, 3-blade whittler, 3" 350

3350, whittle senator, pearl, 3 blade, 3-1/4" 300

3352, senator, pearl, 3-1/2" 300

3002, whittler, green celluloid, 3-3/4"; $375.

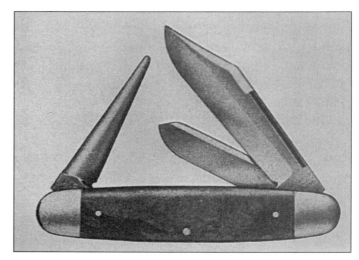

3016, cattle, celluloid, 3-3/4"; $450.

3022, whittler, imitation tortoiseshell, 3-1/4"; $350.

3353, senator, pearl, 2-5/8" 225

3360, bartender, pearl, 3-1/4" 400

3361, equal-end cattle, pearl, LP, 3-3/4" 500

3366, whittler senator, pearl, 3 blade, 3-3/8" 350

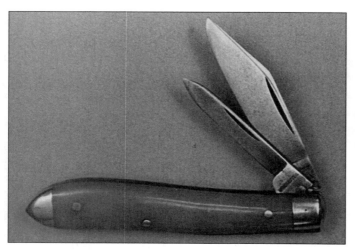

2999, dog-leg jack, white smooth bone, 3-1/8"; $225.

3370, lobster, pearl, 3" 200
3371, lobster, pearl, 3" 225
3373, whittler senator, pearl, 2-7/8" 275
3377, sleeveboard, pearl, 3-3/8" 300
3378, sleeveboard whittler, pearl, 3" 300
3379, senator whittler, pearl, 3" 300
3380, sleeveboard, pearl, 2-3/4" 200
3381, lobster, pearl, 3-1/8" 200
3625, cattle, ebony, 3-5/8" 300
3902, swell center, stag, 3-1/2" 400
3903, swell center, stag, whittler,
   3 backsprings 1,000
3905, swell center cattle, stag, 3-1/2" 400
3906, premium stockman, stag, 4" 450
3907, premium stockman, stag, 4" 500
3908, 3-3/4" 400
3909, senator, stag, 3-3/8" 300

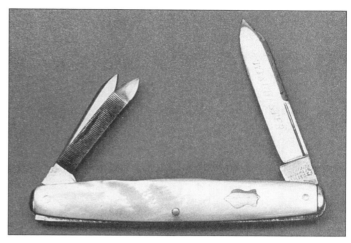

3357, whittler, pearl, 3-1/8"; $400.

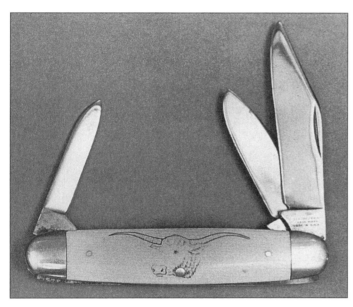

3049, cattle knife, imitation white bone, 3-5/8"; $400.

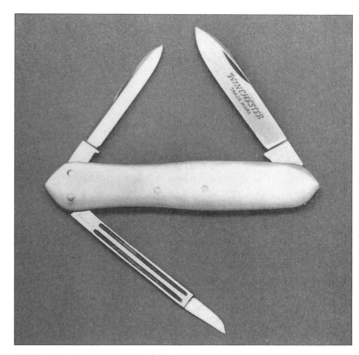

3382, lobster, pearl, 3"; $200.

3345, whittler, pearl, 3-1/4"; $400.

3904, whittler, brown bone, 3-5/8"; $1,000.

3911, senator whittler, stag, 3"............................300
3915, swell center cattle, stag, 3-1/2"................325
3917, premium stockman, stag, 3-1/2".............300
3924, senator, stag, 3"..225
3925, swell center, stag, 3-5/8".......................400
3927, serpentine pen, stag, 3-3/8"....................300
3928, premium stockman, stag, 4"...................450
3929, congress, stag, whittler, 3-1/4"...............400
3931, sleeveboard, stag, 3".................................200
3932, senator, stag, 3-blade whittler, 3-3/8".......325
3933, senator, stag, 3-blade whittler, 3-3/8".......300
3936, cattle, stag, 3-5/8".....................................450
3938, senator, stag, 3-blade whittler, 3-3/8".......300
3939, senator, stag, 3-blade whittler, 3-3/8".......300
3949, serpentine cattle, stag, 3" 250
3950, cattle, stag, 3-5/8".....................................400
3951, cattle, stag, 3-5/8".....................................400
3953, bartender, stag, 3-1/4" 300
3960, premium stockman, stag, 4" 450
3961, premium stockman, stag, 4" 450
3962, premium stockman, buffalo horn, 4" 400

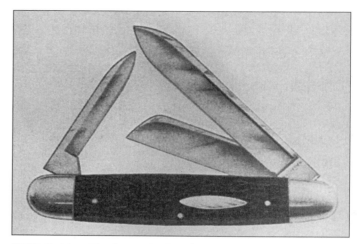

3942, light cattle, bone, 3-3/8"; $325.

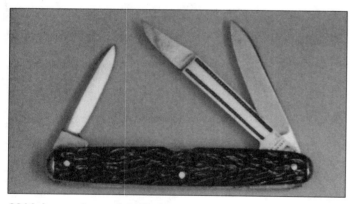

3914, brown bone, 2-3/4"; $225.

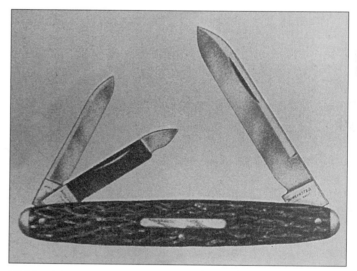

3944, whittler, bone, 3-1/4"; $300.

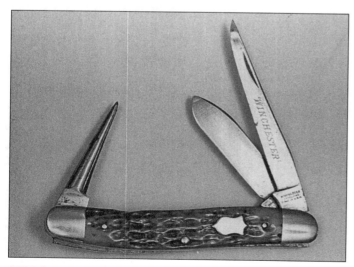

3916, brown bone, 3-1/2"; $325.

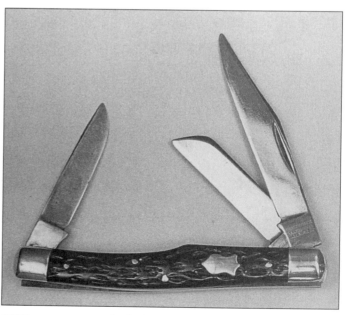

3948, reverse gunstock, brown bone, 3-5/8"; $600.

3952, cattle, brown bone, 3-3/4"; $400.

3963, stockman, stag, 4" 450
3964, premium stockman, stag, 4" 450
3965, premium stockman, stag, 3-1/4" 350
3966, premium stockman, stag, 3-1/4" 350
3967, premium stockman, stag, 3-1/4" 350
3968, stag, whittler, 3-1/4" 350
3969, premium stockman whittler, stag, 3-1/4" ... 350
3971, swell center, stag, whittler, 3-5/8" 400
3972, swell center, stag, whittler, 3-5/8" 400
3973, cattle, stag, 3-1/2" 350
3975, cattle, stag, 3-3/8" 400
3977, cattle, stag, 3-3/8" 375
3980, serpentine cattle, stag, 3" 325
3991, sleeveboard, stag, whittler, 3-3/8" 350
3992, senator, stag, slim-line whittler, 3-3/8" 350
3993, premium stockman, stag, 4" 450
4001, premium stockman, celluloid, 4" 450
4301, lobster, pearl, 2-3/4" 225
4313, senator, pearl, 3" 300
4340, senator, pearl, 3-1/4" 300

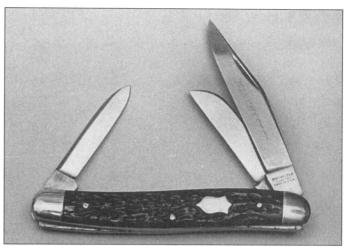

3978, serpentine stockman, brown bone, 3-1/4"; $325.

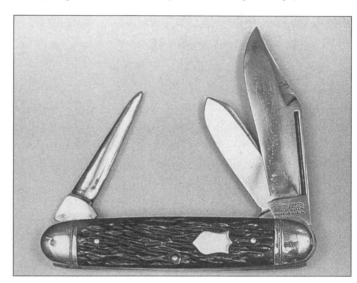

3979, cattle, brown bone, 3-5/8"; $400.

3959, stockman, brown bone, 4"; $450.

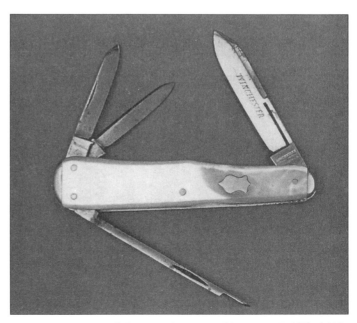

4320, gunstock whittler, pearl, orange blossom, 3-1/8"; $400.

4901, utility, brown bone, 3-3/8"; $400.

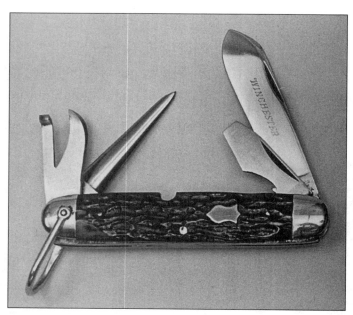

4950, utility, brown bone, 3-3/4"; $500.

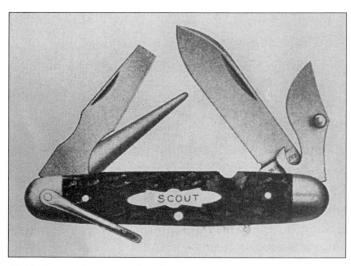

4950, Scout, bone, 3-5/7"; $550.

4961, premium stockman, bone, 4"; $500.

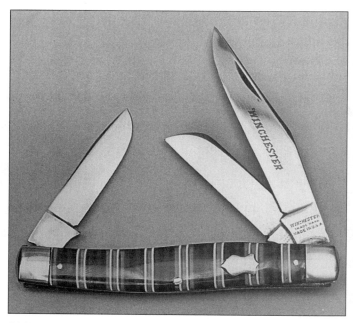

3018, stockman, candystripe, 4"; $500.

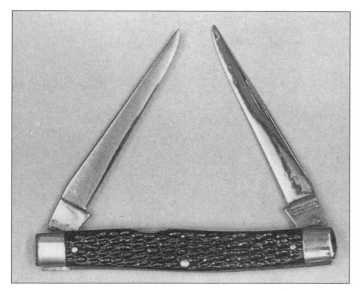

No number, muskrat, imitation jigged bone, 4"; $200.

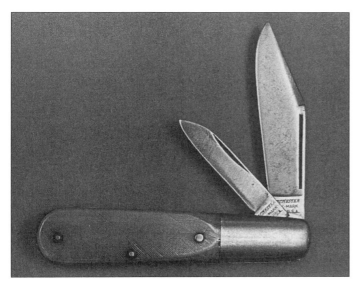

No number, barlow, bone, 3-1/4"; $225.

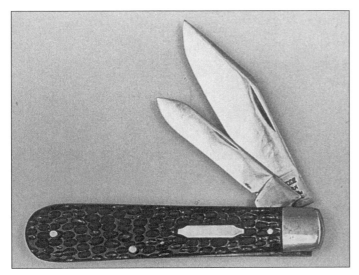

No number, jack, imitation bone, 3-3/8"; $90.

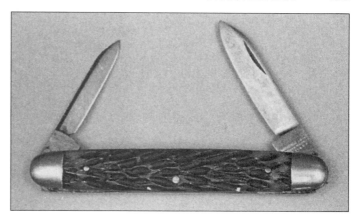

No number, pen, brown bone, 2-5/8"; $90.

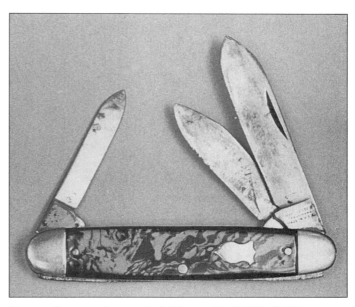

No number, stockman, dark blue swirl, 3-3/8"; $140.

No number, stockman, imitation black bone, 3-7/8"; $200.

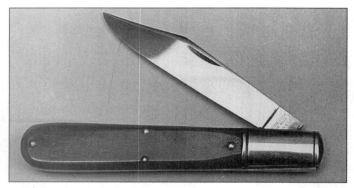

1703, daddy barlow, brown bone, 1 blade, 5-1/8", Winchester USA; $400.

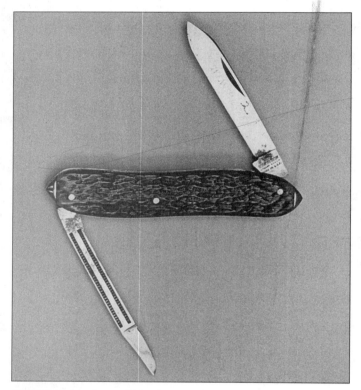

2910, lobster, bone, Winchester; $150.

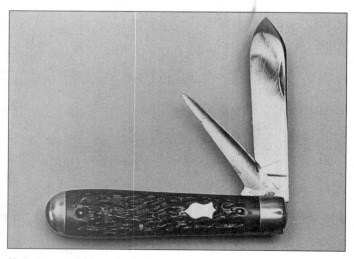

Unknown number, jack, brown bone, 3-1/2"; $200.

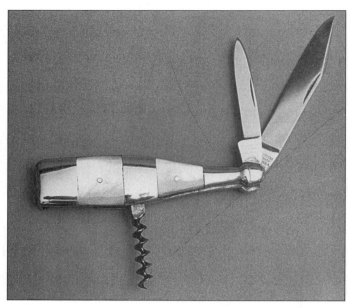

Two-blade bartender knife, pearl and nickel silver, Winchester USA, 3-3/8", very rare; $600.

1704, Daddy easy opener, brown bone; $600.

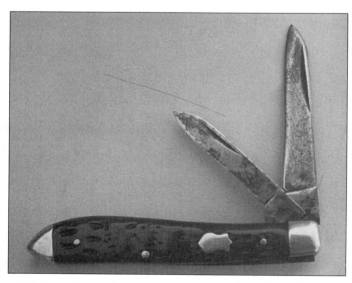

2857, Winchester dog leg, bone, 3-1/8"; $225.